Parents as Partners
in Education

Parents as Partners
in Education

The School and Home Working Together

Second Edition

Eugenia Hepworth Berger
Metropolitan State College

Merrill Publishing Company
A Bell & Howell Information Company
Columbus   Toronto   London   Melbourne

Cover Photo: © Merrill Publishing Company, Tim Cairns

Published by Merrill Publishing Company
A Bell and Howell Information Company
Columbus, Ohio 43216

This book was set in Garamond.

Administrative Editor: Jeff Johnston
Production Coordinator: Anne Daly
Cover Designer: Cathy Watterson

Photo credits: All photos copyrighted by individuals or
companies listed. Debra Berger McClave, Elena Machina
Berger, John Berger, or Eugenia Hepworth Berger, pp. 2, 4, 8,
12, 14, 43, 47, 50, 52, 53, 55, 60, 62, 63, 67, 77, 78, 81, 82, 88,
97, 100, 112, 121, 135, 142, 147, 158, 165, 175, 197, 210, 219,
223, 227, 234, 238, 245, 251, 271, 279, 353, 355, 359, 361, 362,
373; National Gallery of Art, pp. 24, 28, 29, 30, 31, 33, 34, 35,
37, 38, 40, 42, 45, 46, 54; Metropolitan Museum of Art, pp. 26,
27, 41, 44, 48, 51.

Library of Congress Catalog Card Number: 86–61188
International Standard Book Number: 0–675–20711–8
Printed in the United States of America

5 6 7 8 9—91 90 89

To my extended family

my parents, **Gladys** and **Richard Hepworth**
            and **Anna** and **Henry Berger**
my sisters, **Cora, Marian,** and **Jo**
my aunt, **Cora**
my cousins, **Ethelynn** and **Marion**
my children, **Dick, Debra,** and **John**
and my husband, **Glen**

It was through my participation in an extended family that I became aware of the importance of support, nurturance, and love.

PREFACE

Since I wrote the preface to the first edition of *Parents as Partners in Education, schools* have become more committed to collaborating with parents. Federal reports emphasize that parental involvement with a child's education makes a great difference in the child's success. Do any two institutions have more to gain from working together to help children become productive adults than the family and the school? They need the help and support of one another.

This text was written to help school personnnel and parents work together more effectively. It is meant to be a "hands-on" approach to bringing about a real partnership between the professional in the field and the parent at home. It includes strategies that will help teachers, paraprofessional caregivers for children, community workers in children's services, and professionals who implement programs of parent involvement.

As a parent educator and sociologist, I have observed the increase in parent involvement programs. Head Start, Follow Through, and Home Start, first established in the 1960s and 1970s, recognized the need for parent involvement and initiated parent advisory councils. Parents, the primary caregivers and teachers of children, are partners with professionals whether or not they are accepted as such by the school system. It is the schools' responsibility to develop or to strengthen a positive relationship with parents to ensure the continuity and developmental environment that children need.

Chapter One, The Need for Parent Involvement, establishes the rationale behind the current concern for parent education. Research shows that parent involvement is essential for optimum development of children. The fast pace of society, the change in the extended family, and economic reality have forced change in family patterns and have increased the need for support systems.

Chapter Two, Historical Overview of Family Life and Parent Involvement, summarizes the history and trends of parent education. Parent involvement is not new; parents have always been prime educators of their children. But through the years parents as partners in education have changed the emphasis of their involvement. Since the 1960s increased concern for matching school and home has resulted in parent participation in schools, home visitation programs, health and education service programs, child care training programs for mothers, diagnostic and prescriptive centers, parent resource centers, and many other programs designed to fit particular needs.

Chapter Three, The Parent Community, describes families in the United States today. The 15 traits of a healthy family as described by Curran are listed. Many more women are now working outside the home and the number of single parents has increased. This chapter discusses why it is difficult for some families to achieve the success they desire within their family. Poverty and out-of-wedlock teen-age mothers are discussed. Cultural diversity, with a focus on African-Americans, Hispanics, and the Indochinese, completes the chapter.

Chapters Four, Five, and Six answer quesions concerning parent involvement in schools and child care centers. Chapter Four, Effective Home-School-Community Relationships, covers activities to improve parent-teacher rapport, parent conferences, parents as partners in education, and parent resource centers in the schools. Chapter Five, Parent Education and Leadership Training, includes techniques used to organize and develop parent groups. Chapter Six, School-based Programs, describes effective programs for infants through young adults that originate in the school.

Working with parents in their homes is covered in Chapter Seven, Home-based Programs. With the home environment used as the educational base, the chapter discusses the means available to support the parent in their homes and for encouraging the use of materials found in the home to enrich the child's experiences.

There has been increased recognition of the needs of the handicapped child. Chapter Eight, Working with Parents of the Exceptional Child, was written by Jo Spidel, an educator who holds advanced degrees in special education, with the main emphasis on learning disabilities. The chapter includes mainstreaming, the development of the Individual Education Program, and the unique needs of handicapped children and their families.

One can read the daily newspaper and find in detail the problems of child abuse in the United States. Teachers and child care workers need to be able to recognize child abuse and to relate to the parents of the abused child. Knowledge of available resources or support systems that will help the family in dealing with its problems is essential. Chapter Nine, the Abused Child, includes data on abuse and recommends procedures for dealing with this problem.

Chapter Ten, Rights and Responsibilities, was co-authored with G. B. Berger, whose background includes vocational rehabilitation counseling, teaching, and law. It delves into the concerns of student and school rights and responsibilities.

Chapter Eleven, Resources for Home and School Programs, contains a bibliography of resources, films, books, pamphlets, and materials for use by the parent, paraprofessional, or professional. A reader of this book can combine the ideas in Chapers Five and Eleven to develop programs and workshops that meet the needs of parents and their children, from infancy through young adulthood. The resources are designed to enable students, teachers, parent educators, administrators, or parents develop comprehensive and varied home-school programs. These resources, along with the theory and material in the remainder of the book, will be useful for active professionals as well as students preparing to be educators.

I would like to thank all those who willingly allowed me to use their works. They were cooperative and gracious, and their encouragement helped me to continue. Professional friends, Virginia Plunkett, Willow Brzeinski, Gwen Hurd, Elmer Choury, and my colleagues at Metropolitan State College counseled and shared with me. I am indebted to my MSC students who have been wonderful in their suggestions, discussions, and responses to my class presentations.

Unless credited to a museum, the photographs were taken by Debra Berger McClave, Elena Machina Berger, John Berger, or me. Even the best photographer could not get such winning smiles without charming subjects. Most of the children photographed attended the Metropolitan State College Child Development Center or the Auraria Child Care Center. We are very appreciative of the staff at both centers for the cooperation and help they gave us. Our thanks goes to Walter Hazelbaker for the care he took in processing the prints.

I wish to thank the editors at Merrill Publishing Company, who supported and guided me in the production of this second edition, Phyllis Crandall, who answered my various questions, and those who offered critiques and suggestions. My friend Martha Piper Aune, a fellow educator, gave me invaluable support through suggestions, criticisms, and editing in the first edition.

My family was an essential ingredient in the entire project. My three children, Dick, Debra, and John were responsible for my entrance into the field of parent education. My husband, Glen, supported me throughout the endeavor of revising this book. My parents, who were my first educators, set an unexcelled example of supportive child rearing.

Eugenia Hepworth Berger

CONTENTS

Contents

8 Working With Parents of the Exceptional Child 279

Jo Spidel

Development of Special Education 280 / Legislation for the
Handicapped 282 / Development of the IEP 284 / Who is the
Exceptional Student? 292 / Rights and Services Available to
Parents 294 / Parent Involvement in Education 295 / Maslow's
Hierarchy of Needs 298 / Special Problems of Parents of Exceptional
Children 299 / Parental Reactions 300 / Reaching the Parent of the
Young Exceptional Child 301 / Exceptional Children in Head
Start 302 / Technical Assistance for Parent Programs 302 / Child Find
Project 302 / Advocacy in Special Education 303 / Involving Parents of
Very Young Handicapped Children 303 / Normal Activities for
Preschoolers 303 / Play Is Important 304 / A Shared Concern 304 /
Burnout 305 / Communicating With Parents of Exceptional
Children 305 / How Parents Can Help at Home 307 / Charting 308 /
Rules of Learning 308 / A Few Things to Remember 309 / How Parents
Can Tutor at Home 309 / What the Parent Expects of the
Professional 310 / Learning Is Hard 310 / Keepers of the Flame 310 /
Summary 311

9 The Abused Child 314

Background 315 / Abuse and Neglect 317 / Identification of Physical
Abuse 319 / Identification of Sexual Abuse 319 / Talking with
Families 321 / Development of Policies 321 / Breaking the Abusive
Cycle 324 / What Precipitates Child Abuse? 324 / Who Are the Abused
and the Abusers? 325 / Who Reports the Maltreatment Cases? 328 /
Behaviorial and Attitudinal Traits of Parents and Children That May Indicate
Child Abuse 328 / Training 333 / How to Talk With Children and
Parents 334 / Support Systems for the Child, Parents, and
Professional 338 / Preventing Abuse 338 / Response by Schools and
Child Care Centers 339 / United Nations Declaration of the Rights of the
Child 340 / Summary 341 / Appendix 345

10 Rights and Responsibilities 353

G. R. Berger, co-author

Origin of Parents' and Children's Rights 353 / Parent's Right to Select
Their Child's Education 354 / Student Records—Open Record
Policy 355 / Rights and Responsibilities of Students 357 / Developing
Criteria Together 360 / A Sleeping Giant: The Child Advocate 362 / An
Example of Advocacy and Collaboration 363 / Summary 369 /
Appendix 372

Parents as Partners
in Education

CHAPTER ONE

The Need for Parent Involvement

If we want to educate a person in virtue we must polish him at a tender age. And if someone is to advance toward wisdom he must be opened up for it in the first years of his life when his industriousness is burning, his mind is malleable, and his memory is strong. (Comenius, *The Great Didactic*)

What works to educate children? "Parents are their children's first and most influential teachers. What parents do to help their children learn is more important to academic success than how well-off the family is" (U.S. Department of Education, 1986, p. 7). *What works: Research about teaching and learning,* a synthesis of research findings, published by the U.S. Department of Education, emphasized the importance of parents' involvement in their child's education. "Parental involvement helps children learn more effectively" (U.S. Department of Education, 1986, p. 19).

These findings reinforce the challenge made to parents by the National Commission on Excellence in Education. The report, *A nation at risk: The imperative for educational reform,* told parents:

. . . you bear a responsibility to participate actively in your child's education. You should encourage more diligent study and discourage satisfaction with mediocrity and the attitude that says "let it slide"; monitor your child's study; encourage good study habits; encourage your child to take more demanding rather than less demanding courses; nurture your child's curiosity, creativity, and confidence; and be an active participant in the work of the schools. (1983, p. 35)

It is almost impossible to overemphasize the significance of parenthood. Society would not survive if a culture stops either procreating or rearing its young. Infants cannot survive without being nurtured by someone who feeds them and gives them minimal care. The manner in which infants are nurtured varies within each subculture as well as across cultures. The well-being of the child is affected by both quality of care and the resiliency of the child. One child may thrive, while another may deteriorate in environments that seem identical. The child, the caregiver, and the environment intertwine in the child-rearing process, making every child's experiences unique. The essential bond between child and caregiver emphasizes the significance of the parents' role. Although other roles such as breadwinner, food-gatherer, or food-producer are necessary, they can be fulfilled in a variety of ways, depending upon the culture. In child-rearing, however, certain obligations and responsibilities transcend all groups of people.

Parents nurture their children's growth and development.

Every child must be fed, touched, and involved in communication, either verbal or nonverbal, to continue to grow and develop. Child-rearing, whether by natural parents or alternative caregivers, requires a nurturing environment. Perhaps the ease with which most men and women become parents diminishes the realization that parenthood is an essential responsibility. It has been assumed that parenthood is a natural condition and that becoming a parent or caregiver transforms the new mother or father into a nurturing parent. As a result, society has not demanded that parents have the prerequisite knowledge that would ensure competence in one of the most important occupations—child-rearing. Some basic understanding of child development on which to base parenting skills, allowing for individualization and cultural diversity, should be expected.

The ability to nurture does not automatically blossom when one gives birth to a child. It involves many diverse variables, ranging from parent-child attachment, previous modeling experiences, and environmental conditions that allow and encourage a positive parent-child relationship to support systems of family, friends, or professionals. Many new parents have not had the good fortune to learn from a role model, or they are faced with a difficult situation that makes the rearing of children an overwhelming burden rather than a joy. These parents need parenting information as well as a support system. With the birth of a child, the need for parenting skills has just begun.

CONTINUITY

Throughout childhood, many caregivers—teachers, child care workers, doctors, administrators—are involved with the child and family. They can provide a stable environment where each of society's institutions contributes to the child's growth in an integrated and continuous approach. *Continuity* is defined as a coherent whole or an uninterrupted succession of development. From a population that finds strength in its diversity, it would be impossible to produce a curriculum that assures perfect continuity for all, but it is possible to work toward support systems that foster the child's continuous development. The family and home as the primary support system, supplemented by schools, child care centers, and social agencies, could try to provide the necessary ingredients for a nurturing environment. This is much easier to state as a goal than to accomplish. Various behaviors and characteristics can be observed among children when they come to centers and schools. They may be happy, depressed, alert, lethargic, tall, short, self-actualized, dependent on direction, secure, outgoing, or reticent. They find a wide variety of teachers: creative, structured, open, closed, authoritarian, self-actualized, or discouraged. Families are just as varied—disorganized, stable, nuclear, extended, enriching, restrictive, verbal, nonverbal, or bilingual. All of these variables need to fit into the sequence of development. The aim for families and schools is not perfection, but adjustment to each other in a close, productive working unit. This is an enormous challenge to families, schools, and communities and is an issue that will need continued investigation. "Families and social institutions are part of the ecology which influences the development of children over time" (Grotberg, 1977, p. 419). Grotberg raised the following questions:

1. What is the role of the parents in assuring continuous development of their children?
2. What kinds, sequences, and lengths of interventions are needed to assure continuous development of children?
3. What institutional and family changes are needed to assure continuous development of children?
4. How are cultural differences preserved and cultural linkages promoted to assure continuous development of children?
5. What is the effect of early and/or periodic intervention programs on adolescent development? (pp. 418–419)

When parents are involved with the education of their children, continuity is possible. A study of parent involvement in four federal programs—Follow Through, Title I, Title VII Bilingual, and the Emergency School Aid Act—found that parent involvement does help:

- Children whose parents help them at home do better in school. Those whose parents participate in school activities are better behaved and more diligent in their efforts to learn.
- Teachers and principals who know parents by virtue of their participation in school activities treat those parents with greater respect. They also show more positive attitudes toward the children of involved parents.
- Administrators find out about parents' concerns and are thus in a position to respond to their needs.
- Parental involvement allows parents to influence and make a contribution to what may be one of their most time-consuming and absorbing tasks—the education of their children. (Lyons, Robbins, & Smith, 1983, p. xix)

This book focuses on the roles of parents and schools or centers in the continuing development of children. Research cited later in this chapter indicates that the home has an enormous impact on the developing child and that a partnership between home and school is supportive of the developing child. Although all of the evidence is not yet gathered, the concept is supported by enough data to encourage educators to include parents as partners in the educational process. This dictates that parents be active participants—real partners—in the process. It also requires that teachers know what children do at home and which special interests and talents they have. It requires that they teach with a knowledge of what went before and what is to follow, but without the limitations of discrete levels and curriculum restrictions. It focuses on a common effort by the school, home, and community to provide for the student's growth through integrated successive learning experiences that allow for variation in skills, cognitive development, creative abilities, and physical development.

PARENT PROGRAMS

From infancy to young adulthood, varying needs require different types of programs. Brief descriptions of programs related to age levels are discussed to provide the reader with an overview of current parent involvement. Following these descriptions is the rationale for parent involvement and the research that supports it.

Infancy

If continuity is to be achieved, the teamwork of parents, schools, and the community begins before the child is born. Prenatal and postnatal care of the mother and subsequent early stimulation and initial bonding of the infant require the cooperative effort of medical care systems and families. The need for parent

Parents of infants need programs that illustrate the stages of development and emphasize the importance of human contact and relationships.

education during the child's infancy may be critical if the new family does not have an extended family that is knowledgeable about child development and child care. Even with a support system within the extended family, new developments in the field of infant stimulation and care are able to enrich traditional child care. Infant programs include the following:

1. Parent education and infancy (Infant-toddler Programs, Chapter 6; Reaching the Parent of the Young Child, Chapter 8; and New Parents as Teachers Project, Chapter 7)
2. Home visitations (Chapter 7)
3. Comprehensive health-education institutions (Brookline Early Education Project, Chapter 6)

Preschool

A second period calling for effective parent education and involvement is when the child is toddler through preschool age. During these years, parent education and preschool programs meet the educational needs of and lend emotional and social support to the family of a young child. Center-based programs have been joined by home visitation. Typical preschool programs for parents include:

1. Parent education and preschool (See Chapters 5, 6, and 10 for information on parent education and preschool programs.)
2. Head Start (Chapter 6)
3. Home visitations (Chapter 7)

Primary and Intermediate Grades

While the child is in elementary school, a wide variety of activities is available. Parents are involved as tutors, teaching assistants, policymakers, and partners with the school. The following programs represent opportunities for parent involvement:

1. School participation (Chapters 4 and 6)
2. Policy board (Chapters 7 and 10)
3. Partnership in educational planning (See Chapter 4 for closer school-home partnership. Chapter 8 gives details for developing an Individual Education Program [IEP].)
4. PTA/PTO (Chapter 4)

Secondary Schools

Historically parents have participated less in school activities during their child's junior-senior high years than they did during the elementary school years. In this period of tremendous social change, however, child development specialists and parents recognize that parent involvement may be more necessary than previously believed. Increasing numbers of teenage pregnancies mandate more child and family education. Peer pressure and easy availability encourage students to use drugs and alcohol. Many students have difficulty obtaining satisfying jobs. These pressures and problems set the stage for discontinuity in development. Lack of self-direction in and opportunity for the meaningful use of spare time set adolescents adrift. A unified effort by school, home, and community could develop appropriate programs both during and after school for young adults. Needed programs include:

1. Support groups (Chapter 4)
2. Curriculum in school (Chapter 6)
3. Education and support for young parents (Chapter 6)
4. Drug education (Chapter 10)

A full circle of support services has been developed, beginning with the family of an infant and continuing to the time when that infant becomes a new parent. Special programs have emerged in many areas of the country that speak to the infant, preschool, elementary, and secondary levels. These programs will be discussed in detail in later chapters.

RENEWED INTEREST IN PARENT INVOLVEMENT

Parent involvement in the education of children is not a new concept. Its history goes back many centuries, as the discussion in Chapter 2 will show. Interest in parents as partners in the education of their children has been rekindled by modern research.

Theories Concerning Intellectual Development

One of the first theorists to raise questions concerning the development of intelligence in children was J. McVicker Hunt. In his book, *Intelligence and Experience* (1961), he challenges the assumptions of fixed intelligence and predetermined development. The belief in fixed intelligence had far-reaching implications for education and child rearing. If IQ were fixed, intellectual growth could not be affected. The role of parents, therefore, had been to allow intellectual growth to unfold naturally toward its predetermined capacity. Hunt (1961) cites that, during the decades between 1915 and 1935, parents were even warned against playing with their small infant, lest overstimulation interfere with the child's growth. Hunt's belief that IQ is not fixed, led to a change in perception of the parental role from one of passive observation to one of facilitation.

Hunt's book focuses on the outcome the title implies—the effect of experience on the development of intelligence. In it he thoroughly reviews studies and research concerning the development of intelligence in children. He devotes a large portion of his book to the works of Jean Piaget, a genetic epistemologist who wrote a prodigious number of books and articles on knowledge and cognitive development. Piaget emphasizes that development involves the interaction of the child with his environment. Piaget's book, *To Understand Is to Invent* (1976), succinctly illustrates his basic concept of the importance of activity on the part of the learner—the need to act or operate upon the environment in the process of developing knowledge. It is through this process of interaction with the environment that the child develops intelligence. Piaget sees this as an adaptive process that includes assimilation of experiences and data into the child's understanding of the world; accommodation, by which the child's thought processes are adjusted to fit the new information into the schemes or models already constructed; and finally equilibrium that results from the adaptive process. This model of acquiring new knowledge was important to the cognitive theorists and had an impact on the educator's curriculum development because it emphasized the importance of experience to the developing child. A child without a rich environment was at a disadvantage.

Another aspect of Piagetian theory that reinforces his description of the developmental process of learning is his analysis of the developmental stages of the child's thought. Children, in the process of acquiring intellect, do not have the same concepts as adults. They relate to experience at their own levels of understanding. Hunt (1961) described these three major stages—sensorimotor, preconceptual, and formal—in this way:[1]

The first period of intellectual development, the sensorimotor, lasts from birth till the child is roughly between 18 months and 2 years old. The reflexive sensorimotor schemata are generalized, coordinated with each other, and differentiated to become the elementary operations of intelligence which begin to be internalized and which correspond to the problem-solving abilities of sub-human animals. During this period, the child creates through his continual adaptive accommodations and assimilations, in six stages, such operations as "intentions," "means-end" differentiations, and the interest in novelty (Piaget, 1936). On the side of constructing reality, the child also develops the beginnings of interiorized schemata, if not actual concepts, for such elements as the permanence of the object, space, casuality, and time (Piaget, 1937).

The second period of concrete operations in intellectual development, beginning when the child is about 18 months or 2 years old, lasts till he is 11 or 12 years old. It contains, first, a preconceptual phase during which symbols are constructed. This lasts to about 4 years of age, and during it the child's activity is dominated by symbolic play, which imitates and represents what he has seen others do,

and by the learning of language. The accommodations forced by the variation in the models imitated along with the assimilations resulting from repetitions of the play-activities gradually create a store of central processes which symbolize the actions imitated (Piaget, 1945). As the images are established, the child acquires verbal signs for those which correspond to the collective system of signs comprising language. At this point the child comes under dual interaction with the environment, i.e., with the world of things and the world of people. The child's action-images greatly extend the scope of his mental operation beyond the range of immediate action and momentary perception, and they also speed up his mental activity, for the sensorimotor action is limited by the concrete sequence of perceptions and actions. This period contains, second, an intuitive phase. This is a phase of transition that lasts till the child is 7 or 8 years old. In the course of his manipulations and social communications, he is extending, differentiating, and combining his action-images and simultaneously correcting his intuitive impressions of reality (space, causality, and time). It contains, third, the phase of concrete operations. As the child interacts repeatedly with things and people, his central processes become more and more autonomous. Piaget (1945, 1947) speaks of his thought becoming "decentred" from perception and action. With greater autonomy of central processes come both differentiations and coordinations, or groups, of the action-images into systems which permit classifying, ordering in series, numbering. . . . The acquisition of these "concrete operations," . . . bring a distinctive change in the child's concrete conceptions of quantity, space, causality, and time.

The third period of formal operations starts at about 11 and 12 years when the child begins to group or systematize his concrete operations (classifications, serial ordering, correspondences, etc.) and thereby also to consider all possible combinations in each case.

Piaget's theories clearly indicate that intellectual development is a *process* that commences in infancy and continues throughout childhood. The early years are important even though the development of intelligence in the young child differs from that of an older child. Hunt's book kindled interest in Piaget and in

---

1. From Hunt, J. M. *Intelligence and experience.* New York, 1961, pp. 113-115. Copyright © 1961, John Wiley & Sons, Inc. Reprinted by permission of John Wiley & Sons, Inc.

the importance of experience for young children during a time when their prime caregivers or teachers are the parents. Hunt (1960) stated:

It is no longer unreasonable to consider that it might be feasible to discover ways to govern the encounters that children have with their environments, especially during the early years of their development, to achieve a substantially faster rate of intellectual development and a substantially higher adult level of intellectual capacity. (p. 363)

The time was ripe for consideration of intervention and parent involvement. Equal educational opportunity was a high priority. The nation had been aroused by the U.S.S.R.'s launching of Sputnik in 1957. Many people wondered if children were learning as well as they should. There was concern that the United States was falling behind Russia in scientific discovery. It was hoped that an emphasis on early childhood education would help overcome learning and reading deficiencies. These considerations supported arguments for early intervention in education.

Benjamin Bloom's book, *Stability and Change in Human Characteristics,* added fuel to the fire and had great impact on establishing the importance of early childhood education. If early childhood is a prime time for children's learning and development, their caregivers have the opportunity to be their primary teachers. Bloom (1964) described the importance of the home:

It would seem to us that the home environment is very significant not only because of the large amount of educational growth which has already taken place before the child enters the first grade, but also because of the influence of the home during the elementary school period. (p. 110)

Bloom investigated many aspects of human development, including general intelligence, general achievement, specific aptitudes, reading comprehension, vocabulary, sociometric status, aggression, and dependence, as well as such physical aspects as height, weight, and strength. His statements about intellectual development in the very young attracted national attention. He and his colleagues analyzed many classic research studies. Based on information from Bayley's correlation data and/or Thorndike's absolute scale, Bloom (1964) made the following astounding observations on general intelligence:

It is possible to say, that in terms of intelligence measured at age 17, at least 20% is developed by age 1, 50% by age 4, 80% by about age 8 and 92% by age 13. Put in terms of intelligence measured by age 17, from conception to age 4, the individual develops 50% of his mature intelligence, from ages 4 to 8 he develops another 30%, and from ages 8 to 17 the remaining 20%. (p. 68)

With this in mind, he questioned the concept of absolute constant IQ and suggested that intelligence was a developmental trait similar to other characteristics such as height or strength. His figures suggest that the early years, particularly between the ages of 1 and 5, are very important in the development of intelligence. Again, he pointed out the impact of environment on the child's development.

In addition to general intelligence, Bloom (1964) also related general achievement or learning to age. Again, the early years are of the utmost importance. Between birth and age 6, 33 percent of the child's achievement at age 18 can be accounted for. Another 17 percent of growth, which takes place between the ages of 6 and 9, results in 50 percent of general achievement accomplished by age 9. Although the achievement pattern is not as extreme as with intelligence, both place the early years as a "crucial" time for children. Bloom suggested that the remaining 9 years of schooling are affected by what the child has gained by the end of third grade. His findings indicated that early extreme deprivation has a greater effect on children than deprivation in later years. During the first 4 years of life, environmental deficiency can stunt the development of intelligence approximately 2.5 IQ

Bloom's research suggests that this child, aged four, has developed about 50 percent of his intelligence (as measured at age 17).

points per year. During the years from 8 to 17, extreme environmental deprivation can depress average IQ growth by only 0.04 points a year. Bloom did not discount the importance of heredity in the development of intelligence; rather, he and his colleagues focused on change and stability in human characteristics and in so doing, recognized that some of the variations in IQ must be attributed to environment. Since parents have great control over their child's environment in the early years, they are an integral part of the educational system.

Studies Related to Schools and Families

The social climate of the nation during the 1960s mandated a concerted effort to provide equality of opportunity, as reflected in the Civil Rights Act of 1964. One result was a comprehensive national survey of 645,000 students in 4000 schools. These findings were revealed in *Equality of Educational Opportunity* by James S. Coleman et al. in 1966. Although the main thrust of the report was to investigate the effects of de facto and de jure segregation on educational achievement, the report had implications for educators who might effect early intervention. The researchers found that school curricula and expenditures on facilities and materials do not affect school achievement, but that the quality of teachers does. The students who achieved felt that they had some control over their own destiny. "Minority pupils, except for Orientals, have far less conviction than whites that they can affect their own environment and futures" (Coleman et al., 1966, p. 23). The most important single factor shown to affect achievement is family background. Important variables include the home's effective support of education, number of children in the family, and parents' educational levels.

Continued interest in explaining inequality in the United States and varying impact that family and schooling have on a child's later occupational and financial achievement led Jencks and his colleagues (1972) to study contributing factors to success. They studied inequality in schools, cognitive skills, educational attainment, occupational status, income, and job satisfaction. Some of the variables they analyzed included family background, socioeconomic background, effects of race, and school quality. They found that schools alone cannot affect the child; family background "explains nearly half of the variation of educational attainment" (Jencks et al., 1972, p. 143). Evidence from studies on educational institutions and data on the importance of early childhood on intellectual development together pointed to the importance of schools and parents becoming partners in the education of children.

Studies on Human Attachment

During the 1930s, questions about the importance of human attachment in the young child were raised. Harold Skeels, a member of the Iowa group of child researchers, studied the effect of environment on the development of children during a period when most researchers were studying maturation or behaviorism (e.g., Gesell and Watson). One of Skeels' studies, a natural history investigation, had startling findings. Skeels placed 13 infants and toddlers from an orphanage in an institution for the mentally retarded. Each subject fit the following criteria: (1) under 3 years of age, (2) ineligible for placement for legal reasons, (3) not acutely ill, and (4) mentally retarded. The 13 children, 10 girls and 3 boys, ranged in age from 7.1 to 35.9 months and had IQs from 36

to 89, with a mean IQ score of 64.3. Each child in the control group of 12, also chosen from children in the orphanage, fit these criteria: (1) had taken an IQ test when less than 2 years of age, (2) was still in the orphanage at age 4, (3) was in the control group of the orphanage preschool study, and (4) had not attended preschool. These children had IQs of 50 to 103, with a mean IQ of 86.7 points, and were 12 to 22 months old. The children placed in the wards for the feebleminded were showered with attention by the attendants and supervisors. They were cared for, played with, loved, and allowed to go along on excursions. Almost every child developed an attachment to one person who was particularly interested in the child and the child's achievements. The control group of children in the orphanage, however, received traditional care with no special treatment. When retested, after varying periods from 6 to 52 months, the children in the mental institution had gained 27.5 IQ points, but the ones left in the orphanage had lost an average of 26.2 IQ points.

Although the research could be criticized because variables were not controlled (there were more girls than boys placed in the wards) and changes in IQ can partially be explained by statistical regression, the results were so dramatic and unexpected that the impact of early environment had to be considered. Skeels (1966) followed up the subjects of this research and almost 20 years later found evidence to reinforce the initial findings. Of the 13 children who had been transferred to the mental institution, 11 had been adopted and reared as normal children. Twelve of the experimental group had become self-supporting adults, who achieved a median educational level of 12 years of schooling. Of the 12 who had been left in the orphanage, 4 were still in institutions; 1 was a gardener's assistant; 3 were employed as dishwashers; 1 was a floater; 1 was a part-time worker in a cafeteria, and 1 had died. Only 1 had achieved an educational level similar to that of the experimental group, and he had received different treatment from the others. He had been transferred from the orphanage to a school for the deaf, where he received special attention from his teacher. The children who had been placed in the mental institution and later adopted received personal love and developed human attachments; they had achieved a typical life-style, while those left in the orphanage had only a marginal existence. Evidence strongly supports the importance of a nurturing early environment and also indicates that poor initial environment can be reversed by enriched personal interaction (Skeels, 1966).

René Spitz, a physician, also became involved in the observation of infants during the 1930s. In his book, *The First Year of Life,* published in 1965, he described his research and observations of the psychology of infants. He studied babies in seven situations, which included private families, foster homes, an obstetrics ward, an Indian village, a well-baby clinic, a nursery, and a foundling home. Both the nursery and foundling home were long-term institutions that guaranteed constancy of environment and dramatically illustrated the necessity of human attachment and interaction. Both institutions provided similar physical care of children, but they differed in their nurturing and interpersonal relationships. Both provided hygienic conditions, well-prepared food, and medical care. The foundling home had regular daily visits by a medical staff, while the nursery called a doctor when needed. The nursery was connected to a penal institution where delinquent girls, pregnant on admission, were sent to serve their sentences. Babies born to them were cared for in the nursery until the end of their first year. The mothers were primarily delinquent, psychopathic, feebleminded, or socially maladjusted minors. In contrast, some of the children in the foundling home came from well-adjusted mothers who were unable to support their children; others were children of unwed mothers whose children were admitted on the condition that they come to the home and

nurse their own and one other child during the first 3 months.

Spitz filmed a representative group of the children he studied in both institutions. In the nursery, he studied 203 children, and in the foundling home, 91. The major difference in the care of the two sets of children was the amount of nurturing and social interaction. The nursery, which housed 40 to 60 children at a time, allowed the mothers or mother-substitutes to feed, nurse, and care for their babies. The infants had at least one toy; they were able to see outside their cribs and to watch the activities of other children and mothers caring for their babies. These babies thrived. In the foundling home, however, the babies were screened from outside activity by blankets hung over the sides and ends of their cribs, thus isolating them from any visual stimulation. They had no toys to play with, and the caretakers were busy tending to other duties rather than mothering the children. During the first 3 months, while the babies were breast fed, they appeared normal. After separation, they soon went through progressive deterioration. Of the 91 foundling home children, 34 died by the end of the second year. Spitz (1965) continued to follow up 21 of the children who remained in the foundling home until they were 4 years of age. He found that 20 could not dress themselves; 6 were not toilet trained; 6 could not talk; 5 had a vocabulary of two words; 8 had vocabularies of three to five words; and only 1 was able to speak in sentences. Spitz attributed the cause of the deterioration of the infants to lack of mothering. The children in the nursery had mothering, while those in the foundling home did not:

Absence of mothering equals emotional starvation . . . this leads to progressive deterioration engulfing the child's whole person. Such deterioration is manifested first in an arrest of the child's psychological development; then psychological dysfunctions set in, paralleled by somatic changes. In the next stage this leads to increased infection liability and eventually, when the emotional deprivation continues into the second year of life, to a spectacularly increased rate of mortality. (p. 281)

In 1951 John Bowlby reviewed the literature on studies of deprivation and its effect on personality development. He then made a systematic review for the World Health Organization in which he described those works that supported theories on the negative aspects of maternal deprivation. The research was classified into three categories: (1) direct observation studies, which included works by Goldfarb, Spitz, and Wolf; Roudinesco and Appell; Burlingham and Freud, and others; (2) retrospective studies by Bender, Goldfarb, Levy, Bowlby, and others; and (3) follow-up studies of Goldfarb, Lowrey, and others. In his monograph Bowlby (1966) stated:

It is submitted that the evidence is now such that it leaves no room for doubt regarding the general proposition that the prolonged deprivation of the young child of maternal care may have grave and far-reaching effects on his character and so on the whole of his future life. (p. 46)

Bowlby (1966) emphasized that the greatest effect on personality development is during the child's early years. The earliest critical period is during the first 5 or 6 months while mother-figure and infant are forming an attachment. The second vital phase lasts until near the child's third birthday, during which time the mother-figure needs to be virtually an ever-present companion. During a third phase, the child is able to maintain his attachment even though the nurturing parent is absent. During the fourth to fifth year, this tolerable absence might extend from a few days to a few weeks; during the seventh to eighth years, the separation could be lengthened to a year or more. Deprivation in the third phase does not have the same destructive effect on the child as it does in the period from infancy through the third year.

The 1951 monograph by Bowlby was republished in 1966. Articles by Prugh and Harlow, Andry, Mead, Wooton, Lebovici, and Ainsworth clarify, re-evaluate, elaborate upon, and reassess the significance of maternal deprivation. Those articles and later publications, such as Rutter's *Maternal Deprivation Reassessed* (1972) and Bower's *Development in Infancy* (1982), questioned whether the severe warnings by Bowlby were justified. There were criticisms that the term maternal deprivation was too restrictive to cover a wide range of abuses and variables. Questions regarding the irreversibility of deprivation were raised. It was suggested that maternal deprivation was too limited a concept—that human attachment and multiple attachment should be considered and that warmth as well as love be regarded as a vital element in relationships (Rutter, 1972). Some of the criticisms were an outcome of misinterpretation of Bowlby's original thesis, but others resulted from the complexities of studying and understanding human relationships. In spite of these differences among specialists and theorists, none of them doubted the importance of nurturance in the early years. The questioning did not discredit the importance of human attachment. It indicated the need for more specific research and the identification of basic variables involved in the effect of the environment on infant development (Rutter, 1972; Yarrow et al., 1975).

Obstetricians and pediatricians continued the investigation of parent-child relationships and the attachment of infant and parents. Klaus and Kennell (1976), who worked extensively with parents and premature infants, defined attachment as a "unique relationship between two people that is specific and endures through time" (p. 2). They believe that there is a "sensitive period in the first minutes and hours after an infant's birth which is optimal for parent-infant attachment" (Klaus & Kennell, 1976, p. 66). Brazelton also emphasized the attachment between parent and child and

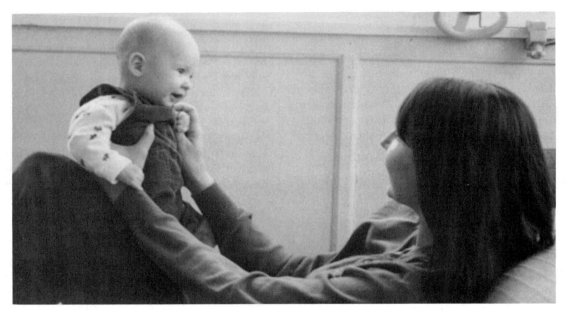

Eye to eye contact helps develop human attachment, a necessary component for the healthy development of young children.

noted the tremendous effect the mother and child have on one another. All three physicians stressed eye-to-eye contact of the mother with the newborn. "Eye-to-eye contact serves the purpose of giving a real identity or personification to the baby, as well as getting a rewarding feedback for the mother" (Brazelton in Klaus & Kennell, 1976, p. 70).

Although there are questions of how critical and absolute early bonding is for infant and parent (Bower, 1982; Rutter, 1972), the recognition of the benefits of human attachment has great consequences for those involved in child rearing, including professional parent educators, teachers, and parents. In *Working and Caring* Brazelton (1985) describes four stages vital to the parent-infant attachment process that lasts from birth to four months. In the 1973 *Review of Child Development Research,* Ainsworth called for "a new kind of child development counselor," who would help promote infant-mother figure attachment as a necessary prerequisite for healthy social development in the young. After

surveying theoretic literature and research on attachment, Ainsworth drew 11 inferences concerning attachment. She recognized that parent-child attachment is necessary for the development of a healthy personality and that this attachment may occur beyond the early "sensitive period." She noted that no system for development of attachment has replaced the family-type environment. A prolonged separation of parent and child is stressful for a child, with the period from 6 months to 3 years being the most tenuous. Attachments may be formed with more than one parent figure. Parents who foster attachment do not spoil the child; instead, it is very desirable to be responsive and sensitive to the "infant's signals." A good infant-mother attachment tends to result in a more secure child.

These implications for child rearing illustrate a challenge for parent educators. New parents should be encouraged to become actively involved with and responsive to their infants. To achieve these goals, child development and family life courses that include information on attachment and bonding should be offered in all high school curricula. Continuing or adult education classes should offer child-rearing classes for parents who are no longer in school. Innumerable channels exist for disseminating information to a wide audience through health services, schools, television, or social agencies.

Educational Intervention Programs

Various reports shattered the idea that intelligence was fixed and that the home environment had nothing to do with a child's intellectual success (Skeels, 1966; Spitz, 1965; Hunt, 1961; Coleman et al., 1966). These reports along with the national mood of the mid-1960s, supporting equal rights and opportunity, propelled the country to respond to the needs of the poor and disadvantaged. One of the most effective responses was to provide educational intervention for the children of the poor.

These experimental programs emphasized the value of an enriched environment for the child and were designed to show the impact that the environment has on the intellectual development of young children. Very high hopes for the changing of intelligence existed. Could a very short program change children's lives? Whereas the research on attachment was based primarily on ethological studies and psychoanalytic examination of the influences on the child's emotional growth, the research on educational intervention programs initially focused on cognitive development of children. It was thought that intervention in the normal programs of economically disadvantaged young children would help them become equal. Therefore, a program for these children had to be instituted. Likewise, since the environment was recognized as important, programs were designed to include the parents.

The projects would have a two-pronged approach. The child would benefit from an enriched early education program, and the parents would be included as an integral part of the programs as aides, advisory

council members, or paraprofessional members of the team. In the summer of 1965, as part of the War on Poverty, the first Head Start centers were opened. Head Start was a comprehensive program of health, nutrition, and education as well as a career ladder for economically disadvantaged families. Rather than wait for results of the long-range effects of early intervention, numerous Head Start programs, funded by the federal government and developed at the local level, sprang up over the nation. The question of whether these programs would result in sustained intellectual development could not be answered at that time.

Researchers in the 1960s demonstrated startling gains in IQ in children enrolled in their programs (Caldwell, 1968; Deutsch & Deutsch, 1968; Gray & Klaus, 1965; Weikart & Lambie, 1968). Those looking for sustained intellectual gains, however, were disappointed with the results of one of the first studies, the so-called Westinghouse Report/Ohio State University Study, that indicated no sustained intellectual development (see Lazar et al., 1977; Consortium for Longitudinal Studies, 1983). From the beginning, early childhood researchers criticized the Westinghouse Report (Campbell & Backer, 1970; White, 1970). Other studies that followed, based on federally funded programs and analyzed by other early childhood researchers, had optimistic findings. It was not until the Consortium for Longitudinal Studies was formed in 1975, however, that researchers united to determine if indeed there were gains from educational intervention. But gains were not to be determined solely by improvement in IQ scores; reduction in special education placements and drop-out rates, health improvement, and families' ability to cope were also indicators of success.

The Consortium for Longitudinal Studies set out to determine the effect that experimental early intervention programs of the 1960s had on the children in their programs. The task was challenging. All the researchers, both those connected to Head Start programs and those who worked on individual early childhood projects, had assessment designs in their projects. However, each program was developed independently of the others, so the task of analyzing the data was tremendous. The programs differed according to the children's ages, the curriculum involved, the duration of the program, and the amount of parent involvement. The Consortium selected a total of 11 research groups for analysis. Principal investigators included Beller, Deutsch and Deutsch, Gordon and Jester, Gray, Karnes, Levenstein, Miller, Palmer, Weikart, Woolman, and Zigler (see Table 1-1.) Each researcher agreed to send raw data to an independent analytic group in Ithaca, New York, to be recorded and analyzed. Although the programs differed, they were all well-designed and monitored, so there was an excellent data base.

The Consortium's findings were positive; early childhood intervention affected five areas (The Consortium for Longitudinal Studies, 1983):

1. Ability in early to middle childhood
   a. Improved scores on Stanford-Binet Intelligence Test
   b. Improved scores on achievement tests
2. Greater school competency in the middle to adolescent years
   a. Special education placement reduced
   b. Less grade retention
3. Improved attitude toward achievement in adolescence
   a. Pride in activity
   b. Mother/child occupational aspiration
   c. Self-evaluation of school performance
4. Educational attainment
   a. High school completion related to competence at grade 9
   b. High school completion/educational expectations
5. Occupational attainment
   a. Employment/school competence
   b. Occupational aspiration

The data imply that five characteristics are important for successful intervention

Early childhood education programs allow children to meet and play with other children and gain self-esteem.

programs (Royce, Darlington, & Murray, 1983, p. 442). Three of the items relate to parent involvement.

1. Begin intervention as early as possible.
2. Provide services to the parents as well as to the child.
3. Provide frequent home visits.
4. Involve parents in the instruction of the child.
5. Have as few children per teacher as possible.

In a discussion of the Consortium's findings, Lazar summarized two important points. First, a good preschool program pays off in two ways: benefits for children's development and financial savings as a result of less special education placement. Secondly, "closer contact between home and school and greater involvement of parents in the education of their children are probably more important"

TABLE 1-1
Characteristics of early education programs and ages of subjects for each data set

Principal[1] investigator	Project name and location	Delivery system	Birth year	Age at entry	Program length	Years of program
Beller[2]	Philadelphia Project, Philadelphia	Center	1959	4 yrs	1 yr	1963–64
Deutsch	Institute for Developmental Studies, New York	Center	1958–66	4 yrs	5 yrs	1963–71 (8 waves)
Gordon/Jester	Parent Education Program, North Central Florida	Home	1966–67	3–24 mos	1–3 yrs	1966–70 (3 waves)
Gray	Early Training Project, Tennessee	Center/home	1958	3.8 or 4.8 yrs	14 or 26 mos	1962–65
Karnes	Curriculum Comparison Study, Champaign-Urbana, Ill.	Center	1961–63	4 yrs	1–2 yrs	1965–67 (2 waves)
Levenstein	Mother-Child Home Program, Long Island, N.Y.	Home	1964–68	2 or 3 yrs	1–2 yrs	1967–72 (5 waves)
Miller	Experimental Variation of Head Start Curricula, Louisville, Ky.	Center and center/home	1964	4 yrs	1 yr	1968–69
Palmer	Harlem Training Project, New York	Center	1964	2 or 3 yrs	1 or 2 yrs	1966–68
Weikart	Perry Preschool Project, Ypsilanti, Mich.	Center/home	1958–62	3 or 4 yrs	1 or 2 yrs	1962–67 (5 waves)
Woolman	Micro-social Learning System, Vineland, N.J.	Center	1966–68	4–5 yrs	1–4 yrs	1969–73
Zigler	New Haven Follow-Through Study, New Haven, Conn.	Center	1962–64	5 yrs	4 yrs	1967–71 (2 waves)

1. Many researchers have developed projects for early childhood education. Some have been home-based, some center-based, and some a combination of home- and center-based.
2. Beller used a different designation of program group from the one shown here. In his own study, this group received 2 years of preschool while his second group received 1 year of preschool (i.e., kindergarten).
Source: From I. Lazar, R. Darlington, H. Murray, J. Royce, & A. Snipper, Lasting effects of early education: A report from the Consortium for Longitudinal Studies. *Monographs of the Society for Research in Child Development, 47* (2–3). Chicago: The University of Chicago Press, 1982.

than generally realized by administrators (Lazar, 1983, p. 464).

The research findings have been substantiated (see Gray, Ramsey, & Klaus, 1982; Lazar & Darlington, 1982; Spodek, 1982; Consortium for Longitudinal Studies, 1983).

More data followed the Consortium report. A follow-up study on Weikart's Perry Preschool Program vividly illustrated the impact that early educational intervention can have on children's lives (Berrueta-Clement et al., 1984). The Perry Preschool Program continued to follow the children to age 19, four years beyond the report published by the Consortium. Berrueta-Clement et al. compared children who had attended the Perry Preschool with children who did not. The researchers found that former Perry Preschool students grew up with more positive school success, placed a higher value on school, had higher aspirations for college, had fewer absences, and spent fewer of their school years in special education than the children in the control group. But though Weikart's program had a strong parent involvement component, the contributions of parents to the program's success were not analyzed because the researchers were unable to separate parent involvement from the preschool effect. In fact, however, the influence of caregivers, whether teachers or parents, cannot be separated from the well-being of the child and the success of a program.

HOME-BASED COMPARED TO CENTER-BASED PROGRAMS

Bronfenbrenner (1976) examined two types of early intervention programs: the typical center-based intervention program, and home visitation programs where paraprofessionals or professionals worked with parents and child as either a complement to a center or as a separate program. Upon analysis, seven center programs satisfied the research criteria. These included Howard University Preschool Program, Elizabeth Herzog; Ypsilanti Perry Preschool Project, David Weikart; Early Training Project, Susan W. Gray; Philadelphia Project, Temple University, Kuno Beller; Indiana Project, Walter L. Hodges; Infant Education Research Project, Earl Schaefer; and Verbal Interaction Project, Phyllis Levenstein. After examining these programs, Bronfenbrenner came to the conclusion that although there were considerable gains in IQ during the first year of operation, these gains "washed out" after the child left the program. He insisted that this evidence should not be interpreted to mean that the programs were not beneficial to the child, family, and community because many of the goals of the program had a wider focus than intelligence quotient scores.

Of significance to the supporters of parent involvement were the data on home-based programs. "In contrast to group intervention projects, the experimental groups in these home-based programs not only improve on their initial gains but hold up rather well 3 to 4 years after intervention has been discontinued" (Bronfenbrenner, 1976, p. 21). Bronfenbrenner drew not only from Schaefer's Infant Education Research Project, Levenstein's Verbal Interaction Project, Gray's Early Training Project, and Weikart's Ypsilanti Perry Preschool Project, whose center programs had a home-based complement, but also examined Karnes' Experimental Programs for Disadvantaged Mothers and Ira Gordon's Florida Project. Citing from these studies, Bronfenbrenner made the following generalizations: the effects of intervention were cumulative, the younger the child at entrance (aged 1 or 2, as opposed to 3 or 4), the greater the gain, and intervention helped not only the child registered in the program, but also his younger siblings. These benefits hinged upon inclusion beyond the child, since "the involvement of the child's family as an active participant is critical to the success of any intervention program" (pp. 52-55).

EVIDENCE FOR
PARENT INVOLVEMENT

In a review of cross-sectional and longitudinal research on intervention (including the work of Karnes, Teska, Hodgins, and Badger, 1970; Klaus and Gray, 1968; Levenstein, 1970; and others), Schaefer (1972) concluded that the

accumulating evidence suggests that parents have great influence upon the behavior of their children, particularly their intellectual and academic achievement, and that programs which teach parents skills in educating are effective supplements or alternatives for preschool education. (p. 238)

Schaefer continued to research the collaboration between families and institutions. In 1983 he emphasized the use of an ecological systems approach to child care. Professionals, community, and parents have shared and reciprocal roles. He found that professionals need to know how to support and work with parents. Few elementary school teachers have training and orientation to help them collaborate with parents in their child's education.

Studies conducted in the 1970s consistently demonstrated the importance of an enriched early home environment to the child's school success (Hanson, 1975; Shipman et al., 1976; White et al., 1973). In Shipman's (1976) study of black, low socioeconomic status children, the mother's educational aspirations and expectations were higher for children in high reading groups than for those in low reading groups. A higher level of parental education was also associated with academic success of children:

Thus, a higher level of parental education is associated with greater academic knowledge, increased awareness of public affairs and popular culture, more informed perceptions of school, and continued seeking of new knowledge as in reading books and magazines (cf. Hyman, Wright, and Reed, 1975), all of which may have impact on the child's knowledge and motivation for learning. (p. 34)

Others continued the concern for children in the 1980s. As mentioned previously, the *Nation at Risk* report challenged parents to be responsible for their children's education. The Association for Childhood Education International promoted the linkage among home, school, and community; "we believe that teachers and parents need to establish a stronger bond with one another" (Umansky, 1983, p. 263).

Closer contact between parents and teachers will give each a more complete picture of the child's abilities and improve consistency in working toward desired goals. Most important, perhaps, the child will identify both the school and the home as places to learn, and parents and teachers as sources of learning. (Umansky, p. 264)

The Frank Porter Graham Child Development Center (University of North Carolina at Chapel Hill) has reported on over 180 research reports concerning the understanding and prevention of retarded development. Among the major projects that the Center directed were the Carolina Abecedarian Project and Project CARE. The Carolina Abecedarian Project found that educational intervention of home/school teachers was effective. The home/school teacher filled the following roles: curriculum developer, teacher of parents on use of activities, tutor of children, provider of supplemental classroom materials, advocator for child and family, and provider of summer experiences and activities (Ramey, 1985, pp. 4–5). Another longitudinal study, Project CARE, taught problem-solving techniques to parents as one of their intervention approaches. The program aimed to help parents act more responsively to their children, to view the problem, and to be able to work on it (Wasik, 1983).

Research in the 1980s on parent involvement focuses on infancy through high school. The New Parents as Teachers Project, developed in Missouri, worked with parents beginning in the third trimester of pregnancy and continuing until the child's third birthday. Research results showed significant achievement in language and intelligence (White, 1985). Elementary schools joined in researching parent involvement. A study of 250 California elementary schools found parent involvement related to both parent satisfaction and student achievement (Herman and Yen, 1980). The "curriculum of the home" that includes parent/child discussions about everyday occurrences, monitoring and viewing television together, encouragement and discussion of reading, and emotional support and interest in the child's world led to greater academic achievement. In 29 controlled studies 91 percent of the children in the program benefitted when the learning environment at home improved. The control children were compared to children who did not participate in the program. The home environment affected the outcome twice as much as socioeconomic status (Walberg, 1984). The discussion of the "curriculum of the home" in *What Works,* emphasizes a similar environment in the home. It states:

Parents can do many things at home to help their children succeed in school. . . . They do this through their daily conversations, household routines, attention to school matters, and affectionate concern for their children's progress.

Conversation is important. Children learn to read, reason, and understand things better when their parents:

- read, talk, and listen to them,
- tell them stories, play games, share hobbies and
- discuss the news, TV programs, and special events.

In order to enrich the "curriculum of the home," some parents:

- provide books, supplies, and a special place for studying,
- observe routine for meals, bedtime, and homework, and

- monitor the amount of time spent watching TV and doing after-school jobs.

Parents stay aware of their children's lives at school when they:

- discuss school events,
- help children meet deadlines, and
- talk with their children about school problems and successes.

Research on both gifted and disadvantaged children shows that home efforts can greatly improve student achievement. For example, when parents of disadvantaged children take the steps listed above, their children can do as well at school as the children of more affluent families. (U.S. Department of Education, 1986, p. 7)

DEVELOPMENT OF READING

One of the most promising directions of parent partnership with schools involves the ability to read. *What Works* reports that "the best way for parents to help their children become better readers is to read to them—even when they are very young. Children benefit most from reading aloud when they discuss stories, learn to identify letters and words, and talk about the meaning of words" (U.S. Department of Education, 1986, p. 9).

The report stresses that there are many ways parents can encourage reading, but reading to them and relating stories to everyday events are most significant. Just talking together and having conversations while reading is as important as the reading itself. When parents don't discuss the story or ask questions that require thinking, the children do not achieve as well in reading as children of parents who do involve the child.

Other studies concerned with reading ability support the importance of parents reading to and with their children. Investigations of the importance of parent encouragement of and interest in their children's reading have found that the children who achieve well in reading have parents who actively guide and help their children develop reading ability. Their homes contain available reading material and parents use encouragement rather than punishment. Parents also assist their children in setting realistic goals, elicit questions about their reading, and spend time with their children (Silvern, 1985).

BENEFITS FOR PARENTS AND CHILDREN

Meier (1978) reported on benefits of parent participation for both parents and children. Parents who participated in an early education program gained a sensitivity to their child's emotional, social, intellectual development and needs; greater acceptance of their children; the ability to respect individual differences; a greater enjoyment of their children; an ability to sense and reduce their children's distress; more affection; use of more elaborate language patterns; more communication through reasoning and encouragement rather than through authority; development of parental educational goals; and effective use of community agencies. Children were (1) more aware and responsive, (2) equipped with better skills for problem solving, (3) able to vocalize in early years and develop more complex language skills in second and third years, (4) more successful in both short-term and long-term intellectual development, and (5) stronger socially and emotionally with improved attachment to parents; there was also increased and richer interaction with the mother and, later, others.

WORKING WITH PARENTS

Including parents as partners in the educational process involves many dimensions. The resolution of social problems will not be accomplished solely by instituting a parent program, but even in the most difficult cases, a response to the problems and issues is better than ignoring the situation. Consider the suggestions and curricula in the following chapters as a guide to working with parents, be they parents who need an opportunity to use their talents or those who need support. Parent involvement is not new, but the need continues. Parent education and involvement are not a panacea for all the ills of society, but they comprise one component in the system that works to ameliorate those problems. Join in the exploration of parents as partners in the educational process. Expand and adapt the ideas presented in this book, and develop an individual way of working with parents.

SUMMARY

Parenthood is an essential role in society. The support given by parents, interrelated with other agencies—particularly the school—should be integrated and continuous. Parent programs that respond to parent needs range from infancy, preschool, and primary and intermediate grades to secondary and young adult programs.

The renewed interest in parent involvement, which manifested itself with concern over the child's intellectual development, was reinforced by the writings of Hunt, Bloom, and Coleman. The time was ripe for consideration of intervention and parent involvement. Concurrently, the concern for equal opportunities resulted in the initiation of Head Start, Follow Through, and Chapter I programs.

Studies on human attachment (Skeels, Spitz, Bowlby, Ainsworth, and others) emphasized the significance of a parent figure, nurturing and warm. Many intervention programs included parent involvement as an integral part of the process.

Research on the intervention results of Head Start home visitation and parent involvement programs showed that parents were an important component in a child's development. Researchers emphasized the value of an enriched environment for the child and the importance of parents as part of that environment. Positive changes in parent behavior not only resulted in improved conditions for the child during the program but also continued after its completion. In addition, parenting skills helped subsequent children in the family.

In studies involving children at all levels, from infancy through high school, parent involvement made a difference. Reading specialists stressed the importance of parents reading to and with their children, encouraging, eliciting questions, and setting realistic goals for their child's learning.

SUGGESTIONS FOR CLASS ACTIVITIES AND DISCUSSIONS

1. Survey a preschool, elementary school, or junior high or high school in your area and find out how each involves parents.
2. Invite a social worker to discuss the problems involved in foster home and institutional placements.
3. Discuss Bloom's findings. What is the difference between intellectual potential and achievement?
4. Give Piagetian-type tests to children age 3 months to 9 years.
5. Discuss the importance of Hunt's book, *Intelligence and Experience*. How has it helped change the belief in fixed IQ?
6. Visit an infant center or nursery. Observe children actively involved in their environment. Are some more actively involved in their environment than others?
7. Visit a Head Start center. How are parents involved in the program?
8. Keep a log of brief encounters where you observe parents and children, infancy through young adulthood. Which kinds of interactions did you find at the grocery store, in the park, at the zoo, in the department store, or at home? Which interactions were most positive?
9. Can you defend the importance of parents as teachers of their own children and parents as partners with the school?
10. Look into the research on attachment. How are both parents important to the infant?
11. Which research points to involving parents in the education of their children?
12. Investigate types of parent responses that facilitate their child's intellectual and emotional growth. Discuss them.
13. Explain why educators work with the whole child (emotional, social, physical, and intellec-

tual) rather than separating intellectual and other domains.
14. Discuss the ways parents who participated in early education programs gained from the experience.
15. Visit a parent cooperative. Talk with some parents about their responsibilities for the preschool program. Interview the director and discuss the roles parents play in the total program.

BIBLIOGRAPHY

Ainsworth, M. D. The development of infant-mother attachments. In B. M. Caldwell and H. N. Ricciuti (Eds.), *Review of child development research.* Chicago: University of Chicago Press, 1973.

Ainsworth, M. D., Andrv, R. G., Harlow, R. G., Lebovici, S., Mead, M., Prugh, D. G., & Wootton, B. *Deprivation of maternal care.* New York: Schocken Books, 1966.

Berrueta-Clement, J. R., Schweinhart, L. J., Barnett, W. S., Epstein, A. S., & Weikart, D. P. *Changed lives: The effects of the Perry Preschool program on youths through age 19* (Monograph of the High/Scope Educational Research Foundation No. 8). Ypsilanti, Mich.: The High/Scope Press, 1984.

Bloom, B. *Stability and change in human characteristics.* New York: Wiley & Sons, 1964.

Bower, T. G. R. *Development in infancy* (2d ed.). San Francisco: W. H. Freeman, 1982.

Bowlby, J. *Maternal care and mental health.* New York: Schocken Books, 1966.

Brazelton, T. B. *Working and Caring.* Reading, Mass.: Addison-Wesley, 1985.

Bronfenbrenner, U. *Is early intervention effective? A report on longitudinal evaluations of preschool programs.* (U.S. Department of Health, Education, and Welfare, Office of Human Development, Office of Child Development). Washington, D.C.: U.S. Government Printing Office, 1976.

————. *Who needs parent education?* Paper presented at the Working Conference on Parent Education, Mott Foundation, Flint, Mich., Sept. 29 and 30, 1977.

Brown, B. (Ed.) *Found: Long-term gains from early intervention.* Boulder, Colo.: Westview Press, 1978.

Caldwell, B. The fourth dimension in early childhood education. In R. Hess and R. Bear, *Early education: Current theory, research, and action.* Chicago: Aldine Publishing, 1968.

Campbell, D. T., & Backer, A. How regression artifacts in quasi-experimental evaluations can mistakenly make compensatory education look harmful. In J. Hellmuth (Ed.), *Disadvantaged child. Vol. 3: Compensatory education: A national debate.* New York: Brunner/Mazel, 1970.

Coleman, J., Campbell, E. Q., Hobson, C. J., McPartland, J., Mood, A. M., Weinfeld, F. D., & York, R. L. *Equality of educational opportunity.* Washington, D.C.: U.S. Government Printing Office, 1966.

The Consortium for Longitudinal Studies. *As the twig is bent.* Hillsdale, N.J.: Lawrence Erlbaum Associates, Publishers, 1983.

Deutsch, C. P., & Deutsch, M. Brief reflections on the theory of early childhood enrichment programs. In R. Hess & R. Bear, *Early education: Current theory, research, and action.* Chicago: Aldine Publishing, 1968.

Goodson, B. D., & Hess, R. *Parents as teachers of young children: An evaluative review of some contemporary concepts and programs.* Stanford, Calif.: Stanford University Press, 1975.

Gordon, I. Parent education and parent involvement: Retrospect and prospect. *Childhood Education,* 1977, *54*(2), 71–79.

Gray, S. W., & Klaus, R.A. An experimental preschool program for culturally deprived children. *Child Development,* 1965, *36*(4), 887–898.

Gray, S. W., Ramsey, B. K., & Klaus, R. A. *From 3 to 20: The Early Training Project.* Baltimore: Baltimore University Park Press, 1982.

Grotberg, E. Child development. In E. Grotberg (Ed.), *200 years of childhood.* (U.S. Department of Health, Education, and Welfare, Office of Child Development, Office of Human Development). Washington, D.C.: U.S. Government Printing Office, 1977.

Hanson, R. A. Consistency and stability of home environmental measures related to IQ. *Child Development,* 1975, *46*, 470–480.

Hellmuth, J. (Ed.). *Disadvantaged child.* Vol. 3: *Compensatory education: A national debate.* New York: Brunner/Mazel, 1970.

Herman, J. L., & Yen, J. P. *Some effects of parent involvement in schools.* Paper presented at the AERA (American Educational Research Association) meeting, Boston, April 1980.

Hess, R. D., & Bear, R. M. *Early education: Current theory, research, and action.* Chicago: Aldine Publishing, 1968.

Hunt, J. M. *Intelligence and experience.* New York: Ronald Press, 1961.

Hyman, H. H., Wright, C. R., & Reed, J. S. *The enduring effect of education.* Chicago: University of Chicago Press, 1975.

Jencks, C., Smith, M., Acland, H., Bane, M. J., Cohen, D., Gintis, H., Heyns, B., & Michelson, S. *Inequality: A reassessment of family and schooling in America.* New York: Basic Books, 1972.

Karnes, M. C., Teska, I. A., Hodgins, A. S., & Badger, E. D. Educational intervention at home by mothers of disadvantaged infants. *Child Development,* 1970, *41*, 925–935.

Klaus, M. H., & Kennell, J. W. *Maternal-infant bonding: The impact of early separation or loss on family development.* St. Louis: C. V. Mosby Co., 1976.

Klaus, R. A., & Gray, S. W. The educational training program for disadvantaged children—a report after five years. In *Monographs of the Society for Research in Child Development* (Vol. 33). Chicago: University of Chicago Press, 1968.

Lazar, I. Discussion and implications of the findings. In the Consortium of Longitudinal Studies, *As the twig is bent.* Hillsdale, N.J.: Lawrence Erlbaum Associates, Publishers, 1983, p. 464.

Lazar, I., Darlington, R., Murray, H., Royce, J., & Snipper, A. *Lasting effects of early education: A report from the Consortium for Longitudinal Studies.* Monographs of the Society for Research in Child Development, *47*, 1982.

Levenstein, P. Cognitive growth in preschoolers through verbal interaction with mothers. *American Journal of Orthopsychiatry,* 1970, *40*, 426–432.

Lyons, P., Robbins, A., & Smith, A. *Involving parents in schools: A handbook for participation.* Ypsilanti, Mich.: The High/Scope Press, 1983.

Mann, A. J., Harrell, A. V., & Hurt, M., Jr. A review of Head Start research since 1969. In B. Brown (Ed.), *Found: Long-term gains from early intervention.* Boulder, Colo.: Westview Press, 1978.

Meier, J. H. Introduction. In B. Brown (Ed.), *Found: Long-term gains from early intervention.* Boulder, Colo.: Westview Press, 1978.

National Commission on Excellence in Education. *A nation at risk: The imperative for educational reform.* Washington, D.C.: U.S. Department of Education, 1983.

Piaget, J. *To understand is to invent.* New York: Penguin Books, 1976.

Ramey, C. T. *Does early intervention make a difference?* Paper presented at the National Early Childhood Conference on Children with Special Needs, Denver, Colo., October 1985.

Royce, J. M., Darlington, R. B., & Murray, H. W. Pooled analysis: Findings across studies. In the Consortium for Longitudinal Studies, *As the twig is bent.* Hillsdale, N.J.: Lawrence Erlbaum Associates, Publishers, 1983.

Rutter, M. *Maternal deprivation reassessed.* Harmondsworth, England: Penguin Books, 1972.

Schaefer, E. S. Parents as educators: Evidence from cross-sectional, longitudinal and intervention research. *Young Children,* April 1972, pp. 227–239.

———. Parent-professional interaction: Research, parental, professional and policy perspectives. In R. Haskins (Ed.), *Parent education and public policy.* Norwood, N.J.: Ablex, 1983.

Shipman, V. C., Boroson, M., Bridgeman, B., Gart, J. and Mikovsky, M. *Disadvantaged children and their first school experiences.* Princeton, N.J.: Educational Testing Service, 1976.

Silvern, S. Parent involvement and reading achievement: A review of research and implications for practice. *Childhood Education,* September/October 1985, *62,* 44–49.

Skeels, H. Adult status of children with contrasting early life experiences: A follow-up study. In *Monographs of the Society for Research in Child Development* (Vol. 31). Chicago: University of Chicago Press, 1966.

Spitz, R. A. *The first year of life.* New York: International Universities Press, 1965.

Spodek, B. (Ed.). *Handbook of Research on early childhood education.* New York: Free Press/Macmillan, 1982.

Stone, J. C., & Schneider, F. W. *Foundations of education, commitment to teaching.* (Vol. 1). New York: Thomas Y. Crowell, 1971.

Umansky, W. On families and the re-valuing of childhood. *Childhood Education,* March/April 1983, *59,* 260–266.

U.S. Department of Education. *What works: Research about teaching and learning.* Washington, D.C.: U.S. Department of Education, 1986.

U.S. Department of Health, Education, and Welfare. (Office of Human Development Services, Administration for Children, Youth, and Families, Children's Bureau, National Center on Child Abuse and Neglect). *Selected readings on mother-infant bonding.* Washington, D.C.: U.S. Government Printing Office, 1979.

Walberg, H. F. Families as partners in educational productivity. *Phi Delta Kappan,* February 1984, *65,* 40.

Wasik, B. H. *Teaching parent problem solving skills: A behavioral-ecological perspective.* Paper presented at the American Psychological Association Meeting, Anaheim, Calif., August 1983.

Weikart, D. R., & Lambie, D. A. Preschool intervention through a home teaching program. In J. Hellmuth (Ed.), *Disadvantaged child.* Vol. 2: *Head Start and early intervention.* New York: Brunner/Mazel, 1968.

Westinghouse Learning Corporation and Ohio State University. *The impact of Head Start. An evaluation of the effects of Head Start on children's cognitive and affective development.* Springfield, Va.: Clearinghouse for Federal Scientific and Technical Information, 1969.

White, B. The center for parent education newsletter. Newton, Mass.: Center for Parent Education, October 1985.

White, B. L., Kaban, B. T., Attanucci, J., Shapiro, B. B. *Experience and environment: major influences on the development of the young child* (Vol. 1). Englewood Cliffs, N.J.: Prentice-Hall, 1973.

White, S. H. The National Impact Study of Head Start. In J. Hellmuth (Ed.), *Disadvantaged child.* Vol. 3: *Compensatory education: A national debate.* New York: Brunner/Mazel, 1970.

White, S. H., Day, M.C., Freeman, P.K., Hantman, S.A., & Messenger, K. P. *Federal programs for young children: Review and recommendations.* Vol. 3: *Recommendations for federal program planning.* (Department of Health, Education, and Welfare Publication No. Os 74–103). Washington, D.C.: U.S. Government Printing Office, 1973.

Yarrow, L. J., Rubenstein, J. L., & Pederson, F. A. *Infant and environment.* New York: Wiley & Sons, 1975.

CHAPTER TWO

Historical Overview of Family Life and Parent Involvement

How long have you been aware of or concerned about parent involvement in education? The eruption of parent education and parent involvement programs in recent decades tended to erase the historic roots of the parent education movement. Schools and government agencies stressed the importance of teachers working with parents as if a new strategy were emerging.

Actually, a traditional concept was being re-emphasized. The many new programs that resulted were rich in design and control and produced additional knowledge about the whys and hows of programs involving parents. There have been periods in the past, however, when parents *were* the natural advocates of their children and partners in the educational process.

It is meaningful to compare the emergence of educational programs to the economic conditions and social thought of the corresponding historic periods, for there is a relationship between societal developments and the child-rearing practices and educational theories of the times. Note the impact of the Russian Sputnik on the emerging emphasis on cognitive development during the 1960s. Or go back into history and relate the needs of the poverty-stricken children in Switzerland in

the 1700s to the educational beliefs and practices of Pestalozzi. The history of parent education and involvement can be pictured as the constant ebb and flow of the ocean's tide. Some eras portray a calm; others are characterized by tumult. As rapid changes, social problems, poverty, and political unrest produce turbulence for families, their need for stabilizing forces increases. So in the 1960s with the call for a "War on Poverty" and the achievement of a "Great Society," there emerged a focus on the family as one institution that could affect the lives of millions of disadvantaged children. The call was strong and resulted in renewed interest in programs in child care centers, home-based education, and combined home-school intervention projects. The emphasis on individualism and families in the 1980s has called for increased parent involvement. Concentrating on the fabric of recent programs, we tend to overlook the threads of the past.

PREHISTORIC PARENT EDUCATION

Since the beginning of civilization, family groups and parents have been involved with the rearing of their young. Before the develop-

Paintings depict the feeling of society toward the young. Poussin's painting is one of the earliest to show infants as plump babies rather than small adults. The Assumption of the Virgin. *Nicolas Poussin. (National Gallery of Art, Washington, D.C. Alisa Mellon Bruce Fund.)*

ment of written records, which is believed to have occurred between 6000 and 5000 BC, early humans had developed a primitive culture. To ensure survival they had to develop means to obtain food and water for sustenance and provide protection from harsh weather and predators. Picture a primitive family group with children modeling their parents' actions. Children accompanied their parents on food forays and learned to obtain their food supply, whether through hunting, fishing, producing crops, or gathering wild foods. Parents also taught them rules and regulations for participating as a member of both the family group and of a larger society. A study of contemporary primitive groups in Brazil substantiates the fact that nonliterate people use the oral tradition to pass on accumulation of time-tested wisdom and practices.

Primitive education aims to transmit unchanged from the adults to the young, the beliefs, practices and attitudes that have stood the test of time and proved successful in the environment in which one's ancestors lived. (Frost, 1966, p. 8)

Primitive societies did not develop schools; the prime educators were the family and community. "The pressures of the group plus the need to survive and to be accepted are powerful incentives to learning" (Frost, 1966, p. 9). Children were valued for both their contribution to survival and for their implied continuance of society. They were the future— they would carry on the traditions of the culture as well as provide the basic needs of the group.

An important education agency in every culture is the family. Here is to be found both formal and informal education. Parents teach their children by merely living with them in the family group. They are examples which children follow instinctively. They also teach directly by telling and showing, by praising when the children conform and punishing when they fail to measure up to the standards set by the family group. The family is first in time, and in many ways the most important teaching agency in any society. (Frost, 1966, p. 12)

For thousands of years the society's important customs, rules, values, and laws were learned and internalized by children so that they could function within their cultural groups. This process of socialization is prevalent in all groups, primitive or highly developed. Without it, children do not develop into functioning human beings as defined by the culture in which they live.

There continue to be cases in highly developed societies where children have not been socialized. Isolated children who have been forced into closets and neglected exhibit characteristics that are not recognized as human. They may speak in croaking noises, waddle instead of walk, exhibit intense fear, and react in a manner atypical of a socialized child. Informal learning and socialization are necessary ingredients in human development. Emile Durkheim declared: "Education consists of a methodical socialization of the young generation" (as cited in Brembeck, 1966, p. 12). During prehistoric times, just as today, the first teachers—the socializers—were parents and families.

FORMAL EDUCATION IN EARLY SOCIETIES

Our knowledge of education in cultures of ancient civilizations with written records is more extensive. In the valleys of the Tigris-Euphrates and the Nile Rivers, where the ancient civilizations of Sumeria, Babylonia, Assyria, and Egypt flourished, formal learning joined forces with informal learning. Concern for formal education emerged when there was a need to "preserve order in communities of mankind and to maintain a stable society and a viable state . . . and to help man become more fully and completely himself, more attuned to God, the possessor of greater personal fullness of being" (Braun & Edwards, 1972, p. 4). During the Old Kingdom in Egypt, 5510 to 3787 BC,

Egyptian boys were educated at home during the Old Kingdom. During the Middle Kingdom, schools developed outside the home. Portrait Panel from a mummy. Encaustic on wood panel, Second Century A.D. *(The Metropolitan Museum of Art. Gift of Edward S. Harkness, 1917–18.)*

children were educated in their homes. During the Middle Kingdom, 3787 to 1580 BC, there were indications that school outside the home developed (Frost, 1966). As in Sumeria, both boys and girls were important to the fam-

ily and were given opportunities to learn (Chambliss, 1982). Formal systems of education also existed in ancient India, China, and Persia, as well as in the pre-Columbian New World, particularly in the Indian cultures of the Mayas, Aztecs, and Incas. The system that had greatest carry-over and effect on Western thought, however, was the educational system of ancient Greece (Braun & Edwards, 1972).

PARENT INVOLVEMENT IN EDUCATION AND FAMILY LIFE IN GREECE

The Athenian state produced philosophy and social thought that is still studied in schools. As far back as the sixth century BC regulations governed schools: parents were responsible for teaching their sons to read, write, and swim; schools were to be in session for a certain number of hours; a public supervisor was to be appointed; and free tuition was provided for sons of men killed in battle. Schools were nonetheless private, and parents had the right to choose the pedagogue or school they desired for their children.

Real concern over education blossomed during the golden age of Greece. Plato (427 to 347 BC) questioned theories of child rearing in his dialogues in the *Republic*.

Do you not know, then, that the beginning in every task is the chief thing, especially for any creature that is young and tender? For it is then that it is best molded and takes the impression that one wishes to stamp upon it.

Quite so.

Shall we, then, thus lightly suffer our children to listen to any chance stories fashioned by any chance teachers. . . .

By no manner of means will we allow it.

We must begin, then, it seems by censorship over our storymakers and what they do well we must pass and what not, reject. And the stories on the accepted list we will induce nurses and mothers to tell to the children and so shape their souls by these stories far rather than their bodies by their hands. But most of the stories they now tell we must reject. (as cited in Hamilton & Cairns, 1971, p. 624)

In the *Republic,* "an exercise in philosophic imagination" (Becker & Barnes, 1961, p. 180), Plato designed an ideal city-state in which genetics and procreation would be controlled by the state to produce children who, when grown, would be capable of administering affairs of state (Chambliss, 1982). Parent education was not for the benefit of the family or its individual members; it was designed to strengthen the communal state.

Although Aristotle (384 to 323 BC) disagreed with Plato's thoughts about the desirability of a communal ideal state, he, too, felt education was too important to leave to the financial ability of the parents. Aristotle did not place the privilege or the burden on the parents. In providing education by the state, he attempted to control the socialization and education of children to fit the needs of the state (Chambliss, 1982; Frost, 1966).

PARENT INVOLVEMENT AND FAMILY LIFE IN ROME

During approximately the same period, family life in Rome was flourishing, and parents were actively involved with their children's education. The high priority placed on children resulted in concern for their development, with the parents being their first educators. Polybius (204 to 122 BC) and Cicero (106 to 43 BC) both wrote of the importance of the family in the development of good citizens. Cicero declared:

For since the reproductive instinct is by Nature's gift the common possession of all living creatures, the first bond of union is that between husband and wife; the next, that between parents and children, then we find one home, with everything in common. And this is the foundation of civil government, the nursery, as it were, of the state. (as cited in Chambliss, 1982, p. 226)

Families were important to Romans, and fathers placed high priorities on their sons' educations. Francesco Sassetti and His Son Teodoro. *Fifteenth Century portrait by Domenico Ghirlandaio. (The Metropolitan Museum of Art. The Jules Bache Collection, 1949. [49.7.7])*

Cicero believed, as Aristotle had, that man was a social and political creature and that human virtues are developed through social participation.

In Rome, as in Sparta, the mother was the first teacher of her children, but she had a greater role in academic education than the Spartan mother and taught the children to read. The father soon encouraged his sons to learn business acumen and citizenship. The mother taught her daughters the obligations, responsibilities, and skills necessary to be a homemaker (Frost, 1966).

It should be noted that from the era of primitive cultures, through Greco-Roman days, to modern times, laws and customs illus-

Christianity held that all lives were sacred in the eyes of God. This reduced the practice of infanticide and abandonment of young children. Madonna and Child. *Fra Filippo Lippo. (National Gallery of Art, Washington, D.C. Samuel H. Kress Collection.)*

trate that infanticide, abandonment to exposure, and sale of children were common practices. (Read deMause, 1974, pp. 25–33.) Children had few rights. Roman fathers held power of determination over their children, even to the extent of deciding upon life or death. In primitive societies, when the population became too large for the limited food supply, infanticide or exposure was used to reduce the population (Bossard & Boll, 1966). The need for survival became a guide for prac-

tices of infanticide. "Sometimes it was under the direction of the state, as in ancient Sparta, or among the Romans, whose Twelve Tables forbade the rearing of deformed children, or at the discretion of the parents, as among the Athenians" (Bossard & Boll, p. 491). In most societies where infanticide or similar practices occurred, once the decision to keep children was made, they were raised as other children within the culture.

Concern for eradication of child desertion, infanticide, and the selling of children began to grow around the first century AD. Rewards were offered to those who reared an orphan. Refuge and asylum for abandoned children were offered by the church, which further testified to the emergence of concern for children (Bossard & Boll, 1966).

Education and family life during the golden civilizations of Greece and Rome and in early Christian times had become important. A subsequent decline in the importance of the family occurred during the Middle Ages, and the concern for parent involvement did not emerge again until many centuries later.

EUROPEAN CHILDREN DURING THE MIDDLE AGES

As the Roman Empire declined, a feudal system emerged, which provided a protective though restrictive social order for the people. During the Middle Ages, approximately 400 to 1400 AD, children were very low among society's priorities. Children of serfs and peasants learned what they could from their parents and peers. There was no system of education and, due to the lack of privacy, very little family life. Living conditions did not provide the poor with an opportunity for privacy or time with their families. Thus, learning was accomplished by working with parents in fulfilling the menial tasks required to subsist on the feudal estates (Aries, 1962; Frost, 1966). As children worked and participated in everyday life, they were socialized into the way of life—the

Peasant children worked the fields with their parents. Landscape with Peasants. *Louis Le Nain. (National Gallery of Art, Washington, D.C. Samuel H. Kress Collection.)*

values, customs, and means of existence for the poor.

On the other hand, children of noblemen were reared and taught in their homes until the age of 7. They, too, were socialized into the values and social graces of their families, but beyond that they were also taught reading, ciphering, and the art of penmanship. Because the men were often away on missions and women were left to run the estates, both sexes were taught the practical needs of caring for the household and land. After the age of 7, children were sent to apprentice in another family. Boys from the upper classes learned skills and duties befitting a nobleman and the art of chivalry, while commoners were apprenticed to learn a craft, trade, or agriculture.

The custom of education by apprenticeship existed for many centuries.

EARLY PARENT EDUCATION BOOKS

The invention of the printing press around 1450 made books available to a much larger segment of the population. Only the wealthy, however, were able to purchase them for personal use.

Savonarola (1452–1498), a physician and teacher, gave advice on teaching children to talk:

Around the age of 2, when the infant begins to talk and to have some knowledge, one should skillfully

Noble children, dressed as young adults, were reared to run estates by other noble families rather than their own parents. Edward VI as a Child. *Hans Holbein, the Younger. (National Gallery of Art, Washington, D.C. Andrew Mellon Collection, 1937.)*

and alluringly encourage the child to utter different words, while saying "My little baby" and calling him by name; and at that time you should have a certain thing that he likes and say, "I will give you this if you repeat what I say," and then similarly vary from one word to another. In this, women are usually quite experienced. (as cited in Demaitre, 1977, p. 476)

The change in children's lives between the fifteenth century, when children were still tied to apprenticeship systems, and the seventeenth century, when the family was organized around children, is illustrated by the change in etiquette books. Those published in the 1500s were restricted to etiquette, while *La civilitie nouvelle,* written in 1671, included children as part of the family system. One of the very early parent education books contained directives for parents to use as they taught children their letters. It even included the proper way to discipline and control children (Aries, 1962). For the first time in history, authors were speaking directly to parents.

CHILDREN OF THE REFORMATION

Throughout the Middle Ages, the Catholic church was a primary influence on people's behavior. When Martin Luther (1483–1540) introduced his Ninety-five Theses, he opened the floodgate for religious change. The most important aspect of the Protestant Reformation was the concept of a priesthood of believers, where people were expected to learn to read and study the Bible for themselves and thereby find their own salvation. Luther believed that people should be able to read the Bible in their own language. He brought his beliefs to the people and wrote the Sermon on the Duty of Sending Children to School, in which he pointed out to parents that they should educate their children. He recommended that children learn their catechisms, and he encouraged the use of Aesop Fables for the teaching of morals.

The importance of Christianity in the Middle Ages is reflected in the enormous number of paintings featuring the Madonna and the infant Jesus. The Small Cowper Madonna. *Raphael. (National Gallery of Art, Washington, D.C. Widener Collection, 1942.)*

The Catholic Counter-Reformation saw the founding of the Jesuit Order, which made much progress in religious education. These advancements in education permeated educational practices both in Europe and the United States. The religious tenor of the times also influenced social thought and, consequently, child-rearing practices for centuries.

THE BEGINNINGS OF THE MODERN PARENT EDUCATORS AND CHILD DEVELOPMENT THEORISTS

The modern parent educator began to emerge during the seventeenth century, but the general population was not affected until the nineteenth century. New ideas about education and the importance of the home in the education of children were developed by social thinkers such as Comenius of Moravia, Locke of England, Rousseau of Switzerland and France, Pestalozzi of Switzerland, and Froebel of Germany.

John Amos Comenius (1593–1670)

Comenius, born in Moravia in 1592, was a member and bishop of the Moravian Brethren. A religious man, he believed in the basic goodness of each child as opposed to the concept of original sin. This idea is reflected in his writing about education methodology; his thinking was more advanced than that of others who lived during the same period. In *Didactica Magna,* a large treatise on education, he discussed the importance of the infant's education, stressing that children, when young, can be easily bent and shaped. In the *School of Infancy,* written in 1628, he emphasized that education began at home and described in detail the manner in which young children should be educated. Comenius also wrote textbooks for children. *Orbis Pictus* (The World in Pictures) is considered to be the first picture book for children (Morrison, 1983). Although a prolific writer, he was unable to change the direction of education during his lifetime.

John Locke (1632–1704)

John Locke, an Englishman who was educated at Christ Church College, Oxford, had far-reaching and innovative ideas concerning government and education. Probably, he is best known for the concept that the newborn's mind is a *tabula rasa,* or blank slate, at birth. All ideas develop from experience; none are innate. It is incumbent upon family and teacher to provide optimum environment and valuable experiences for the thriving of the child's mind.

Locke, who lived during the period when hardening of the child was in vogue, was a staunch supporter of the concept. If children were exposed to cold baths and other methods of hardening, they were supposed to be more resilient to diseases and ailments. A strong body would house a quick and able mind.

Although Locke recognized the home as the optimum environment for children, he suggested, as Commissioner of the London Board of Trade, that orphans and children of the poor be taken from homes at 3 years of age and placed in working schools until they were 14, at which time they would be apprenticed to learn a trade (Frost, 1966). Although the plan might seem harsh, indigent families of the late 1600s did not have the means or family system to provide an adequate environment for growing children. Locke devised the plan so mothers could help secure an income and children would receive a basic education of religion, vocational training, and discipline.

Jean Jacques Rousseau (1712–1778)

Rousseau was another giant in the development of changing European social thought. As thoughts of greater freedom for humans evolved, stirrings of freedom for children also emerged. As a political analyst, Rousseau wrote *Social Contracts* in 1762, in which he described government through consent and contract with its subjects. This desire for freedom extended into his writings concerning children. Although Rousseau allowed his five children to be placed in foundling homes soon after birth, he wrote charming books about child development. In *Emile,* written in 1762, he charged, "Tender and provident mothers . . . cultivate, water the young plant ere it die; it will one day bear fruit delicious to your taste. Set up a fence betimes round your child's soul, others may mark its circuit, but you must build the barrier" (as cited in Archer, 1964, p. 56). In *Julie* and *La Nouvelle Heloise,* he expressed concern that children be allowed freedom: "Nature means children to be children before they become men" (as cited in Archer, p. 28). Rousseau's writings resounded with the child's need to grow free and untainted by society.

Johann Heinrick Pestalozzi (1747–1827)

Johann Heinrick Pestalozzi was a Swiss educator and a sensitive social activist influenced by the writings of Rousseau. After his father died when he was only 5, he was reared by his mother and nurse in a sheltered restrictive environment. His greatest joy came during his visits to his grandfather, Andrew Pestalozzi, pastor at Hoenigg near Zurich. Here he accompanied his grandfather on pastoral calls and saw the mean and hungry depths of abject poverty starkly contrasting with the accumulated luxuries of wealth. These impressions and his later work at the university fermented into a zeal for righting the wrongs inflicted on the poor.

He read Rousseau's *Emile* and was so impressed that he used it as a guide for the education of his own child. Pestalozzi believed in the natural goodness of children and struggled for many years teaching and caring for poor children in his home.

Pestalozzi based his teaching on use of concrete objects, group instruction, cooperation among students, and self-activity of the child. To teach mathematics, he used beans

Pestalozzi wanted to help the poor and give their children an opportunity for education. The Cottage Dooryard. *Adriaen van Ostade. (National Gallery of Art, Washington, D.C. Widener Collection, 1942.)*

and pebbles as counters and divided cakes and apples to demonstrate fractions. The child's day also included recreation, games, and nutritious snacks and meals (Gutek, 1968). Pestalozzi is remembered primarily for his writings; in his first successful book, *How Gertrude Teaches Her Children*, he declared: "Dear Gessner, how happy shall I be in my grace, if I have contributed something towards making these springs known. How happy shall I be in my grave, if I can unite Nature and the Art in popular education, as closely as they are now separated" (Pestalozzi, 1915, p. 29). His statement rings of the free and natural education of children as professed by Rousseau.

The first modern theorist to stress the parents' vital roles in the education of their children, Pestalozzi can be hailed as the "Father of Parent Education." He stridently emphasized the importance of the home. "As the mother is the first to nourish her child's body, so should she, by God's order be the first to nourish his mind" (Pestalozzi, 1951, p. 26). He saw the effects of the environment on the young charges he taught and noted the significance of parents in this way: "For children, the teachings of their parents will always be the core, and as for the schoolmaster, we can give thanks to God if he is able to put a decent shell around the core" (Pestalozzi, 1951, p. 26).

Friedrich Wilhelm Froebel (1782–1852)

The "Father of Kindergarten," Friedrich Froebel, was born in 1782, 35 years after Pestalozzi. Although Froebel is most noted for his development of a curriculum for the kindergarten, he also recognized the importance of the mother in the development of the child. He saw the mother as the first educator of the child and wrote a book for mothers to use with their children at home. The book, *Mother Play and Nursery Songs with Finger Plays,* included verses, pictures, songs, and finger plays still used today, such as "pat-a-cake, pat-a-cake." Froebel's plan for education grew

around a concept of unity. He organized his curriculum to follow the natural unfolding of the child with the mother assisting in the development. The child and mother enjoyed the language and interaction. Visualize the small child and mother playing the following game:

> *Count your baby's rosy fingers.*
> *Name them for him, one by one.*
> *Teach him how to use them deftly.*
> *Ere the dimples all are gone;*
> *So, still gaining skill with service,*
> *All he does will be well done.*

(Blow & Eliot, 1910, p. 147)

Froebel recognized the importance of the mother's interaction and play with her children. Lady Templetown and Her Son. *Sir Thomas Lawrence. (National Gallery of Art, Washington, D.C. Andrew W. Mellon Collection, 1937.)*

The mother was involved in teaching her child, guided by Froebel's curriculum.

The development of the kindergarten had significant impact on the current philosophy of education. Instead of a prescribed curriculum designed by the adult to teach the child to read, write, and be moral, the curriculum was developed from the needs of the child. The concept of child development and teaching to the individual levels of each child was a radical departure from lockstep education.

CHILDREN IN THE SEVENTEENTH AND EIGHTEENTH CENTURIES

Ambivalent feelings about children and their place in the social system were reflected during the seventeenth and eighteenth centuries. Montaigne reflected this attitude in the following statement:

Our jealousy in seeing children appear and enjoy life when we are about to part with it makes us more grudging and strict with them. We resent it when they step on our heels as if to urge us to be gone. And if we are afraid because, to tell the truth, it is in the order of things that they can exist and live only at the expense of our existence and our life, then we should not get mixed up in the business of being fathers. (as cited in Hunt, 1970, Preface)

Child rearing during this era was analyzed by Hunt (1970) in *Parents and Children in History.* He examined the life of Louis XIII, son of Henri IV and heir to the French throne. Relying on Heroard, who recorded Louis' childhood in *Journal,* Hunt studied the socialization of the young dauphin. The use of a wet nurse to nourish and provide milk for the child was a necessary and common occurrence during this period. Another characteristic of the period was the swaddling of young infants, which seems to have been done primarily to provide warmth, since buildings were damp and drafty. The infants were bound from head to toe in a cloth band (maillot) approximately 2 inches wide with their

Van Dyck's painting of Filippio Cattaneo illustrates the manner in which children were dressed and treated as adults. Filippo Cattaneo, Son of Marchesa Elena Grimaldi. *Sir Anthony van Dyck. (National Gallery of Art, Washington, D.C. Widener Collection, 1942.)*

arms at the sides and legs extended. Later, between the first and fourth month, the arms were released, and the child could use them. Usually at around 8 or 9 months, the infant was unswaddled. Babies were unwrapped when it was necessary to clean them. Although it may seem that swaddling might have retarded growth and development, this does not appear to be the case. After they were unswaddled, babies were soon encouraged to walk. Louis was running by 19 months of age and playing the violin and drum at approximately 1½ years (Hunt, 1970).

Strict discipline and physical punishments were the mode of child guidance. Children could be physically punished for crying, lying, and being obstinate, or headstrong. Louis' father wrote to Madame de Montglat, who was caring for Louis, and requested punishment:

I have a complaint to make; you do not send word that you have whipped my son. I wish and command you to whip him every time that he is obstinate or misbehaves, knowing well for myself that there is nothing in the world which will be better for him than that. (Hunt, 1970, p. 135)

While swaddling fell into disfavor in France in the late 1700s, the belief in physical punishment in France and England persisted through the eighteenth century and beyond.

The eighteenth century was one of tremendous upheaval, filled with social change and restlessness. In France this political and social unrest resulted in the French Revolution. In England growth and industry created a demand for labor. Toward the latter half of the eighteenth century and during a major portion of the nineteenth century, the Industrial Revolution created an atmosphere of poverty and misuse of children as laborers.

Families tended to fit into three categories: the wealthy, who allowed others to rear their offspring and who exhibited indifference to children; the emerging middle class, who wanted to guide, direct, and mold their children in very specific patterns (Lorence, 1974); and the poor and poverty-stricken, who lacked the means to have much semblance of family life.

The disinterest of the wealthy in their children encouraged the continuation of placing babies to be fed and reared by a wet nurse. In France and England mothers placed their children with countrywomen to be cared for until they were 2 or 3 years of age. Or, if very wealthy, they hired nurses to come into their homes.

The use of wet nurses was not condoned by authorities in England and France. The French physician, Guillemeau, in *De La Norriture et Government des Enfans,* stated "there is no difference between a woman who refuses to nurse her own children and one that kills her child as soon as she has conceived" (as cited in Lorence, 1974, p. 3). William Cadogan criticized the practice when he wrote in 1748, "I am quite at a loss to account for the general practice of sending infants out of Doors to be suckled or dry-nursed by another woman. . . . The ancient Custom of exposing them to wild Beasts or drowning them would certainly be much quicker and humane ways of despatching them" (as cited in Lorence, 1974, pp. 3, 4).

These writings and those of Comenius, Rousseau, Pestalozzi, and Froebel illustrated a new spirit of humanism and a recognition of children as human beings with some rights. Sometimes these rights were subjugated to the belief that children must be totally obedient to their parents in order to grow properly. These parents represent the second category, those who wanted to guide, direct, and mold their children in very specific patterns.

Susanna Wesley, mother of John Wesley, the founder of the Methodist religious movement in England, could never be criticized for overindulgence. Regarding her child-rearing beliefs, she wrote:

I insist upon conquring the will of children betimes, because this is the only strong and rational foundation of a religious education, without which both precept and example will be ineffectual. But when this is thoroughly done, then a child is capable of being governed by the reason and piety of its parents, till its own understanding comes to maturity, and the principles of religion have taken root in the mind. (as cited in Moore, 1974, p. 33)

Children of poor families were often sent to workhouses and foundling homes, and these were hardly nurturing environments for the young. As soon as the child was old

It was not all work and no play in earlier days. Children and adults found pleasure in games and outdoor activities as depicted in this ice-skating scene. A Scene on the Ice. Hendrick Avercamp. *(National Gallery of Art, Washington, D.C. Alisa Mellon Bruce Fund, 1967.)*

enough to work, apprenticeships were found, and, most often, the child was misused as a source of cheap labor.

Despite the strict discipline imposed on the young of all classes, there was a degree of light and free times for some children in England. There were many recreational diversions. The theater was immensely popular and occasionally upper-class children accompanied parents, but, more often, children attended puppet shows. They also played organized games, including many that are still popular today such as blindman's bluff, hide-and-seek, teeter-totter, cricket, hockey, and football (Bossard & Boll, 1966). Rhymes and fairy tales prevailed. Mother Goose tales, published in 1697, gave parents a collection of rhymes and stories to read to their children. Many of the favorite nursery rhymes read to children today originated during this period, including, among others, "To Market, To Market"; "Little

Boy Blue"; "Baa, Baa, Black Sheep"; "Jack and Jill"; "Who Killed Cock Robin?"; "Tom, Tom, the Piper's Son"; and "The House That Jack Built." Many of the rhymes were political statements of the times but were used then, as today, as favorite poems for children.

Such were the diverse methods of child rearing in Europe at the time of the settling and colonization of the future United States. Depending on their station in life in the old country, settlers had varied child-rearing practices, but there was some homogeneity within the colonies. More consistency developed as colonists faced common conditions in a new frontier.

THE FAMILY IN COLONIAL NORTH AMERICA

Colonists settled three major areas: New England, the middle colonies, and the southern

Cards were another popular pastime in the eighteenth century. The House of Cards. *Jean-Baptiste-Simeon Chardin. (National Gallery of Art, Washington, D.C. Andrew W. Mellon Collection, 1937.)*

colonies. In the new country, the concept of the family had unique importance. Children were valued in the frontier because cutting homesites from raw land, constructing houses and outbuildings, tilling the soil, and harvesting the crops required great physical efforts. Eager hands were needed to survive.

The religious zeal of the New England Puritans permeated family life and influenced child-rearing practices as it defined the duties of parents and children, husbands and wives, and masters and servants. Benjamin Wadsworth, in a 1712 essay entitled *The Well Ordered Family or Relative Duties,* gave directives on proper marital relationships. Husbands and wives were to be supportive of and loving toward one another. "Though they owe duty to one another, yet to God's Law that declares and prescribes what that duty is; when therefore they fail in duty, they not only wrong each other, but they provoke God by breaking his Law" (p. 41).

Wadsworth further advised parents on their relationships with their children. He also outlined the duties of the children to their parents. Both mothers and fathers should love their children as Abraham had loved Isaac. Mothers were expected to nurse their children. Parents were required to provide religious instructions, pray for their children, and see that they were well "settled in the World." Although parents were to care for their children, they were not to be overindulgent. Children were to be brought up with diligence and to have respect for the law.

Children were not "to laugh or jear at natural defects in any, as deafness, blindness, lameness, or any deformity in any person but teach them rather to admire God's mercy; that they themselves don't labour under such inconveniences." Children were to love, fear, revere, and honor their parents. They were to be obedient and faithful, for "when children are stubborn and disobedient to Parents, they're under awful symptoms of terrible ruine (sic)."[1]

Wadsworth's essay was followed in 1775 by Eleazar Moody's *The School of Good Manners.* In the preface, his theme was supported by a quote from Proverbs 22:6—"Train up a Child in the Way he should go, and when he is Old he will not depart from it." The complete title, *Composed for the Help of Parents in Teaching their Children how to carry it in their Places during their Minority,* explains the purpose of the essay. Indeed, this was a parent education book for the colonies. Chapter 2 contained 163 rules for children, which included those governing behavior at the meeting house, at home, at school, or in the company of others. Following are a few of the rules:

Be not hasty to run out of the Meeting-house when the Worship is ended, as if thou wer't weary of being there.

Never sit in the presence of thy Parents without bidding, tho' no stranger be present.

Approach near thy Parents at no time without a Bow.

Dispute not, nor delay to Obey thy parents Commands.

There were many rules of behavior to be followed in company. Children were not to sing, hum, cough, or sneeze. They were not to gnaw their nails, lean upon the chair, spit on the fire, cross their legs, or play with their fingers. As if these requirements were not enough, the child was to speak clearly and not drawl or stumble. Perhaps it was easier for them to be seen and not heard! Parents were not without ample guidance in the rearing of their children.

---

1. Quotations from Wadsworth are from Rothman and Rothman, 1972, pp. 55, 58, 87, and 97.

Families were important to the settlement of the United States. Children were expected to obey their parents and follow specific rules of conduct. The Copley Family. *John Singleton Copley. (National Gallery of Art, Washington, D.C. Andrew W. Mellon Fund.)*

New England schools reinforced stern discipline and instruction in good manners, as well as providing religious teachings. Breaking the will of obstinate young pupils was handled through corporal punishment. The birch rod, the flapper (a 6-inch-wide leather strap with a hole in the center), ferules (flat pieces of wood used to smart the palms of students' hands), and the cat-o'-nine-tails were used in schools to enforce discipline (Bossard & Boll, 1966).

The essays of Cotton Mather, Benjamin Wadsworth, and Eleazar Moody, all published in Boston, reflected the life-style in New England. Childhood in the northern colonies implied adherence to a strict and complicated code. The families in the middle colonies were a more heterogeneous group ranging from the Dutch in New York to the Quakers in Pennsylvania. Those who settled in the south, though as concerned about their children, were more gentle and solicitous in their guidance.

The families in all three regions were patriarchal, and the father's word was an ultimatum for children. Colonial laws supported parental authority. An early New York law exemplified the extreme to which demands for respect of parental authority could be carried.

If any Child or Children, above sixteen years of age, and of Sufficient understanding, shall smite their Natural Father or Mother, unless provoked and forct for their selfe preservation from Death or

Mayming, at the complaint of said Father or Mother, and not otherwise, they being sufficient witness thereof, that Child or those Children so offending shall be put to Death. (as cited in Bossard & Boll, 1966, p. 504)

The early settlers had brought a diversified and rich cultural heritage from Europe.

They were still influenced by European social thought, but they were developing their own individual life-styles and educational systems. Through the colonial years, the "family carried the greatest burden. . . . The family continued to be an important center of training even after colonial society developed" (Middlekauff, 1969, p. 281).

The voyage to the Americas was difficult and the mortality rate was high. Many children arrived parentless in the new land. The Steerage. *Alfred Stieglitz, twentieth century. (The Metropolitan Museum of Art. The Alfred Stieglitz Collection, 1933.)*

EARLY EDUCATION IN THE SPANISH SOUTHWEST

While family life on the eastern seaboard of North America was developing, Spain was extending its settlement of Mexico and the American Southwest. To seek wealth was Spain's initial reason for exploring north of the Rio Grande. Later, settlements were established to claim the land for Spain and spread the Catholic faith.

Life in these settlements developed quite differently from the structures of the eastern colonies of the northern Europeans. Some of the Spaniards had been given land for their military service; others obtained their land by "squatters' rights." Spanish colonists included continentals (those born in Spain),

The Spanish brought their value of strict supervision of their daughters to the Southwest. A Girl and Her Duenna. *Bartolome Esteban Murillo. (National Gallery of Art, Washington, D.C. Widener collection, 1942.)*

Spaniards born in the New World, mestizos (offspring of Spanish and Indian marriages), and Indians and slaves. Each of the first three classes looked down on the classes below it. Wealthy Spaniards, who received land grants from the viceroys, seldom mixed with the mestizos or Indians, except to employ them as overseers for their haciendas. The major educational force was the family, with religious guidance coming from Catholic missionaries. Families resulting from intermarriage, however, tended to mix religious customs. The parents of the Indian child, as well as the parents of the mestizo and the Spanish child, served as the major educators of their children. Parents and the extended family were responsible for what was largely the informal education of their children into the customs and work ethic of the area.

The Jesuit and Franciscan priests, who wanted to convert all people to Catholicism and teach Spanish to the Indians, were not encouraged by the viceroys from Spain to establish schools, so no formal system of education was developed during the early days in the Southwest. Children did not need to learn to read the scriptures because priests cared for their religious needs.

DEVELOPMENT OF THE FAMILY CONCEPT

Concurrent with thoughts of the child as a unique individual was the development of the family into a more cohesive and private unit. In eighteenth century Europe, however, this evolution was limited to families of means. In the early nineteenth century, the greatest proportion of families, those who were poor, lived as they had in medieval days, with children separated from their parents. Living conditions were crowded, and there was little privacy. Children were either apprenticed at a young age or remained with their parents and labored from dawn to dusk to earn their keep.

The family was strong and had the opportunity to develop as a basic unit in the United States.

World as slaves. Family life was not allowed to develop; mothers and children were separated from fathers by the whim of their owners. It was not until after the Civil War that former slaves were free to redefine their family roles and structures. This early loss of human rights had a complex and continuing effect on the economic and social history of the black family in the United States.

CHILD REARING IN THE 1800s IN THE UNITED STATES

The colonies were now the United States. The first hard years of recovering from a war for independence, of building a new nation, and fighting the War of 1812 were over. Instead of looking to Europe or relying solely on the religious guides of the clergy, families began to read from steadily increasing publications in the United States.

Robert Sunley analyzed this period by drawing from original works concerning child rearing in nineteenth century magazines, journals, reports, children's books, medical books, and religious texts. Some of the earliest included *Advice to Mothers on the Management of Infants and Young Children,* written by W. M. Ireland in 1820, and *Hints for Improvement of Early Education and Nursery Discipline* by Louise Hoare, published in 1829. *Mother's Magazine* published "To Mothers of Young Families" and "Hints for Maternal Education" in 1834 and "Domestic Education" in 1838 (Sunley, 1955). *Parents' Magazine* (not related to the current publication) was published from 1840 until 1850. Child-rearing advice consistently emphasized the significance of the mother's role in the care and upbringing of the child. Fathers were, for the most part, ignored in the child-rearing literature.

Mothers were encouraged to breastfeed their children. Babies were to be weaned between 8 and 12 months of age, and mothers were not to extend the period by many

Between the eighteenth and twentieth centuries, the European concept of family did not change, but the ability to have a family life extended to those who were not wealthy (Aries, 1962).

In this respect, the pattern in the colonies differed from that in Europe. Families were able to become cohesive social entities in early colonial life. They were able to establish homes and work together to provide food for the table. The Puritans took their roles as parents especially seriously and, in their zeal, developed strong family patterns and rigid goals and guidelines.

The land of opportunity did not exist, however, for persons brought to the New

Even after emancipation, black families had a difficult life and worked long hours while they attempted to keep their families together and cared for. The Cabbage Patch. *Thomas Pollock Anschutz, 1879. (Courtesy of the Metropolitan Museum of Art. The Monnis K. Jesup Fund, 1940.)*

months. Loose, light clothing was recommended, but heavy overlayers seemed to be prevalent, and swaddling was customary in some areas. Cradles were used, although mothers were not to rush to the side of the cradle if the baby cried. Immediate response to a baby's crying was thought to encourage more crying.

Early toilet training was recommended as a means of "establishing habits of cleanliness and delicacy." Standards for personal neatness and cleanliness were high, and children were expected to wash often (Sunley, 1955, p. 157).

Articles advised strict moral training, reflecting the Calvinist doctrine of infant depravity, which required strict guidance reminiscent of earlier days. Children were not to be spoiled, and parents were to expect total and immediate obedience. "It was considered fatal to let the child win out" (Sunley, 1955, p. 160). Breaking children's wills freed them of basically evil natures. European influence was thereby evident and reflected a strong cultural carryover.

Mothers were intent on their responsibilities of child rearing. Brim (1965) cited parent group meetings as early as 1815 in Portland, Maine. Mother study groups were formed before 1820 in other parts of the country as well. Called Maternal Associations, these parent groups generally consisted of middle-class members of Protestant-Calvinist religious groups (Brim, 1965). They were interested in proper moral training and discussed methods of child rearing that included discipline and breaking the child's will.

Sunley pointed out that there were two other theories besides the religious moral emphasis discussed earlier. One was the idea of "hardening" the child, which probably stemmed from Locke and Rousseau. "Children should become strong, vigorous, unspoiled men like those in early days of the country" (Sunley, 1955, p. 161).

A third theory had a more modern ring of nurturing. Sunley cited the theory as having "its roots in English and European movements." Children were treated in a gentle and persuasive manner with "understanding and justice" and with "consistency and firmness" underlying the nurturing (Sunley, 1955). This guidance was thought to enable children to reach their potential.

Mothers sought child-rearing advice and even formed parent groups as early as 1815. Baby at Play. *Thomas Eakins. (National Gallery of Art, Washington, D.C. John Hay Whitney Collection.)*

During the nineteenth century, three theories of child-rearing prevailed: strict child-rearing as reflected in the Puritan ethic; hardening of the child suggested by Locke; and looking at children as flowers that needed to be nurtured. Miss Willoughby. George Romney. (National Gallery of Art, Washington, D.C. Andrew W. Mellon Collection.)

It seems that the third theory reflected thoughts of Pestalozzi and Froebel. Their influence was felt in the United States through the interest of professional educators and new prominent German immigrants. In 1856 Mrs. Carl Schurz founded the first kindergarten in the United States in Watertown, Wisconsin (Weber, 1969). This school, based on Froebelian theory, was in marked contrast to the authoritarian and rigid traditional schools of the period.

Economic upheavals made the young country ripe for change. "The Industrial Revo-

lution was one of the most severe social crises which had thus far taken place in the history of human society" (Becker & Barnes, 1961, p. 598). There was great misery and suffering among the poor, and those concerned with human lives either sought to improve or ignore the paralyzing conditions. Those who wanted to remedy the dire plight of the poor came from a school of philosophic thought represented by Owen, Robertson, and Mill, English social scientists who advocated improvement of the human condition. The other attitude was exemplified by Herbert Spencer, who felt that government interference and social reforms would not help the poor but would produce greater social ills (Becker & Barnes, 1961). On the other hand, education for parenthood was essential for direct and indirect self-preservation and was considered more significant than preparation for citizenship (Spencer, 1900). Although parenthood was considered of great importance to Spencer, government intervention to improve the quality of family life was not. Although not the originator of Social Darwinism, his thought echoed the belief in the survival of the fittest and was reflected for years in the lack of government programs for the poor. The use of private philanthropic programs to ease the burdens of the poor was acceptable to Spencer, because those who were giving received satisfaction from their contributions and were doing a social "good."

In the 1860s, the country was torn apart by the Civil War. During the war and Reconstruction, change came about for women. Women began to take over farmwork and to carry out all the obligations generally reserved for their husbands. Women also filled the void left by men who resigned from teaching (Calhoun, Vol. 2, 1960), and their prior experience with children brought forth a more nurturant environment in the educational system.

After the Civil War, women did not return to the same subservient positions they had held previously. Calhoun described the change:

The Civil War tore the Nation apart. Women were called upon to teach in the schools and assume the place of the men fighting the war.

The whole movement signifies an extension of woman's economic independence of man, and the breaking down of that barrier of inequality that had so long served to keep woman in a subordinate place in the household. While the Civil War did not start the movement, it did greatly stimulate, and . . . helped to unsettle the foundation of "mediaeval" family which was now passing out and through a transition of storm and stress yielding to the new family of equality and comradeship. (Vol. 2, pp. 361 and 362)

The change in woman's role in the family and the new feeling of equality encouraged later formation of women's clubs and the resultant emphasis within those organizations on parent education.

Change was coming to education as well as to family life. During this same period, the mid-1800s, the kindergarten movement was gaining strength. Henry Barnard, Secretary of the Connecticut Board of Education and later United States Commissioner of Education, became enthused by Froebelian materials at the International Exhibit of Education Systems in London in 1854. Information was disseminated by Barnard in the *American Journal of Education* and a volume, *Kindergarten and Child Culture Papers,* edited by him. He became recognized as the father of the kindergarten movement in the United States. Elizabeth Peabody, a sister-in-law of Horace Mann, was also a staunch supporter of the kindergarten movement and helped to spread the "good word" about the kindergarten methods of Froebel. Most importantly, Elizabeth Peabody crusaded to introduce the kindergarten throughout the land and spread her beliefs about the natural goodness of children. Throughout her life, she was an apostle of Froebelian kindergarten. She believed that the system had come to him through revelation (Weber, 1969). Since she and Henry Barnard had great stature in educational circles, they were able to make a substantial impact on educational thought. Pestalozzi and Froebel considered the parents an integral component of early education, and the kindergarten movement involved parents from its inception.

THE PARENT EDUCATION MOVEMENT

1870 to 1890

The decades between the 1870s and the 1890s were ones of extension of the kindergarten movement and parent education. Froebel's *Mother Play and Nursery Songs* was translated into English. This gave parents an opportunity to use Froebelian activities in their homes. In 1870 there were only four books on kindergarten, but by the end of the decade five more books had been translated, four more written, many articles printed and distributed, and two journals, *The Kindergarten Messenger* and *The*

New Education, were flourishing (Vande-walker, 1971).

There was a growing belief in the perfectability of man and society. Thus, kindergarten was believed to be an excellent instrument to reach children while they were still young enough to be guided in their moral development. Settlement houses were established in the 1880s and 1890s for the urban immigrant groups who arrived in the new land, destitute and without sufficient means to earn a livelihood. The kindergarten was used by the settlement houses as a means of alleviating the suffering of young children. They were also able to reach parents with information about child rearing and Froebelian curriculum. "Industry, neatness, reverence, self-respect, and cooperation were seen as results of the properly directed Froebelian kindergarten, and these moral benefits were linked to both individual and societal advancement" (Weber, 1969, p. 39).

The Women's Christian Temperance Union (WCTU) also supported the kindergar-

An upswing in the influence and activities of women began in the 1880s. Many groups were interested in child development and recognized the importance of parent involvement as shown in this painting. Jungle Tales. *James J. Shannon. (The Metropolitan Museum of Art. Arthur Hoppock Hearn Fund, 1913. [13.143.1])*

ten movement and education of parents by establishing WCTU kindergartens in at least 20 cities (Weber, 1969). Free Kindergarten Associations were formed throughout the United States. By 1897, there were over 400 actively involved in the education of young children and parents. The WCTU developed a course using Froebel's belief in unity with a sequential curriculum for use with mothers of young children. Settlement houses and Free Kindergarten Associations worked with the lower socioeconomic groups and new immigrants. The concern and interest shown the poor and the philanthropic commitment to alleviate suffering reflected the awakening of renewed social conscience. The kindergarten movement and parent education benefited from the development of humanism and the belief in the child's innate goodness (Weber, 1969).

By the 1880s, this growing emphasis on child-rearing and education emerged from two additional sources. Associations organized by women in the late 1800s were the first source and included The Child Study Association of America, formed in 1888 by a group of interested New York City mothers; The American Association of University Women, founded in 1882 by college graduates; The Congress of Parents and Teachers, the PTA, organized by women who gathered from across the nation at a meeting in 1897; and The National Association of Colored Women established in 1897.

The associations founded in the 1880s made a lasting impact on parent education in the United States. Throughout its history, the Child Study Association of America has emphasized child study and parent education; it is the earliest and largest organization solely committed to the study of children. Their earliest programs were studies of authorities of the time, that is, Spencer, Rousseau, Froebel, and Montessori (Brim, 1965). The organization has since engaged in a wide variety of activities and services—all related to children and parents. These have included child study groups, lectures and conferences, consultation services, lending libraries, publications on subjects of interest to parents, a monthly magazine, and leadership training (Brim, 1965; Fisher, 1933; National Society for the Study of Education, 1929; Schlossman, 1976). The second group, The American Association of University Women, has implemented a diverse educational program, including the study of children and parent education. The third, PTA, has been concerned with parent-school relationships since its inception. The National Association of Colored Women focused on civic service, social service, and education with committees on home and the child, mothers, and legislation. Another group, the General Federation of Women's Clubs, formed in 1889, ushered in an even greater interest in women's roles as leaders. These organizations are still actively involved in the field of education in the 1980s.

Working alongside the associations, these professionals in the social sciences were represented by G. Stanley Hall, a charismatic psychologist at Clark University. When elected president of Clark in 1889, he founded a child study center. Children had not been the center of scientific research to a great extent prior to that time. Hall wanted to determine what was in children's minds. Using a questionnaire method of research, he first used associates and assistants at the university to gather data. As his research progressed, he extended the use of questionnaires to teachers throughout the country and then to thousands of parents. To answer the questions, parents needed to observe their child's speech and behavior. This natural observation was a learning experience for the observer as well as a device for collecting data. Although many of the completed questionnaires contained questionable answers, Hall and his associates (Patty Smith Hill and Anna Bryan studied under him) compiled some very provocative recommendations. "Above all, he counseled parents, be indulgent with young children; treat them as young animals, who simply have to behave as they do. Childhood was an easygoing, cavorting stage which youngsters must pass through

Most families lived in small rural communities or on farms such as the one pictured here.

peaceably if they were eventually to become mature, self-controlled adults" (Schlossman, 1976, p. 443). Even though his child study movement was short lived and was replaced by the research of Thorndike, Cattell, and Watson in the 1900s, he remains important to parent education for his institutionalization of child study and his influence on the founding of the PTA.

From this period forward, the development of effective child-rearing practices and parent education was not the effort of just a few interested individuals. Child study had been made a part of a college program by Hall, and strong organizations, founded and sustained by dedicated, interested women, are actively involved in parent education today.

1890 to 1910

The 1890s and the first decade of the twentieth century were centered around the family, with defined roles for mother, father, and children. The father's duty was to financially support the family while the mother controlled the home. Women's clubs were flourishing. Well-to-do mothers were able to join one of the many clubs available to them. Those who were on a lower socioeconomic level were served by settlement houses and the Free Kindergarten Association.

Stendler (1950)—who analyzed the first year of every decade from 1890 until 1950 from articles in three popular magazines, *Good Housekeeping, Ladies' Home Journal,* and *Woman's Home Companion*—found an immense amount of interest in child rearing in the 1890s and early 1900s. The home environment was recognized as very important in the formation of character. Mothers were idolized as the epitome of purity and goodness, and children were thought to model after the mother in their character development. It was important then that the mother be the right kind of person. The father was earning the family fortune, and the mother was looked up to as knowledgeable and capable of rearing children. If these magazines reflected the interests of their readers, the subjects of physical development and character formation were overwhelming in their appeal, for 73 percent of the articles were written on these two subjects in 1890 and 50 percent in 1900. It was

very important to provide a good home environment for the rearing of children, as reflected by 61 percent of the articles in 1890 and 53 percent in 1900. To achieve this environment, young children were given tender loving care, and infants were fed on demand. Character was best formed through provision of a good home with love and affection between mother and child, although 15 percent of the articles said that divine aid was also a help.

This style of child rearing suggests G. Stanley Hall's belief in the goodness of the child. Hall's study on children indicated that the young child should not be overdirected but allowed to grow easily and naturally. Hall thought that children should be kept out of school until they were 7 or 8 and allowed freedom to explore or be given a kindergarten

Country schools educated many of the youth in primarily rural nineteenth century America. This famous picture depicts young men playing crack the whip during a recess. Crack The Whip. *Winslow Homer. (The Metropolitan Museum of Art. Gift of Christian A. Zabriskie, 1950.)*

experience in an unstructured environment (Schlossman, 1976).

During these decades Hall's influence was strongly felt due to espousal of his theories by the PTA. The organization was active in political affairs and worked toward passing child labor laws, pure food and drug acts, and housing legislation (Schlossman, 1976). The PTA was always concerned about child study, and study groups were formed in connection with the public schools. Publications about children and education were issued, and there was a strong focus on interaction and coopera-

The period between 1890 and 1910 witnessed an explosion of popular interest in children as evidenced by the great number of magazine articles on child development. G. Stanley Hall, who felt children should be kept out of school until they were 7 or 8, represented the growing academic interest in children.

tion between parents and teachers. Parent education and involvement became an institutionalized part of the school through action of the PTA.

Two additional organizations related to parent education were created during the first decade of this century. In 1908 the American Home Economics Association was formed. Primarily an organization of teachers of home economics in colleges, public schools, and, after 1914, extension programs, the organization emphasized home management related to homemaking and parenthood such as food preparation and nutrition. As teachers of extension specialists, their mission was to share their expertise with students and families. They did this through county extension classes for homemakers, parent groups, conferences, public school and college classes, and publications. Emphasis gradually included child development and family enrichment (Brim, 1965; National Society for the Study of Education, 1929). In 1909, the second organization, the National Committee on Mental Hygiene, was formed. Because there was concern with improving mental hygiene, the emphasis on mental health increased during succeeding decades. In 1950 this group merged with others to form the National Association of Mental Health.

The period from 1890 to 1910 saw change emerging in education as well as in child rearing. John Dewey, along with Hall, emphasized the need for change in childhood education. Dewey, William Kilpatrick, Francis Parker, and Patty Smith Hill drew away from traditional structured educational practices toward a curriculum that included problem solving, learning by doing, purposeful activity, and social aspects of education.

While educators in the United States were moving toward a child-oriented, problem-solving curriculum, Maria Montessori was establishing another educational form in Italy. Concern for poverty-stricken children caused Montessori, an Italian physician, to establish

Families were important in the late 1800s and early 1900s. Mothers were revered. The extended family supported and helped one another.

Casa dei Bambini, a children's home in a tenement section of Rome. In 1907, she designed a specific program, structured so that children learn by doing. By teaching children precisely how to use equipment, she was able to help children overcome their impoverished environment. Her methodology—more structured than that of American theorists—did not find wide acceptance in the United States until the 1960s.

There were also poverty-stricken children in the United States. Forced to work under horrendous conditions at a very young age, children who were undernourished, neglected, or abused prompted a rising social concern. As a result, the first White House Conference on Care of Dependent Children was called in 1909. The Children's Bureau was created in 1912 as a consequence of the conference, a first step in government concern for children.

1910 to 1920

Soon after the first White House Conference on Care of Dependent Children in 1909, the government began disseminating information on child care. The first *Infant Care,* a popular parent education book on child care for infants, was published in 1914. The Smith-Lever Act of 1914 provided 2000 County Home Demonstration agents. This county extension program included education in homemaking, improved nutrition, and child care. Later, the Smith-Hughes Act of 1917 established "homemaking" as a vocation and included a provision for education in child care and nutrition through extension classes, demonstrations,

In well-to-do families, children were cherished and allowed to be children during the 1890s and 1900s. Girl with a Hoop. Auguste Renoir. (National Gallery of Art, Washington, D.C. Chester Dale Collection, 1962.)

and institutions under the auspices of the Office of Education. The next year, the United States Public Health Service began programs for parents on children's health (Brim, 1965). Government entered the field of parent education through creation of the Children's Bureau, provision for county demonstration agents, and concern for children's health.

Colleges and universities also entered the field by establishing research and teaching centers devoted to the study of children. The State University of Iowa instituted a child study center in 1911. In 1917, the Iowa Assembly appropriated funding for the establishment of the Iowa Child Welfare Research Station at the State University of Iowa. Its purpose was the "investigation of the best scientific methods of conserving and developing the normal child, the dissemination of the information acquired by such investigation, and the training of students for work in such fields" (as cited in National Society for the Study of Education, 1929, p. 286). Thus, preschool laboratories for psychologic studies and an infant laboratory for study of nutrition were established. The first concerted effort to distribute findings to parents did not occur until the 1920s, when programs in parent education were offered throughout the state. The Yale Psycho-Clinic and The Merrill Palmer School of Homemaking were also pioneers in the study of children and made valuable contributions to the understanding of children and to the development of parent education (National Society for the Study of Education, 1929).

Twelve faculty wives at the University of Chicago—with guidance from the university—established the first parent cooperative in the United States in 1916. The women wanted quality child care for their children, parent education, and time to work for the Red Cross during the war (Taylor, 1981). This cooperative, the only one established in that decade, followed the tradition of English nursery schools established in 1911 by Margaret McMillan. McMillan originally designed an open air school for the poor in England. She emphasized health, education, play, and parent education, rather than mere child watching. The concept of the nursery school was welcomed by middle-class American families, as illustrated by the first parent cooperative in Chicago. Thus, parent cooperatives and the growth of nursery schools in the United States strengthened and promoted parent education.

Although authorities during the 1890s and early 1900s had emphasized love and af-

The government became interested in children. The Children's Bureau was created in 1912.

fection in the formation of character, a new trend suggested that discipline through punishment was necessary to assure character development. Parents were advised to use more discipline in the establishment of character in their children. Discipline (reward or punishment) was discussed in 14 percent of the magazine articles in 1900 and jumped to 34 percent in both 1910 and 1920. Providing a good home influence, which had commanded the attention of 53 percent of magazine articles in 1900, was the focus of only 30 percent in 1910 and dropped to 12 percent in 1920 (Stendler, 1950). The increased attention to strict child rearing was illustrated by the first issue of *Infant Care*. Autoerotic activities, such as thumb-sucking and masturbation, were thought to be

extremely dangerous. It was felt that if such activities were not brought under control, they could permanently damage the child. "While he was in bed, he was to be bound down hand and foot so that he could not suck his thumb, touch his genitals, or rub his thighs together" (Wolfenstein, 1953, p. 121). During the day, thumb-sucking was handled by covering the hand with cotton mittens or making the hand inaccessible to the child (Wolfenstein, 1953).

A drastic change in attitude was reflected by scheduling the infant's activities rather than responding to the baby's needs. In 1890, the infant's life was loosely scheduled. By 1900, 22 percent of the articles recommended tight scheduling for infants, and by 1910, 77 percent of the articles called for rigid scheduling of infants (Stendler, 1950). While breast-feeding was still highly recommended, a supplemental bottle could be given at 5 months, and the child was supposed to be completely weaned by the end of the first year (Wolfenstein, 1953). Mothers were told to expect obedience, to ignore temper tantrums, and to restrict physical handling of their children. These severe attitudes continued into the 1920s when all magazine articles recommended strict scheduling of infants (Stendler, 1950).

Throughout these periods there were exceptions to every trend (Brim, 1965). Although strict scheduling began around 1910 and continued through the 1920s and early 1930s, a book published in 1894, Holt's *The Care and Feeding of Children,* recommended "strict, routinized care of the child" (Brim, 1965, p. 169). Watson's *Psychological Care of Infant and Child* stated, "There is a sensible way of treating children. . . . Let your behavior always be objective and kindly firm. Never hug and kiss them, never let them sit in your lap. If you must, kiss them once on the forehead when they say goodnight. Shake hands with them in the morning" (as cited in Vincent, 1951, p. 206). Published in 1928, Watson's book appeared "when Freudian theory was well in its ascendancy" (Brim, 1965, p. 169). Between 1910 and 1920 the Child

Study Association of America was emphasizing "love, support, and intelligent permissiveness in child care, based on the work of Freud, G. Stanley Hall, and other leaders in the clinical movement" (Brim, 1965, pp. 169–170). Vincent (1951) also noted that overlaps in theories occurred with reference to "tight scheduling" as late as 1948, and preference for self-regulation appeared as early as 1930. Even though the period of 1890 to 1910 stressed love and freedom and the period of 1910 to 1930 emphasized strict scheduling and discipline with self-regulation appearing in the late 1930s and 1940s, there were other theories interwoven with these during the same periods.

1920 to 1930

Early childhood as an important period for character formation was stressed in the 1920s. This belief was on the other end of the pendulum from Hall's belief in allowing the child to grow free and unrestricted. Behaviorists warned that parents should "do it right early or else" (Schlossman, 1976, p. 462).

During the 1920s many teen-agers and young adults were viewed as reckless, overindulged, and spoiled (Schlossman, 1976). To reverse this scandalous situation, children were to be trained early to be responsible, well-behaved individuals. Watsonian behaviorism was beginning to be felt. This child-rearing theory was mixed in the 1920s with the learning-by-doing theories of Dewey, a small portion of Freudian psychology, and Gesell's belief in natural maturation and growth. Although each theorist had a different approach, all recognized the importance of early age and the influence of the environment on the child's development.

Infant Care, issued by the Children's Bureau in 1923, admonished parents that "toilet training may begin as early as the end of the first month. . . . The first essential in bowel training is absolute regularity" (as cited in Vincent, 1951, p. 205). Although breast-feeding was recommended for 6 to 9 months, once

weaning was commenced it was to be accomplished in 2 weeks. If the parents insisted on substitution to "artificial food," "the child will finally yield" (Wolfenstein, 1953, p. 125).

An explosion of parent programs accompanied the prosperity of the 1920s. The era reflected a swing from parent education offered by settlement houses for immigrants and free kindergartens for the underprivileged to the involvement of many middle-class parents in study groups for their own enlightenment and enjoyment. Yu studied the growth of parent education and reported that the decade of the 1920s brought forth 26 significant parent education organizations (as cited in Brim, 1965).

Abagail Eliot, who had worked with the McMillan sisters in London, started the Ruggles Street Nursery in Boston in 1922. Eliot was especially interested in working with parents as well as their children. The nursery school movement emphasized the family as partners in education (Osborn, 1980).

Parent cooperatives emerged at the following five locations in the 1920s: (1) Cambridge, Massachusetts, (2) the University of California at Los Angeles, (3) Schenectady, New York, (4) Smith College, and (5) the American Association of University Women at Berkeley, California. The last, called Children's Community, has continued to flourish over the years and is the oldest continuous parent cooperative program in the United States (Taylor, 1981).

The parent cooperative movement, which developed rapidly in California but grew more slowly elsewhere until after World War II (Osborn, 1980), was a way for parents to obtain quality education for children. To participate, parents must share responsibilities—an excellent example of parent involvement.

Membership growth also illustrated increased interest in parent education. PTA membership expansion depicted, in terms of sheer numbers, the growth in interest in parent programs. The organization grew from 60,000 in 1915 to 190,000 in 1920, to 875,000 in 1925, to nearly 1,500,000 in 1930 (Schlossman, 1976). American Association of University Women (AAUW) membership rose to 35,000 in the 1920s, and each issue of its journal contained a column on parent education. Concurrently, the Child Study Association, recognized as the educational leader in parent education during the 1920s, grew from 56 parent groups in 1926 to 135 in 1927 (National Society for the Study of Education, 1929).

In 1922 Benjamin Gruenberg published *Outlines of Child Study: A Manual for Parents and Teachers.* This text on child rearing was used as a study guide for many parent groups. Succinct discussions on issues of child development were included in each chapter; for example, speech development, early years, habitual and emotional aspects of development, heredity, obedience, freedom and discipline, mental tests, adolescence, and emotional and intellectual development. Following each discussion was an outline and references for further reading (Gruenberg, 1927). Parents, along with a professional or lay leader, could read and discuss the issues. A need for trained leaders resulted in the Child Study Association of America's (CSAA) sponsorship of the first university course in parent education held at Columbia University in 1920.

Across the country many school systems implemented parent education and preschool programs. The Emily Griffith Opportunity School (Denver public school system) initially funded a parent education and preschool program in 1926. The early emphasis was on health education for families and expanded to child-rearing theories and other parent skills as interests and needs changed.

The mushrooming of new parent organizations resulted in the CSAA's initiation of the National Council of Parent Education as a clearinghouse for parent education activities. The National Council was formed in October 1925. Representatives of 13 organizations attended and expressed concern that greater coordination was needed. Seventy organizations joined together in a concerted effort to coordinate various parent education efforts throughout the nation. The Council had a significant influence during its existence (1925 to 1938) on the expansion of parent programs through federal agencies, conference leadership, and advisement to parent education groups (Brim, 1965; Fisher, 1933; Gruenberg, 1940).

The tremendous strides in parent education that occurred in the 1920s could not have happened without financial support. Federal programs initiated from 1900 to 1920 continued to be funded through state and federal appropriations. The emergence of parent education in the schools was largely supported by local tax money and tuition or fees paid by the participants. Two private foundations, however, enabled many unique and innovative programs to progress. The Laura Spelman Rockefeller Memorial and the Spelman Fund contributed to private and public associations for the development of research and programs in parent education. Both funds were devoted to child study and parent education, and, as a result, many unique opportunities for research and implementation were offered associations and institutions. They contributed to child development study and parent education training programs, research centers for child study, and self-study programs by associations, such as the Home Economics Association and the National Congress of Parents and Teachers (Brim, 1965; Fisher, 1933; Gruenberg, 1940).

Colleges and universities received money from the Memorial and Spelman Fund for research, teaching, and dissemination of findings from their child study centers. Prominent during the 1920s were state universities in California, Minnesota, and Iowa; private universities (Yale and Columbia); and private institutions like Merrill Palmer Motherhood and Homemaking School and the Washington Child Research Center. In Canada, programs were established at McGill University and the University of Toronto. The goals of the universities and other institutions varied, but primarily they focused on three purposes: (1) research on the development of children, (2) training of professionals for services for and research on children, and (3) dissemination of information and education of parents (National Society for the Study of Education, 1929).

Most educational institutions established nurseries to be used in connection with their research and training. These nurseries involved parents and their children in an interactive process with the institution. With the exception of the parent cooperative established at the University of Chicago in 1916, the nursery school movement did not become a part of the early childhood scene until the 1920s. Three were in operation in 1920, 25 in 1924, and 89 by 1928 (Goodykoontz, Davis, & Gabbard, 1947). The spokesmen for early childhood during this period saw the nursery school as a descendant of the English nursery. In England, however, the nursery fulfilled a need for the poor, while in the United States, the early nurseries were connected with universities and involved middle-class parents (Schlossman, 1976).

Concern for the mentally retarded emerged during the 1920s with separation and custodial care seeming to be the answer. "In regard to all mentally deficient children, it may be said that while we cannot improve their mentality we have reached the point where, by recognition of their capabilities and limitations, we can so place them in our social scheme that they may lead happy and useful lives" (Gruenberg, 1927, p. 230). This thinking has gradually changed over the years to the position of mainstreaming for the handicapped in the 1970s and 1980s, and increased parent involvement and advocacy by parents of exceptional children.

The impact of early childhood concerns and parent education was so great during the 1920s that the *Twenty-Eighth Year Book* of the National Society for the Study of Education was devoted to preschool and parent education. This issue described the programs and listed conferences and agencies engaged in parent education during the 1920s.

Refer to the *Twenty-Eighth Year Book* for a comprehensive report on the 1920s.

As the 1920s drew to a close, middle-class parents were active in parent groups, optimistic about the future, and concerned about health, nutrition, and shaping their children's actions. The financial crash of 1929 brought a tremendous change in the life-style of many families and set the stage for the 1930s.

1930 to 1940

The 1930s ushered in the depression era with a necessary response to the needy and a broadening of concern for the family and family relationships as well as for the individual child (Fisher, 1933; Gruenberg, 1940).

The decade began with a White House Conference on Child Health and Protection in November 1930. Attended by over 4000 specialists, the conference produced the following statement on parent education:

In view of the responsibilities and obligations being laid upon the family as the primary agency for child health and protection, as revealed by the recommendations of the various sub-committees of the White House Conference, this Committee strongly recommends that various educational associations and organizations and the educational departments of the parent education as part of the system of public instruction and that the professional groups and organizations concerned with children to be asked to study their opportunities and obligations for parent education. (as cited in the Pennsylvania Department of Public Instruction, 1935, pp. 9 and 10)

The 1930s reflected varying viewpoints on child rearing, ranging from strict scheduling to self-regulation. Fewer articles were written in the early 1930s than in the early 1920s, and when published, they emphasized physical development, nutrition, and character formation. Character formation began to take on broader meanings. Whereas it had meant moral development earlier in the 1900s, articles in magazines now included personality development (Stendler, 1950). Thumb-sucking was still considered dangerous, but parents were admonished to divert the child's attention, rather than use restraints. "It is a natural habit . . . it should not excite parents unduly" (Wolfenstein, 1953, p. 123).

Parent education continued at a high level of participation during the first half of the decade. Bulletin 86, *Parent Education* by the Pennsylvania Department of Public Instruction reported that parents were being reached through study groups, with more than 700,000 parents involved in group participation. Parents were also receiving information through the mass media: radio series, lectures, magazines, and distribution of over 8 million copies of *Infant Care.* The following statement from the Bulletin emphasized the importance of parent education:

More and more it is being recognized that educators have a responsibility for providing professional leadership and for furthering the coordination of parent education activities in their communities. The job of the school is only half done when it has educated the children of the nation. Since it has been demonstrated beyond doubt that the home environment and the role played by understanding parents are paramount in the determination of what the child is to become, it follows that helping the parent to feel more adequate for his task is fully as important from the point of view of public education and the welfare of society as is the education of the children themselves. Moreover, an educated parenthood facilitates the task of the schools and insures the success of its educational program with the child. (Pennsylvania Department of Public Instruction, 1935, p. 12)

This high priority on parent education in the early 1930s extended across the United States. Parent education courses were offered in at least 25 states in 1932 (Brim, 1965). Aims and objectives published in the Pennsylvania Department of Public Instruction (1935) reflected the following high ideals:

1. To aid parents to interpret the findings of specialists in regard to various aspects of child and family life.

2. To give parents an opportunity to modify or change their attitudes toward their children and their behavior.

3. To serve as a device for personal adjustment.

4. To give an opportunity to consider civic problems affecting family living, and the relation of these problems to social and economic life in the community.

5. To provide a forum in which parents may verbalize their conceptions of the mores and attempt to adapt them to present conditions and trends.

6. To help develop a better understanding of the functions and purposes of education of various types and needs for these services. (p. 15)

These aims and objectives illustrate the trend toward environmental considerations and inclusion of the family as a part of parent education. Social and economic conditions were having an impact on family life and, consequently, the children within the family. The depression and a need to support families by offering information on budget, clothing, health, physical care, and diet precipitated parent education for the poor. Rehabilitation projects of the 1930s (Works Progress Administration) offered a forum for parents who were not active in women's clubs or parent-teachers associations to learn about home management practices. Established in October 1933, the Federal Emergency Relief Administration (FERA) authorized work-relief wages for unemployed teachers and others to organize and direct nursery schools; approximately 75,000 children were enrolled during 1934 and 1935 (Goodykoontz et al., 1947). It was the intention of FERA that the nursery programs be taken over by the schools when funds from the federal government were terminated. "It is my desire that . . . schools shall be so administered in the states as to build toward a permanent and integral part of the regularly established public school program" (Goodykoontz et al., 1947, pp. 60 and 61). Few, however, were taken over by the schools.

Parent education continued during the 1930s, and additional programs were available

This mother, reading to her children, illustrates the emphasis on parent education that expanded in the 1920s and continued through the 1930s.

for the needy. Skeels and the Iowa group commenced their study of the effect of the environment on child development (Chapter 1). Toward the end of the decade there was reduced emphasis on child development research in most areas and withdrawal of foundation support. The National Council of Parent Education had coordinated parent education programs and published a professional journal, *Parent Education,* from 1934 to 1938, but the support of the Spelman Fund was terminated in 1938, and this organization and the publications were disbanded.

In the early 1930s mothers were strongly influenced by scientific opinions from psychologists. The scientific method of discovering truths gave immense credibility to Watsonian psychology and behaviorism as opposed to the sentimentality of earlier child-rearing practices. During this same period, the Freudian view of infantile fixation and the need for expression of repressed emotion by the child began to influence beliefs about children. This set the stage for the concern about emotional development prevalent in the 1940s.

1940 to 1950

The parents of the 1920s and early 1930s who followed the specific rules of the behaviorists changed in the 1940s to persons who recognized that no one answer could work for all situations (Brim, 1965). The emotionally healthy child was the goal for professionals and parents. Stendler (1950) pointed out that in 1940, 33 percent of the articles on infant discipline favored behaviorism, while 66 percent endorsed self-regulation. "The swing from the 'be-tough-with-them, feed-on-schedule, let them cry-it-out' doctrines of the twenties and thirties was almost complete" (Brim, 1965, pp. 130, 131). Self-regulation allowed the development of trust and autonomy in the young child.

Vincent (1951) suggested that the decade between 1935 and 1945 could be called "baby's decade" with the mother "secondary to the infant care 'experts' and the baby's demands" (p. 205). By the early 1940s, mothers were told that children should be fed when hungry, and bowel and bladder training should not begin too early. Babies were to be trained in a gentle manner after they developed physical control. *Infant Care* depicted the child as interested in the world around him and viewed exploring as natural. "Babies want to handle and investigate everything they see and reach. When a baby discovers his genital organs he will play with them. . . . A wise mother will not be concerned about this" (as cited in Wolfenstein, 1953, p. 122).

Wolfenstein described the change in attitude toward the basic nature of humans as follows:

One of the most striking changes in American thinking about children from the nineteenth and early twentieth centuries to the more recent past and the present is the radical change in the conception of the child's nature. From the nineteenth-century belief in "infant depravity" and the early twentieth-century fear of the baby's "fierce" impulses, which, if not vigilantly curbed, could easily grow beyond control and lead to ruin, we have come to consider the child's nature as totally harmless and beneficient. (Mead & Wolfenstein, 1955, p. 146)

Shifts in beliefs about children were reflected in the child-rearing practices of the period.

In 1946 Benjamin Spock, a national best-selling author and parent educator, published *The Common Sense Book of Baby and Child Care*. He responded to the change from strict scheduling to self-regulation, for he believed the rules and regulations imposed on parents during the 1920s and 1930s caused undue pressure. He advised parents to enjoy their children and the role of parent. Spock pointed out the following in the 1957 edition of his book:

When I was writing the first edition, between 1943 and 1946, the attitude of a majority of people toward infant feeding, toilet training, and general child management was still fairly strict and inflexible. However, the need for greater understanding of children and for flexibility in their care had been made clear by educators, psychoanalysts, and pediatricians, and I was trying to encourage this. Since then a great change in attitude has occurred, and nowadays there seems to be more chance of a con-

scientious parent's getting into trouble with permissiveness than with strictness. So I have tried to give a more balanced view. (pp. 1–2)

Spock's book answered questions on feeding, sleeping, clothing, toilet training, management, and illnesses; he had an answer for almost all of the questions a new parent would have. No wonder it was a best seller. It is an example of widespread parent education through the media, and because it was used by many parents as their educational guide, it continued to have great influence on child rearing through the 1950s and 1960s.

The 1940s, although consumed by the outbreak of World War II, saw no reduction in offerings for parent education. Parent groups continued in public schools, and county extension programs prospered. Three states, Mississippi, South Carolina, and Georgia, expanded their state-supported programs. While services continued and emergency-relief nursery schools for workers involved in the war effort expanded, research and training in child development declined (Brim, 1965). Both the depression and World War II brought federal support for children at a younger age. The Federal Emergency Relief Administration regulated the child care funds originally, followed by the Works Progress Administration, and, during World War II, the Federal Works Agency (Goodykoontz et al., 1947). The need for support for families during the depression emanated from the necessity for parents to work to support their families. During World War II women needed child care services so they could join the war effort.

Parent education found added direction in the 1940s through the mental health movement. In 1946 the National Mental Health Act was passed. States were authorized to establish mental health programs and related parent education (Goodykoontz et al., 1947). The need to understand oneself and one's children was recognized as necessary for healthy parent-child interaction.

The decade ended quietly. The war was over, and the establishment of families, delayed by the war, was in full swing.

1950 to 1960

The 1950s were years of relative calm, with emphasis on children and family life. Schools were feeling the increase in numbers of children and were rapidly expanding to meet the needs. Many young adults had postponed marriages and the starting of families during the war. With its completion, however, the "baby boom" began. The PTA had more than 9 million members and thousands of study groups among its 30,000 local chapters. Study groups used material on child rearing and special concerns of parents published by the PTA. Parents

Having delayed having children during the Depression and World War II, couples quickly made up for lost time and the Baby Boom began.

were involved with the schools as room-parents and fund-raisers for special projects. The view, "Send your child to school, we will do the teaching; your responsibility as a parent is to be supportive of the teachers and schools" prevailed as the basic philosophy between school and parents. The formal learning of reading, writing, and arithmetic started when the child entered first grade, the same as it had for many decades.

In a survey by the National Education Association, 32 percent of adult education classes were on family life (Brim, 1965). Parent education and preschool programs, part of adult education in many school districts, continued as a vital source of child-rearing information. Pamphlets from the Child Study Association, Public Affairs Committee, Science Research Associates, and Parent Education Project of Chicago, plus books by authorities such as Arnold Gesell, Erik Erikson, B. F. Skinner, Benjamin Spock, Lawrence Frank, and Sidonie Gruenberg, were used as curriculum guides. During the 1950s James L. Hymes wrote his first book on home-school relations.

Orville Brim, sponsored by the Russell Sage Foundation and the Child Study Association, examined the issues involved in parent education in his book, *Education for Child Rearing.* His analysis of the effects of parent education continues to be relevant to the study of parent education today.

Your Child from 6 to 12, published by the U.S. Department of Health, Education, and Welfare in 1949, illustrated the attitude that prevailed in the 1950s and subsequent years. The preface of the booklet reflected the change from the absolutism of the 1920s and 1930s: "There are many more things that we don't know than we know about children." "Every child is unique in temperament, intelligence, and physical make-up" (U.S. Department of Health, Education, and Welfare, 1949, p. 39).

In the early 1950s thumb-sucking was viewed as a natural rather than a negative occurrence. A baby "may try to get pleasure out of his thumb or fingers. Sucking is a poor substitute for being held, or talked to, or fed; but it is better than nothing" (as cited in Wolfenstein, 1953, p. 124).

Concern for mental health gave parents double messages; it was difficult to combine firm guidance and advice on emotional health. One such view on emotional health stated, "Any action that causes children to feel guilty . . . should be avoided. It is often better to say nothing whatever to the children, for fear of saying too much, or the wrong thing. Instead, divert their minds, give them new interests" (U.S. Department of Health, Education, and Welfare, 1949, p. 38).

Erikson popularized the eight stages of man in a book, *Childhood and Society,* first published in 1950. His neo-Freudian theories emphasized social and emotional development based on interdisciplinary theories from biology, psychology, and sociology. Humans develop through eight stages from infancy to old age, beginning with trust and ending with ego integrity. His theories and the child-rearing practices of the 1950s reflected the belief that social and emotional health were of utmost importance to the child.

In a content analysis of *Ladies' Home Journal, Good Housekeeping,* and *Redbook,* 1950 to 1970, Bigner (1985) found literature primarily concerned with parent-child relations, socialization, and developmental stages. Spanking was condoned by some in the early 1950s, but by the end of the decade it was consistently discouraged and described as an inefficient and barbaric method that does no more than show the youngster that parents can hit. Most articles encouraged self-regulation by the child. Parents were told it was important that children feel loved and wanted. Parents were advised to hold, love, and enjoy their children and rely on their own good judgment for child-rearing decisions.

Parents were encouraged to provide a home life that was supportive of individual differences and allowed each child to grow into a well-adjusted adult. Development was a natural process, and maturation could not be pushed. Gesell's work on development in psychomotor and physical areas supported theories that children proceed through innate developmental stages. As a consequence, parents were encouraged to provide a well-balanced

In the late 1940s and 1950s, children were fed on demand, loved, and cherished.

nutritional diet and an environment that allowed children to grow and learn at their own rate.

To carry this idea a step further, the Parent Education Project of the University of Chicago, with financial aid from the Fund for Adult Education, developed a study curriculum, *Parenthood in a Free Nation*. The curriculum was concerned with rearing children to become "mature, responsible citizens of a free nation" and was based on six characteristics: "(1) feelings of security and adequacy, (2) understanding of self and others, (3) democratic values and goals, (4) problem-solving attitudes and methods, (5) self-discipline, responsibility, and freedom, and (6) constructive attitudes toward change" (Kawin, 1969, p.v). The series of books discussed basic concepts for parents; early, middle, and later childhood; and adolescence. It also included a manual for group leaders and participants.

The Department of Health, Education, and Welfare (HEW), established in 1953 with the Social Security Administration, Office of Education, and Public Health Service under its jurisdiction, continued a diversified approach to parent education. The Office of Education was involved with parent education through state and local school systems and through the Home Economics Branch, whose specialists served as consultants and teachers at the state and local levels (Brim, 1965). The Children's Bureau, part of the Social Security Administration, had three sections related to parent education: the Research Division, Health Services, and Nursing. The Research Division was responsible for the publication of *Infant Care*. Over 60 million copies had been distributed to parents by 1955. The Division of Health Services, working through state social services and maternal and child health programs, supported parent education through training of nurses for leadership in parent education (Brim, 1965). Within the Public Health Service the National Institute of Mental Health continued education and developed research studies to evaluate the effects of parent education.

Federal concern for and involvement in child rearing were reflected in the establishment of HEW and the subsequent development of more programs.

Toward the end of the 1950s the nation's calm was disturbed. Russia's success in placing Sputnik into space caused a ripple effect across the United States. Why had the Russians achieved a feat not yet accomplished by the United States? In the 1960s Americans looked for an answer.

1960 to 1970

The 1960s was a decade of sweeping changes in parent involvement, social and civil rights, and family characteristics. The family had been gradually changing since the early part of the century when the family was viewed with great sentimentality. Mothers were revered; the family was a sacred institution that few dared to question. By the 1960s it was common for all institutions—family, education, religion, economics, and government—to be criticized and questioned. Great changes in the American family developed from 1890 until 1960 when the country changed from a basically rural nation to an urban nation. The majority of families, which had been self-sufficient rural families with authoritarian parents, became dependent on others for income. As a mobile society evolved, one person in five moved each year as better jobs and better education became available. Children were no longer economic assets who helped their parents with the family farm or business; instead, they became financial liabilities, costing $20,000 to raise from infancy to 18 years of age (Hill, 1960). The many women who had continued working after World War II were joined in the 1960s by many more who returned to the labor force to supplement their husband's income or to increase their own economic freedom. For many women, who were single parents or were a supporting member of a two-parent family, working was an economic necessity.

The 1960s began a period of concern for intellectual and cognitive development in the young, but little change was noticed between the 1950s and 1960s concerning social and emotional child-rearing practices. Acceptance of the child was still emphasized. "Your pleasure in him as an infant and child will be the most precious gift you can give. Through your enjoyment of him as an infant and child, he becomes an adult who can give enjoyment to others and experience joy himself" (U.S. Department of Health, Education, and Welfare, 1963, p. 1).

The importance of the father's relationship with his children was stressed, and although his obligations to his children were not the same as the mother's, early interaction with his newborn baby was recognized as very beneficial. "Fathers who feel comfortable giving physical attention to their babies at the start are lucky" (U.S. Department of Health, Education, and Welfare, 1962, p. 29).

Parents had many child care books or booklets from which to choose. Publications from the Child Study Association and Science Research Associates and public affairs pamphlets covered many of the problems parents faced. Benjamin Spock continued to publish books on child care, and in them he advised firm, consistent guidance of the child. "A child needs to feel that his mother and father, however agreeable, have their own rights, know how to be firm, won't let him be unreasonable or rude. He likes them better that way. It trains him from the beginning to get along reasonably with other people" (Spock, 1957, p. 326).

Spock was joined by a psychologist, Haim Ginott, who offered parents a method for talking about feelings and guiding the child in a manner that avoided placing guilt and helped the child understand the parents' feelings, thus disciplining the child in a positive manner.

Professionals working with children and parents were greatly influenced by Piaget's theories of cognitive development. His ideas, clearly discussed by Hunt in his book, *Intelligence and Experience* (Chapter 1), emphasized active involvement of the child with the environment. Parents became much more concerned about their child's intellectual development and were no longer satisfied that development would unfold naturally.

When the Golden Anniversary White House Conference on Children and youth convened, it delved into the concerns of the family and social change, development and education, and problems and prospects for remediation (Ginsberg, 1960). This conference was followed by a White House Conference on Mental Retardation in 1963. The time was ripe to meet the needs of all people—not just the dominant social class. The depression of the 1930s and World War II of the 1940s had kept the country occupied with emergencies. The affluent 1950s, impaired by the Korean War and the Cold War with Russia, gave cause for reflection. The 1960s brought forth many questions. Was the United States able to provide advantages for all its people? Was democracy and the free enterprise system capable of providing the best life for the most people? Could the United States surpass the Russians in the space challenge? These were the difficult questions, concerning millions of people, that faced the nation.

Although prosperity was available for most of the United States and the standard of living had steadily improved to the highest in the world, minorities, the handicapped, and the economically disadvantaged were still underemployed, poverty stricken, and ignored. The United States government had high hopes for a Great Society where poverty could be eliminated for all citizens. In the War on Poverty programs, children of the poor, who were undernourished, in poor health, without proper housing, and lacking educational opportunities, were chosen as a major hope for the future. The works of behavioral scientists and educators presented overpowering evidence that early environment has a profound effect on a child's development (Bloom, 1964; Hunt, 1961; Skeels, 1966). If children could be given equal environmental opportunities, the cycle of poverty could be broken. The stage was set for the birth of Head Start. As research indicated that parent involvement and family background were positively correlated with academic success, the inclusion of parents in their child's education program was entrenched from the beginning of the Head Start program.

In 1965 the Office of Economic Opportunity began an 8-week summer program for disadvantaged preschool children. In the fall the trial program was enlarged to encompass many Head Start programs, funded by federal money but administered by local agencies. Its name described its aims. Children who were disadvantaged would be given an opportunity to have a head start on school. The objectives included a comprehensive approach to child development centering on (1) strengthening and improving the child's physical health, social and emotional development, self-concept, mental processes, and cognitive development; (2) strengthening family relationships; and (3) encouraging self-help and self-determination by the family through career development and parent education. To accomplish these objectives the specialists who planned the programs included a comprehensive approach with six major components: education, social services, health services, career development, administration, and parent education. A center-based program for children 4 to 5 years of age with outreach for parents through parent education, participation by parents on advisory boards, and career opportunities within Head Start made this an innovative and developmentally strong program for parents. The expectation of changing the cycle of poverty for all Americans was unrealistic, but many success stories of parents and their families who were helped by Head Start can be related, and research supports the educational benefits. Head Start's influence was also felt in the public schools where parent components were mandated in many federally funded programs.

Shortly after the formation of Head Start, the Office of Education, Department of Health, Education, and Welfare undertook direction for the Elementary and Secondary Education Act (ESEA) of 1965. Suddenly, twice the amount of federal money poured into schools that applied for and received grants. Public schooling, although still controlled by local boards of education, began to be influenced by federal spending. The federal money, funded through state agencies, was used to help eliminate the educational disadvantages of children in the public schools. Some of the Title (now entitled Chapter) projects under ESEA included:

1. Title I, which assists local school districts in improving the education of educationally deprived children. From its inception parents were involved in the program.
2. Title IV C (formerly Title III), which promoted the innovative programs that enrich educational opportunities. Many of these projects included home visitation programs for preschool children, identification of handicapped children prior to school entry, and working with these parents for the benefit of their children.

Concern over continuity of educational success after Head Start resulted in the implementation of the Follow Through program as part of the 1967 Economic Opportunity Act. Designed to carry benefits of Head Start and similar preschool programs into the public school system, parent participation was a major component of the program, and as with the Head Start program, parent advisory councils were mandated.

Although not directly connected with parent education, the Civil Rights Act of 1965 had great influence on the role of minorities and women during subsequent decades and, through this, had an impact on the family. Affirmative action, requiring minorities and women to be treated equally in housing, education, and employment, resulted in psychological as well as empirical changes in conditions for these populations. Although the increase in equality was not accomplished as the Civil Rights Act demanded, heightened awareness on the part of minorities and women had profound effects on their understanding of themselves, their relationships within the family unit, and their concern for equal opportunities.

Throughout most of this decade the Vietnam War affected family relationships, value clarification, and social change. The war diminished the opportunity for success of the Great Society by funneling money and energy away from domestic programs. It also had immense impact on family unity because many families were torn apart over diverse value orientation concerning drug use, participation in the war, and moral responsibilities. The parent of the adolescent cried for direction and guidance when confronted with overwhelming value changes in their children. Television, peer group influence, lack of consistent social and moral guidance, and involvement in the Vietnam War thrust parents into an arena for which they were not prepared by previous modeling of their parents or by education.

The decade closed with greater emphasis on parent involvement and education for low socioeconomic families than in any other era. Services for the disadvantaged were the concern of Montessori's work in Rome, Pestalozzi's school in Switzerland, Froebel's kindergarten, and, around the turn of the century in the United States, the settlement houses and Free Kindergarten Association's programs. Parent involvement of the 1960s, although reminiscent of these earlier programs, overshadowed them in scope, size, and participation. Backed by federal money rather than philanthropists, the War on Poverty attacked many areas. Whereas early programs were structured to inculcate immigrants and the poor into the values and customs of the dominant culture, the 1960s attempted to recognize the importance and viability of diverse cultural backgrounds and draw from the strengths of diversity with parents as active advocates for their children and themselves. Blacks, Chi-canos, Puerto Ricans, underprivileged whites, and others of low socioeconomic background had the opportunity to express their needs and desires, and the Head Start program reflected each community.

1970 to 1980

The enormous number of programs implemented in the sixties came of age in the 1970s. Development occurred in both private and public sectors with churches, local agencies, public schools, and clubs, as well as state and federal agencies, showing concern for families caught in the stream of social change. The country was still confronted with the Vietnam War at the beginning of the decade. With its end in 1973, one of the major disruptive forces on family unity was resolved.

The decade could be described as the era of advocacy. Groups were no longer willing to sit and wait for someone to do something for them; they had learned in the 1960s

Grandfather, father and child enjoy a moment while pretending to ride in a car. The importance of fathers and grandparents has been emphasized in the 1970s and 1980s.

that the way to help is through self-help and self-determination. Parents of handicapped children, individually and through organizations such as the Association for Retarded Children, the Council for Exceptional Children, and the Association for Children with Learning Disabilities, advocated equal rights for the special child and won (Chapter 8). Advocate groups for children sprang up across the land with training sessions on political power and means to implement change and protection for children. Child abuse and neglect were recognized as debilitating and destructive forces against children, and the concerns of the 1960s became a mandate to report all suspected cases of child abuse and neglect (Chapter 9).

The public schools were not immune. Parents began to question programs and their participation with schools and teachers. Forced integration and required busing was an issue confronting schools and parents. Without family cooperation the schools were powerless to find an appropriate solution. In some cities parents who were not supportive of the schools were destructive to the integration process. Parents and schools had to work together in a partnership to have the educational system work, and parents were interested in participating.

Over the years parent-school decision making had diminished. Originally families had the prime responsibility for education of their children. When formal education joined with informal education, parents still had decision-making rights in regard to their child's schooling. In colonial days the church and family were the major institutions for the socialization of children. During the eighteenth and nineteenth centuries the community school increased in importance, but parents were still involved in decision making. Schools were small. Many country schools were dispersed across the nation, and schoolteachers were hired by the local school board, lived in the community, and were responsible to the local school district. Between 1890 and 1920 there

was a shift from community to urban schools (Butts & Cremin, 1953; Goodson & Hess, 1975). The dramatic change from a rural society to an urban society resulted in a change in the control of schools. The process transferred control of schools from the community to professionals. Consolidation of rural schools into a larger, centrally located school improved equipment, facilities, and diversity of staff, but it took away parent influence. From the 1920s until the 1970s the steady flow from rural to urban areas increased the separation of school and families. Minorities and the poor were most alienated from the educational process. In the 1960s with the recognition that the powerless must be instruments of their own change, parents were included on advisory councils, in career development programs, and in education of children. Parents had become involved in the educational process again.

In 1972 16 Home Start programs serving 1200 families were launched. Eleven Child and Family Resource Programs serving 900 families were started in July 1973. "These programs, all built around a Head Start program, promote continuity of service by including all children in the participating family from prenatal stage through age 8, and broaden the program focus from the age-eligible child, to the entire family" (U.S. Department of Health, Education, and Welfare, 1974, p. iii).

Concern over the link between Head Start and the public school resulted in funding for developmental continuity. Two types of program designs were investigated. One was based on a cooperative model with both Head Start and the schools working out a continuous educational program for the child. The other caused change within the existing school system and included programs for children 3 years and up as part of the school system as well as a curriculum structured for ages preschool through age 8. Both programs involved parents throughout preschool and school years.

Head Start and Follow Through continued to flourish with increasing emphasis on parent participation. The involvement of parents in the Follow Through program had an effect on public schools. Schools could model parent participation and use the same ideas in other school programs. The concept of partnership rather than intervention reflected the belief that it is only through parents, school, and agencies working together that lasting change in education is possible.

Children in the 1970s, if raised according to the experts, continued to need love, consistent guidance, and an enriched and responsive environment. Concern over parent-child separation, particularly in a required hospital stay, was evident in advice given to parents. They were told to stay with the child if hospitalization were necessary. Bonding and the importance of early child-parent interaction was reflected in the research of Spitz, Bowlby, Ainsworth, Brazelton, and Klaus and Kennell.

Sexist referrals in texts, which implied innate differences between boys and girls or referred to children in masculine terms, became noticeable by their absence. Feminists joined civil rights activists and advocates of rights for the handicapped in elimination of stereotypes and inequality of opportunity. The 1970s moved forward, slipped backward, and consolidated gains for many who were not a part of the mainstream of life in the United States.

Mass media, affluence, the fast pace of life, employment of both parents, and unemployment or underemployment put a strain on family life. To complicate matters, children were maturing at a younger age. Communication among family members became more essential than ever because values and customs were changing so rapidly.

Concern over teen-age pregnancies and the lack of parenting skills of young parents resulted in the development of two curricula for young adults. *Exploring Childhood* was published in 1974, and *Education for Parent-hood,* a compilation of curricula from youth organizations, was distributed in 1978.

Government publications ranged from the traditional *Infant Care* and *Your Child from One to Six* to curriculum materials for Head Start, Home Start, Follow Through, and two new series, *Family Day Care* and *Caring for Children.* Attention continued to focus on the total family rather than the individual child. The Office of Child Development became the Administration for Children, Youth, and Families.

The decade closed with school, government, social agencies, and families concerned with educational programs and support systems for children and parents. Plans for the White House Conference for Families were underway. The diversity of underlying philosophies was exemplified in the concern for a definition of family composition. Differing opinions ranged from those who believed families were composed of two parents and children to those who believed any unit living together was a family. These heterogeneous groups met at state conferences where they selected issues and elected delegates to the conference. The White House Conference, held in three locations in July 1980, was attended by representatives from many ethnic origins, handicapped persons, single parents, and the elderly. The times were difficult; inflation was causing great hardships. From among the many issues, one concern raised hope for the future—parents were vitally concerned about the future of the family.

1980s

While the 1960s and the 1970s were times for expansion of family programs, the 1980s have been a time for retrenchment. Money for social programs has been reduced dramatically; publications concerning child growth and education have been reduced. The Head Start program has survived the budget cuts and continues to receive funding, but at a less than optimum rate. Two million children need Head Start, but less than half a million have been served (Children's Defense Fund, 1985, p. 216).

The trend toward greater parent involvement in the education of their children continues. Participation of parents is encouraged in preschool programs and in elementary and secondary schools.

In more than half of the families in the United States, both parents work. This fact has given families greater monetary ability. However, time has become a precious commodity, and some families are finding it difficult to save time for themselves and their children. Articles on handling stress and programs for stress reduction continue to grow in popularity.

Young people are increasingly faced with unstructured free time, coupled with the influence of available drugs and alcohol. Parents have started to join forces with the schools to reduce the use of drugs and alcohol by the young.

Great affluence in the United States is accompanied by great poverty. One in five children lives in poverty. The poorest families are those headed by single women. Estimates of homeless persons range from 300,000 to 3 million (Children's Defense Fund, 1985, p. 130).

Refer to Chapter 3 for a more complete analysis of the family in the 1980s.

SUMMARY

Parental involvement in the education of children has been present since prehistoric times. (Table 2-1 presents a brief overview of important ideas about children over the centuries.) The family provided the first informal education for the child through modeling, teaching, and praise or discipline. From the times of early Egyptian, Sumerian, Hebrew, Greek, and Roman days, parents were actively involved in the selection of teachers and the education of their children.

During the Middle Ages (400 AD to 1400 AD), at 7 years of age, children were sent to live in another noble's home or to apprentice in a trade. Chil-

dren were treated as miniature adults rather than children. It was not until the fifteenth to seventeenth centuries that the concept of family began to develop.

Strict discipline was imposed on all classes of children. This philosophy prevailed until the writings of Rousseau, Pestalozzi, and Froebel in the eighteenth and early nineteenth centuries brought a touch of humanism to the rearing of children.

Family life in the United States was able to flourish from the early days. Child-rearing practices varied according to the location of the founders but were basically tied to the religious background of the family. The major exceptions were the black families, brought from Africa to serve as slaves, who were not allowed to have a normal family life.

Child-rearing practices were reflected by the Puritan belief in breaking the will of the child and the need for perfect behavior. The parent education groups in the early 1800s were based on the need to rear children according to these religious principles.

The modern parent education movement began in the 1880s and 1890s. Prominent women founded the National Congress of Mothers (PTA), the Child Study Association, and the American Association of University Women. Each included child rearing as a part of its program. Stanley Hall created the first child study center in the United States at Clark University. In addition, philanthropic organizations included parent education in their settlement schools and Free Kindergarten Association programs.

The federal government became involved in family life with the first White House Conference on Care of Dependent Children in 1909. As a result, the Children's Bureau was established in 1912, and the first issue of *Infant Care* was published in 1914.

Colleges and universities showed their concern for research in child development by the establishment of research and child study centers.

The years during the 1920s were the most productive in terms of the establishment of parent education programs. Twenty-six parent education organizations were founded during the decade, and many parent education groups emerged across the nation. Change had also come in terms of child-rearing practices. Although authorities in the 1890s and the early 1900s emphasized love and affection in the formation of character, the 1920s focused on strict scheduling and discipline.

TABLE 2-1
A brief outline of important people and events influencing ideas about children and childrearing

6000–5000 BC	Primitive cultures developed. Children learned by modeling their parents.
5510–3787 BC	Egyptian children were educated in their homes in the Old Kingdom of Egypt.
3787–1580 BC	Schools outside the home developed in Egypt.
427–347 BC	Plato questioned theories of childrearing. He suggested that young children's environment should be controlled so that they would develop the right habits.
	Infanticide was practiced by Greeks, Romans, and others.
384–323 BC	Aristotle, the father of the scientific method, promoted childrearing and education by the state.
204–122 BC	Polybius marked the importance of the family in the development of good Roman citizens.
106–43 BC	Cicero emphasized the family in the development of the Roman citizen.
318 AD	Emperor Constantine declared infanticide a crime.
400–1400 AD	Roman Empire declined and the feudal system emerged. There was loss of family life. Wealthy children were apprenticed to nobles. Commoners were apprenticed to learn trades. Peasants worked in fields as common laborers.
1450 AD	The printing press was invented. Books were available but were reserved for the wealthy.
1500–1671	Etiquette books changed from strictly adult etiquette to include children.
1483–1540	Martin Luther introduced the Ninety-five Theses and began the drive for all to learn to read the Bible. He also recommended Aesop Fables.
1592–1670	Comenius, a Moravian educator, wrote books with progressive educational theories.
1632–1704	John Locke believed the newborn's mind was like a blank slate. Nothing was innate; everything must be learned.
1697	Mother Goose tales published.
1712–1778	Rousseau, author of *Emile,* wrote that children need to grow free and untainted by society.
1747–1827	Pestalozzi, father of parent education, developed a curriculum based on concrete objects and group instruction, cooperation among students, and self-activity of the child. Among his work is *How Gertrude Teaches Her Children* (published in 1801).
1782–1852	Friedrich Froebel developed an education for the young child based on the concept of unity. He is regarded as the father of kindergarten.
1703–1791	John Wesley, founder of Methodism, was reared quite strictly by his mother, who believed in breaking the child's will.
17th & 18th Centuries	Wealthy European children were reared by wet nurses.
	Colonial American children followed Puritanical religious beliefs, were disciplined, and trained to be obedient and faithful.
	Children in the Southwestern United States were reared in extended closeknit Spanish-Indian Catholic families.
19th Century	American parents began to rely on American publications in addition to European ideas and the tenets of the church.
1815	Parent group meetings were held in Portland, Maine.
1854	Henry Barnard, United States Commissioner of Education, supported Froebelian concepts.

TABLE 2-1, *continued*

1856	The first kindergarten was established in Watertown, Wisconsin, by Margaretha Schurz. (It was a German-speaking kindergarten.)
1860	Elizabeth Peabody established the first English-speaking kindergarten in America. Peabody, sister-in-law of Horace Mann crusaded for kindergartens.
1860–1864	During the Civil War women were encouraged to replace men as teachers.
1870	The National Education Association was founded.
1870–1880	A great extension of kindergarten movement and parent education occurred.
1871	First public kindergarten in North America was established in Ontario, Canada.
1873	Susan Blow directed the first American public kindergarten, opened by Dr. William Harris in St. Louis, Missouri.
1882	The American Association of University Women was established.
1884	The American Association of Elementary, Kindergarten, and Nursery School Educators was established under the auspices of National Education Association.
1888	The Child Study Association was founded.
1889	The General Federation of Women's Clubs was founded.
	G. Stanley Hall started the first child study center.
1890–1900	Settlement houses were established to aid the poor and new immigrants.
1892	The International Kindergarten Union was established.
1895	Patty Smith Hill and Anna Bryan studied with G. Stanley Hall.
1896	The Laboratory School at the University of Chicago was started by John Dewey.
	The National Association of Colored Women was established.
1897	The Parent Teachers Association (PTA) was founded.
1898	*Kindergarten Magazine* was first published.
1905	Maria Montessori established Casa dei Bambini in Rome.
	Sigmund Freud wrote *Three Essays of the Theory of Sexuality.*
1909	The First White House Conference on Care of Dependent Children was held.
1911	Margaret McMillan designed an open air nursery for children of the poor in England.
	Gesell started Child Development Clinic at Yale University.
1912	The Children's Bureau was established.
1914	First *Infant Care* was published by the Children's Bureau.
1916	First parent-cooperative was established in Chicago.
1917	Smith Hughes Act was passed. Homemaking became a vocation.
	Iowa Child Welfare Research Station was established.
1920s	Emergence of 26 parent education programs occurred.
1920	Child Welfare League of America was founded.
	Watson, a behaviorist, emphasized that children were to be strictly scheduled and were not to be coddled.
1922	Nursery school was established in Boston, Massachusetts, by Abigail Eliot.
	Benjamin Gruenberg wrote the *Child Study Manual.*
1925	National Council of Parent Education was established.
	National Committee on Nursery Schools (now the National Association for the Education of Young Children) was started by Patty Smith Hill.

TABLE 2-1, *continued*

1927	First black nursery school in United States was founded by Dorothy Howard in Washington, D.C.
1928	The nursery school movement expanded from 3 in 1920 to 89 in 1928.
1930	Depression hit the United States.
	White House Conference on Child Health and Protection recommended parent education as part of the public school system.
	The International Kindergarten Union became the Association for Childhood Education.
1932	Parent education courses were offered in 25 states.
1933	Federal Emergency Relief Administration authorized work-relief wages for nursery school teachers.
1934	*Parent Education,* journal of National Council of Parent Education, published from 1934 until 1938.
1940s	A new emphasis on mental health for children emerged.
1940	The Lanham Act provided money for child care so that mothers could join the war effort. Most of the money went for child care centers.
1946	Benjamin Spock published *The Common Sense Book of Baby and Child Care.*
1949	*Your Children from 6 to 12* was published by the Children's Bureau.
1950	Erik Erikson wrote *Childhood and Society,* which included the eight stages of growth.
	James Hymes wrote *Effective Home School Relations.*
1952	Jean Piaget's work, *The Origins of Intelligence in Children,* was translated into English.
1957	Russia launched Sputnik. New emphasis was placed on the intellectual development of children.
	Parenthood in a Free Nation was published by Parent Education Project of the University of Chicago.
1960	Golden Anniversary White House Conference on Children and Youth was held.
	The Parent Cooperative Preschools International was founded.
1960	Day Care and Child Development Council of America was founded.
1962	J. McVicker Hunt wrote *Intelligence and Experience,* one of the first books to question the concept of fixed IQ
1963	White House Conference on Mental Retardation was held.
1964	Economic Opportunity Act of 1964 began the War on Poverty.
1965	Civil Rights Act was passed.
	Head Start was established.
	Elementary and Secondary School Act was passed. Title I provided money for educationally deprived children.
1967	The Follow Through Program was initiated to provide continuity of service to former Head Start students in elementary school.
1970	White House Conference on Children and Youth was held.
1972	The National Home Start Program was initiated. It involved parents in the teaching of their children.
1975	The Education for All Handicapped Children Act, P.L. 94-142, was passed. It mandated free and appropriate education for handicapped children.
1980	The White House Conference on Families was held.

During the 1940s parent education programs continued, bolstered by child care money for mothers working in the war effort.

The 1950s showed more concern for the mental health of the child. Freud's and Erikson's writings on social-emotional growth, plus Benjamin Spock's famous child care book, helped shift attitudes from the strict scheduling of the 1920s to the "on demand" feedings and concern for mental health of the 1950s.

In the late 1950s the U.S.S.R. launched Sputnik. Suddenly, there was concern for intellectual development in the young. This forecast the emphasis toward cognitive development in the 1960s and 1970s. The total child—emotional, social, intellectual, and physical—was the focus of many professionals, and although cognitive development was emphasized and Piaget's theories on cognitive development had great impact on education, this developmental theory complemented the belief in the need for physical, social, and emotional health. Head Start, Follow Through, and Title I programs looked toward the child's total needs. The family was brought into the development and ongoing commitments of federal programs.

In the 1960s and 1970s Americans were confronted with great social change. The 1980s began with the First White House Conference on Families, which was attended by men and women representing diverse philosophic beliefs about families.

Parent involvement was recognized as an important element in a child's success at school. Monetary support for family support programs, however, has decreased in the 1980s. Head Start continues but serves less than one-fourth of the eligible children. Societal problems include increased drug and alcohol abuse by school-aged children and poverty for one in five children. Families are faced with a shortage of time and increased stress in a turbulent world.

SUGGESTED CLASS ACTIVITIES AND DISCUSSIONS

1. Visit an art museum. Explore the artists' portrayals of children. See if you can find pictures in which children were depicted as miniature adults. Are there time periods when children were idealized? Are there time periods when children were painted realistically? Discuss.

2. Ask the librarian for books from art museums throughout the world. Examine these for trends in child-rearing practices and beliefs.

3. Divide into groups. Each group chooses a prominent figure in parent education, for example, Pestalozzi, Froebel, Locke, or Rousseau. Investigate their lives, beliefs, and the impact they had on education. Obtain copies of their original works. When reporting back to class, pretend you are a product of the relevant time period and defend the educator's beliefs.

4. Find a library that has federal publications. Look through books published by the Children's Bureau. Examine the changes in beliefs in child development.

5. Get a copy of the *Twenty-Eighth Year Book, Parts I and II, Preschool and Parent Education* by the National Society for the Study of Education. Compare the programs on parent education in the 1920s to the programs in the 1980s.

6. The periods of 1890s, early twentieth century, 1930s, and 1960s were ones when there was concern about the poor. What were the differing causes of poverty? Why did the concern seem to lessen in intervening decades?

7. Why did nursery schools serve the poor in England? Why do they tend to serve middle-class parents in the United States? How did their origins differ?

8. Discuss federal intervention. Trace its history from the "hands off" approach of Spencer to the start of the Children's Bureau. How has federal involvement grown since 1910?

9. Who are the current leaders in early child education? Read materials by James Hymes, Ira Gordon, David Weikart, Bettye Caldwell, Merle Karnes, and others. Obtain copies of *Childhood Education, Young Children,* and *Children Today.* Listen to the *Living History* tapes by James Hymes. Do you find a trend in the direction of early childhood education today that will be history tomorrow?

10. Examine your community. How many new types of programs have been started since Head Start was initiated in 1965?

BIBLIOGRAPHY

Archer, R. L. (Ed.). *Jean Jacques Rousseau. His educational theories selected from Emile, Julie and other writings.* Woodbury, N.Y.: Barron's Educational Series, 1964.

Aries, P. *Centuries of childhood.* New York: Vintage Books, 1962.

Becker, H., & Barnes, H. E. *Social thought from lore to science.* (Vol. 1. and Vol. II). New York: Dover Publications, 1961.

Bigner, J. J. *Parent-child relations.* New York: Macmillan Publishing Co., 1985.

Bloom, B. *Stability and change in human characteristics.* New York: Wiley & Sons, 1964.

Blow, S. E., & Eliot, H. R. *The mottos and commentaries of Friedrich Froebel's mother play.* New York: D. Appleton, 1910.

Bossard, J. H. S., & Boll, E. S. *The sociology of child development.* New York: Harper & Row, 1966.

Braun, S. J., & Edwards, E. P. *History and theory of early childhood education.* Worthington, Ohio: Charles A. Jones Publishing, 1972.

Brembeck, C. S. *Social foundations of education.* New York: Wiley & Sons, 1966.

Brim, O. *Education for child rearing.* New York: Free Press, 1965.

Butts, R. F., & Cremin, L. A. *A history of education in American culture.* New York: Holt, Rinehart & Winston, 1953.

Calhoun, A. W. *A social history of the American family* (Vols. 1, 2, & 3). New York: Barnes & Noble, 1960.

Chambliss, R. *Social thought.* New York: Irvington Press, 1982.

Children's Defense Fund. *A children's defense budget: An analysis of the President's FY 1986 budget and children.* Washington, D.C.: Children's Defense Fund, 1985.

Demaitre, L. The idea of childhood and child care in medical writings of the Middle Ages. *Journal of Psychohistory,* 1977, 4(4), 461–490.

deMause, L. (Ed.). *The history of childhood.* New York: Psychohistory Press, 1974.

Education Development Center. *Exploring childhood.* Newton, Mass.: EDC School & Society Program, 1977.

Erikson, E. *Childhood and society.* New York: W. W. Norton, 1963.

Fisher, M. Parent education. In *Encyclopedia of the social sciences* (Vol. 2). New York: Macmillan, 1933.

Frost, S. E., Jr. *Historical and philosophical foundations of Western education.* Columbus, Ohio: Charles E. Merrill, 1966.

Ginsberg, E. (Ed.). *The nation's children* (Vols. I, II, III). New York: Columbia University Press, 1960.

Godfrey, E. *English children in the olden time.* Darby, Pa.: Folcroft Library Editions, 1977. (Originally published, New York: E. P. Dutton, 1907.)

Goodson, B. D., & Hess, R. *Parents as teachers of young children: An evaluative review of some contemporary concepts and programs.* Stanford, Calif.: Stanford University Press, 1975.

Goodykoontz, B., Davis, M. D., & Gabbard, H. F. Recent history and present status in education for young children. In *National Society for the Study of Education, 46th yearbook, part II.* Chicago: National Society for the Study of Education, 1947.

Gruenberg, B. C. (Ed.). *Outlines of child study.* New York: Macmillan, 1927.

Gruenberg, S. Parent education: 1930–1940. In W. B. Grave (Ed.), *Annals of the American Academy of Political and Social Sciences.* Philadelphia: American Academy of Political and Social Sciences, 1940.

Gutek, G. L. *Pestalozzi and education.* New York: Random House, 1968.

Hamilton, E., & Cairns, H. *Plato: The collected dialogues.* Princeton, N.J.: Princeton University Press, 1971.

Hill, R. The American family today. In E. Ginsberg, *The nation's children.* New York: Columbia University Press, 1960.

Hunt, D. *Parents and children in history.* New York: Basic Books, 1970.

Hunt, J. *Intelligence and experience.* New York: Ronald Press, 1961.

Hymes, J. L. *Effective home-school relations.* New York: Prentice-Hall, 1953.

Kawin, E. *Parenthood in a free nation. Early and middle childhood* (Vol. 2). Lafayette, Ind.: Purdue Research Foundation, 1963.

Lorence, B. W. Parents and children in eighteenth century Europe. *History of Childhood Quarterly: The Journal of Psychohistory,* 1974, 2(1), 1–30.

Mead, M., & Wolfenstein, M. *Childhood in contemporary cultures.* Chicago: University of Chicago Press, 1955.

Middlekauff, R. Education in colonial America. In J. A. Johnson, H. W. Collins, V. L. Dupuis, & J. H. Johansen (Eds.), *Foundations of American education: Readings.* Boston: Allyn & Bacon, 1969.

Moody, E. The school of good manners: Composed for the help of parents teaching children how to behave during their minority. In D. J. Rothman & S. M. Rothman, *The colonial American family.* New York: Arno Press, 1972.

Moore, R. L. Justification without joy: Psycho-historical reflections on John Wesley's childhood and conversion. *History of Childhood Quarterly: The Journal of Psychohistory,* 1974, *2*(1), 31–52.

Morrison, G. S. *Early childhood education today* (3d ed.). Columbus, Ohio: Charles E. Merrill Publishing Co., 1983.

National Society for the Study of Education. *Twenty-Eighth Year Book. Preschool and Parent Education (Parts 1 and 2).* Bloomington, Ill.: Public School Publishing, 1929.

Osborn, D. K. *Early childhood education in historical perspective.* Athens, Ga.: Education Associates, 1980.

Pennsylvania Department of Public Instruction. *Parent education.* Bulletin 86. Harrisburg: Pennsylvania Department of Public Instruction, 1935.

Pestalozzi, F. J. *How Gertrude teaches her children.* London: Allen & Unwin, 1915.

_____. *The education of man.* New York: Philosophical Library, 1951.

Rothman, D. J., & Rothman, S. M. *The colonial American family.* New York: Arno Press, 1972.

Schlossman, S. L. Before Home Start: Notes toward a history of parent education in America. 1897–1929. *Harvard Educational Review,* 1976, *46*(3), 436–467.

Skeels, H. Adult status of children with contrasting early life experiences: A follow-up study. In *Monographs of the Society for Research in Child Development* (Vol. 31). Chicago: University of Chicago Press, 1966.

Spencer, H. *Education: Intellectual, moral, and physical.* New York: Appleton, 1900.

Spock, B. *Baby and child care.* New York: Pocket Books, 1957.

Stendler, C. B. Sixty years of child training practices. *Journal of Pediatrics,* 1950, *36,* 122–134.

Sunley, R. Early nineteenth-century American literature on child rearing. In M. Mead & M. Wolfenstein, *Childhood in contemporary cultures.* Chicago: The University of Chicago Press, 1955, pp. 150–163.

Taylor, K. W. *Parents and children learn together: Parent cooperative nursery schools.* New York: Teachers College Press, 1981.

U.S. Department of Health, Education, and Welfare. (Welfare Administration; Children's Bureau). *Your child from 6 to 12.* Washington, D.C.: U.S. Government Printing Office, 1949.

_____. *Your child from 1 to 6.* Washington, D.C.: U.S. Government Printing Office, 1962.

_____. *Infant care.* Washington, D.C.: U.S. Government Printing Office, 1963.

_____. *Home Start/child and family resource programs. Report of a joint conference—Home Start, child and family resource program.* Washington, D.C.: U.S. Government Printing Office, 1974.

Vandewalker, N. C. *The kindergarten in American education.* New York: Arno Press, 1971.

Vincent, C. E. Trends in infant care ideas. *Child Development,* September 1951, 199–209.

Wadsworth, B. The well-ordered family: Or relative duties. In D. J. Rothman & S. M. Rothman, *The colonial American family.* New York: Arno Press, 1972.

Weber, E. *The kindergarten.* New York: Teachers College Press, 1969.

Wolfenstein, M. Trends in infant care. *American Journal of Orthopsychiatry,* 1953, *23,* 120–130.

CHAPTER THREE

The Parent Community

FAMILIES

Families in the United States and around the world are living with change. But the essence of the family remains stable with members of the family sharing a certain amount of commitment and support for each other. "Changes in family forms will come and go as economic and political conditions change but . . . the sense of connectedness is the essence of family" (Howard, 1980, p. x).

The family is the most stable component of society. Countries have emerged and disintegrated, but the family remains, changed in form, but not in essential functions. If there is a bond among its members, with young children receiving necessary nurturing as well as shelter and food, then the family will survive. If the family is close knit, thereby reducing a feeling of isolation among its members, then the family and those within it will flourish. As provider for and socializer of children, the family has no match. A family may be a nuclear two-parent family, a single-parent family, or an extended family, but as long as it provides nurturance and support to its members, it is a viable, working unit.

If you walked down a street in the United States today and knocked on a door, would you be likely to find a mother, father, and child living in the house? Children live with parents in almost 4 out of every 10 houses. We are a nation made up of many persons; some are young; some are senior citizens; some are middle-aged and any of these may be single, divorced, widowed, or married. Eighty-one

A family may be one-parent, two-parent, or extended. As long as it can provide connectedness and underlying support, it is a viable family.

Our nation comprises many persons—young, mature, and of many different ethnic backgrounds.

percent are white; 11 percent are classified as black; 1½ percent are Asian or Pacific Islanders and 6 percent are of Spanish origin (calculated from Department of Commerce, Bureau of Census, 1982, p. 47). One-fourth of households are inhabited by unrelated persons and three-fourths by related families.

Marriage and a happy home life are important to both women and men. When answering polls, those questioned placed importance on the family and were willing to adapt and make sacrifices to keep the family together. Although over 47 million children (75 percent) lived in two-parent families, over 12 million (20 percent) lived in one-parent homes in the 1980s. Only 11 percent of families fit the concept of a father as provider, mother as homemaker, and two children (Washington & Oyemade, 1985, p. 13). The 12 million single-parent homes represent an increase of over 44 percent between 1970 to 1980. These figures do not negate the desire for a happy family life. Many one-parent families have strong permanent families based on the parent and child. The rate of remarriage illustrates the desire to continue the traditional life style of two parents in the family with children. The ability to form a happy family depends on many things,

but it is not dependent upon the form of the family.

GROWTH OF A NATION

The first United States census in 1790 reported a population of 3,939,326. By the 1940s, the country had grown to a bustling, heterogeneous land of 131,409,119 persons (Kaplan & Van Valey, 1980, p. 25). During this period, the nation changed from a rural population to a large, industrialized and urbanized population. From 1940 until 1980 approximately 95 million more inhabitants were added to the population. From 1790 until 1940, 150 years, the population increased by 128 million persons; from 1940 until 1980, only 40 years, the population increased by 73 percent (U.S. Department of Commerce, Bureau of the Census, 1982, p. 4). Most of the increase was from the net increase of births over deaths rather than from immigration. Infant mortality was reduced and senior citizens were living longer. During the 1970s the birthrate declined to 13,027,000, but with the arrival of refugees and immigrants, and with the increased number of senior citizens, the population steadily increased.

A look at one year illustrates the continued growth. In 1981 the population increased by 2.3 million persons, incorporating a natural increase (net births over deaths) of 1.7 million and legal immigration of approximately 600,000. Similar increases in the late 1970s were affected by large numbers of refugees from Indochina, Cuba, and Haiti. The population figures cited do not include the estimated 500,000 illegal immigrants (many from Mexico) who enter the United States each year (Population Reference Bureau, 1982, pp. 3–5).

In the 1980s children of the baby-boom era—1947–1964—began having more children. By 1990, it is estimated that 23.3 million preschoolers will need child care (Children's Defense Fund, 1982, p. 1). The children of the baby-boom era, having delayed marriage and childrearing, now want to have children. In the 1980s the pressure to marry has steadily decreased (Thornton & Freedman, 1983, p. 5). Only 36 percent of women aged 20 to 24 were not married in 1970, whereas 56 percent of the women, 20 to 24, were not married in 1980. The baby-boom generation continues to set trends rather than follow them.

The number of families in the United States is on the increase; there were 58.4 million families in 1980 compared to 38.8 million in 1950. The Census Bureau projects 68.5 million families by 1990 (Children's Defense Fund, 1982, p. 1). In 1985 there were 62.7 million families in the United States. Of these families, 50.4 million were composed of married couples, 10.1 million were headed by women, and 2.2 million were headed by men (U.S. Department of Commerce, 1985).

Following is an overview of American families:

- Marriage and a happy family life are important.
- Three-fourths or 47 million children live in two-parent—original or reconstituted—families.
- Twenty percent or over 12 million children live in one-parent families.
- Fifty-three percent of women with children work outside the home.
- Over one million children are affected by divorce each year.
- Average number of children per family is 1.7.
- Eighteen percent of births in 1980 were out of wedlock.
- Half of all recent first marriages will end in divorce.
- Poverty is on the increase and many are "new poverty" situations. (Thornton & Freedman, 1983)
- One in every 6 Americans or 16 to 17 percent move annually.
- Continued population growth is expected. (Population Reference Bureau and Guest Experts, 1982)

Education of Parents

Parents today are better able to work with and are more comfortable dealing with the school. In 1940 only 36 percent of men and 40 percent of women, who were 24 to 25 years old, had completed high school; and only 7 percent of the men and 5 percent of the women had completed college. In 1979, 85 percent of both men and women in the 24 to 29-year-old age group had completed high school, and 25 percent of the men and 20 percent of the women had completed college (Thornton & Freedman, 1983, p. 6). Parents who have not had educational opportunities are often very supportive of the schools and desire an education for their children, but some parents who have had to quit school or have had an unpleasant experience in their own schooling may fear the schools and find it difficult to become partners with the professional. The school must reach out to these reticent parents. Educated parents usually collaborate with the schools.

Working Mothers

Today working mothers outnumber homemakers. Fifty-six percent of the children have mothers in the work force. Sixty-two percent of single-parent mothers work outside the home. The greatest change in the working population is in the number of working mothers who have preschool children. Today, women are not as likely to leave the labor force when they have children as they once were. Working mothers with children under one increased from 24 percent in 1970 to 46.8 percent in 1984 (see Table 3-1).

If one looks at the period a decade earlier, the change is even greater. Working mothers with children under 3 more than doubled from 17 percent in 1959 to 42 percent in 1980; and those with children from 3 to 5 doubled from 27 percent in 1959 to 55 percent in 1980 (Children's Defense Fund, 1982, p. 2).

The trend for greater employment of women outside the home while their children are young is illustrated by Table 3-1, which compares percentages of mothers who worked in 1970 with those in 1984. By 1984 employment rates of single divorced parents were 67.9 percent for parents with children under 6 years old, and 55.5 percent for single parents with children under 3 (Hayghe, 1984, p. 32). Mothers with one or two children were most likely to work outside the home; as family size increased, outside employment decreased.

IMPACT OF DAYCARE ON YOUNG CHILDREN

Is it harmful for both parents to work outside the home? The answer depends in part upon the quality of the substitute care. If the child is in a good setting, 8 out of 10 studies suggest there is no appreciable difference in maternal/child bond or the child's development between children in daycare and children at home. Children from low-income homes had greater success in school and required placement in special education less often if they had a good preschool experience (Berrueta-Clement, 1984). Burton White (1980) encouraged mothers to care for their children at home at least

TABLE 3-1

Percent of mothers who work, grouped according to their children's ages

Age of youngest child	March 1970	March 1984
1 year and under	24.0%	46.8%
2 years	30.5	53.5
3 years	34.5	57.6
4 years	39.4	59.2
5 years	36.9	57.0

Source: Hayghe, H. Working mothers reach record number in 1984. *Monthly Labor Review,* December 1984, p. 31.

for the first 3 years, but parents who need or want to work, can feel comfortable that their children will not be adversely affected if they select good daycare. Parents should visit centers or daycare homes and find one that has a positive environment and fits their needs.

GREATER INVOLVEMENT OF FATHERS WITH THEIR CHILDREN

Fathers have long been identified as providers. In some families the roles of provider and authority were the only ones evident to the children. The role of the father as a nurturant parent was virtually ignored until the 1970s. Since then the interest in fathers as more active parents has exploded.

This new emphasis on the father role involves him even from the child's infancy. Lamb (1976) found that fathers who took their roles seriously and showed warmth in their relationship with both daughters and sons helped their children develop. Girls were affected most if their fathers were absent during adolescence, while boys found the father's absence more difficult at an earlier age. Fathers needed to have extensive interaction with their children because "masculinity of sons and femininity of daughters are greatest when fathers are nurturant and participate extensively in child rearing" (Lamb, p. 23). Stereotypical masculine types were not as influential as role models for their sons as were the fa-

Fathers need to be warm and loving parents, interacting with their children in a nurturing manner.

a way of fulfilling their own lives with meaningful relationships.

In spite of recent trends, however, mothers still carry the heaviest load of the homemaking tasks. In studies of middle-aged blue-collar workers, men generally refused the responsibility of equal care for children (LeMasters & DeFrain, 1983). Though some of the "new" breed of fathers did participate in child rearing if their wives worked, the majority did not assume greater homemaking responsibilities.

Swick and Manning (1983) offered ways in which fathers can participate positively in the family. Their suggestions ranged from the father reinforcing the mother's efforts in child care and communicating with her about the children, to his playing, listening, and exploring with the children at all ages, and being involved in their schooling from preschool through the upper grades.

thers who spent quality time with their children. Children model those about whom they feel positive more than those of whom they are afraid. Children did not see their father's involvement in child rearing as unmasculine. Warmth of the father-child relationship also correlated with children's academic performance and ability to feel good about themselves (Lamb, 1976).

This heightened interest in fatherhood correlates with the increasing number of working mothers. More than ever mothers need a cooperative husband to help with child care and homemaking. Single parents often substitute a network of friends and kin to handle emergencies and everyday obligations. But need has not been the only reason fathers have expanded their role. Many young fathers see the expression of love toward their children as

OUT-OF-WEDLOCK BIRTHS

The recent increase in out-of-wedlock births, especially for young teen-agers, is alarming. Eighteen percent of all children are now born to unmarried mothers. Increased births outside of marriage does not mean that there are more teen-age mothers. Girls do not now marry as early as their counterparts in the 1950s, so there was a decline in births to teen-age mothers. Out-of-wedlock births among white teen-agers increased by 50 percent during the 1970s decade. The young age of both black and white teen-age mothers caused concern. Although the birthrate for unmarried black teen-agers was six times higher than that for white teen-agers, the rate of out-of-wedlock births for black teen-agers declined in the 1970s at the same time it increased for the white teen-agers. Teen-age girls aged 13 to 19 were the largest child-bearing group in the world.

Two factors—the increase in out-of-wedlock births and the decrease or delayed births for married women—increased the percentage of births to unmarried mothers from 5 percent in 1970 to 18 percent in 1980 (Thornton & Freedman, 1983, pp. 20, 21). This startling figure points out the need for more family life education in the schools. Higher mortality rates and greater risk to the child are two of the problems associated with teen-age pregnancies. Very young women are not prepared emotionally, economically, or physically to take on the challenge of child rearing.

SINGLE-PARENT FAMILIES

Single-parent families are not a new phenomenon. From the 1860s until the mid-1960s there was no increase in the number of single parents because the growing divorce rate was offset by the declining death rate. Generally, however, children in the last half of the 1800s and first half of the 1900s were raised in single-

Children are charming, but young teenagers are not ready physically or emotionally for the responsibilities implicit in parenthood.

parent families because the mother was widowed. By the 1960s, however, the number of single-parent families was increasing because of divorce rather than death (Thornton & Freedman, 1983, p. 8). The divorce rate doubled from 1963 until 1979, but appears to have stabilized in the 1980s. Still, half of all recent first marriages will end in divorce. And though increasing numbers of divorced parents remarry, making it possible for 79 percent of the children to live in two-parent homes, almost half live with a single parent sometime during their childhood.

Today single parents have more opportunities, but discrepancies between wages paid to women and paid to men still exist. Four out of five families receiving Aid to Dependent Children are single-parent families, and many more families headed by women live at the poverty level. The average age when parents obtain a divorce has consistently lowered from the 1950s. While only 29 percent of couples married in 1952 were divorced by the 25th wedding anniversary, 28 percent of those married in 1967 were divorced after 10 years of marriage (Thornton & Freedman, 1983, p. 8).

Teachers may expect to see more children affected by divorce because of the continuing high rate of divorce and because more parents now divorce while their children are very young. Over a million children are affected by divorce each year. One of every three white children and two of every three black children will experience their parents' divorce before age 16, and of the parents who remarry, one-third of the white children and one-half of the black will experience a second divorce (Thornton & Freedman, 1983, p. 8).

Infants are not as affected by divorce as preschool children, who tend to blame themselves for their parent's divorce and are frightened and confused by it (Lowery and Settle, 1985). According to Wallerstein and Kelly (1980), some attitudes and feelings last for a long time. In elementary schools children tend to feel ashamed of the divorce and feel rejected because of their fathers' departures. Younger children seem to suffer most at the time of the divorce, but in a 10-year follow-up, older girls still harbored feelings of betrayal and rejection by men that made commitment to their own relationships difficult. If the quality of life after the divorce is good, children do well. If parents continue to fight over the children or burden their children with too much responsibility, "in short, if stress and deprivation continue after the divorce—then children are likely to suffer depression and interrupted development" (Wallerstein, 1985). Divorce may improve the situation for the child if a successful re-established single family or a re-marriage provides the child with a good quality of life.

What does this mean for a teacher? First, if school personnel consider the function of a family, they will immediately recognize that single-parent families *can* supply the components necessary for a flourishing, functioning family. They will also recognize that during the period of divorce, the family will be in some turmoil. Children bring their distress with them to the classroom. The school can offer children a stable and sensitive environment during that period. If parents and teachers communicate, it helps children overcome the isolation and distress that they feel.

Although only one in every five children will probably be from a one-parent family at any given time, one in every two children will spend part of their childhood in a one-parent family. Parents tend to remarry fairly soon after a divorce and the child will gain a new stepparent and often step-siblings. This adds to the complexity of the family and will probably be a period of adjustment for the children in the new blended families. Even after remarriage many children still hope and dream that their original family will get back together. Again, schools are the one stable part of the child's life. Children of reconstituted families who are able to stay in their same

school have some stability in teachers and friends. Those who have to move to a new school face a new mixture in their family plus an unknown at school. Many children withdraw into themselves at the very time they need support. (See Chapter 4 for more detail on working with families.)

Adapting for Single Parents

Single parents need special acknowledgment as well as special accommodation. First, unless they have established a strong network of friends or family, they may have difficulty accomplishing all the requests and obligations they have in their involvement with the school. What are some of their problems?

1. *Times for parent-teacher conferences.* Single parents (and many two-parent families) need special times for their conferences. If you use a form such as suggested in Chapter 4 (Fig. 4-7), you can find out when they are available. Single parents may also need a baby-sitting service to care for their children while they attend a conference. This service is also nice for two-parent families so that both parents may attend.

2. *Acknowledgment of and communication with noncustodial parents.* If noncustodial parents receive report cards and other reports, they will be more interested in the child's work and better able to be involved with the child. Since most single parents are women, the noncustodial parent is generally the man. The percentage of men who supply child support is low; the schools can help increase the father's interest by keeping him informed. Other fathers already have a keen interest in their child's schooling. They want to know what is happening without questioning the child. Honor their position; send them frequent reports.

3. *Awareness of parents' names.* Always check the records to determine the names of the children and the mother, since

they may not be the same. This is also necessary for two-parent families, because half of the families will have had a divorce at sometime in their married life. Try to call the parents by their correct names.

4. *Parent involvement.* Find ways that single parents can be involved without putting great stress on the family. Early morning breakfasts allow working parents to attend meetings before work. Plan to have child care during the breakfast and provide breakfast for the children. Keep the number of parents at each breakfast small so you can talk with each parent individually. Find out how they would like to be involved, what their needs are, and if they have any ideas for their partnership with the school. Acknowledge their suggestions for improved home/school collaboration.

5. *Communication between parents.* Establish a newsletter that allows parents to communicate with other parents. Let the parents include what they want to say in the newsletter. Make it a parent-to-parent newsletter, so that they can establish a network. The single parent may be able to establish a network among the other parents in the class.

6. *Care in communication.* Take care when preparing invitations to programs. Perhaps you may wish to emphasize one group, but make sure the child and parent know that they do not need to have a father, mother, or grandparent to attend. For example, "Bring your grandparent or a grand friend to class next week" implies that the visitors, not their qualifications, are important. At the program make sure you have some get-acquainted activities so that no one feels left out or alone. (See Chapter 4 for more school activities and Chapter 5 for ways to make group meetings work.)

POVERTY

Poverty is the greatest child killer in 1985, affluent America. More American children die each year from poverty than from traffic fatalities and suicide combined. Twice more children die from poverty than from cancer and heart disease combined. (Children's Defense Fund, 1985, p. 1)

Poverty is as prevalent in the 1980s as it was when the War on Poverty began in 1966. At that time one in every five families—39.5 million—were below the poverty level. This was reduced to one in eight by 1969—24.1 million families. The level of poverty-level households remained fairly constant throughout the 1970s until 1979–1981 when 4.8 million more became impoverished. By 1983 35.3 million persons lived below poverty level, including almost one in every five—11.4 million—children.

Poverty may be defined as "a physical and sociopsychological environment in which individuals have severely limited amounts of power, money, and social status" (Farran, Haskins & Gallagher, 1980, p. 47). To exist in the culture of poverty means to feel depressed, powerless to make change, and unable to control your own destiny. Alienation, isolation, and depression are common partners with poverty. Parents, who are depressed and unable to control their own world, pass that feeling on to their children.

It is estimated that 10,000 American children die each year from poverty. More than 13.3 million poor children live in the United States. Of these 7.2 million are white and their poverty rate is 47 percent; 4.6 million are black and their poverty rate is 69 percent. The increase in poverty since 1979 has been 3.3 million children, or 33 percent.

According to Kenniston (1977), it is a myth that all families are self-sufficient. Nor does the United States provide equal opportunity for all. "One child out of four in America is 'being actively harmed by a stacked deck' created by the failings of our society" (p. 18).

Poverty is defined in the United States according to the income of the person or family. In 1983 a family of four who made under $10,178, a single person over 65 who made $4,775, and a family of nine or more who earned less than $20,310 before taxes were considered below poverty level. Of these, 35 percent received cash welfare benefits (O'Hare, 1985, pp. 4–6). In the United States those in poverty live surrounded by affluence, a more difficult situation than that which occurred during the depression when the majority of people were poor. Being hungry and cold hurts and kills no matter who or where you are.

The two groups that were hardest hit by poverty in the United States were black children and children of female-headed households. Forty-two percent of black children and over 50 percent of all children in single-parent families headed by women lived in poverty. Blacks and Hispanics have a higher proportion of single-parent families than whites. More than 60 percent of single-parent Hispanic and black families and 36 percent of white single-parent families were below the poverty level. Two-parent families fared better; 20 percent of black and Hispanic families and 9 percent of white families were under the poverty threshold (Hayghe, 1984, p. 33). Children living in the United States have one chance in four of being on welfare sometime during their lives (Children's Defense Fund, 1982, p. 3).

It is evident that one of the greatest problems that half of single mothers face is their insufficient income. When working with these mothers, it is well to recognize not only their time constraints, but also their financial bind, and avoid pressuring them in either area. You may be able to help some by providing information on social services available. Find alternative activities and ways in which they could be involved, for they need to know that they are wanted and are important.

If you teach in the inner city, you are likely to have many children who are in low socioeconomic levels in your classes. However, only 5 million, or 14 percent, of the poor live in inner-city ghettos. More of the children— 7.9 million—live in central cities outside the poverty areas. In 1983, about one in four of the poor lived in suburban areas. The rest lived in rural areas and small towns (O'Hare, 1985, pp. 15, 16). Teachers may expect to find children from families having financial problems no matter where they teach.

Contrary to popular opinion only a portion of the impoverished (estimates range from .7 percent, up to 10 percent) are consistently poor, that is, poor for 8 or more years (O'Hare, 1985, p. 21). Most people who become poverty stricken move back out of poverty in 1 or 2 years.

Many younger adults were living at the poverty level in the 1980s. They found themselves competing in an overcrowded employment market at the same time there was a loss of jobs to automation, an increase in female labor force, and increasing competition from foreign products. The greatest increase in unemployment has been among males, 18 to 44 years of age. In 1983 nearly 20 percent were unemployed; for young black males the percentage was double (O'Hare, 1985, p. 14).

Families who have always been self-sufficient and who find themselves without employment have tremendous psychological adjustments as well as difficulty in providing shelter and food. For some, using social welfare is acknowledgment of defeat. Before viewing a child as being neglected, find out the source of the problem.

Table 3-2 illustrates the number of poor according to race or cultural origin, and family status. The black family has a particularly difficult time obtaining employment. This is true in both the North and the South. In 1983, 35.7 percent of the blacks were below poverty level. Persons of Spanish origin had a 28.4 percent poverty rate, while the white population had a 12.1 percent rate. In 1980, the racial characteristics of families who made less than $5,000 per year were as follows: 3 million were white; 1.2 million, black; 68 thousand, Asian and Pacific Islanders, and 455 thousand, Spanish origin (U.S. Department of Commerce, 1982, p. 47). Even though the percentage rate of whites at poverty level is lower than that of

TABLE 3-2
Number of poor and poverty rate, by age, sex, race or cultural origin, and family status:
1959, 1978, 1983

Characteristics	Number of poor (in 1,000s)			Poverty rate (percent)		
	1959	*1978*	*1983*	*1959*	*1978*	*1983*
Total	39,490	24,497	35,266	22.4	11.4	15.2
Age						
Under 18	17,208	9,931	13,807	26.9	15.9	22.2
18–64	16,801	11,333	17,748	17.4	8.7	12.4
65 and over	5,481	3,233	3,711	35.2	13.9	14.1
Race and cultural origin						
White	28,484	16,259	23,974	18.1	8.7	12.1
Black	9.927	7,625	9,885	55.1	30.6	35.7
Spanish origin[a]	—	2,607	4,249	—	21.6	28.4
Sex						
Males	—	10,017	15,182	—	9.6	13.5
Females	—	14,480	20.084	—	13.0	16.8
Family status						
In families	34,562	19,062	28,434[b]	20.8	10.0	14.1
In male-headed families	27,548	9,793	15,940	18.2	5.9	9.3
In female-headed families	7,014	9,269	12,494	49.4	35.6	40.5
Unrelated individuals[c]	4,928	5,435	6,832	46.1	22.1	23.4

Sources: From W. P. O'Hare, *Poverty in America: Trends and New Patterns.* Washington, D.C. Population Reference Bureau. June 1985, p. 17. O'Hare's study was adapted from Bureau of the Census, 1959 and 1978: "Characteristics of the Population Below the Poverty Level: 1978," Tables 1 and 11; 1983: "Characteristics of the Population Below the Poverty Level, 1983", Tables 1 and 11.
[a]Persons of Spanish origin may be of any race.
[b]The 1983 family data have been adjusted to include 630,000 persons living in "unrelated subfamilies" below the poverty line who are not included in these categories in the published Census Bureau report on poverty for 1983.
[c]Unrelated individuals are persons not living with persons related to themselves by blood or marriage.

blacks, the total number of whites under the poverty level is 68 percent of the total.

To counteract the stress of poverty, families need to have

1. A decent standard of living (minorities and women should be able to hold jobs that pay enough to adequately rear children),
2. More flexible working conditions so that children can be provided for,
3. An integrated network of family services, and
4. Legal protection for children outside and inside families.

WORKING WITH CULTURALLY DIVERSE GROUPS

Since the end of the Vietnam War, refugees from Indochina—including Laotians, Hmongs, Thais, Cambodians, and Vietnamese—have entered our schools. In addition many new arrivals have come from Mexico, Latin America, and South America. Immigration has continued from other countries as well, so you may find children in the schools speaking languages from Europe, Asia, Africa, and the Americas. It is estimated that by 1990 one-fourth of our population will be minority members.

[handwritten: Culture - all rules of appropriate behaviors that are learned. These rules must be common to large % of pop + they must be shared.]

Because of the influx of new minority groups into the United States, teachers will have to increase their understanding of many cultures. This is not an easy task, but it requires an essential commitment.

The first and most important thing to remember when working with culturally diverse groups is to avoid stereotyping. Although it is essential to understand the minority children's culture, it is also necessary to allow them to be individuals. Every group is composed of individuals, and those individuals may not fit the norm.

To be successful in working with minority parents then, involves three steps. The first involves understanding oneself. The second necessitates understanding other attitudes and value systems. The third requires commitment through expression and curriculum. Insights and curriculum ideas are suggested in this chapter and in the books and references listed in Chapter 11.

African-American Students

The black child is an excellent example of the need to eliminate stereotyping. African-Americans have a marvelous heritage that includes a high development of music, art, literature, and an emphasis on religion. Blacks have a strong commitment to their churches, and children grow up in families where faith and religion are important aspects of their lives. Many of the black leaders (for example, Martin Luther King and Jesse Jackson) have been ministers. Music in their religion as well as the development of jazz by black musicians illustrate a remarkable creative ability in the field of music. However, this does not mean that all blacks are great musicians, nor that all blacks use the church as a focal point in their lives.

African-American people have been a part of the Americas since Diego el Negro first came over with Columbus in 1492. Blacks helped Coronado explore present-day Kansas in 1541, and helped establish St. Augustine, Florida, in 1565 (Banks, 1984, p. 218). As in-

Most children have great potential for academic success.

dentured servants, they landed on the eastern shores of the United States in 1619. It was only later that they were brought over as slaves. At that time their culture was eradicated as much as possible, and they were conditioned to work for others. Family life was discouraged and families were broken up if the master wanted to sell one member of the family and not the other. Children were most often left with their mother until they were old enough to be on their own. Most were not taught to read; schooling was usually forbidden. After the Civil War times changed, but blacks were still not allowed to exist as first-class citizens. Not until 1965 and the passage of the Civil Rights Act was the beginning of equality allowed. Today, covert discrimination still exists.

Insights for Teachers

What then should teachers know about black children? The answers are diverse. Black culture depends in great part upon the location and socioeconomic status of the family. The culture—black or white—in a lower class neighborhood is much different from that in a middle-class or upper-class area. Middle- and upper-class blacks assume the culture of middle- and upper-class society in the United States. If anything, black parents require their children to be more perfect and behave better than corresponding parents in the white society.

Impoverished black families have different strengths and different problems. Parents of black children in a ghetto area in a core city face poverty, powerlessness, alienation, and a negative environment. Over a third of the black population is poor; almost half of black children live in poverty. These children do not see models of financial success due to education and hard work. A good standard of living is not possible if the parent is unemployed or earning minimum wage. These children are raised in a culture of dropouts and school failure in spite of love of their extended family. In 1983 black urban youth were handicapped by a 70 percent unemployment rate in some metropolitan areas.

Teachers should realize that children who speak Black English at home will come to school knowing different language patterns than children who speak standard English. They will have to "learn" a second language—standard English—not always an easy task. It is much easier to write standard English if it is your original dialect. Black children from middle-class and upper-class homes will come to school with the benefit of enough financial backing, better social environment, and a greater chance of speaking standard English.

Black families often have strong networking among family members and friends. Aunts, uncles, and grandparents help and support one another (Stevens, 1982). Most black parents are very interested in their children.

Until prejudice and discrimination are reduced or eliminated in the United States, most Black children will receive mixed messages throughout life. They need to receive encouragement that they will succeed and that they are first-class citizens. Teachers have an important role in conveying that message to all the children in their classrooms.

Spanish-surnamed Students

Although the Spanish-surnamed residents of the United States share some linguistic and cultural traditions, each wave of immigrants from Spain, Cuba, and Mexico has brought unique customs and attributes to the new American environment. Their varied social status and educational levels in their countries of origin, the isolation or hardships encountered on arrival, their desire to acculturate, and even the length of their family's residence in the United States all contribute to a heterogeneous Hispanic-American population. Teachers must

Spanish-surnamed children may be from families that have been in the United States for years or that have just recently immigrated.

work to dispel any stereotypical ideas they may have about their Spanish-surnamed students.

Who are the many people who have contributed to this varied group? The Southwest United States was Spanish territory until 1821, when Mexico gained independence from Spain; later Texas was annexed by the United States in 1845. Arizona, New Mexico, Nevada, and parts of California and Colorado were acquired by the United States as the result of the Mexican-American War. Thus, by 1848 many persons whose ancestors had lived in traditionally Spanish speaking areas since the 1600s had suddenly become citizens of the United States and minorities in an overwhelmingly Anglo culture. The first group of Spanish-surnamed citizens in the United States had ancestors who had been in America before the Pilgrims arrived on the east shore. Hardly immigrants, they had settled and lived with the Pueblo Indians of the area long before United States was interested in the territory. These Spanish colonialists, given land grants by the Spanish viceroys, continued their Spanish lifestyle, albeit controlled by the new environment in which they lived. Their culture is still visible today in Santa Fe, San Antonio, and San Diego. Missions and Spanish-style architecture along with their methods of ranching and their irrigation systems show their contributions to the life-style of the Southwest. Many of their descendants do not want to be called Mexican-American or Chicano; their heritage is Spanish, and the term, Spanish-American or Hispanic, better fits their culture and their heritage.

The greatest influx of Mexican-Americans began around the time of the Mexican Revolution in 1910. Many of the first immigrants were upper-class Mexicans who were refugees, escaping for political reasons. Their assimilation into American society was relatively easy; a second influx occurred in 1916 when Mexicans were hired to help maintain the railroad system across the United States. They were expected to work and return home, but

many remained. They suffered bitter discrimination, especially from those who felt that they were taking jobs from U.S. citizens. Nonetheless the descendents of this group of Mexican-Americans are now assimilated into American society.

During World War II the United States needed help with its farm crops. Therefore, the bracero program was instituted—Mexicans were invited to work temporarily in the United States. The workers benefited the gardens of California and other states. In 1951, the Migratory Labor Agreement (Public Law 78) established a new bracero program (Banks, 1984, p. 258).

After World War II, many Spanish-surnamed persons migrated to cities and northern states to work. Some came from Mexico, but many were American citizens from New Mexico, Texas, and southern Colorado who wanted to work in northern cities and on ranches. Some had been forced off their land when the mines of the Southwest began to close and automation took over. They were a rural people, trying to assimilate into an urban culture.

The use of braceros and migrant workers set a pattern of Mexican workers coming to the United States. Many began crossing the border illegally. In 1954, immigration authorities began deporting illegal Mexicans, but thousands of Mexican-Americans continued to pour across the border as illegal immigrants (Banks, 1984, p. 258). Illegal immigration continues today. The Mexican economy was and is poor. Many Mexicans grasp at an opportunity to provide for their families. Mexican children arrive at our schools with very little or no English and need special care and help to succeed in our educational system. Children of Mexican nationals born while their parents live in the United States are citizens. This new group of Mexican-Americans, coupled with the rural to urban movement of long-time citizens of Hispanic background, provide a challenge to the schools to provide both bilingual education and a strong program in language enrichment.

Not all Spanish-surnamed persons nor all Anglo-Americans fit the cultural traits listed in Table 3-3. Hispanics whose families have lived in the United States for some time and who have wanted to acculturate into the dominant culture, fit the Anglo-American cultural traits more than they do the Mexican-American traits. Compare the general traits of the two cultures to increase your understanding of yourself and others.

Insights for Teachers

Teachers can expect Spanish-surnamed children having difficulty in school to be the ones who do not receive recognition at home for school achievement. Hispanic children are loved whether they achieve in school or not and although this attitude reflects a positive value, parents need to be encouraged to acknowledge their children's effort and encourage them in their school work. Teachers may have some difficulty getting recently arrived immigrants involved in the school. Many fear being identified as illegal immigrants even though schools are required to educate all children and are not responsible for determining who is legal and who is not. Many parents of established families who moved from rural to urban communities have not had a good school experience themselves and feel threatened by the school. Involving the reticent Spanish-surnamed parent is a challenge, but it can be accomplished. (See Chapters 4, 6, and 7 for ideas.) Children of Spanish-surnamed families who are acculturated into the dominant society will work with you as any other parent of the dominant culture.

Spanish-surnamed children will probably work best in a cooperative rather than a competitive atmosphere. School activities should include opportunities for cooperative work.

Lack of extended language rather than no language at all seems to be the biggest problem for the Mexican child. Opportunities for language expression need to be encouraged at all levels of education. Small-group discussions, games that increase language skill, use of language on the computer, role playing, creative dramatics, puppetry, and general encouragement are all essential in language development. Classrooms in which children are allowed to talk quietly or at specific time periods also encourage language development. Whenever you see a lunchroom in which children are not allowed to talk, their teachers do not understand the importance of language development. If the school provides opportunities for language development, the benefits will outweigh the difficulties.

TABLE 3-3

Cultural traits of Mexican-American and Anglo-American families

Mexican-American	Anglo-American
Extended family	Nuclear family
Ascribed position	Achieved position
Work for a reason	Work ethic
Cooperation	Competition
Subsistence	Profit Making
Present orientation	Future orientation
Dependence on patron	Independent
Resistance to change	Favorable view towards change
Strong religious orientation (primarily Catholic)	Variety of religious orientations
Religious-magical interpretations	Scientific method
Resignation-fatalism to superior order	Master of own destiny
Sense of being	Sense of doing

As is the case with all children, teachers working with Spanish-surnamed children need to get to know the parents and work with them and their children at their level of need. Some will need a lot of encouragement, some will need a great deal of help, and some will be able to help you.

Indochinese Students

The easiest mistake for teachers to make is to presume all Indochinese students share a common background.

The first major group of refugees arrived from Vietnam in 1975 after the fall of the country to the North Vietnamese. This group included wealthy and poor, highly educated scholars and professionals, as well as the unskilled. Most were literate but 18 percent had no education (Banks, 1984, p. 18). The second wave of Indochinese refugees were more diverse and included Hmong, Laotians, and Kampucheans (Cambodians). They were homogeneous in their lack of education and their inability to speak English.

French Indochina, first proclaimed the Indochinese Union by the French in 1893, was made up of Vietnam, Cambodia, and Laos. Until that time, the countries were separate political entities; after the union they continued to differ from one another in language, history, and culture. Throughout their long history, these countries were often enemies, controlled by one or the other as one empire thrived and was then destroyed. When working with children from Indochina, do not assume they are from Vietnam; ask them about their homeland.

Differences in Indochinese culture can be shown by language differences as illustrated in Figure 3-1. Do not expect Vietnamese children to be able to communicate with or teach Hmong children in their native language. They will have to use English as a second language (ESL) the same as you. Indochinese families may also have different placement of names (see Figure 3-2), although many immigrants have adapted their names to fit traditional name placement found in the United States, so schools may not find as great a problem in the 1980s as they did in the 1970s.

During the 2,000 year history of Indochina, its inhabitants were influenced by the Chinese, Indian, and Oceanic peoples. In the last 500 years European cultures have also influenced their native heritages. The great variety of religious traditions are indicative of the many cultures represented by the term *Indochinese.* Buddhism spread to Indochina from India; Taoism and Confucianism originated in China. Christianity was introduced much later. An Indochinese person may believe in more than one religion, for unlike Christianity, Eastern religions are based on philosophies of behavior more than deification of their leaders. In addition to the major religions, animism and ancestor worship are practiced in many rural areas. Polytheism is accepted. Most East-

Families of Asian-descent children have been assimilated in varying degrees into the dominant culture of the United States.

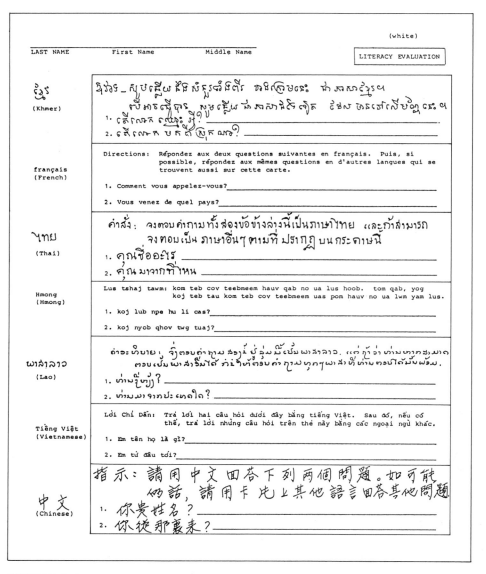

FIGURE 3-1

These examples illustrate the wide variety of written language of the Indochinese people. (*Source:* From Language and Orientation Resource Center. *Indochinese students in U.S. schools: A guide for administrators.* Washington, DC: Center for Applied Linguistics, 1981, pp. 60, 61.

ern religions share an emphasis on the individual's search for peace and harmony, a reverence for ancestors, and a respect for the elderly.

Insights for Teachers

If children come from a culture where there was no formal education, they may have greater problems adjusting to school. The Hmong, for

	Last name	Middle name	First name	Addressed as*
Vietnamese				
Nguyen Hy Vinh (M)	Nguyen	Hy	Vinh	Vinh
				Mr. Vinh
Hoang Thi Thanh (F)	Hoang	Thi	Thanh	
1. Married (to Mr. Vinh)				Thanh
				Mrs. Thanh
				Mrs. Vinh
2. Unmarried				Thanh
				Miss Thanh
Cambodian				
Sok Sam Bo (M)	Sok	(none)	Sam Bo	Sam Bo
				Mr. Sam Bo
Rith Bopha (F)	Rith	(none)	Bopha	
1. Married (to Mr. Sam Bo)				Bopha
				Mrs. Sam Bo
2. Unmarried				Bopha
				Miss Bopha
Lao				
Vixay Siharath (M)	Siharath	(none)	Vixay	Vixay
				Mr. Vixay
Douangkeo Malaythong (F)	Malaythong	(none)	Douangkeo	
1. Married (to Mr. Vixay)	Siharath	(none)	Douangkeo	Douangkeo
				Mrs. Douangkeo
2. Unmarried				Douangkeo
				Miss Douangkeo
Hmong				
Chu Sao Thao (M)	Thao	Chu	Sao	Chu
	(clan name)			Mr. Chu Sao
May Xee Vang (F)	Vang	May	Xee	
	(clan name)			
1. Married (to Mr. Chu Thao)				May Xee
				Mrs. Chu Sao
2. Unmarried				May Xee
				Miss May Xee

*Adding *Mr., Mrs., Miss* makes the form of address more formal.

FIGURE 3-2
Name placement varies among the Indochinese ethnic groups. (*Source:* From Language and Orientation Resource Center. *Indochinese students in U.S. schools: A guide for administrators.* Washington, DC: Center for Applied Linguistics, 1981, pp. 49, 50.

instance, did not have a written language until the 1960s. Children without an ability to write and read in their native language are at a disadvantage when they attempt school in the United States. They are sometimes called double illiterates, because they have no written language base from which to draw. Teachers need to recognize the children's experience and background and plan a curriculum based on their strengths and needs.

Most Indochinese families value education, and generally Indochinese students will work hard to obtain an education. Their respect for education extends to teachers. In fact, Indochinese parents do not question the teacher's decisions or expertise. They leave their child's education up to the teacher.

Those who were in school before coming to the United States were taught largely through lecture and memorization; active participation in the learning process may be new to them. Others may not have attended school at all. Often parents or siblings will tutor young children or others before school.

Indochinese families are close-knit extended families. They often try to reunite when they arrive in the United States. They also work hard to save money and bring other members of their families to their new home.

Many Indochinese students suffered extreme trauma in their escape to freedom. Use journals for older children and creative art for younger and older children to help them express feelings.

It is important for teachers to be sensitive to gestures and mannerisms that may have unintended meanings for themselves or their students. For example, Indochinese students may not look at the teacher steadily in the eye since such behavior is a sign of disrespect. A pat on the head may be meant kindly, but is likely to offend. Children should not be called by a hand motion with fingers up since such mannerisms are reserved for animals. To call a student with your hand, place your palm and fingers down. Be sure not to criticize the Indochinese children in front of others; they need to be able to "save face."

Indochinese pupils may come to school with small round bruises on the arm, but "coining" (pressure by coins) is used to reduce illness or pain and is not a sign of abuse.

Parents and children may not let you know if they do not understand. They are more likely to agree and smile rather than to question. Indochinese children fit smoothly into a school system. They tend to value good grades, are well-behaved, and industrious.

Teachers need to be concerned about the stress children are under in their desire to achieve. Teachers should give these students assignments that are realistic.

WHAT PARENTS LIKE ABOUT TEACHERS

Parents, in describing the ideal teacher, stressed the following qualities:

1. Ability to communicate, to understand, to relate
2. Patience
3. Ability to discipline, to be firm and fair
4. High moral character
5. Friendliness, good personality, sense of humor
6. Dedication to teaching profession, enthusiasm
7. Ability to inspire, motivate students
8. Intelligence
9. Caring about students (Gallup, 1983, p. 44).

This chapter points out many of the diverse challenges that face teachers, parents, and schools. The changing world accompanied by the birth and growth of new generations and the arrival of newcomers from other lands requires dedication to the task.

Children are like snowflakes
At first they appear to be alike
But on close examination they are
*   all different*
Focus on their similarities
But understand their differences

SUMMARY

Family structure is changing, but the family is still the most stable component of society. Marriage and family life are important to Americans.

The population of the United States has increased dramatically in the last 40 years. Along with growth there have been new trends. More mothers are working outside the home. More people are completing high school and college. There has also been an alarming increase in out-of-wedlock births, and the highest growth has been with teen-agers. Eighteen percent of children live with single-parent mothers. Over 2 percent of the children live with single-parent fathers. Fathers are becoming more involved with their children.

Poverty in the United States has increased, and almost one in five children lives in poverty—most the children of single mothers and black families.

Black families still face covert prejudice, although strides have been made to reduce overt discrimination. An increase in the number of illegal Mexicans has added to the workforce. Spanish-surnamed residents, along with blacks, find it difficult to find satisfactory occupations.

The recent wave of Indochinese immigration has made an impact on the schools. The influx of Vietnamese, Hmong, Laotians, and Cambodians, each with a different culture, is a challenge to the schools. Although it is important to understand cultural differences, the teacher should focus on the strengths of all children, regardless of their financial or racial background.

7. Interview a single parent. Find out the advantages and disadvantages of rearing children alone. Which support systems do they need?
8. Interview social agencies concerned with families, for example, a welfare agency, child care association, or Head Start. Find out their income-level requirements. Which services do they provide?
9. How is family life changing in the United States? How does this affect parent education programs? Discuss the changes that have occurred during your lifetime.
10. What is an ideal family? Discuss. List the values and strengths you look for in an ideal family. Why did you choose them?
11. Call several schools and find out about their programs for teen-age mothers. Visit one of the programs. Talk with the teen-age mothers. What are they learning? How do they feel about motherhood?

SUGGESTED ACTIVITIES AND DISCUSSIONS

1. Interview parents in your neighborhood, school district, or college community. Which kinds of support systems and types of activities do they want?
2. Count the number of moves the members of your class have made. Why have they moved? Where have they moved? How many times have they moved?
3. Survey your class members. How many lifestyles are represented in your class? Discuss.
4. Obtain the busing plan in your community. How would you need to adapt your plans for working with parents because of busing? For example, would you need to visit different neighborhoods or hold meetings at alternate locations?
5. Investigate methods school districts are using to help Vietnamese, Cambodians, Cubans, Laotians, Chicanos, and other immigrants acculturate into the school system. Ask for materials from your school district that are being used by teachers.
6. Visit agencies that work with single parents. Find out about available resources.

BIBLIOGRAPHY

Banks, J. A. *Teaching strategies for ethnic studies.* Boston: Allyn & Bacon, 1984.

Berrueta-Clement, J. R., Schweinhart, L. J., Barnett, W. S., Epstein, A. S., & Weikart, D. P. *Changed lives: The effects of the Perry preschool program on youths through age 19.* Ypsilanti, Mich.: The High/Scope Press, 1984.

Cherlin, A. J. *Marriage, divorce, remarriage.* Cambridge, Mass.: Harvard University Press, 1981.

Children's Defense Fund. *America's children and their families: Key facts.* Washington, D.C.: Children's Defense Fund, 1982.

———. *A children's defense budget: An analysis of the President's FY 1986 budget and children.* Washington, D.C.: Children's Defense Fund, 1985.

Farran, D. C., Haskins, R., & Gallagher, J. J. Poverty and mental retardation: A search for explanations. In J. J. Gallagher (Ed.), *New Directions for Exceptional Children,* 1980, *1,* 47–65.

Gallup, G. H. The eleventh annual Gallup Poll of the public's attitudes toward the public school. *Phi Delta Kappan,* September 1979, pp. 33–45.

———. The fifteenth annual Gallup Poll of the public's attitude toward the public schools. *Phi Delta Kappan.* September 1983, pp. 33–47.

Hayghe, H. Working mothers reach record number in 1984. *Monthly Labor Review,* December 1984, pp. 31–33.

Howard, A. E. *The American family myth & reality.* Washington, D.C.: National Association for the Education of Young Children, 1980.

Kaplan, G. P., Van Valey, L., & Associates. *Census '80: Continuing the factfinder tradition.* (U.S. Bureau of the Census.) Washington, D.C.: U.S. Government Printing Office, 1980.

Kenniston, K. & The Carnegie Council on Children. *All our children.* New York: Harcourt Brace Jovanovich, 1977.

Lamb, M. E. *The role of the father in child development.* New York: A Wiley-interscience Publication, 1976.

Language and Orientation Resource Center. *Indochinese students in U.S. schools: A guide for administrators.* Washington, D.C.: Center for Applied Linguistics, 1981.

LeMaster, E. E., & DeFrain, J. *Parents in contemporary America: A sympathetic view* (4th ed.). Homewood, Ill.: Dorsey Press, 1983.

Lowery, C. R., & Settle, S. A. Effects of divorce on children: Differential impact of custody and visitation patterns. *Family Relations,* October 1985, pp. 455–461.

O'Connell, J. C. Research in review. *Young Children,* February 1983, pp. 63–70.

O'Hare, W. P. *Poverty in America: Trends and new patterns. Population Bulletin* (Vol. 40, No. 3). Washington, D.C.: Population Reference Bureau, 1985.

Population Reference Bureau and guest experts. *U.S. population. Where we are; where we're going* (Vol. 37, No. 2). Washington, D.C.: Population Reference Bureau, 1982.

Stevens, J. H., Jr. Support systems for black families. In J. D. Quisenberry (Ed.), *Changing family lifestyles.* Washington, D.C.: Association for Childhood Education International, 1982.

Swick, K. J., & Manning, M. L. Father involvement in home and school settings. *Childhood Education,* November/December 1983, pp. 128–134.

Thornton, A., & Freedman, D. *The changing American family* (Population Bulletin Vol. 38, No. 4). Washington, D.C.: Population Reference Bureau, 1983.

U.S. Department of Commerce (Bureau of Census). *Current population reports. Population characteristics.* Series P-20 No. 402, Washington, D.C.: U.S. Department of Commerce, 1985.

———. *1980 census of population and housing: Provisional estimates of social, economic, and housing characteristics: Supplementary report.* Washington, D.C.: U.S. Department of Commerce, 1982.

Wallerstein, J. Effect of divorce on children. *The Harvard Medical School Mental Health Letter,* 1985, *2*(3).

Wallerstein, J. S., & Kelly, J. B. The effects of parental divorce: Experience of the child in later latency. In A. Skolnick & J. H. Skolnick, *Family in transition.* Boston: Little, Brown, and Co., 1980.

Washington, V., & Oyemade, U. J. Changing family trends. *Young Children,* September 1985, pp. 12–20.

White, B. L. *A parent's guide to the first three years.* Englewood Cliffs, N.J.: Prentice-Hall, 1980.

CHAPTER FOUR

Effective Home-school-community Relationships

If you had three wishes, what would you wish for that would ensure a pleasant effective home-school-community relationship? Would you wish for a supportive working relationship with your colleagues, teachers, administrators, and parents? Perhaps you would wish for the answer to the learning difficulties of your students. Would you want freedom to express your concerns regarding schools, children, and curriculum without fear of misinter-

pretation? You might make one grand wish that the cooperative effort of teacher, parents, administrators, and community would provide a continuous supportive educational program for the diverse children trying to grow into productive adults. This chapter looks at the home-school-community relationship and suggests procedures, ideas, and methods to help you realize those wishes. Choose those ideas that fit your needs. Incorporate them into your

As volunteers in the classroom, parents can support and help the teacher while they learn new activities to share with their children at home.

teaching or parenting style, and you will enjoy a more open, constructive environment.

At a workshop involving parents, teachers, and administrators, the participants were asked to raise their hands if they were parents. Almost every person in the room raised a hand. Suddenly the teachers and administrators were in their parental rather than professional roles. Teachers described how different their feelings were when their roles were reversed from teachers to parents. As they thought about the change of roles, they recognized the difference in emotions present in each position. The teacher's understanding of parents' feelings and concerns is a giant step toward creating effective home-school relationships. Picturing parents as a group separate from the school sets up an artificial barrier. Parents are no special breed. We are the parents of the current generation of young people. To understand ourselves as parents is to begin to understand others. What makes us effective participants in home-school-community relationships are those same qualities that make others productive members of the home-school-community team.

SCHOOL CLIMATE AND PARENTAL ATTITUDES

When you walk into a school, are you able to sense its spirit? Does it seem to invite you to visit? Does it make you feel unwelcome? Can you pinpoint the reasons for your feelings? Each school differs in its character (usually set by the administrators) and reflects the morale and attitudes of the personnel. Some say, "Come, enjoy with us this exciting business of education." Others say, "You are infringing on my territory. Schools are the professional's business. Send us your children. We will return them to you each evening, but, in the meantime, let's each keep to our own responsibilities." In the first instance, there is joy in the educational spirit. In the second, fear or avoidance overrides all sense of joy.

Although schools have an obvious climate, one must always consider that parents also bring their attitudes into the home-school relationship. One parent may feel excitement and anticipation over a forthcoming visit to the school, while another may be struck with dread over a required conference. Parents come from diverse backgrounds. If their past school experiences were pleasant and successful, they are likely to enjoy visiting schools again. If their experiences were filled with failure and disappointments, whether real or imagined, the thought of school is foreboding and depressing; if they do approach the school, they do so with trepidation.

Coupled with the parents' past experiences are present pressures. In some districts the burden of poverty will consume the parents. Parents concerned with mere subsistence have little energy left for self-fulfillment or for meeting their children's emotional and educational needs. Maslow's (1968) hierarchy of needs stresses that basic needs must be met before persons can climb to higher rungs of the ladder toward self-actualization. Parents contending with unemployment, inflation, and social change will need special understanding. "Humans of all ages get caught in a powerful web spun of two strong threads; the way they were treated in the past, and the way the present bears down on them" (Hymes, 1974, p. 16). The school must be a support system working cooperatively with the home rather than another agency viewing the parents as failures.

Add the parents' concerns for their children's welfare and you will recognize why school-home relationships can be either negative encounters or effective partnerships. Hymes (1974) eloquently described the parent-child-teacher relationship when he said that parents love their children, and if the teacher

feels this same love, then parents are your friends. Show your interest in a child and parents are on your side. Be casual, be off-handed, be cold toward the child and parents can never work closely with you. . . . To touch the child is to touch the parent. To praise the child is to praise the parent. To criticize the child is to hit at the parent. The two are two, but the two are one. (pp. 8, 9)

Debilitating experiences with schools, feelings of inadequacy, poor achievement by children, and pressures of the present can cause some parents to stay away from the school. On the other hand, some parents tend to dominate and to be compulsively involved with the schools. Between these two extremes are parents who need encouragement to come to school, parents who readily respond when invited, and parents who are comfortable about coming to school and enjoy some involvement in the educational process. (See Figure 4-1.) Each group requires a different re-

sponse from the professional staff. The first group will need time to overcome past negative experiences and to appreciate current circumstances that prove the school can be trusted to help their children. If the school has an inviting and responsive climate, the second, third, and fourth groups of parents will feel welcome. These three middle groups (which encompass the largest portion of parents) will soon become contributing resources to the school's activities. They can also form a supportive advocacy for future school plans. Parents in the fifth group may need to be delegated tasks that encourage them to work more cooperatively with the school. Offering a variety of tasks and different degrees of involvement assures parents that they may contribute according to their talents and available time and al-

FIGURE 4-1

Parents respond to schools based upon past experience and current situation.

lows all of them to be comfortable about coming to school and enjoying involvement in the educational process.

THE CASE FOR IMPROVED RELATIONSHIPS

Schools have more contact with families than any other public agency. Almost every child over 6 spends 9 months a year, 5 days a week, 5 or 6 hours a day, in school. If daycare centers and preschools are included, the school-home-community relationship begins at an even earlier age. Locally controlled, schools can respond to the needs of the community. If schools and community join forces in a co-ordinated effort to support families and children, they can have an enormous impact. The school and home also have a natural opportunity to work together. With the community, they can achieve their goals for children.

In an extensive research project, Williams (1984) finds both school personnel and parents concerned about the necessity of parent involvement in schools. A majority of school staff, administrators, and parents feel that parent involvement in education is both important and necessary.

Williams' study includes a sample of 950 teacher educators, 2,000 teachers, 1,500 principals, 4,800 parents, 2,500 school superintendents, 2,500 school board presidents, and 36 state department of education officials. Parents are very interested in all aspects of their child's education. They differ with school administrators and teachers in their desire for more involvement in decision making. School staff want more educational involvement at home and support for the school program but little parental involvement in school decision making. Both groups agree that training teachers to work with parents is important. The study recommends that parents be involved as real partners, beginning with the traditional roles and progressing until they function as partners in the educational process (Williams, 1984).

Parent-school-community partnership has been recognized in such national programs as Head Start and the Elementary and Secondary School Act, Chapter I, III, IV, or VIII. Follow Through and Right-to-Read programs, like Head Start, recommend that parents participate in policymaking. Parents became partners in program design when Public Law 94-142 required Individualized Education Programs (IEP) for special education students to be written by educators with parental input and approval. Across the nation, school districts have started new alliances with parents and the community. Those involved in programs where parents have been active components have found that the partnership is a success. "I don't feel that I'm competing with the teacher any longer. For the first time I feel that I'm contributing to the education of my child," said one gratified parent (Benet, 1976, p. 31). In Chapter I, Head Start, and Chapter

Parents working as partners with the teacher are more effective than parents as observers.

IV programs, in-service conferences where parents, teachers, and administrators work, study, and discuss together have made parents partners in educational process.

Seefeldt (1985) has called for parent involvement in which there is concern for the welfare of the parents along with the children. She has asked for being sensitive to the needs of families, focusing on offering real support for families and providing true collaboration between home and school (p. 99). She sees parent's decision-making powers as including "decisions about the school's budget, selection of staff and general operating procedures" (p. 102).

A 1979 Gallup Poll delves into the cooperative relationships among parents, community, and schools. It solicited recommendations for improving community relations and summarized the responses to the survey.[1]

1. Better communication. The local community cannot be expected to take a keen interest in the schools if people know little about them. The media should carry much more school news, especially news about the achievements of students and the schools, the means being taken to deal with school problems, and new developments in education. Media research has shown that there is far greater interest in schools and in education than most journalists think. At the same time, the schools should not rely solely on the major media. Newsletters are important to convey information that media cannot be expected to report.
2. More conferences. Many of those included in the survey recommend that more conferences about the progress and problems of students be held with parents—both father and mother. Special monthly parent meetings and workshops are also suggested as a way to bring teachers, administrators, and parents together. Survey respondents also recommend courses for parents and special lectures. PTA meetings, some suggest, could be more useful to parents if school

problems and education developments were given more attention.
3. Invite volunteers. Some respondents suggest that, if more members of the community could serve in a volunteer capacity in the classrooms and elsewhere in the school, they would further better community understanding of the problems faced by the schools. In addition, their involvement in school operations would increase their own interest in educational improvement at the local level.
4. Plan special occasions. Interest in the schools and in education could be improved, some suggest, by inviting members of the community—both those who have children in the schools and those who do not—to attend meetings, lectures, and social events in the school buildings. . . . Only one person in three across the nation attended a lecture, meeting, or social occasion in a school building during the last year. In 1969, when the same question was asked, a slightly higher proportion said they had attended a lecture, meeting, or social occasion in a school building.

Private schools, and virtually all colleges and universities, plan many occasions to bring their alumni back to their campuses in order to keep them interested in the school. The public schools could adopt the same policy to their advantage, inviting not only alumni to attend such events but members of the community who have attended schools in other areas.

REASONS PARENTS VISIT SCHOOLS

Another questionnaire (Berger, 1979, Appendix, Chapter 4) addresses questions not included in the Gallup Poll—why parents visit schools. Most parents visit the schools for specific reasons—to attend special events, such as PTA meetings, the school carnival, parent-teacher conferences, back-to-school night, conferences with teachers, a mother-daughter tea, and fathers' night. Some indicate a general interest in what is going on in school. They come to school to become informed; they want to watch their children interact with other children, to observe what is going on in the classroom, and to see which activities are

1. From Gallup, G. The eleventh annual Gallup Poll of the public's attitudes toward the public schools. *Phi Delta Kappan,* September 1979, p. 41.

available to children. Others feel they want to get to know the teachers. Most important, parents want to encourage their child, and the child encourages the parents to visit school. Parents have a personal interest in what their child is learning and doing. They want the child to know how interested they are. Some of them want the teacher to know, too.

Several respondents to the questionnaire mention volunteer activities in the classroom. Some parents go to school to aid teachers in the classroom, to do volunteer work in the office, library, or clinic, and to attend volunteer aide conferences. This co-working appears to be a major breakthrough in professional-lay relationships.

One parent in the study mentioned the openness of the faculty and a feeling of freedom to visit school, but was the only parent who mentioned feeling welcomed. Most indicated that the schools had done nothing to encourage them to participate. Most parents respond to notices of programs and meetings; they visit for a specific reason rather than because they feel that the school is a part of the family social system. That the majority of parents attend schools only when requested indicates that there is still a great deal schools and parents can do to become partners in the educational process.

HOME-SCHOOL CONTINUITY

Continuity between home and school is a necessary and important support system for families today. Look at the facts. One in five families has a single-parent mother; one in two children has both parents working outside the home. This was not the case 30 years ago. Over half of school-aged children now go home to empty homes or alternative child care. Families cannot afford to be caught in an adversarial position with the school. They need cooperation, support, and facilities that make it possible to supply their children with a stable environment.

Split sessions, classes finishing at 2:30 P.M., and a lack of after-school programs illustrate a society that has little concern for the family of the 1980s. Tradition controls the time school is held as well as how the school buildings are used. You may wonder why the schools do not work with other social agencies in offering the support that families need. The burden for providing continuity cannot be placed on individual teachers. Working with children for 6 hours a day, preparing class materials, grading papers, and comforting and supporting children is a full-time job. Other groups such as recreation programs, library services, special after-school teachers, and artists in residence should be enlisted to help extend the school day to accommodate parents' schedules. Parents who are not employed outside the home could volunteer or be paid to help with after-school and before-school programs. Enrichment activities, physical development, and social opportunities should be provided for children who have working parents and for others who wish to partake of the opportunities.

ROLES OF PARENTS

Within each school parents may assume a variety of roles (Figure 4-2). Most commonly parents are spectators who merely observe what the school does with their children in the educational process. They view the school as an authority figure, best able to handle the education of their children. But parents may also assume other roles simultaneously.

The room-parent, for example, who provides treats and creates parties is an accessory volunteer. Accessory volunteers can provide needed services unrelated to the educational process, and their children are pleased if the event is a success, but their involvement is geared only to a specific time and task. After the event is over, the room-parent withdraws from the educational environment to await the next assignment.

FIGURE 4-2
Parents are involved as teachers of their own children, spectators, volunteers, paid employees, and policymakers.

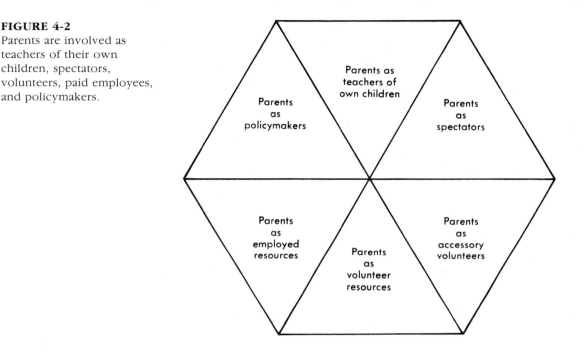

Parents sometimes serve as resources in the school's instructional program. As volunteers they may develop materials and curriculum ideas or occasionally share their expertise. Schools that have encouraged innovative development of resource materials by parents emphasize the benefits schools may receive (Gilmar & Nelson, 1975; Harris, 1978).

Parents may also serve as policymakers. Local school boards have been composed of community leaders charged with education policymaking for many years. Although early control of schools was accomplished by local community leaders who were generally the elite of the area, at least 50 percent of the Parent Advisory Councils required by Chapter I and Head Start should be composed of parents served by those programs. With this representative membership, policy control has reached down to the grass roots of the constituency being served. The decisions of policymaking parents directly affect the schools their own children attend.

Finally parents are teachers of their own children. Whether sufficiently appreciated or not, parents have always reared and educated their children until informal education was supplemented by formal education. There is now emerging an increasing awareness of the link between informal and formal instruction. Parents can enhance the informal education of their children by knowledge of the formal educational process, and although they are encouraged to teach in an informal manner, the steppingstones of early formal education are being realized. Daily incidental teaching of language and problem solving encourages the development of intelligence in the young child. As the parent lets the child select socks that match the color of the child's shirt, the child is learning color discrimination and matching. Setting the table and putting away the dishes involve classification of articles. Programs to help parents in their role as the child's early educator have been successful. Chapter I has encouraged parents to teach reading and reinforce the school's program. Parents who are aware of their roles in the educational development of their adolescent children promote the successful completion of their formal education. Parents are the one continuous force in the education of their children from birth to adulthood.

THE TEACHER'S ROLE IN PARENT INVOLVEMENT

The teacher is central to parental involvement in the educational process. Teacher roles include facilitator, teacher, counselor, communicator, program director, interpreter, resource developer, and friend. These roles are illustrated through the activities described later in the chapter, for example, parent-teacher conferences, volunteer programs, and program development.

THE ADMINISTRATOR'S ROLE IN PARENT INVOLVEMENT

Administrative leadership is evident in four aspects of school-parent interaction. First, the spirit of the school and the enthusiasm of its staff reflect the administrator's role of morale builder. Supportive guidance, with freedom to develop plans based on individual school needs, allows the principal to function with productive autonomy. The principal builds staff morale by enabling staff to feel positive, enthusiastic, and secure in their work with children and parents.

A second leadership role, program designer, involves the implementation of the educational program. The principal needs to recognize the importance of home-school-community relationships in the success of the educational program and strive toward implementation of such a working relationship. If the principal allows teachers the autonomy to work with parents, using volunteers and aides in the development of individualized curricula, the school is on its way to an effective program of parent involvement.

The administrator's third role requires the development of an effective principal-parent relationship. The principal determines if the school atmosphere makes parents feel welcome. Besides influencing the general spirit and morale of the school, the principal is responsible for maintaining an open-door policy, scheduling open houses, providing and equipping resource areas for parents, arranging parent education meetings, developing parent workshops and in-service meetings, and supporting the PTA or PTO.

Finally, the principal serves as a program coordinator. Individual teachers may develop unique programs using the talents of parents, but the achievement of continuity requires the principal's coordination of parent-involvement programs.

A WORD OF CAUTION

A word of caution must be injected into this bright picture. If we depend upon improved home-school-community relationships to solve all educational and social problems, we are expecting too much. Improving home-school-community relationships is important, but we cannot expect such improvement to be the panacea for all educational ills.

TEACHERS' FEELINGS ABOUT PARENT INVOLVEMENT

The school needs personnel who demonstrate acceptance of parents, but sometimes teachers and administrators are unaware of how they feel toward parents. Value clarification questionnaires can bring out these feelings, but are even more beneficial when professionals use them as guides to effecting change. Several effective and well-illustrated books can aid the educator in developing value clarification exercises (Curwin & Fuhrmann, 1975; Kniker, 1977; Kroth & Simpson, 1977; Raths, Harmin, & Simon, 1978; Simon, Howe, & Kirschenbau, 1985). By determining whether statements agree or disagree with their beliefs, professionals can begin to understand their attitudes about parents. If they know they prefer working alone, they may maintain that attitude or they may examine why they feel better working by themselves and decide that this can be changed. Staff members need to understand their values about their relationships with families so they can interact with children and parents more effectively and objectively.

The clarification tools shown in Figure 4-3 were developed to help teachers assess their attitudes toward parents. Kroth and Simpson (1977) used similar tools as teacher value clarification instruments. They suggest that you might want to add or delete statements and share the clarification instrument with a co-worker. Discussion with another person, evaluation of your apparent values by a close colleague, and comparisons of your real with your ideal values will help focus your attitudes about working with parents. There are no right or wrong answers; the purpose is to recognize your values and attitudes.

As a teacher I . . .	*How you see yourself*		*How you wish you were*	
	Yes	*No*	*Yes*	*No*
1. Feel that parents are more work than help.	☐	☐	☐	☐
2. Tense when parents enter my room.	☐	☐	☐	☐
3. Prefer to work alone.	☐	☐	☐	☐
4. Compare brothers and sisters from the same family.	☐	☐	☐	☐
5. Feel threatened by parents.	☐	☐	☐	☐
6. View parents as a great resource.	☐	☐	☐	☐
7. Believe that disadvantaged children have parents who do not care.	☐	☐	☐	☐
8. Enjoy working with several outside persons in the classroom.	☐	☐	☐	☐
9. Have prejudiced feelings about certain groups.	☐	☐	☐	☐
10. Feel that parents let children watch too much television.	☐	☐	☐	☐
11. Feel parents are not interested in their children.	☐	☐	☐	☐
12. Work better with social distance between the parent and myself.	☐	☐	☐	☐
13. Believe parents who let their children come to school in inappropriate clothing are irresponsible.	☐	☐	☐	☐
14. Feel that a close working relationship with parents is necessary for optimal student growth.	☐	☐	☐	☐
15. Am pleased when all the parents are gone.	☐	☐	☐	☐
16. Anticipate parent conferences with pleasure.	☐	☐	☐	☐
17. Feel that parents have abdicated the parental role.	☐	☐	☐	☐
18. Enjoy working with parents.	☐	☐	☐	☐

FIGURE 4-3
Teachers can tell how they feel about collaboration with parents by answering this questionnaire.

	As a teacher I believe that I should . . .		As a teacher I . . .	
	Essential	Not important	Always	Never
1. Listen to what parents are saying.	☐	☐	☐	☐
2. Encourage parents to drop in.	☐	☐	☐	☐
3. Give parents an opportunity to contribute to my class.	☐	☐	☐	☐
4. Have handouts written that enable parents to participate in the classroom.	☐	☐	☐	☐
5. Send newsletters home to parents.	☐	☐	☐	☐
6. Contact parents before school in the fall.	☐	☐	☐	☐
7. Listen to parents 50% of the time during conferences.	☐	☐	☐	☐
8. Contact parents when a child does well.	☐	☐	☐	☐
9. Allow for differences among parents.	☐	☐	☐	☐
10. Learn objectives parents have for their children.	☐	☐	☐	☐
11. Learn about interests and special abilities of students.	☐	☐	☐	☐
12. Visit students in their home.	☐	☐	☐	☐
13. Show parents examples of the student's work.	☐	☐	☐	☐
14. Enlist parent volunteers for my classroom.	☐	☐	☐	☐
15. Accept differences among parents.	☐	☐	☐	☐
16. Encourage both mother and father to attend conferences.	☐	☐	☐	☐
17. Make parents feel comfortable coming to school.	☐	☐	☐	☐
18. Include parents in educational plans for their children.	☐	☐	☐	☐
19. Try to be open and honest with parents.	☐	☐	☐	☐
20. Send notes home with children.	☐	☐	☐	☐
21. Include students along with parents during conferences.	☐	☐	☐	☐
22. Let parents sit at their child's desk during back-to-school night.	☐	☐	☐	☐
23. Keep both parents informed if parents are separated.	☐	☐	☐	☐
24. Consider parents as partners in the educational process.	☐	☐	☐	☐

FIGURE 4-3, *continued*

OPEN COMMUNICATION

Improving communication is a necessary step in the right direction for improved home-school-community relationships. "Communication begins with a source, an individual or group whose purpose is to convey a message" (Chinn, Winn, & Walters, 1978, p. 45). Communication ranges from the simplest note sent home by the teacher to a complicated news report in the media. Parents want to know what is happening at school and are interested in program development and curriculum decisions.

One-way communication informs parents about the school's plans and happenings. Two-way communication allows parents to feed into the school their knowledge, concerns, and desires and requires interaction between the participants. Both the school and parents gain. The steps to achieve effective communication among school, home, and community are easy to implement once the importance of effective communication is acknowledged. A number of strategies for establishing improved communication are described on the following pages. Choose the ones that fit your individual needs, and add others that work for you.

One-way Communication

A newsletter may be used by the school as a message from the principal, or it may be sent home by each teacher. It is a simple form of one-way communication, and the format varies with the goals and objectives of each newsletter. Design ranges from a very simple notice to an elaborate and professional letter.

Simple Newsletters

At the beginning of the year, teachers may duplicate a small sheet bearing a title and including sections marked off for classroom news. Items may include the children's activities in curriculum areas such as math contracts or contests, reading projects, group presentations in social studies, hands-on-work in science, practice in music skills, and art experiences. A section may be left for remarks about field trip excursions, care of classroom pets, contributions by resource persons, creative drama experiences, and accomplishments or remarks by individual children. Newsletters may also be used at the secondary level with

sections blocked for each course of study. Communication between home and secondary schools is essential. At that level as well as lower levels, students may be given the responsibility of writing the periodic newsletter. As soon as enough news is accumulated, publish. You may wish to select a regular publication day. The more newsletters you write, the easier it becomes. Not every newsletter contains all information, for it is an ongoing communication. The design may vary from a very simple newsletter, printed by hand and duplicated at the school office or neighborhood library, to a letter printed by the school's duplicating services. You may allow each student to write an individual newsnote to accompany the newsletter. In this way, the newsletter serves two purposes: curriculum and communication. The students have a challenge to write neatly, spell correctly, and construct a readable newsletter. In classes where composition of the complete newsletter would be an overwhelming task for students, leave only one section blank for their individual contributions. Figure 4-4 may be used as a guide. Tips for producing and publishing an appropriate newsletter for preschool, elementary, intermediate or middle, and secondary levels are listed here.

Preschool.   Parents love to hear about happenings in the preschool. Newsletters at this stage are your responsibility. Although children can contribute drawings and stories, you will need to publish the newsletter. It is a good idea to collect newsletter ideas throughout the year. State home economic extension agencies will probably have some excellent ideas to contribute to your collection. See Chapter 11 on resources for additional sources of newsletter material. Subjects interesting to parents include nutrition, child development, communication, and activities for rainy days, as well as events specific to your center. As you collect interesting comments by the children or complete special projects, make a short notation for

FIGURE 4-4
Newsletters can take many forms, ranging from this informal design to very sophisticated publications.

the newsletter. When time comes for publication, you will have more than enough news. If you include articles about individual children, be sure to include each child before the end of the term.

It is more important to have a newsletter than to worry about its design. If typing isn't possible, write in your neatest script. A picture drawn by a child to accompany the news is an attractive addition.

Elementary. A newsletter is an excellent curriculum tool in elementary school. Although children in the first grade may not be able to produce their own newsletter, you will be surprised at how well young children can write and edit their news. Make the newsletter an ongoing project, with a center set up to handle the papers and equipment. Assign a group in each subject area to be responsible for the newsletter. Let them collect the news and determine the content and design of the letter. If you cut and paste, the children can be allowed to type their own copy. Photocopy the master and print it by Thermofax, Xerox, or the most convenient method of duplication. If it is necessary to use a professional company, check the prices of a fast photocopying center; you will probably find that reproducing a one-sheet newsletter is inexpensive.

Middle and Secondary. Although seldom used at this level, the newsletter is an excellent mechanism for secondary students to gain experience in writing, composition, and making layouts. You receive dual benefits; students learn through the process of doing, and a communication system between school and home is established.

A sophisticated newsletter may be the goal for upper-level students, but the importance of the newsletter as a communication tool should not be overlooked. If producing a sophisticated newsletter is too time-consuming, write the newsletter in a simple, informative style. The major objective is communication between the teacher and home. What is the class studying? What types of assignments are the students expected to do? Is there any problem solving being done in class? Which problems seem the most difficult? Are there any parents who would like to contribute to the subject being covered?

The newsletter is a short, practical form of newspaper. It is easily produced and is able to relate to a smaller and, therefore, more specific group of students. It can address current

concerns and interests and can inform a select group of parents of the happenings that impact their children's lives.

Spontaneous Notes and Happy-grams

Notes written on the spur of the moment to be carried home by the student are a very effective means of communication. An especially pretty picture, an interesting comment by the child, an unsolicited helpful gesture, or a report particularly well done is reason enough for a short note.

It is a good idea to buy small sheets of paper with a space large enough for a one- or two-line note. If you write too much, you may be forced by time limitation to postpone the incidental note, and the positive impact of timeliness is lost.

It has become popular to use happy faces, "glad-grams," or similar notes for teachers to periodically report something positive about each child. The concept behind each of these formats is the same—to communicate with the parent in a positive manner, thereby improving both parent-teacher relations and the child's self-concept. Make a concerted effort to send these notes in a spirit of spontaneous sincerity. A contrived, meaningless comment, sent because you are required to do so, will probably be received as it was sent. Preserving good relations requires that the message have meaning.

Newspapers

Most school districts have newspapers, yearbooks, and other school-sponsored publications. These, along with the district newsletter, are important school traditions and effectively disseminate information. Don't stop publishing them, but always remember that the newsletters that touch their children and, thereby, touch them are of greater importance to parents. Those parents most affected by yearbooks are those whose children are pictured in them. Parents most affected by newspapers are those who find articles in them concerning activities in which their children are involved.

Relying solely on newspapers and yearbooks for communicating with parents may promote complacency since some administrators and teachers assume that communication is complete because a newspaper comes out periodically and a yearbook is published when seniors graduate. Yearbooks have very little impact on school-home relationships. They arrive after the student's school career ends, they often picture a small segment of the school population, and they are generally the product of a small, select group of outstanding students. The majority of students may be omitted or ignored. The school newspaper cannot take the place of individual class newsletters. Parents are more interested in their particular children than in the school leaders and star athletes. Newspapers and yearbooks meet different needs and are both significant in their own way, but to establish a real working relationship between parents and schools, the school's publication must concern the parents' number one interest—their own children.

District Newsletter

Many school districts use newsletters to keep the community up-to-date on school events. Often produced by professional public relations firms, they may display excellent style and format and contain precise information, but they may also lack the personal touch and tend to be viewed as a formal communiqué from the administration. District newsletters do have a place in building effective home-school-community relations, however, and, if supplemented by individual class reports (newsletters), the parent will receive both a formal and personal communication regarding their child's schooling.

Media

A formal and effective means of reaching parents is through the community newspaper, television, or radio. Television and radio often make public service announcements. Use them to inform the community about events at school.

Enlist the TV station as a partner in education. Some stations sponsor tutoring programs. Students are encouraged to call designated numbers (e.g., 000-HELP, 000-PASS or 000-AIDE) and talk to someone about homework. The station commits funds to hire tutors to answer questions children or parents might have about homework. It also works to have recognizable personalities take turns on the telephone. Watch the tutor service take off if parents and children know that local celebrities are willing to help.

Handbooks

Handbooks sent to homes before the child enters school are greatly appreciated by parents. If sent while the child is a preschooler, the school's expectations for the child can be met early. If given to parents at an open house during the spring term, it can reinforce the directions given by the teacher at that time. Handbooks can help parents new in the area if they include information on community activities and associations available to families. A district handbook designed to introduce parents to the resources in the area, with special pages geared to each level of student, can be developed and used by all teachers in the district. Consider the following items in the compilation of your handbook:

- Procedures for registration
- Invitations to visit school
- Conferences and progress reports
- Special events
- Testing and evaluation programs
- Facilities at the school (e.g., cafeteria, clinic, library)
- Special programs offered by school (e.g., band, chorus, gymnastics)
- Summer programs
- Recreation programs
- Associations related to families and children
- Community center

- Special section related to child's grade level and academic program
- Child's assignment—teacher's name and short autobiography

The special section related to the child's grade level can be developed by classroom teachers at each level and inserted for children assigned to them. If a handbook does not give individualized, personal information, a note from the teacher mailed to the home during the summer will be appreciated by the family and will set the tone for a successful home-school relationship.

Two-way Communication

Although one-way communication is important, two-way communication is essential, and it is possible only when school personnel meet the children and their parents. The school principals or center directors set the climate of acceptance within their institutions. Their perceptions of the role of the school in communicating with parents permeates the atmosphere, making parents feel welcome or unwanted.

Open-door Policy

An open-door policy is more an attitude of the school than a series of activities, although periodic open houses, forums, coffee hours, and interactive seminars can add to the receptive climate of the school. Parents are welcome at any time in schools with an open-door policy. Schools that have unpleasant announcements rather than welcome on their doors and that require appointments to visit the principal, teachers, or classrooms are saying, "Come only by request or when you want to discuss a problem." Schools and parents need to avoid the problem-conference syndrome. Dialogue between parents and schools should occur before a problem develops. This can be done through coffee klatches and seminars. Parents can give suggestions and get answers; school personnel can ask questions and clarify school

procedures and curriculum long before an issue might arise. By establishing two-way communication before a problem emerges, the climate is set for parents and school to work together in behalf of, rather than suffer a confrontation over, a child.

Contacts Early in the Year

Many teachers have found that early communication is well worth the time it takes during summer vacation. It is quite common for kindergarten teachers to invite the new kindergarten class and their parents to a spring orientation meeting. Generally, these functions have been held in the hope that the strangeness of school will diminish and that, as a result, subsequent entry into kindergarten will be more pleasant. The message to the parents that the school cares is just as important. This idea can be carried over into other levels of education with results that are just as gratifying.

Letters in August

Some teachers send letters, with pictures of themselves enclosed, to each new student coming to their classes. The student and parents learn the teacher's identity and know that the teacher cares enough to write. A good rapport between teacher and home is established before school begins.

Neighborhood Visits

Rather than waiting until the regular conference period arrives or a problem has arisen, teachers should contact each parent early in the year. Visits to the neighborhood are excellent ways to meet parents.

Block Walk. Try a block walk while the weather is warm and sunny. Map the location of all your students' homes (this may be a class project) and divide the area into blocks. Schedule a series of block walks and escort the children living in each block area to their homes on a selected day. Letters or notes indicating that you will visit a particular block can be written by the students before the appointed

Two-way communication makes it possible for this child and his parents to work most effectively with his school.

day. Choose an alternate day in case of rain. On the appointed day, walk or ride the bus to the chosen block. Meet the parents outside and chat with them about school. You may also accumulate some curriculum materials such as leaves, sidewalk rubbings, or bits of neighborhood history to be used later by the children in the classroom. This initial contact with parents will be positive, and possibly make a second meeting even more productive. You can reinforce the positive aspect of an early meeting by making an interim telephone call to inform the parents of an activity or an interesting comment made by their child.

Bus Trip and Coffees.   An all-school project, with teachers riding a bus to tour the school's enrollment area, allows parents and teacher to meet before the opening of school. If prior ar-

rangements are made for coffees at parents' homes, other parents may be invited (Rich & Mattox, 1977).

Picnic
A picnic during the lunch hour or while on a field trip during the early part of the year will afford teachers the opportunity to meet some parents. Plan a field trip to the park or zoo and invite the parents to a "bring-your-own-lunch." Have another picnic after school for those who could not come at lunchtime. After the lunch or picnic, call to thank those who came. Since some parents work and will be unable to attend either picnic, you might wish to phone them for a pleasant conversation about their child.

Telephone Calls
Begin the dialogue with parents on a positive note. If it is impossible to visit, rely on a telephone call. An early telephone call produces many benefits from appreciative parents. Most parents wonder what is wrong when their child's teacher calls; this is quite an indictment of our communication system. Parents are generally contacted only when something is amiss. Change that tradition by setting aside a short period each day for making telephone calls to parents. Early in the year, calls can include information about who you are, why you are calling, and a short anecdote about the child. If each call takes 5 minutes and you have 30 children in your class, the calls will consume 2½ hours—a small amount of time for the results the calls bring. Divide the time into short segments of 20 to 30 minutes each evening. It saves time and is more considerate of the parent if you send a note home saying that you hope to call and asking for a convenient time. A sample letter is shown in Figure 4-5.

Home Visits
Some teachers make the effort to visit their students' homes early in the fall. This may be the only way to reach parents who have no tele-

---

Dear Mr. and Mrs. _____ ,

   During the school year, I will be making periodic telephone calls to parents of my students. I am able to call on Wednesday afternoon from 3:30 PM to 5 PM or on Tuesday evening from 7 PM to 9:30 PM. Could you mark the time that would be most convenient for you?

   Should you want to call me, you will find me available on Thursday evenings from 7 to 9 PM. Feel free to call my home at _____ if you have questions or would like to talk.

   I am looking forward to visiting with you this year.

Best wishes,

_____

- -

Telephone call preference

   Tuesday: ☐ 7:00 to 8:00   Wednesday: ☐ 3:00 to 4:00
   　　　　 ☐ 8:00 to 9:00 　　　　　　 ☐ 4:00 to 5:00

If none of these times is convenient, please let me know.

FIGURE 4-5

Asking parents when they are available for telephone calls and letting them know when they can call you encourages communication.

phone and are unable to attend the picnic or block walk. It is also a rewarding experience for any teacher who can devote the time required. All parents are not receptive to home visits, however, and some are afraid that the teacher is judging the home rather than coming as a friendly advocate of their child. Take precautions to avoid making the family feel ill at ease. Always let the family know that you are coming. It is a good idea to write a note in which you request a time to visit, or you may give parents the option of holding the visit at another place. Once home visits become an accepted part of the parent involvement program, they become less threatening, and both parents and children look forward to them. Chapter 7 gives suggestions for making home visits successful.

Breakfasts

If you have a cooperative cafeteria staff or volunteers who are willing to make a simple breakfast, you can invite parents to an early breakfast. Many parents can stop for breakfast on their way to work. Plan a breakfast meeting early in the fall to meet parents and answer questions. Breakfast meetings tend to be rushed because parents need to get to work, so hold a series of breakfasts and restrict the number of parents invited to each. In this way, real dialogue can be started. If a group is too large, the personal contact that is the prime requisite of two-way communication is prevented.

   Contacts early in the year prove beneficial throughout the year. Telephone calls are an excellent addition to all planned activities. Choose any of the suggested ideas or use them in combinations, and an early two-way communication system will be established.

COMMUNICATION THROUGHOUT THE YEAR

Although many ideas for making initial contact should be continued during the year, increased involvement is necessary for a true partnership. Visits to school, parent-teacher conferences, and school activities encourage continued parental involvement. Visits to the classroom allow parents to become acquainted with their child's educational environment, the other children in the room, and the teacher. Conferences held periodically continue the dialogue on the educational progress of the child. Participation in school activities allows parents to become working members of the educational team.

Visits to the Classroom

The traditional visit with parents invited for a specific event works very well in some school systems. In other schools, special events are complemented by an open invitation to parents to come and participate in ongoing educational programs.

Outside the room or just inside the door, hang a special bulletin board with messages for parents. It might display assignments for the week, plans for a party, good works children have done, requests for everyday items to complete an art project, requests for special volunteer time, or just about anything that would promote the welfare of the room. Parents can plan and develop the bulletin board with the teacher's guidance.

Participation Visits

Directions for classroom participation are necessary if the experience is to be successful. Parents or other visitors feel more comfortable,

teachers are more relaxed, and children benefit more if parents or visitors are given pointers for classroom visits. They can be in the form of a handout or a poster displayed prominently in the room, but a brief parent-teacher dialogue will make the welcome more personal and encourage specific participation.

The best welcome encourages the visitor to be active in the room's activities. Select activities that are easily described, require no advance training, and contribute rather than disrupt. You may want to give explicit directions on voice quality and noise control. If you do not want the parent to make any noise, request that a soft tone be used when talking with students in the room. Or you might want to ask the parent to work in one specific area of the room. Most visitors are happiest when they know what you want. If it bothers you that some parents tend to give answers to students rather than help the students work out their own problems, suggest the method of instruction you prefer. You might give them a tip sheet for working with students that describes your favorite practices. Keeping activities simple for the "drop-in" participant will keep problems to a minimum. If some parents prefer to sit and observe, don't force participation. As they become more comfortable in your room, they may try some activities. Selecting and reading a story to a child or group, listening to a child read, supervising the newsletter center, playing a game chosen from the game center with a student, supervising the puzzle table, or talking with students about their work are appropriate activities for new volunteers.

Visits by Invitation

A special invitation is sent to parents of a different child each week asking them to visit as "Parents of the Week" or VIPs, Very Important Parents. The invitation, written by the child or teacher, is accompanied by a memo from the administration that explains the objective of the visit. Have the child bring in information about brothers and sisters, favorite activities, and other interesting or important facts about the family. Place a picture of the family on the bulletin board that week. The family could include parents, grandparents, or special friends (young or old), and younger children. Parents and guests are asked to let the teacher know when they plan to visit. Trail (1971) suggested that ushers, selected from the classes, meet the parents at the principal's office and escort them to their child's classroom. An alternative plan allows the student whose parents were invited the opportunity to be the escort. Lunch might be a special treat.

You could also improve the child's self-concept by making the child "Student of the Week." Not only do the children have a chance to feel good about themselves on their special day, it helps organize the class to have one special person be in charge of lunch count, leading the line, and doing the teacher's errands.

Feedback from parents after a visit is important. A reaction sheet is given to parents with the request that they write their impressions and return it to the school. Comments range from compliments to questions about the school. This process allows two-way communication.

Parent-teacher Conferences

Parent-teacher conferences are personal opportunities for two-way communication between parent and teacher or three-way communication among parent, teacher, and student. Parents, as well as teachers, recognize the conference as an excellent opportunity for clarifying issues, searching for answers, deciding on goals, determining mutual strategies, and forming a team in the education of the student. In an informal questionnaire (Berger, 1979), parents chose the parent-teacher conference as the most important opportunity for parent-teacher communication. Teachers also recognize the conference as an excellent opportunity to talk with parents about their child's progress in school. Most schools sched-

ule conferences tw How can conference sible and yet nonthre ers, and students?

The invitation i sets the tone. If it is con ness of parents' busy live. gives the parent time op. the conference, the teache. eration of the parents and a desire to meet with them. Most school systems have worked out procedures for scheduling conference periods. Release time is usually granted teachers. Originally, most conferences were held during afternoons. Children attended school in the mornings, and classes were dismissed at noon, with conferences between parents, usually mothers only, and school personnel held in the afternoon. With the increase in the number of working parents and single-parent families, plus the increasing number of fathers interested in their children's education, many schools are scheduling more evening conferences and retaining some afternoon conferences. Schools recognize the importance of daytime conferences and still allow release time during the day for teachers, but conference schedules now include more evening appointments.

To prepare the schedule, notes are sent to parents asking for their time preference. The formal note should be direct and specific as to time and place of the conference. A sample note is found in Figure 4-6. After the responses have been returned, staff members, including those teachers in special areas of education, meet to schedule back-to-back conferences for parents with more than one child attending school there.

A telephone call to each parent from the teacher adds a personal note. These calls, made either before or after the invitation has been sent home, may clarify questions and let the parents know they are really welcome.

Notes, with the time and date of the conference clearly indicated, should be sent home, whether the parent has been contacted

Dear Mr. and Mrs. _____,

We are looking forward to meeting with you and discussing _____ experiences and progress at school. Will you please let us know when a conference would be most convenient for you? Please check the date and time of day you could come.

Thank you,

_____
Teacher or principal's name

	Afternoon 1 to 4 PM	Evening 6 to 9 PM
Tuesday, November 12	_____	_____
Wednesday, November 13	_____	_____
Thursday, November 14	_____	_____

Could you give a first and second choice? Please write "1" for your first preference and "2" for your second.

Please return by _____.

FIGURE 4-6
A note sent home to schedule a conference.

or not. This ensures that both teacher and parent have the same understanding of the conference time. This confirmation note to each parent from the teacher could be personal, or a form could be used (see Figure 4-7). A personal note might read:

I am looking forward to meeting _____ parents. I enjoy his/her contribution to the class through his/her great interest in _____. The time and date of the conference is _____.

Private and Comfortable Meeting Place

How often have you gone into a school, walked down the halls, and seen parents and teachers trying to have a private conversation in the midst of children and other adults? To achieve open two-way communication, it is essential that the parent and teacher talk in confidence. Select a room designed for conferences or use the classroom, with a note at-tached to the door so people won't interrupt. Give the parents adult-size chairs so everyone can be comfortable and on the same level as the teacher. Place a table in front of the chairs so materials, class projects, and the student's work can be exhibited. The parent, teacher, and student (if it is a three-way conference) can sit around the table and talk and exchange information. The room should be well ventilated and neither too warm nor too cold.

Persons conducting interviews can set up psychological and physical barriers to maintain social distance or imply a status relationship. For example, an executive may sit behind a desk and talk with a subordinate; teachers who sit behind their desks opposite parents need to ask if this barrier facilitates communication. Teachers sensitive to the "space language" that barriers imply will not put barriers between them and the parents (Chinn, Winn, & Walters, 1978).

Dear _____ ,

    Thank you for your response to our request for a conference time. Your appointment has been set for _____ (time) on _____ (day) _____ (month and date) in room _____ .

    We have set aside _____ minutes for our chance to talk together. If the above time is not convenient, please contact the office, and we can schedule another time for you.

    We are looking forward to meeting with you.

                              Best wishes,

                              _____

                              Teacher

FIGURE 4-7
A note sent home to confirm a conference.

Effective Communication

The most essential ingredient to the success of parent-teacher interaction is effective communication. School and home relationships concern the school staff's relationship to parents, peers, students, and the administration.

    Some school administrators and teachers make the mistake of seeing parent-school communication as the school informing the parent about the educational process, rather than as a two-way system. During the conference a teacher should speak only 50 percent of the time. If teachers recognize the conference as a sharing time, half the burden has been lifted from their shoulders. They can use half the time to get to know the parent and child better.

    Listening has been known to be an effective tool of communication since the early 1960s when Rogers made an impact on methods of psychological counseling with his concept of reflective listening. The concept has been extended and reinterpreted in the day-to-day world of teaching parents and children. Gordon talked about the language of acceptance and the use of active listening as essential for improved parent-child relationships. Whether called "active" (Gordon, T., 1970), "effective" (Dinkmeyer & McKay, 1983), "responsive" (Chinn et al., 1978), or "reflective"

(Rogers, 1963), this kind of listening works. It helps open up the communication process.

    Receptive listening is essential because no one can accurately respond to another's statement unless that statement has been heard and understood. To listen effectively the teacher must pay attention to both stated content and implied feelings. Paying attention to the message and following with a reflective response will set the stage for further communication, while a quick, closed response, which places blame or shows a negative reaction to the statement, will stop productive communication. A reflective response is an empathetic response that speaks verbally and physically to the specific feelings of the speaker at that moment (Chinn et al., 1978).

Several qualities can be observed in effective responsive listening: (1) It is empathetic. (2) It utilizes labeling of specific feelings, not general ones. (3) It begins by focusing on current feelings in the here and now. (4) The listener's nonverbal messages—visible in facial expressions and gestures, audible in voice tone and volume—are congruent with his or her expressed verbal response. (Chinn et al., 1978, p. 84)

    Reflective listening in a parent-teacher conference or in response to a concerned parent encourages communication rather than a confrontation. Fortunately many excellent books describe in detail the concept and process of reflective listening. Chinn, Winn, and Walters' *Two-Way Talking with Parents of Special Children: A Process of Positive Communication,* Gordon's *Teachers Effectiveness Training,* and Roger's *Freedom to Learn* contain discussions of teacher communication. Gordon in *P.E.T.: Parent Effectiveness Training* and Dinkmeyer and McKay in *S.T.E.P.: Systematic Training for Effective Parenting* clearly illustrate the same concept in communication between parent and child. Using either book in parent groups encourages effective and reflective listening by both you and the parents. A better understanding of effective communication should result in more productive dialogue between you and the parents.

Some basic guidelines can help you achieve effective communication and listening:

1. Listen to the speaker; hear the feeling and meaning of the message.

2. Give your total commitment to the speaker. Establish eye contact and clearly demonstrate by body language that your attention and interest are focused on what is being said.

3. Respond with an open statement that clarifies what has been said and reflects the speaker's meaning and feeling.

4. Avoid closed responses or answering as a critic, judge, or moralist.

5. Show respect for the other person; recognize that his concerns, opinions, and questions are significant to mutual understanding and communication.

6. Recognize the parents' feelings. How much can you discuss with the parents during this conference? Perhaps you need to establish a better parent-teacher relationship before you can completely share your concerns for the child. Set up a time for another conference.

7. If possible, know the parents' ability to accept criticism. Protect the parents' ego by working with them to plan for the child.

8. Tailor your discussion with parents to fit their ability to handle the situation. Do not touch off a fuse of a parent who might not be able to handle their child's inadequacies or misbehavior. Don't accuse; spend more time with the parents in other communication and additional conferences.

9. Emphasize that the concerns are no one's fault. The teacher and parents have to work on problems together and help the child.

10. Remember, no one ever wins an argument. Calmly, quietly, and enthusiastically discuss the *good* points of the child before you bring up any concerns.

11. Protect the parents' ego. Don't blame them or let them believe that they are to blame for their child's deficiencies. Focus on plans for the future. On the other hand, give them credit for their child's achievements.

Respect requires acceptance of another's rights to a feeling or belief, whether you agree with the interpretation or not. A person must be allowed to express views without being shut out or rejected (Chinn et al., 1978; Dinkmeyer & McKay, 1983; Gordon, T., 1970; Rogers, 1963, 1969).

Recognizing closed and open responses helps clarify the concept of reflective listening. Open responses invite continued dialogue. Closed responses, whether through derision or an answer that requires no more elaboration or thought, stop further discussion or inquiry.

Closed Response
PARENT: I'm concerned about John's progress in arithmetic.
TEACHER: If John would work harder, he would not have a problem.

Open Response
PARENT: I'm concerned about John's progress in arithmetic.

TEACHER: You're worried that John is not progressing in arithmetic?

Closed Response

TEACHER: I'm concerned about John's progress in arithmetic.

PARENT: That's your job. Can't you teach him?

Open Response

TEACHER: I'm concerned about John's progress in arithmetic.

PARENT: You're worried that John is falling behind in math?

The first rule for effective communication is to *listen and reflect* and answer with an open response that keeps the dialogue going.

Choice of Words. The second rule for effective communication is to make an acceptable response. If your answer reflects your understanding of parents' concerns, the conversation will remain open, but the words you choose can bring either desirable or disastrous results. A teacher who had good intentions and great concern for a child once opened a conference with a reference to a child's "problem." "I think you're obnoxious!" spat back the antagonized parent, overwrought by family strain and worry over the child. The remainder of the conference time had to be devoted to rebuilding a working relationship, allowing no time for productive dialogue about the child and leaving both teacher and parent with emotional scars. Bradley (1971) suggested avoiding certain words and phrases and substituting more positive words during an interview.

Words to avoid in interview	More positive words to substitute
Shy	Reserved
Below average	Works at his or her own level
Steals	Takes without permission
Cheats	Depends too much on others
Lazy	Can do more
Uncooperative	Should develop better skills
Mean	Has difficulty getting along
Selfish	Lacks sharing skills
Show-off	Strives for attention
Is going to fail	A chance to pass, if

The words should also be used within a context that promotes cooperation.

Avoid	Say instead
1. Your boy is lazy.	1. I find it difficult to challenge your child. _____ could do more. Do you think these things I am doing are helpful? What more can we do?
2. Your boy has a problem.	2. I need your suggestions for working with _____. What do you think would help?

(Modified from Bradley, 1971, p. 114)

Attentive Behavior. Have you ever had a conversation with a friend who you believed was miles away in thought? During conferences communicators need to believe that what they have to say is important to the listener. Body language can reflect feelings contrary to the spoken word so the verbal message may be misunderstood or missed altogether. It is important to be aware of what you are communicating. If you are rushed, pressured, or concerned about your own family, you will have to take a deep breath, relax, and concentrate on the conference.

Just as some physical gestures communicate distraction or disinterest, so does some body language convey your interest and attention to parents' concerns. Use appropriate nonverbal language to relay your interest.

1. *Eye contact.* Make sure you look at the person as you communicate. Failure to do

so could imply evasion, deception, or lack of commitment.

2. *Forward posture.* Leaning forward creates the image of interest in what is being said. Be comfortable, but do not slouch to indicate that the whole process is boring or unimportant.

3. *Body response.* A nod in agreement, a smile, and use of the body to create an appearance of interest promote empathy. If you act aware and interested, you will probably become interested. If you do not, perhaps you are in the wrong profession.

4. *Touch.* Sometimes a touch to the arm or a clasp of the hand assures the other person that you care and understand.

Understandable Language. Specialized language gets in the way of communication. Although medical terminology is familiar and efficient to the doctor, it often sounds like a foreign tongue to the patient asking for an explanation of a diagnosis. Each year new terms and acronyms become common language in the schools, but they freeze communication when used with persons not familiar with the terms. Imagine a teacher explaining to a parent that the school has decided to use the SRA program this year in second grade, but the first grade is trying the ITA. "I've been using behavior modification with Johnny this year, and it has been very effective, but with Janet I find TA more helpful." Jargon can create misunderstanding and stop communication.

Sometimes terms have meaning for both communicators, but the meanings are not the same. Hymes (1974) declares that lack of communication, superficial communication, and "words and vocabulary, without friendship and trust and knowledge, get in the way of understanding" (p. 33).

Look, for example, at "progressive education." Use those words and you have a fight on your hands. People get emotional and wild charges fly. Yet parents will be the first to say: "Experience is the best teacher" and there you have it! Different words but

a good definition of what progressive education stands for. (Hymes, 1974, p. 33)

Practice. To achieve the ability to listen reflectively and to respond in a positive manner, practice until it becomes natural. You can practice alone, but it is more effective if you can role play the conference. Having an observer present allows both practice and feedback. Teachers can choose a typical case from among their records or invent a hypothetical one. For example,

Andy, a precocious third grade child, spends most of the class period doodling ideas in a notebook. Although he completes his assignments, Andy takes no pride in his work and turns in messy papers. Special enrichment centers in the classroom do not attract him. Andy participates positively during recess and in physical education and music.

Each participant has basic information (real or hypothetical)—the child's sex, grade assigned, and background information. Assign one participant to act as the parent, another as the teacher. The third member of the team observes the interaction between the parent and teacher to check on

1. reflective listening
2. attentive behavior (eye contact, forward posture, etc.)
3. sensitivity to parent's feelings
4. positive language
5. cooperative decision making

Since no two teachers or parents are identical, there is no prescribed way to have a conference. The dialogue will be a constant flow, filled with emotions as well as objective analysis. You can prepare yourself, however, by practicing good reflective listening and positive communication. Look forward with pleasure to sharing together.

Preparation for the Conference
Two types of preparation will set the stage for a successful conference. The first, an optional

Keep records, papers, and anecdotal notes to have the material needed for parent-teacher conferences.

program, involves training teachers and parents for an effective conference. The second is the essential—analyzing the child's previous records, current performance and attitude, and relationship with peers and gathering examples of work along with recent standardized test results.

Workshops and Conference Guides. Workshops for parents, teachers, or a combination of both are fruitful. A discussion of what makes a conference a success or a calamity can bring forth an enormous number of tips for both parents and teachers. If parents and teachers form small groups, many ideas will emerge that can be recorded on the chalkboard for later discussion by the total group. Encourage parents to ask questions about their part in conferences. Clarifying objectives for

conferences and what the school expects from the parents will help parents understand their responsibilities. Parents and teachers attending a workshop together can learn the art of reflective listening and communication. Role playing during conferences can elicit discussion. Many participants will see themselves in the roles portrayed and will attempt to find alternative methods of handling conference discussions. Films that illustrate common communication problems can also be used as starters for discussion.

At the close of the workshop, handouts or conference guides may be distributed to the participants. The guide should be designed with the school's objectives in mind. Parents can be told what to expect in the school's report and what the school expects from them. The following are questions selected from an article by Landau (1971), that parents might expect to have answered:

How is your child progressing academically? Try to learn something about both the quantity and the quality of his work. Ask to see sample tests and other records.

What are his talents and aptitudes, both evident and submerged?

How does your child get along with others?

How good is his mental health? . . . Should your child display emotional conduct that seems to be interfering with his school progress, it would be well for you to know about it. (p. 207)

Rather than scheduling workshops, some schools send a memo home before conferences suggesting questions that the parents might come prepared to answer. Typical questions include:

1. Which activities does the student talk about at home?
2. Which activities seem to stimulate his intellectual growth?
3. What does the student enjoy?
4. What does the student dread?
5. What are your child's interests and hobbies?

A similar memo suggests questions that the parents might want to ask:

1. How does my child react to discipline?
2. Does my child select books at the proper reading level from the library?
3. Do you expect me to help my son or daughter with homework?

Supplying questions before the conference is helpful in preparing parents, but it can also limit questions that develop naturally; and if these questions are strictly adhered to during conferences, they can limit the scope, direction, and outcome of the conference.

Teacher Preparation. Throughout the year teachers should make a practice of accumulating anecdotal records, tests, workbooks, art projects, and papers that represent both academic and extracurricular areas. Folders created by students, an accordion file, or a file box or cabinet can store the papers until conference time. Students may then compile a notebook or folder of samples of their work to share with their parents during conferences. If the file is worked on periodically throughout the term, papers can be placed in chronologic order, thus illustrating the progress in each subject. The child's work is an essential assessment tool.

Standardized tests that reveal the child's potential compared to actual performance level are useful in determining an education program that fits the students. The McGraw-Hill Comprehensive Test of Basic Skills (CTBS), given along with the Short Form Test of Academic Aptitude (SFTAA), gives results that indicate actual grade equivalent of performance, along with the anticipated grade equivalent based on aptitude. With this information, parents and teacher can discuss whether the student is performing above or below potential. Parents and teachers can use the information to plan for the future.

One word of caution on the use of standardized tests must be included. Tests are not infallible. Children may not feel well on the day of testing, some may freeze on tests. Use standardized test results as a supplement to informal assessment tools such as class papers, notebooks, class observation, and informal tests, not as a replacement for them. If standardized test results and your informal assessment are congruent and the child scores high on aptitude tests and shows moments of brilliance in class but consistently falls down on work, you can be fairly certain that the child is not working up to ability. If the child scores low but does excellent work in class, observe closely before deciding that the child is under too much pressure to achieve. In that case, the test may not indicate the child's true potential. Should the child score low on the test and also show a high level of frustration when working, you may want to make plans to gear the work closer to the child's ability. The standardized test, used as a backup to the informal assessment, can help teachers and parents plan the child's educational program.

Congruent Beliefs About the Child. Have you ever had a disruptive child in a class only to discover that the child was retiring and well behaved during Scouts? Sometimes the disparity makes one wonder if it is the same child. It is difficult to discuss a child on common ground if the parents' and teachers' perceptions of the child are completely different. The Q Sort gives teachers and parents a means of comparing their perceptions of the child. It is often meaningful to have students sort their own views so the perceptions of teacher, parents, and student can be compared.

The Q Sort was developed by Stephenson (1953) as a self-referent technique to measure self-concept and was extended to be used by parents, teachers, and students in the measurement of "perceptions of behavior at home and in the classrooms" (Kroth, 1975, p. 43). Figure 4-8 is an adaptation of Kroth's tool as illustrated in *Communicating with Parents of Exceptional Children.* You can buy the Q Sort

Asks for help when needed 1	Is friendly 2	Squirms in seat 3	Excels in reading 4	Talks with other students constantly 5
Keeps busy 6	Is unhappy 7	Hands in messy work 8	Finishes work on time 9	Does poorly in academic classes 10
Excels in artwork 11	Has poor coordination 12	Enjoys music 13	Writes with poor penmanship 14	Pays attention to instruction 15
Disturbs others while they are working 16	Never finishes work 17	Walks around room without permission 18	Cooperates with students and teachers 19	Gets along well with other students 20
Excels in math 21	Pesters other children 22	Works well in group 23	Constantly gets out of seat 24	Works persistently until finished 25

FIGURE 4-8
Q sort cards, with one-half positive and one-half negative items, can be designed to answer any type of behavior. (*Source:* Modified from R. L. Kroth, *Communicating with parents of exceptional children.* Denver: Love Publishing, 1975.)

form or develop your own. You may want to check the list of items before adding your own and adapting the instrument for your use. Make sure that half the items are positive and half are negative when you develop your list.

1. List 25 behaviors on small cards (Figure 4-8).
2. Make a sorting board with squares for the 25 cards (see Figure 4-9).
3. Sort the cards according to how truly descriptive they are of the subject. In this

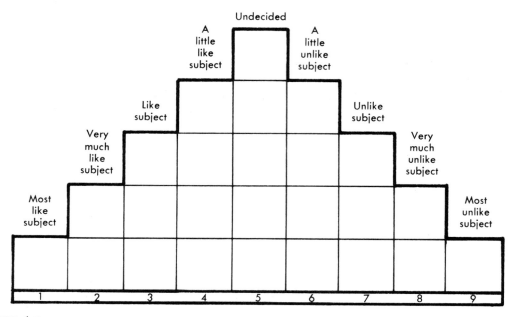

FIGURE 4-9
Enlarge the Q sort board in order to allow the parent to use it easily. (*Source:* Modified from R. L. Kroth, *Communicating with parents of exceptional children.* Denver: Love Publishing, 1975.)

case, the subject is the student. Place only one card on each space.

4. Record the scores of each card on the recording form (Figure 4-10).
5. Record scores for both parent and teacher. If the difference between the scores is more than four, your perception of the child is significantly different than the parent's. Discuss incongruent items and clarify your views.

The Q Sort is a nonthreatening means of recognizing differences in perceptions. Quickly and easily administered, the Q Sort can be completed by parents while waiting for the conference. With the results parents and teachers can clarify situations that would otherwise remain cloudy or unrecognized. For areas of discrepancy they can determine if each needs to use a different strategy when interacting with the child.

Conference Membership

When children are taught by more than one teacher or have contact with numerous specialists (i.e., speech teacher, physical therapist), including all professionals involved with the child is appropriate and involves prior cooperative planning. Beware of the impact on the parent, however, because four professionals to one parent may be awesome and foreboding. If special care is taken to assure parents that all specialists are there to clarify and to work with the teacher and parent as a team, the cooperative discussion and planning can have worthwhile results. An alternative plan allows the parent to talk individually with each involved specialist. In some schools the homeroom teacher reports for all the specialists, but personal contact with all persons involved with the child's education is more satisfying to the parents. If time is short, the entire group could meet with the parents once in the

	Name *John*	Teacher	Parent	Difference
1.	Asks for help when needed	8	3	5
2.	Is friendly	2	2	0
3.	Squirms in seat	4	3	1
4.	Excels in reading	6	6	0
5.	Talks with other students constantly	7	2	5
6.	Keeps busy			
7.	Is unhappy			
8.	Hands in messy work			
9.	Finishes work on time			
10.	Does poorly in academic classes			
11.	Excels in artwork			
12.	Has poor coordination			
13.	Enjoys music			
14.	Writes with poor penmanship			
15.	Pays attention to instructions			
16.	Disturbs others while they are working			
17.	Never finishes work			
18.	Walks around room without permission			
19.	Cooperates with students and teacher			
20.	Gets along well with other students			
21.	Excels in math			
22.	Pesters other children			
23.	Works well in a group			
24.	Constantly gets out of seat			
25.	Works persistently until finished			

FIGURE 4-10
The record sheet illustrates the differences in opinions about the child's behavior.

fall and assure the parents they will be accessible whenever the parents have a concern.

Consider including the child. Who is better equipped to clarify why the child is doing well or needs extra help? Who has more at stake? Preschoolers make poor conference members, but as soon as the child becomes interested in assessment and evaluations and recognizes the goal of parent-teacher conferences, the teacher should consider including the child in the process. Initially, the child may attend for a short portion of the conference, but as interest and attention span increase, it is realistic to have the child present during the complete conference. If portions of the conference need to be conducted without the child present, have a supervised play area available. Older students are natural team members who can help clarify. If students are included as members of the team, issues can be clarified and goals set. The student is a part of the discussion and helps in setting realistic goals.

Congruent Conferences

Conferences go more smoothly when expectations held by the teacher and parents are congruent with the performance of the child. If the child is an excellent student and both teacher and parents are pleased with the evaluation, it is easy to accept the report. If the child is handicapped and both teacher and parents recognize the handicapping condition, they can work together to plan an appropriate program for the child.

Too often the outward signs of good marks and pleasant personality and behavior fail to uncover how the child feels and whether the teacher can make the educational experience more satisfying and challenging. In working with a successful student, parents and teachers may fail to communicate about the child's potential and need to have a good self-concept. Special interests of the child, friends, reading preferences, experiences, and needs are important for the teacher to know. Bring the child into the decision-making process. Together, the parents, teacher, and child can plan activities that will encourage growth and improve self-concept. Let these parents and children communicate, too.

The Day of the Conference

The day of the conference has arrived. Review your objectives, maintain effective communication skills, discuss concrete examples of work, and plan together.

Clear Statement of Objectives. Some objectives may be universal; others will be specific for the individual conference. Use the following objectives as a guide:

1. To gain a team member (the parent) in the education of the child

2. To document the child's progress for the parent
3. To explain the educational program you are using as it relates to the individual child
4. To learn about the environment in which the child lives
5. To allow the parents to express feelings, questions, and concerns
6. To get a better understanding of the expectations the parent holds for the child
7. To set up a lasting network of communication among parent, teacher, and child
8. To establish cooperative goals for the education of the child

Recognition of the Parent As Part of the Team. After you have made sure that the room is comfortable, that two-way communication will be uninterrupted, and that you are ready to listen and be responsive to the parent, it is easy to recognize the parent as a part of the educational team. Parents arrive at conferences as experts on their children's history, hobbies, interests, special likes and dislikes, friends, and experiences. You, as the teacher, have a great deal of knowledge and understanding of the child to gain from the parents.

Besides being adept at reflective listening, you need to listen intuitively to determine if parents have oppressive problems within their homes or are themselves emotionally immature. Such problems make it difficult for the child to have the home support needed for educational success. When indicated, bring other professionals, such as the school social worker or principal, into the conference to support and help the family and child. You can be more understanding of the child's needs if you understand the child's home (Grissom, 1971).

Why is it that parents enter into parent-teacher conferences with apprehension? Some parents are worried because they want the best for their child but do not know how to achieve it. They are unsure of themselves in the discussion and are threatened by terminology. If parent and teacher can throw away their roles during the conference and look at it as a meeting place for the exchange of ideas and information and a chance to support each other, both can enter into the conference with anticipation and confidence.

Explain to the parents that you don't want them to think of you as a teacher and you don't want to think of them as parents, but that all participants in the conference are members of a team looking at the progress of the child and working together to benefit the child. How can *we* help the child who is having a difficult time? How can *we* enrich the program for the child who is accelerated? How can *we* get the child to do the tasks at hand? How can *we* promote self-esteem? These questions, when answered as a team, can be more productive than when answered by a teacher who is questioning a parent. Here are some tips that will help the parent feel a part of the team:

- Know the parent's name. Do not assume that the child's last name is the same as the parent's. Look in the record for the correct name.
- Insure the privacy of the conference.
- Know the time limitations.
- Do not use terminology that has meaning for you but not for the parent.
- Do not refer to organizations, forms, tests, materials, or ideas by their initials. Do not assume that everyone knows what the initials mean.
- Have some questions about and show interest in the child.
- Remind the parents that they may ask questions at any time and that you will be pleased to explain anything that is not clear.
- Begin on a positive note. Start by praising an accomplishment of the child or a contribution the child has made to the class.
- Review your file and know enough about the child before the parent arrives that the parent can tell you have taken a personal interest in the child's welfare.
- Keep on the subject—the child's schooling and development.

- Encourage the parents to contribute. Allow parents to talk for at least 50 percent of the conference.
- Show that you understand the parent by checking with him periodically during the conference, for example, "Would you agree with this?" or "Do you have suggestions to add about this?"
- Make a note of an idea suggested by a parent, but do not get so involved in writing that you lose the flow of the conversation.
- Maintain eye contact.
- Use attending behaviors, that is, lean forward, look interested, and nod when in agreement.
- Do not ignore a parent's question.
- Be honest, yet tactful and sensitive, to the parent's feelings.
- Base your discussion on objective observation and concrete examples of work.
- Deal in specifics more than generalities.
- Evaluate needs and select methods of remediating deficiencies.
- Evaluate strengths and select methods of enriching those strengths.
- Plan together for future educational goals.
- Clarify and summarize the discussion.

Concrete Examples of Child's Work and Behavior. Both the parent and teacher are interested in the child's accomplishments. Objective observation of the child's classroom behavior, with anecdotal notes collected in a loose-leaf notebook throughout the reporting periods, documents the child's social as well as intellectual achievements. Anecdotal records of significant behaviors are particularly valuable for conferences with parents of young children. Here papers and tests may not be available, and the anecdotal records become tools for evaluating the child's social, intellectual, and physical progress. In the case of children with behavioral problems, it is also important to be able to report specific incidents rather than vague generalizations about disturbances.

The accumulated examples of the child's work with a few words from the teacher also illustrate to parents what their child is doing. It is not necessary to state that the child has not progressed, for it will be obvious. If the child has made great progress, it will be evident from the samples collected. Consider asking the parents if they have come to the same conclusion as you when comparing early and subsequent papers.

Some teachers supplement papers and anecdotal records with videotapes of children in the room. Although time-consuming, a film report is enjoyed by parents and encourages interaction between parent and teacher on the child's classroom participation.

Bringing to the conference concrete examples that illustrate the child's work eliminates a teacher-parent confrontation and allows parent and teacher to analyze the work together. Include anecdotal records and examples of the child's work significant in comparison to expected behavior at that age level. In preschool this may be fine motor control, large muscle activities, art, problem solving, etc. With school-age children include papers, artwork, projects, work in academic subjects, tests, notebooks, workbooks, and anecdotal records. It is also helpful to parents for the teacher to collect a set of unidentified average papers. If the parents want to compare their child's work with that of the average child, they have a basis for this comparison.

The tone of the conference should be comfortable. Parents have related that they feel accepted when the teacher says to them, "Come in, let's meet. Don't think of me as the teacher, and I won't think of you as parents. Let's be a team that looks at John's, Carol's, Ann's, or Tom's work and see what we can do together to best develop this child's potential." The child may be one who is accelerated, or the child may need special help to catch up. The child may be progressing right on schedule. Whatever the level of the child's performance, the parent and teacher need to form a team as they evaluate the child's educational progress and work together for the good of the child. A checklist may be used for self-evaluation:

Conference checklist

Yes	No	*Did you*
☐	☐	1. Prepare ahead by collecting anecdotal records, tests, papers, notebooks, workbooks, and art materials from the beginning to the end of the reporting period?
☐	☐	2. Provide book exhibits, displays, or interesting reading for parents as they wait for their conferences?
☐	☐	3. Make arrangements for coffee or tea for parents as they waited for their conferences?
☐	☐	4. Prepare your room with an attractive display of children's work?
☐	☐	5. Welcome the parents with a friendly greeting?
☐	☐	6. Start on a positive note?
☐	☐	7. Adjust your conference to the parents' needs and levels of understanding?
☐	☐	8. Have clear objectives for the conference?
☐	☐	9. Say in descriptive terms what you mean? Did you avoid educational jargon and use of initials?
☐	☐	10. Listen reflectively?
☐	☐	11. Keep the communication lines open? Were you objective and honest?
☐	☐	12. Avoid comparing students or parents? Discuss other teachers only if it was complimentary?
☐	☐	13. Check your body language? Were you alert to the parents' body language?
☐	☐	14. Plan the child's educational program together?
☐	☐	15. Summarize your decisions?
☐	☐	16. Begin and end on time? If you needed more time, did you set up another appointment?

If you are able to answer yes to these questions, you are ready to have productive parent-teacher conferences.

Quick conferences

Preschool teachers find that a quick interchange with parents when they pick up their child is beneficial. If you have a basic plan, you can systematically talk with each parent every month. Some parents will seek you out, and the communication network with them will be even more effective. Look for the others and make a special point of talking with them. Tell them about an activity their child seemed to enjoy or one in which the child did exceedingly well. An interesting anecdote about the child is always in order. You can also ask the parents which part of the program their child enjoys most. This short interchange keeps the communication lines open.

School Activities

Following are school activities that encourage parent participation.

Back-to-school Nights

A time-tested school event, the back-to-school night, has proven very successful. Teachers often complain that the parents who need to come to learn about the educational program are the very ones who do not come, but this type of evening program has proven successful in improving home-school relationships from preschool through secondary schools. Parents enjoy sitting in the desk normally occupied by their child, viewing the curriculum materials, observing the displays in the room, and listening to the teacher. Parents expect the teacher to tell them about school programs. Following a presentation of the course objectives, there is usually a period for questions and answers. Back-to-School night is not a time for talking about individual children, although the teacher should identify which parents belong to which students. It is a good time to set up a special conference if you have concern about the progress of a student.

A variation on the back-to-school night is the Saturday morning session. Some working parents have difficulty attending evening programs. Offering an alternative time invites increased parental participation. The Saturday morning activity can be a workshop with parents participating in their children's normal activities, or it can be a presentation-discussion similar to the evening session. Saturday morning programs can become a meaningful educational experience for children and families by having a series of parent-child programs.

Parent Education Groups

Parent education groups are discussed in detail in Chapter 6. Meetings range from a 1-day workshop to an organized series of workshops throughout the year. Individual teachers use the parent group meetings for in-service training of volunteers in their rooms, dissemination of information to parents, or presentation of programs that answer parents' needs. Parents become real resources for the school through parent education meetings, which teach them to become effective tutors and volunteers in the school.

Parent education meetings offered by schools are viable for those with children at any age level. The parent of a young child may be interested in child development, enrichment activities, and promotion of creativity. It was noted in Chapter 5 that parents of children of all ages are concerned about drugs and alcohol. Parent education groups that allow parents to meet and discuss common concerns are a very essential part of the educational program. Interestingly, junior highs and high schools have very few parent education groups, but the parents of these students are vitally concerned about their children's futures. They need information, but, even more important, they need the support system that a parent education group offers. If parents of adolescents can discuss problems and understand that other parents have the same concerns, they are able to cope with pressures better. An advocacy group for children and parents can be formed. Responsibilities and guidelines for students, determined by parents and students in a specific community, can support parents in the rearing of their children. Schools need to offer parent education. In doing so, they strengthen parent-school-community relationships.

School Programs and Workshops

Remember when the introduction of "modern math" made it impossible for some parents to help their children with math? Parent workshops that explained the new terminology and processes were appreciated. Schools can offer programs and workshops to the community with the same success. Parents from the community can plan and implement some of the workshops; speakers can be obtained; projects can be started.

A bookmaking project can be a great success. Although a limited number of parents can make books at one time, the workshop can be repeated. If parents make books from their own child's work, they can create remembrances to be kept for years. Simple construction paper books, as well as hardback books, can be developed. Books containing stories and poems composed by parents or children can be placed in the library and classroom for use by students.

Try to arrange alternate times to offer workshops. If you have meetings during the day, in the evening, and on Saturday, parents will be able to come to the ones that fit their schedules.

School Projects

Enlist parent help if you plan to add to the playground or build a reading loft in your classroom. Parents enjoy contributing their time for something permanent. Children will be proud that their parents helped build the jungle gym or planted the elm tree in the schoolyard. Saturday sessions give ample time

to develop, plan, and build. Many fathers find this the most comfortable way to contribute to the school. It starts a relationship that brings them into a partnership with the school.

PTO or PTA

The tradition of parent-teacher associations extends back to the 1890s. Their influence on parent-school relationships has been demonstrated over the years. PTA publishes material for parents and strives for parent-school cooperation. Many parent-teacher groups (generally called Parent-Teacher Organizations—PTOs) do not join the national PTA but have similar structure and interaction with the schools. Both PTA and PTO can serve as an avenue toward greater parent-school interaction.

Fairs, Carnivals, and Suppers

Traditionally the PTO or PTA sponsors spaghetti suppers, potluck dinners, dinner theaters, or similar activities that promote a community spirit, give families a night of fun together, and usually increase the treasury. Parents and children flock to school to attend a carnival produced by parents and school staff. Money earned is generally spent on materials or equipment for the school program.

Exchanges

Children grow; toys get tiresome; books are read. Why not have an exchange? A popular exchange is one where boots, heavy jackets, and raincoats are brought to school to be traded or sold. Boots seldom wear out before they're outgrown, so a boot exchange works very well.

Toys can also be exchanged. Some schools have children bring two toys, one for exchange and one to give to another child. Children swap the toy they brought for a new one. How often have you seen Christmas toys sit for months without being used?

Children tire of some books and can exchange their old ones for books they have not read. A parent volunteer checks in the books and issues tickets to be used to buy another one. Children can look through the books until they find what they want. Then they buy the books with the tickets.

Suggestion Box

The suggestion box brings suggestions from parents to school. Placed in the hallway, it encourages parents to share their concerns and their pleasures with the school anonymously. Although this is really a one-way communication system, it effectively tells parents, "We want your suggestions. Let us know what you feel," and encourages the parent to respond.

Learning Centers

Parents can be in charge of learning centers. Use the resource room to furnish ideas and supplies for parents, or have a workshop to demonstrate how they can plan and prepare a learning center. Learning centers can include (for example):

1. a place for games
2. a reading center
3. a writing-and-making book center
4. a puzzle center
5. a center for problem-solving activities
6. a science area
7. a talk-and-listen center
8. a place for music and tapes
9. a weaving center
10. an art project center

Rules and regulations for using the center should be posted.

Telephone Tutor

Take advantage of call-forwarding, which is now available in most communities. With call-forwarding, the school can set up a tutor or homework aid program via telephone calls in the evening. Volunteers or teachers could answer the telephone in the afternoon at the school. Later telephone calls may be forwarded to the homes of the volunteer or paid aide working with the children that night. In a well-coordinated program the volunteer could know what homework each teacher had as-

signed. If the entire district uses the telephone tutor, special numbers could be assigned for mathematics and language arts.

If call-forwarding is not available, a telephone answering machine (with names and numbers of tutors on call for that night) could direct the student to help. An excellent way to draw attention to the needs of the school district is to enlist important people in the community to serve as volunteer tutors. Their leadership will provide publicity and credibility to the volunteer program.

RESOURCE ROOM

When parents see they can contribute to a project that has obvious benefits for their children, some will become actively involved. A resource room can be beneficial to both school and parents. Resource materials located in an empty room, storage closet, corner of a room, or metal cabinet can be a great help to teachers. Involve parents in developing a resource center by holding a workshop to describe and discuss the concept. Brainstorm with parents and other teachers on ideas that might be significant for your school. Parents can take over after the workshop to design, stock, and run the center. Later, as assistants in the classroom, they will make use of it.

Articles on Teaching. Parents can check old magazines related to teaching and classify useful articles according to age level and subject, that is, art, math, language arts, music, and science. These can be filed for use by teachers and aides. In searching for and classifying the articles, parents learn a great deal about teaching activities for home and school so the activity is beneficial for the parent and the school.

Games. Parents can check books, magazines, and commercial catalogues for ideas for games and adapt them to the school's needs. Volunteers can make universal game boards for reading, spelling, and math from poster card or tagboard. Felt markers are used to make lines and note directions; games are decorated with artwork, magazine cut-outs, or stickers from novelty stores. Game materials should be laminated or covered with clear contact paper.

Recycled Materials. Volunteers can collect, sort, and store materials for classroom teachers. Items such as egg cartons, wood scraps, wallpaper books, cardboard tubes, felt, fabric remnants, and plastic food holders are used for many activities. Egg cartons, for example, are used to cover a dragon, make a caterpillar, hold buttons for classification activities, and hold tempera paint for dry mixing. Milk cartons can be used for making items from simple computers to building blocks.

Science activities are enriched by a collection of machines, for example, motors, radios, computers, clocks, and typewriters. The articles can be used as they are or taken apart and rebuilt. Recycling is limited solely by the imagination.

Library

A collection can be made of magazines and books useful to parents or teachers in the development of teaching aids (e.g., games and learning activities) or for information on how children learn. From ideas therein, a toy lending library and an activity lending library, as well as a book and magazine library, can be developed. Items can be checked out for a week or two. Checkout and return are supervised by parent volunteers.

Toy Lending Library. The toy lending library is developed from educational toys for young children (Nimnicht & Brown, 1972) or from a collection of toys for older children. The toys for young children can be built and collected by parents. Toys for older children can be collected from discarded toys after the toy exchange or built by parents and children.

Activity Lending Library. Games and activities developed by parents and children can be checked out for a week or two.

Book and Magazine Library. Discarded magazines and books can be collected and used to build a comprehensive lending library. Professional magazines have many articles on child development, education, and learning activities. Booklets distributed by numerous organizations can also be loaned. Refer to Chapter 11 for lists of organizations that handle pertinent books. Pamphlets and articles cut from magazines can be stapled to file folders and loaned to parents. To keep track of the publications, glue a library card pocket in each book or on each folder. Make a card that states the author and title of the publication, with lines for borrowers to sign their names. As each is taken, have the borrower sign the card and leave it in the card file. When the publication is returned, the name is crossed out, and the card is returned to the pocket.

FAMILY CENTER

Parents need a place within the school where they can meet, share information, work, and relax. Ideally, parents will have a room similar to that traditional haven, the teachers' lounge, as well as a space within each classroom.

The family room can be equipped and stocked by the parents. Typical items include a sofa, comfortable chair, table, coffeepot, hot plate, telephone, typewriter, duplicator, bulletin board, storage area, supplies, and reading materials. If a room is not available, a small area shared in a workroom, an area in an unused hall, or a large closet would give minimal space. In each, both storage space and a bulletin board for notices should be available.

Teachers can help parents develop a base in each room. An extra desk, a corner, or a bulletin board can give parents the feeling they can claim a spot within their child's classroom. If the area contains information on current assignments, new curriculum ideas, activities to be used at home, taped messages from the teacher, or a display of children's work, parents will make a point to stop by. Parents of preschool, kindergarten, and elementary children can use the corner to find activities that will continue the educational experience in the home or to talk or work with individual children or small groups. Teachers can use the corner to hold a short conference with a parent.

The parents' room implies that parents are expected to be in the building. There is a place for them to stop and a base from which they can reach out in their involvement.

PARENTS AS RESOURCES

Parents should be asked early in the year if they have any talents or experiences they would like to share with classes. Parents may share their careers with children. Perhaps they have a hobby that would spark student interest or supplement learning programs. Storytelling is an art often overlooked. Invite some senior citizens to tell about their childhoods. The resources in the community are unlimited. More ideas on use of these resources will be discussed in Chapter 6.

Career Day

Plan a day or a series of days when parents come in and explain their careers. Rather than have parents talk to the whole class, let them work at a center. Let them explain their careers, the pros and cons, the necessary skills, and the satisfaction obtained from their work. If feasible, the parent would provide some activities the children could do related to the career. For example, a carpenter could bring in tools, demonstrate their use, and let the children make a small project, supervised by the carpenter and an aide or another parent.

Talent Sharing

Let parents tell stories, sing folk songs, lead a creative dramatics project, or share another talent. You might persuade some to perform before the class; some may wish to work with a few children at a time and let the children be involved.

Some parents may have a collection or a hobby to share. Quilting is popular and could be followed by a lesson in stitchery. Basketmaking, growing orchids, stamp collecting—all provide opportunities for enriching the classroom learning experiences. Bring those educational and fun lessons out to enjoy.

PARENT ADVISORY COUNCILS

All schools can establish parent advisory councils. Chapter I components establish two parent advisory councils, a district-wide and a local council for each involved school. The councils give input on the planning, implementation, and evaluation of the Chapter I program. Head Start and Home Start have had participatory advisory councils since the 1960s, but the public schools were not required to have such parent participation until 1974. Fifty percent of council members should be selected from among parents of students receiving Chapter I services.

The success of parent advisory councils in Head Start, Home Start, and Chapter I programs has demonstrated that parents can be involved in policy and decision making in a meaningful and constructive way. "PAC [Parent Advisory Council] members must know the program well and keep abreast of how it is operating in each project" (U.S. Department of Health, Education, and Welfare, 1978, p. 26).

In establishing a parent advisory council, school districts should consider six components:

1. Preparation—districts work toward improved home-school relationships with

school personnel recognizing the positive attribute of parent involvement and parents feeling comfortable in their participation.

2. Membership—parents are solicited, and their consent to run is obtained prior to an election of PAC members.

3. Training—continuous training on participation in the Chapter I program and the organization and implementation of an advisory council is provided.

4. Organization—the basic structure of the PAC is left up to the individual council.

5. Support—support of school districts includes money for supplies, transportation, and baby-sitters, as well as provision of a meeting place and availability of school officials for information about the school system.

6. Evaluation—the evaluation of success or failure of the PAC will bring out strengths and weaknesses and direct the council in the future (U.S. Department of Health, Education, and Welfare, 1978).

Although other schools can implement a parent advisory council with a less formal structure, they can also learn from the Chapter I experience, which actively solicits parent participation, and gives them the information and training needed to become effective policy and decision makers.

Parents surveyed by a Gallup Poll also indicated a strong interest in being involved as members of educational advisory councils or policy boards. In the 1976 Gallup Poll survey, 90 percent of the respondents indicated willingness to serve on one or more committees.

Advisory committee[2]	*Percent who would like to serve on such a committee*
1. Discipline and related problems	47
2. Student/teacher relations	31
3. Career education	29
4. Student dropouts	29
5. Teacher evaluations	28
6. The handicapped student	26
7. Educational costs/finances	22
8. The curriculum	21
9. Education for citizenship	19
10. Work-study programs	19
11. Home study and work habits	19
12. Community use of school buildings	16
13. Pupil assessment and test results	15
14. School facilities	14
15. Public relations of schools	13
16. School transportation	12
17. The athletic program	12
18. Educational innovations	12
19. Extracurricular activities	11
20. Progress of recent graduates	9
21. None	4
22. Don't know/no answer	6

MEETING THE NEEDS OF YOUR SCHOOL AREA

Schools can make a special effort to help families function more effectively. Some fathers travel constantly; mothers in those families have many of the same problems that a single parent has (see Chapter 3). A family with a handicapped parent may need help with transportation or baby-sitting. An early survey of families will disclose what parents need and suggest ways the school can encourage participation.

Telephone Tree

A telephone tree set up by the PTO or PTA can alert parents quickly to needs in the community. One caller begins by calling four or five persons who each in turn calls four or five more. Soon the entire community is alerted.

Transportation

If the parent group is active, it can offer transportation to those who need help getting to

2. From Gallup, G. The eighth annual Gallup Poll of the public's attitudes toward the public school. *Phi Delta Kappan*, September 1976, p. 194.

The teacher establishes the climate in the classroom that either encourages parents to participate or induces them to withdraw.

the school or to the doctor's office. Those in need include the handicapped, a mother with small children, or someone who has an ill child in the family.

Parent-to-parent Support

Parents who do not have an extended family can find other parents with whom to team. If the parent organization organizes a file on parents that includes their needs, interests, children's ages, and location, a cross-reference can be set up for parents to use. Parent education group meetings often promote friendships within the group. Parents who isolate themselves are often the ones who need the help of another parent the most. One parent may be able to manage the home efficiently, while the other needs tips and help. Some parents have never been exposed to a stable

home environment and need a capable parent to use as a model. Although educators may want to stay out of the lives of parents, they must remember that they meet and work with all parents and have the greatest access to the most parents of any community agency.

Child Care

Child care during conferences can be offered to families with young children. Older children could participate in activities in the gymnasium, while young children could be cared for in a separate room. It is difficult for some parents to arrange for child care, and a cooperative child care arrangement with parent volunteers would allow greater participation at conferences.

Crisis Nursery

A worthwhile project for a parent organization is the development of a crisis nursery. Schools would have to meet state regulations for child care to have a nursery within the school. If able to do this, schools would provide a great service as well as meet parents and children prior to school entrance. An assessment program, similar to Child Find, might alert parents and schools to developmental problems, such as a hearing loss or poor sight.

A neighborhood home can also be used as a crisis base. If a parent needs to take a child to the doctor, the crisis center can care for the other children during the parent's absence. Abusive parents can use the crisis center as a refuge for their children until they are in control of their emotions.

After-school Activities

Schools can become centers for the community. One step toward greater community involvement is the after-school program. With so many working parents, many children are "latch key kids," who go home to an empty house. If schools, perhaps working with other agencies, provide an after-school program for children, preschool through secondary, a great service would be done. Teachers should not be expected to be involved in an after-school program. However, recreation workers and volunteers can implement a program that supplements the school program. Children can be taught how to spend leisure time through participation in crafts, sports, and cultural programs. Although it is generally recognized that young children need supervision, the needs of secondary students are ignored. Older students have 3 to 4 unsupervised hours between the time they are out of school and the time their parents arrive home. In studies of secondary school drop outs, the greatest number who did not complete school were not involved in school activities. If you look at community structure, it becomes clear that schools are the major link between the family and the community.

SUMMARY

Understanding parents' feelings and concerns provides the basis for creating effective home-school relationships. Schools have character; some invite parents to participate; others suggest that they stay away. Parents have feelings about schools that range from a desire to avoid schools to such a high interest that they are overly active. Parents participate in schools as spectators, accessory volunteers, volunteer resources, paid resources, policymakers, and teachers of their children.

Schools can develop attitudes that welcome parents and conduct activities that invite them into the school. First, personnel in the school need to know what their attitudes toward parents are. Use of value clarification instruments helps in the recognition of feelings toward parents.

Second, the schools must set up one-way communication systems. One-way communication includes newsletters, spontaneous notes, happygrams, newspapers, media announcements, newspaper columns, telephone messages, and handbooks.

Third, two-way communication must be established. An open-door policy with open forums, coffees, and seminars invites comments from parents. Initial contact should be made early in the year or during the summer before the school year begins. Suggestions for early contact include neighborhood visits, telephone calls, home visits, and breakfasts. Two-way communication continues through the year with classroom visits and participation, back-to-school nights, parent education groups, school programs, projects, workshops, PTA carnivals, exchanges, and a suggestion box.

One of the most effective methods of two-way communication is the parent-teacher conference. Check with parents for convenient times for them to meet. Find a private and comfortable meeting place where you will not be disturbed. Establish effective open communication with the parent by listening for feeling and content and responding with an open statement. Show respect for the parent without shutting out their opinions. Choice of words, attentive behavior, and understandable language help in developing effective communication.

Prior to conferences collect anecdotal records, tests, workbooks, art projects, and papers that demonstrate the student's work. A Q Sort allows parents and teachers to see if they perceive the child in the same way. Recognize the parent as a member of the educational team. Consider including the student as the third member of the team. Through an analysis of examples of the student's work, design the educational program together. When parents and schools work together, education can move forward.

A resource room, established and staffed by parent volunteers, makes parents significant educational resources. The resource room includes articles on teaching, games, recycled materials, and a lending library for toys, books, and games. A family center gives parents a place to stop and a base from which they can reach out to help children.

Parents today are more involved as policymakers than in former times. Parent advisory councils are part of Chapter I, and parents confer with school administrators on program planning, implementation, and evaluation.

Schools can become community centers and meet the needs of families in the area by organizing parent volunteers for parent-to-parent groups, child care centers, crisis centers, and after-school programs.

SUGGESTED ACTIVITIES AND DISCUSSIONS

1. Visit a school and inquire about parent programs. Interview the principal, teachers, and counselors or social workers. Ask them about parent involvement. What are their tips for getting parents actively involved? What recommendations do they have for working with a variety of parents?
2. Make a list of suggestions in this chapter. Use it as a checklist to test your school's response to parents.
3. Contact the president of the PTA or PTO in a neighborhood school. What are their goals for parent involvement in the school? Which programs have they planned for the year? Which direction would they like the PTO or PTA to take?
4. Plan an ideal school for administrators, teachers, and parents. Which roles would each play? Which activities and programs would the school have?
5. Discuss why parents may feel intimidated by the schools and why teachers may be reluctant to have parents involved. Role play teacher and parent roles and share your feelings.
6. Describe an ideal parent-teacher relationship. List five things a teacher can do to encourage such a relationship. List five ways parents can work with the school.
7. Write out three situations that call for a parent-teacher conference. Play the part of parent, teacher, specialist, or child. Try your approaches using both closed and open responses and authoritarian or cooperative roles. Was there a change in the effectiveness of the conference? Discuss.
8. List what makes you feel comfortable or uncomfortable when you visit a center or school.
9. Construct a value clarification tool for your class. Have the members take the test. Break the class into groups and have them discuss where and how they developed their values. How much influence did their families have on the development of their values?
10. Construct a Q Sort appropriate for your own age-group. Take the test with a friend. Did you differ in your analysis of your actions? Discuss.
11. Write guidelines for parents to use when they visit or work in the classroom. Describe the guidelines on a poster and/or handout.
12. Examine your community and develop a list of field trips and home-learning activities. Plan a packet for parents to use with their children during spring break.

BIBLIOGRAPHY

Benet, J. Parents and a dream school. In D. Davies (Ed.), *Schools where parents make a difference.* Boston: Institute for Responsive Education, 1976.

Berger, E. H. *Parent questionnaire.* Unpublished questionnaire, Denver, Colo., 1979.

Bradley, R. C. *Parent-teacher interview.* Wolfe City, Tex.: University Press, 1971.

Brown, P. Picture a parent conference. *Early Years,* October 1975, pp. 48–50.

Carberry, H. H. Parent-teacher conferences. *Today's Education,* January-February 1975, pp. 67–69.

Carlson, J., & Hillman, W. Facilitating parent-teacher conferences. *The School Counselor,* March 1975, pp. 128–132.

Cary, S. Forming a partnership with parents. *Day Care and Early Education,* September 1974, pp. 11–14.

Chattanooga Public Schools. *Home/school education learning products.* Chattanooga, Tenn.: Chattanooga Public Schools.

Chinn, P. C., Winn, J., & Walters, R. H. *Two-way talking with parents of special children: A process of positive communication.* St. Louis: C. V. Mosby, 1978.

Curwin, R. L., & Fuhrmann, B. S. *Discovering your teaching self: Humanistic approaches to effective teaching.* Englewood Cliffs, N.J.: Prentice-Hall, 1975.

Da Silva, B., & Lucas, R. D. *Practical school volunteer and teacher-aide programs.* West Nyack, N.Y.: Parker Publishing, 1974.

Dinkmeyer, D., & McKay, G. D. *Parent's handbook.* Circle Pines, Minn.: American Guidance Service, 1983.

_____. *S.T.E.P.: Systematic training for effective parenting.* Circle Pines, Minn.: American Guidance Service, 1983.

Gallup, G. H. The eighth annual Gallup Poll of the public's attitudes toward the public schools. *Phi Delta Kappan,* October 1976, pp. 187–196.

Gallup, G. H. The eleventh annual Gallup Poll of the public's attitudes toward the public schools. *Phi Delta Kappan,* September 1979, pp. 33–45.

Gilmar, S., & Nelson, J. Resources for learning: Parents get into the act. *Childhood Education,* February 1975, pp. 208–210.

Gordon, I. J. Reaching the young child through parent education. *Childhood Education,* February 1970, pp. 247–249.

Gordon, T. *P.E.T. parent effectiveness training.* New York: Peter H. Wyden, 1970.

Grissom, C. E. Listening beyond words: Learning from parents in conferences. *Childhood Education,* December 1971, pp. 138–142.

Harris, J. A. Parents and Teachers Inc. *Teacher,* September 1978, pp. 85–87.

Hogan, J. R. The three-way conference: Parent-teacher-child. *The Elementary School Journal,* February 1975, pp. 311–315.

Hymes, J. *Effective home-school relations.* Sierra Madre: Southern California Association for the Education of Young Children, 1974.

Kniker, C. R. *You and values education.* Columbus, Ohio: Charles E. Merrill, 1977.

Kroth, R. L. *Communicating with parents of exceptional children.* Denver: Love Publishing, 1975.

Kroth, R. L., & Scholl, G. T. *Getting schools involved with parents.* Reston, Va.: Council for Exceptional Children, 1978.

Kroth, R. L., & Simpson, R. L. *Parent conferences as a teaching strategy.* Denver: Love Publishing, 1977.

Landau, E. D. Preparing for a teacher-parent conference. In R. C. Bradley, *Parent teacher interviews.* Wolfe City, Tex.: University Press, 1971.

Maslow, A. H. *Toward a psychology of being.* Princeton, N.J.: D. Von Norstrand, 1968.

Miller, B. L., & Wilmshurst, A. L. *Parents and volunteers in the classroom: A handbook for teachers.* San Francisco: R. E. Associates, 1975.

Nimnicht, G. P., & Brown, E. The toy library: Parents and children learning with toys. *Young Children,* December 1972, pp. 110–116.

Raths, L. E., Harmin, M., & Simon, S. B. *Values and teaching.* Columbus, Ohio: Charles E. Merrill, 1978.

Rich, D., & Mattox, B. *101 activities for building more effective school-community involvement.* Washington, D.C.: Home and School Institute, 1977.

Rogers, C. R. *On becoming a person.* Boston: Houghton Mifflin, 1963.

_____. *Freedom to learn.* Columbus, Ohio: Charles E. Merrill, 1969.

Seefeldt, C. Parent involvement: Support or stress. *Childhood Education,* November/December, 1985, pp. 98–102.

Simon, S. B., Howe, L. W., & Kirschenbaum, H. *Values clarification.* New York: Dodd Publishing, 1985.

Stephenson, W. *The study of behavior: Q technique and its methodology.* Chicago: University of Chicago Press, 1953.

Trail, O. A. Are you keeping parents out of your schools? In R. C. Bradley, *Parent-teacher interviews.* Wolfe City, Tex.: University Press, 1971.

U.S. Department of Health, Education, and Welfare. (Office of Education). *Title I ESEA: How it works: A guide for parents and parent advisory councils.* Washington, D.C.: U.S. Government Printing Office, 1978.

Williams, D. L., Jr. *Highlights from a survey of parents and educators regarding parent involvement in education.* Paper presented at the Seventh National Symposium on Building Family Strengths, Lincoln, Neb., May 1984.

Appendix

PARENT QUESTIONNAIRE

This questionnaire is written to give you, the parents, an opportunity to express your needs and desires in your relationships with schools or child care centers. What could the school or child care center do to make your role as a parent easier, more nurturing, and more possible to achieve?

1. Area in which you live: ☐ Urban   ☐ Suburban   ☐ Rural
2. Address: _____
3. Number of children: _____
4. Ages of children: _____   _____   _____   _____   _____
5. Sex of children: _____   _____   _____   _____   _____
   (Please place the sex designation under the correct age.)
6. Status of parent: ☐ Two parents   ☐ Divorced and remarried   ☐ Divorced and single   ☐ Single
7. Parent answering questionnaire: ☐ Mother   ☐ Father
8. Age of parent: ☐ Under 18   ☐ 18 to 21   ☐ 21 to 45   ☐ Over 45
9. Have you visited your child's school or child care center? ☐ Yes   ☐ No
10. Why did you visit?

11. What encourages you to visit?

12. Which aspects of the school or child care center did you like best?

If you were principal of the school or director of the child care center, which programs and activities would you have for parents and their children? Which of these programs would you use as a parent?

	School should offer		I would use	
	Yes	No	Yes	No
13. Parent education and preschool program	☐	☐	☐	☐
14. Parent education and toddler program	☐	☐	☐	☐
15. Child care during conferences	☐	☐	☐	☐
16. Resource or parent room	☐	☐	☐	☐

Continued.

PARENT QUESTIONNAIRE—cont'd

	School should offer		I would use	
	Yes	*No*	*Yes*	*No*
17. Crisis nursery	☐	☐	☐	☐
18. Newletters	☐	☐	☐	☐
19. PTA or PTO	☐	☐	☐	☐
20. After-school programs for children whose parents work	☐	☐	☐	☐
21. Parent volunteers	☐	☐	☐	☐
22. Parents as resource persons in the room	☐	☐	☐	☐
23. Parents as tutors	☐	☐	☐	☐
24. Parents Anonymous	☐	☐	☐	☐
25. Parent-to-parent support groups	☐	☐	☐	☐
26. Special support groups for single parents	☐	☐	☐	☐
27. Activities and guides for parents to use with children during holidays and spring break	☐	☐	☐	☐
28. Parent advisory committee	☐	☐	☐	☐
29. Home visits by teachers	☐	☐	☐	☐
30. Home visits by parent aides	☐	☐	☐	☐
31. Parent-teacher conferences	☐	☐	☐	☐

Other suggestions: _____

_____

_____

32. Would you like programs to be held at alternative times? ☐ Yes ☐ No
33. Would you like programs during: ☐ Day ☐ Evening ☐ Saturday
34. Would you like after-school services for your child and self? ☐ Yes ☐ No
35. How long each day do you need child care or education for your children?
    ☐ 2 hr ☐ 3 hr ☐ 4 hr ☐ 5 hr ☐ 6 hr ☐ 7 hr ☐ 8 hr ☐ 9 hr
36. How long each day would you like kindergarten to be?
    ☐ 2 hr ☐ 3 hr ☐ 4 hr ☐ 5 hr ☐ 6 hr
37. In which areas do you need help for your child/children?

38. In which areas do you need help for yourself as a parent?

39. Where would you go for help? Can you give a source for each of the following?
    Health care: _____
    Information: _____
    Evaluation of child
    　　Educational: _____
    　　Gifted or handicapped: _____
    　　Emotional: _____
    Emotional support for parent: _____
    Emergency child care: _____
    Child care placement: _____
    Educational enrichment for child/children: _____
    Other needs: _____
40. What would you like to know about your center or school's program?
    Preschool: _____
    _____

    Primary: _____
    _____

    Intermediate: _____
    _____

    Secondary: _____
    _____
41. What would you like to know about your center or school's facilities?

42. Which qualities in a director or principal make you feel "at home" and give you confidence in the school or center?
    Preschool:_____
    _____

    Primary: _____
    _____

    Intermediate: _____
    _____

    Secondary: _____
    _____
43. Which qualities make a good teacher?
    Preschool: _____
    _____

    Primary: _____
    _____

    Intermediate: _____
    _____

    Secondary: _____
    _____
44. Additional comments:

CHAPTER FIVE

Parent Education and Leadership Training

Have you ever attended a relaxed meeting where everyone was accepted and encouraged to participate and still the objectives of the meeting were accomplished? Each person participated in the meeting and, in turn, developed higher self-esteem and had the opportunity to be a part of a productive group. A well-led parent group is representative of such a meeting and accomplishes its goals by educating parents and clarifying and responding to their questions and concerns.

The principles and practices of parent group education . . . offer a dynamic learning experience, which grows out of the parents' interests and needs and in which they participate in their own individual ways. (Auerbach, 1968, p. 5)

Leadership in parent group education may be viewed as a continuum (see Figure 5-1) that ranges from the lay leader, to the non-professional with little training, to a knowledgeable expert trained to expedite group

The goal of education is to help parents become familiar with the phases of a child's growth and to become more effective parents.

Parent leader with no training	Parent leader with leadership training	Parent leader with a structured curriculum	Parent leader with professional support	Professional leader with parent support	Professional teacher

FIGURE 5-1
Continuum of leaders in parent education.

processes, to the professional who lectures as an authority. As you begin a parent education program, keep in mind that groups can be organized in different fashions. A trained professional should not dominate the interaction within the group with specific didactic teaching, nor should the lay group be left without direction.

The use of lay leaders—parents leading their own groups—encourages parents to be actively involved. Since educational growth and positive change is what is wanted in parent education groups, active involvement is highly desired. More change will occur if the parent formulates some of the educational suggestions and acts upon the information. Parents are more able to develop their own ways of handling parent-child relationships if they develop their expertise from their own research and interact with other members of the group. This does not mean that experts in the field should not be used. At times it is necessary to have an authority give background material. After the information is received, however, parents need to discuss it and act upon it themselves. Professional leadership does not have to be overbearing and authoritarian. This concept is illustrated by the proverb credited to Lao-tze, an ancient Chinese philosopher.

> *A leader is best*
> *When people barely know that he exists*
> *Not so good when people obey and acclaim him*
> *Worst when they despise him*

> *Fail to honor people,*
> *They fail to honor you,*
> *But of a good leader, who talks little*
> *When work is done, his aim fulfilled*
> *They will all say, "we did this ourselves."*

A professional who can support and motivate the group can accomplish the goals of the group without undermining the responsibilities of the participants. Likewise, when "guided interaction is the key to effective learning, then a knowledgeable educator, skilled in group process, is needed for maximum individual learning" (Pickarts & Fargo, 1971, p. 78). The style of the leader will be determined by the individual's training and personality as well as the makeup of the group. Group management can be enhanced by leadership training sessions where professional members of the parent group can be introduced to group methods, curriculum, and resources.

A parent group organized and led by a lay leader can be effective if the leader is able to develop leadership skills and has traits such as sensitivity to and acceptance of others, flexibility, and an outgoing personality (Hereford, 1963). All parent education groups need basic understanding of group processes and communication, whether led by parent leaders or professionals.

This chapter describes various types of meetings and group processes as a guide in the development of new parent group programs. The programs discussed here range from those led by the unskilled person without curriculum guides on the left of the continuum to the authoritarian meeting on the right. The center of the continuum contains the parent education group that is most appropriate for achieving parental self-determination, attitudinal change, competency, and educational gains—that of parent leadership with professional support. Descriptions of programs that illustrate each of the types include:

1. Unstructured meetings with no goals, curriculum, or trained leader
2. Meetings led by lay leaders to get feedback, solve a problem, study an issue, or become better acquainted (for example, Hereford's research into a program that involved trained lay leaders with a curriculum devised according to parent needs)
3. Meetings led by lay leaders who follow a curriculum devised by professionals (e.g., Parent Effectiveness Training, Systematic Training for Effective Parenting)
4. Meetings called by a parent and/or a professional that involve members and respond to their concerns with professional support
5. Meetings called and led by a professional, with participation by lay members, and
6. Meetings called, led, directed, and controlled by the professional, with members of the audience being observers only

Although parent education programs differ in the underlying structures—some are led by professionals, others by lay leaders—they are similar in their goal to develop decision-making abilities in parents (Auerbach, 1968; Hereford, 1963; Pickarts & Fargo, 1971; U. S. Department of Health and Human Services, 1980.) Allowing parents to evaluate child-rearing practices in the light of their own situations, values, and beliefs is an extension of democratic principles. Belief in the autonomy of parents inspires the promotion of their decision-making abilities and thus underscores the need for active involvement of parents in the programs.

Auerbach (1968) reinforced the need for parent involvement in her discussion of the following theories:

1. Parents can learn
2. Parents want to learn
3. Parents learn best what they are interested in learning
4. Learning is most significant when the subject matter is closely related to the parents' own immediate experiences
5. Parents can learn best when they are free to create their own response to a situation
6. Parent group education is as much an emotional experience as it is an intellectual one
7. Parents can learn from one another
8. Parent group education provides the basis for remaking experiences
9. Each parent learns in his own way

Parents, when involved in a study that interests them and one in which they are active investigators, tend to learn more and change more in attitude than parents who merely attend lectures. As H. H. Stern pointed out:

An authoritarian form of instruction and passive receptivity by the pupil is too restricted in interpretation of the concept of education. The principles and practices of parent group education in marked contrast offer a dynamic learning experience which grows out of the parents' interests and needs and in which they participate in their own individual ways. (as cited in Auerbach, 1968, p. 5)

With the recognition that parent education discussion groups are one of the most effective forms of parent education, organizational and planning skills, complemented by the ability to communicate with and to support parents in group discussions, become essential qualities for teachers, administrators, and parent educators.

NEEDS ASSESSMENTS

Before you begin a parent education program, and periodically during the program, make evaluations to determine the interests and needs of the community. First, meet with a group of parents representative of the diversified ethnic and socioeconomic levels within the community. Jot down the ideas or questions that concern and interest them. A brainstorming session is an ideal mechanism for eliciting many ideas. To facilitate the brainstorming session, duplicate and distribute a handout of the problems recognized by parents in the ninth Gallup Poll described on page 146.

Once you have developed your basic list of interests and concerns, give it to a trial group, and have them add new ideas and concerns. Next, construct a needs assessment tool (assessment of needs) for wide distribution, and disseminate the needs assessment questionnaire to adults through the school or center community. Finally, choose from the questionnaire those items that received the most requests, and develop a program to meet the needs of the community.

Be sensitive to minorities and single parents and incorporate their responses to such needs and desires into the parent program. "Among the parents who indicate greatest need for help . . . are the single parents and parents from minority races" (Yankelovich, Skelly, & White, Inc., 1977, p. 120).

The Appalachian Educational Laboratory has designed a comprehensive needs assessment to determine curriculum for a parent education course for television (Coan & Gotts, 1976). Parents of children in 186 classrooms in 26 schools located in 10 states across the United States were surveyed. From the answers of the needs assessments six factors were clustered and factored: family care, child growth and development, child management, self as parent, treating your child like a person, and baby care. This needs assessment is illustrated in the Appendix to this chapter and can be used as a guide when you construct an instrument for your locality.

According to a 1985 Gallup Poll parents regarded discipline as the greatest problem facing the schools. Their next greatest concern was the use of drugs. Curriculum, standards in the schools, and getting good teachers were also prominent concerns (Gallup,

1985, p. 42). The 1977 Gallup Poll questioned parents on needs and concerns that could be addressed by parent education programs. By a four to one margin, parents favored parent education courses. In the survey, the statement, "What to do about drugs, smoking, and use of alcohol" was of greatest concern to the parents (Gallup, 1977, p. 42). Although later polls did not address the need for parent programs, the list generated by the concerns of parents of elementary school-age children in 1977 is relevant for use in developing a needs assessment in the 1980s. Since these lists are used to help generate ideas and the concerns are selected on the basis of what the current group of parents indicate as their greatest needs, the final selection of interests and concerns will be based on individual needs of each group. If you are working with parents of young children, include some of the items from the Appalachian Education Laboratory needs assessment in the Appendix of this chapter when you establish your initial list. The following list from the 1977 Gallup Poll will help form a total interest listing.

Parents whose eldest child was 12 years or younger ranked the items as follows:

1. What to do about drugs, smoking, use of alcohol
2. How to help the child set high achievement goals
3. How to develop good work habits
4. How to improve the child's school behavior
5. How to improve the child's thinking and observation abilities
6. How to deal with the child's emotional problems
7. How to increase interest in school and school subjects
8. How to help the child organize his/her homework
9. How to improve parent/child relationships
10. How to help the child choose a career
11. How to use family activities to help the child do better in school
12. How to encourage reading
13. How to help the child get along with other children

14. How to reduce television viewing
15. How to deal with dating problems
16. How to improve health habits[1]

Needs assessments at the individual small-group level can be less formal:

1. Brainstorm ideas for concerns and interests.
2. Collect as many ideas as your group may generate.
3. Show the group a similar list that might add to the list they have generated.
4. Form buzz groups and let the participants discuss the lists.
5. Let the members list their choices in order of importance to them.
6. Generate your programs for the year from the responses of the group.
7. If a new issue arises that concerns most of the group, find a space or add a session to cover the important topic.

Needs assessments are necessary when new programs are developed as well as when established parent groups reassess their needs. Less formal assessments are used frequently by ongoing groups.

INTEREST FINDERS

If a parent group is already established, members may use a number of informal methods to indicate their interests. These range from brainstorming among the members to soliciting suggestions in a question box.

Brainstorming.   A brainstorming session can be held. Choose a recorder and encourage all members to contribute ideas for programs. A list of programs successful in former years may be distributed. Write ideas on a chalkboard or

on a transparency on an overhead projector. After all the suggestions are listed, have members choose in writing three to six ideas that interest them most. Develop your program from the interests that receive the most votes (or are most frequently mentioned). If the group has difficulty thinking of items, you may be able to generate responses by having participants complete statements such as the ones in this example:

My greatest concerns are _____.
My greatest happiness comes from _____.
If I had three wishes, I would _____.
If I could eliminate one problem from my home, it would be _____.
Questions that concern me about my child's education are _____.
Questions that concern me about my child's development are _____.
As a parent I hope to be _____.

Annoyance Test.   An annoyance test is relevant for parents. The leader writes the following on a chart or blackboard:

My children annoy me when they _____.
I annoy my children when I_____.

The parents then list points under each, and the results are tabulated. The four or five most popular topics may then be discussed in subsequent meetings (Denver Public Schools, 1978).

Charts.   "The Worried Mother"—the leader draws a picture of a worried mother. The leader introduces the meeting by pointing to the worried mother and saying, "How many of you would like to get rid of your worries so you can be a happy mother? Let's each make a list of all the reasons for our worries and then see what we can do about them." After listing all the causes for worries, count the most common ones. Plan meetings using these topics (Denver Public Schools, 1978).

Open-Ended Questions.   Soliciting requests for a wider knowledge of the community and

---

1. From Gallup, G. H. The ninth annual Gallup Poll of the public's attitudes toward the public schools. *Phi Delta Kappan,* September 1977, p. 42.

What questions might this mother have as she cares for her young child?

suggesting ways for parents to become more involved in schools and the community is relevant for parents' groups. The leader asks parents to respond to such topics as:

1. What I want to know about my school
2. What I want to know about my community
3. What I would like to do about my school and/or community

Question-Answer Sheets. Question-answer sheets, such as *Test Your Know-How as a Parent,* bring out differences in opinions in the group and show where interests and room for learning occur.

Question Box. Some parents are hesitant to make suggestions in an open meeting. It is advantageous to have a question box available in which members can place questions and comments throughout the year.

During early planning it may also be advisable to let the members write their ideas on a small sheet of paper anonymously. Parents may be very concerned about drugs and alcohol, for example, but be hesitant to mention them lest they reveal that they have that problem in their homes.

DEVELOPMENT OF OBJECTIVES

After the group's interests have been assessed, program development proceeds. Within most programs at least two aspects should receive attention: the content of the meeting and the behavioral and attitudinal changes of the participants. Table 5-1 may be helpful in illustrating how objectives in these two areas intertwine. Social and emotional objectives are as important as content objectives. If knowledge is not implemented in changed behavior, then it is useless. Table 5-1 is merely suggestive and illustrates one program's needs.

PARENT EDUCATION PROGRAMS

Many parent education programs incorporate the resources of child-rearing suggestions from the curricula furnished by Parent Effectiveness Training (PET) or Systematic Training for Effective Parenting (STEP). Brief excerpts from these programs illustrate the materials and communication techniques each uses. As you read the materials, check the content in Table 5-1. Note that some topics are related to family relations, communication, interpersonal relations, and behavior and misbehavior. These topics are typical of those which parent groups request.

PET

In PET Thomas Gordon discusses active listening, "I messages," changing behavior by changing environment, parent-child conflicts, parental power, and "no-lose" methods for resolving conflicts as well as other parent-child

TABLE 5-1

Parent education program objectives

Choose any or all of the content aspects of this chart, then decide what objectives you want to accomplish related to the chosen issues. For example, in dealing with social problems the program represented in this table chose drug/alcohol and violence as necessary topics and determined that all the behavioral objectives were relevant.

Content aspects of the objectives	*Behavioral aspects of the objectives*					
	Use of facts and materials	*Familiarity of resource materials*	*Decision making and critical thinking*	*Influence of values on perceptions of daily living*	*Improved communication and interpersonal relations*	*Development of sensitivity to social problems*
Home and the school						
1. New classroom teaching methods						
2. Home-school relationships						
3. Readiness for learning						
4. Parent involvement						
Child development						
1. Growth						
a. Physical	X		X			
b. Mental						
c. Social						
d. Emotional						
2. Behavior and misbehavior						
3. Individual differences						
a. Special children (gifted or retarded)						
b. Diagnosis						
c. Building self-concept						
4. Sexuality						
a. Sex education						
b. Nonsexist education						

Category					
Family relations					
1. Communication	X	X	X	X	
2. Interpersonal relations					
3. Sibling rivalry					
Social problems					
1. Drugs/alcohol	X	X	X	X	X
2. Violence	X	X	X	X	X
3. Smoking					X
4. Stress					X
5. Living with change					X
Enrichment activities of childhood					
1. Creativity/exploration, imagination, music, art					
2. Experiences					
3. Literature and reading					
4. Influence of television					
Mental and emotional health					
1. Value clarification					
2. Self-understanding					
Living in a democracy					
1. Decision making					
2. Responsibilities					
3. Moral values					
4. Critical thinking					

*On the chart check the appropriate content aspects and behavioral aspects that are needed in your parent education program. For example, in dealing with social problems the program represented above chose drug/alcohol and violence as necessary topics and determined that all the behavioral objectives were relevant.

issues. The excerpt here relates to problem ownership and active listening.

In the parent-child relationship three situations occur that we will shortly illustrate with case histories:

1. The child has a problem because he is thwarted in satisfying a need. It is not a problem for the parent because the child's behavior in no tangible way interferes with the parent's satisfying his own needs. Therefore, *the child owns the problem.*
2. The child is satisfying his own needs (he is not thwarted) and his behavior is not interfering with the parent's own needs. Therefore, *there is no problem in the relationship.*
3. The child is satisfying his own needs (he is not thwarted). But his behavior is a problem to the parent because it is interfering in some tangible way with the parent's satisfying a need of his own. *Now the parent owns the problem.*

It is critical that parents always classify each situation that occurs in a relationship. Which of these three categories does the situation fall into? It helps to remember this diagram [Figure 5-2] . . .

When a parent accepts the fact that problems are owned by the child, this in no way means he, the parent, cannot be concerned, care, or offer help. A professional counselor has real concern for, and genuinely cares about, each child he is trying to help. But, unlike most parents, he leaves the responsibility for solving the child's problem with the child. He allows the child to own the problem. He accepts the child's having the problems. He accepts the child as a person separate from himself. And he relies heavily upon and basically trusts the child's own inner resources for solving his own problem. Only because he lets the child own his problem is the professional counselor able to employ active listening.

Active listening is a powerful method for helping another person solve a problem that he owns, provided the listener can accept the other's ownership and consistently allow the person to find his own solutions. Active listening can greatly increase the effectiveness of parents as helping agents for their children, but it is a different kind of help from that which parents usually try to give.

Paradoxically, this method will increase the parent's influence on the child, but it is an influence that differs from the kind that most parents try to exert over their children. Active listening is a method of influencing children to find their own solutions to their own problems. Most parents, however, are tempted to take over ownership of their children's problems, as in the following case:

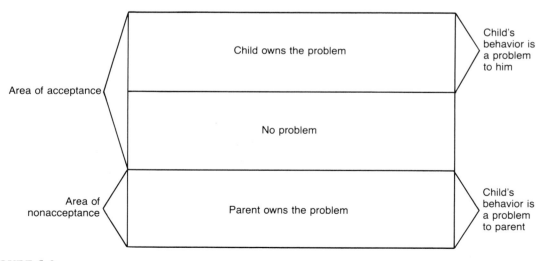

FIGURE 5-2

When the child's behavior is a problem to the parent, the parent owns the problem. (*Source:* T. Gordon, *P. E. T./Parent effectiveness training.* New York: Wyden, 1975, p. 64).

JOHNNY: Tommy won't play with me today. He won't ever do what I want to do.

MOTHER: Well, why don't you offer to do what he wants to do? You've got to learn to get along with your little friends. *(advising; moralizing)*

JOHNNY: I don't like to do things he wants to do and besides I don't want to get along with that dope.

MOTHER: Well, go find someone else to play with then if you're going to be a spoilsport. *(offering a solution; name-calling)*

JOHNNY: He's the spoilsport, not me. And there isn't anyone else to play with.

MOTHER: You're just upset because you're tired. You'll feel better about this tomorrow. *(interpreting; reassuring)*

JOHNNY: I'm not tired, and I won't feel different tomorrow. You just don't understand how much I hate the little squirt.

MOTHER: Now stop talking like that! If I ever hear you talk about one of your friends like that again, you'll be sorry. *(ordering; threatening)*

JOHNNY: (walking away and sulking): I hate this neighborhood. I wish we would move.

Here is how the parent can help the same boy with active listening.

JOHNNY: Tommy won't play with me today. He won't ever do what I want to do.

MOTHER: You're kinda angry with Tommy. *(active listening)*

JOHNNY: I sure am. I never want to play with him again. I don't want him for a friend.

MOTHER: You're so angry you feel like never seeing him again. *(active listening)*

JOHNNY: That's right. But if I don't have him for a friend, I won't have anyone to play with then.

MOTHER: You would hate to be left with no one. *(active listening)*

JOHNNY: Yeah. I guess I just have to get along with him someway. But it's so hard for me to stop getting mad at him.

MOTHER: You want to get along better, but it's hard for you to keep from getting mad with Tommy. *(active listening)*

JOHNNY: I never used to—but that's when he was always willing to do what I wanted to do. He won't let me boss him anymore.

MOTHER: Tommy's not so easy to influence now. *(active listening)*

JOHNNY: He sure isn't. He's not such a baby now. He's more fun though.

MOTHER: You really like him better this way. *(active listening)*

JOHNNY: Yeah. But it's hard to stop bossing him— I'm so used to it. Maybe we wouldn't fight so much if I let him have his way once in a while. Think that would work?

MOTHER: You're thinking that if you might give in occasionally, it might help. *(active listening)*

JOHNNY: Yeah, maybe it would. I'll try it.

In the first version, the mother used eight of the "Typical Twelve" categories of responding. In the second, the mother consistently used active listening. In the first, the mother "took over the problem"; in the second, her active listening kept ownership of the problem with Johnny. In the first, Johnny resisted his mother's suggestions, his anger and frustration were never dissipated, the problem remained unresolved, and there was no growth on Johnny's part. In the second, his anger left, he initiated problem solving, and took a deeper look at himself. He arrived at his own solution and obviously grew a notch toward becoming a responsible, self-directing problem solver.[2]

Gordon clarifies active listening and problem ownerships through examples such as these. Parent groups follow up the printed page with a parent notebook and discussion within the group. Open discussion, led by a person knowledgeable about PET, allows parents to apply the methods to their own experiences in child rearing.

STEP

The STEP program furnishes cassettes, a parent manual, and a leadership manual to facilitate parent meetings. Figure 5-3 is taken from the parent manual.

---

2. From Gordon, T. *P.E.T. Parent effectiveness training.* New York: Wyden, 1975, pp. 64 and 66–68.

These programs fit under the category of meetings with a parent leader with a structured curriculum, illustrated in Figure 5-1. There is great leeway, however, in the structure of the meetings. Following the structured presentation or during the presentation, the leader may open the meeting to discussion for the whole group or may form buzz groups, thus allowing group interaction. Many parent groups have incorporated these programs into their plans for the year. For example, 12 meetings may be devoted to the STEP program, and 18 meetings may be planned to cover the other aspects of the group's objectives.

GROUP DISCUSSIONS

Most meetings involve group discussion, which can range from the use of open discussion as the total meeting format to a short discussion following a formal presentation.

Group discussion can follow various formats: an informal discussion plan, which varies with the needs of the group and emanates from the interests of the members and the direction of its leader; a meeting with an underlying structure based on problem solving; and a discussion based on the use of experience as a learning tool (Pfeiffer & Jones, 1979).

Informal Discussion Plan

A. Stems from interest or needs of group
EXAMPLE: How can parents be more involved in their child's school?
B. Establishes goals and objectives
EXAMPLE
1. Goal—parental involvement
2. Objectives
   a. To determine why parents do not feel comfortable coming to school
   b. To encourage parents to participate in schools
   c. To initiate a plan for getting parents involved

d. To suggest activities in which parents can be involved
C. Provides for informal group meetings
1. Allows parents to speak freely
2. Emphasizes the clarification of feelings and acceptance of ideas
3. Encourages participation
4. Includes keeping a record of suggestions
D. Selects and analyzes relevant information that emerges during the discussion
E. Outlines plan for action, if group desires

Problem-solving Format

A. Recognition of the problem—state the hypothesis
1. The problem should be one that is selected by the group and reflects its needs and interests.
   EXAMPLE: How can we monitor television programs and television viewing for the benefit of children and families?
2. The leader writes the question or problem for discussion on chart or chalkboard.
B. Understanding the problem—discuss the nature of problem
EXAMPLE: Is television viewing a problem and, if so, why?
C. Data collection—gather a wide range of ideas and determine which are relevant
1. Prior development of expertise—identify resources and read prior to meeting
2. Nonjudgmental acceptance—accept and record comments and ideas from participants
D. Analysis of the problem
1. Focus the subject so that it can be discussed thoroughly by participants
2. Establish criteria for evaluation of a solution
3. Keep participants focused on problems
E. Conclusion and summary
1. Suggest solutions
2. List possible conclusions
3. Seek an integrative conclusion that reflects the group's goals and thinking
F. Appropriate action
1. Develop a timetable
2. Determine a method of accomplishing task
3. Delegate tasks

CHILD'S FAULTY BELIEF	CHILD'S GOAL*	PARENTS' FEELINGS AND REACTIONS	CHILD'S RESPONSE TO PARENTS' ATTEMPTS AT CORRECTION	ALTERNATIVES FOR PARENTS
I belong *only* when I am being noticed or served.	Attention	**Feeling:** annoyed **Reaction:** tendency to remind and coax	Temporarily stops misbehavior; later resumes same behavior or disturbs in another way	Ignore misbehavior when possible; give attention for positive behavior when child is not making a bid for it; avoid undue service; realize that reminding, punishing, rewarding, coaxing, and service are undue attention
I belong *only* when I am in control or am boss, or when I am proving no one can boss me!	Power	**Reaction:** tendency to fight or to give in **Feeling:** angry; provoked; as if one's authority is threatened	Active- or passive-aggressive misbehavior is intensified, or child submits with "defiant compliance"	Withdraw from conflict; help child see how to use power constructively by appealing for child's help and enlisting cooperation; realize that fighting or giving in only increases child's desire for power
I belong *only* by hurting others as I feel hurt. I cannot be loved.	Revenge	**Feeling:** deeply hurt **Reaction:** tendency to retaliate and get even	Seeks further revenge by intensifying misbehavior or choosing another weapon	Avoid feeling hurt; avoid punishment and retaliation; build trusting relationship; convince child that she or he is loved
I belong *only* by convincing others not to expect anything from me. I am unable; I am helpless.	Display of inadequacy	**Feeling:** despair; hopelessness; "I give up" **Reaction:** tendency to agree with child that nothing can be done	Passively responds or fails to respond to whatever is done; shows no improvement	Stop all criticism; encourage any positive attempt, no matter how small; focus on assets; above all, don't be hooked into pity, and don't give up.

A

*To determine your child's goal, you must check your feelings *and* the child's response to your attempts to correct him or her. Goal identification is simplified by observing:

1. Your own feelings and reaction to the child's misbehavior
2. The child's response to your attempts at correction

By considering your situation in terms of the chart, you will be able to identify the goal of the misbehavior.

FIGURE 5-3
The STEP program gives illustrated guidance for ways of helping parents relate positively with their children. *A.* The goals of misbehavior. *B.* Communication: listening. *C.* Effective listening. (*Source:* reproduced by permission of American Guidance Service from *Systematic training for effective parenting* by Don Dinkmeyer and Gary McKay.)

B

POINTS TO REMEMBER

1. Communication begins by listening and indicating you hear the child's feelings and meanings.

2. Effective listening involves establishing eye contact and posture that clearly indicate you are listening.

3. Avoid nagging, criticizing, threatening, lecturing, probing, and ridiculing.

4. Treat your children the way you treat your best friend.

5. Mutual respect involves accepting the child's feelings.

6. Reflective listening involves hearing the child's feelings and meanings and stating this so the child feels understood. It provides a mirror for the child to see himself or herself more clearly.

7. Learn to give open responses that accurately state what the other person feels and means.

8. Avoid closed responses that ignore the child's feelings, relaying that we have not heard or understood.

9. Let the child learn. Resist the impulse to impose your solutions.

FIGURE 5-3, *continued*

154

Closed response	Denies children a right to their feelings by demonstrating listener's unwillingness to accept and understand

Open response	Acknowledges children's right to their feelings by demonstrating that the listener accepts what they feel as well as what they say; indicates that the listener understands

Child's remark:	Closed response:	Open response:
I'm never going to play with her again!	Why don't you forget it; she probably didn't mean it.	You're really angry with her.
I can't do it!	Now, don't talk like that! You just got started!	It seems very difficult to you.
I wish I could go along. He always gets to go everywhere.	We've discussed this before, so stop fussing.	It seems unfair to you.
Look at my new model!	That's nice . . . now will you please go.	You're pleased with your work on it.
I don't want to go to school today. Billy is mean!	Everyone has to go to school. It's the law.	You're afraid Billy will pick on you.
You're the meanest mother in the whole world!	Don't you ever talk to me that way!	You're very angry with me.

C

For each remark, give an example of a CLOSED response and an OPEN response.

1. I don't *like* vegetables, and I'm not going to eat them. _____

2. Our teacher is crabby. _____

3. I don't *want* to go to bed! It's too early. _____

4. I'm not going to wear my raincoat. Nobody in my class wears a stupid old raincoat. _____

FIGURE 5-3, *continued*

Experiential Learning Cycle

The experiential learning cycle is most often used when members of the group have been involved in an activity such as role playing or a similar sensitizing experience. Pfeiffer and Jones illustrated the role-playing activity.

The role playing activity is the beginning of a five-step experiential model (Pfeiffer & Jones, 1979, p. 305) which is based on a cyclical learning process of five separate but interlocking procedures. As implied by the name of the model, the emphasis is on the vicarious experiences garnered through didactic approaches.

The experiential model is also an inductive rather than a deductive process: the participant discovers for himself the learnings offered by the experiential process. His discovery may be facilitated by a leader, but in the end the participant finds and validates his own experience.

This is the "laboratory" . . . approach to learning. It is based on the premise that experience precedes learning and that the learning, or meaning, to be derived from any experience comes from the learner himself. Any individual's experience is unique to himself; no one can tell him what he is to learn, or gain, from any activity. Probable learnings can, of course, be devised, but it is up to the participant to validate these for himself.

Five revolving steps are included in the experiential model.

Experiencing. The process usually starts with experiencing. The participant becomes involved in an activity; he acts or behaves in some way or he does, performs, observes, sees, says something. This initial experience is the basis for the entire process.

Publishing. Following the experience itself, it becomes important for the participant to share or "publish" his reactions and observations with others who have either experienced or observed the same activity.

Processing. Sharing one's reactions is only the first step. An essential—and often neglected—part of the cycle is the necessary integration of this sharing. The dynamics that emerged in the activity are explored, discussed, and evaluated (processed) with other participants.

Generalizing. Flowing logically from the process step is the need to develop principles or ex-

tract generalizations from the experience. Stating learnings in this way can help participants further define, clarify, and elaborate them.

Applying. The final step in the cycle is to plan applications of the principles derived from the experience. The experiential process is not complete until a new learning or discovery is used and tested behaviorally. This is the "experimental" part of the experiential model. Applying, of course, becomes an experience in itself, and with new experience, the cycle begins again.

Each step of the experiential learning cycle can be related to role playing. In the experiencing phase, the focus is on the role play itself. Here it is important to recognize that this phase creates the data base of human interaction for later discussion. Thus much of the emphasis in preparing a role play has to be on later phases, i.e., what after the role play is completed. In the publishing phase, i.e., the observers' reports and the role players' expression of feelings, attitudes, and experiences are the significant aspects. Here the emphasis is on sharing reactions experienced in the role play.

The publishing phase of the role play experience flows into the next phase—processing. Observers can report the patterns of behavior that they observed. At this point role players often are still emotionally in their roles, and it is important to make an intervention that will help to "de-role" them and make them more receptive to cognitive integration of the experience. Often a simple announcement—"All role players may now resume being and acting themselves"—is adequate. Sometimes, however, a meeting may be required with support or reference groups for the purpose of finishing the unfinished business of the role play.

The next phase is generalizing from the role-play experience to "real-world" situations. There are a variety of techniques for developing generalizations: individuals and/or groups can be instructed to write declarative statements based on their experiences outside the training situation; and participants can be encouraged to develop cause-and-effect hypotheses about the dynamics that emerge in the role-play experience.

The final phase of the role-play process is the most important one: applying. In this part of the design participants are led to explore two crucial questions: "So what?" and "Now what?" These discussions can take place between goal-setting partners, within natural subgroups of the training group, between participant-observer pairs, and by repeating the role play and applying the generalizations that came out of the first round. It is important that the facilitator, in devising a role play, think very carefully about how participants are to be led from playing a role to integrating their learning into practical, everyday, significant changes in behavior.[3]

Questions and statements that facilitate the group's discussion and clarification of the five steps were suggested by Gaw in the *1979 Annual Handbook for Group Facilitators.* These comments can be used to clarify issues and to promote learning in other types of discussion groups, as well as in a learning cycle.

Stage One: *Experiencing*
(Questions aid the group in moving either more deeply into the stage at hand or on to another stage.)
* What is going on?
* How do you feel about that?
* What do you need to know to . . . ?
* Would you be willing to try?
* Could you be more specific?
* Could you offer a suggestion?
* What would you prefer?
* What are your suspicions?
* What is your objection?
* If you could guess at the answer, what would it be?
* Can you say that in another way?
* What is the worst/best that could happen?
* What else?
* And?
* Would you say more about that?

Stage Two: *Sharing or publishing*
(Questions are directed toward generating data.)
* Who would volunteer to share? Who else?
* What went on/happened?
* How did you feel about that?
* Who else had the same experience?
* Who reacted differently?
* Were there any surprises/puzzlements?

* How many felt the same?
* How many felt differently?
* What did you observe?
* What were you aware of?

Stage Three: *Interpreting*
(Questions are directed toward making sense of that data for the individual and the group.)
* How did you account for that?
* What does that mean to you?
* How was that significant?
* How was that good/bad?
* What struck you about that?
* How do those fit together?
* How might it have been different?
* Do you see something operating there?
* What does that suggest to you about yourself/your group?
* What do you understand better about yourself/your group?

Stage Four: *Generalizing*
(Participants work toward abstracting from the specific knowledge they have gained about themselves and their group to superordinate principles. Questions are directed toward promoting generalizations.)
* What might we draw/pull from that?
* Is that plugging into anything?
* What did you learn/relearn?
* What does that suggest to you about ____ in general?
* Does that remind you of anything?
* What principle/law do you see operating?
* What does that help explain?
* How does this relate to other experiences?
* What do you associate with that?
* So what?

Stage Five: *Applying*
(Participants are concerned with utilizing ideas in real world situations. Questions are directed toward applying the general knowledge they have gained to their personal and/or professional lives.)
* How could you apply/transfer that?
* What would you like to do with that?
* How could you repeat this again?
* What could you do to hold on to that?
* What are the options?
* What might you do to help/hinder yourself?
* How could you make it better?
* What would be the consequences of doing/not doing that?

---

3. From J. W. Pfeiffer & J. H. Jones. *The reference guide to handbooks and annuals* (3rd ed.). San Diego, Calif.: University Associates, 1979, pp. 189–191.

Members of your parent groups work more effectively if they have information about group leadership and group dynamics.

- What modifications can you make work for you?
- What could you imagine/fantasize about that?[4]

LEADERSHIP TRAINING

Lay leaders benefit from guidelines in the development of their leadership skills. The leader's goal is to establish an environment that facilitates and guides members in achieving the objectives.

Leaders need to take a pro-active and influencing role, but the thrust of these actions should be power diffusing and helpful to the self-enhancing processes of the individual, organization and society. . . . Leaders establish a model for behavior by their participation, acceptance of criticisms, non-evaluative comments, willingness to deviate from pre-planned procedures, ability to listen with understanding, ability to capture and reflect feelings, by their clarifying comments and by the method of expressing their own feelings. (Gardner, 1974, p. 72)

Some suggestions that help a group become cohesive and productive follow:

1. Group responsibility is shared by all the members.
2. Policies should be decided by the group.
3. Meetings should be informal.
4. Methods which allow participation by as many as possible should be used.
5. Leaders should be flexible in the handling of the meeting. Modify and change if it helps the group move forward.
6. The group should not be a threat to its members.
7. The group should evaluate its progress throughout the year.
8. Members of the group should know the importance of roles within the group.
9. Form the group so that all members can see the faces of other group members.
10. Encourage freedom to be active participants, allowing movement and verbal participation. (Gibb, Platts, & Miller, 1959, pp. 58, 59)

Group members can participate more effectively if they are aware of their rights and responsibilities within the group. A handout, given to the membership early in the school

4. Reprinted from J. B. Jones and J. W. Pfeiffer (Eds.). *The 1979 annual handbook for group facilitators.* San Diego, Calif.: University Associates, 1979, pp. 150 and 151. Used with permission.

term, helps eliminate problems and encourages a relaxed, productive group (see Figure 5-4). Use the handout as a guide.

This handout, along with a description of group roles chosen from the list given later in this chapter, will enable the group members to grow into productive participants in group interaction. As a leader it is your responsibility to share these communication tips with the group membership.

General Qualifications. The following pointers emphasize the leader's personality, interpersonal relationships, and skill in handling group discussions:

A. Leader's personality
   1. Ability to think and act quickly. The leader may need to change plans on the spur of the moment.
   2. Ability to get along with others, to be well liked, and not have a tendency to "fly off the handle."
   3. Respect for the opinions of others. The leader should be a good listener and avoid trying to "tell" others what to think.

   4. Willingness to remain in the background. Instead of voicing opinions, asks questions and guides but does not dominate.
   5. Freedom from prejudice.
B. Leader's knowledge and skills
   1. Knowledge of the discussion method. The leader must know the why and the how, the purpose and the procedure, agreed upon for the meeting to be successful.
   2. Knowledge of the opinions of authorities on the subject so that conclusions may be based on evidence rather than on the leader's opinion.
   3. Skill in asking questions. The leader should present questions that bring out the opinions of others. Avoid hasty decisions or the acceptance of conclusions not based on good evidence by the use of questions. Throwing out a question to the group can help avoid expression of personal opinions. Some examples of how to handle certain situations that arise in a discussion by the use of a question follow:
      a. To call attention to a point that has not been considered: "Has anyone thought about this phase of the problem—or about this possible solution?"

CRITERIA FOR GROUP COMMUNICATION

1. Come to the meeting ready to ask questions and share your ideas.
2. Once your ideas and thoughts are given to the group, do not feel compelled to defend them. Once shared, they become the group's property to discuss and consider. Clarify meaning if it would help the group proceed but don't feel responsible for the idea just because you suggested it.
3. Speak freely and communicate feelings. Listen to others with consideration and understanding for their feelings.
4. Accept others in the interchange of ideas. Allow them to have opinions that differ from yours. Do not ignore or reject members of the group.
5. Engage in friendly disagreements. Listen critically and carefully to suggestions others have to offer. Differences of opinion bring forth a variety of ideas.
6. Be sincere. Reveal your true self. Communicate in an atmosphere of mutual trust.
7. Allow and promote individual freedom. Do not manipulate, suppress, or ridicule other group members. Encourage their creativity and individuality.
8. Work hard, acknowledge contributions of others, and focus on the objectives of the group's task.

FIGURE 5-4
Criteria for group communication.

b. To evaluate the strength of an argument: "What reasons do we have for accepting this statement?"

c. To get back to causes: "Why do you suppose a child—or a parent—feels or acts this way?"

d. To question the source of information or argument: "Who gathered these statistics that you spoke of?" or "Would you care to name the authority you are quoting?"

e. To suggest that no new information is being added: "Can anyone add a new idea to the information already given on this point?"

f. To register steps of agreement or disagreement: "Am I correct in assuming that all of us agree on (or disagree with) this point?"

g. To bring a generalizing speaker down to earth: "Can you give us a specific example?" or "Your general idea is good, but I wonder if we can't make it more concrete. Does anyone know of a case . . .?"

h. To handle the member who has "all the answers": "Would your idea work in all cases?" or "Let's get a variety of opinions on this point."

i. To bring an individual back to the subject: "I wonder if you can relate your ideas to the subject we are discussing?"

j. To handle a question directed to the leader.
  (1) If the leader knows the answer but does not wish to be set up as an authority, the question can be redirected to the group.
  (2) The leader can quote from resource material and ask for additional opinions.
  (3) If the leader is a specialist in the area, occasional questions may be answered.
  (4) The leader can say, "I don't know. Who does? Shall we research this?"

k. To cut off a speaker who is too long-winded: "While we're on this point, let's hear from the others" or "Shall we save your next point until later?"

l. To help the members who may have difficulty expressing themselves: "I wonder if I am interpreting you correctly; were you saying . . . ?" or "Can we tie in what you are saying with our subject something like this . . . ?"

m. To encourage further questions: "I'm glad you raised that question. Can anyone answer?"

n. To break up a heated argument: "I'm sure all of us feel strongly about this. Would some of the rest of you care to express opinions?"

[o] [To be sensitive to body language of the group, watch for persons wanting to speak, and bring out their contributions.][5]

ARRANGEMENTS FOR THE MEETING

In parent group meetings and PTA meetings, there are necessary procedures, regardless of the meeting format. Parents need to feel physically and emotionally comfortable at every meeting, whether formal or informal. To assure this, the person in charge of the meeting should do the following:

1. Check the meeting room to be sure the temperature is appropriate, the ventilation and lighting are adequate, and the room will accommodate the group.

2. As members or guests arrive, make them feel welcome. Greet them, offer name tags, and suggest they have refreshments, look at a book display, or participate in an icebreaker activity before the meeting begins. Call members or guests by name as soon as possible.

3. Have refreshments before the meeting, during the break, or at both times. A 15-minute refreshment period before the meeting

---

5. Modified from Denver Public Schools. Pointers for discussion group leaders. In *Parent education and preschool department leadership handbook*. Denver: Denver Public Schools, 1978, pp. 19–21.

gives late-comers an opportunity to arrive before discussion commences. It also sets a relaxed tone and gives members a forum for informal interaction.

4. As participants arrive, involve them in an informal discussion through an icebreaker activity. Get-acquainted activities are important but choose an appropriate one. For meetings where very few people know one another, a signature sheet may prove beneficial, or have the entire group form pairs; each partner introduces the other one to the group.

5. In large groups where icebreakers are not appropriate, the participants can respond to group questions—where they live, what they do, how many children they have, what their interests are and so on. Responses to the questions (by a show of hands or verbal answers) help the speaker to know more about the audience to be addressed, and the audience feels that it has been recognized.

6. After the group feels comfortable, the meeting can commence. Open discussion is part of all but the most formal meetings, so it is important that all group leaders are able to conduct discussion sessions. Debates, panels, audiovisual aids, buzz sessions, workshops, role playing, book reviews, dramatizations, and observations can precede open discussion. The leader should gauge the time and conclude the meeting.

7. After the presentation and discussion (or question and answer section), thank the presenters and give appropriate recognition for their contributions.

8. Announce any specific instructions necessary for the next meeting before the group disperses.

Icebreakers

In meetings where it is important to have an accepting, warm atmosphere, get-acquainted activities help persons relax and become involved in the group. These icebreakers range from introductions of the person to the right to mixers during the refreshment period.

While Members Gather

Signature Sheets. Make a form before the meeting that includes statements about people. Following each statement is a signature blank. These sheets can be made specifically for the group or can be broad enough to be used in any group. The kinds of signature sheets are not limited—create original ones. As the group arrives, give one to each participant. Encourage mixing and meeting new people. By the time the period is completed, the members will have an opportunity to meet and talk with a large number of people. A typical signature sheet is shown in Figure 5-5.

Bingo Card. Make a card that contains 12 to 24 squares. Ask each member to fill each blank with a signature. Signatures may not be repeated. This encourages interaction with all members.

A variation of the bingo card includes letters within each blank. Find someone with a name that begins with that letter. Check the roster ahead of time and use initials of the membership.

Who Am I? Attach a piece of paper with the name of a famous person to the back of each person. Members go from person to person asking questions until they determine who they are. Questions must be phrased so that a yes or no answer is adequate. Variations include changing the famous person to an event, an animal, or an educational statement.

Scrambled Name Tags. Make up name tags with letters out of order, for example, Ilaehs (Sheila). Have the members try to figure out each name as they talk with each person. Obviously, this has to be done at the first or second meeting before the group becomes acquainted.

```
Find persons who meet the qualifications listed below and have them sign their
names.

  1.  Find someone who is wearing the same color clothes as you _____

  2.  Find someone who has the same color eyes as you _____

  3.  Find someone who has the same number of children as you _____

  4.  Find someone who lives in the same area as you _____

  5.  Find someone who has a child the same age as yours _____

  6.  Find someone who likes to go hiking _____

  7.  Find someone who plays the piano _____

  8.  Find someone who has the same hobby as you _____

  9.  Find someone who has lived in this state as long as you have _____

 10.  Find someone who was brought up in the same area you were _____
```

FIGURE 5-5
Use a get-acquainted activity such as a signature sheet at the beginning of meetings.

After Members Are Seated

Dyad Introductions. Have every two members talk together, with the idea that they will introduce each other. You may give specific instructions, such as ask the number of children the person has and what the member expects from parent education, or you may leave the discussion completely up to the two individuals. Following the discussion, go around the room and have members introduce their partners.

It is interesting to have the dyad discuss memory questions such as something their partner remembers that happened before the age of 5 or their happiest experience. This activity can be used later in the year as well as at the beginning.

Allow Members to Introduce Themselves. Topics they might include are:

My secret hiding place was _____.
As a child I liked to _____ best.

Summertime was _____.
If I had my wish, I would be _____.
What I liked best about school was _____.
What I remember about walking or riding the bus home from school was _____.

I've Got a Secret. After people have become acquainted, each participant can write a secret on a piece of paper. (Be sure that the person does not mind having the secret revealed.) Place the pieces of paper in a bag, and as they are drawn and read, the group tries to guess who has that secret.

Activities that promote good human relations and allow members to get acquainted are limited only by the planner's imagination. The chairperson or leader may be in charge of this part of the program, or may delegate the responsibility to a number of persons charged with the task of discovering new means of interaction.

GROUP ROLES

In *Dynamics of Participative Groups,* Gibb et al. (1959) state:"Group members should be conscious of the importance of the roles they play in the group. Study the different roles that people can play, analyze the roles you play, consciously play roles that are helpful to group process" (p. 59). Group members should be given descriptions of group roles chosen from the list that follows later in this chapter to help them identify their participatory roles or roles they would like to develop (see Table 5-2). Within each group roles emerge that are functional and task-oriented, which move the group forward; group-sustaining, which are expressive and maintain the group; and negative and dysfunctional, which reduce the effectiveness of the group.

Analysis of the interaction process illustrates the expressive (socioemotional) and task areas within a group. The center of Bales' interaction theory (Figure 5-6) includes task questions and task responses, which are both directed toward completing the task at hand as well as the socioemotional areas that involve the feelings and integration of the group (both positive and negative).

Although Bales' group interaction theory has been used primarily as a research tool to study communication and interaction in groups, it can also be used to clarify group interaction in the training of parent groups. An examination of the interaction process reveals a continuum of productive to negative interaction. The positive socioemotional reactions—for example, showing solidarity, giving help, and rewarding others—are helpful in effecting group integration. At the other end of the spectrum showing antagonism, deflating another's status, and asserting oneself are destructive to the group's integration. In the center all the task-oriented questions and answers support the objectives of completing a task assignment. Although the answers of members are more productive than the questions, both help move the interaction process along—the first by providing direction and information while accepting another member's autonomy, the second by asking for eval-

TABLE 5-2

Role interaction. Both task and maintenance roles are necessary for effective group participation.

Task roles	Group-building or maintenance roles	Dysfunctional roles
Initiator-leader	Encourager	Dominator
Information giver	Harmonizer	Aggressor
Information seeker	Listener	Negativist
Clarifier	Follower	Playboy
Questioner	Tension breaker	Blocker
Asserter	Compromiser	Competitor
Energizer	Standard setter	Deserter
Elaborator	Observer	
Orientator	Recorder	
Opinion giver	Gatekeeper	
Opinion seeker		
Summarizer		

Source: Modified from Beal, G., Bohlen, J. M., & Raudabaugh. *Leadership and dynamic group action.* Ames, Iowa: Iowa State University, 1962, pp. 103-109; Benne, K., & Sheets, P. Functional roles of group members. *Journal of Social Issues,* 1948, *4*(2), 41-49; King, C. E. *The sociology of small groups.* New York: Pageant Press, 1962, pp. 108-109.

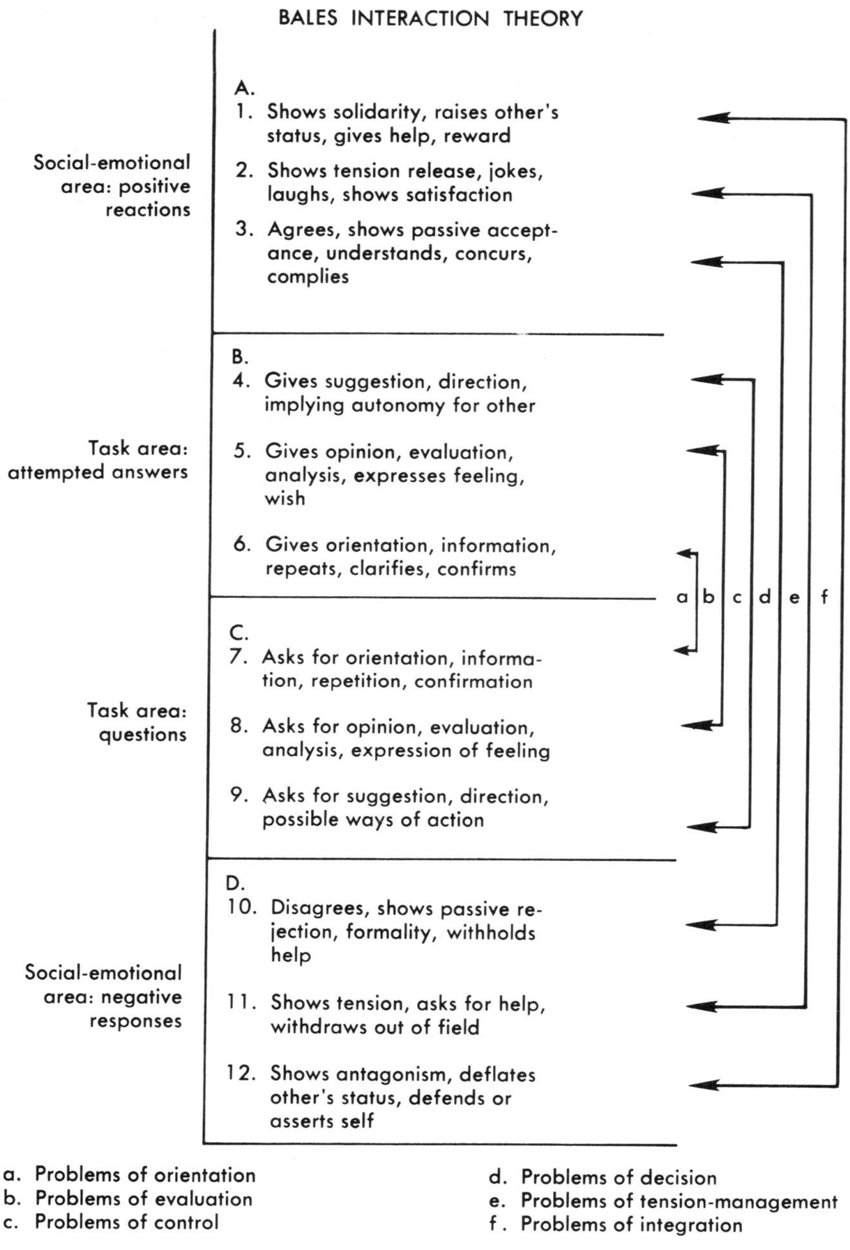

BALES INTERACTION THEORY

Social-emotional area: positive reactions

A.
1. Shows solidarity, raises other's status, gives help, reward
2. Shows tension release, jokes, laughs, shows satisfaction
3. Agrees, shows passive acceptance, understands, concurs, complies

Task area: attempted answers

B.
4. Gives suggestion, direction, implying autonomy for other
5. Gives opinion, evaluation, analysis, expresses feeling, wish
6. Gives orientation, information, repeats, clarifies, confirms

Task area: questions

C.
7. Asks for orientation, information, repetition, confirmation
8. Asks for opinion, evaluation, analysis, expression of feeling
9. Asks for suggestion, direction, possible ways of action

Social-emotional area: negative responses

D.
10. Disagrees, shows passive rejection, formality, withholds help
11. Shows tension, asks for help, withdraws out of field
12. Shows antagonism, deflates other's status, defends or asserts self

a | b | c | d | e | f

a. Problems of orientation
b. Problems of evaluation
c. Problems of control
d. Problems of decision
e. Problems of tension-management
f. Problems of integration

FIGURE 5-6

The Bales Interaction Theory illustrates social-emotional and task areas related to group interaction. Problems in each area are defined (a through f). The theory ranges from positive reactions in A to negative reactions in D. (*Source:* reprinted from *Interaction process analysis: A method for study of small groups* by Robert F. Bales by permission of The University of Chicago Press. Copyright 1950 by the University of Chicago.)

Leaders emerge from the group if they have not been formally selected.

uation, direction, and possible forms of action.

Roles emerge within groups and influence the interactive process. A *role,* defined as the behavior characteristic of a person occupying a particular position in the social system, influences the actions of the person and the expectations of others toward that person. Parent groups (in this text) are the "social system"; members of the group expect certain norms or standards of behavior from the perceived leader of the group. These role expectations are projected in members' role behavior toward the leader. Likewise, the leader's own interpretation of the role influences the resulting role behavior or role performance. Should members of the group hold different expectations of behavior for the leadership role from those held by the occupant of that role, inter-role conflicts may arise (Applbaum et al., 1979; Berger, 1968; Biddle & Thomas, 1979; Gross, Mason, & McEachern, 1958.) For these reasons, it is beneficial to discuss or clarify standards and duties of roles within a group.

Role continuity is easier to obtain in parent education groups that have ongoing memberships. Parents are encouraged to participate for at least 2 years. New officers and leaders, already familiar with the standards of the group, may be elected in the spring and be ready to take over leadership in the fall. Although this system ensures greater continuity than the establishment of a new group each year, the returning members must be careful to be flexible, open to new ideas, and sensitive to the desires of new members. Early in the year a session may include a discussion of roles and group dynamics. Role playing is an excellent mechanism for clarifying role behavior. If group members are aware of the effect roles have on the functioning of a group, they do not fall into dysfunctional roles as readily. By discussing group dynamics with the group prior to establishment of role patterns, group production is often increased (Beale et al., 1962).

A leader can deter or eliminate the problem of domination or withdrawal by group members if members are aware of roles and how each member of the group can influence the group's functioning, either positively or negatively. Most members do not want to be viewed as dysfunctional members and will, therefore, refrain from acting in ways that are detrimental to group interaction. I have used a discussion of roles in parents' groups and classes since the early 1960s and have found that a group discussion and role playing of group roles have greatly enhanced the productivity of the group. Although this knowledge will encourage some members, it can also inhibit others who worry about which role theory they are enacting. Although this is a possible negative result of a discussion of group roles, role definition is, on the other hand, a benefit to the total group in the elimination of one common problem in groups—domination of the discussion by a few participants. It is also beneficial to reticent communicators to learn that inability to express themselves does not mean that they cannot be productive group members. Asking questions, being an active listener, and being a positive member of the group are shown to be valuable contributions to a well-functioning discussion group. When balanced out, the positive aspects of discussing group roles overshadow the negative ones. One word of caution, however—do not wait until the problem has become obvious before discussing dysfunctional roles. You will embarrass and alienate the person who has been a negative contributor. It is best to handle such a problem through the leadership techniques discussed on pp. 159–160.

Dynamics of Roles Within Groups

Observation of interaction within groups shows that role behavior influences the cohesiveness and productivity of the group. Observation will be facilitated if analysis of the group is based in Bales' interaction process (Figure 5-6) or role interaction (Table 5-2), wherein behaviors within a group are divided into task, maintenance and building, and dysfunctional roles.

Task Roles. The roles related to the task area in Table 5-2 are attributed to the members of the group who initiate, question, and facilitate reaching the group's goals or objectives. These tasks correspond to Bales' task areas.

Group-building and Maintenance Roles. The roles related to group-building or maintenance are attributed to members of the group who support and maintain the cohesiveness, solidarity, and productivity of the group. These roles include Bales' socioemotional positive reaction area and, in addition, add a maintenance aspect.

Dysfunctional or Individual Roles. The roles in this area are attributed to members who place their own individual needs, which are not relevant to group goals, above group needs. These individual goals are not functional or productive to group achievement, but if such members are brought into the group process, they can become contributing participants. These roles correspond to Bales' socioemotional negative reaction area.

Members of groups generally do not fit into only one role category. Members may participate in a task role and switch to a maintenance role with the next action or comment. For example, Helen is anxious about absenteeism and suggests that the group might improve attendance by organizing a car pool. May responds to the comment by suggesting a telephone network to contact members. Helen welcomes the idea, "Good thought, May. We might be able to start right away." Helen, within the space of 2 minutes, has initiated an idea, acting in a task-oriented role, and has then supported May's contribution with a group-building or maintenance statement. There may be moments when members lapse into a dysfunctional role. As long as the mix of interaction remains primarily positive and productive, the group will be effective.

The following role descriptions were based on Beal, Bohlen, and Raudabaugh (1962), Benne and Sheets (1948), and King (1962).

ROLE DESCRIPTIONS

Task

initiator-leader: Initiates the discussion, guides but does not dominate, contributes ideas or suggestions that help move the group forward *information giver:* Contributes information and facts that are from authoritative sources and are relevant to the ongoing discussion

information seeker: Asks for clarification or expansion of an issue by additional relevant authoritative information

clarifier: Restates the discussion of an issue so that points are made clear to the group

questioner: Asks questions about issues, requests clarification, or offers constructive criticism

asserter: States position in a positive manner, may take a different point of view and disagree with opinions or suggestions without attacking them

energizer: Stimulates and facilitates the group to action and increased output and problem solving

elaborator: Expands an idea or concept; brings out details, points, and alternatives that may have been overlooked

orientator: Takes a look at the group's position in relation to the objectives of the meetings and where the discussion is leading

opinion giver: States own opinion on the situation, basing the contribution on personal experiences

opinion seeker: Requests suggestions from others according to their life experiences and value orientation

summarizer: Brings out facts, ideas, and suggestions made by the group in an attempt to clarify the group's position during the meeting and at the conclusion

Group-building and Maintenance

The first six roles will emerge within the group; the last four are appointed or elected maintenance roles.

encourager: Supports, praises, and recognizes other members of the group; builds self-confidence and self-concept of others

harmonizer: Mediates misunderstandings and clarifies conflicting statements and disagreements; adds to the discussion in a calming and tension-reducing manner

listener: Is involved in the discussion through quiet attention to the group process; gives support through body language and eye contact

follower: Serves as a supportive member of the discussion by accepting the ideas and suggestions of others

tension breaker: Uses humor or clarifying statements to relieve tension within the group

compromiser: Views both sides of the questions and changes solutions or suggestions to fit into conflicting viewpoints

standard setter: Sets standards for group performance; may apply standards as an evaluative technique for the meeting

observer: Charts the group process throughout the meeting and uses the data for evaluation of group interaction

recorder: Records decisions and ideas for group use throughout the meeting

gatekeeper: Regulates time spent and membership participation during various parts of the program; keeps the meeting on a time schedule

Dysfunctional

dominator: Monopolizes the meeting and asserts superiority by attempting to manipulate the group

aggressor: Shows aggression toward group in a variety of forms, for example, attacks ideas, criticizes others, denigrates others' contributions, and disapproves of solutions

negativist: Demonstrates pessimism and disapproval of suggestions that emerge within the group; sees the negative side of the issue and rejects new insights

playboy: Refuses to be involved in the discussion and spends time showing this indifference to the members by distracting behavior, for example, talking to others, showing cynicism, making side comments

blocker: Opposes decision making and attempts to block actions by introducing alternate plans that have already been rejected

competitor: Competes with other members of the discussion group by challenging their ideas and expressing and defending his own suggestions

deserter: Leaves the group in spirit and mind but not in body; doodles, looks around room, makes a show of disinterest, and stays aloof and indifferent to the group process

Role Playing Group Roles

Early in the growth of a group, a session in which members role play task, maintenance, and dysfunctional roles while discussing an is-

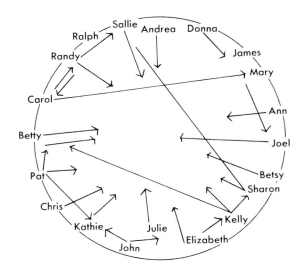

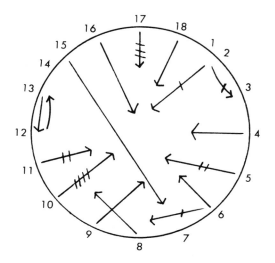

FIGURE 5-7
Group interaction recorded on an observation wheel.

FIGURE 5-8
Group interaction anonymously recorded on an observation wheel. Each time a person speaks a mark is added to the interaction line. In this manner one can see how often and to whom each participant communicates.

sue of high interest will illustrate to the members how role performance can support or destroy a group. It is practical to use a concentric circle, allowing the inner circle to discuss an issue in the light of the role assigned, while the outer circle observes and analyzes which roles are being demonstrated. The session will be humorous, with members enthusiastically playing dysfunctional roles but it should end with the understanding that each member is important to the effectiveness of the group process.

Observer

Analysis of group interaction reveals patterns that are not always obvious to the casual observer. A systematic observation can pinpoint problems or illustrate strengths to the members. One simple technique for analytic observation is the construction of a discussion wheel. A diagram of the participants, with names or numbers reflecting individual members, is made. If the participants are sitting in a

circle, the diagram would be similar to the one in Figure 5-7.

As members speak, the observer records the interaction. A double-sided arrow indicates that the communicator is speaking to the group; and one-sided arrow represents a statement made to an individual rather than to the group (Beal, Bohlen, & Raudabaugh, 1962). A quick glance at Figure 5-7 shows that Ralph did not make a suggestion and had either withdrawn from the group or lacked its supportive encouragement. Most members contributed to the group process, rather than making side comments to individual communicators. If the observer continues making notes throughout the meeting, cross marks on the arrows, which reflect duplication of communication, eliminate an overabundance of lines in the observation circle (Figure 5-8).

A more detailed observation sheet may be adapted from Bales' interaction process illustrated earlier in this chapter. The three task

Date_____ Time_____ Meeting_____

Topic_____ Method_____

UNIT-ACT ROLES

Task roles	Group maintenance and group-building	Dysfunctional roles
1. Initiator-leader	13. Encourager	19. Dominator
2. Information giver	14. Harmonizer	20. Aggressor
3. Information seeker	15. Listener	21. Negativist
4. Clarifier	16. Follower	22. Playboy
5. Questioner	17. Tension breaker	23. Blocker
6. Asserter	18. Compromiser	24. Competitor
7. Energizer		25. Deserter
8. Elaborator		
9. Orientator		
10. Opinion giver		
11. Opinion seeker		
12. Summarizer		

Member participation record

Speaker	Spoken to	Role	Time	Comments	Speaker	Spoken to	Role	Time	Comments

FIGURE 5-9
Group observer's summary sheet for recording unit-act roles and amount and orientation of participation. (*Source:* modified from G. Beal, J. M. Bohlen, and J. N. Raudabaugh. *Leadership and dynamic group action.* Ames, Iowa State University, 1962, p. 330.)

areas also provide a framework for an excellent role analysis. Beal, Bohlen, and Raudabaugh illustrated a summary sheet for recording unit-act roles; an adaptation of their form is shown in Figure 5-9.

An analysis that includes roles, speakers, and order of comments allows group leaders to study interaction within the group and emphasizes the positive areas of communication while eliminating negative aspects. Many insights may be gained by studying what actually happened during group interaction. The summary sheet illustrates that interaction.

END-OF-MEETING EVALUATIONS

Evaluations are used effectively by many groups to see if the needs of the group are be-

ing met. Since every group is somewhat different, evaluations should be constructed to meet the needs of that group and should be based on the goals and objectives of the meet-

---

Topic _____   Date _____

Group _____

Check along the continuum

1. Was the meeting of interest to you?

| Very much | Some | Very little |

2. Did you receive any pertinent ideas that will be helpful to you?

| Many ideas | Some | No ideas |

3. Did the group participate and seem involved in the meeting?

| Very involved | Some | No involvement |

4. Did the meeting give you any new insights, or did you change any of your attitudes as a result of the meeting?

| New insights | Some | No effect |

5. Were you encouraged to contribute as much as you wanted?

| Participation encouraged | Neutral | Left out |

6. Did the leader respond to the needs of the group?

| Good leadership | Neutral | No leadership |

7. Was there adequate preparation by the members?

| Excellent preparation | Some | Poor preparation |

8. Was there enough time for discussion?

| Too much | Just right | No time |

9. Was the atmosphere conducive to freedom of expression?

| Safe environment | Neutral | Felt threatened |

10. Do you have any suggestions for improvement?

11. What were the strong points of the meeting?

12. Comments

You do not need to
sign this sheet

FIGURE 5-10

A meeting evaluation form lets you know exactly how the participants viewed the program.

ing. Sample evaluations are helpful, however, to guide the group in its development of evaluative methods that work for that particular group. The example in Figure 5-10 may be adapted to any group's needs.

TYPES OF MEETINGS

Meetings range from formal lectures to informal buzz sessions. In parent groups, informal meetings are used most often to reinforce the active involvement that proves so critical to understanding concepts and attitude changes. The formal meeting has its place, however, if the group needs a specialist to give an organized background lecture on a specific topic. Figure 5-11 illustrates types of meetings that can be used as needs, time, space, subject, and resources dictate. On the right are those meetings that are the most informal and require active involvement by the participants; in the center is the panel meeting; on the left is the most formal lecture where the only audience participation is listening to the speaker. Although all of these types of meetings have their place in parent group meetings, the informal meetings elicit more participation by group members—a necessary ingredient for attitude clarification, learning, and change.

The descriptions of the types of meetings that follow are compiled from my experiences with parent education and information found in Applbaum, et al. (1974), Denver Public Schools (1978), and Kawin (1970). Resources that support the curricula are found in Chapter 11.

Roundtable (Open Discussion)

Although the roundtable is not the most informal meeting available, it is a true open discussion, the mainstay of group interaction. It is used to complement most meetings, for example, panels, symposiums, role-playing sessions, or buzz sessions. (See Figure 5-12.)

In a roundtable discussion all members are encouraged to participate throughout the meeting. Care must be taken to promote good communication among all members of the group. To facilitate good group interaction, leaders should keep in mind the following suggestions from the Denver Public Schools (1978):[6]

1. Have a clear understanding of the topic as defined by the group.
2. Obtain materials.
3. Get a general knowledge, through reading, to be able to direct and add to the contributions from the group.
4. Be sure to plan an introduction which will stimulate interest of the group.
5. Prepare a logical progressive list of questions to start the ball rolling and keep it moving.
6. Keep discussion on the track; keep it always directed, but let the group lay its own track to a large extent. Don't groove it narrowly yourself.
7. Be alert to adjust questions to needs of group . . . omit, change, reword.
8. Remember—the leader's opinion doesn't count in the discussion. Keep your own view

---

6. From Denver Public Schools. *Parent education and preschool department leadership handbook.* Denver: Denver Public Schools, 1978, pp. 12, 13.

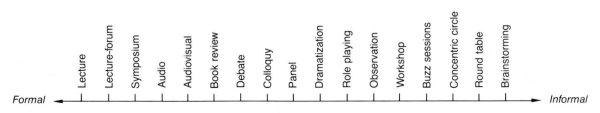

FIGURE 5-11
Meetings range from informal to very formal.

FIGURE 5-12
The roundtable is the basic open discussion group.

out of it. Your job is to get the ideas of others out for airing.

9. If you see that some important angle is being neglected, point it out; "Bill Jones was telling me last week that he thinks. . . . What do you think of that?"

10. Keep the spirits high. Encourage ease, informality, good humor. Let everybody have a good time. Foster friendly disagreement. Listen with respect and appreciation to all ideas, but stress what is important, and turn discussion away from what is not.

11. Take time every 10 minutes or so to draw the loose ends together; "Let's see where we've been going." Be as fair and accurate in summary as possible. Close discussion with summary—your own or the secretary's.

12. Call attention to unanswered questions for future study or for your reference back to speakers. Nourish a desire in group members for continuing study and discussion through skillful closing summary.

Problems that could emerge in a roundtable meeting include domination of the discussion by one or two members, withdrawal from the group and side discussions by two or three people, or lack of preparation by the membership. Good leadership makes it possible to avoid these pitfalls. If the leader is prepared for the meeting, and if the membership come to the meeting prepared, have relevant experiences, or have background expertise on the subject, the meeting can be a most effective means of changing attitudes and educating members. It allows all members to contribute and become involved in discussion, clarification of issues, and decision making.

Arrangements prior to meeting

1. Select a topic for open discussion and announce it to the membership.
2. Provide members with materials and bibliography.
   a. Duplicate and distribute background information on the topic through a distribution system or at the meeting prior to the roundtable.
   b. Select members to read relevant material prior to meeting.
   c. Come to meeting well-prepared and ready to guide but not to dominate.
3. Review the Arrangements for the Meetings (pp. 160–161) and make appropriate preparations.

Setup

1. Arrange chairs in a circle or semicircle or around tables in such a manner that all participants can see each other and eye contact is possible.
2. Check the room for comfort—ventilation, lighting, and heat.

Procedure

1. The leader starts the meeting with a thought-provoking question or statement of fact. Throughout the discussion, the leader tries to keep the meeting from wandering. Prior to the meeting, the leader has prepared a list of questions or statements that may keep the discussion moving forward.
2. During the meeting the leader avoids dominating the discussion. Instead, the leadership role brings others into the discussion, helps clarify, and keeps the meeting on the topic.
3. The leader summarizes at the conclusion.
4. If the members want to take action on the conclusions, the leader should call for appropriate action, help the group make plans, and assign tasks.

Appropriate topics

1. Learning activities that work
2. Teamwork between mothers and fathers
3. What to do on a rainy day
4. Behavior and misbehavior
5. Influence of television on children
6. Rivalry between brothers and sisters

Concentric Circle

The concentric circle is a variation of the open discussion or roundtable meeting where, instead of one circle, there are two circles, one inside the other and all facing the center. The dialogue among members is similar to that of the open discussion, but only the smaller circle within the larger circle contains the communicators at first. (See Figure 5-13.) Divide the group so that the smaller group is the size of a buzz session (6 to 8 persons) or up to 12 persons. The members within the small group discuss the issue; those in the larger group listen to the discussion. After a designated time of 5 to 10 minutes, the meeting is opened to the entire group. If you have a group of 24 to 30 persons, which contains persons who are reticent to speak out in a large group, the concentric circle will help solve the problem. Those within the inner circle form a small group with which to interact. This arrangement precipitates more discussion from them and succeeds in getting the total group interested in the discussion. Those sitting in the outer circle are required to listen, but the statements, questions, and ideas offered usually promote their interest as they listen. This method is surprisingly effective in getting groups to discuss. By the time the discussion is opened up to the entire group, many ideas have emerged.

Arrangements prior to meeting

1. Announce the subject of the meeting to the group prior to the meeting.
2. Distribute handouts and/or reference materials suggested. (Concentric circles may also be used on the spur-of-the-moment.)
3. Review the Arrangements for the Meetings (pp. 160–161) and make appropriate preparations.

FIGURE 5-13
Concentric circles encourage those who might not participate freely to get involved.

Setup

1. Arrange chairs with one large circle on the outside and a smaller circle within the larger circle. The smaller circle can be anywhere from the size of a buzz session (6 to 8 persons) up to 50 percent of the total group of 24. The chairs should be spaced fairly close together so the meeting is informal and all participants are able to easily hear the discussion of the inner circle.

Procedure

1. The leader of the total group may request a volunteer leader for the concentric circle, or the leader may take that role.
2. The session is started with a statement or question to promote interest and dialogue.
3. The inner circle discusses, using a small group open discussion format. The outer circle listens. At the end of a designated period, for example, 6 minutes, the discussion may be opened to all in the room. At that time the leader continues to control the meeting but not to dominate.
4. For variation, reverse the roles. Those in the outer circle now move to the inner circle and have the opportunity for more involved discussion, while those from the outer circle listen to this discussion. A separate issue or different questions concerning one issue may be used for each group in its discussion.

Appropriate topics

1. How to build self-esteem in children
2. What do you expect of 2-, 3-, 4-, or 5-year-olds
3. Value clarification
4. Living with change
5. Positive uses of television

Buzz Sessions

Buzz sessions, an excellent means of eliciting participation from all members of the group, are very small open discussions. They must be small enough to allow interaction among all participants. The smallest buzz session consists of 2 persons, and the maximum size should be 6 to 8 persons. This makes it possible for all members to have the chance to express their opinions easily. Buzz sessions can be used in small or large groups. In the small group of 24 persons, the membership divides up into 4 or more groups and discusses the issue. In a large group in an auditorium, the audience can also divide into groups and discuss. The latter is called a 6-6 discussion, with 6 people discussing for 6 minutes. Since the buzz session time is limited, it does not allow thorough examination of issues, but it does bring

Buzz groups give everyone an opportunity to talk.

forth ideas from all involved in a very short period of time—an objective that is not accomplished in an open discussion with a large group.

Arrangements prior to meeting

1. Buzz sessions are usually used in conjunction with other meeting formats. The buzz session itself does not need special preparation, but the leader may prepare the questions and issues in advance. The value of the buzz session lies in an optimal participation by all.
2. Review the Arrangements for the Meetings (pp. 160–161) and make appropriate preparations.

Setup

1. Small group (up to 24)
   a. Arrange chairs in circle or semicircle.
   b. When the buzz session is to begin, 6 persons turn their chairs to form their buzz session group. It is also possible for a group to remove itself from the total group in order to have a more quiet meeting.
2. Large auditorium buzz sessions
   a. In the auditorium meeting persons are sitting in rows. Three persons in front turn around and discuss with 3 persons behind them.
   b. Form groups of 6 throughout the auditorium.

Procedure

1. Buzz sessions may be at the beginning of the meeting, or they may be initiated later in the meeting. The leader announces the formation of buzz groups, which are formed either by proximity of chairs, a common interest in specific discussion areas, or by a mechanism to distribute the membership, such as counting off one through six and having each number for a buzz group.
2. Each group chooses a leader and a recorder.
3. The topic is introduced to the group for discussion, and persons are encouraged to participate much as they would in a small-group discussion.
4. The recorder keeps relevant thoughts ready to report back to the larger group. In the smaller group meeting (24 persons), each buzz group may have the time to give a short report to the total group. In an auditorium 6-6 meeting, it may not be possible to have everyone report back. Allow a specific number of groups who indicate interest in doing so to report back to the total audience.

Appropriate topics

1. Home management tips
2. Emotions and feelings about child rearing
3. Discipline
4. Moral values
5. Vacation ideas
6. Solving problems around home

Brainstorming

Brainstorming is a unique method of active interaction by all members of the group. It promotes interchange, encourages lateral thinking, and facilitates expansion of thought. In brainstorming, all contributions are accepted. Everyone is encouraged to suggest ideas and solutions. The participants may add to, combine, or modify other ideas, or they may introduce something completely new into the interchange. There are no value judgments on the quality of suggestions. Osborn (1957) suggests that the "average person can think of twice as many ideas when working with a group than when working alone" (pp. 228–229). The free and open brainstorming session provides an environment that facilitates the production of a variety of ideas from the participants. Members who have been reticent about contributing during an open discussion because they were not sure their ideas were worthy have a guaranteed-safe environment in which to contribute during brainstorming. Quantity of ideas is the object. Later, the ideas may be analyzed, judged as to quality, and reduced to selected items. The brainstorming technique, therefore, is excellent for stimulation of diversified thought and solutions to issues and problems. It also reinforces the socioemotional aspects of a group by accepting the contributions of all persons freely.

Arrangements prior to meeting

1. Because the major purpose of brainstorming is the encouragement of fresh ideas, no study program need be initiated prior to the session.
2. Review Arrangements for the Meetings (pp. 160–161) and make appropriate preparations.

Setup

1. Arrange chairs in a circle if the group has less than 30 members. A small group allows for more interaction.
2. Brainstorming, however, may be used in a larger group with an auditorium arrangement of chairs. In that case, the entire group has difficulty participating, but the mechanism is effective for bringing forth a quantity of ideas and thoughts.

Procedure

1. The brainstorming session requires a leader and a recorder.
   a. Appoint a recorder or request someone to volunteer.
   b. Appoint a leader or assume the leadership role.
2. The leader begins the brainstorming session by explaining the rules and emphasizing that all contributions are wanted and accepted. Even if ideas seem unusual, members should contribute. Ideas should be interjected as they occur.
3. The topic or issue is explained to the group.
4. The session is opened to contributions from the group.
5. The recorder writes on a chalkboard or piece of paper all the ideas that come from the group.
6. After a selected amount of time—4, 6, or 10 minutes, depending on the issue and the flow of ideas—the group may turn to analyzing all the suggestions and pulling out the ones that seem to answer the issue or problem best.
7. A summary of the solutions and ideas gained from brainstorming is reported by the leader.
8. If this is an action meeting, plans for action should be identified at this time.

Appropriate topics

1. Ideas to solve problems, for example, subjects for meetings, summer activities
2. How to get your child to study (eat, go to bed, etc.)
3. Creative activities
4. Exploring your environment
5. Nutrition

Workshops and Centers

Workshops are a superb means of achieving involvement by members. Most useful as a demonstration of programs and curricula, they can be used as an effective means of explaining procedures, illustrating the learning process, and developing understanding by "doing." The major ingredient in a workshop is active participation by the membership, whether through making puzzles and toys, working on mathematics, painting, modeling with clay, editing a newspaper, composing music, writing poetry, or planning an action.

Although often confused with workshops, centers are different from workshops in that they do not require the participant to be actively involved in the project. Centers allow subgroups of the membership to gather simultaneously in various areas of the room, where they may see a demonstration, hear an explanation of an issue or program, or watch a media presentation. If time allows, more than one center may be visited. The variety of centers is limited only by the imagination and productivity of the planning group. The advantages of this diversified meeting are (1) it reduces group size and thus promotes more interaction and allows individual questions; (2) participants are able to select topics of interest to them; and (3) tension and anxiety of the presenters are reduced because of the informal format.

Arrangements prior to meeting

1. Review the Arrangements for the Meetings (pp. 160–161) and make appropriate preparations.
2. Choose topics or areas for presentation, for example, how to make a toy, improvement of reading, editing a newspaper, or arts and crafts. If participants are going to go from workshop to workshop or center to center, designate a time limit for each center.
3. Designate persons to obtain materials and prepare and present each session.
4. Make samples of finished projects for illustration at workshop.
5. Obtain and assign space for presenters.

Setup

1. Depending on available space, workshops and centers may be held in separate rooms or in one large room with designated areas.
2. Each presenter may have different requirements. Amount of space, tables, and chairs previously requested should be set up according to those requirements.

Procedure

1. The chairperson explains the variety of workshops and/or centers available and procedures to be used.
2. Participants choose a workshop or center. These may be assigned according to several procedures: free choice, numbers on name tags, or preregistration.
3. Participants attend one or more workshops depending on time available. If plans have included a time limit for each, the groups proceed from one to the next at a signal.
4. Members may gather together for closing the meeting, or it may conclude with the final workshop.

Appropriate topics

1. Learning activities
2. Art activities
3. Making books
4. Games and toys
5. Math activities to do at home
6. Science activities to do at home
7. What to do on a rainy day

Observations and Field Trips

Although observations and field trips can be quite different in their objectives, they are similar in theory and procedure. The active viewing of a classroom, like the visit to the community, encourages the member to be involved in observing activities. The opportunity to see activities in process clarifies that process as no written or spoken word can. It is imperative, however, to discuss objectives with points to consider prior to the field trip or observation. It is also essential to analyze and discuss following the visits, in order to clarify the experience and bring it into focus. Many times the conclusion of a field trip can be the beginning of a new expanded project for the individual or group.

Arrangements prior to observation or field trip

1. Select the time and place for the observation or field trip.
   a. Plan classroom visits in advance. Specific objectives may be discussed prior to the observation.
   b. If the classroom has an observation area, observers can easily watch without disturbing the class. If there is no observation area, those going into the classroom should know the preferred procedure requested by the teacher.
   c. Field trips must be planned in advance and permission for visiting obtained.
2. Participants learn more and receive more satisfaction from field trips if background information and items to be aware of are discussed prior to the visit.

3. If the membership is going to a meeting place different from their regular meeting area, arrangements should be made for travel by car pool or bus.
4. Review the Arrangements for the Meetings (pp. 160–161) and make appropriate preparations.

Procedure

1. The leader plans and conducts a previsit orientation.
2. The observation or field trip is completed.
3. Discussion of the experience clarifies the issues and focuses on the learning that has taken place. Many field trips tend to be an end in themselves, but this omits the most important follow-up where new ideas and greater understanding are generated.

Appropriate observations

1. In classroom observation, look for the following:
   a. How children learn
   b. Play—child's work
   c. Interpersonal relations
   d. Aggression
   e. Fine and gross motor control
   f. Hand-eye coordination
   g. Stages and ages

Appropriate field trips

1. Children's museum
2. Art museum
3. Park
4. Special schools
5. Newspapers
6. Hospital

Role Playing

Role playing is a dramatization of a situation where group members put themselves into a designated role. Role playing is a very informal type of meeting, similar to presenting a drama, so it can be adapted to a wide variety of situations. The roles that persons play can be completely initiated by the players, or there can be a set format or specific situation that players are to enact. In either situation, the persons playing the roles are to put themselves into those roles. They are to feel that they are the "role" and respond with appropriate reactions and emotions. For this reason, spontaneous role playing is advantageous over the planned drama. Figure 5-14 depicts a typical role-playing situation.

Role playing can be used to demonstrate a problem or to develop participants' sensitivities to a situation. In the first, demonstration of a situation, the group members discuss their feelings and reactions and offer solutions to the role. It is an excellent means for getting many people involved in a particular situation and is easily used to illustrate parent-child interaction. In the second, development of sensitivity, role reversal is often used. An example of role reversal is when the teacher plays the role of the principal while the principal plays the role of the teacher. Not only do participants begin to understand the obligations of the other role, but through their playing of the role, they are able to demonstrate what their feelings are. This clarifies feelings for both parties. Another role reversal situation that can be used is the parent-child relationship, with one participant playing the child's role and the other playing the parent's role. The parent in the child's role develops sensitivity to the child's position.

Participants in role playing feel free to communicate their feelings and attitudes because they are not portraying themselves. This encourages greater openness and involvement. When group members begin role playing, they tend to be hesitant to get involved emotionally with the part. After using role playing for a period of time, hesitancy and reluctance to be involved disappear, and people enjoy the opportunity to participate. If the group progresses to a therapeutic enactment, professional counselors should be included and consulted.

Arrangements prior to meeting

1. Review the Arrangements for the Meeting (pp. 160–161) and make appropriate preparations.

FIGURE 5-14
Dramatizations like role
playing illustrate the
dynamics of hypothetical
situations.

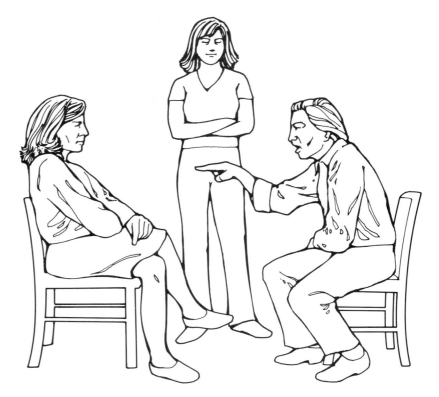

2. Prepare descriptive situations illustrating particular problems or issues prior to the meeting, if specific role assignments are planned.

Setup

1. Role playing can be used in a variety of formats: (1) the role playing is conducted within the circle of participants; the center of the circle can then be the stage; (2) when used with a larger group, participants may have the chairs formed into semicircles, with a stage in front of the group; (3) role playing may also be used in a large group meeting with an auditorium stage for the actors.

2. If the role playing is planned for participation by the entire group, allow members to meet first in a circle arrangement and to break into smaller groups after an introduction.

Procedure

1. A short discussion of the topic or situation is introduced by the leader or panel.

2. The situation that needs to be role played is introduced. This may be accomplished by (1) volunteers, (2) persons selected prior to meeting to start the initial role play, or (3) breaking up the total group into groups of four or five, who are given a topic with an outline of the role situation or are challenged to develop their own role situations.

3. The role can be played in two ways:

   a. Roles can be played in front of the entire group with the membership watching and listening to the dramatization and interaction. Following the role play, the members use the open discussion method to clarify issues, study the problem, and make decisions.

   b. If the membership is divided into smaller groups, it is beneficial to let each of the groups play its roles simultaneously within the room and have each small group discuss the feelings and attitudes that arose while they were playing their roles. Following this, the small groups may discuss alternative means, ideas, and solutions.

4. If the small groups have all met and developed specific situations, it is also meaningful to have each group perform its role playing in front of the total group. Following the performance of the groups, the larger group is allowed to discuss the role playing openly. Clarification, questions, and solutions are brought forth at this time.

5. The leader thanks those who participated in role playing.

Appropriate topics

1. Parent-teacher conferences
2. Behavioral problems
3. Building self-esteem
4. Reflective listening
5. Roles within groups

Dramatizations

Short plays, written by group members or selected from those available from commercial companies, mental health organizations, or social agencies, can be used as springboards to discussions. There is an advantage to skits composed by the membership. First, the length can be kept short and the parts easily learned. Second, the action may be specifically related to the group's needs. Third, the preparation of the skit encourages the group participants to become actively involved in the process and in the material that is presented.

A variation of the drama can be the use of puppets. Many participants are able to use puppets more freely than to perform themselves, because using puppets takes away the threat of performing.

Arrangements prior to meeting

1. Select a group to plan a drama (a play chosen or developed by group).
2. Select the cast or allow members to choose their own parts.

3. Encourage participants to study the parts and work together on the presentation.
4. Review the Arrangements for the Meeting (pp. 160–161) and make appropriate preparations.

Setup

1. Depending on the number of persons at the meeting, the room can be arranged as follows:
   a. Use a circle for a small group, with the dramatization performed as a play in-the-round.
   b. If the group is small, the chairs may be formed in a semicircle with the stage at the opening. The stage may be raised or on the same level as the group members.
   c. If the group is large, an auditorium arrangement is appropriate. The dramatization can be held on a stage.

Procedure

1. The leader convenes the meeting and introduces the drama and the cast of characters.
2. The dramatization is presented.
3. Open discussion ensues, which clarifies feelings, emotions, and information presented.
4. The leader thanks the performers.

Appropriate topics

1. Family violence
2. Handling the stubborn child
3. Rivalry between children
4. Family rivalry
5. Family conferences
6. Communication among family members

Panel

A panel is an informal presentation by approximately four to six presenters who discuss an issue or idea. Panel members come prepared with background material on a selected subject and, seated behind a table or in a semicircle, discuss the subject among themselves. The presentation allows informal interaction and conversation among the members of the panel.

A chairperson, although a member of the panel, has different responsibilities from the other members. The chairperson introduces members, presents the topic, and then encourages participation by the other members. Like a leader, the chairperson can clarify, keep the panel focused on the topic, and summarize the closing.

Arrangements prior to meeting

1. Review the Arrangements for the Meeting (pp. 160–161) and make appropriate arrangements. In a panel meeting with informal conversation among panel members, it is important to set the stage.
2. Choose four to six participants to discuss a specific topic.
3. The panel thoroughly researches the topic. Notes are kept for reference and introduction of ideas during the panel presentation.

Setup

1. Place a table or two tables slightly turned toward one another in front of the audience. Set chairs for the panelists behind the table, which allows members to see and converse with each other easily.
2. Seat the audience or remaining members of the group in a semicircle, with the panel facing them. If the audience is large, auditorium-style seating may be used with a panel presentation.

Procedure

1. The chairperson clarifies the panel procedure to the audience.
2. The chairperson presents the topic for discussion and the relevance of the topic to the group's concerns.
3. The chairperson introduces the panel members.
4. The chairperson starts the discussion by a question or statement, and the panelists begin a discussion, freely interacting and conversing with one another.
5. The chairperson asks for questions from the audience. Questions are discussed among panelists.

6. The chairperson summarizes the major points and the conclusions of the panel.
7. The chairperson thanks the panel members for their contributions.

Appropriate topics

1. Child development—social, intellectual, emotional, and physical
2. New classroom teaching methods
3. Nonsexist education
4. Exceptional children
5. Drugs and alcohol—influence on children
6. Discipline
7. Emotions in children
8. Managing a home with both parents working
9. Nutrition

Colloquy

The colloquy is a panel discussion by an informed or expert panel where members of the audience are encouraged by the chairperson to interject a question or comment during the presentation. This allows information specifically pertinent to the audience to be discussed during the main part of the presentation instead of waiting for the question-answer period after the presentation.

A second form of the colloquy includes two sets of panels, an expert panel and a lay panel. The lay panel uses the procedures for a panel discussion. The expert panel gives advice when called upon by the lay panel or when it feels some pertinent information is being overlooked.

Arrangements prior to meeting

1. The lay panel is selected, or if the expert and lay panel forum is being used, two panels are selected.
2. Necessary preparations of topic material is completed. The subject is researched, and notes are developed for discussion.
3. Review the Arrangements for the Meeting (pp. 160–161) and make appropriate arrangements.

Setup

1. For a single panel, place chairs behind tables turned so the members of the panel can make eye contact with one another.
2. For two panels, lay and expert, seat the chairperson in the center with one panel on the left and one on the right, both slightly facing the center so that the presenters can see each other and the audience.

Procedure

1. Colloquy—single panel
   a. The leader or chairperson explains and clarifies the colloquy procedure to the audience.
   b. The topic for discussion is introduced.
   c. Panel members are introduced.
   d. The chairperson offers a stimulating comment or question to start the discussion.
   e. The chairperson encourages free interaction among panel members and takes questions and comments from the audience.
   f. An open forum follows the conclusion of the panel discussion.
   g. The leader summarizes and concludes meeting.
2. Colloquy—dual panel
   a. The chairperson explains and clarifies the two-panel colloquy to the audience.
   b. The chairperson introduces the subject for discussion.
   c. The expert and lay panels are presented to the audience.
   d. The leader starts the discussion with a stimulating remark or question.
   e. As expert advice is needed, the second panel is called upon to contribute.
   f. A question-answer period follows the presentation, with comments and questions from the audience answered and discussed by both the lay and expert panel.
   g. The chairperson summarizes, thanks the participants, and concludes the colloquy.

Appropriate topics

1. Dealing with your child's fears
2. Handling stress
3. Drug addiction and alcoholism
4. Helping exceptional children
5. Nutrition

Debate

When an issue is of a pro-and-con nature, a debate is an effective means of presenting both sides. The debate team presents opposing views of a controversial issue.

Arrangements prior to meeting

1. Select two to six members for the debate team. Divide into two teams and give each group one side of the issue.
2. The debaters research the background material on the issue and develop a 2- to 4-minute speech.
3. Review the Arrangements for the Meeting (pp. 160-161) and make appropriate arrangements.

Setup

1. Place enough chairs for the debate team on each side of a podium or table.
2. Place chairs in a circle for a small audience; if the group is large, use an auditorium formation.

Procedure

1. The question to be debated is announced by the chairperson, and then the issue is turned over to the speakers for each side.
2. One speaker for the affirmative begins with a 2- to 4-minute speech. The next speaker is from the opposing position. The teams alternate until each member has spoken.
3. Rebuttal following each speech is optional, or leaders of both debate teams may conclude the debate section with rebuttals.
4. The chairperson entertains questions from the audience, and the debate teams answer and discuss the issue.

Appropriate topics

1. Sex education—home or school?
2. Behavior modification vs. logical consequences
3. Open education vs. traditional education
4. Encouragement toward achievement vs. "Don't push my child"

Book Review Discussion

Book reviews by members of the group or experts provide a format that brings out stimulating new ideas or acknowledges expertise. The review may be given by one presenter or a number of members. An open discussion by the entire group follows.

Arrangements prior to meeting

1. Select the book and expert or members to give the book reviews.
2. Plan with the group how the review will be done, that is, each presenter taking one section of the book, one person doing the entire book, or a panel discussion of issues in the book.
3. Each presenter must read the book and prepare the review or a specific portion of the review.
4. The group is told about the upcoming book review and encouraged to read the book.
5. Review the Arrangements for the Meeting (pp. 160–161) and make appropriate arrangements.

Setup

1. Place chairs for book reviewers behind a table in front of the group.
2. Arrange chairs for the audience in a circle or semicircle.

Procedure

1. The chairperson tells about the book to be reviewed and introduces the book reviewer or book review panel.
2. The book reviewer gives information about the author of the book.
3. The book review is given.

a. If the book is to be reviewed by a panel discussion, the group discusses issues and ideas in a conversational format.
b. One person may give the book review.
c. Each of two or three persons may give a review of a portion of the book.
4. Following the review, the entire group joins in an open discussion of the book.

Appropriate Topics

1. Value clarification
2. Decision making
3. Building self-concept
4. Communication
5. Divorce
6. Role identification
7. Single parents
8. Refer to Chapter 11 for a list of books

Audiovisual

Visual stimuli, programmed material, and film presentations can be used as catalysts for a good open discussion. The audiovisual format is directed toward two senses, hearing and sight, whereas an audio presentation relies solely on hearing. The addition of visual stimuli is beneficial to those who learn better through sight than through sound. Charts, posters, and/or pictures accompanying any presentation help to clarify ideas. Films, filmstrips, and video presentations can present information in an interesting and succinct manner.

Techniques

1. Audio—tapes and records
2. Audiovisual
   a. Filmstrips with records or tapes
   b. Sound films
   c. Videotapes
   d. Slides with running commentary
3. Visual
   a. Charts
   b. Posters
   c. Chalk drawings
   d. Filmstrips with printed information

e. Opaque projector images

f. Overhead projector transparencies

Arrangements prior to meeting

1. The teacher and/or group decides on information needed by the membership through interest finders.
2. Films, slides, or tapes are reviewed and selected. (Choose only programs that are relevant, interesting, and presented well.)
3. Choose a member to give a presentation.
4. Films, video, or tapes must be reserved and equipment ordered—tape or record players, projectors, chart stands, projection carts, extension cords, outlet adapters, screen, etc.
5. Previewing of audiovisual and audio materials is necessary to be sure of quality and to develop questions and comments relevant to the presentation. Do not use audiovisual materials as fillers; use them only as relevant additions to curricula.
6. Review the Arrangements for the Meeting (pp. 160–161) and make appropriate preparations.

Setup

1. Check and prepare equipment prior to meeting. Have film, slides, or filmstrips ready to begin and have charts and posters up.
2. Arrange chairs so membership can see the presentation.

Procedure

1. The chairperson introduces the topic and the presenter.
2. The presenter gives background information on audiovisual material and points out important aspects of the showing.
3. Following the presentation, the presenter leads an open discussion and question-answer period.

Appropriate topics

1. Foundations of reading and writing
2. Emotional growth
3. Dealing with fears
4. Exceptional children, for example, learning disabled, autistic, mentally retarded, and gifted

5. Chapter 11 lists a number of films and filmstrips that would make excellent starting points for a discussion

Symposium

A symposium is a formal presentation on various aspects of a topic given by several speakers. Each symposium presenter develops a specific talk of 5 to 15 minutes. The symposium is similar to a lecture, but information is given by several lecturers rather than just one. Its value, to share expert information, is the same.

Arrangements prior to meeting

1. Symposium presenters are selected.
2. A set talk, based on research of appropriate authorities and relevant articles, is prepared by each symposium member.
3. A chairperson or leader is chosen from the symposium presenters.
4. Review the Arrangements for the Meeting (pp. 160–161)) and make appropriate preparations.

Setup

1. Place chairs for the presenters behind a table in front of the audience.
2. Chairs for the audience may be in circle or semicircle for a small group, or auditorium arrangements can be made for a large group.

Procedure

1. The chairperson or leader introduces the symposium speakers.
2. Each presenter gives a set talk.
3. The chairperson or leader provides transitional statements between each speaker's presentation.
4. At the end of the presentations, questions directed to a specific speaker or to the entire symposium are entertained by the chairperson. A discussion of questions follows.
5. The chairperson summarizes the main points of the meeting.
6. Symposium presenters are thanked for their contributions.

Appropriate topics

1. Nonsexist education
2. Single parenthood
3. Sex-role identification
4. Multicultural understanding
5. Consumer education
6. Death and dying
7. Safety in the home (e.g., toys, poison, home arrangement)

Lecture

A lecture is a talk or speech prepared by an expert or lay presenter. During the presentation, there are no interruptions or questions allowed, but there may be a question-answer period following the address. The lecture without a forum following it results in a formal presentation with no interaction between speaker and audience. A lecture forum that includes a period for questions and answers at the end of the address permits some interaction and allows the audience an opportunity to have relevant questions answered, to clarify points, and to make comments.

Lectures are an excellent vehicle for dissemination of specific information. As a result, care must be taken to choose a speaker who not only knows the subject but who presents unbiased material.

Arrangements prior to meeting

1. Select a topic and obtain a speaker who is recognized as an unbiased authority.
2. Communicate with the speaker on group interests and needs, time limit for speech, and forum period.
3. Prepare an introduction that is based on the speaker's background and expertise.
4. Review the Arrangements for the Meeting (pp. 160–161) and make appropriate preparations.

Setup

1. Place a podium or table at the center of the stage if the audience is large. Place chairs in a circle with a small table in front of the speaker if the audience is small.

2. Check the sound system if area is large.
3. Obtain a glass or pitcher of water for the speaker's use.

Procedure

1. The chairperson introduces the speaker and topic.
2. The speaker gives a talk for a specific period of time.
3. The chairperson conducts a forum for questions, with the guest speaker responding to comments and answering questions.
4. The speaker is thanked by the chairperson, and the meeting is concluded.

Appropriate topics

1. Money management
2. Specialists, for example psychiatrist, pediatrician, dentist, nutritionist, obstetrician, special educator, speech therapist, physical therapist
3. How to manage stress
4. Dealing with illness and death
5. Preventive health measures
6. Childhood diseases

Select the meeting format that fulfills your needs and is most appropriate for the topic.

SUMMARY

Parent group meetings are one of the most efficient and viable forms of parent education. Positive leadership skills are essential to facilitate productive functioning of parent groups. Included in this chapter are a description of a needs assessment and a discussion of the formation of parent groups. Leadership skills and good group interaction can be developed if groups are aware of leadership and group roles. Roles that emerge within groups have an impact on the interaction of the participants. A knowledge of task, maintenance, and dysfunctional roles improves the productiveness of group interaction through the concerted elimination of nonfunctional roles. An analysis of group discussion illustrates the interaction in process.

Group meetings use a variety of meeting formats, either individually or in combination. The formats include roundtable, concentric circle, buzz session, brainstorming, workshop, field trip, role playing, dramatization, panel, colloquy, debate, book review, audiovisual, lecture, and symposium. Choice of topics for the meetings should fit the interest and needs of the groups.

Evaluations are necessary in ongoing parent groups because they provide a basis for improvement of group interaction and suggestions for the continuing program.

SUGGESTED ACTIVITIES AND DISCUSSIONS

1. Generate some innovative icebreakers. Try them out on your classmates.
2. Develop a needs assessment for your community of parents. Ask parents to complete the needs assessment. Discuss their answers.
3. Conduct an opening period of a parent meeting. Include icebreakers and interest finders.
4. Choose roles from the dysfunctional and maintenance categories. Role play these roles while the group holds an open discussion or concentric circle discussion. Let the members of the group guess which roles the others are playing. If you use a concentric circle, have each member of the inner circle role play a group role. The outer circle can record the interaction and analyze the roles being played.
5. Make an interaction pattern on an observation wheel. Discuss the interaction pattern.
6. Obtain parent education programs such as STEP, PET, *Parents' Magazine* tapes and filmstrips, PAR (Parents as Resources) filmstrips, or other programs. Conduct meetings using the curricula from these programs.
7. Conduct a needs assessment within the total group. From the results pick one topic for each of the formats, that is, panel, debate, symposium, workshop, buzz session, etc. Let each group be responsible for a meeting using these topics and formats.
8. Attend a parent education meeting in your community. Visit with the members. Note how the meeting is conducted, the involvement of

the parents, and the feelings of the members. Talk with the director about the goals and objectives of the group. Talk with the parents concerning their desires for the group.
9. Engage a group in an experiential activity such as role playing. Using the experiential stages as a guide, ask questions that carry the group forward.
10. Administer a needs assessment. From the responses, develop a curriculum plan for the semester.
11. Construct a program evaluation. Have students complete the questionnaire after a class session or a "parent" meeting. Evaluate the questionnaire. Did you get the type of feedback that you needed?
12. Develop a workshop or meeting for parents. Include the objectives of the meeting, questions to be answered, background material on the questions, and a list of additional resources.

BIBLIOGRAPHY

Applbaum, R. L., Bodaken, E. M., Sereno, K. K., & Anatol, K. W. E. *The process of group communication* (2d ed.). Palo Alto, Calif.: Science Research Associates, 1979.

Auerbach, A. B. *Parents learn through discussion: Principles and practices of parent group education.* New York: John Wiley, 1968.

Bales, R. *Interaction process analysis: A method for the study of small groups.* Chicago: University of Chicago Press, 1951.

Beal, G., Bohlen, J. M., & Raudabaugh, J. N. *Leadership and dynamic group action.* Ames, Iowa: Iowa State University, 1962.

Benne, K. D., & Sheets, P. Functional roles of group members. *Journal of Social Issues,* 1948,4(2), 41–49.

Berger, E. H. *Mature beginning teachers: Employment, satisfaction, and role analysis.* Unpublished dissertation, University of Denver, 1968.

Biddle, B. J., & Thomas, E. J. *Role theory: Concepts and research.* Melbourne, Fla.: Robert E. Kreiger Publishing Co., 1979.

Coan, D. L., & Gotts, E. E. *Parent education needs: A national assessment study.* Charleston, W. Va.: Appalachia Educational Laboratory, 1976. (ERIC

Document Reproduction Service No. ED 132 972).

Denver Public Schools, Emily Griffith Opportunity School. *Parent education and preschool department leadership handbook.* Denver, Colo.: Denver Public Schools, 1978.

Dinkmeyer, D., & McKay, G. D. *STEP (systematic training for effective parenting).* Circle Pines, Minn.: American Guidance Service, 1983.

Gallup, G. H. The ninth annual Gallup Poll of the public's attitudes toward the public schools. *Phi Delta Kappan,* September 1977, pp. 33–48.

_____. The 17th annual Gallup Poll of the public's attitude toward public schools. *Phi Delta Kappan,* September 1985, pp. 35–47.

Gardner, N. D. *Group leadership.* Washington, D.C.: National Training & Development Service Press, 1974.

Gaw, B. A. Processing questions: An aid to completing the learning cycle. In J. E. Jones and J. W. Pfeiffer (Eds.), *The 1979 annual handbook for group facilitators.* La Jolla, Calif.: University Associates, 1979.

Gibb, J. R., Platts, G. N., & Miller, L. F. *Dynamics of participative groups.* Washington, D.C.: National Training Laboratories, 1959.

Gordon, T. *P.E.T.: Parent effectiveness training.* New York: Wyden, 1975.

Gross, N., Mason, W. S., & McEachern, A. *Explorations in role analysis.* New York: John Wiley, 1958.

Hereford, C. F. *Changing parental attitudes through group discussion.* Austin: University of Texas Press, 1963.

Jones, J. E., & Pfeiffer, J. W. (Eds.). *The 1979 annual handbook for group facilitators.* La Jolla, Calif.: University Associates, 1979.

Kawin, E. *Parenthood in a free nation. Basic concepts for parents* (Vol. I), *Early and middle childhood* (Vol. II), *Later childhood and adolescence* (Vol. III). Lafayette, Ind.: Purdue University, 1969.

_____. *A manual for group leaders and participants.* Lafayette, Ind.: Purdue University, 1970.

King, C. E. *The sociology of small groups.* New York: Pageant Press, 1962.

Osborn, A. F. *Applied imagination.* New York: Scribner, 1957.

Pfeiffer, J. W., & Jones, J. H. *The reference guide to handbooks and annuals* (3rd ed.). San Diego, Calif.: University Associates, 1979.

Pickarts, E., & Fargo, J. *Parent education.* Englewood Cliffs, N.J.: Prentice-Hall, 1971.

U.S. Department of Health and Human Services (Office of Human Development Services, Administration for Children, Youth, and Families, Head Start Bureau). *A leader's guide to exploring parenting.* Washington, D.C.: U.S. Government Printing Office, 1980.

Yankelovich, Skelly, & White, Inc. *Raising children in a changing society: The General Mills American family report, 1976-1977.* Minneapolis: General Mills, 1977.

*Appendix**

Dear Parent:

Our Laboratory is preparing a new instructional series for parents. It is called "Education for Effective Parenthood."

Your local school has agreed to help us. Now we need your help. You will find a four (4) page form with this letter. The form will tell you "what to do." You can help by telling us on the form about your own needs as a parent. We hope you will talk with your husband or wife as you give your answers on the form. If you are a single parent, please let us know of your needs from this point of view.

When you finish answering, put your form in the envelope. Then seal it and return it to the school. Do not put your name on the outside of the envelope. We will not tell anyone what you said. We will use your answers to help us plan the "Education for Effective Parenthood" series.

We would like to know your answers. But you do not have to answer. Even if you do not answer, please seal your form in the envelope and return it to the school.

Soon you will hear from the school about the new instructional series. Watch for this news.

Thank you for your help.

Sincerely,

_____

*The material in this appendix is from Coan, D. L., & Gotts, E. E. *Parent education needs: A national assessment study.* Charleston, W. Va.: Appalachia Educational Laboratory, Inc., 1976, pp. 75–84. (ERIC Document Reproduction Service No. ED 132 972); *Learning to be a better parent* was developed by E. E. Gotts, D. L. Coan, & C. E. Kenoyer, 1975.

LEARNING TO BE A BETTER PARENT

Name: _____

My city and state: _____

My children's ages (in years): _____

Name of nearest grade school: _____

What to do: First, read what it says below about each thing you might learn more about. Then decide how much you feel you need or want to learn more about that. For example, if you feel you already know all or just about as much as you need or want to know about "How Children Grow and Develop," then mark the box *Nothing more at all*. However, if you feel you need or want to learn *more* about that, then you may wish to answer *A little more* or *A lot more*. Put a check mark (√) in the box under *A lot more, A little more,* or *Nothing more at all* for each question. We are interested in what you feel. You may, of course, feel that you need or want to learn more about some things, and nothing more about others. No one will judge you as a parent, whatever your answers are. If you do not want to answer a question, then leave it blank.

	A lot more	A little more	Nothing more at all
A. How children grow and develop			
How much do you feel you need or want to learn more about:			
1. Where you can find out about how children develop.	☐	☐	☐
2. What your child should be able to learn at his age, so as not to "push" your child too much.	☐	☐	☐
3. How children grow into special, one-of-a-kind people.	☐	☐	☐
4. How the world looks and sounds to your child, and how to help him learn about it.	☐	☐	☐
5. How your child's personality is formed.	☐	☐	☐
6. How your child learns to use his body by playing (runs, jumps).	☐	☐	☐
B. Taking better care of your baby			
How much do you feel you need or want to learn more about:			
1. What happens before the baby comes (what to eat; what drugs not to take; how long to wait before having another baby; things that can happen to the baby).	☐	☐	☐
2. How babies learn to talk (what the baby hears; what it learns from what you do and say).	☐	☐	☐
3. Helping the baby feel good (not too warm or cool; enough to eat; food that might upset the baby; giving the baby room to move around).	☐	☐	☐

	A lot more	A little more	Nothing more at all
C. Treating your child like a person			
How much do you feel you need or want to learn more about how to:			
1. Tell what children are doing by watching them.	☐	☐	☐
2. Help your child see and accept his or her own feelings.	☐	☐	☐
3. Show love and care to your child.	☐	☐	☐
4. Talk with your child about his problems and answer his questions.	☐	☐	☐
5. Help your child to behave when he starts to fight.	☐	☐	☐
6. Help your child learn to get along with family and friends.	☐	☐	☐
7. Help your child see why rules are good.	☐	☐	☐
D. Taking care of your family			
How much do you feel you need or want to learn more about how to:			
1. Pick things for the child's bed and for him to wear (so that they last and are easy to take care of).	☐	☐	☐
2. Find and take care of a home for your family (how to shop and pay for housing and furniture).	☐	☐	☐
3. Pick the right foods and take care of them so they will not spoil (fix meals that are good for your family's health).	☐	☐	☐
E. Teaching and training your child			
How much do you feel you need or want to learn more about:			
1. What ways of teaching will work best with your child (the way you teach; use of books, TV).	☐	☐	☐
2. How to control your child by using reward, praise, and correction in a loving way (how to help your child control himself).	☐	☐	☐
3. How to teach your child to be neat and clean and to show good manners.	☐	☐	☐
4. How to get your child to go to bed on time (and to rest or take naps).	☐	☐	☐
5. How to get your child to change from doing one thing to doing something else.	☐	☐	☐

Continued.

LEARNING TO BE A BETTER PARENT—cont'd

	A lot more	A little more	Nothing more at all

E. Teaching and training your child

How much do you feel you need or want to learn more about:

	A lot more	A little more	Nothing more at all
6. How to plan your child's use of TV (picking TV programs, not watching too much TV).	☐	☐	☐
7. How to place your chairs, tables, and other things so that your child will have room to play and learn (and keeping some things out of sight so your child will not want them).	☐	☐	☐
8. How to feed your child; teach him to feed himself; and make eating fun for your child.	☐	☐	☐
9. How to teach your child to dress and undress.	☐	☐	☐
10. How to help your child think for himself (choose what he wants to do; make plans).	☐	☐	☐
11. How to teach your child to tell right from wrong (to be moral).	☐	☐	☐

F. Keeping your family safe and well

How much do you feel you need or want to learn more about:

	A lot more	A little more	Nothing more at all
1. How to keep your child from getting hurt (and how to give first aid).	☐	☐	☐
2. How to keep your child well (get shots and have the doctor check your child).	☐	☐	☐
3. How to know if something is wrong with your child (is not learning; cannot walk well; cannot see or hear well).	☐	☐	☐
4. How to know when your child is sick (has a fever or says he hurts some place).	☐	☐	☐
5. How to pick things that are safe to play with.	☐	☐	☐
6. How to tell if your child is growing right (body size, height, weight).	☐	☐	☐

G. Taking care of things at home

How much do you feel you need or want to learn more about:

	A lot more	A little more	Nothing more at all
1. Making good use of your time (plan your time for child care, house work, school or job, time for yourslf and your friends).	☐	☐	☐
2. Getting good help with child care (day care, baby sitter, nursery school).	☐	☐	☐

	A lot more	A little more	Nothing more at all
3. How your child deals with the way that your family lives (people in the home, what they do together, how they get along).	☐	☐	☐
4. Finding help for people who don't take care of their children, or who hurt their children.	☐	☐	☐

H. Yourself as a parent

How much do you feel you need or want to learn more about:

	A lot more	A little more	Nothing more at all
1. Your own feelings and habits and how these help or hurt your child care (how they affect your child care).	☐	☐	☐
2. Your need to make your child mind you (how your own needs can affect how your child feels about himself, and your child's learning).	☐	☐	☐
3. Why your child will not mind you and how this bothers you (how to get over being upset).	☐	☐	☐
4. How to be sure that you are doing what is best for your child (or your worries about what other people think).	☐	☐	☐

What to do: Just as before, read what it says about each thing from which you can learn. That is, if you think you would enjoy learning about being a better parent from "reading books," then you may wish to answer *A lot* or *A little*. But if you would *not* enjoy learning from "reading books," then mark the box *Not at all*. You may, of course, think that you would like to learn from some things and not from others. Put a check mark (√) in the box under *A lot*, *A little* or *Not at all* for each question.

I. How to learn about being a better parent

How much would you like to learn about being a better parent from:

	A lot	A little	Not at all
1. Reading books.	☐	☐	☐
2. Talking with parents in group meetings.	☐	☐	☐
3. Watching a special TV series.	☐	☐	☐
4. Seeing movies near my home (at a school).	☐	☐	☐
5. Having a person visit my home and talk with me each week.	☐	☐	☐
6. Seeing slides and hearing a person tell about them.	☐	☐	☐
7. Reading about this in magazines or in small newspapers (4 to 8 pages long).	☐	☐	☐
8. Hearing a special radio series.	☐	☐	☐
9. Listening to records or tapes.	☐	☐	☐
10. Playing games that teach me to be a better parent.	☐	☐	☐

Continued.

LEARNING TO BE A BETTER PARENT—cont'd

	A lot	A little	Not at all

I. How to learn about being a better parent

On TV or radio or in the movies, how much would you like to learn from:

	A lot	A little	Not at all
1. A funny show (humor, comedy, jokes).	☐	☐	☐
2. A talk show with well-known guests and parents.	☐	☐	☐
3. Stories about real people (not humor).	☐	☐	☐
4. Special stories done by actors (not humor).	☐	☐	☐
5. An M.D. (doctor) or other expert.	☐	☐	☐
6. A show that goes into real people's homes.	☐	☐	☐

Other ideas

What else do you think you need or want to learn more about in order to be a better parent? Print so that your ideas will be easy to read.

_____

_____

_____

_____

CHAPTER SIX

School-based Programs

Can you visualize your school as the center of a wheel with the spokes stretching out to the homes in the community through programs, resources, family centers, and support systems? Figure 6-1 illustrates some of the many components possible for a school.

Head Start can be illustrated by a similar wheel, with spokes for parent involvement, dental and medical care, a nutritional program, psychological support, and community resources. Comprehensive health and educational centers also rely on a variety of components to offer families the support they need. An example is the Brookline Early Education Project, which is described later in this chapter. Outreach from school-based programs takes a variety of forms, each with its own strengths. This chapter discusses many programs and ideas that reach out from the school to meet the needs of parents and children.

A WALK THROUGH A SCHOOL

Assume the role of a parent who visits a school that is committed to the involvement of parents. As you open the school door, you notice a sign that welcomes you. The office staff also greet you with smiles when you check into the office. If you want to have a cup of tea or cof-

fee, look through the school's curricula, or read an article, you can visit the family center. There, several parents are developing curriculum material for the school's resource room. One parent is making a game for the third and fourth grade classes. Another is clipping curriculum-related articles to be filed for reference. As you sip your coffee, the sounds of young children echo down the hall from the west wing of the building. Parents and their children are arriving for their parent education and/or parent-child meetings. This school offers programs for parents of infants, toddlers, and preschool children. Both parents are invited and included in the programs. For those who cannot come during the week, a Saturday session is added.

You came to school today, however, to visit your child's classroom so, after a brief visit in the family center, you walk to your child's room. Outside the door you pause as you read a welcome notice on the bulletin board that shows in detail what the children have been accomplishing. Here the teacher has described the happenings for the week, listed the volunteer times for parents, and has asked for contributions of plastic meat containers to be used in making tempera paint prints. Immediately aware of what is happening in the room, you promise to start collecting "scrounge materi-

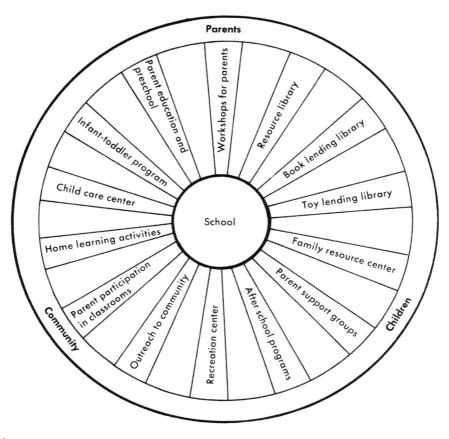

FIGURE 6-1
The spokes of the wheel radiate from the school and reveal opportunities for involvement of parents, children, and community.

als" for recycling in the classroom. An invitation to an evening workshop reminds you that you have saved next Tuesday evening for that very event. On the space for notes to and from parents, you write a short response to the message you received from the teacher last week. Attached to the bulletin board are "Tips for Visiting." These let you know that you can become involved in a classroom activity rather than spend your time in passive observation. The teacher smiles and acknowledges your presence but, if involved with the class, continues teaching. The class greeter, a child chosen as a very important person this week, comes up and welcomes you. Later, during a

center session or break, you have an opportunity to talk with the teacher and your child.

Recruitment for volunteers is underway so you are encouraged, but not forced, to contribute. Flexible hours, designated time periods, child care services, and a variety of tasks make it easy to share some time in this classroom.

Knowing that the principal holds an open forum each week at this time, you stop by and join a discussion of school policy. Parents are being encouraged to evaluate the "tote bag" home learning activities that have been sent home with children. In addition, plans are underway for an after-school recreation program. The principal will take the com-

Preschools as well as before and after-school programs located in the public schools help fill a need for many parents.

ments to the Parent Advisory Board meeting later this week.

After listening to others and expressing your recommendations and appreciation, you glance at your watch and realize that you must go. As you leave the school, you feel satisfied that this school responds to the needs of both you and your child.

INFANT-TODDLER PROGRAMS

As you walk down the corridors of some public schools, you may view the unusual sight of mothers, fathers, or grandparents exercising with infants and toddlers on the floor. No, they are not in the wrong building. These parents or grandparents are fortunate to have a school that extends its welcome to future students and their parents by providing an infant-toddler development program for parents of children from birth to age 3. One such program, in Prairie View Elementary School, Gainesville, Florida, provides the following classes for parents:

Your new baby and you	Birth to 6 months
Your infant and you	6 to 12 months
Your toddler and you	12 to 24 months
Your young child and you	24 to 36 months

In addition to weekday programs, once-a-month Saturday meetings are held for those parents who cannot attend during the week. Six to eight families at a time has proved optimal for the best interaction and results. Parents attend the classes with their children so, with six families, there may be 16 or 17 people in the room, including babies, mothers and/or fathers, teachers, and assistants (Packer et al., 1979).

Parenting classes are organized around four components:

1. Learning activities and exercises
   a. To encourage positive interaction between parent and child while basic caregiving activities such as diapering, bathing, and feeding occur
   b. To facilitate language and communication
   c. To promote sensorimotor development
2. Relaxation exercises and postnatal conditioning for the mother
3. Sharing period when common concerns are discussed
4. Consultation from interdisciplinary professionals such as nutritionists, pediatricians, psychologists, and nurses

This program has additional outreach components (similar to the spokes of the wheel). Complementary offerings of the Parenting-Family Development Education program include:

- Parent advisory council
- Toy lending library
- Home visits as needed
- Referral services to other agencies
- Supplementary materials for parent use

Initial assessment of the program suggests that parents are better able to handle stress at the end of the first year than they had been at the beginning of the program. Parents' responses to the program were positive and reflected appreciation. This outreach by the school to new parents and their children provides preventive educational services. "It is believed that parents and children who participate in these parenting classes will have a better opportunity to understand and relate to each other in ways that will enhance their mutual growth and development" (Packer et al., 1979, p. 9).

NEW PARENTS AS TEACHERS PROJECT

Programs based primarily in the home often have their origin in the schools. The spokes from the school radiate out, helping, supporting, and caring about families in the area. One of the most isolated families in an area may be the beginning family that has recently rented or bought their first home; they begin on a real adventure after the birth of their first child. These and established couples who were having their first child were the parents selected for the New Parents as Teachers Project that was developed in four districts in Missouri. The research project reaffirmed the importance of parents in the education of their children.

First-time parents are usually very receptive to guidance. If the mother or father is not working out of the home, she or he usually has a need to visit and socialize with others as well as a desire to learn how best to raise the child. Contact and support reduces the loneliness felt by a parent who is totally responsible for an infant. In addition, new parents have no preconceived ideas gained by their experience in rearing other children that would be contrary to the research design.

Three hundred and eighty families participated in the New Parents as Teachers Project. Beginning in the third trimester of pregnancy and continuing until the child was 3, each family received the following:

- Information and guidance before the child was born that helped the parents prepare for the new arrival.
- Information on child development that fosters cognitive, social, motor, and language development. Clearly written handbooks describing what the parents should expect during each phase of development were published. The phases based on Burton White's *The First Three Years of Life* were:
  Phase 1 – birth to 6 weeks
  Phase 2 – 6 weeks to 3½ months
  Phase 3 – 3½ months to 5½ months
  Phase 4 – 5½ months to 8 months
  Phase 5 – 8 months to 14 months
  Phase 6 – 14 months to 24 months
  Phase 7 – 24 months to 36 months (Ferguson-Florissant School District, 1985).
- Periodic hearing and vision checkups provided for the children in order to screen for possible problems.
- Parent resource center at the school that was available for the parent meetings.
- Individualized parent conferences each month.
- Monthly group meetings with other parents.

The research validated the parents' positive responses. It showed that children participating in the New Parents as Teachers Project scored significantly higher on all measures of verbal ability, intelligence, language ability, achievement, and auditory comprehension than did comparison children.

BROOKLINE EARLY EDUCATION PROJECT (BEEP)

The Brookline Project is an outstanding example of a public school system working with other agencies. Brookline Public Schools and Children's Hospital Medical Center, Boston, joined to develop a coordinated plan for physical checkups and educational programs for young children, birth to kindergarten. Together, the hospital and school supplied a reassuring support system for 285 children and their families in Brookline during this pilot program in the late 1970s. "The family was seen as the basic child-rearing unit and BEEP's role is to be responsive to the needs and life-style of each family" (Brookline Early Education Project, 1979, p. 3). Three types of services offered included:

1. A diagnostic program consisting of early and periodic detection screening and follow-up for each child, including physical and developmental assessments, beginning shortly after birth and continuing up through entry into school.
2. Support for parents in the rearing of their children by providing knowledge and human resources.
3. Direct educational programs for children beginning at 24 months of age with a playgroup experience and, later on, entering a preschool program. (Brookline Early Education Project, 1979, p. 3)

The Brookline outreach included these services and resources in addition to the diagnostic and educational program:

- Family center
- Consultants
- Library books and pamphlets
- Films and videotapes on child development
- Series of special events—workshops, films, and lectures
- Transportation for parents to BEEP

Figure 6–2 illustrates the extent of the involvement of families, school, and the medical center.

Children joined a playgroup when they reached the age of 2. Attendance was varied; most met once a week. While their children attended the playgroup, the parents observed the children's play and interaction with others. Parents also met in small groups and discussed child development and parent concerns.

The diagnostic program included compilation of complete medical and life events data as well as dental examinations and lead and anemia screenings in order to monitor each child's health and development in the early years. Examinations were made at 2 weeks, 3½ months, 6½ months, 11½ months, 24 months, 30 months, and 42 months. Monitoring assured parents and educators that the child's learning would not be hindered by undetected health problems.

Additionally, the project developed materials for replication by other schools that wished to join with the medical field in a similar joint effort to provide services for families. The comprehensive approach by the BEEP program demonstrates that educational programs and health services, working together, can assist the growing family.

BIRMINGHAM MODEL FOR PARENT EDUCATION

The Birmingham Model, based on the premise that mothers learn from other mothers, provided new experiences and skills through modeling, role playing, discussion, and self-evaluation. Whereas the Brookline project

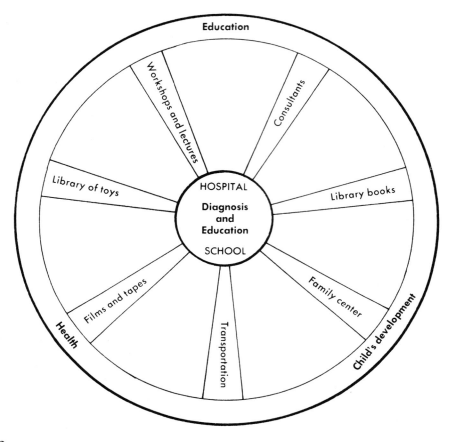

FIGURE 6-2
The hospital and school work together to provide for the child's health, education, and development.

worked with middle and upper-middle class parents, the Birmingham model worked with mothers from low-income neighborhoods and public housing projects who were recruited by door-to-door canvassing. The participants were randomly assigned to either the program or a control group. Those in the program were given stipends to enable them to attend. Experienced mothers, who encouraged and trained mothers with less experience, learned in the process also. Extensive curriculum material was provided, but the primary resource was the mothers.

The Birmingham Model required participation of the infant from age 3½ months until 36 months of age. Mother and child attended sessions at the center from 9 AM to 1:30 PM, 3 days each week for 9 months. Attendance, thereafter, was increased to 5 days a week. As mothers gained experience, they took on more responsibility in the center, and with this came an increase in pay.

The program had positive results for the children in both cognitive and socioemotional areas. The use of parents as trainees and models reinforced the mother's learning. The program mothers showed a greater degree of sensitivity and responsiveness to their children than did those in the control group. The most interesting aspect of this program, from an educational viewpoint, is that mothers learned from experience and by modeling, as well as from teaching in the program. These are effective learning strategies (Lasater et al., 1975).

SCHOOL ON SATURDAY

School on Saturday? How can it work? Follow the example set by the Ferguson-Florissant School District, St. Louis, Missouri, where home and school have joined hands with 500 to 700 families yearly since 1972 to provide a program for all 4-year-olds. The program has four major components:

1. Diagnostic and prescriptive testing
2. Half-day preschool held each Saturday in a public school kindergarten
3. Active participation by both parents
4. Outreach to the home

The outreach provides activity sheets or booklets for both the 4-year-olds and younger siblings, beginning at birth. Parents, involved in home activities, continue activities on their own during the week by using guidesheets left by the teacher.

Saturday School works! Children gain in intellectual, language, and visual motor skills. Their parents gain in ability to communicate with their children, use appropriate reinforcement techniques, and sense a child's learning readiness.

The handicapped child, or the child with special problems, progresses just as significantly. Several children, who at age 4 had problems with learning, when tested in fourth grade, were at the same level as those without learning disabilities except in the area of spelling (Ferguson-Florissant School District, 1978).

The program reaches out to fathers as well as mothers as revealed in a special section for the father. The curriculum, dealing with motor coordination development, goes hand in hand with positive interaction between child and father (Figure 6-3).

What can other programs gain from the success of the Saturday School? These aspects seem particularly important:

1. Active participation by both parents in teaching their own children
2. Diagnostic and prescriptive activities for children with handicaps
3. Observation and participation by parents in a school setting
4. Guidance and activities that support the parents' efforts
5. Teacher visits to home, which establish a team rapport between teachers and parents
6. Opportunities for the child to experience routine school activities and an enriched curriculum each week
7. Home learning activity booklets to be used by parents of children from birth through age 3

The varied approaches of the Saturday School meet many more needs than does a program that has only one dimension (e.g., preschool without the parent component). This was recognized by the district, and although this program was initially funded with federal money, it proved its value and is now financed by the local school district and supplemented with education funds for the handicapped.

CHATTANOOGA PUBLIC SCHOOLS

The Chattanooga Public Schools wanted to develop material to be used by Head Start, Chapter I, and Follow Through with coordinated sets for children, parents, and teachers. The style and presentation promote a positive and enjoyable activity for the child and parent (Figures 6-4 and 6-5.) These activities illustrate

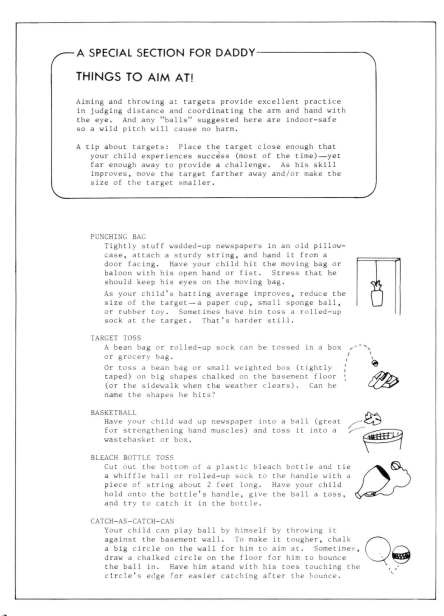

A SPECIAL SECTION FOR DADDY

THINGS TO AIM AT!

Aiming and throwing at targets provide excellent practice
in judging distance and coordinating the arm and hand with
the eye. And any "balls" suggested here are indoor-safe
so a wild pitch will cause no harm.

A tip about targets: Place the target close enough that
    your child experiences success (most of the time)—yet
    far enough away to provide a challenge. As his skill
    improves, move the target farther away and/or make the
    size of the target smaller.

PUNCHING BAG
    Tightly stuff wadded-up newspapers in an old pillow-
    case, attach a sturdy string, and hand it from a
    door facing. Have your child hit the moving bag or
    baloon with his open hand or fist. Stress that he
    should keep his eyes on the moving bag.
    As your child's batting average improves, reduce the
    size of the target—a paper cup, small sponge ball,
    or rubber toy. Sometimes have him toss a rolled-up
    sock at the target. That's harder still.

TARGET TOSS
    A bean bag or rolled-up sock can be tossed in a box
    or grocery bag.
    Or toss a bean bag or small weighted box (tightly
    taped) on big shapes chalked on the basement floor
    (or the sidewalk when the weather clears). Can he
    name the shapes he hits?

BASKETBALL
    Have your child wad up newspaper into a ball (great
    for strengthening hand muscles) and toss it into a
    wastebasket or box.

BLEACH BOTTLE TOSS
    Cut out the bottom of a plastic bleach bottle and tie
    a whiffle ball or rolled-up sock to the handle with a
    piece of string about 2 feet long. Have your child
    hold onto the bottle's handle, give the ball a toss,
    and try to catch it in the bottle.

CATCH-AS-CATCH-CAN
    Your child can play ball by himself by throwing it
    against the basement wall. To make it tougher, chalk
    a big circle on the wall for him to aim at. Sometimes,
    draw a chalked circle on the floor for him to bounce
    the ball in. Have him stand with his toes touching the
    circle's edge for easier catching after the bounce.

FIGURE 6-3
Fathers are an integral part of the Saturday School. (Reprinted with permission from
the Ferguson-Florissant School District, St. Louis, Mo.)

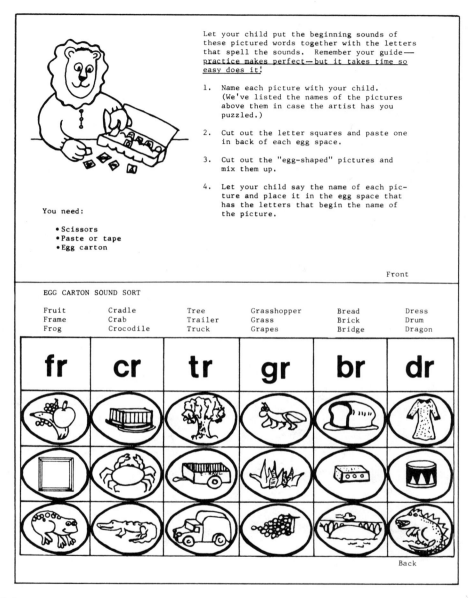

Let your child put the beginning sounds of these pictured words together with the letters that spell the sounds. Remember your guide— <u>practice makes perfect—but it takes time so easy does it</u>!

1. Name each picture with your child. (We've listed the names of the pictures above them in case the artist has you puzzled.)

2. Cut out the letter squares and paste one in back of each egg space.

3. Cut out the "egg-shaped" pictures and mix them up.

4. Let your child say the name of each picture and place it in the egg space that has the letters that begin the name of the picture.

You need:

• Scissors
• Paste or tape
• Egg carton

Front

EGG CARTON SOUND SORT

Fruit	Cradle	Tree	Grasshopper	Bread	Dress
Frame	Crab	Trailer	Grass	Brick	Drum
Frog	Crocodile	Truck	Grapes	Bridge	Dragon

| **fr** | **cr** | **tr** | **gr** | **br** | **dr** |

Back

FIGURE 6-4

Games at home reinforce the school's curriculum. (Reprinted with permission. Chattanooga Public Schools. Copyright 1976 by the city of Chattanooga, Tenn.)

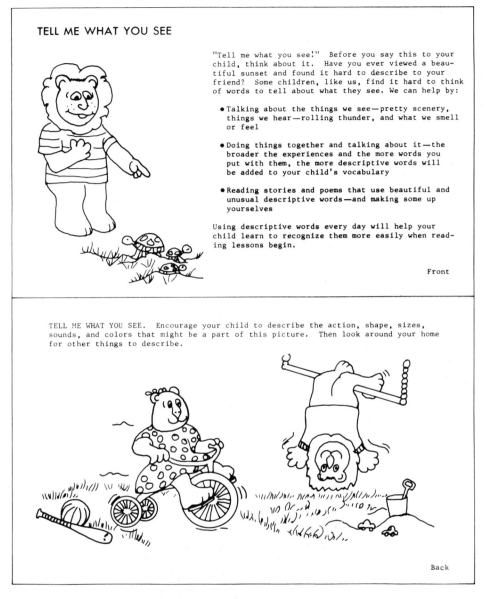

FIGURE 6-5

Young children can be encouraged to observe and describe. (Reprinted with permission. Chattanooga Public Schools. Copyright 1976 by the city of Chattanooga, Tenn.)

two levels of educational attainment through home learning activities.

Materials, geared to satisfy the objectives of the program, were developed and field-tested. These include:

1. A preschool competency profile checklist
2. A set of parent/child activity cards relating to general skills, prereading skills, and premathematics skills
3. A set of parent booklets, one a series in itself containing the units or separate booklets on ways to learn; others are individual booklets about teaching behaviors, parenting behaviors, health habits, and social development
4. A guide for teachers and parent coordinators to help them involve parents in their children's education and to implement the newly-developed activity card system for parents (Parent Education Demonstration Project, 1976, p. 77)

Although originally developed for Head Start, Chapter I, and Follow Through, the guidelines and activity sheets are helpful to teachers and to parents of children in traditional classrooms.

HEAD START

Head Start, a federal program with such credibility that the funding has continued since 1965, is a fine example of a program that involves parents. From its inception Head Start involved the family in its outreach, with spokes of the wheel radiating from the Head Start Center to include dental and health care, resources in the community, nutritional food for the children, and information on career opportunities.

Before initiating any parent program, it is wise to ask parents how they perceive their needs. Although needs will change throughout the life of any program, early assessment with periodic review will show the initial needs and the progression of later needs. A sample assessment suggests areas to investigate, as illustrated in a questionnaire directed to parents of Head Start children (Figure 6–6).

After Head Start parents complete the needs assessments, plans for parent participation can be devised with better understanding. As parents become more familiar with the program and more sophisticated in their learning, their needs and requests will vary, so provide a current assessment by continued use of questionnaires. In initial planning, involve parents as:

• Decision makers
• Participants in the classroom
• Teachers of their own children
• Participation in parent activities (Hubbell, 1983, p. 57)

In decision making the average Head Start program involves parents at two or three levels, that is, the Head Start Center Committee, Head Start Policy Committee for the delegate agency, and/or the Head Start Policy Council (for the grantee funded by the federal government). The first is initiated by each center, which should have a committee composed of parents whose children are enrolled. The center committee has the following responsibilities:

1. To assist teachers, center director, and all other persons responsible for the development and operation of every component, including curriculum, of the Head Start program
2. To work closely with classroom teachers to carry out daily activities
3. To plan, conduct, and participate in informal, as well as formal, programs and activities for center parents and staff
4. To participate in recruiting and screening of center employees within guidelines established by HEW, the Grantee Council and Board, and the Delegate Agency and Board (Littlejohn & Associates, 1976, pp. 1–1 and 1–2)

The policy committee is set up at the agency delegated to administer the Head Start

PARENT NEEDS ASSESSMENT QUESTIONNAIRE*

Name: _____ Date: _____

Address: _____ Center: _____

Phone: _____ Child's name: _____

1. In my job as a parent I have the hardest time in:

	Very difficult	Somewhat difficult	No problem
a. Being an only parent	☐	☐	☐
b. Teaching my child to obey	☐	☐	☐
c. Providing proper nourishment	☐	☐	☐
d. Making time to listen and play with my child	☐	☐	☐
e. Disciplining my child	☐	☐	☐
f. Having patience and understanding	☐	☐	☐
g. Understanding my child's growth	☐	☐	☐
h. Other (specify) _____	☐	☐	☐

2. To do my job better as a parent I would like training in:

	Very important	Somewhat important	Not important
a. Child growth and development	☐	☐	☐
b. Bilingual-bicultural education	☐	☐	☐
c. Nutrition	☐	☐	☐
d. Child behavior and discipline	☐	☐	☐
e. First aid	☐	☐	☐
f. Self-improvement	☐	☐	☐
g. Home improvement	☐	☐	☐
h. Techniques in working with the handicapped child	☐	☐	☐
i. Other (specify) _____	☐	☐	☐

3. What I expect Head Start to do for my child:
   a. Learn to get along with other children _____
   b. Develop self-confidence _____
   c. Obtain medical and dental screening _____
   d. Other (specify) _____
4. What I expect Head Start to do for me as a parent:
   a. Get to know and understand my child better _____
   b. Become aware of services available for me and my family _____
   c. Develop patience with my child _____
   d. Understand what my child is learning at school and how I can help him at home _____
   e. Get acquainted with teachers and other parents _____
   f. Other (specify) _____

FIGURE 6-6

Parent Needs Assessment Questionnaire. (*Source:* modified from R. Littlejohn & Associates. *Involving parents in Head Start: A guide for parent involvement coordinates* [final draft]. Washington, D.C.: Office of Human Development, 1976.)

PARENT NEEDS ASSESSMENT QUESTIONNAIRE—cont'd

5. As a parent, my interest in becoming involved with the Head Start Center is:
   - a. ☐ In the classroom working with children
   - b. ☐ In decision-making committees
   - c. ☐ In working with my child and teacher
6. As a parent my special interests are:
   - a. ☐ Working with young children
   - b. ☐ Cooking
   - c. ☐ Typing
   - d. ☐ Working on fund raising activities
   - e. ☐ Planning special occasion parties for the children
   - f. ☐ Planning parent activities
   - g. ☐ Music—playing piano, guitar, other
7. When would be the most convenient time for you to attend parent training and meetings:

	Morning	*Afternoon*	*Evening*
Monday	☐	☐	☐
Tuesday	☐	☐	☐
Wednesday	☐	☐	☐
Thursday	☐	☐	☐
Friday	☐	☐	☐
Weekends	☐	☐	☐

8. At home we speak mostly:
   - a. ☐ Engligh
   - b. ☐ Spanish
   - c. ☐ Both English and Spanish
   - d. ☐ Other (specify)
9. Would you prefer parent meetings, workshops, in-service training held in:
   - a. ☐ English
   - b. ☐ Spanish
10. Which day would be most convenient for you to volunteer to ride the bus or volunteer in the classroom:

	Morning	*Afternoon*
Tuesday	☐	☐
Wednesday	☐	☐
Thursday	☐	☐
Friday	☐	☐

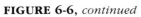

FIGURE 6-6, *continued*

program. At least 50 percent of the membership must be parents of children presently enrolled in Head Start. This committee is responsible for "planning general administration, personnel administration, grant application, and evaluation" (Littlejohn & Associates, 1976, p. 1–2). The Head Start Policy Council may be this same committee if the agency responsible for running the program is also the grantee. If there are two levels involved, that is, the grantee designates another agency to run the program, both levels must have policy councils, formed and run similarly. The essential feature of policy committees and/or policy councils is that guidelines for both require that 50 percent of the membership be composed of parents. This requirement has had immense impact on increased involvement of parents in decision making, not only in the Head Start program but also in programs that followed.

In order to implement the objectives of the parent involvement component of Head Start, parent coordinators were included in the staff. Suggestions for the parent coordinator include the following:

- Give parents a purpose for getting involved.
- Demonstrate the benefits their involvement will bring.
- Plan with them, not for them.
- Develop programs to meet parents' needs as they see them.
- Focus on real problems and concerns, not on abstract theory.
- Recognize parents' knowledge and skills and learn from them. (Littlejohn & Associates, 1976, p. 7–16)

Parent Satisfaction and Participation

A study of 467 Head Start parents (Service Delivery Assessment study as cited in Hubbell, 1983) showed that most parents were very satisfied with the accomplishments their children made in Head Start. A study by the Abt Associates, Cambridge, Massachusetts, found parents pleased with the help Head Start gave them and their children, and 97 percent indicated that they would send their younger children to Head Start (Hubbell, 1983).

Head Start's services to families resulted in high satisfaction for parents. Parents benefitted most from their improvement of life skills, job training, employment, and satisfaction with life (Hubbell, 1983). The more involved the parents, the greater the return. Those parents felt happier, more satisfied, and more successful. It was easier to involve parents who were better educated and had higher salaries than it was to involve other parents. Those who did not participate fully felt less control over their own lives and powerless to influence their child's school (Hubbell, 1983). Another study (Lamb-Parker as cited in Hubbell, 1983) compared the mothers' psychological well-being. Those mothers who participated most had less depression and anxiety. Their trust in others increased too. Those mothers who lived in better housing and who were less depressed, participated more in the Head Start program. These findings point out a problem for all parent programs. Those who are most able, participate the most; those who need the most help, do not participate as fully.

Parent coordinators can help overcome this lack of participation by making a special effort to involve the reticent parent. Show parents that you accept them and their children from the very first day:

- Provide experiences and activities which lead to enhancing the development of their skills, self-confidence, and sense of independence in fostering an environment in which their children can develop to their full potential.
- Provide experiences in child growth and development which will strengthen their role as the primary influence in their children's lives.
- Train parents in observing the growth and development of their children in the home environment and in identifying and handling special developmental needs.

- Help parents understand and use a variety of methods to foster learning and development of their children.
- Include parents in center, classroom, and home program activities.
- Include parents in program planning and curriculum development and have them serve as resource persons.
- Identify and use family and community resources to meet the basic life support needs of the family. (Littlejohn & Associates, 1976, pp. 2–3, 2–6)

Head Start, initially conceived with a parent component, has integrated parents into every aspect of its program. Visualize the degree of parent involvement in the Head Start program. On a visit to a typical Head Start class, you will find a teacher and aide surrounded by 12 eager 3- and 4-year-olds, working, singing, playing, and laughing. Because the center is located in the community, parents usually bring and pick up their children each day. As they enter the school, teacher and parents exchange pleasant greetings. On some days the parents stay and help. The teacher may be a college graduate from another neighborhood, but, just as often, the teacher is a local parent who had children enrolled in the Head Start program several years before. The aide comes up and chats with the parent about something exciting the child did yesterday. The aide knows the child well; she resides in the neighborhood and has children, too. The matron responsible for lunch is another community parent. Busy preparing the food or serving catered meals, the matron begins a career ladder that might see her become a teacher someday. (Through a Head Start career ladder, many low-income parents are hired to assist in the program.) After lunch the parent coordinator drops in to check on a child who has been ill. The parent coordinator was chosen by the policy committee because the parents respected and liked this neighbor. This person has not failed in establishing rapport with and support for the neighbors. Two of the most essential

and greatest strengths of the Head Start philosophy are the involvement of parents and the belief that parents can achieve.

VALIDATED FEDERALLY FUNDED PROGRAMS

Programs that have been validated as exemplary by the Joint Dissemination Review Panel involve parents in a variety of ways. The Richmond, Virginia, Follow Through program is "based on the active involvement of parents in the education of their children. This concept is founded on the premise that patterns of and motives for academic achievement and personal development in primary grade children (K–3) are largely the result of home study influence" (Far West Laboratory, 1983, p. B5-32). Two paraprofessional parent educators are assigned to each Follow Through class. Their time is divided between aiding in the school and visiting the homes of Follow Through children. Each week the classroom teacher demonstrates a home learning activity to the parent educator, who, in turn, teaches the activity to the parent. Ten guiding principles of the teaching-learning process support the teaching behaviors of the teacher and parent. These include using "open-ended questions, positive reinforcements, and the discovery approach to stimulate and expand the intellectual processes of the learner" (Far West Laboratory, 1983, p. B5-32).

Chapter Programs

Chapter programs, federal programs funded under one of several titles, also illustrate innovative use of parents as partners in the educational process. Needs assessments, parent advisory councils, conferences, and home-school activities are included in typical programs. The Child Parent Center program located in Chicago, Illinois, describes its parent involvement:

CPC activity heavily emphasizes parent involvement, recognizing that the parent is the child's first teacher and that home environment and parental attitude toward school influence a child's academic success. A parent-resource teacher is provided to work solely with parents. Parents are trained to instruct their children at home and are also involved in the school program. Potential adopting school districts may be interested in adopting the parent component in conjunction with their existing early childhood program. (Far West Laboratory, 1983, p. B5-9).

In Huntington Beach, California, a Child Development Center identifies developmental needs of children and provides intervention before they enter school. The center is based on the belief that "the sooner educators identify young children's developmental needs and work together with parents to achieve effective intervention, the stronger the chance of children's early success in school" (Far West Laboratory, 1983, p. B5-8).

"Programs that Work" offers innovations that benefit the infant and preschool child as well as the older child.

Developmental Play, a Title III project, uses a unique approach toward children. The program is based on a "relationship-focused activity-based intervention program for young children and a training model in child development and behavior for participating adults" (Far West Laboratory, 1983, p. B5-16). Children and adults are paired; they get to know each other through play and expression of warmth and caring. One half hour of one-to-one child-adult play is followed by group play during "circle time." The program is described in *Finding Your Way to Helping Young Children through Developmental Play*. The basis for this program stems from a belief in human attachment. "Children mature through an intimate or attachment relationship with specific adults. Relationship is everything. Without it, children do not mature and they certainly do not function well in a school setting" (Brody, 1976, p. 1).

These successful programs represent the best in curriculum development. Their concern for parent involvement illustrates the significance of parents in the successful education of their children.

OTHER PROGRAMS THAT WORK

If you want to pursue a study of other programs throughout the United States, purchase the most recent edition of *Educational Programs That Work* from the Far West Laboratory for Educational Research and Development[1] or check with the regional U.S. Department of Education for a copy. In the 1983 edition, 35 programs geared to young children, parent readiness, and parent involvement are described. Ranging from the Added Dimensions to Parent and Preschool Education to the Weeksville School/Bank Street College Follow

---

1. 1855 Folsom Street, San Francisco, CA 94103. For more information write to the Southern Association of Colleges and Schools, 795 Peachtree Street, Atlanta, GA 30308.

Through program, each program is described, and the contact person is listed.

HELPING PARENTS WORK WITH THEIR CHILDREN

In *Tested Ways to Help Your Child Learn* (1963), Warren lists many excellent ideas for parents to use in working with their children or in working with the schools. In the introduction she states:

You will notice, not one of the methods in this book involves parents taking over the job of teacher. Not one sets the parent to work doing complicated mathematics problems or actually teaching the child to read. That is the teacher's job, and unless you have been trained to teach, educators say, you may do your child more harm than good by trying. (p. x)

Warren was reflecting the beliefs of the time. In the 1980s attitudes have changed; parents are encouraged to help their children learn but are cautioned to use productive techniques. Children learn best when they are actively involved. The idea of home-school cooperation does not include viewing the parent as a taskmaster intent on forcing the child to learn. Instead, the parent is viewed as a responsive, alert facilitator. Piaget illustrates this point well. In *To Understand Is to Invent* (also discussed in Chapter 1), Piaget (1976) insists that learning stems from the active involvement of the person doing the inventing; once invented, the theory and/or steps are not forgotten. Piaget recommends:

The use of active methods which give broad scope to the spontaneous research of the child or adolescent and require that every new truth to be learned be rediscovered or at least reconstructed by the student and not simply imparted to him. (pp. 15, 16)

Experiential activities that afford children an opportunity to learn by discovery are facilitated best in a relaxed, natural, and rich learning environment. The setting can be either in the home or in the community. The steps to developing a home learning activity, based on Gordon's program in Florida, reflect the use of the natural environment (Chapter 7). Many of the illustrated ideas for home learning activities can be enjoyed by both parents and children. Most of the summer activities suggested by Saturday School are based on situations and opportunities that emerge or are always present if the parent just takes the time to spend a moment with the child (Figure 6-7). Although the kitchen and workshop activities require special supplies, the activities to do when the sun comes out are based on events or materials available to everyone. Most important is the attitude that learning is possible everywhere for the child.

Resources in the Home

The home is a learning center. Children learn to talk without formal instruction. They learn as they interact with others and participate in exciting events. Learning tasks at home can and should be an intriguing activity rather than difficult paperwork. A parent who reads stories to children is actually teaching reading. The development of an interest in and love of reading is the first step toward acquisition of proficient reading skills. Projects around the home can furnish experiences in math, language, art, music, science, and composition. The process of exploring an idea and carrying it to fruition requires problem solving. Ideas for activities around the home and in the community are restricted only by the imagination.

Activities at Home

Brainstorm for a moment about all the learning opportunities available in a home. Record the ideas to use with your children or to share with parents. The following ideas may lead to many more:

- *Art.* Have tempera paint, crayons, and clay available for spontaneous art projects. Try painting outdoors with water.

FIGURE 6-7
When vacation time comes the Ferguson-Florissant schools send children home with a booklet that explains the purpose of suggested summer activities A B and C illustrate suggested indoor activities; D and E offer ideas for outdoor pursuits. F and G show ideas for math, memory, letters, and language. The final page (not shown here) thanks the parents for their cooperation. (Reprinted with permission from Ferguson-Florissant School District, St. Louis, Mo.)

A

- *Magnifying glass.* Explore the world through a magnifying glass. Look at leaves, dirt, bugs, and any other objects in the yard.
- *Dramatics.* Produce a play. Let the children write or describe the script, as well as plan and design costumes.
- *Circus.* Collect all the circus activities available around your home, yard, or neighborhood. Sell popcorn, lemonade, or peanuts. Imitate circus acts. Pretend household pets are circus animals. Sing, dance, and be merry. If the circus project seems too involved, try a lemonade stand.
- *Start a story.* Begin a story and let the next person continue it. When an easy conclusion comes, let the story end and start another.

- *Write a family newsletter.* Write a cooperative newsletter for the neighborhood or relatives. Make a form with areas for writings by each person or descriptions of each project. Let someone fill in the information.
- *Games.* Take time to play games. The list is long; use commercial games or homemade games such as Concentration, hopscotch, jacks, jump rope, basketball, Ping-Pong, toss a ball, Lotto, Monopoly, Boggle, anagrams, and matching.
- *Garage sale.* Have a garage sale and let your child be the cashier.

Activities Away from Home

Trips away from home can also be adventures.

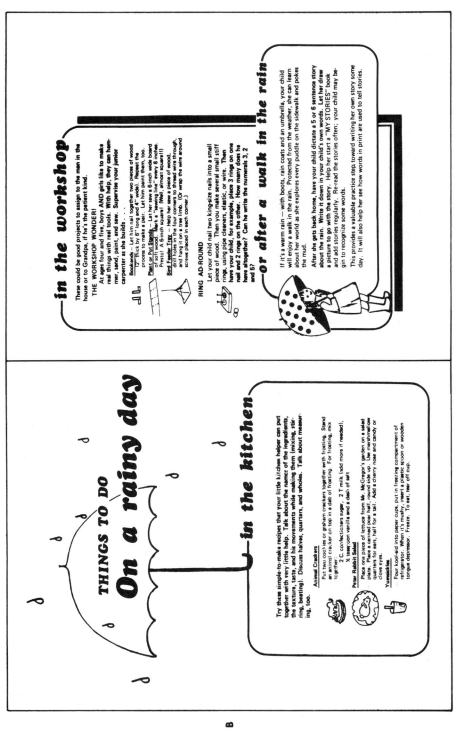

FIGURE 6-7, continued

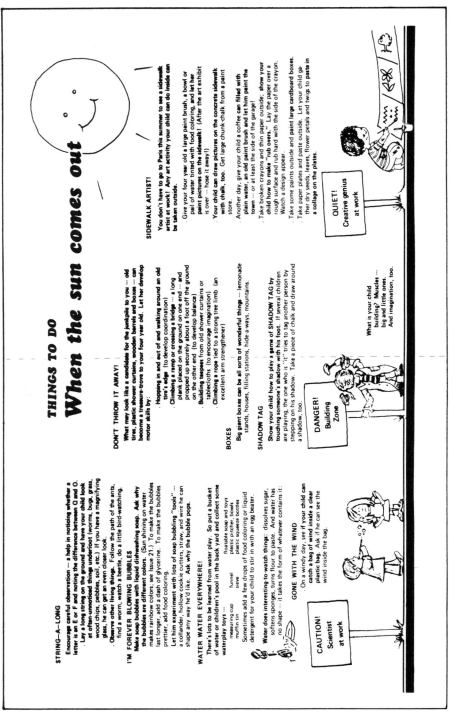

THINGS TO DO
When the sun comes out

STRING-A-LONG

Encourage careful observation — a help in noticing whether a letter is an E or F and noting the difference between Q and O.

· Lay a long string on the ground and have your child look at often-unnoticed things underfoot (worms, bugs, grass, wood chips, pebbles, soil, etc.) If you have a magnifying glass, he can get an even closer look.

· Observe other living things. Follow the path of the ants, find a worm, watch a beetle, do a little bird-watching.

I'M FOREVER BLOWING BUBBLES

Make soap bubbles with liquid dishwashing soap. Ask why the bubbles are different colors. (Sun shining on water makes rainbow colors; see Issue 21.) To make the bubbles last longer, add a dash of glycerine. To make the bubbles prettier, add food coloring.

· Let him experiment with lots of soap bubbling "tools" — a collander, hollow cookie cutters, straw, and wire he can shape any way he'd like. Ask why the bubble pops.

WATER WATER EVERYWHERE!

There's lots to be learned from water play. So put a bucket of water or children's pool in the back yard and collect some waterplay toys —

measuring cup	floatable soap and toys
muffin tin	plastic pitcher, bowls
funnel	plastic squeeze bottles
sieve	

Sometimes add a few drops of food coloring or liquid detergent for your child to stir in with an egg beater.

Water does interesting-to-watch things: dissolves sugar, softens sponges, turns flour to paste. And water has no shape — it takes the form of whatever contains it:

GONE WITH THE WIND

· On a windy day, see if your child can catch a bag of wind inside a clear plastic bag. Ask if he can see the wind inside the bag.

CAUTION!
Scientist at work

DON'T THROW IT AWAY!

What may look like a candidate for the junkpile to you — old tires, plastic shower curtains, wooden barrels and boxes — can become a treasure-trove to your four year old. Let her develop motor skills by:

· Hopping in and out of and walking around an old tire's edge (to develop coordination)

· Climbing a ramp or crossing a bridge — a long plank placed on the ground on one end — and propped up securely about a foot off the ground on the other end (to develop balance)

· Building teepees from old shower curtains or tablecloths (to encourage imagination)

· Climbing a rope tied to a strong tree limb (an excellent arm strengthener)

BOXES

Big giant boxes can be all sorts of wonderful things — lemonade stands, houses, filling stations, hide-a-ways, mountains.

SHADOW TAG

Show your child how to play a game of SHADOW TAG by touching someone's shadow with his foot. If several children are playing, the one who is "it" tries to tag another person by stepping on his shadow. Take a piece of chalk and draw around a shadow, too.

DANGER!
Building Zone

What is your child building? Muscles — big and little ones. And imagination, too.

SIDEWALK ARTIST!

You don't have to go to Paris this summer to see a sidewalk artist at work! Any art activity your child can do inside can be taken outside.

· Give your four year old a large paint brush, a bowl or pail of water tinted with food coloring, and let her paint pictures on the sidewalk! (After the art exhibit is over — hose it away!)

· Your child can draw pictures on the concrete sidewalk with chalk, too. Get large chunk-chalk from a paint store.

· Another day, give your child a coffee can filled with plain water, an old paint brush and let him paint the town — or at least the side of the garage!

· Take broken crayons and thin paper outside; show your child how to make "rub overs." Lay the paper over a rough surface and rub hard with the side of the crayon. Watch a design appear.

· Take some paints outside and paint large cardboard boxes. Take paper plates and paste outside. Let your child gather dry seeds, leaves, flower petals and twigs to paste in a collage on the plates.

QUIET!
Creative genius at work

FIGURE 6-7, *continued*

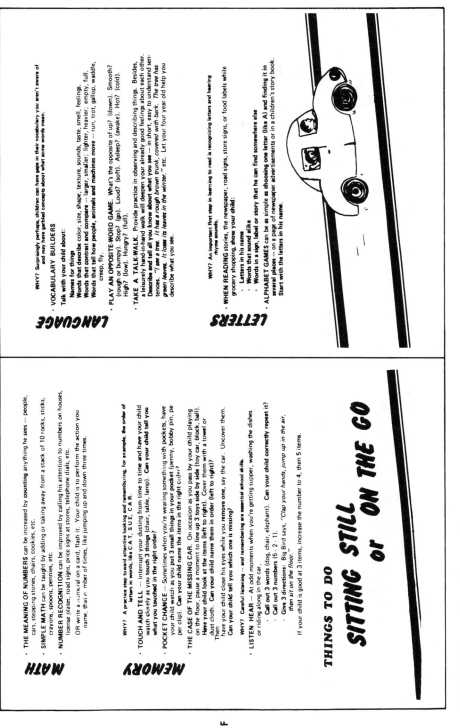

LANGUAGE

WHY? Surprisingly perhaps, children can have gaps in their vocabulary you aren't aware of and may have garbled concepts about what some words mean.

· **VOCABULARY BUILDERS**

Talk with your child about:

Names for things

Words that describe color, size, shape, texture, sounds, taste, smell, feelings.

Words that contrast and compare — larger, smaller; lighter, heavier; empty, full.

Words that tell how people, animals and machines move — run, trot, gallop, waddle, creep, fly.

· **PLAY AN OPPOSITE-WORD GAME.** What's the opposite of up? (down). Smooth? (rough or bumpy). Stop? (go). Loud? (soft). Asleep? (awake). Hot? (cold). High? (low). Hungry? (full).

· **TAKE A TALK-WALK.** Provide practice in observing and describing things. Besides, a leisurely hand-in-hand walk will deepen your already good feelings about each other. Describe and tell all you know about what you see — in short, easy to understand sentences. *"I see a tree. It has a rough brown trunk, covered with bark. The tree has green leaves. It loses its leaves in the winter."* etc. Let your four year old help you describe what you see.

LETTERS

WHY? An important first step in learning to read is recognizing letters and hearing rhyme sounds.

· **WHEN READING** stories, the newspaper, road signs, store signs, or food labels while grocery shopping, show your child:

· Letters in his name
· Words that sound alike
· Words in a sign, label or story that he can find somewhere else

· **ALPHABET GAMES** can be as simple as choosing one letter (like A) and finding it in several places — on a page of newspaper advertisements or in a children's story book. Start with the letters in his name.

MATH

· **THE MEANING OF NUMBERS** can be increased by counting anything he sees — people, cars, stepping stones, chairs, cookies, etc.

· **SIMPLE MATH** can be taught by adding or taking away from a stack of 10 rocks, sticks, crayons, spoons, pennies, etc.

· **NUMBER RECOGNITION** can be improved by calling his attention to numbers on houses, license plates, road signs, price signs at stores, telephone dials, etc.

OR write a numeral on a card, flash it. Your child is to perform the action you name, that is, number of times, like jumping up and down three times.

MEMORY

WHY? A practice step toward attentive looking and remembering, for example, the order of letters in words, like C A T, S U E, C A R.

· **TOUCH AND TELL** — Interrupt your dusting from time to time and have your child watch closely as you touch 3 things (chair, table, lamp). **Can your child tell you what you touched in the right order?**

· **POCKET CHANGE** — Sometimes when you're wearing something with pockets, have your child watch as you put 3 small things in your pocket (penny, bobby pin, paper clip). **Can your child name the items in the right order?**

· **THE CASE OF THE MISSING CAR.** On occasion as you pass by your child playing on the floor, pause a moment to line up 3 toys side by side (toy car, block, ball). **Have your child look at the items** (left to right). Cover them with a towel or dust cloth. **Can your child name them in order (left to right)?**

Then have your child close his eyes while you remove one, say the car. Uncover them. **Can your child tell you which one is missing?**

WHY? Careful listening — and remembering are essential school skills.

· **LISTEN HEAR** — At odd moments when you're getting supper, washing the dishes or riding along in the car.

· Call out 3 words (dog, chair, elephant). **Can your child correctly repeat it?**
· Call out 3 numbers (5 - 2 - 1).
· Give 3 directions: Big Bird says, *"Clap your hands, jump up in the air, then sit on the floor."*

If your child is good at 3 items, increase the number to 4, then 5 items.

THINGS TO DO
SITTING STILL or ON THE GO

FIGURE 6-7, *continued*

215

- *Take a walk.* Collect water from a stream or puddle. Examine the water through a microscope when you return home. Describe or draw the creatures found in a drop of water.
- *Visit the grocery store, post office, department or hardware stores.* Before going to a store, make out your shopping list with your child. Keep it simple. Let the child help with selection and cost of the products. After you get home, figure out if the bill is correct.
- *Explore art, natural history, historical, or specialty museums.* In museums you may find pictures or artifacts that lend themselves to artwork at home. To increase observation powers, let the child look for colors. Choose a configuration. How many circles can the child find? Focus on a color or shape that can help the child observe the pictures or displays.
- *Visit historical buildings.* Take along your paper, pen, and crayons. Engage in art activities as you visit. Draw the shape of the building. Make a crayon rubbing of the placard that tells about the building's dedication.
- *Garage sale.* Visit garage sales and figure how many articles you could buy for $5 or $10.

Using activities that are intriguing and exciting benefits the family in two ways: (1) learning is accomplished and (2) the parent-child relationship is enhanced. Parents need to know the importance of a rich home environment; they need to be reinforced for their positive teaching behaviors. Although good times together may be reinforcement enough, schools can help support productive parent-child interaction by encouraging parents, offering workshops, and supplying home learning activities.

Workshops for Parents

A workshop is one vehicle for introducing parents to home-school learning activities. Ann

Grimes, first grade teacher, invited the parents of her students to such a workshop. She greeted them, gave out nametags, and passed out a get-acquainted signature sheet (Chapter 5). The evening went by quickly. After the signature game, during which parents enthusiastically talked with one another, the make-and-take workshop began. Mrs. Grimes explained the program, its philosophy, and what the school expected of the parents. She assured the parents that close two-way communication helps ensure that the program is meeting the needs of the child, parent, and school. If parents were interested in participating in a home-school learning project, she assured them that she would like to work with them as a member of the team.

Mrs. Grimes reminded the parents of how important it is to listen to children, to ask open-ended questions, and to allow the children the opportunity to predict and problem solve. She also reminded the parents that children, like adults, work best when they have a nice, quiet, private work area and a regular time in which to work. She stressed that children are expected to enjoy and be successful at home assignments. If the child fails more than 20 percent of the projects or problems, reassessment of the activities enables the selection of appropriate activities geared to the child's level. Many home activities can be recreational and enriching to family life. As she concluded her talk, she explained the plans for the evening. Parents were asked to participate in the center activities located in different areas throughout the room. "If you will look at your nametag, you will find a number. Go to that activity first," she instructed the parents.

The centers in the room included games and activities as well as directions on how to play them. Materials and guidelines were also available for activities that could be constructed by parents and taken home. Parents played Concentration (Figure 7-2, *C*), and made game boards. They found that game boards could be constructed easily on cardboard, posterboard, or a file folder. Mrs. Grimes furnished stickers that the parents could place on the game boards for decoration. To protect the completed board, some parents used the laminating machine, and others spread contact paper over their work. Each board was different, yet each was based on the same format, that is, squares on which the children placed symbols as they used a spinner or die to tell them how many spaces to go forward. Some parents wrote letters or numbers on the spaces; others developed cards that children could take as they had a turn. If the spaces were left empty, the board could be used for many skill activities by developing sets of cards for phonics, numbers, or other basic skills. Figure 6-8 illustrates a completed game board that can be used to develop many different skills. While some parents were busy with the game boards, others worked on language and math concepts, constructed books, or plied their creativity at the art center.

After a busy 2-hour session the group met again, and an animated discussion of the activities began. Two parents volunteered to make canvas "tote bags" for the class, and another promised to make a silk-screen print of the class emblem on each. They decided that the "tote bags" would be reserved for home learning adventures.

"Please be sure to evaluate the home learning activities as you use them. And, please contribute your own ideas," encouraged Mrs. Grimes. "I'll keep track of each child's activities on these record sheets. If you have any questions, be sure to write or call me."

After refreshments the parents began to leave. Some stopped by the table to sign up to volunteer in the program. Mrs. Grimes recognized that she would need help in implementing the home learning program and that she could use help in the room as well. A volunteer training session was planned for the next week; the work toward a productive home-school endeavor had just begun.

Implementation of Home Learning Activities

Home learning activities can be useful as enrichment projects, such as those described above in the section Activities at Home, or they can be valuable as a sequential educational curriculum. If they are used to complement the learning that is occurring simultaneously in the school, it is necessary to monitor the child's work at home and, thereby, keep track of what is accomplished.

The process varies according to the availability of a parent coordinator. If parent coordinators are available, it will be their responsibility to keep track of the home learning activities. They can contact parents, make home visits, and report on the progress of each child. It is the teacher's responsibility to advise the parent coordinator about the child's progress in school and to recommend appropriate learning activities. If a parent coordinator is not available, a parent volunteer can help with record keeping and provide contact between the parents and the teacher. The following steps are appropriate for either situation:

1. Offer an orientation workshop.
2. Send learning activities home in a "tote bag," deliver them personally, or give the responsibility of the delivery system to a parent coordinator.
3. Keep records of activity cards the child has taken home. Make a record card for each child with a space to indicate when each activity went home and a space for response to the activity. In this way you will know which activity the child should be given next.
4. Get feedback from parents via notes, reports, phone calls, or visits. Find out their reactions to the activities and their assessments of their child's success.
5. Continue dialogue with parents. Include supplemental ideas and activity sheets on a skill that proved difficult for a particular

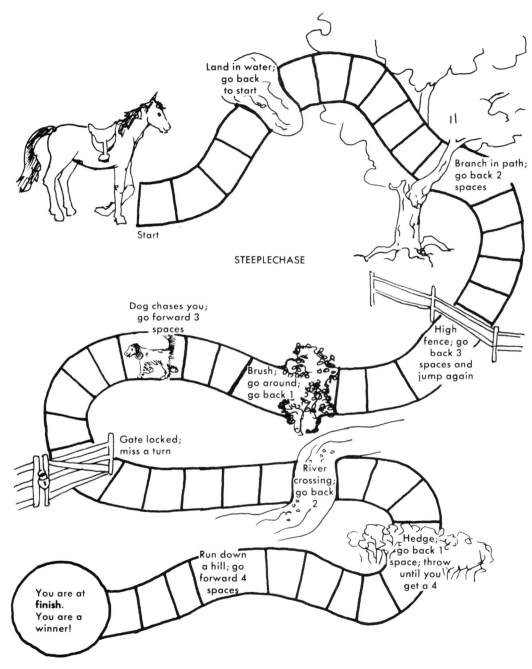

Land in water;
go back
to start

Branch in path;
go back 2
spaces

Start

STEEPLECHASE

High
fence; go
back 3
spaces and
jump again

Dog chases you;
go forward 3
spaces

Brush;
go around;
go back 1

Gate locked;
miss a turn

River
crossing;
go back
2

Hedge;
go back 1
space; throw
until you
get a 4

Run down
a hill; go
forward 4
spaces

You are at
finish.
You are a
winner!

FIGURE 6-8

A steeplechase sets the theme for this game board. Children can suggest their special
interests, and games can be developed from their ideas.

student. Ask parents to reinforce skills leading up to the "missed" level. Have them refer to previous activity cards for readiness projects.

6. Diversify your program to meet the needs of the parents and keep the interest level high.

7. Have an occasional meeting with parents or make home visits to support the monitoring system.

Communication is a basic ingredient in the success of home-school cooperation. Through talking with parents, you will know whether they consider home learning activities to be a joy or a threat. You will want to adapt your program according to each parent's desires.

REACHING RETICENT PARENTS

Perseverance, patience, and true interest in the parent are the three best ingredients to overcome parent reticence. Understanding, support, and interest will usually encourage the retiring parent to take that first step toward collaborating with the teacher for the good of the child. In every situation, a few parents may refuse to be involved. Some may have serious social adjustment problems and need profes-

sional help in that area. One difficult parent or one bad experience should not color the home visitor or teacher's commitment of working with others. Teachers should not expect to be 100 percent successful. Do what can be done and acknowledge possible inability to reach all parents. Do this with grace, understanding, and no recriminations. Work with the children and involve the parents who want to be involved.

If you follow the ideas presented in Chapter 4, you will probably have no difficulty in communicating with parents. Remember, a call from the teacher or home visitor should not always mean that a child is in trouble. If good communication and support has been established, that call could mean that the child is terrific.

Involving parents may be difficult because of the following reasons:

1. *Families and parents may be under a lot of stress.* Problems can range from lack of money, illness of a loved one, unemployment, to an argument with a friend. In our high-charged society, many parents are under stress. It is possible that they cannot be actively involved at the time of hardship. They should not be made to feel guilty. Let them know you are supportive and whenever they want to be

Teachers enrich their school programs by collaborating with parents.

more actively involved, they may. Keep communication open through telephone calls.

2. *Many hard-to-reach parents feel out of their element whether coming to school or receiving home visitors*. They are not sure of themselves. They do not have confidence in their own ideas, or they feel that someone else will not value them. They need their self-esteem raised. If they have the time, let them contribute in a small way. Accept their ideas. Enlist their help in an activity at which they will succeed. Build slowly; it takes time to make a change.

3. *The parents do not recognize their importance in the education of their child*. Many parents, both those in special programs such as Home Start and Head Start, and those who live in very affluent areas do not recognize their importance as an educator. Their interest and involvement are important to the child. Starting with parent-teacher conferences or home visits, the teacher needs to reflect that the parent is a true partner. The parents' knowledge about the child is important; they are the best experts on their child. Their interaction with the child is part of the child's education.

4. *"The parent doesn't believe anyone has no ulterior motives"* (Honig, 1979, p. 58). According to Honig, these parents do not believe that anyone can value their ideas. Trust will build slowly. Find out the parents' goals and help them accomplish them.

5. *In working with parents, you need to know them well*. Be able to suggest projects and activities that lend themselves to the capabilities of the parent. In one program where a home visitor was working with an abusive parent, it was suggested that the child was not using the right arm enough. At the next week's class, the home visitor found bruises up and down the child's arm. The parent, who was concerned about the teacher's comment, was "developing" the child's arm! This may seem extreme, but the response was geared to the parent's ability to cope with everyday problems. The parent actually wanted the child to do well. Some parents cannot work well with their children or help

with school work. They become frustrated and angry; the child responds with dejection and hurt. Rather than helping the child, the parent creates a battleground.

In working with reticent parents, develop effective strategies. Honig (1979) suggested the use of a 24-hour Crisis Center with project staff, perhaps psychiatric interns, recruited to give telephone counseling, reassurance, and referrals. A second idea was a retreat house in the countryside where families could go and, under the guidance of a staff, discuss and learn as well as have fun and food. Honig's third suggestion described a workshop where, working together, new trust could be promoted (p. 58).

It is helpful to have training sessions for parents where techniques and suggestions for working positively with the child are discussed. The STEP and PET programs give methods for communicating with children (Chapter 5). These programs have planned programs for parents. *Parents' Magazine* filmstrips and *Active Parenting* and *Parents as Resources* videotapes also illustrate parenting skills and parents as teachers. These resources can serve as a guide in setting up sessions on working with children. Parents also learn through modeling. Aiding in the classroom can be an effective learning experience. Methods of teaching that provide for observation, demonstration, and role playing prove useful. Parents, like children, learn best through active participation.

Prevention is better than a cure. That is why it is important to reach reticent parents when their children are young. If parents can be involved from the start, their resistance to programs and partnerships can be reduced or eliminated.

PARENT EDUCATION FOR TEEN-AGERS

A powerful time for reaching new parents and parents-to-be is during adolescence. The alarming rise in the number of teen-age pregnancies and the lack of parenting education directed to that age group prompted funding for development of appropriate curricula for teen-age students and passage of the Adolescent Health, Services, and Pregnancy Prevention and Child Care Act of 1978. Since that time many schools have responded by offering programs for young mothers that include daycare for the children and special classes for the parents.

Between 1971 and 1979 the number of premarital pregnancies for teen-agers doubled from 8 to 16 percent. During the same period the number of premarital pregnant women who married prior to the birth of their baby decreased from 33 to 16 percent (Thornton & Freedman, 1983). In 1982 there were 715,200 births to unmarried women. Approximately 8,700 of these births were to children under 15 years of age; 260,600 were to unmarried teen-agers, 15 to 19 years of age. These figures reflect two trends. First, the number of pregnancies for very young mothers under the age of 15 has been declining; the numbers reduced from 11,000 in 1975 to 8,700 in 1982. The second is an increase in pregnancies among teen-agers, 15 to 19 years of age; these numbers increased from 222,500 in 1975 to a high of 262,800 in 1980 at which time the number leveled. At the same time, teen-agers, aged 15 to 19, had more abortions, which increased from 325,000 in 1975 to 433,000 in 1981 (U.S. Bureau of the Census, 1985).

The number of births to teen-agers increases when figures for married teen-agers are included. In the group of mothers 15 to 17 years of age, 57.4 percent were unmarried when their child was born; 24.2 percent of the babies were premaritally conceived, and 18.4 percent were postmaritally conceived. Older teen-agers are more likely to be married prior to having their first baby. In the group of 18- and 19-year-old mothers, 36.3 percent were married at the time of conception, 24.1 percent married prior to birth, and 39.6 percent were unmarried when their child was born.

These figures point out the large number of young parents, married and unmarried, who need parent education. This need was felt during the 1970s when a hearing before the Committee on Human Resources drew many professionals together to express their concern. The data collected at that time stated that nearly 20 percent of all adolescent girls face pregnancy and its associated problems each year. Lack of education makes assuming financial responsibilities more difficult for the young parent. Alarmingly, 25 percent of these young mothers became pregnant again within 1 year (Hearings before Committee on Human Resources, 1978). Half of the pregnant teenagers between 15 and 17 years of age received no prenatal health care until the second trimester of their pregnancies and 6 percent received no prenatal care at all. Teen-age mothers run a greater risk of producing infants with neurological problems, mental retardation, or an infectious disease. Additionally, there is a higher mortality rate for baby and mother (Osofsky & Osofsky, 1979 as cited in Teen Parents Project). Low birth weight of the infant occurs in 6 to 20 percent of pregnancies of young girls. Studies indicate that low birth weight, with its accompanying medical problems, is related to the gynecologic age of the mother. The gynecologic age is computed from time of menarche. Some investigators have found that a higher incidence of low birth weight is found in the group of mothers less than 2 years beyond menarche (Hearing before Committee on Human Resources, 1978). These figures and other impressive data supported the establishment of "a program for developing networks of community-based services to prevent initial and repeated pregnancies among adolescents, to provide care to pregnant adolescents, and to help adolescents become productive independent contributors to family and community life" (Hearing before Committee on Human Resources, 1978, preface).

Over the years individual school systems have developed excellent family life programs for their students, usually in home economics and sociology classes. Schools are beginning to recognize that human development courses and child care experiences are an essential part of the curriculum. In addition, schools are mandated to allow pregnant girls to attend classes. Title IX of the Education Amendments of 1972 prohibits their exclusion from any school receiving federal money on the basis of pregnancy or related conditions (Population Reference Bulletin, 1976). As indicated earlier in this chapter, only 25 percent of teen-age mothers graduate despite this ruling. Some schools, through child care centers, allow new parents in their student bodies to bring their children to school with them. Such schools are facing the realities and needs of the time and establishing a child care laboratory in the process. Bolstered by encouragement and understanding and equipped with knowledge of parenting skills, the young parents are better able to care for their infants. Teen-agers without these opportunities and without positive models in their own homes face the enormous task of child rearing unprepared. Expectations by some young parents for their infant's development are often unreasonable; for example, some teen-agers believe that infants should be completely toilet trained by 8 months. Understanding and knowledge of child development smooth the way for effective child rearing. Providing support and mechanisms that allow teen-agers to become self-sufficient parents is essential. The problems are evident; teen-age parents need special attention, skillful direction, and sensitive support.

Curriculum Development

A funding approach by the Department of Health, Education, and Welfare in the 1970s was three-pronged. One program, *Exploring Childhood*, developed by the Education Development Center, has specific curricula for junior and senior high students. The second, *Exploring Parenting*, has 20 sessions for par-

ent education groups. The sessions range from Getting Involved in Your Child's World to Coping with Fear and Child's Play (U.S. Department of Health and Human Services, 1980). In addition, *Education for Parenthood—Curriculum and Evaluation Guide* uses the wisdom and experience of organizations that have traditionally worked with youth—that is, Boy Scouts of America, Boys' Club of America, National 4-H Club Foundation of America, Girl Scouts of USA, National Federation of Settlements and Neighborhood Centers, Salvation Army, and Save the Children Federations—to develop a resource book for use by agencies and schools in working with young parents. The third component was the establishment of a Parent/Early Childhood and Special Program center for resources and help in the development of individualized programs across the nation.

The first component, *Exploring Childhood*, divides the curricula into three modules: family and society, seeing development, and working with children. Each module has booklets, films, posters, records, cassettes, filmstrips, and records to support parts of the curricula. The techniques and materials are shown in Figure 6-9. By examining the titles within each module, you may see the development of a curriculum that illustrates family life, the development of children, and how to work with children.

School Programs for Young Parents

Agnes, age 15, is pregnant. Her mother is not aware of the impending birth, and Agnes, in tears, confides to her friend at school. Where should she turn? Mary, age 14 and pregnant, wants to marry her boyfriend, Tom, also 14. Tom is still in school. "If I quit," he says, "where will I get a job? Are you sure you want to have the baby?" Problems and early teenage pregnancies go hand in hand. The young teen-ager who lives in a city with adequate facilities and programs geared to the young mother is very fortunate. If Agnes and Mary lived in Albuquerque, they could attend the New Futures School for school-age parents, a program geared for young mothers, grades 8 through 12. Daycare for the children is provided while the young mothers attend classes. The program also provides health services, instruction in health care, nutrition, family living, child development, family planning, and homemaking (Hearings Before Committee on Human Resources, 1978).

Planned Parenthood and public health departments offer additional support systems for the young parent. Health departments are also available to schools as educational resources. Working together, these programs offer the support system needed by young parents.

Opposition to School Involvement

A major deterrent to the widespread success of parent education and family life courses is public opposition to teaching values in the schools. State legislators, concerned with the rising number of teen-age pregnancies and the high divorce rate among young people, have presented bills that would require family life education. Such bills, however, have been defeated by fear of and opposition to such courses. The perennial question of responsibility emerges. Should the school step in and require programs, or are parents responsible for teaching their children about sex and family life? At which level should programs be implemented? A surprising number of elementary school students are becoming pregnant. Elective courses in family life tend to be accepted by the public; sex education for younger children faces brisk opposition. If parents are shown the material to be presented and are given the right to determine whether their child should participate, the sex education program usually wins approval.

Schools and social agencies do not oppose parent involvement in the education of the child in family life, sex education, or child rearing. Instead, they applaud such efforts. The stalemate exists, however, because many

Young children need parents who understand their growth and development.

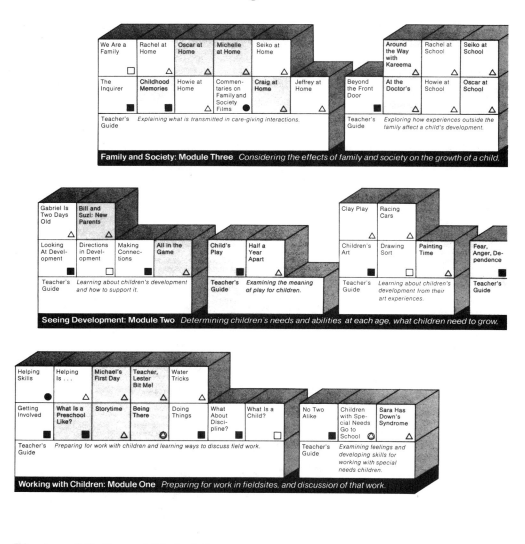

Display of Units and Materials

Key

■ Booklet	△ Film	Filmstrip ◓ and Record
□ Poster	● Record	
☑ Cards	▲ Cassette	

FIGURE 6-9

The basic curriculum and material available for implementation of the Exploring Childhood program. (*Source:* Exploring Childhood. *Program overview and catalog of materials.* Education Development Center, Newton, Mass., 1979.)

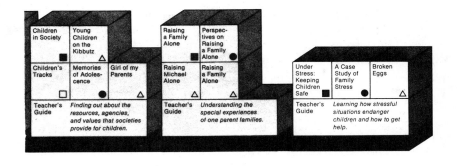

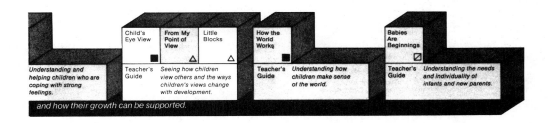

Classroom Set
(Full Year Course Selection)

Supplementary Materials

Individual items of print and media are arranged into three modules for classroom use. The white boxes represent items included in the "classroom set" as listed on page 34.

FIGURE 6-9, *continued*

parents do not assume the responsibility or feel comfortable doing so, yet they are unwilling to let the schools assume it. The problem continues; its solution is thwarted by a vicious circle of fear, inaction, apathy, and resistance.

Perhaps in the future the crisis will be met by enlightened school districts, clubs, churches, parents, and agencies such as those who prepared the *Education for Parenthood* program. Three outcomes, although possible, seem improbable:

1. Citizens will recognize the problems and educate themselves and their children.
2. Schools will be mandated to provide family life and sex education.
3. Schools will make family life and child-rearing courses so exciting and relevant to the students' lives that the students will insist on taking them.

None of these outcomes looks as though it will be realized in the near future. Schools, however, can and are developing courses that are attracting a number of secondary students; other agencies also are responding to the challenge.

MAKING PROGRAMS HAPPEN

"How can parent programs be started?" This question can be answered from two different approaches, both related to financing. Funding can be obtained to initiate a parent program, or the individual district, school, or teacher can design a program with or without financial support.

Funding

Funding for school-related programs primarily comes from three major sources, that is, federal and state grants, private foundations, and local school budgets. A public school's budget is based on local taxes and state distribution of funds. Private schools rely primarily on tuition and private sources to provide their budgets although some grants from federal moneys can be obtained. Current information on funding and grant possibilities can be obtained from your regional Department of Education or Department of Health and Human Services.

The most stable funding source for public schools is the local school board. As schools begin to view the parent component as worthwhile or essential, more programs will be implemented and funded through local support. The Parent Education Demonstration Project found that local support increased as the parent programs proved themselves. Private foundations also fund special projects for parents and children. Local businesses and foundations are probably the best source of funds and/or information on moneys available in your community.

Most grants are provided for a particular time period, usually 3 years. If the program is dependent on the extra grant funding, plans must be made for financing after the grant runs out, or the program will either deteriorate or no longer exist. The major importance of grants is the impetus they provide for developing programs, materials, and services. Many programs, now a permanent part of the community, were started on grants. Try to obtain funding and grants, but if your efforts are not rewarded, consider parent involvement as an integral part of the school program and develop your unique approach to fulfill the potential partnership. Using volunteers in a positive, useful way can help the teacher and enable the school to enrich its educational offerings. Volunteers can be an alternative to funding in making programs happen.

VOLUNTEERS

Have you ever wondered why some teachers have extra help around their schools while you struggled valiantly by yourself? One answer lies in the recruitment of volunteers and the subsequent interaction with them. With 53 percent of parents employed, a large number of parents will not be able to volunteer during working hours, but with 47 percent occupied primarily with home management, many are able to volunteer. The cup is half full rather than half empty. Parents want the best for their children; most will respond to an opportunity to volunteer if the options for working are varied and their contributions are meaningful. When both parents work, short-term commitments geared to their working hours will allow and encourage participation from this group. Although the world is a busy place, time spent at school can bring satisfaction and variety to a parent's life.

Volunteers: Used or User?

Volunteerism has been criticized by some as inequitable and an exploitation of "woman power." Try to choose volunteers who can afford the time, or allow busy parents to contribute in such a way that they enjoy the time away from their other obligations. If education and training are included in your volunteer program, the participants can gain personally from the experience. For many, volunteering in school may be the first step toward a career.

If you are alert to the needs of your parents, using them as volunteers can become a means of helping their families. If you work with them over a period of time, listen and use your knowledge of community resources to support the families in solving their problems. Volunteerism should serve the volunteer as well as contribute to the school.

Who Should Ask for Volunteers?

Although all teachers can benefit from the services of volunteers, teachers should determine the extent to which they are ready to use assistance. Volunteer programs vary in their scope and design. Individual teachers may solicit volunteers from among parents; individual schools can support a volunteer program; or school districts can implement a volunteer program for the total system.

The opportunity to volunteer can be beneficial to the teacher as well as to the volunteer.

A teacher who has not used aides, assistants, or volunteers should probably start with help in one area before expanding and recruiting volunteers for each hour in the week. In preschools, the free-choice or free-work period is a natural time to have added assistance. In elementary schools assistance during art projects is often a necessity. Add to this initial use of volunteer help by securing extra tutors for reading class. In secondary schools recruitment for a special project provides an excellent initial contact.

Easing into use of volunteers may not be necessary in your school. Since most preschools and primary grades have used assistance for many years, their teachers are ready for more continuous support from volunteers. Yet involving other persons in the classroom program is an art, based on good planning and the ability to work with and to supervise others. Successful involvement of a few may lay the groundwork for greater involvement of others at a later time.

Recruitment of Volunteers by Individual Teachers

Many teachers have been successful in implementing their own volunteer programs from among the parents of their students. If you have used volunteers previously and parents in the community have heard about your program from other parents, recruitment may be easy. Early in the year, an evening program where the curriculum is explained and parents get acquainted is an effective time to recruit parents into the program. If parents have not been exposed to volunteerism, encourage them to visit the room and give them opportunities to participate in an easy activity such as reading a story to a child or playing a game with a group while they are visiting. Ask them back for an enjoyable program so that they begin to feel comfortable in the room. Sharing their hobbies with the children introduces many parents to the joys of teaching. Gradually the fear of classroom involvement will disappear, and parents may be willing to spend several hours each week with the children in the classroom.

Invitations to Visit School That Work. Suppose you have written parents notes or have published an invitation to visit school in the newsletter, but nobody comes. If this has happened to you, you need a "parent-getter." Judge your activity and invitation by the following questions:

1. Does the event sound as though it is enjoyable?
2. Is there something in it for the parents?
3. Are the parents' children involved in the program?
4. Does the program have alternate times for attendance?

The first criterion should be met by the wording of the invitation. The second and third vary in importance; one or the other should be answered in each bid for parent attendance. Scheduling alternate times depends on your parents' needs.

Recently a teacher mentioned that her school had parents who just were not interested in helping. Only three had volunteered when they were asked to clean up the playyard. When asked if there were any other enticements for the parents to volunteer to help, the teacher answered, "No." "Would you have wanted to spend your Saturday morning cleaning up the playground?" she was asked. As the teacher thought about the invitation, she recognized that she would not have participated either if she had been one of the parents. An excellent means of determining the drawing power of a program or activity is your own reaction to the project. Would you want to come? Had the Saturday cleanup project included the children, furnished refreshments, and allowed time for a get-together after the work was completed, the turnout would have been much better. Make it worth the parents' time to volunteer.

Performances. Many schools have children perform in order to get parents to turn out. The ploy works; parents attend! Some professionals discourage this method because they believe that children are being exploited to attract parents. However, it is probably the manner in which the production is conceived and readied rather than the child's involvement that is unworthy. What are your memories of your childhood performances? If the experiences were devastating, was it the programs themselves or the way they were handled that led to disappointment? If the performance is a creative, worthwhile experience for the child and does not cause embarrassment, heartache, or a sense of rejection for the child who does not perform well and if all children are included, this method of enticing parents can be valuable for both the child and parents. Experience in front of an audience can lead to poise, heightened self-concept, and pleasure for the child. Parents invited to unpolished programs enjoy the visit just as much as if they had attended refined productions. Small, simple classroom functions, held often enough so that every child has a moment in the limelight, are sure to have high parent turnouts. The more parents come to school and get involved with the activities, the better chance you have of recruiting assistance.

Field Trips. Use a field trip to talk with parents about volunteering in the classroom. Parents will often volunteer for field trips, during which teacher and parent can find time to chat. See if the parents' interests include hobbies that can be shared with the class. Be receptive to any ideas or needs that parents reveal. The informal atmosphere of a field trip encourages parents to volunteer.

Hobby Week. Miller and Wilmshurst (1975) suggested a hobby week as one successful method of involving parents. During this time, parents share their hobbies with the children. The invitation, sent to the home, has a tear-off portion at the bottom of the page on which the parents respond with hobby, agreeable time period, and space required. Each parent is scheduled into the week at a time convenient for parent and teacher. If possible, a follow-up in class of the ideas presented will make the week even more meaningful. Following the presentations, thank-you notes from the teacher with suggestions that parents might come to class again become a means of recruiting potential volunteers.

Workshops. A make-and-take workshop effectively fulfills the second criterion (Is there something in it for the parent?). Parents enjoy both being involved and taking home a product. If the make-and-take workshop offers a choice of curriculum-based tasks, such as constructing game boards, bookmaking, or fashioning the components for home learning activities, you can fulfill two objectives. Parents are helping to expand resources for the school, and parents are learning to develop activities for the home.

Workshops, based on learning centers, are effective learning experiences for parents. Through active participation in the child's curriculum, the parent better understands the school's educational program. An open invitation to help with learning centers can be issued, and those who are especially interested are invited back for a specific time. The experience of doing the activities first gives the parent the confidence to attempt to help the students. Workshops fulfill the first two criteria listed; use them to get parents involved.

Invitations to share. Sending home invitations with the children that ask parents if they are interested in volunteering is a direct way to recruit. Each teacher should design the invitation to fit the needs of the class. A letter that accompanies the form should stress to parents how important they are to the program. Let them know the following:

- Teachers and children need their help.
- Each parent is already experienced in working with children.
- Their child will be proud of the parents' involvement and will gain through their contributions.
- Volunteers can work in an area where they feel comfortable and productive. (Modified from Miller & Wilmshurst, 1975, p. 7)

Friendly requests along with suggestions enable parents to respond easily. School want ads, modified from the volunteer notice of Hawthorne School, Boise, Idaho, suggest needs and request contributions (Figure 6–10).

Other programs design a recruitment flyer, which lists specific activities that the parent checks. Be sure to ask parents for their ideas and contributions. You have no way of knowing what useful treasures you may find! Let parents complete a questionnaire, such as the one in Figure 6–11 to indicate their interests and time schedules. Perhaps one parent cannot visit school but is willing to make calls

TIME TO SHARE

Situations Wanted

I have the following talents, skills, interests that I would like to share:

_____

_____

_____

Position Available

Tutor wanted to help with reading class.

_____

Room mother needed to work with teacher. Light duties. Help serve three classroom parties annually. Goodies provided by PTO.

_____

Give an hour a week (or more) to help children improve their skills. Excellent teacher supervision available.

_____

Situation Wanted

I have no particular talents, but I would like to help. Please call me.

_____

Off-Broadway Talent Scout

Now hiring persons interested in assisting with theater production: direction, makeup, costumes, etc.

_____

Big Building Boom!

Donate your carpentry skills.

_____

Working Parents Special

Spend 3 hours on a Saturday afternoon assisting with a PTO carnival. Sell candy, popcorn, cider, etc.

_____

Please check any of the above ads that interest you. Fill in your name, address, and telephone number and return this sheet to school with your child PROMPTLY. Thank you for your involvement.

Name _____ Phone _____ _____
                                                                Principal
Address _____
                                                    Volunteer coordinator
Available: AM ____ PM ____

FIGURE 6-10
Solicit school volunteers through a want ad. (*Source:* modified from *Notebook for Boise school volunteers.* Boise, Idaho: The Independent School District of Boise City, 1978.)

and coordinate the volunteer program. This parent can find substitutes when regular parent volunteers, who must be absent, call in. Others who are homebound can aid the class by sharing baby-sitting, making games and activities at home, writing newsletters, and telephoning. Parents who are able to work at school can perform both teaching and non-teaching tasks. Relate the task to the parent's interests. Nothing is as discouraging to some

PLEASE SHARE WITH THE SCHOOL

Dear Parents:

We need volunteers to help us with our school program. You can share your time by helping while you are at home or at school. If you want to share in any way, please let us know.

Are you interested in volunteering this year? _____Yes _____ No

Check the ways you want to help.

_____In the classroom
_____In the resource center
_____At home

WHAT WOULD YOU LIKE TO DO?

_____Share your hobby or travel experience   _____Tell stories
_____Help children in learning centers   _____Check papers
_____Be a room mother   _____Check spelling
_____Work in resource room   _____Help with math
_____Supervise a puppet show   _____Read to children
_____Go on field trips   _____Make games
_____Babysit for others   _____Listen to children read
_____Substitute for others   _____Play games with children
_____Supervise learning center   _____Make books
_____Tutor reading   _____Share your recipes

Any other suggestions? _____

_____

Comments _____

When can you come?

	Monday	Tuesday	Wednesday	Thursday	Friday
	AM | PM	AM | PM	AM | PM	AM | PM	AM | PM

Name _____ Telephone _____

FIGURE 6-11
Questionnaires are one way to obtain parents' interests and time schedules.

volunteers as to be forced to do housekeeping tasks continually with no opportunity for interaction with the children. The choice of tasks should not be difficult, however, because the opportunities are numerous and diversified as the following lists indicate:

- **Teaching tasks**
  Tutor
  Supervise learning centers
  Listen to children
  Play games with students
  Tell stories
  Play instructional games
  Work with underachievers or learning disabled students
  Help select library books for children
  Teach children to type
  Help children prepare and practice speeches
  Help children improve handwriting

Take children to resource center
Read to children
Help children create a play
Supervise the making of books
Show filmstrips
Supervise the production of a newsletter or
  newspaper
Assist in learning centers
Share a hobby
Speak on travel and customs around the world
Demonstrate sewing or weaving
Demonstrate food preparation

- **Nonteaching tasks**
Make games for class
Prepare parent bulletin board
Repair equipment
Select and reproduce articles for resource
  room
Record grades
Take attendance
Collect lunch money
Plan workshop for parents
Prepare worksheets
Run off material on copier
Grade and correct papers
Straighten cupboards

- **Contributions from home**
Serve as telephone chairperson
Collect recycling materials
Furnish refreshments
Furnish dress-up clothes and costumes
Wash aprons
Make art aprons
Repair equipment
Make games
Baby-sit
Write newsletters
Coordinate volunteers

Teaching embraces creative ideas and
methods; volunteers, responding to the challenge, can provide a vast reservoir of talent
and support.

Management Techniques
Use management skill in organizing and implementing your volunteer program. A parent

coordinator can be very helpful in developing
effective communication between teacher and
parent. Two charts, time schedules and volunteer action sheets, clarify the program and
help it run more smoothly.

Time Schedules.   Time schedules can be adjusted if weekly charts are both posted and
sent home. When parents can visualize the
coverage, the class will not be inundated by
help in one session and suffer from lack of
help in another.

Volunteer Sheet.   Because volunteers are
used in a variety of ways, developing an action
sheet that describes each person's contribution is helpful. Figure 6-12 illustrates the scope
of involvement within one classroom. With
this list the parent coordinator can secure an
effective substitute for someone who must be
absent. If the teacher needs games constructed,
the parent coordinator can call on the parents
who have volunteered for that activity. Special
help at a learning center or with a student project can be found by calling one of the parents
who has indicated an interest in helping in
these ways. The responsibility for the volunteer program does not need to rest solely on
the teacher's shoulders. Parents and teachers
become partners in developing a smoothly
working system.

Increasing Volunteer Usage
Although permanent volunteers are more effective in establishing continuity in a program
than periodic contributions by occasional volunteers, both are needed. As the year progresses, some parents may find that they enjoy
teaching immensely. These parents may extend their time obligation and, in doing so,
will bring more continuity to the program.
Ideally, an assistant should tutor a reading
group or a child for several sessions each week
rather than just one. When initiating a program, it is better to start out with easily handled time slots and enlarge the responsibilities
of the parents after they become secure and fa-

Name	Telephone	Classroom regularly	Classroom substitute	Special presen-tation	Babysit	Make games at home	Work in resource center Help students	Develop resources Type	Develop resources Make games
Names of volunteers	555-5555	X							X
" "	"		X	X					
" "	"		X	X					
" "	"	X		X					
" "	"		X	X		X			
" "	"	X				X			
" "	"				X	X			
" "	"						X	X	
" "	"	X							
" "	"	X							
" "	"	X		X					
" "	"						X	X	X
" "	"	X							
" "	"			X		X		X	X
" "	"				X				
" "	"		X						
" "	"		X						
" "	"		X			X			
" "	"		X						
" "	"		X			X			
" "	"				X				
" "	"				X				
" "	"			X	X				
" "	"		X						
" "	"					X			
" "	"		X				X	X	X
" "	"		X						
" "	"		X		X				
" "	"		X	X					

FIGURE 6-12
Volunteer action sheets help organize an orderly volunteer program.

miliar with the class, the objectives, and the material.

Volunteer Training

Several parents have indicated interest in becoming permanent volunteers in your classroom. What is your next step? The time spent explaining your routine, expectations, and preferences for teaching will be well worth the effort in the parents' abilities to coordinate with you in your classroom. Most teachers have specific preferences for teaching that they will want to share with the volunteers helping them. These, in addition to some general guidelines, will help prepare the volunteer. The following humanistic guidelines for working with children are appropriate for all volunteers:

1. A healthy, positive self-concept is a prerequisite to learning.

2. The act of listening to a child implies that you accept him as a worthwhile person.
3. The child will develop a better sense of self-worth if you praise him for his efforts rather than deride him for his failure.
4. Provide him with tasks at which he can succeed. As he masters these, move on to the next level.
5. Take time to know the student as a person. Your interest in him bolsters his confidence in your relationship. (DaSilva & Lucas, 1974, p. 110)

Many children who need extra help with their work also need their self-concepts strengthened. Volunteers can provide an extra touch through kindness, interest, and support.

Teacher's Responsibilities to the Volunteer

As teachers enlist the help of volunteers, certain responsibilities emerge. Following are the teacher's responsibilities:

Volunteers can help children develop a better sense of worth.

1. Make volunteers feel welcome. Smile and reassure them.
2. Explain class rules and regulations.
3. Introduce volunteers to the resources within the school.
4. Explain the routine of the class.
5. Describe your expectations for their participation.
6. Remember that volunteers are contributing and sharing time because of satisfaction received for self and/or child.
7. Give volunteers reinforcement and recognition.
8. Meet with volunteers when class is not in session to clarify, answer questions, and, if needed, give instruction and training.
9. Appreciate, respect, and encourage volunteers.

Awareness of these points will make the cooperative effort of teacher and volunteer more fulfilling for both.

Volunteer's Responsibilities to Teacher

If parents or persons from the community volunteer to help in the school, they accept certain responsibilities, which include the following:

1. Be dependable and punctual. If an emergency requires that you miss a session, obtain a substitute or contact the volunteer coordinator.
2. Keep privileged information concerning children or events confidential. Do not discuss children with persons other than school personnel.
3. Plan responsibilities in the classroom with the teacher.
4. Cooperate with the staff. Welcome supervision.
5. Be ready to learn and grow in your work.
6. Enjoy yourself, but do not let your charges get out of control.
7. Be fair, consistent, and organized.

Volunteer aides are not helpful if they continually cancel at the last moment, disrupt the room rather than help it run smoothly, or upset the students. They are immensely helpful if they work with the teacher to strengthen and individualize the school program.

Recruitment by Schools and School Systems

Many schools and school districts assist teachers by recruiting volunteers for their classes. The first step in initiating a volunteer program for a school or school system is the development of a questionnaire to ascertain the teachers' needs. The teachers complete a form, based on the curriculum for each age level. After the forms are completed, the coordinators can determine the requirements of each room.

After teachers have indicated their needs, the coordinator begins recruitment. Many avenues are open for the recruiter. A flyer geared to the appropriate age or level of children, which requests people to share their time with the schools, can bring about the desired results. Organizations can also be contacted. The PTA or PTO, senior citizen groups, and other clubs have members who may want to be involved as volunteers in the school.

The points discussed earlier for obtaining volunteers for the individual classroom are also appropriate for volunteers who are solicited on a larger scale. The major differences are organizational. They include the following:

1. Teachers contact or reply to the volunteer coordinator's questionnaire if they want a volunteer.
2. Districts usually require that volunteers fill out an application stating background, giving references, and listing the hours they are available.
3. An extensive compilation of resource persons can be obtained by the school district. These resource persons and/or experts can share their knowledge with classes throughout the school district. Lists of topics with resource persons available to share expertise can be distributed throughout the district. Teachers request the subject and time they want a presentation. The central office handles the arrangements and obtains the volunteer presenter for the teacher (Boise School Volunteer Office, 1978; Minneapolis Public Schools, 1974).
4. Outreach such as a community study hall can be initiated and staffed by the volunteer program. Volunteers can tutor and work with children after school hours in libraries, schools, or other public facilities (Denver Public Schools).
5. Certificates of awards distributed by the district offer a way to thank the volunteer for effort and time shared with the schools.

Individual teachers tend to use parents as aides and resource persons in the room. The district most often furnishes resource persons, drawn from the total population, to schools throughout the district. The school volunteer coordinator uses both approaches and recruits volunteers to tutor and aid in the classroom and resource persons from residents of the school's population area to enrich the curriculum. At all three levels, however, volunteers can be used in a diversified and meaningful manner, and they can contribute through both roles, that is, resource person and volunteer aide.

SUMMARY

School-based programs that involve parents are varied. After describing a walk through a school committed to parent involvement, this chapter explores school-based programs ranging from those at the infant-toddler age level to those for young adults. These projects include the Gainesville Infant-Toddler Program, Brookline Early Education Project, Birmingham Model for Parent Education, Ferguson-Florissant Saturday School, Chattanooga Public Schools, Head Start, and Chapter I, and Chapter III programs.

Parents must be supported in home-school involvements. Teachers should share methods of working with children, hold make-and-take workshops, and develop a home learning activity program. Teachers must work closely with parents in the development of a home-school program. They should know their parents and adapt the program to each family.

Teen-age pregnancies and the need for family life education during adolescent years resulted in the development of *Exploring Childhood and Education for Parenthood* to supplement traditional programs.

Ways that home-school programs can be started are discussed. Many programs are started with grants. If this monetary support is not available, schools can try to increase personnel support by soliciting volunteers. Volunteers can help by aiding the teacher, producing materials for the classroom, and serving as resource specialists. Suggestions for recruiting and using volunteers and the responsibilities of both volunteers and teachers are included.

School-based programs are diversified, but each type of involvement is essential if the needs of families are to be met.

For more information contact the following sources:

National School Volunteer Program, Inc.
300 North Washington Street
Alexandria, VA 22314

Director, Volunteers in Education
U.S. Department of Education
400 Maryland Avenue, SW
Washington, DC 20202

Retired Senior Volunteer Program
ACTION
806 Connecticut Avenue, NW
Washington, DC 20520

School systems that have used volunteers successfully, such as those in Boise, Idaho; Minneapolis, Minnesota; Denver, Colorado; and Ferguson-Florissant School District, St. Louis County, Missouri, can also be contacted for more information.

SUGGESTED ACTIVITIES AND DISCUSSIONS

1. Visit a Chapter I program in a public school. Talk with the principal about the parent involvement specifically developed for the Chapter I program.
2. Survey three or four schools that have federal funding. How do the schools differ in their approaches to parent involvement? What are the commonalities? Are there different responses to the various types of funding, for example, Chapter I, Chapter IVC, Chapter VII, Follow Through, or Right to Read.
3. Develop a list of Dos and Don'ts to guide a volunteer in your classroom.
4. Design a want ad or letter that invites parents to become volunteers in the classroom.
5. Design a parent bulletin board that illustrates the various components of the parent program in your classroom.
6. Develop a resource file of games, articles, books, and recycled materials.
7. Hold a workshop in which you have various learning centers, for example, reading readiness, sorting and classifying, problem solving,

creativity, self-esteem, and language development.
8. Conduct a brainstorming session on tasks for parent volunteers. How many ideas are you able to list? Categorize them according to type of involvement, that is, tutoring, teaching, developing materials, housekeeping tasks, or busywork. Why is it important to allow parents to participate in meaningful work?
9. Make a universal game board and a series of cards to be used with it.
10. Develop activities that parents can use with their children at home.
11. Search the community for resources that can be used in the school. Include specialists, materials, and places to visit.

BIBLIOGRAPHY

Boise School Volunteer Office. *Notebooks for Boise school volunteers*. Boise, Idaho: The Independent School District of Boise City, 1978.

Brody, V. *Developmental play*. St. Petersburg, Fla.: All Children's Hospital, 1976.

Brody, V., Fenderson, C., Stephenson, S., Bailey, R. (Ed.). *Sourcebook for finding your way to helping young children through developmental play*. St. Petersburg, Fla.: Pupil Personnel Services Demonstration Project, 1976.

Brookline Early Education Project. *A brief description of the Brookline Early Education Project: Overview*. Brookline, Mass.: Brookline Early Education Project, 1979.

DaSilva, B., & Lucas, R. D. *Practical school volunteer and teacher-aide programs*. West Nyack, N.Y.: Parker Publishing, 1974.

Denver Public Schools. *For VIPs only: Volunteers in public schools*. Denver, Colo.: Denver Public Schools, 1974.

Eaton Public Schools. *Eaton School volunteer handbook*. Eaton, Colo.: Eaton Public Schools, 1979.

Education Development Center. *Exploring childhood, program overview and catalog of materials*. Newton, Mass.: EDC School and Society Programs, 1979.

Far West Laboratory. *Educational programs that work*. San Francisco: Far West Laboratory for Educational Research and Development, 1983.

Ferguson-Florissant School District. *Parents as first teachers.* Ferguson, Mo.: Ferguson-Florissant School District, 1985.

_____. *Saturday School: A success story.* Ferguson, Mo.: Ferguson-Florissant School District, 1978.

Hearings before committee on human resources. Adolescent's Health Services and Pregnancy Prevention and Care Act of 1978. Washington, D.C.: U.S. Government Printing Office, 1978.

Honig, A. S. *Parent involvement in early childhood education.* Washington, D.C.: National Association for the Education of Young Children, 1979.

Hubbell, R. *A review of Head Start research since 1970.* (Administration for Children, Youth and Families, Office of Human Development Services, Department of Health and Human Services). Washington, D.C.: U.S. Government Printing Office, 1983.

Lasater, T. M., Briggs, J., Malone, P., Gilliam, C. F., & Weisburg, P. *The Birmingham Model for parent education.* Paper presented before the Society for Research in Child Development, Denver, Colo., April 1, 1975.

Littlejohn, R., & Associates. *Involving parents in Head Start: A guide for parent involvement coordinators* (final draft). Washington, D.C.: Office of Human Development, 1976.

Miller, B. L., & Wilmshurst, A. L. *Parents and volunteers in the classroom: A handbook for teachers.* San Francisco: R & E Research Associates, 1975.

Minneapolis Public Schools. *How to initiate and administer a community resource volunteer program.* Minneapolis, Minn.: Minneapolis Public Schools, 1974.

Packer, A. B., Resnick, M. B., Resnick, J. L., & Wilson, J. M. An elementary school with parents and infants. *Young Children*, January 1979, pp. 4–9.

Parent Education Demonstration Project in Region IV. *Together is best: Families and schools.* Atlanta, Ga.: Southern Association of Colleges and Schools, 1976.

Piaget, J. *To understand is to invent.* New York: Penguin Books, 1976.

Plunkett, V. Personal communication. Denver, Colo., April, 1980.

Population Reference Bureau. Adolescent pregnancy and childbearing—growing concerns for America. In *Population Bulletin* (Vol. 31, No. 2). Washington, D.C.: Population Reference Bureau, 1976.

Teen parents project. Child Development Center, Department of Pediatrics and Child Health and the Institute for Child Development and Family Life. Washington, D.C.: Howard University, 1977.

Thornton, A., & Freedman, D. The Changing American family. *Population Bulletin,* (Vol. 38, No. 4). Washington, D.C.: Population Reference Bureau, 1983.

U.S. Bureau of the Census. Statistical Abstract of the United States: 1985 (106th ed.). Washington, D.C., 1985.

U.S. Department of Health and Human Services (Office of Human Development Services, Administration for Children, Youth and Families, Head Start Bureau). *A leader's guide to exploring parenting.* Washington, D.C.: U.S. Government Printing Office, 1980.

Warren, V. B. *Tested ways to help your child learn.* Englewood Cliffs, N.J.: Prentice-Hall, 1963.

CHAPTER SEVEN

Home-based Programs

As a concerned parent of preschool-age children, did you ever want an educational support system? Would a visit by a paraprofessional home teacher have made you feel less isolated? Perhaps you have never experienced the trials and joys of being a parent of one or more preschool children. Or if you had preschool children, you may have lived near a child development center that your children attended. Yet imagine yourself as a mother of two preschoolers living in the country at least a mile from the next home. Or pretend that you are a parent in a core-city apartment house. Some parents in urban and suburban areas have no more contact with supportive friends than those isolated by distance in the country. Both urban and rural residents as the first teachers of their children, need the support and knowledge necessary for them to provide an enriched positive environment for their children.

Home visitors are sometimes the only contact a parent has with anyone outside the home.

HOME-BASED EDUCATION

In the 1960s several programs chose the home-based parent as their target: HOPE—Appalachia Educational Laboratory home-oriented preschool education; David Weikart's Ypsilanti High/Scope Infant Education Project, Ypsilanti, Michigan; Phyllis Levenstein's Mother-Child Home Program, New York City; Ira Gordon's Florida Parent Education Program; Susan Gray's home-based program, DARCEE, Nashville, Tennessee; and Ronald Lally's home visitor program, Children's Center, Syracuse University, New York. Some of these focused on families who lived away from the population center, for example, Gordon's home-based program and HOPE. Others worked with parents as an outreach of their center programs (High/Scope Educational Research Foundation). All recognized parents as the child's most important teacher during the formative years.

One Home-based Program

A program initiated in 1971 in Yakima, Washington, acknowledged the importance of parents as their children's first teachers as the following article written by Carol Jackson and Vivian Hedrick vividly illustrates:

The Winning Play at Home Base

The Rochas's home, neat and attractive, is modest by almost anyone's standards. A few fall flowers brighten the gravel walk, and a small tricycle that has seen better days lies on its side in the grass announcing the presence of at least one preschooler. From under a bush the family's gray-striped cat lifts an eyelid as a visitor approaches.

Plump, dark-haired Mrs. Rochas responds immediately to the knock, hampered only slightly by her 2½-year-old son Benjie, who manages to cling to her knee while keeping one finger in his mouth. "Hi, Jean. Come in," says Mrs. Rochas, with a smile almost as wide as the door she swings open to permit her caller to enter the small living room. As Mrs. Rochas gently eases Benjie back toward his toy collection in the corner, she tells Jean that Margaretta, her daughter who is almost 4, is still napping.

"That's fine, don't disturb her," Jean, a paraprofessional parent-educator, replies before she settles on the davenport and begins pulling some materials from her shopping bag—a stack of index cards, several old magazines, a pair of scissors, and a tube of glue.

The casual banter notwithstanding, some serious business is at hand: Mrs. Rochas is about to undergo a lesson that marks the beginning of her second "school year." She is one of 200 parents in

Yakima, a central Washington community of 49,000, who are learning how to teach their own preschool children through Project Home Base, a pioneer early-childhood education program. Depending on how well she learns her weekly lessons, she could have a positive and lasting effect on her child's performance in school.

Like many Home Base families, the Rochases were lured to the area from northern California during the previous fall by the promise of better wages in Yakima's fruit industry. Soon afterward they were visited by a representative from the Home Base project, who explained that all parents of children aged 8 months to 4 years in their neighborhood were being given an opportunity for special, federally sponsored training to enable them to help their preschoolers prepare for school. The Rochases were enthusiastic, but even while accepting the invitation, Mrs. Rochas had a number of doubts. Among them, her daughter (then 3 years old) did not always "take to strangers" and Benjie was still "just a baby." But as the weeks passed and the home-visitor became a familiar and friendly face, the doubts disappeared.

A half hour goes by and Margaretta awakens from her nap. Still sleepy, she enters the living room to find her mother busily engaged in a game of "Concentration." This particular exercise calls for pasting pictures of "like" objects, cut from magazines, onto cards to create a series of pairs. The cards, bearing pictures of various animals and buildings, are then shuffled and placed face down in rows. The game begins with a player picking up a card and trying to match it with a second. If no match results, both cards are returned to their original positions and a second player tries. When all the cards are matched, the player with the most pairs is the winner.

It is important, Mrs. Rochas knows from past experience, that she learns exercises like this one thoroughly before trying them with her children. Then she can become more comfortable in the unfamiliar role of "Teacher."

Before Margaretta plays the game after dinner that day and frequently during the remainder of the week, she will be encouraged to look at the cards and then talk—in complete sentences—about the pictures. As she gains a familiarity with the objects pictured and the exercise by adding more cards or, to keep the lessons fresh, change the object of the exercise to matching pairs of colors rather than pictures. It may be just fun to Margaretta, but all the while she is playing, she is acquiring some important skills, including the ability to think logically. She is thus preparing to become a better learner when she enters kindergarten the following year.

Little Benjie, meanwhile, is an important part of the action, too. Before leaving that afternoon, Jean shows Mrs. Rochas how a small hand mirror and a full-length mirror can transform him into "The Most Wonderful Thing in the World."

Examining his face in the mirror, Benjie is helped to identify his most prominent physical characteristic, such as his curly hair, bright brown eyes, and white teeth. Then he tries to figure out what makes him "special," what makes him different from everyone else in his family. He observes that one eyebrow is straighter than the other, and his ears are round. Then there are all the tricky things he can do with his face: he can squint, wrinkle his nose, and pucker his lips. He is encouraged to talk about how a smile is different than a frown. Before the full-length mirror in the bedroom, Benjie studies his posture and imitates various commonplace activities such as eating a hamburger or kicking a football. He and Margaretta look together into the mirror and discover how their appearances are different and how they are alike. The purpose? To help a child realize he or she is special and to feel good and confident about the discovery.

Although the allotted hour has flown by, Jean takes a few more minutes to discuss some new pamphlets on nutritious snacks for children she has brought along from the County Extension Office, and to confirm her appointment for next week.

The exercises for Margaretta and Benjie just described are only two drawn from more than 200 individual "tasks" for various age levels identified and developed by the Home Base staff. Each exercise has a specific goal or aim. Since most learning handicaps in the target population—preschoolers in the Yakima area—relate to language development, Home Base stresses conversations between parents and their children. There is no special significance attached to the activities' sequence. Tasks become more complex as the child's needs and intellectual capacity grow.

Parents are continually encouraged to adhere closely to a number of effective teaching techniques such as eliciting questions from the learner, asking questions that have more than one correct answer, asking questions that require more than a one-word reply, praising the learner when he or she does well, urging the child to respond according to evidence instead of guesswork, allowing the child time to think out a problem before receiving assistance, and helping him or her to become familiar with the learning situation and materials.

"As we teach parents what to expect from their children in each situation and how to respond to their child's successes or failures, we find that the parents become stronger and more confident in their teaching role," project director Carol Jackson says. "When they understand the necessity for teaching skills like problem solving, they realize the time is well spent."

Project Home Base, a National Developer/Demonstration Project, started in 1971 with funding under Title III of the Elementary and Secondary Education Act (ESEA). This year it is funded under Title I. The project, operating on the premise that the parent is the child's first and most significant teacher, is adapted from Ira Gordon's Follow Through Parent Education Model. Currently, Home Base serves the parents of about 300 preschool children, all of whom reside in a Title I-identified neighborhood of Yakima, the center of a major agricultural and agri-business area with its resulting highly transient population among lower-income families. The city population is made up of about 10% ethnic minorities, with a 30% minority representation in the Home Base program.

Home Base employs ten parent-educators as home-visitors. These paid paraprofessionals attend a 2-week training class in the fall and receive in-service instruction throughout the year during planning sessions each Friday morning. The home-visitor's workday spans from 8:30 to 4, with about an hour spent at each home. "The most important qualification for a parent-educator is genuine desire to work with and help others," Mrs. Jackson says. "This is an emotionally demanding job." It also helps to have a driver's license and an available vehicle. Fortunately, language problems are avoided because one of the home-visitors is bilingual; her services are in constant use translating tasks into Spanish and attending meetings to serve as interpreter for Spanish-speaking parents.

A great deal of role playing is used in the training of parent-educators during which they try for themselves all of the activities scheduled. "An unusual aspect of our program is that we use no commercial learning games," Judy Popp, the Home

Base demonstration coordinator, says. "Wood scraps from a local mill are our building-block materials. We buy flannel to make flannel boards, and we mix flour and water and salt to make playdough. Of course we also made good use of ordinary items found in every home—coffee cans with plastic lids, measuring spoons—anything that will help to stimulate a young mind." And what Home Base doesn't have on hand, the community usually provides. Owing to more than 30,000 home visits logged to date, the community has become increasingly intimate with the project staff and has been the source of a constant stream of donated materials.

The program is comparatively economical. All costs, including salaries, special services from a psychologist, an outside auditor, and secretarial support and materials, come to about $200 per learner per year. Because of its field-centered operation only minimal office space is required, and that is provided at Eisenhower High School. In return, the high school's students who are enrolled in a course called "Exploring Childhood" may accompany a Home Base parent-educator on her visits to see how academic learning can be applied to real life settings.

In the Friday morning staff sessions, home-visitors discuss their problems and successes and plan new strategy for the coming week. At one such meeting, a Home Base parent-educator reported that her persistence in persuading a family to have their child's hearing checked had paid off—a 40% hearing loss had been detected. The child would be referred to the appropriate community agency for medical help. Another observed that even parents new to the program "feel reassured to discover and understand their children's needs." She added that one mother had admitted that she's experienced numerous problems with her oldest child, but, thanks to Home Base, she believes she can avoid them with the younger one. And she added that all the emphasis on language is clearly helping the younger child's speech; he has begun to speak in sentences rather than fragments, and at an appreciably younger age than his brother.

Home Base is not without benefit for the rest of the family, too. "A father told me that being involved in Home Base has made a difference in his wife," reports another of the parent-educators. "She's found out she has ability and she is using it. Her opinion of herself has been greatly improved." Keeping an otherwise isolated family in touch with the community is another valuable aspect of the Home Base program. "Instead of my feeling alone and all tied up by my problems," a woman told her visitor, "you help by just being a friend that I can talk to once a week."

Beyond the parent and home-visitor interaction, parents also get together in small neighborhood groups and in larger sessions to swap information about child development and discuss mutual concerns. They are also a lot of fun; a recent gathering was called a "Small World Smorgasbord," a triumph for the cause of culinary diplomacy. Between performances of native dances, long-time Yakimans and their Japanese, Chicano, and Indian neighbors spent an evening of getting to know one another over plates full of their favorite foods.

There are always a few dropouts from the Home Base program, but the rate of attrition is much less than one might expect from a population that accepts transiency as a condition of employment. The director feels that's chiefly because of the "nonthreatening" approach the staff use, which removes any suggestion of the remedial stigma. The program's psychologist is a key figure in this regard, for both parent training and staff development. A high percentage of the participating families either request or are referred to the psychologist for a home visit sometime during the year. The Home Base psychologist is careful not to interpret such a request as an indication that a serious problem exists but simply offers an opportunity to share experiences and talk about children in a relaxed and familiar setting.

One concern early in the program was whether training parents systematically to teach developmental skills to their children during the early formative years could really be statistically measured. And how would Home Base children perform compared with children of similar economic status on nationally used school-readiness tests? To gauge the effects of the Home Base program, a realistic set of objectives was established. One requires mothers to teach at least 82.5% of the tasks presented to them. A composite figure of the percentage taught for the period between 1971 and 1975 shows the results at 83.6%, slightly above the goal established. Another objective—since attained— was for mothers to increase their use of desirable teaching behaviors when teaching their children.

Data collected by the Home Base staff reveal that the project's third objective, requiring children to perform 92.5% of the tasks taught to them by their parents, was attained and in fact exceeded during each of the first 3 years of operation. The youngsters fell short of the target only once, in 1974–75, when the percentage of tasks performed was 90.4. A fourth objective, to improve the youngsters' potential for learning, requires that the Home Base children perform significantly better on the Educational Testing Service's Preschool Inventory exam than comparable children who have not participated in the program. They've done just that. Against a national norm of 50, the Home Base children scored 87% during the period between 1972 and 1975, while the non-Home Base control group earned a composite score of only 55%.

As a national demonstration project, Home Base has frequently been in the spotlight. During the past year alone, 44 demonstrations of the program were held in Yakima, 16 more at other locations in the state, and another 32 at selected communities throughout the country. Since 1971, spinoff programs have been started in Indiana, Alaska, California, and Minnesota, and several other municipalities are planning to launch projects this year.

Evaluation in 1975–76, a locally devised measurement of developmental skills, showed an average increase from 1.80 tasks (performed at age level) in the fall, to 3.63 tasks accomplished by the end of the program year. The Developmental Profile has been used during the past school year to measure parents' perceptions of their children's development from birth to age 10 in five categories—physical, self-help, social, academic, and communication. Results are now being tabulated, and Mrs. Jackson believes the profile will provide a more complete picture of each child's progress as encouraged by home instruction.

"But these are only statistics," Mrs. Jackson concludes. "The important and encouraging part of our work is that we have established that children can be immeasurably helped during their earliest years by their potentially best teacher, their parents. The parents are already involved. They love their children and want the best for them. What we hope is to enable them to transfer this love and concern into practical ways of helping their youngsters that will pay off in later years."[1]

The Yakima Home Base program illustrates how schools or centers can use the home as a teaching center. The emphasis is on practices that encourage the child's educational growth: (1) learning communication skills; (2) reasoning logically; (3) developing self-concept; (4) becoming nutritionally aware; (5) using developmental activity sequences; (6) employing effective teaching techniques such as eliciting questions, asking questions that have more than one answer, praising the child for accomplishments, providing problem-solving situations, and urging the child to respond to evidence rather than guessing; (7) using easily obtained play materials such as playdough made from flour, salt, and water, wood scraps from the lumberyard, and homemade flannel boards; and (8) extending new expertise and knowledge about parenting to other members of the family. This program responds to the individual requirements of the community from which it evolved, but many of the techniques of effective parenting and teaching are appropriate for any home-based program.

Chapter I Programs

The Yakima program was originally funded by a Title III, Elementary and Secondary School Act grant. Later the school district received Title I (now called Chapter I) funding to continue the program. Across the nation similar demonstration projects were initially funded by the U.S. Office of Education, Department of Health, Education, and Welfare. When successful, the projects might be chosen as exemplary, suitable for dissemination to and duplication by other school districts such as the Home Start programs in Waterloo, Iowa, and a Parent Education and Preschool program with Added Dimensions in Jefferson County, Colorado.

Home Start

Head Start added Home Start demonstration programs in 1972. The success of earlier

---

1. From Hedrich, V., and Jackson, C. Project Home Base. *American Education,* July 1977, pp. 27–30.

home-based programs, plus the belief that parents were the "first and most important educators of their own children" (U.S. Department of Health, Education, & Welfare, 1976, p. 5), resulted in the funding of 16 Home Start projects during a 3-year demonstration period from March 1972 until June 1975. Programs were founded in San Diego, California; Wichita, Kansas; Gloucester, Massachusetts; Binghamton, New York; Reno, Nevada; Huntsville, Alabama; Fairbanks, Alaska; Dardanelle, Arkansas; Fort Defiance, Arizona; Franklin, North Carolina; Laredo, Texas; Logan, Utah; Parkersburg, West Virginia; Houston, Texas; Cleveland, Ohio; and Harrogate, Tennessee. The Home Start program differed from Head Start in its location of services and its emphasis on parents as teachers in the home. Although Head Start included parents in decision making and included home visits, Home Start's purpose was to use the home as base and, through home visitors, help parents to become teachers of their children. The diverse locations of the Home Start programs ensured the implementation of the program among different ethnic and cultural groups and varying social conditions.

ADDITIONAL FEDERAL PROGRAMS GEARED TO PARENT INVOLVEMENT

A number of comprehensive resource programs that had outreach to parents were funded approximately at the same time as Home Start. These included (1) Parent Child Development Centers (PCDC), (2) Parent and Child Centers (PCC), and (3) Child and Family Resource Programs (CFRP).

Parent Child Development Centers

Although PCDC evolved from the recognized need for parent involvement, the three programs chosen for demonstration (Birmingham, Alabama; New Orleans, Louisiana; Hous-

ton, Texas) worked with different populations and used different delivery systems. Birmingham's project was center-based, while Houston had a combination of home-based and center-based programs, and New Orleans had two models: one, home-based, and the other, center-based (Ricciuti, 1975). The projects were designed to determine the effects of intervention on the following:

1. Whether a parent intervention program would attract the attention of parents
2. What kind of programs could best help parents understand the dimensions of growth in infancy
3. How the program effects could be measured appropriately
4. What kinds of growth in children were related to what kinds of growth in parents (U.S. Department of Health, Education, and Welfare, 1976, p. 19)

The Houston Model for Parent Education geared its program toward change in the mother's behavior. Working with low-income Mexican-American mothers, the home educators visited the home once a week for approximately 1½ hours and held four Saturday family workshops during the first year of the program. During the second year mothers and their 2-year-old children attended a 3-hour program at the center 4 days a week. Evening sessions were held for both parents twice a month. The model worked toward and gained greater verbal interaction between parent and child, granting more autonomy to the child, and increased warmth in parental interaction with the child (Leler et al., 1975).

Parent and Child Centers (PCC)

The 36 Parent and Child Centers were intially funded in 1967. The models varied. Some were home-based; some were center-based, and others were a combination of the two. Goals and objectives for the programs included:

1. Improving the overall developmental progress of 0- to 3-year-old children

2. Increasing parents' knowledge of their roles as teachers of their own children
3. Strengthening the family and its functions through parent involvement
4. Creating community awareness in the parents of infants
5. Serving as a locus of research (U.S. Department of Health, Education, and Welfare, 1976, p. 18)

Child and Family Resource Program (CFRP)

Funded in June 1973, the CFRP, as a part of Head Start, coordinated comprehensive services for families at 11 projects. The CFRP enrolled families rather than just the children and provided a child-centered family service program. By working with the total family, the program reached all children ages 0 through 8 and included the children in programs related to their ages. Following were the objectives of the programs:

1. To individualize and tailor programs and services to children and their families
2. To link resources in the community so that families may choose from a variety of programs and services while relating primarily to a single resource center for all young children in the same family
3. To provide continuity of resources available to parents, enabling each family to guide the development of its children from the prenatal period through their early school years
4. To enhance and build upon the strengths of the individual family as a child-rearing system, with distinct values, culture, and aspirations; the CFRP will attempt to reinforce these strengths, treating each individual as a whole and the family as a unit (U.S. Department of Health, Education, and Welfare, 1975, pp. 3 and 4)

CFRP offered the following minimum services:

1. Comprehensive individual assessment of family and child needs, based on consultation with the family

2. Preventive, treatment, and rehabilitative services as required for the individually diagnosed medical, dental, nutritional, and mental health needs of children up to 8 years of age
3. Prenatal medical care and educational services for pregnant mothers
4. Developmental services for families and children
   a. Programs to assist parents in promoting the total (emotional, cognitive, language, and physical) development of infants and toddlers through age 3
   b. Preschool comprehensive Head Start services for children from ages 3 to 5
   c. Programs designed to ensure smooth transition for children from preschool into the early elementary grades
   d. Group activities and family development programs for parents
   e. Special development programs for handicapped children
5. Family support services
   a. Individual and group counseling for children and adults
   b. Referral services for life support needs
   c. Emergency services in crises
   d. Family planning assistance and counseling
   e. Information regarding food assistance programs

The CFRP programs were expected to consider the families' cultural and ethnic backgrounds and their language patterns. Understanding of the families' needs was essential, and needs assessments were conducted prior to design of each family's program and throughout the implementation of the program.

Services for children in the family beyond the 8-year level were not unusual. Scouts were encouraged for school-age children. Tutoring was provided for school children and adults if needed. The CFRP attempted to provide a comprehensive service for participating families.

Effectiveness of Services

These three programs demonstrated that home-based education is a viable undertaking for educators and, along with Home Start, Title I, and Title IV C programs, contributed research data and suggested procedures for implementation. The ESEA demonstration programs (Titles I, III, IV C) and those funded through the Office of Child Development (later the Administration for Children, Youth, and Families) were developed with the hope of disseminating and developing similar programs, wherever needed, across the nation. It was recognized that each locality would have individual needs and that individualized programs for children and their families would be both necessary and beneficial.

The variety of approaches—that is, outreach to homes as the only service, center-based operations, and home-based in combi-

Outreach can touch mothers and fathers as they raise their children.

nation with center programs—allowed communities that were planning to implement a home-based program many options from which to develop unique programs. The demonstration programs devised methods of implementation and developed curricula that could be modeled by schools, centers, and agencies starting home-based programs. Many Head Start agencies have added a Home Start component to their center-based program. School districts have also begun to involve parents prior to the time their children commence school. Although only a few demonstration programs still exist, their influence is felt through the implementation in Head Start and schools. Some of the suggestions will be discussed.

DECIDING ON A HOME-BASED PROGRAM

Before a particular home-based program is considered, the reasons for and needs of such a program must be examined. The primary goals of home-based programs include the following:

1. To enable parents to become more effective teachers of their children
2. To support the parents in the roles of caregivers and homemakers
3. To strengthen the parents' sense of autonomy and self-esteem
4. To reach the child and family early in the child's formative years
5. To respond to the family's needs and thus improve the home environment

The overriding goal of educators is the impact of the program on the child. Desirable results are the child's increased sense of well-being, a more successful educational experience in school, and the realization of the child's potential for optimum development.

Goals for programs vary according to the needs of the area. For instance, in one area, health may be an overriding concern, in another, language development, and in still another, nutrition. Although all three are probably important in varying degrees in every home-based program, the intensity of involvement may vary.

NEED FOR A PROGRAM

In certain school communities the need for a home-based program is blatantly clear. Whether it will be accepted by parents is not as obvious, however. In other communities, although the very real need may be hidden, a home-based program may be readily accepted by parents. Federal moneys are provided for areas that have a high density of economically disadvantaged families. Home Start's 16 demonstration grants were made to communities with evident economic needs. Under Title III, ESEA, which funded innovative education programs and schools, economic need was not a prerequisite for funding. School districts were encouraged to integrate costs of the programs into local school budget after federal grants were depleted. Initial financial support was a significant motivation for schools to develop innovative programs with parent involvement as a component, just as federal money was an incentive for communities to initiate Head Start, Home Start, Child Development Centers, and Child and Family Resource Programs. Research, which indicated that family involvement in the educational process resulted in fewer retentions and special placements of children after they entered school, gave evidence that the programs were cost effective for the school districts. This is true for any area where some children may be educationally disadvantaged, whether their socioeconomic level is high or low. Although federal money is still available for existing Head Start and Chapter I programs, new funds are primarily earmarked for demonstration programs and remediation, rather than for long-term financial support.

Schools and centers should consider parent involvement and home-based programs within the framework of their own needs. They should examine all approaches carefully and share a commitment to the child and family before embarking on a home-based program. These questions can serve as guidelines for choosing a program.

1. Are there children in current school classes who could have been helped by early intervention in the home?
2. What can the school do in a home visitation program that cannot be accomplished through other programs?
3. Could early remediation reduce the number of retentions when children go to school?
4. Are there handicapped children in the area who could be diagnosed and given service before they enter school?
5. Will the preventive program help eliminate later educational problems and thereby offset the cost to the public?
6. Will the prevention of later educational problems reduce later emotional problems and thereby offset the cost to the public?
7. Can the personnel needed to staff the program be obtained?
8. Is there willingness to attempt an outreach program?
9. Is there evidence that a need exists in the community?

If "yes" was answered to a majority of the questions, then determine both need for service and feasibility of providing it. The following factors, which were suggested by participants at a national conference on Home Start and other programs, should be considered:

1. The clientele must be identified, as to rural/urban, ethnic/cultural groups, age, income, and involvement in any existing similar programs.
2. Family and community needs must be identified. Existing census or welfare data and data

from social service agencies may be used. A questionnaire may be devised, and a sample group from existing programs may be interviewed as part of this identification process.

3. Existing and needed services and resources must be identified in areas such as health (medical, dental, and mental health), education, transportation, housing, and legal services.
4. Costs of purchasing available services, providing new services, and transporting clients or staff must be considered.
5. The need for and feasibility of the program must be documented. The feasibility of going partially or completely home-based must be determined, as must the feasibility of affiliating with existing programs or agencies, and the program must be geared to family needs. (U.S. Department of Health, Education, and Welfare, 1976, p. 35)

Many answers will come from the identification of needs mentioned in factor two. Before a questionnaire or needs assessment is devised, data should be gathered from school files, social service agencies, city surveys, or census reports. Social services will be particularly helpful in determining services and number of children in disadvantaged families. School figures, questionnaires, and surveys will supplement that data so that services may be offered to all those who desire or need them. Make every effort to establish a good working relationship with the various agencies. You will need to coordinate your efforts at a later time, and initial communication and rapport are essential to later implementation of the program.

INVOLVING OTHERS IN THE PROGRAM

The four components of a Home Start program are education, social services, health services (physical and mental health, dental care, nutrition, and safety), and parent involvement. Although the project will be fully responsible for education and parent involvement, social and health services will need the support of other agencies. "Knowing what agencies are willing to handle the various family problems that will be found, and getting them involved with the program early in the planning, pay great dividends when the program swings into operation" (U.S. Department of Health, Education, & Welfare, 1974, p. 12).

Social agencies may be contacted individually, or representatives may be invited to a meeting where goals, objectives, and initial plans for the programs are discussed. Elicit suggestions from the agencies as well as find out how they can contribute.

PARENT ADVISORY COUNCIL

Parents to be served should be actively involved in the initial planning. Many schools and preschool programs have parent advisory councils or citizen advisory councils that can give input on the needs of the community and suggest relevant questions that might be asked. If a council is not functioning in your area, it may be advisable to implement one. You can work through the existing PTO or PTA, or you can establish an entirely new council based on the parents you will serve. The formation or election of the board is advertised. Parents have an opportunity to nominate themselves or others, and an election is held to determine who will represent the community on the council. You may advertise the formation of an advisory council by sending notes home with children from school, by explaining the council at area meetings of organizations such as Boy Scouts, Camp Fire Girls, PTA, YMCA, and YWCA, and by distributing flyers throughout the community. All nominations should be accepted. If you use a democratic process, you will have to rely on the intelligence of the parents in the selection process.

Distinct advantages to using a democratic selection process rather than appointment in the formation of an advisory council are the creation of the following: (1) interest in the program, (2) a sense of self-determination and autonomy on the part of the parents, (3) a source of relevant information and feedback from those being affected, and (4) increased cooperation between school and parents.

SELECTION OF HOME VISITORS

Before selecting home visitors, the choice must be made whether to use professional parent teachers, paraprofessionals, or volunteers. Although the director, coordinator, and special services specialists will probably be professionals, many programs use paraprofessionals or volunteers for the home visit specialists. Criteria for selection will be determined by the needs of your specific program.

When recruiting paraprofessional home visitors, the available positions should be advertised widely throughout the community. Announcements must be clear and include the following:

1. Explanation of the program. Explain what your specific home-based program entails. Indicate what the goals and objectives are.
2. Job description of the position. List the duties and responsibilities, hours of work, salary range, and benefits.
3. Qualifications required. Indicate whether high school, college, and/or specific competencies are required.
4. Equal opportunity employment announcement. Make a statement of nondiscrimination.
5. Instructions for applying. Give instructions on how to apply, whom to contact, and the deadline for application.

The announcement of openings should be posted in public places, for example, libraries, schools, stores, and agencies such as Head Start. Telephone canvassing will alert many persons to the new program. To reach a large population, advertise in the newspaper and distribute flyers. Wide dissemination of information about available positions encourages individuals in the community to become involved and alerts others to the upcoming home-based program.

SELECTION COMMITTEE

Although schools and centers have sometimes questioned the policy of parental decision-making, the use of such councils in Head Start, Home Start, and Chapter I programs has produced benefits that strongly recommend this policy. Parents join administrators and teachers who may work with the home visitors on the selection committee.

Bernard (1976) points out four purposes for using parents in screening applicants for home visitors:

First, the sharing of decision breaks down the artificial barrier between the administration and parents concerned about the program.

Second, the development of selection criteria by parents will reveal their concerns.

Third, parents, rather than being more lenient in the selection process, often are tougher and more perceptive and attentive to concerns about who visits in the home than are administrators.

Fourth, parents may know the applicants' personality characteristics, attitudes, social relationships in the community, and philosophical beliefs. They are, therefore, able to help the administrator look beyond the traditional application form in choosing the "best" applicant. (p. 41)

Existing Staff

If the home-based program will reduce staff from other programs, these persons should be considered for the home-based positions. It is important, however, to select persons able to work well with diverse people under varying circumstances.

Selection Criteria

The Home Start guide lists criteria for selection of home visitors. Although the Home

Start program used paraprofessionals as home visitors, each program will determine whether it should use paraprofessionals, professionals, or volunteers. Additionally, because the Home Start guide eliminated academic requirements for home visitors, each program will have to determine its own educational criteria for home visitors. The following selection criteria are from the Home Start guide:

There is still much to be learned about selecting persons who, with good training, will be able to cope most effectively with all of the situations they will meet as home visitors. In general, the emphasis in hiring in the Home Start program has been on friendly attitudes, suitability of culture and language backgrounds to those they will serve, and successful experiences as parents, rather than on academic background or degrees.

Thus, home visitors are usually selected because of exceptional personal qualities which they have shown in their past work, the reputation they have established in the community, and the impressions that they make in the hiring interviews.

Some of the personal qualities that have been found by home-based programs to relate particularly well to the success of home visitors include:

"Personality." Many different types of people with widely different personalities have been highly successful as home visitors. For example, some outstanding home visitors are talkative, energetic persons. They have many valuable characteristics—such as eagerness, energy, and enthusiasm. At the same time, there are many highly successful home visitors who are quiet, dignified, low-key people. They impart a serenity and a sense of security that children and the families find very important. Which is the "best" personality? None is best, but a balance is good, including the ability to adapt one's personality to meet varying needs.

Relating effectively with many different people. It has been found that successful visitors understand and relate easily and effectively to many different people and many types of behavior. They tend to be outgoing people and listen well and communicate readily with almost everyone.

Maturity. Visitors need some maturity to have learned that there is no single right or wrong way to approach all the situations they will face. They benefit from the confidence that comes with experience. Maturity helps one see the many possibilities for "multiplying yourself"—getting other people to do things (older siblings, grandparents), and getting the entire family involved in the program, rather than trying personally to do most of the job. It is a particularly important quality in helping home visitors with the mother, showing her in turn how to work with her children.

Sensitivity. A person who is sensitive to the actions and reactions of others, who can sensitively and objectively see the strengths of the individual families, who listens well and sympathetically, and who changes strategies easily when subtle signals indicate resistance or nonacceptance, usually becomes a successful home visitor.

Flexibility. Home-based programs are generally quite new. Home visitor positions are new to almost everyone, and these positions may evolve into something different as time goes by. There is a great deal new to be learned. Methods used one day may not be appropriate the next. Home visitors need a certain amount of flexibility to meet the needs of an experimental program, as well as the changing needs of families and communities.

They will also need to be flexible when visiting families. If the mother is washing her hair, cooking supper, or caring for the baby, visitors must be able to change their plans, and be ready to make their approach fit the agenda of the family. Not everyone is able to manage a job that calls for changing behavior and modifying plans frequently, and still enjoy the work.

Empathy. Visitors need constantly to listen attentively to and respond sympathetically to parents and children. As a home visitor, it is an advantage to be able readily to see the other person's point of view, and to want to work out solutions that are not only the "right" solutions, but also ones that are particularly acceptable to each family. To do this, it is important to be able to see things from the other person's situation and background.

Motivation. An eager interest in the job of home visitor and the motivation to work hard and long hours, have been identified as important considerations in the selection process. A person who is anxious to learn, able to change, and committed to learning and developing new skills will be easy to train in the new skills that will be needed.

Cultural background. Whatever the culture and background of the families to be served, home visitors must be able to win their confidence quickly, and to be accepted and trusted. Being a resident of the community helps facilitate the job of the home visitor, for they may already know the families, and understand the values and attitudes of the community.

Many of the most successful home visitors identify readily with the cultural and social preferences and interests of the families being served. Individuals who are "foreign" to the local families because of economic status, or some other reason, can be handicapped in getting close to and winning the confidence of the low-income families of the community, whereas a respected long-time resident of the community will have established rapport with many of the families living there. Such a person will understand the community and be able to communicate in the manner and at the level of those living there, and complement the qualifications of other staff members.

Other considerations that reflect field experience, and that have been shown to be important in selecting people capable of becoming outstanding home visitors include:

Language facility. The ability to converse with the families in their own language is important. This may mean in some cases that home visitors will have to be bilingual.

Availability to work some evenings and weekends. When families depend on visitors for guidance, friendship, and support, visitors must be readily available to respond. This means that home visitors may need to make some visits or attend meetings on weekends, or during the evening hours when both mother and father are available. Home visitors must be free enough so they can respond to the families' needs as they arise.

Sex of visitor. Most often the home visitor will be a woman, one who has been a mother, who possesses the skills of a mothering person. And often the cultural backgrounds of the families served indicate that home visitors should be women. Some of the families served, in certain areas of the country, feel that a man's place is in the working world, out of the home, and that the woman's place is at home, caring for the children. Home-based programs must be sensitive to these cultural biases, when they occur.

On the other hand, men can be very successful home visitors. Both boys and girls need to identify with a male, and having at least one male home visitor can help when the children have no father figure. Also, some fathers may relate more readily to a man than a woman.

Age/health/energy. Since home visitors need maturity and should have had successful experience of their own in child rearing, very young people are not usually selected, although there have been some exceptions, and a few in their early twenties, for example, have performed very well. However, the average age of most home visitors is around 30, or slightly older. Regardless of their age, they need to possess eagerness to learn, lots of energy, and must be in good health.

Driving a car. In most areas, transportation is a problem. Families seldom live within walking distance and home visitors will generally be carrying equipment and materials which would be too cumbersome and difficult to handle either on foot or on public transportation. In addition, relying on public transportation schedules makes planning for even routine home visit schedules almost impossible. For these reasons, it is essential that home visitors have or be able to obtain a driver's license, and that they have regular access to a car that is in good working order.

Discretion. Home visitors need to keep privileged information confidential, particularly when they're dealing with their neighbors.

Even seemingly unimportant information gained in a home is personal to the family and must not be shared with anyone other than authorized personnel—perhaps the program director or specialists. . . . This attention to preservation of confidentiality helps to establish a firm pattern of respect for the privacy of families.[2]

The personality traits discussed by the Home Start guide imply some of the benefits of a home visitation program. If the home specialist has these qualities, families will be reached in a sensitive and supportive manner. The locus of education is the home, and the outreach goes to the entire family. The missing

2. From U.S. Department of Health, Education, and Welfare. (Office of Child Development). *A guide for planning and operating home-based child development programs.* Washington, D.C.: U.S. Government Printing Office, 1974, pp. 33–37 and 62.

components—knowledge of educational goals for the particular program, curriculum expertise, and ability to refer to appropriate services—will be gained from preservice workshops and continuous in-service training and discussion.

HOME LEARNING ACTIVITIES

Each project funded by federal money has developed a unique approach to home learning activities. The Portage project developed a systematic program for its home visitors that can be used by others who plan programs. Levenstein's Home Child Program chose commercial games and books as the basis for verbal interaction between parent and child. Gordon's parent program in Florida devised a method of curriculum development that can be replicated in any program, each time re-

sponding to the individual needs of the specific program. With the Gordon method, home learning activities, both active and thoughtful, are based on the children's interests. The program differentiates between thinking and doing. The thinking skills include:

1. Observing people, places, and things
2. Comparing similarities and differences
3. Sorting and classifying objects and ideas
4. Organizing information
5. Anticipating outcomes to situations
6. Hypothesizing solutions to problems
7. Solving problems
8. Using language to label the environment; to say what, why, and how something happens; to say how and why one feels and does; to express creative ideas (Packer et al., 1976, p. 133)

The doing skills include:

1. Caring for self—dressing, feeding, washing
2. Caring for personal property—putting away toys, clothes
3. Making things work—tying shoes, buttoning buttons, working puzzles
4. Moving easily and well—walking, jumping, running, skipping, climbing
5. Using tools—hammers, scissors, forks, and spoons (Packer et al., 1976, p. 133)

Learning occurs within a family when parents and children interact in everyday activities. When joining the family at breakfast, the child may contribute by placing four napkins at four plates, at the same time solving a problem of one-to-one relationships. Choice of napkin color to match the tablecloth or dishes increases learning by adding a matching problem. After sitting at the table, the napkin is placed "in" the child's lap. During breakfast, butter and jam are spread "on" the toast, or butter may be placed "between" and syrup poured "over" the pancakes. Children can be given options of a half or a whole glass of juice or a half or a whole cup of milk. Concepts and understanding of abstract relationships are being developed.

Parents can devise curriculum ideas from everyday activities in the home.

Commercial and School Home Learning Activities

In the implementation of a home-school program both teachers and parents may be supported by learning activities developed by commercial companies and school districts. Appropriate learning activities can be purchased or found in the library. Refer to the references and suggested readings in Chapter 11 for additional activity books for young children. Samples of activities are illustrated in Figure 7-1.

Development of Activities

As the home visitor becomes involved with each family, appropriate activities to accommodate the individual strengths and needs of the family will become apparent. Some home visitors will use suggested and sequential activities for their teaching curriculum such as the Portage Program, which is discussed later in this chapter. Others will use the commercial books illustrated in Figure 7-1, A-B or the sample from the Yakima Home Base program (Figure 7-1, C). Another alternative is to develop activities related to the particular interests of the child and parent.

The Florida Parent Education Program recommends the following framework in the development of home activities.

Idea. The concept or idea emerges from the child, parent, home visitor, or special interests of the family. What does the family enjoy? Which experiences have been interesting and fun? Which collections, toys, or materials are available around the home?

Ideas are also shared among the staff—teachers, other home visitors, and curriculum specialists. When an idea occurs, a memo is jotted down to remind the home visitor of the activity.

Reason. Each idea is used for a reason. The reasons may range from learning experiences to developing self-concept. After an idea or ideas are collected, examine the skills that can be associated with each. For example, if the child picks a leaf from one of the trees in the neighborhood, start a collection of fallen leaves that can be classified according to size, color, and shape. The child can make texture and outline rubbings of them. "How many kinds of trees are represented by the variety of leaves?" you might ask the child. "Put each kind of leaf in a separate pile and count the kinds of leaves." The many learning opportunities available from collecting leaves make this a worthwhile project for as long as the child's interest continues.

Materials. Implementing a reasonable idea requires available materials. Some experiences can be developed around materials commonly found in the home. The Utah program developed a unit on gardens and vegetables that uses materials readily found in the home (see Figure 7-2). If the idea requires special equipment and materials, make sure they are easily available. One of the main objectives of home visits is to involve the parent as the teacher. If parents do not realize that they have readily available teaching materials or if the learning activities are not furnished for them, part of the parental autonomy and subsequent success of the program is lost.

Action. Follow the child's lead and let the activity develop. If the child chooses something to explore that is different from your plans for the activity, vary your plans, take a detour, and enjoy the inquiry and discovery the child is experiencing. Your ideas may be brought up later or eliminated altogether. Remember the objectives of the learning process. If they are being fulfilled, it does not matter which action brought about the learning.

Extension. Are there other activities related to this idea? If so, expand the action, follow the interest, and extend the learning (modified from Packer et al., 1976).

FOCUS ON

    Recognizing colors
    Classifying
    Classifying by multiple attributes
    Developing basic language concepts:
        alike, different, with, without,
        big, little, large, small

MATERIALS

    All available keys
    Egg carton

INDEPENDENT LEARNING CENTER

1. Ask the child to put the keys into egg carton sections in groups that are *alike* in some way.
2. When the child has finished, ask him to tell you how each group of keys is *alike.*
3. Mix the keys, and ask the child to find some *different* ways to put them in groups.
4. When the child has gone as far as he is able on the basis of exploration and discovery, help him expand his classification skills by suggesting new categories, a few at a time.

        Some ways to sort keys:
            Color, shape, size
            Broken, not broken
            Rusty, not rusty
            With numbers, without numbers
            With letters, without letters
            Not cut, cut on one side, cut on both sides
            One color, more than one color
            One hole in the top, more than one hole in the top
            Hole in the top that is round, hole in the top that is not round

MEETING INDIVIDUAL NEEDS

1. The ability to classify is interrelated with the development of language. For children with learning problems, it is often helpful and sometimes necessary to suggest categories after initial exploration if language development is to be facilitated. Left to discovery, many of these children will not develop categorizing skills or expand their language usage.
2. To make the task more challenging, suggest categories based on multiple attributes or characteristics, for example, red keys with square tops, blue keys with numbers, silver keys with more than one hole in the top.

A

FIGURE 7-1
A sample of learning activities. A, Dozens of keys. (*Source:* J. S. McElderry, & L. E. Escobedo. *Tools for learning.* Denver, Col.: Love Publishing, 1979, p. 21.)

Toy Lending Library

A home visitor can incorporate the development of curriculum ideas along with a lending library. Toys, games, books, and patterns for making toys can be loaned for set periods of time. Other toys and books may be given to the participants. Guidelines may be obtained from the plans used by the toy lending library (Nimnicht, 1972).

    Home visitors become capable of designing appropriate curriculum for young chil-

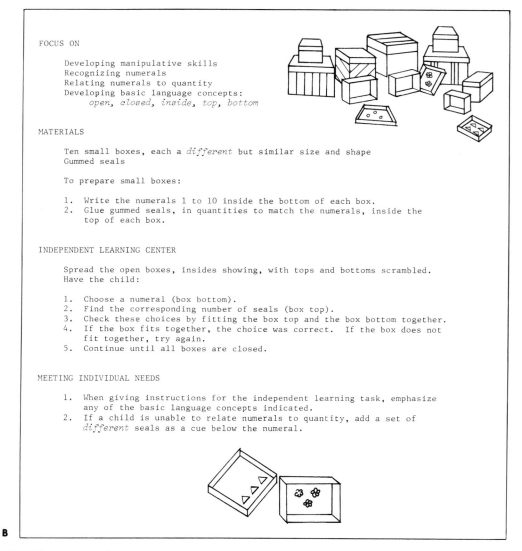

FOCUS ON

Developing manipulative skills
Recognizing numerals
Relating numerals to quantity
Developing basic language concepts:
open, closed, inside, top, bottom

MATERIALS

Ten small boxes, each a *different* but similar size and shape
Gummed seals

To prepare small boxes:

1. Write the numerals 1 to 10 inside the bottom of each box.
2. Glue gummed seals, in quantities to match the numerals, inside the top of each box.

INDEPENDENT LEARNING CENTER

Spread the open boxes, insides showing, with tops and bottoms scrambled. Have the child:

1. Choose a numeral (box bottom).
2. Find the corresponding number of seals (box top).
3. Check these choices by fitting the box top and the box bottom together.
4. If the box fits together, the choice was correct. If the box does not fit together, try again.
5. Continue until all boxes are closed.

MEETING INDIVIDUAL NEEDS

1. When giving instructions for the independent learning task, emphasize any of the basic language concepts indicated.
2. If a child is unable to relate numerals to quantity, add a set of *different* seals as a cue below the numeral.

B

FIGURE 7-1, *continued*
B, If the top fits. (*Source:* J. S. McElderry, & L. E. Escobedo. *Tools for learning.* Denver, Col.: Love Publishing, 1979, p. 86.)

TASK SAMPLE—"CONCENTRATION"

TASK SAMPLE—"CONCENTRATION"

AIM: to play a matching game with pairs of cards.

WHY: to practice visual memory, remembering the position of matching cards. To follow rules and take turns are skills used in most games.

MATERIALS: grocery sack or small cards, five pairs of matching pictures, magazines, sales pamphlets, paste, scissors.

PROCEDURE:

1. Cut pairs of like pictures (10) from magazine and paste on circles cut from paper sacks or cards.

2. Encourage child to talk about pictures and name them. Then, together, place them in pairs.

3. Collect cards, turn them face down, and mix them.

4. Place cards in rows without looking at pictures.

5. Have child pick up one card and turn it over and say what it is. (Repeat the name for child if he cannot say the name.) Then choose another card trying for a match. If no match, then both cards are turned over. Say, "That's your turn; now it's my turn."

6. The play continues until all the cards are matched. Count the "pairs" to see who is the winner.

EXTENDING THE CONCEPT:

1. Add more picture cards for pairs.

2. Play game using colors instead of pictures.

3. Use pictures of sets of objects.

C

FIGURE 7-1, *continued*
C, The game of concentration. (*Source:* Project Home Base, Yakima, Wash.)

UTAH HOME VISITOR GUIDE*
April—1st week

Unit title: Gardens and Vegetables

With the high cost of living, it's important to grow your own fresh vegetables because they are so much needed in our daily diets. Homegrown vegetables are also healthier (less chemicals, fertilizers and more nutritious). Families need information on how to store, preserve and prepare fresh vegetables. Gardening is an excellent learning and sharing experience for families.

Specific objectives:
1. To help parents realize the economical benefits gained through home gardening
2. To give parents help with methods of food preparation and preservation
3. To stress the importance of vegetables to good nutrition
4. To reinforce Basic 4

Activities:
1. Discussion on growing a garden
   a. Why grow a garden
   b. How to grow a garden
   c. How to store and preserve food from the garden
   d. Handout on food storage and preserving
   e. How to involve children in gardening
   f. Children will often eat more when they grow it themselves
   g. Gardening is good exercise and teaches responsibility
   h. Handouts on planting times, spacing, what grows in this area (information from county agents)
2. Choose a garden site
3. Plan a garden
   a. What do you want to grow/like to eat?
   b. How much space, water, and time do you have?
   c. What will grow in your area?
   d. Is this to be a permanent site?
4. If no garden space, use boxes, crates, and flower beds
5. Take fruits and vegetables into home for snack/look, feel, and taste
   a. Cleanliness in handling food
6. Look at seeds and compare or match with vegetable
7. Snack tray of raw vegetables and cottage cheese dip
8. Sprout seeds
9. Plant seed in plastic bag with wet paper towel
10. Plant seed in egg carton
11. Grow plants from sweet potatoes and avocado seed in water
12. Seed collage
13. Start your own tomato plants, green pepper, and cantaloupe plants indoors in cardboard cartons
14. Count seeds
15. Pop popcorn
16. Classify vegetables and fruits—cut pictures from magazines
17. Stories and books
    a. Carrot seed
    b. Turnip seed
    c. Peter Rabbit—Mr. McGregor's Garden
    d. The Little Seed
18. Creative movement—germination and growth of seed
19. Tell parents where to get information and handouts
    a. County extension office
    b. Seed stores
20. Sprinkle grass on wet sponge
21. Print with vegetable or weed leaves
22. Talk about seeds you can eat and eat some for a snack
23. Talk about food that people and animals eat
24. Make a vegetable salad
25. Handouts on vegetables

Follow-up for positive reinforcement:
1. Show seeds—sprouted in bag or planted
2. How do you wash vegetables?
3. What did you decide about your garden?

FIGURE 7-2

The Utah Home Visitor Guide. The unit on gardens and vegetables illustrates how ordinary activities around the home can be used for education. (*Source:* U. S. Department of Health, Education, and Welfare. *Partners with parents.* Washington, D.C.: U. S. Government Printing Office, 1978, pp. 72 and 73.)

dren. By using a screening test like those that follow, they are able to refer children who need special programs.

SCREENING FOR BETTER UNDERSTANDING

Parent educators need to be able to recognize if the families under their guidance need special help. Screening for potential problems in both the developmental status of children and the children's environment—especially if they are growing up in a low socioeconomic area—will help the parent educator identify problems early and more effectively serve children and their families (Fandal, 1986).

Several instruments are available to screen the developmental progress of children. Two of the most widely used are the Denver Prescreening Developmental Questionnaire (PDQ) and the Denver Developmental Screening Test (DDST). There are also standardized methods of assessing the home environment of children, such as the Home Screening Questionnaire (HSQ) and the Home Observation for Measurement of the Environment (HOME).

Environment

Home Observation for Measurement of the Environment (HOME)

The HOME Inventory is used by schools, child care centers, and other social service agencies to help them determine the quality of the home environment as it relates to the child's development. "Although a child may appear to be developing at a normal rate early in life, the environment begins to either enhance or 'put a lid' on developmental progress within the first year or two" (Fandal, 1986). The HOME Inventory was developed by Caldwell and Bradley in order "to get a picture of what the child's world is like from his or her perspective—i.e., from where he or she lies or sits

or stands or moves about and sees, hears, smells, feels, and tastes that world" (Caldwell & Bradley, 1984, p. 8). In addition to the standardized HOME Inventories for 0–3 and 3–6 year olds, an inventory for elementary school children is being developed.

When using the program, the interviewer should

- Know the HOME Inventory well before using it
- Contact the parents and let them know that you want to visit
- Visit during a period while the child is awake and available
- Start the interview with some friendly, relaxed interaction

A suggested technique for starting the interview is described by the following statement:

You will remember that we are interested in knowing the kinds of things your baby (child) does when he is at home. A good way to get a picture of what his days are like is to have you think of one particular day—like yesterday—and tell me everything that happened to him as well as you can remember it. Start with the things that happened when he first woke up. It is usually easy to remember the main events once you get started. (Caldwell & Bradley, 1984, p. 3)

The administration and scoring of each of the items in the inventory is clearly described in the Administration Manuals, so the interviewer can make correct judgments on the scoring of HOME. For example, see Figure 7-3, item 4, which states, *"Parent's speech is distinct and audible."*

A positive score on this item is determined by whether the interviewer is able to understand what the parent says. This item should not be interpreted as meaning that dialect usage mandates a negative score. What is important is whether the interviewer can understand and communicate with the parent. (Caldwell & Bradley, 1984, p. 15)

13

HOME Inventory for Families of Infants and Toddlers

Bettye M. Caldwell and Robert H. Bradley

Family Name _____ Date _____ Visitor _____

Child's Name _____ Birthdate _____ Age _____ Sex _____

Caregiver for visit _____ Relationship to child _____

Family Composition _____ (Persons living in household, including sex and age of children)

Family Ethnicity _____ Language Spoken _____ Maternal Education _____ Paternal Education _____

Is Mother Employed? _____ Type of work when employed _____ Is Father Employed? _____ Type of work when employed _____

Address _____ Phone _____

Current child care arrangements _____

Summarize past year's arrangements _____

Caregiver for visit _____ Other persons present _____

Comments _____

SUMMARY

Subscale	Score	Lowest Middle	Middle Half	Upper Fourth
I. Emotional and Verbal RESPONSIVITY of Parent		0-6	7-9	10-11
II. ACCEPTANCE of Child's Behavior		0-4	5-6	7-8
III. ORGANIZATION of Physical and Temporal Environment		0-3	4-5	6
IV. Provision of Appropriate PLAY MATERIALS		0-4	5-7	8-9
V. Parent INVOLVEMENT with Child		0-2	3-4	5-6
VI. Opportunities for VARIETY in Daily Stimulation		0-1	2-3	4-5
TOTAL SCORE		0-25	26-36	37-45

For rapid profiling of a family, place an X in the box that corresponds to the raw score on each subscale and the total score.

14

HOME Inventory*

Place a plus (+) or minus (–) in the box alongside each item if the behavior is observed during the visit or if the parent reports that the conditions or events are characteristic of the home environment. Enter the subtotal and the total on the front side of the Record Sheet.

I. Emotional and Verbal RESPONSIVITY

1. Parent spontaneously vocalized to child twice.
2. Parent responds verbally to child's verbalizations.
3. Parent tells child name of object or person during visit.
4. Parent's speech is distinct and audible.
5. Parent initiates verbal exchanges with visitor.
6. Parent converses freely and easily.
7. Parent permits child to engage in "messy" play.
8. Parent spontaneously praises child at least twice.
9. Parent's voice conveys positive feelings toward child.
10. Parent caresses or kisses child at least once.
11. Parent responds positively to praise of child offered by visitor.

Subtotal

II. ACCEPTANCE of Child's Behavior

12. Parent does not shout at child.
13. Parent does not express annoyance with or hostility to child.
14. Parent neither slaps nor spanks child during visit.
15. No more than one instance of physical punishment during past week.
16. Parent does not scold or criticize child during visit.
17. Parent does not interfere or restrict child more than 3 times.
18. At least ten books are present and visible.
19. Family has a pet.

Subtotal

III. ORGANIZATION of Environment

20. Substitute care is provided by one of three regular substitutes.
21. Child is taken to grocery store at least once/week.
22. Child gets out of house at least four times/week.
23. Child is taken regularly to doctor's office or clinic.
24. Child has a special place for toys and treasures.
25. Child's play environment is safe.

Subtotal

IV. Provision of PLAY MATERIALS

26. Muscle activity toys or equipment.
27. Push or pull toy.
28. Stroller or walker, kiddie car, scooter, or tricycle.
29. Parent provides toys for child during visit.
30. Learning equipment appropriate to age—cuddly toys or role-playing toys.
31. Learning facilitators—mobile, table and chairs, high chair, play pen.
32. Simple eye-hand coordination toys.
33. Complex eye-hand coordination toys (those permitting combination).
34. Toys for literature and music.

Subtotal

V. Parental INVOLVEMENT with Child

35. Parent keeps child in visual range, looks at often.
36. Parent talks to child while doing household work.
37. Parent consciously encourages developmental advance.
38. Parent invests maturing toys with value via personal attention.
39. Parent structures child's play periods.
40. Parent provides toys that challenge child to develop new skills.

Subtotal

VI. Opportunities for VARIETY

41. Father provides some care daily.
42. Parent reads stories to child at least 3 times weekly.
43. Child eats at least one meal per day with mother and father.
44. Family visits relatives or receives visits once a month or so.
45. Child has 3 or more books of his/her own.

Subtotal

TOTAL SCORE

*For complete wording of items, please refer to the Administration Manual.

FIGURE 7-3

Home visitors may use the HOME Inventory to analyze the home environment of their charges. (*Source:* B. M. Caldwell & R. H. Bradley. *Administration manual: Home observation for measurement of the environment.* Little Rock, Ark.: University of Arkansas, 1984.)

The inventory for 3 to 6 year olds has similar directions. For example, item 4 states, *"Toys or games permitting free expression.* Examples of toys allowing free expression would be clay, finger paints, play dough, crayons and paint and paper"* (Caldwell & Bradley, 1984, p. 28).

Home Screening Questionnaire (HSQ)

Frankenburg recognized the value of the HOME Inventory but was concerned about the length of time needed for a skilled interviewer to make a home visit, so he developed a questionnaire, the HSQ, that could be answered by parents. With the cooperation of the authors of the HOME, items were selected and reconstructed into questionnaire format as illustrated by Figure 7-4. Two questionnaires were developed that correspond to the two HOME scales (for children from birth to 3 years and from 3 to 6 years of age). They take approximately 15 minutes for a parent to complete. The questionnaire has been validated as an effective screening tool to identify those environments that would benefit from a more intensive assessment. "The HSQ Manual gives complete instructions for scoring the questionnaires. As with all suspect screening results, questionable HSQ results should be followed with a visit by a trained home interviewer to assure that the result of the screening test is accurate and that appropriate intervention can be planned" (Fandal, 1986).

Development

Denver Prescreening Developmental Questionnaire (PDQ)

The PDQ is a brief, parent-answered questionnaire for children from birth to 6 years of age that can be completed by parents as they sit in a doctor's office or attend a parent education meeting. Parents answer questions about their child's current developmental skills. The questions, written on a sixth-grade reading level, are illustrated in Figure 7-5. As children mature, they may perform some of the tasks. When the results of the PDQ are suspect, it should be followed by a DDST. The PDQ has been widely used since 1976 and a revision of the questionnaire (PDQ-R) is currently being field tested.

Denver Developmental Screening Test (DDST)

The DDST screens the child's development from infancy to 6 years of age. It is a more time-consuming developmental screening tool than the PDQ and takes from 10 to 20 minutes to administer. A person giving the DDST (Figure 7-6) needs to study the manual and administer the test according to precise directions in order to assure validity of the test results. Another form which includes identical information is also available. Suspect results on the DDST, as designated in the test manual, should be followed by an appropriate assessment and, when indicated, intervention should be planned (Fandal, 1986).

"Either the PDQ or the DDST, when used to routinely screen a child's development serves to alert parents to what they may expect next in their child's developmental progress. This seems to increase the parents' interest in activities that they can pursue to encourage the next stages of development" (Fandal, 1986).

RECRUITMENT OF FAMILIES

Many families will be identified by existing local facilities, such as Head Start, schools and social service agencies. Articles in newspapers about the new home-based program will alert other parents, and flyers can be delivered by school children. The most effective method, however, is a door-to-door canvas. Home visitors can go from house to house and chat with parents of young children and explain the program and its benefits. This personal approach

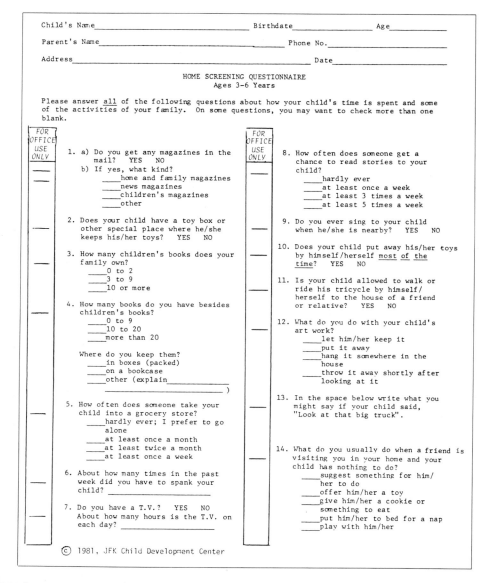

Child's Name_____ Birthdate_____ Age_____

Parent's Name_____ Phone No._____

Address_____ Date_____

HOME SCREENING QUESTIONNAIRE
Ages 3–6 Years

Please answer <u>all</u> of the following questions about how your child's time is spent and some of the activities of your family. On some questions, you may want to check more than one blank.

FOR OFFICE USE ONLY

1. a) Do you get any magazines in the mail?   YES   NO
   b) If yes, what kind?
      ____home and family magazines
      ____news magazines
      ____children's magazines
      ____other

2. Does your child have a toy box or other special place where he/she keeps his/her toys?   YES   NO

3. How many children's books does your family own?
   ____0 to 2
   ____3 to 9
   ____10 or more

4. How many books do you have besides children's books?
   ____0 to 9
   ____10 to 20
   ____more than 20

   Where do you keep them?
   ____in boxes (packed)
   ____on a bookcase
   ____other (explain_____
   _____)

5. How often does someone take your child into a grocery store?
   ____hardly ever; I prefer to go alone
   ____at least once a month
   ____at least twice a month
   ____at least once a week

6. About how many times in the past week did you have to spank your child? _____

7. Do you have a T.V.?   YES   NO
   About how many hours is the T.V. on each day? _____

FOR OFFICE USE ONLY

8. How often does someone get a chance to read stories to your child?
   ____hardly ever
   ____at least once a week
   ____at least 3 times a week
   ____at least 5 times a week

9. Do you ever sing to your child when he/she is nearby?   YES   NO

10. Does your child put away his/her toys by himself/herself <u>most of the time</u>?   YES   NO

11. Is your child allowed to walk or ride his tricycle by himself/herself to the house of a friend or relative?   YES   NO

12. What do you do with your child's art work?
    ____let him/her keep it
    ____put it away
    ____hang it somewhere in the house
    ____throw it away shortly after looking at it

13. In the space below write what you might say if your child said, "Look at that big truck".

14. What do you usually do when a friend is visiting you in your home and your child has nothing to do?
    ____suggest something for him/her to do
    ____offer him/her a toy
    ____give him/her a cookie or something to eat
    ____put him/her to bed for a nap
    ____play with him/her

© 1981, JFK Child Development Center

FIGURE 7-4
The HSQ is a shortened version of the questionnaire about home environment designed for parents to answer. (*Source:* C. E. Coons, E. C. Gay, A. W. Fandal, C. Ker, and W. K. Frankenburg. *Home screening questionnaire.* Denver, Col.: JFK Child Development Center, 1981).

The form (right panel):

DENVER PRESCREENING DEVELOPMENTAL QUESTIONNAIRE

Child's Name _____
Date _____
Birthdate _____

Please read each question carefully before you answer. Circle the best answer for each question. YOUR CHILD IS NOT EXPECTED TO BE ABLE TO DO EVERYTHING THE QUESTIONS ASK.

YES - CHILD CAN DO NOW or HAS DONE IN THE PAST
NO - CHILD CANNOT DO NOW, HAS NOT DONE IN THE PAST or YOU ARE NOT SURE THAT YOUR CHILD CAN DO IT.
R - CHILD REFUSES TO TRY
NO-OPP - CHILD HAS NOT HAD THE CHANCE TO TRY

© Wm. K. Frankenburg, M.D., University of Colorado Medical Center, 1975.

4 YEAR - 4 YEAR, 9 MONTH

4 year check - Answer 71 through 80

71. Can your child pedal a tricycle at least ten feet? If your child has never had a chance to ride a tricycle his size, circle NO-OPP.　YES　NO　R　NO-OPP

72. After eating, does your child wash and dry his hands well enough so you don't have to do them over? Circle NO-OPP if you do not allow him to wash and dry his hands by himself.　YES　NO　R　NO-OPP

4 year, 3 month check - Answer 73 through 82

73. Does your child put an "s" at the end of his words when he is talking about more than one thing such as blocks, shoes or toys?　YES　NO　R　NO-OPP

74. Without letting your child hold onto anything, have him balance on one foot for as long as he can. If necessary, encourage him by showing him how. GIVE HIM THREE CHANCES. Estimate seconds by counting slowly. Did your child balance 2 seconds or more?　YES　NO　R　NO-OPP

75. Without letting your child take a running jump, ask him to jump length-wise over this paper. Did he do this without landing on the paper?　YES　NO　R　NO-OPP

76. Have your child draw this figure in the space below. DO NOT SAY "CIRCLE". Do not help or correct your child. Say to your child, "Draw a picture just like this one", and point to the picture on the right.

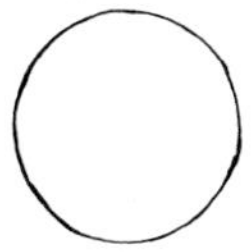

Look at these examples when scoring your child's drawing.

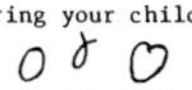

Answer YES

Answer NO

Did your child draw a circle?　YES　NO　R　NO-OPP

4 year, 6 month check - Answer 77 through 86

77. Can your child put eight blocks on top of one another without the blocks falling? This applies to small blocks about 1 inch in size and not blocks more than 2 inches in size.　YES　NO　R　NO-OPP

4 year, 9 month check - Answer 78 through 87

78. Does your child play hide-and-seek, cops-and-robbers or other games where he takes turns and follows rules?　YES　NO　R　NO-OPP

79. Can your child put jeans, shirt, dress or socks on without help except snapping, buttoning and belts?　YES　NO　R　NO-OPP

80. Without your coaching or saying his name so he can repeat it, does your child say both his first and last name? Circle NO if he only gives his first name or is not easily understood.　YES　NO　R　NO-OPP

The instructions (left panel):

DENVER PRESCREENING DEVELOPMENTAL QUESTIONNAIRE

Instructions

EXPLANATION

The Denver Prescreening Developmental Questionnaire (PDQ) is a brief questionnaire to be answered by the parent. As a "prescreening" tool, it is designed to identify those children ranging in age from three months to six years who will require further screening with the Denver Developmental Screening Test (DDST). The PDQ also can be used as a systematic method of logging a child's development. Although the PDQ is designed to detect developmental lags, it should be understood that failures on the PDQ do not necessarily indicate an abnormality, but only suggest that more detailed screening with the DDST is required. It takes only a few minutes to prepare the parent and interpret the results.

Directions

A. Steps in Administering the PDQ:

1. Calculate the child's age to the nearest month. For instance, if a child is 3 months and 16 days round off to 4 months. When rounding to the nearest month consider all months to have 30 days and round off 15 days to the next higher month.

2. Select the appropriately colored questionnaire by referring to the reverse side of these instructions.

3. On the questionnaire, locate the age category which corresponds most closely with the age of the child.

4. Bracket the ten age appropriate questions and INDICATE THE DATE (see the sample).

5. Instruct the parent to read the instructions at the top of the page and answer all ten questions enclosed within the brackets. If a parent is uncertain about any answer ask her to select the best answer.

B. Scoring the PDQ:

1. Review the results to be certain that all ten bracketed questions were answered.

2. Count only the number of "Yes" responses.

3. If the child has 9 or 10 "Yes" answers, the results are negative (nonsuspect).

4. If less than 9, the results are positive or suspect, therefore:

   a. Check your age calculations;

   b. Check to be sure you bracketed the correct questions.

   c. If there are 7 or 8 "Yes" responses, schedule for rescreen with the PDQ within one month and if still less than 9 "Yes" schedule for DDST.*

   d. If there are 6 or fewer "Yes" responses perform the DDST without repeating the PDQ.

C. Repeated Use of PDQ:

If the results are negative, the PDQ should be administered every three months during the first year of life, every six months during the second year and yearly after age two.

*The ten appropriate questions on this rescreen may be identical to those on the initial screen, or there may be a few new questions depending upon the lapse of time between the first and second PDQ.

FIGURE 7-5

Parents can answer the PDQ quickly as they wait in the doctor's office or the school's parent room and recognize suspect results or feel comfortable in their child's development. (*Source:* W. K. Frankenburg. *Denver prescreening developmental questionnaire.* Denver, Col.: JFK Child Development Center, 1975.)

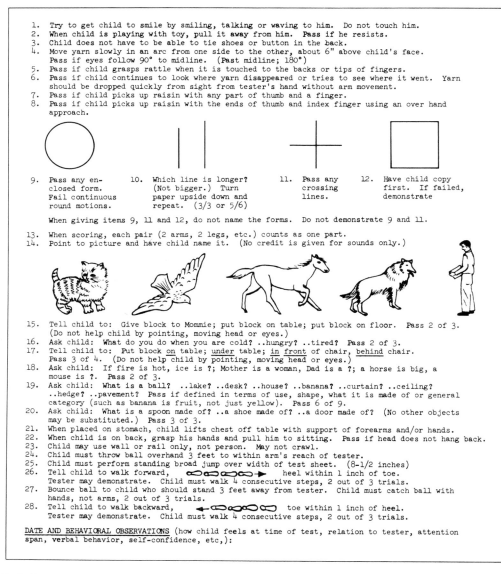

1. Try to get child to smile by smiling, talking or waving to him. Do not touch him.
2. When child is playing with toy, pull it away from him. Pass if he resists.
3. Child does not have to be able to tie shoes or button in the back.
4. Move yarn slowly in an arc from one side to the other, about 6" above child's face. Pass if eyes follow 90° to midline. (Past midline; 180°)
5. Pass if child grasps rattle when it is touched to the backs or tips of fingers.
6. Pass if child continues to look where yarn disappeared or tries to see where it went. Yarn should be dropped quickly from sight from tester's hand without arm movement.
7. Pass if child picks up raisin with any part of thumb and a finger.
8. Pass if child picks up raisin with the ends of thumb and index finger using an over hand approach.

9. Pass any enclosed form. Fail continuous round motions.
10. Which line is longer? (Not bigger.) Turn paper upside down and repeat. (3/3 or 5/6)
11. Pass any crossing lines.
12. Have child copy first. If failed, demonstrate

When giving items 9, 11 and 12, do not name the forms. Do not demonstrate 9 and 11.

13. When scoring, each pair (2 arms, 2 legs, etc.) counts as one part.
14. Point to picture and have child name it. (No credit is given for sounds only.)

15. Tell child to: Give block to Mommie; put block on table; put block on floor. Pass 2 of 3. (Do not help child by pointing, moving head or eyes.)
16. Ask child: What do you do when you are cold? ..hungry? ..tired? Pass 2 of 3.
17. Tell child to: Put block on table; under table; in front of chair, behind chair. Pass 3 of 4. (Do not help child by pointing, moving head or eyes.)
18. Ask child: If fire is hot, ice is ?; Mother is a woman, Dad is a ?; a horse is big, a mouse is ?. Pass 2 of 3.
19. Ask child: What is a ball? ..lake? ..desk? ..house? ..banana? ..curtain? ..ceiling? ..hedge? ..pavement? Pass if defined in terms of use, shape, what it is made of or general category (such as banana is fruit, not just yellow). Pass 6 of 9.
20. Ask child: What is a spoon made of? ..a shoe made of? ..a door made of? (No other objects may be substituted.) Pass 3 of 3.
21. When placed on stomach, child lifts chest off table with support of forearms and/or hands.
22. When child is on back, grasp his hands and pull him to sitting. Pass if head does not hang back.
23. Child may use wall or rail only, not person. May not crawl.
24. Child must throw ball overhand 3 feet to within arm's reach of tester.
25. Child must perform standing broad jump over width of test sheet. (8-1/2 inches)
26. Tell child to walk forward, ⬤⫘⬤⫘⬤⫘ heel within 1 inch of toe. Tester may demonstrate. Child must walk 4 consecutive steps, 2 out of 3 trials.
27. Bounce ball to child who should stand 3 feet away from tester. Child must catch ball with hands, not arms, 2 out of 3 trials.
28. Tell child to walk backward, ⬅⬤⫘⬤⫘⬤⫘ toe within 1 inch of heel. Tester may demonstrate. Child must walk 4 consecutive steps, 2 out of 3 trials.

DATE AND BEHAVIORAL OBSERVATIONS (how child feels at time of test, relation to tester, attention span, verbal behavior, self-confidence, etc,):

FIGURE 7-6

The DDST is a screening tool to be used to determine a child is not developing appropriately. It should be followed by more prescriptive instruments if the results are suspect. (*Source:* W. K. Frankenburg & J. Dodds. *Denver developmental screening test.* Denver, Col.: University of Colorado Medical Center, n. d.)

FIGURE 7-6, *continued (opposite)*

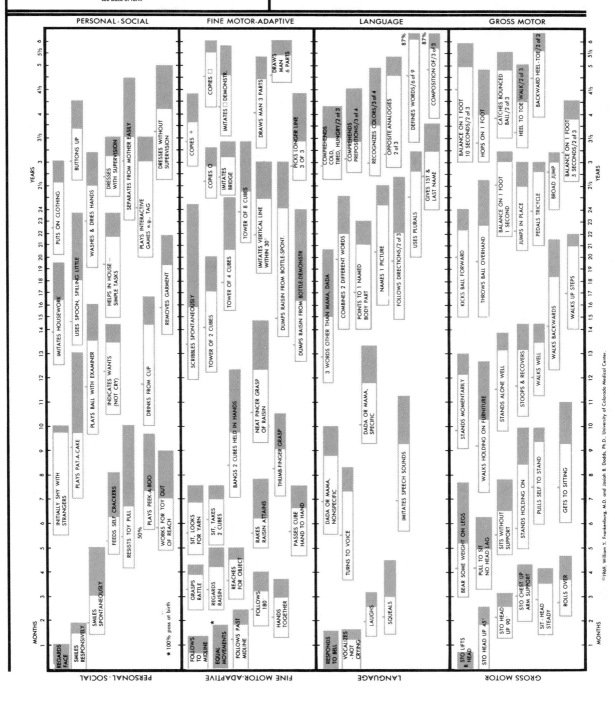

DENVER DEVELOPMENTAL SCREENING TEST

STO.= STOMACH
SIT = SITTING

PERCENT OF CHILDREN PASSING

May pass by report

Footnote No. ──→
see back of form

Test Item

Date
Name
Birthdate
Hosp. No.

©1969, William K. Frankenburg, M.D. and Josiah B. Dodds, Ph.D. University of Colorado Medical Center.

seems to encourage parents to participate when a notice through the mail may not. Families new to the area or unknown to social agencies or Head Start will be contacted by a door-to-door campaign; otherwise, they might not know of the opportunity.

Articles can increase parents' interest. Curriculum and child development may be

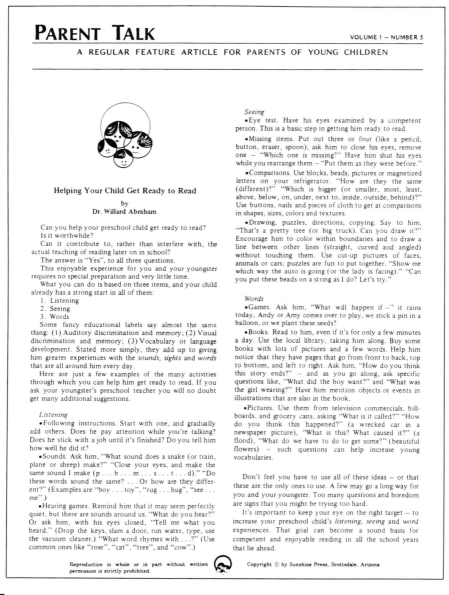

PARENT TALK

VOLUME 1 – NUMBER 5

A REGULAR FEATURE ARTICLE FOR PARENTS OF YOUNG CHILDREN

Helping Your Child Get Ready to Read
by
Dr. Willard Abraham

Can you help your preschool child get ready to read? Is it worthwhile?

Can it contribute to, rather than interfere with, the actual teaching of reading later on in school?

The answer is "Yes", to all three questions.

This enjoyable experience for you and your youngster requires no special preparation and very little time.

What you can do is based on three items, and your child already has a strong start in all of them:

1. Listening
2. Seeing
3. Words

Some fancy educational labels say almost the same thing: (1) Auditory discrimination and memory; (2) Visual discrimination and memory; (3) Vocabulary or language development. Stated more simply, they add up to giving him greater experiences with the *sounds*, *sights* and *words* that are all around him every day.

Here are just a few examples of the many activities through which you can help him get ready to read. If you ask your youngster's preschool teacher you will no doubt get many additional suggestions.

Listening

• Following instructions. Start with one, and gradually add others. Does he pay attention while you're talking? Does he stick with a job until it's finished? Do you tell him how well he did it?

• Sounds. Ask him, "What sound does a snake (or train, plane or sheep) make?" "Close your eyes, and make the same sound I make (p . . . b . . . m . . . s . . . t . . . d)." "Do these words sound the same? . . . Or how are they different?" (Examples are "boy . . . toy", "rug . . . hug", "see . . . me".)

• Hearing games. Remind him that it may seem perfectly quiet, but there are sounds around us. "What do you hear?" Or ask him, with his eyes closed, "Tell me what you heard." (Drop the keys, slam a door, run water, type, use the vacuum cleaner.) "What word rhymes with . . .?" (Use common ones like "rose", "cat", "tree", and "cow".)

Seeing

• Eye test. Have his eyes examined by a competent person. This is a basic step in getting him ready to read.

• Missing items. Put out three or four (like a pencil, button, eraser, spoon), ask him to close his eyes, remove one – "Which one is missing?" Have him shut his eyes while you rearrange them – "Put them as they were before."

• Comparisons. Use blocks, beads, pictures or magnetized letters on your refrigerator. "How are they the same (different)?" "Which is bigger (or smaller, most, least, above, below, on, under, next to, inside, outside, behind)?" Use buttons, nails and pieces of cloth to get at comparisons in shapes, sizes, colors and textures.

• Drawing, puzzles, directions, copying. Say to him, "That's a pretty tree (or big truck). Can you draw it?" Encourage him to color within boundaries and to draw a line between other lines (straight, curved and angled) without touching them. Use cut-up pictures of faces, animals or cars; puzzles are fun to put together. "Show me which way the auto is going (or the lady is facing)." "Can you put these beads on a string as I do? Let's try."

Words

• Games. Ask him, "What will happen if –" it rains today, Andy or Amy comes over to play, we stick a pin in a balloon, or we plant these seeds?

• Books. Read to him, even if it's for only a few minutes a day. Use the local library, taking him along. Buy some books with lots of pictures and a few words. Help him notice that they have pages that go from front to back, top to bottom, and left to right. Ask him, "How do you think this story ends?" – and as you go along, ask specific questions like, "What did the boy want?" and "What was the girl wearing?" Have him mention objects or events in illustrations that are also in the book.

• Pictures. Use them from television commercials, billboards, and grocery cans, asking "What is it called?" "How do you think this happened?" (a wrecked car in a newspaper picture), "What is this? What caused it?" (a flood), "What do we have to do to get some?" (beautiful flowers) – such questions can help increase young vocabularies.

Don't feel you have to use all of these ideas – or that these are the only ones to use. A few may go a long way for you and your youngster. Too many questions and boredom are signs that you might be trying too hard.

It's important to keep your eye on the right target – to increase your preschool child's *listening*, *seeing* and *word* experiences. That goal can become a sound basis for competent and enjoyable reading in all the school years that lie ahead.

FIGURE 7-7
"Suggestions for parents" is a series of feature articles to be used in parent programs. (*Source:* W. Abraham. *Parent talk.* Scottsdale, Arizona: Sunshine Press. Reprinted with permission.)

communicated through newsletters as well as personal visits. It is also a good idea to combine the two and give the parent a handout at the end of a home visit. Write your own newsletter or use a commercial one such as *Parent Talk* (Figure 7-7).

HOME VISITS

If you picture the typical home visit as one where the visitor works solely as a teacher of the young child, you will have to do a complete turnabout. Instead, the home visitor helps parents to become child development experts and teachers of their own children by modeling activities and working with their children. The time spent on each facet of the Home Start program is illustrated in Figure 7-8.

Although 55 percent of the time is spent on education, 24 percent is spent on parental concerns and services. There is more interaction with the child than with the parent—55 percent as opposed to 45 percent—but the emphasis on health, nutrition, and parental concerns illustrates the broad base served by Home Start. Another program located in an affluent area of the city might not include an emphasis on health and nutrition but should still

focus on helping the parents to become more aware of their function as educators of their children and to develop the means to accomplish the task.

The home visitor's work in the field reflects the goals and objectives of the specific program. The following suggestions were adapted primarily from the Home Start guide. Choose those that fit your needs.

- Accept the child and family without reservations; base your visits on their needs. Start where they are and work with them as a team to achieve the goals you work out together.
- Come to the home with an activity or toy that breaks the "ice" and engages the child and parent in an enjoyable pursuit. Hand puppets are sure engagers. Bring extras for mother and child. The extension of self through a charming puppet helps the reticent talker to get started. Bring other special toys and attractive puzzles; place them in full view of the child to initiate the interaction process.
- Bring a toy (or book or creative experience) that will involve the parent in a developmental experience with the child. Leave the toy at the home and encourage the mother to use it with the child during the week.
- Develop activities from the home environment that can be duplicated by parents following the visit.

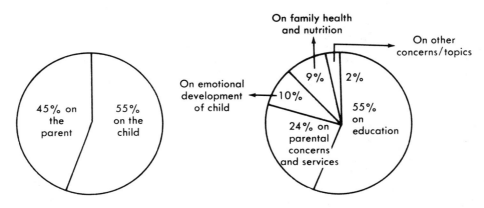

FIGURE 7-8
Focus on home visit activities. (*Source:* J. M. Love et al. *National Home Start evaluation: final report. Findings and implications.* Washington, D. C.: U. S. Government Printing Office, 1976, p. 6.)

- Help the mother improvise toys from household items. Examples of homemade toys include cans filled with pebbles, buttons, or paper clips to produce interesting and varied sounds; stackable measuring cups, pans, or mixing bowls; and building blocks made of empty milk cartons.
- Don't be afraid to help the mother with a household chore (such as washing dishes, making biscuits, or peeling potatoes). By involving the child, demonstrate how activities that normally make up the fabric of each day can be used as constructive learning experiences for children.
- Listen to the parents as they talk about each child and the things they are doing to further their children's development. Praise them for gains made. Make occasional suggestions.
- Include activities that involve the older children or that encourage the older children to work with and to help the younger ones. Such activities may take the form of coloring, pasting, simple crafts, reading to the young ones, etc.
- Budget some time to give the parents an opportunity to talk about their own achievements, needs, or problems. In such conversation, the home visitor may mention adult education classes, parent meetings, available health agencies, or the existence of community services that the family is not using but for which it is eligible. These services are suggested in the context that there are ways in which the parents may be able to do more for the development of their children.
- Take time from more serious purposes for a snack or sociable chat, perhaps while helping a busy mother dry dishes or fold diapers. (Modified from U.S. Department of Health, Education, and Welfare, 1974, p. 58)

IN-SERVICE TRAINING AFTER THE PROGRAM HAS STARTED

Learning by both the family and the home visitor comes to fruition during the development of the program. During this period, the home visitor responds to the individual needs, desires, and styles of the parents and children. Close contact with the program's coordinator or trainers supports the home visitor and allows administrators to keep track of what is happening in the field. Reports on each visit,

filled out in duplicate with one for the home visitor and one for the program's administrators or trainers, will enable persons from both levels of the program to keep in touch with developments and needs (Figure 7-9). In doing so in-service training can be directed to enrich weak areas and clarify procedures.

Small Groups

Throughout the year questions and needs for training will arise. Small groups of home visitors, rather than all members of the program, meeting together as needs emerge encourages effective training sessions. The individualized meeting is beneficial because the session has been set up especially for the participants, and small numbers allow for a more personalized response by the trainer or coordinator.

Community Resources

Although lists of community resources are given to home visitors early in the program, more definite descriptions and procedures are useful when specific problems arise. During the year, specialists from a variety of community agencies can be invited to share their experiences and knowledge of procedures with the staff. Have them come to training meetings, meet the staff, and answer questions concerning use of their programs.

Development of a Home Activities File

The development of a home activities file depends on the objectives and philosophy of the program. Materials and experiences are based on the home environment, the children's interests, and the parents' enthusiasm. You have an excellent opportunity to involve parents in creating learning activities for their children. You may enable the parents to change through your encouragement and acceptance of their contributions.

DENVER PUBLIC SCHOOLS
Division of Education
Office of Federal Projects   Initials _____
Home Based Parent Education Project   School _____
Home Education Language Project   Project _____

No. _____ Individual lesson plan for _____
                                              (Child's name)

on _____ Goal _____
   (Date)

Specific objective: _____

Materials: _____

Lesson schedule

  Initial activity: _____

  Review activity: _____

  Story: _____

  Technique: Flannel board _____ Book _____ Puppet _____ Other _____

Activity to meet specific objective

  1. _____

  2. _____

  3. _____

  4. _____

  5. _____

  Concluding activity: _____

  Parent suggestion for reinforcement of objective: _____

_____

Evaluation
  Child's response   Parental response
  _____ Enthusiastic   _____ Discussed progress
  _____ Interested   _____ Actively participated
  _____ Negative because   _____ Watched with interest
     _____ Ill   _____ Watched passively
     _____ Emotionally upset   _____ Asked questions
     _____ Activity too easy   _____ At home, but not present
     _____ Activity too hard   _____ Discussed suggestion

Other comments: _____

_____

FIGURE 7-9
The Denver home visit report includes activities plus both the child's and the parent's responses. (*Source: Home-based education language project—Tutor's handbook.* Denver, Col.: Denver Public Schools, 1979, p. 15. Reprinted with permission from Denver Public Schools.)

Throughout the year home visitors involve parents in teaching their children at home. As the home visitor suggests activities for the child, additional ideas may occur to both the visitor and the parent. In addition, children themselves may elaborate on old ideas or create new activities. The home visitor should bring these ideas back to the office, where they can be classified and catalogued. Parents receive a boost if home visitors recognize their contributions. They will also continue to develop activities for children if they are reinforced. Write down their suggestions and file them for future use or include them in the program for the coming week.

EVALUATION OF PROGRAM

Ongoing evaluations of contacts made, visits completed, and services rendered are essential. Home visit reports give data that can be used to measure progress. The Denver home visit report illustrates periodic evaluations of both the child's and parent's responses (Figure 7-9). If the home visitor systematically completes each report, the administrator will be able to evaluate throughout the training period.

Parent Questionnaires

Statements by parents and responses to questionnaires concerning the effect of the program on the child and family are valuable in analyzing the impact of the program. Collect these throughout the program as well as at the completion of the year. The Gloucester Parent Evaluation form is a good guide to aid in the construction of a parent questionnaire (Figure 7-10).

Evaluation is a tool to be used during the development of the program as well as a means to assess accomplishments. Include a variety of evaluations to improve the program and to demonstrate its effectiveness.

PRACTICES TO AVOID

Dr. J. Ronald Lally cautions Home Start directors against the following pitfalls:

- Working too much with the child, rather than with the parents
- Seeing emotional and cognitive development in children as separate, when, in fact, they are integral
- Tending to be too rigid in the use of structured cognitive materials intended to promote intellectual development
- Setting up too many formal activities, rather than allowing for more informal give-and-take
- Concentrating too often on reinforcing and rewarding the child, and not providing enough reward and enjoyment for the parents and other children in the family
- Defining the role of the home visitor too narrowly
- Encouraging families to develop an unhealthy dependency on the home visitors when their goal instead should be to help parents become more independent and self-sufficient
- Relying exclusively on a middle-class model of child rearing, rather than attempting to assess the individual situation and strengths of each family (Modified from U.S. Department of Health, Education, and Welfare, 1974, p. 59)

These warnings point out the importance of involving parents in the education of their children. Helping parents become more self-sufficient and nurturing promotes a stable and enriching environment for the child.

PROGRAMS THAT WORK

Numerous methods and approaches have proven effective in a variety of projects funded throughout the United States. Summaries of selected programs illustrate the scope and variety of parent involvement in the educational process. Take from them the ideas and procedures that fit into your specific situation.

Directions: On the following questions put a check in the box opposite the answer that best describes your personal opinion.

1. Since my child started Home Start, he/she
   a. has progressed greatly _____ ☐
   b. has progressed a little_____ ☐
   c. hasn't learned anything_____ ☐
2. Check one
   a. My child really likes Home Start_____ ☐
   b. My child participates because I want him/her to _____ ☐
   c. My child doesn't like Home Start _____ ☐
   d. I don't know how my child feels _____ ☐
3. In my opinion, Home Start
   a. requires too much discipline _____ ☐
   b. there is just the right amount of discipline_____ ☐
   c. there is not enough discipline_____ ☐
4. Do you feel that your child is receiving enough individual attention?
   Yes _____   No _____
5. Do you feel you are receiving enough information about your child's progress?
   Yes _____   No _____
6. Do you find it easy to talk to your Home Visitor concerning your child?
   Yes _____   No _____
7. Would you like to have more opportunity to plan with your Home Visitor about your child?
   Yes _____   No _____
8. Do you like the activities for your child?
   Yes _____   No _____
9. Since my child started in Home Start, I have noticed that he/she
   a. is more independent _____ ☐
   b. is less independent _____ ☐
   c. no difference _____ ☐
10. Since my child started in Home Start, I have noticed that he/she
    a. is more curious _____ ☐
    b. is less curious _____ ☐
    c. no difference _____ ☐
11. Since my child started in Home Start, I have noticed that he/she
    a. gets along better with other children _____ ☐
    b. gets along worse with other children_____ ☐
    c. no change _____ ☐
12. Since my child started in Home Start, I have noticed that he/she
    a. speaks more clearly_____ ☐
    b. speaks less clearly_____ ☐
    c. no change _____ ☐
13. Since my child started in Home Start, I have noticed that he/she
    a. follows directions more easily_____ ☐
    b. follows directions less easily_____ ☐
    c. no change_____ ☐
14. Since my child started in Home Start, I have noticed that he/she
    a. is better behaved _____ ☐
    b. behaves worse _____ ☐
    c. no change _____ ☐
15. Do you think your child will do better in public schools because of Home Start?
    Yes _____   No _____
    What did you expect your child to learn as a result of Home Start?
    a._____
    b._____
    c._____

FIGURE 7-10

The Gloucester parent evaluation form allows parents to analyze their child's growth. (*Source:* U. S. Department of Health, Education, and Welfare. *Partners with parents.* Washington, D. C.: U. S. Government Printing Office, 1978.)

16. In your opinion, what should be done to improve the program for your child?
    a. _____
    b. _____
    c. _____
17. As a result of Home Start,
    a. I know more about my child's development _____ ☐
    b. I know a great deal more about my child's development _____ ☐
    c. I know the same about my child's development _____ ☐
18. As a result of Home Start, I have gained knowledge as the teacher of my child.
    Yes _____   No _____
19. As a result of Home Start, I know more about the services available to me
    in the community.
    Yes _____   No _____

PARENT ACTIVITIES EVALUATION

1. Check one
   a. I attend most of the parent activities _____ ☐
   b. I have attended at least one of the meetings _____ ☐
   c. I have not been able to attend _____ ☐
   Why? _____
2. Which statement best describes your opinion of parent activities?
   a. I find them enjoyable _____ ☐
   b. I like them a little _____ ☐
   c. I find them boring _____ ☐
   d. I haven't attended enough activities to form an opinion _____ ☐
3. As a result of the activities, I have
   a. found out a lot about Home Start _____ ☐
   b. found out a little about Home Start _____ ☐
   c. found out almost nothing _____ ☐
4. Do you feel comfortable sharing concerns and interests with other mothers
   at the activities?
   Yes _____   No _____
5. Have you been able at the activities to discuss the progress of your child?
   Yes _____   No _____

PROGRAM EVALUATION

1. What has Home Start meant to you?
   a. _____
   b. _____
   c. _____
2. What could be improved in Home Start?
   a. _____
   b. _____
   c. _____

FIGURE 7-10, *continued*

Portage Project

The Portage Project is a home teaching program for parents and handicapped preschoolers, ages birth to 6 years. It serves a large rural area of 3600 square miles in south-central Wisconsin. Children who have been diagnosed as either mentally retarded, physically handicapped, hearing impaired, vision impaired, or culturally deprived and children who have speech, language, or behavioral problems are enrolled. The children chosen are referred to the project by local physicians, social workers, public schools, speech therapists, county health nurses, and local guidance teams. In addition, the project was advertised

In many home-based programs professional educators work in the child's home.

on the radio and in newspaper articles, which ask parents to refer children themselves.

Although children could not come a long distance to a center, it was feasible to have a home delivery system with professional educators going to the home on scheduled visits for 9½ months each year. A home teacher visits the home and works with the parents and child each week for 1½ hours on three behavioral goals appropriate to the child's ability level. After the home teacher demonstrates each activity and how to record the child's performance, the parent models the process. The parent continues as the teacher and records the child's performance until the next home visit. At the next home visit the teacher records the child's progress, and the parent-teacher team sets up new goals and activities for the following week.

An extensive diagnostic program is used to assess the children's abilities. Developmental scales and intelligence tests available for evaluation purposes include Bayley Scales of Infant Development (Bayley, 1969), Test of Nonverbal Intelligence, a Language-free Measure of Cognitive Ability (Brown, Sherbenow, & Dollar, 1982), The Culture Fair Series, Scale 1, 1950, Scale 2, 1973, Scale 3, 1973 (Cattell & Cattell, 1973), Expanded Manual for the Peabody Picture Vocabulary Test (Dunn, 1965), Stanford-Binet Intelligence Scale, 3rd edition (Terman & Merrill, 1960), and Wechsler Preschool and Primary Scale of Intelligence Manual (Wechsler, 1976).

The Portage Project staff developed materials that are valuable for use with both handicapped and nonhandicapped children. The materials include:

1. A checklist of behaviors of 580 developmentally sequenced behaviors divided into six areas: infant stimulation, self-help, language, cognition, motor skills, and socialization
2. A card file of 580 cards to match the checklist with suggestions for teaching the behaviors
3. A *Manual of Instruction,* which describes how to use the Portage Guide and develop and implement curriculum goals (Figure 7-11).

Because the program involves the parents in teaching their children, manuals for parents were also developed. The Portage Parent Program includes *Parent Readings and Inventories, Parental Behavior Inventory,* and an *Instructor's Manual.*

The Portage Program uses the parent as the teacher through the week. To facilitate this process, the home teacher supports the parent in the following ways:

1. Demonstrates for the parents what to do and how to do it
2. Helps parents practice teaching the skill
3. Encourages parents when they do well
4. Individualizes the program so it fits the needs of the parents as well as the child

Cognitive 58

AGE 3 to 4

TITLE: Copies series of connected V strokes VVVVVVVV

WHAT TO DO:

1. Draw a series of V strokes. Encourage the child to trace over the
    letter first with his finger and later with a crayon or pencil.
    Help by guiding his hand.
2. Have him draw with you making one line at a time.
3. Make a row of connected V strokes. Then have the child draw more
    rows as you give him verbal directions "up, down, up, down."
4. Have child make a row of V strokes on paper. When he finishes,
    make it into a picture of mountains, grass, trees, etc. for him.

PortageGuide

Cognitive 61

AGE 3 to 4

TITLE: Names objects as same and different

WHAT TO DO:

1. Put three sets of two identical items in a box (two forks, two
    blocks, two combs). Ask child to find two things that are the
    same in the box.
2. Repeat above activity using pictures or textures.
3. Use assortment of paired items telling the child they are the same.
    Mix them up and tell the child they are different. Present pairs
    of same and different items to child and have him tell you if they
    are the same or different.
4. Help the child by giving him clues of the first sound of the word.
    Say, "These are the s-s-s." Let child finish word.
5. If child has difficulty, initially ask him, "Are they same or dif-
    ferent?" Gradually fade this and just ask, "Tell me about these."

PortageGuide

FIGURE 7-11
Two examples from the card deck of the Portage Guide show the type of activities that
parents can do with their children at home. (*Source:* D. Shearer et al. *Portage guide to
early education.* Portage, Wis.: Cooperative Educational Service Agency 12, 1976.)

5. Involves parents in planning and in taking on as much responsibility as they are able

The type of program which stimulates direct involvement of parents in teaching their children can provide parents with necessary skills and techniques to become more effective doing what they already do and being what they already are, the single most important individual in their child's life—parents and teachers. (Shearer et al., 1976, p. 40)

Mother-Child Home Program of the Verbal Interaction Project

Phyllis Levenstein's Mother-Child Home Program (MCHP) is a home-based program that relies on positive verbal interaction between the young child, 2 to 4 years old, and the primary caregiver. The "mother" may be any adult who has the primary nurturing responsibilities of the child. The program is based in the child's home, and home visitors ("toy demonstrators") come twice weekly for half-hour sessions over the 2-year period (ages 2 to 4). The school year covers 7 months, two visits a week for a total of 46 visits to each home each year. The toy demonstrators use 12 books and 11 toys each year. The program progresses developmentally through the 46 visits. Guide sheets cover concepts such as colors, shapes, and sizes and cognitive skills such as matching, pretending, and differentiating. Special features of the MCHP include:

1. Guide sheets that allow the caregiver to have the curriculum in small, easily used portions
2. Training that is based on modeling rather than teaching
3. Permanent assignment of toy demonstrators over the 2 years with each demonstrator using the same 22 toys and 24 books, which ensures a stable curriculum for all participants
4. Techniques that encourage the program to be voluntary and not intrusive upon the caregiver

5. Explicit methods for 2 years that also allow for some flexibility

The goal of the program is to increase the mother's interaction with her child in a natural dialogue that enhances and enriches the child's home environment. By training toy demonstrators who are paraprofessionals with a high school education to demonstrate and model their toys without being didactic, the project facilitates relaxed verbal interaction between parent and child (Levenstein, 1977).

Levenstein (1979) summarizes the importance of reaching parents when she says, "All the mothers wanted this program because they knew we were trying out a method to help their children do better in school. They realize now that their children can do better, that youngsters don't have to be beaten down by 8 years of academic failure" (as cited in *Carnegie Quarterly,* p. 4).

Early Training Project of Gray and Klaus

Susan Gray (1971) wrote that when she and Klaus began working with children in 1961, they planned to bridge the period between spring and fall with a summer home visiting program, a Saturday morning preschool class, and a monthly newsletter for parents. They introduced a home visiting program where a teacher with preschool or social work training met in the home with the parent 1 hour each week. The teacher brought materials and showed the parent how to use the activities with their children. An unexpected result of the program was the beneficial influence it had on younger siblings, who scored approximately 13 points higher on IQ tests than siblings who had not been involved in a program.

Gray and Klaus followed the success of the summer home visiting program with a large study that compared three different types of treatment for young children. The results from these studies indicate that home visits have a positive effect on children.

In the Early Training Project the visitor leaves a series of activities each week. At the beginning of the program the home visitor supplies activities for the entire week, but as the program progresses, parents are expected to add activities and supply their own to complete the week, thus increasing the parents' responsibility for their child's education.

Clinch Powell Educational Cooperative

The Clinch Powell home-based early childhood education program has a varied approach of three components: home visitation, mobile classroom van, and television. During each home visitation the parent educator brings a weekly four-page *Parent Guide,* which contains a one-page discussion of child development, nutrition, or aspects of parenting plus three pages of activities to be used by the parent and child throughout the week. These activities relate to the television program and the objectives of the project. The home visitor explains and/or demonstrates the activities. Toys, books, and materials can be loaned for the week.

The second component, mobile classroom, uses a traveling van equipped as a preschool. A teacher and aide drive the van to different areas each day, and 10 to 15 children in that area attend preschool for 2 or 3 hours.

The children who participated in the Clinch Powell Home Based programs continued to show gains after entering elementary school. Parental attitudes were also more positive than before (Far West Laboratory, 1983).

These programs for preschool children use the home as primary centers for learning. Educational reports in the 1980s focus on home-based work for school-aged students too and emphasize the need for increased homework.

HOMEWORK, HOMESTUDY AND/OR ENRICHMENT AT HOME

Student achievement rises significantly when teachers regularly assign homework and students conscientiously do it. (U.S. Department of Education, 1986, p. 41)

The report *What Works* emphasizes that the home and homework are essential for children to reach their full potential. However, what homework is varies according to the age of the child. First, the home environment, the interaction, and intense work with toys make up the child's learning experience; the home is the child's school and homework. As children become older, the location of school goes outside the home, and suddenly what children do at home is not considered school unless they bring home an assignment from school. But everyone knows the home is still part of the child's learning experiences, and the extra work and advice from school helps to make learning richer.

Homework takes on different dimensions at the preschool, elementary, and secondary levels. At all levels homestudy or homework can form a bridge between home and school that lets parents know what is happening at school. Homework can help form a bond between parent and child. Preschool teachers or parent educators should focus on the child's experiences at home, take advantage of what is already occurring at home, open the parent's eyes to learning opportunities, and enrich the home experience. The program or center should encourage and support parent-child interaction. Asking parents to read to their children is very positive (U.S. Department of Education, 1986). The parent-child partnership should be recognized even though it is often lost in the hustle of the business of life.

At the elementary school level, the use of assigned homework becomes more defined. The following suggestions for involving the parent with the child's schoolwork were pointed out in *What Works:*

- Some teachers ask parents to read aloud to the child, to listen to the child read, and to sign homework papers.
- Others encourage parents to drill students on math and spelling and to help with homework papers.
- Teachers also encourage parents to discuss school activities with their children and suggest ways parents can help teach their children at home. For example, a simple home activity might be alphabetizing books; a more complex one would be using kitchen supplies in an elementary science experiment.
- Teachers also send home suggestions for games or group activities related to the child's schoolwork that parent and child can play together. (U.S. Department of Education, 1986, p. 19)

If the parent is too busy or is unable to help with the home task, dissension may develop between parent and child. The use of a telephone network (see Chapter 4) to assist the child with homework can help eliminate the problem of the child not knowing how to do the assignment and the parent being embarrassed by not knowing how to do it, either.

The 1983 National Commission on Excellence in Education addressed the issue of homework and recommended that more homework be assigned to students. The 1985 Gallup Poll questioned the public on their attitude toward homework for elementary students. The response was almost evenly divided; 40 percent favored and 38 percent opposed. Parents whose children received average or below average grades were more supportive of homework than those whose children received average marks. Nonwhites were more likely than whites to favor homework for their children; 66 percent to 36 percent at the elementary school level and 67 percent to 45 percent at the high school level (Gallup, 1985, p. 42).

Only about 6 out of 10 public school parents required their children to spend a certain amount of time on their homework. In addition, half limited television viewing. This was true regardless of socioeconomic or educational level. When public school parents did require their children to devote time to homework, the average amount was 1 hour and 25 minutes each night (Gallup, 1985, p. 42). A slightly higher amount is reported by teachers, who say they assign about 2 hours of homework per school day. High school seniors say that they spend 4 to 5 hours a week on homework, and 10 percent spend no time at all (U.S. Department of Education, 1986, p. 41).

Preschool and Primary Grades

Research results do not support the use of homework for the very young (LaConte, 1981). On the other hand, research does recognize the importance of home/school involvement. A rich home environment provides homestudy; the parent is interested in and involved with the child's activities; the child does informal study at home and on visits to the store or museum. Talking and reading together foster the child's development. Selecting television programs and viewing television together, followed by discussion, fosters the child's learning and provides interaction between parent and child. Use of home computers, though not a necessity, can give even a preschool child a feeling of success when using a self-correcting activity that allows her to be in command. The time and length of involvement with computers and television must be monitored, because the most important learning takes place between people. Parents who talk, listen, and read to their children learn a lot about the children's feelings, abilities, and interests.

Elementary and Secondary Grades

Traditional homework for elementary and secondary students falls into a three-level taxonomy according to Lee and Pruitt. The categories are *practice, preparation,* and *extension* (as cited in LaConte, 1981).

Practice is the most common type of homework; a skill learned at school is repeated. LaConte recommends that practice drills be limited to the classroom and homestudy be individualized. "The most effective kind of practice assignment asks the student to apply recently acquired learning in a direct and personal way" (p. 9). The able student becomes bored with the repetition; the poor student will probably ignore the assignment. Thus, the more able students are usually given more and more homework while those who need individualized work either do not do the homework or are not assigned the work. If the teacher limits practice drill to the classroom, he can adjust assignments according to individual needs and differences. However, *What Works* reports on one study that reveals that when low-ability students do just 1 to 3 hours of homework, their grades are as high as average students who do no homework (U.S. Department of Education, 1986, p. 41).

Preparation is the assignment of material to be used to lay the groundwork for the next lesson. These assignments should be imaginative and challenging, and should include more than assigning a chapter to read. Interviews, research, gathering information, or development of an original idea could enrich the child's learning experience (LaConte, 1981). Preparation assignments are not appropriate for young children unless you involve the parents. An appropriate example would be a sound walk. Parent and child could walk around their neighborhood and the child could bring back a list of all the sounds that they heard.

Extension is an individualized approach to homestudy that takes the student beyond the traditional classroom assignment. This homework fosters a creative approach to learning and is usually reserved by schools for older children. Younger children would need their parents' help with a project or research. The young child's whole approach to learning could be labeled extension. A child has to reach and grow from the very first day of birth (and even before). The only thing that has not been required is a report on her learning.

Homework is very important in elementary and secondary schools. LaConte suggests assignments that are "(1) necessary and useful, (2) appropriate to the ability and maturity level of students, (3) well explained and motivated, and (4) clearly understood by both child and parent" (1981, p. 20).

A report by the U.S. Department of Education also emphasizes the need for homework to be well planned. The assignments should relate to the classwork and extend the student's learning beyond the classroom.

Effective homework assignments do not just supplement the classroom lesson; they also teach students to be independent learners. Homework gives students experience in following directions, making judgments and comparisons, raising additional questions for study, and developing responsibility and self-discipline (U.S. Department of Education, 1986, p. 42).

Because many homes have computers connected to information services and data banks, cable television classes, videotapes and videodiscs, the home is now widely recognized as a place where school work can be supplemented and reinforced. Home-based education has many facets and will diversify and increase in the future. Methods may vary, but the home is still a primary educator of children.

SUMMARY

Home-based education, initiated in the 1960s, saw continued and increased use in the 1970s. The Home Start demonstration programs, Parent Child Development Centers, Child and Family Resource Programs, and ESEA Chapter I, III, and IV C programs contributed significant research data and suggested procedures for implementation by others. In the 1980s many of the ideas developed by the Home Start demonstration programs were implemented into the Head Start programs.

Selection of personnel and, in particular, the home visitor, has a great effect on the success of the program. Select either paraprofessionals or professionals, but find persons who are pleasant, flexible, and sensitive to the parents' needs. Preservice and in-service training must include participation of the home visitor.

Acquire home learning activities to be used by the home visitor and families through development of individualized activities, commercial offerings, and/or activities developed by demonstration programs. Use materials that are readily available to the parents, for the parent is the primary teacher in the home-based program. The focus in a home-based program is on the parent interacting with and teaching the child after the home visitor is gone.

Concern about excellence in education brought added emphasis on homework. The report *What Works* emphasized the need for homework to supplement the school curriculum. The preschool child's world includes the need for an enriched environment in the home—their homework. Homework for older students includes practice, preparation, and extension. If the school is interested in developing a home-based program, it should (1) show a need for the program, (2) involve others in the planning, (3) develop a parent advisory council, and (4) decide on a program format.

SUGGESTED ACTIVITIES AND DISCUSSIONS

1. Discuss the type of parent-child interaction that best promotes the child's emotional and intellectual growth.
2. Brainstorm home situations that would be positive experiences for children.
3. Itemize household equipment that can be used as home learning tools. How would you use each?
4. Role play a home visit. Use attending behaviors described in Chapter 4. Practice your visit under varying conditions such as (1) a parent who is very eager to cooperate, (2) a parent who is constantly interrupted by the children, and (3) a parent who is threatened by your visit.
5. Imagine many home situations. Write role-playing opportunities based on these families.
6. Develop a home-based curriculum for a 3-, 4-, or 5-year-old.
7. Develop four home learning activities based on Gordon's five steps.
8. Organize a workshop designed to introduce a parent to the learning processes of children.
9. Discuss the dos and don'ts related to home visits.
10. Discuss value systems that may vary from your own. How can you work with parents and refrain from infringing on their beliefs? Discuss.
11. Compare the strengths and weaknesses of home-based, center-based, and home/center-based programs.

BIBLIOGRAPHY

Abraham, W. *Parent talk*. Scottsdale, Ariz.: Sunshine Press.

Appalachia Educational Laboratory. *Home visitor's handbook*. Charleston, W.Va.: Appalachia Educational Laboratory, 1972.

Bayley, N. *Bayley scales of infant development*. New York: The Psychological Corporation, 1969.

Bernard, D. H. Selection and recruitment of home visitors. In I. J. Gordon and W. F. Breivogel, *Building effective home-school relationships*. Boston: Allyn & Bacon, 1976.

Brown, L., Sherbenow, R. J., & Dollar, S. J. *Test of nonverbal intelligence, a language-free measure of cognitive ability*. Austin, TX: Pro-Ed, 1982.

Building concepts through verbal interaction: The key to future success in school? *Carnegie Quarterly*, Winter 1979, reprint.

Caldwell, B. M., & Bradley, R. H. *Administration manual: Home observation for measurement of the environment*. Little Rock: University of Arkansas, 1984.

Carnegie Quarterly reprint. *Building concepts through verbal interaction: The key to future success in school?* Carnegie Corporation of New York, 1979, *25* (1).

Cattell, R. B., & Cattell, A. K. S. The culture fair series. Scale 1, 1950, Scale 2, 1973, Scale 3, 1973. Champaign, Ill.: Institute for Personality and Ability Testing.

Coons, C. E., Gay, E. C., Fandal, A. W., Ker, C., & Frankenburg, W. K. *Home Screening questionnaire.* Denver: JFK Child Development Center, 1981.

Dunn, L. M. *Expanded manual for the Peabody Picture Vocabulary Test.* Circle Pines, Minn.: American Guidance Service, 1965.

Fandal, A. Correspondence. Denver: University of Colorado Medical Center, February, 1986.

Far West Laboratory for Educational Research and Development. *Educational programs that work, 1983.* San Francisco: Far West Laboratory, 1983.

Frankenburg, W. K. *Denver Prescreening Developmental Questionnaire.* Denver: University of Colorado Medical Center, 1975.

Frankenburg, W. K., & Dodds, J. *Denver Developmental Screening Test.* Denver: University of Colorado Medical Center, n.d.

Gallup, A. M. The 17th annual Gallup Poll of the public's attitudes toward the public schools. *Phi Delta Kappan,* September 1985, *67,* 35–47.

Gordon, I. J., and Breivogel, W. F. *Building effective home-school relationships.* Boston: Allyn & Bacon, 1976.

Gray, S. W. Home visiting programs for parents of young children. *Peabody Journal of Education,* 1971, *48,* 106–111.

Hedrich, V., & Jackson, C. Winning play at home base. *American Education,* July 1977, pp. 27–30.

LaConte, R. T. *Homework as a learning experience.* Washington, D.C.: National Education Association of the United States, 1981.

Leler, H., Johnson, D. L., Kahn, A. J., Hines, R. P., & Torres, M. *The Houston Model for parent education.* Paper presented at Society for Research in Child Development Conference, Denver, Colo., April 13, 1975.

Levenstein, P. The mother-child home program. In M. C. Day & R. Parker (Eds.), *Preschool in action: Exploring early childhood programs.* Boston: Allyn & Bacon, 1977.

McElderry, J. S., & Escobedo, L. E. *Tools for learning.* Denver, Colo.: Love Publishing, 1979.

Packer, A. Hoffman, S., Bozler, B., & Bear, N. Home learning activities for children. In I. Gordon & W. F. Breivogel (Eds.), *Building effective home-school relationships.* Boston: Allyn & Bacon, 1976.

Ricciuti, H. N. *Three models for parent-education: The parent-child development centers.* Paper presented at Society for Research in Child Development Conference, Denver, Colo., April 15, 1975.

Shearer, D., Billingsley, J., Frohman, A., Hilliard, J., Johnson, F., & Shearer, M. *Portage Project readings.* Portage, Wis.: Portage Project.

_____. *Portage guide to early education.* Portage, Wis.: Cooperative Educational Service, Agency 12, 1976.

Terman, L. M., & Merrill, M. A. *Stanford-Binet Intelligence Scale* (3rd ed.). Boston: 1960.

U.S. Department of Education. *What works: Research about teaching and learning.* Washington, D.C.: U.S. Department of Education, 1986.

U.S. Department of Health, Education, and Welfare. (Office of Child Development). *A guide for planning and operating home-based child development programs.* Washington, D.C.: U.S. Government Printing Office, 1974.

U.S. Department of Health, Education, and Welfare. *The child and family resource program: An overview.* Washington, D.C.: U.S. Government Printing Office, 1975.

U.S. Department of Health, Education, and Welfare. *Home Start and other programs for parents and children.* Washington, D.C.: U.S. Government Printing Office, 1976.

U.S. Department of Health, Education, and Welfare. (Office of Human Development, Administration for Children, Youth, and Families, Head Start Bureau). *Partners with parents.* Kathryn D. Hewett et al. for Abt Associates and High/Scope Educational Research Foundation. Washington, D.C.: U.S. Government Printing Office, 1978.

Wechsler, D. *Wechsler preschool and primary scale of intelligence manual.* New York: The Psychological Corporation, 1976.

CHAPTER EIGHT

Working with Parents of the Exceptional Child

Jo Spidel

Parents are the most significant influence in an exceptional child's life. Children, raised in close proximity to parents or surrogate par-

Jo Spidel is a certified teacher of learning disabilities, mental retardation, and personal social adjustment and is a qualified director of special education. She has taught public school for 14 years. She is presently associated with the Kansas Elks Training Center for the Handicapped in Wichita, Kansas, as curriculum developer and special education educator.

ents for the first 5 years of their lives, form emotional attachments and their bonding. When children begin school, they are shared with teachers and peer group. As they grow older, children are also affected by the community, but parents continue to influence and shape their development.

Teachers will be wise to listen to parents to learn about the child's background and to discuss concerns. Teachers will gain respect

Fathers need to accept and encourage their children.

and cooperation from parents if they are willing to share their objectives and goals for the child. If teachers will allow the parents to accept some responsibility for the child's learning and will share knowledge of teaching principles and methods of tutoring, the effectiveness of the learning experience can be doubled.

This chapter gives parents and regular classroom teachers techniques that can be used effectively with the exceptional child. There are many ways to solve problems, to communicate with parents, and to teach exceptional children. The methods presented have been proven effective. Take from them those ideas that will work for you.

DEVELOPMENT OF SPECIAL EDUCATION

Many labels were placed on exceptional children in the early part of the twentieth century. One need only review titles of institutions for the mentally ill, the retarded, or the inept to find such descriptions as imbecile, lunatic, crazy, and insane. Such words are indicative of people's perceptions of the problem of exceptionality during that era. Since then, thankfully, parents and professionals have voiced concern over and made real efforts to correct such misconceived labels, which have usually been replaced by the term *exceptional*. The word *exceptional* is used to describe those who are different in some way from the majority of whatever group to which they belong—adults, children, or youth. *Special education* refers to any special needs of or methods required to teach the exceptional child (Hallahan & Kauffman, 1978).

At the middle of this century the term *special education* commonly referred to the education of the mentally retarded. It is proper and helpful that the term is becoming more recognized as open and inclusive. The gifted, retarded, crippled, neurologically impaired, emotionally disturbed, socially maladjusted, speech and language impaired, hard of hearing, deaf, blind, partially seeing, learning disabled, developmentally disabled, and combinations of these are all encompassed by special education. It is significant that the condition of the child was once the labeling factor. The trend now is to label according to the educational needs of the child (Hallahan & Kauffman, 1978; Reynolds & Birch, 1977).

In history there are many tales of cruel and inhumane treatment of people with exceptionalities. Recalling the story of *The Hunchback of Notre Dame* quickly brings to mind these cruelties. The Spartans were known to force parents to abandon imperfect babies by exposing them to the elements (Frost, 1966; Greenleaf, 1978). There are instances, however, in very early history of persons who were more humane toward those who were different. Hippocrates (400 BC) believed that emotional problems were caused not by supernatural powers but by natural forces. Plato (375 BC) defended the mentally disturbed as not being able to account for their deeds as normal people were and, therefore, requiring special judgment for their criminal acts. The temples built by Alexander the Great provided asylum for the mentally ill. In 90 BC the first attempt at classification of mental illness was made by Asclepiades, who advocated humane treatment of mentally ill people. Mania and melancholia were described in 100 AD by Aretaeus. Acceptance did not arrive immediately, however, and mistreatment of those too "different" persisted. The period of 1450 to 1700 was a difficult time for the mentally ill and people with other exceptionalities. Belief in demonology and superstition resulted in the persecution of the mentally ill, the retarded, the developmentally handicapped, and those with any other form of exceptionality (Hallahan & Kauffman, 1978). Significant understanding of and expertise in handling exceptional people was yet to come.

In the late 1700s Jean Marc Gaspard Itard (1775–1838) sought new methods to teach the mentally retarded. He was a physician and an authority on diseases of the ear and education of the deaf. He found a boy in the forest of Auvergne, France, naked and apparently without upbringing, whom he attempted to raise and educate to become a normal person. Influenced by the teachings of Jean Rousseau and John Locke, Itard believed that learning came through the senses and that all persons could develop the ability to learn if given adequate stimulation. He produced behavioral changes in the boy, Victor, but was unable to teach him to talk and to live independently. He felt he was a failure, but his methods were followed, which began a movement in treatment and education that had a profound effect on the development of special education. Edouard Sequin (1811–1880), Itard's student, was much impressed by Itard's work. He immigrated to the United States in 1848 and promoted the European style of residential institution (Hallahan & Kauffman, 1978; Reynolds & Birch, 1977; Reinert, 1980).

In the United States residential schools and asylums very much like those in Europe during the nineteenth century were built. The first American residential school for the deaf was established in 1817 at Hartford, Connecticut, by Thomas Hopkins Gallaudet (1787–1851). Most early schools avoided the severely or multiply handicapped and worked only with the deaf, blind, or retarded. Those more seriously handicapped were often not eligible for admission to any school. Private schools were often expensive, and the state-operated schools were often limited in their facilities (Hallahan & Cruickshank, 1973; Hallahan & Kauffman, 1978; Reynolds & Birch, 1977). This left parents with the nearly total responsibility of caring for their handicapped children at home. I can remember driving through the countryside of the midwestern United States in the 1930s and seeing little houses that were built away from the main house. Upon inquiring what these were, I learned that they were for members of the family who were not "smart," were "off in the head," or "were not controllable."

Perkins School for the Blind, founded in Watertown, Massachusetts, was the first school for sightless people. Samuel G. Howe (1801–1876) proved that the blind could be taught when Laura Bridgemen, blind and deaf, was educated (Hallahan & Kauffman, 1978). Seeking education for his deaf and blind daughter, Arthur H. Keller, father of Helen Keller, consulted many doctors. He consulted Dr. Alexander Graham Bell, who advised him to write to Mr. Anagnos, director of the Perkins Institution. It was from this institution that Anne Mansfield Sullivan came to teach Helen (Keller, 1905; Van Wyck, 1956). The fame of the successful life of this handicapped person did much to persuade parents and professionals that, indeed, the handicapped could be helped.

It was not until the beginning of the twentieth century that community-based programs for exceptional children began to appear. Gallaudet College, the only college for the deaf, started a teacher-training program in the 1890s. In 1904 summer training sessions for teachers of retarded children began at the Vineland Training School in New Jersey (Hallahan & Kauffman, 1978; Reynolds & Birch, 1977). The community-based programs, however, often became "sunshine" rooms, in which activities such as crafts and arts were pursued but little real attempt was made to change the educational status of the children. In some cases expectations were unrealistic, and disappointment in the programs ensued. Many parents and professionals did not hold optimistic outlooks for the education of the handicapped (Hallahan & Kauffman, 1978; Reynolds & Birch, 1977).

The Binét-Simon Scale of Intelligence, translated and revised by Goddard, was cited in 1904 by the National Education Association to be a useful test for exceptional children, especially the mentally retarded. It was used to determine the degree of retardation and, hopefully, to guide individualized instruction. This was the beginning of an era of testing that lasted well into the 1970s (Reynolds & Birch, 1977).

In 1950 Pearl S. Buck wrote of her personal experiences in *The Child Who Never Grew.* Her frank and open discussion of her retarded child and how she learned to accept the problem reached many parents. Her urgings helped to begin the massive movement to provide educational services for handicapped people.

Educators from Europe who immigrated to the United States during World War II also made an impact on the education of the handicapped. Frostig, a psychiatric social worker and rehabilitation therapist, trained in the United States as a psychologist and worked with retarded, delinquent, and learning-disabled children (Hallahan & Kauffman, 1978). Alfred A. Strauss and Laura Lehtinen published *Psychopathology and Education of the Brain-Injured Child,* a test that influenced special education.

Others who have contributed to and influenced the special education movement include Samuel A. Kirk, known for his work on the Illinois Test of Psycholinguistic Abilities, and Barbara Bateman, who developed a linguistic approach to learning problems. In addition, Kephart, author of *The Slow Learner in the Classroom* (1971), presented remedial teaching techniques through a perceptual-motor concept (McCarthy & McCarthy, 1973).

The National Association for Retarded Citizens (previously known as the National Association for Retarded Children) was chartered in 1950 and became active in influencing state legislatures and Congress. Since then, along with other organizations, it has supported such important legislative action as the federal establishment of a national program in the field of special education and governmental support of research and leadership training in mental retardation in 1957 (Reynolds & Birch, 1977). In 1963 support was extended to most other exceptional persons except the gifted, who did not receive support until 1979. The Bureau of Education for the Handicapped was established in 1966 (Reynolds & Birch, 1977).

Another influence on the special education movement was the rehabilitation of World War II and Korean War veterans. Research into and efforts toward rehabilitation have carried over into the areas of working with exceptional persons. For example, with expanded programs for mobility and occupational training, it was found that the blind or deaf did not have to be isolated and dependent upon fate. This philosophy spread to children's programs, and many schools began integrating the blind and deaf into regular classes for part of the day while separating them for the rest of their studies in a resource room with a special teacher (Reynolds & Birch, 1977).

The Kennedys, a powerful and influential family with a handicapped daughter, have done much to help the cause of the handicapped. They established the Joseph P. Kennedy Jr. Foundation—a multimillion dollar effort against mental retardation (The Foundation Center, 1983). The foundation supports research projects and the Special Olympics, a program for the handicapped that is patterned after the International Olympics. Thus, parents, educators, and influential families reinforced the growing concern of all parents with handicapped children; their children should have opportunities to develop to their highest potential.

LEGISLATION FOR THE HANDICAPPED

During the 1960s parents organized effective groups that became vocal and attracted enough attention to result in legislation for their handicapped children. In 1971 the Pennsylvania Association for Retarded Children (PARC) won a landmark case against the Commonwealth of Pennsylvania. It was a decision based on the Fourteenth Amendment, which assures all children, including the handicapped, the right to a free and appropriate education (Reynolds & Birch, 1977). Decisions such as this one led to the passage of other important laws.

Rehabilitation Act of 1973

The Rehabilitation Act of 1973, Section 504, which relates to nondiscrimination under Federal Grant, Public Law 93-112, required that "no otherwise qualified handicapped individual . . . shall solely by reason of his handicap, be excluded from the participation in, be denied the benefits of, or be subjected to discrimination under any program or activity receiving Federal financial assistance" (Sumner County Special Education Services, 1977, p. 5). The rights of the handicapped to equal opportunities were strongly stated.

Buckley Amendment

The Buckley Amendment, written for the rights of all citizens, had great impact on record keeping for the handicapped. It provides the following:

That all "records, files, documents and other materials which contain information directly relating to a student" and which are maintained by an educational agency such as an elementary school, an office of the school district, or university, must be available within 45 days of a request.

The most important work was the development of five principles covering data collection systems for personal data. These can effectively serve to guide school practice. They are as follows:

1. There must be no personal data record keeping systems whose very existence is secret.
2. There must be a way for an individual to find out what information about himself or herself is in a record and how it is used.
3. There must be a way for an individual to prevent information about himself/herself that was obtained for one purpose from being used or made available for other purposes without his/her consent.
4. There must be a way for an individual to correct the record of identifiable information about himself/herself.

5. Any organization creating, maintaining, using or disseminating records of identifiable personal data must assure the reliability of the data for their intended uses and must take precautions to prevent their misuse.[1]

This important amendment is discussed further in Chapter 10.

Education of All Handicapped Children Act of 1975

The most far-reaching and revolutionary legislation in relation to education is Public Law 94-142, the Education of All Handicapped Children Act of 1975. All persons between the ages of 3 and 18 must be provided free and appropriate education. The term *appropriate* means suited to the handicapping condition, age, maturity, and past achievements of the child and parental expectations. The education has to be given in a program that is designed to meet the child's needs in the *least restrictive* environment (von Hippel et al., 1978). This means that the child shall be placed in the classroom that will benefit him the most. If the student will benefit more from a regular classroom, then he will be placed there. The word *mainstreaming* has become synonymous with placing exceptional children into the regular classroom. However, "least restrictive" can also refer to moving the handicapped child out of a regular classroom into a resource room or self-contained special education room. The law requires diagnosis and individualization of the educational program. This is encompassed in Individualized Educational Program (IEP) (von Hippel et al., 1978). The teachers, special teachers, administrators, parents, and others who are concerned with the child's education are involved in the development of the IEP. If appropriate,

---

1. From Sumner County Special Education Services. *Commentary regarding the Individual Educational Plan (IEP).* Wellington, Kan., Sumner County Special Education Services, 1977, p. 5.

the child is also included. Finally, the law provides for a hearing that can be initiated by the parents if they do not agree with the diagnosis of the child, the placement, and/or the IEP. This is "due process," and it is the responsibility of the school to inform the parents of their rights (Sumner County Special Education Services, 1977; von Hippel et al., 1978).

The magnitude of this legislation has been felt across the nation. School boards, administrators, principals, directors of special education, special education teachers, regular teachers, and any others who are concerned are fully aware of the impact on education and the changes that have been made to correct the ills of past neglect. Parents were the driving force in seeing that legislation was passed. Parents, again, will be the force that will see that the intent of the law is achieved and maintained. The Graham/Rudman/Hollings Amendment to the Debt Ceiling Bill passed in January 1986 presents a challenge. Parents, teachers, and educators are concerned that fund reductions will make it impossible to maintain the progress that has been accomplished.

DEVELOPMENT OF THE IEP

Each exceptional child receiving any type of special education services must have an Individual Educational Program prepared by staff in consultation with the parents. The IEP provides the necessary information for the development and statement of a program. It takes into consideration the child's age, handicap, maturity, past achievements, and the parents' expectations. The plan is developed in a meeting of the child's teacher, other school personnel concerned with the child, the parents and, when appropriate, the child (Karnes, 1979; Sumner County Special Education Services, 1977).

The IEP shall include the following:

a. A statement of the child's present performance including where applicable, academic achievement, social adaption, prevocational and voca-

tional skills, sensory and motor skills, self-help skills, and speech and language skills.

b. Justification for the type of educational placement. A description of the extent to which the child will participate in regular classroom education shall be included or, where regular classroom placement is not appropriate, the extent of participation in other "less restrictive environment" activities shall be described.

c. The projected date for the initiation of the prescribed services and anticipated duration of the services.

d. A statement of annual goals which describes the educational performance anticipated in time frames of service.

e. A statement of 9- to 12-week objectives which are measurable intermediate steps between the present level of performance and the annual goals.

f. Objective criteria and evaluation procedures for determining, at least every 12 weeks, whether the short-term objectives are being achieved.[2]

IEPs must be reviewed at least once every 12 weeks and the child's progress reported to the parents. Each year a new IEP must be developed for the child within 30 days of the end of the school year. The child (when appropriate), parents, and staff concerned with the child are included in the yearly revision of the IEP. Federal and state statutes provide guidelines for content, procedures, and time limits. These requirements, specified in Public Law 94-142, are discussed more fully in the rules and regulations of the *Federal Register,* Tuesday, August 23, 1977. A book, *Civil Rights; Handicapped Persons and Education: Section 504 Self-Evaluation Guide for Preschool, Elementary, Secondary, and Adult Education* (von Hippel et al., 1978) is available from the Office for Civil Rights, Office of Program Review and Assistance. Because laws change and specific regulations are subject to frequent change, be sure to check on the current status

---

2. From Kearns, P. (Ed.). *Your child's right to a free public education: Parent's handbook.* Topeka, Kan.: Kansas Association for Children with Learning Disabilities, 1980, p. 9.

of rules and regulations in your state (Sumner County Special Education Services, 1977).

In each school district staff members need to keep informed on sections in their state's plan on delivery models, placement, service continuum, contractual arrangements, evaluation, due process, hearing and appeals, confidentiality, review procedures, and the particular special education program under consideration. Local districts also have their individual philosophies and approaches to implementation of the IEP so those guidelines need to be followed (Sumner County Special Education Services, 1977).

Because this book will be used by teachers and professionals who will be serving in many situations, a factual view of the implementation of Public Law 94-142 must be taken. The intent of the law is explicit, and teachers must be prepared to substantiate their programs. To familiarize teachers with the IEP, complete instructions developed by Sumner County Special Education Services appear in Box 8-1.

BOX 8-1: IEP Instructions

An IEP must be written for a child newly identified and recommended for special education no later than 30 days from the date when it is determined that the child requires special education. BUT, THE IEP MUST BE WRITTEN, PROPERLY EXECUTED, AND ON FILE BEFORE SUCH SERVICES BEGIN. Until the IEP is written such a child shall remain in his current placement.

The basic concept behind the requirement of IEPs is to provide at least minimum communication to the parents as to the PLAN for any child placed in special education. The Bureau of Education for the Handicapped interprets the regulations to establish that IEPs are a contract to provide the services listed in the IEP. The IEP is not a guarantee of objectives to be reached.

The IEP is not a substitute for daily lesson plans and/or teaching prescriptions. Daily lesson plans and teaching prescriptions must be far more detailed and subject to constant and immediate change.

Each staff member, in making a contribution to the IEP, must keep in mind that contractual expectations are created on the part of the parents by the IEP. Statements in the IEP will be subject to interpretation of intent. Care must be taken that proper expectations are conveyed.

A staffing should be held and a written record filed in any instance when regular classroom participation creates unique circumstances. Mainstreaming is such a consideration. Regular class involvement should be considered as a goal for specific children with the ability to profit from existing regular class materials, activities, and schedules. Principals and the regular classroom teacher must be apprised of, contribute to, and agree with such IEPs.

The final content of the IEP shall be by consensus of all parties involved. Minority opinions regarding the IEP shall be made in writing by the dissenter and affixed to the IEP.

Schools have the right and responsibility to provide appropriate educational programs. When differences occur regarding the appropriate program for a child, the administration will determine the final content of the IEP based on the recommendations of professional staff, the parents' wishes, and weighed with the extent of immediate need and degree of accountability.

Participants in the IEP meeting
The IEP meeting will afford the opportunity for the following persons to participate:
A representative of the district other than the child's teacher(s), who is qualified to provide, or supervise the provision of, special education, and who participated in the staffing conference (if a separate meeting was held) and is qualified to interpret the written findings of the comprehensive evaluation to the parents. If the IEP is to consider unique circumstances, this person would be the Director of Special Education, or his designee.

The child's teacher(s), special and/or regular, who has direct responsibility for implementing the child's current individualized educational program. For those children currently receiving special education, the teacher(s) who attends the staffing shall participate in the IEP conference.

One or both of the child's parents or guardian(s). If the parent(s) or guardian(s) are not present, documentation must be provided of the contacts made with the parents to inform them of the meeting. A written record of a minimum of three attempts to involve the parents must be filed with the IEP face sheet and shall be considered a part of the IEP. Copies of any correspondence shall be filed with the contact record.

The child, where appropriate. The decision as to whether or not to include the child should be a joint decision made by the school officials and the parents. The parents' wishes regarding the child's presence should usually be accommodated. In any instance where a child voluntarily expresses the wish to attend the meeting, the child should be allowed to do so. Secondary students routinely shall be encouraged to participate. Any student 18 years of age or older must be involved.

The school psychologist responsible for the evaluation.

The principal who is immediately responsible.

Other individuals at the discretion of the parents or the school. Such individuals might include representatives of school administration, school nurses, medical and supportive medical personnel, and interpreters or other facilitators of communication for parents whose native language is other than English, or for parents who are deaf.

Speech clinicians will be present and will conduct those IEP meetings where speech therapy is the only special education service under consideration.

Scheduling the IEP meeting

The IEP meeting(s) will be scheduled to afford planning from the greatest number of needed participants. Ideally, this will occur in one meeting with all needed participants present. The logistics of the cooperative and the commitments of the various participants may require two or more meetings and/or contacts before the IEP is written in final form. The parents and appropriate school officials must all be advised of the final form of the IEP. The final form must be completed and on file with the Director of Special Education *before* any special education services start for any exceptional child.

The first step in scheduling the IEP meeting will occur at the conference between the school psychologist and the parents at which the evaluation findings are shared with parents. At this time, the school psychologist will present to the parents the completed "Notice of Proposal to Take Action." Also, at this time, the school psychologist will obtain written permission, consenting to the action stated in the "Notice of Proposal to Take Action," from the parents. If the parents choose not to sign the written permission, the parents' refusal will be reported by the school psychologist to the Director of Special Education. Due Process procedures for placement will then be initiated. The IEP will be considered, in such instances, at a later time based on the results of the due process procedure.

When written permission from the parents is obtained at the conference, the school psychologist and the parents will determine a mutually agreeable time at which the IEP meeting will be conducted. The school psychologist will then inform the other needed participants of the date for the IEP meeting. Following this meeting, the school psychologist shall send a letter confirming the date to the parents. A copy of this letter will be sent to the special education teacher who will receive the child. The special education teacher shall file this material with any other IEP material.

In the event parents do not attend the IEP meeting at the agreed upon time, those present will formulate a tentative IEP. The school psychologist shall send a letter to the parents requesting them to contact the RECEIVING special education teacher to arrange a time they might meet to formulate a final IEP. Three such letters shall be sent with no less than 3 days apart. Each time a copy shall be sent to the RECEIVING special education teacher who shall file the material with other IEP material. The third such letter shall establish the date when the "Initiation Date of the Plan" shall be established. A copy of the third letter shall also be sent to the building principal and the Director of Special Education.

The care in contacting parents with three notices and obtaining their input to and acceptance of the IEP illustrates the necessity of parent involvement for every student in the development of the IEP. The "Initiation Date of the Plan" and "Date of Plan" will be determined when the parents have had an opportunity to contribute to the plan. The primary consideration must be that all involved have the opportunity to assist in developing the plan and in communicating to all parties the final plan formulated.

Specific instructions for completing the entries on the Individual Educational Plan

At the top of the form is the notation "Complete all sections without exception." *Each and every part of the IEP must be completed.* [Figure 8-1, *A* shows an example of a completed form.]

Student: Use the child's legal family name, his legal given name, and middle name, if known. If the child is also known by a nickname, place the nickname in parentheses by the given name, e.g. Doe, James, (Jimmie).

Sex: Enter the child's sex.

Born: Enter the child's date of birth (month, day, year, e.g. 1-10-70).

Home District and Building: Identify the home school district in which the child's parents or legal guardian resides.

Grade: All students will be assigned a grade. Usually, the grade assigned will be the grade appropriate for the chronological age. However, if the child has been retained and is just being placed in special education, give the current grade placement.

Some grade assignments will necessarily be determined during the staffing and/or IEP meeting, particularly for students in the Life Skills program. Consideration must be given to those students who will benefit from an extended school program. Grade assignments are particularly important to Basic Skills students in the Senior High School where class rings, junior proms, and graduation activities and planning are important. Grade assignments must also take into consideration the importance to students of the grade they are placed in for the elementary school annual and the Junior and Senior High School annuals.

Parents: Enter the father's given name and the mother's given name followed by the family name, e.g. John and Jane Doe. If the mother's given name is not known, enter Mr. and Mrs. and father's given name. If a parent is not in the home, give only the name of the parent that is, e.g. Jane Doe.

Address: Provide a complete mailing address, e.g. street or box number, city, zip.

Phone: Provide a complete phone number. If the parents do not have a phone, enter "NONE." If none and a phone number is known through which messages can be conveyed to the parents, enter that phone number and the name in which the phone is registered.

Learning Characteristics—Current Intellectual: Identify the general level of intellectual functioning choosing from the terms:

    Superior
    Bright-Normal
    Normal
    Dull-Normal
    Mentally Deficient

Indicate evidence of knowledge, e.g. Mentally Deficient-WISC-R. If the child is receiving *only* speech services, write "Appears Normal."

Learning Characteristics—Projected Intellectual: Choose from the preceding terms as given for "Current Intellectual." Where the Projected (potential) Intellectual varies from the "Current Intellectual," the anticipated change in intellectual ability should be accounted for by statements throughout the Individual Educational Plan. Projected potential must be consistent with the Annual Goals.

Present Level of Educational Performance: This section, which is divided into "Strengths" and "Weaknesses," provides the justification for special education placement. Special Education placement will be based, for the most part, on the "Weaknesses." In every instance, a strength and a weakness shall be noted on the IEP form. If a child has a physical disability such as a visual impairment, record this as a weakness.

Complete all sections without exception

INDIVIDUAL EDUCATIONAL PLAN

Student Schoolgirl   Jane   Sex F   Born 10-21-74
         Last   First
Home district and building Somewhere Jr. High   Grade 7
Parents Schoolgirl, Tom and Mary   Address 600 Grand St.   Phone 701-4718

LEARNING CHARACTERISTICS

Current intellectual: Projected intellectual:
Normal (WISC-R)   Normal

PRESENT LEVEL OF EDUCATIONAL PERFORMANCE
(justification for special education needs)

Include, where applicable, academic achievement, social adaptation, prevocational and vocational skills, sensory and motor skills, self-help skills, and speech and language skills.

Strengths   Weaknesses (requiring special program)

Verbalization   1. Math (PIAT)
(psychologic evaluation)
                                   2. Self-confidence

EDUCATIONAL PLACEMENT

Type of special program needed: LD   Building Jr. High   Level 111
Degree of special program needed (least restrictive): Interrelated resource room
One seventh or approximately 14%; one class period of seven periods
Other special services needed (specify initiation dates for each): None
Regular class participation: 6 class periods of 7 or 86%
Anticipated duration of need for special education 8-23-86 to 5-23-88
Initiation date of this plan 8-23-86   First review date 10-26-86

ANNUAL GOALS
(state according to priority; number each)

1. Math: the student will improve her ability to use addition, subtraction, division, multiplication, sets, fractions, decimals, and percentages to solve math problems.

2. Self-confidence: the student will improve her ability to express herself in situations requiring opinions, participation in classroom activities, and answering questions.

Signatures reflect members of the committee designing the Individual Educational Plan and attest to approval.

Student Jane Schoolgirl   Psychologist J.M. Psychologist
Mother* Mrs. Mary Schoolgirl   Speech therapist Miss Talbot
Father* Mr. Tom Schoolbook   Principal Mary Dumday
Regular teacher Jom Thursday   Principal
Special education teacher
Program coordinator Bill Monday Other
Psychologist   Other

*If parental signatures are not obtained, append notes documenting written, verbal, and telephone contacts made to notify them.

School year 86-87   Date of plan 5-22-86

Short-term objectives are to be attached to this form.

FIGURE 8-1

A. Example of completed Individual Educational Plan. B. Completed Annual Goals form. (Source: Sumner County Special Education Services. Commentary regarding the Individual Education Plan [IEP]. Wellington, Kans.: Sumner County Special Education Services, 1977, pp. 604 and 608.)

In all cases except physical disabilities, the source of knowledge of the weakness shall be indicated. Usually, this will be through the administration of a standardized test. If so, put in parentheses the names of the tests; acronyms may be used. Periodically, it is permissible for "observation" to be the basis of knowledge. A written record of the observation (date, time, behavior observed, by whom) must be made and on file as a part of the evaluation.

Type of Special Program Needed: Identify each student's primary disability and record one of the following labels on the IEP:

Trainable Mentally Handicapped
Educable Mentally Handicapped
Learning Disability
Personal Social Adjustment (emotionally disturbed)
Speech
Physically Impaired
Visually Impaired
Hearing Impaired
Deaf
Blind

Degree of Special Education Needed (least restrictive): State, using the continuum of services concept, which special education program the child will be in:

1. Consultant services
2. Itinerant
3. Interrelated resource room (IRC)
4. Self-Contained
5. Homebound
6. Residential
7. Institutional

State one annual goal for each weakness entered in the section "Present Level of Educational Performance." Correspond the numbers of the annual goals to the order used when listed as weaknesses.

Other Special Services Needed: If the IEP is for a special education placement other than speech therapy and speech is needed, enter speech therapy as a special service needed. Other possibilities may include: physical therapy, occupational therapy, work/study, and so forth. If no other services are needed, write "NONE."

For each entry, a date when that service is to begin must be entered. The amount of time for each service must also be shown. An example would be: Speech (9-27-86) 2 sessions per week.

Regular Class Participation: If none, write "NONE." Otherwise, enter any activity in which the child is participating with regular classes, e.g. lunch, bus ride, assemblies, P.E., field trips.

NOTE! All self-contained students' school programs include the skills developed during the lunch period. (These skills include feeding/eating, drinking, oral hygiene, interpersonal relations, social eating, and any other skills that may be acquired through the lunch period.) The lunch period is part of the school day for all these students and as such must be reflected in the IEP for each of these students. Likewise, the skills learned while riding a bus must be included in the IEPs of each child transported. Teachers will plan appropriate objectives for transportation and lunch and will document an evaluation of the same. If speech is the only service received, write "Regular class participation except for speech."

Anticipated Duration of Need for Special Education: Enter in the first blank the date the plan is to be initiated. In the second blank, enter the most reasonable estimate of the length of time special education will be needed. If indefinite, you may state, "Indefinite."

Initiation Date of This Plan: Give the date that the first services, covered by the Individual Educational Plan, are to begin.

NOTE! This date cannot be prior to "Date of Plan."

First Review Date: Within 12 weeks

Annual Goals: The annual goals are determined by the strengths and weaknesses of the child as entered under the section, "Present Level of Educational Performance." The emphasis will be on the remediation of the weaknesses. Consequently the phrasing should usually include: "improving," "increasing," or "decreasing," for example, 1. She will improve translation of written symbols . . .

Signatures: The regulations stipulate that each IEP shall include the following participants: A representative of the district or state institution, other than the child's teacher, who is qualified to provide or supervise the provision of special education, who participated in the staffing conference (if a separate meeting was held), and who is qualified to interpret the written findings of the comprehensive evaluation to the parents (Psychologist and/or Special Ed. Administrator).

The child's teacher(s), who will be responsible for carrying out the IEP. Generally, this will be the assigned special education teacher.

The child where appropriate. (Involvement of secondary students is encouraged.) The parents, if they are willing. The building principal's involvement is important. The principal is directly responsible for classes within his building. The principal's involvement will help insure needed communication.

Other Individuals at the discretion of the parents or the school.

Parents must be given the opportunity to participate in developing the Individual Educational Program. Documented, reasonable efforts must be made to schedule the IEP meeting at a mutually agreed upon time, so the parents may participate. (Three attempts to involve the parents in the IEP conference must be made prior to meeting without them. These attempts need to be recorded on a "Parent Contact Record" which is forwarded to the Special Education Office with the IEP face sheet.)

School Year: Enter the school year for which the plan is initiated. If a plan is initiated in May of 1986 for the school year 1986-87, enter 1986-87.

Date of Plan: Enter the date the IEP is written and the signatures obtained.

Short Term Objectives Form

These must be maintained and current in the special education classroom [Figure 8-2].

Individual Educational Plan for IEP Initiated _____. In this blank, enter the date found on the first page of the Individual Educational Plan for the section "Initiation Date of This Plan."

From _____ to _____: Enter the time period for which the short term objectives are applicable. Generally, this will be from the date the plan is initiated to the end of the 9 weeks.

Student's Name: Enter the student's name as it is entered on the first page of the IEP form. At a later time, due to confidentiality requirements, it may be necessary to assign identification numbers rather than use the child's name.

Annual Goals: Your annual goals on this page shall correspond directly to the "Annual Goals" form . . . [Figure 8-1, *B*.] Number them identically. Each annual goal need not be restated, but the number of each annual goal for which the objectives on this page are designed to meet must be entered. You may want to use a separate page for each goal if you anticipate adding to it each 9 weeks. Hopefully, this would save you adding nonsequenced pages at a later date.

Review Dates and Reviewed by: (This information is in the upper right hand corner.) Each time the IEP short term objectives are reviewed, enter the date of the review and your signature.

The IEP is reviewed by the classroom teacher to determine the success of the program in meeting the short term objectives (and thus meeting the weaknesses of the child). At each review, the short term objectives will be evaluated. When it is determined that a short term objective is met, the completion date of that objective is entered in the appropriate column. If the short term objectives are not met, extend them until the next review date.

Minimum federal and state requirements would not require supportive data to be attached. But, performance levels at one time may not be met at a future time due to factors of retention. It is highly advisable to append sufficient documentation to establish that the short term objectives

Complete all sections without exception

INDIVIDUAL EDUCATIONAL PLAN

FOR IEP INITIATED ___8-23-86___
(date)

Short-term objectives from 8-23-86 to 10-23-86
extended 10-26-86 to 1-11-87
1-11-87 to 3-14-87
3-14-87 to 5-23-87

Student's name ___Jane Schoolgirl___

Annual goals: 1. Math   2. Self-confidence

Review dates	Reviewed by
10-26-86	_____
1-11-87	_____
3-14-87	_____
5-23-87	_____

Short-term objectives (written in measurable terms) Specify which goal objectives meet	Name and position of person responsible	Special methods/materials	Means for evaluation	Initiated date	Completion date
1.1 The student will improve her ability to perform multiplication combinations and division facts to 9.	IRC teacher	Learning Skills series of math Systems 80	80% accuracy on daily worksheets and tests—pre and post 80% accuracy.	8-23-86	10-23-86; see verification attached.
1.2 The student will improve her ability to multiply and divide 3- or 4-place numbers by 1-place numbers.	IRC teacher	Learning Skills series of math Systems 80	80% accuracy on daily worksheets and tests—pre and post 80% accuracy.	8-23-86	10-23-86; see verification attached.
2.1 The student will improve her ability to express opinions/ perform tasks in new situations in which success is questionable.	IRC teacher	Classroom conversations; regular class sessions	Checklist showing positive or negative reports; regular class grades—increase 15% or better.	8-23-86	5-23-87; see verification attached.
2.2 The student will improve her ability to participate in conversations with teachers and peers.	IRC teacher	Magic Circle discussions; consultation with regular teachers	Checklist of positive reports of regular teachers; 10% increase—pre and post lists.	8-23-86	5-23-87; see verification attached.

As of ___8-23-86___ this is page ___1___ of ___1___ pages
On ___10-23-86___ additional short-term objectives were appended
Form 3/12/86

FIGURE 8-2

Example of Short-Term Objectives form. (Source: *Sumner County Special Education Services.* Commentary regarding the Individual Education Plan [IEP]. *Wellington, Kans.: Sumner County Special Education Services, 1977, p. 608.*)

were met. (For example, if a child masters common homonyms in April of 1986, will he know them 1 year later? Did he actually master the short term objectives as the IEP states he did?) Parents need to be kept apprised of the progress of the child. This would be easiest to handle at regularly scheduled parent conferences.

Special Methods: Indicate the major methods and/or materials to be used, e.g. SRA Math, Level A; Distar, Level 1; flashcards.

Means for Evaluation: The manner of evaluation may be standardized tests, teacher-made tests, or charts. It is permissible to evaluate by means of teacher observation. However, in all cases, including teacher observation, some written record must exist and be filed with the student's objectives for documenting and summarizing evaluations.

The criteria for success must be stated, e.g. "80% accuracy" or specify criteria source. You may want to include the child's current level of performance, for example: Objective—1.1 Reads silently; Evaluation—Improve from 3.4 to 4.5 grade level as determined by PIAT.

Information on Number of Pages: Include the date the objective sheet was initiated and the number of pages for "Short Term Objectives"*

*From Sumner County Special Education Services. *Commentary regarding the Individual Educational Plan (IEP)*. Wellington, Kan.: Sumner County Special Education Services, 1977, pp. 27–38.

The foregoing describes the IEP from the viewpoint of the administration. The following describes exceptional children and approaches the IEP, rights, and services available to parents from the point of informing the parents. It is taken from *Your Child's Right to a Free Public Education: Parents Handbook,*[3] a booklet modeled after a similar publication by the Missouri Association for Children with Learning Disabilities and published by the Kansas Association for Children with Learning Disabilities.

WHO IS THE EXCEPTIONAL STUDENT?

Who meets the criterion of the exceptional student? The following descriptions of exceptional children define and clarify those who need special programs. If a student in a classroom fits into any of the following categories, special services should be provided.

a. Specific Learning Disabilities—Children with specific learning disabilities exhibit a disorder in one or more of the basic psychological processes involved in understanding or in using spoken or written language. Such disorders may be manifested in imperfect ability to listen, think, speak, read, write, spell, or do mathematical calculations. They include conditions which have been referred to as perceptual handicaps, brain injury, minimal brain dysfunction, dyslexia, and developmental aphasia. They do not include learning problems which are due to primarily visual, hearing, or motor handicaps; mental retardation; emotional disturbances; or environmental, cultural, or economic disadvantage. The above definition is made more operational by the delineation of three concepts: Intactness, discrepancy, and deviation.

1. Learning disabled children are primarily intact children. They are not primarily visually impaired, hearing impaired, environmentally disadvantaged, mentally retarded or emotionally disturbed. In spite of the fact that these children have adequate intelligence, adequate sensory processes and adequate emotional stability, they do not learn without special assistance.

3. The preface states: This handbook was edited by Phyllis Kearns, Coordinator of the Dean's Grant, Kansas State University, 1976–1978. The opinions expressed herein do not necessarily reflect the position or policy of Kansas State University or the Bureau of Education for the Handicapped, but do reflect the requirements set forth in the Kansas State Plan for Special Education.

2. Learning disabled children show wide discrepancies of intra-individual differences in a profile of their development. This is often shown by marked discrepancies in one or more of the specific areas of academic learning or a serious lack of language development or language facility. These disabilities may affect his/her behavior in such areas as thinking, conceptualization, memory, language, perception, reading, writing, spelling or arithmetic.

3. The concept of deviation of the learning disabled child implies that he/she deviates so markedly from the norm of his/her group as to require specialized instruction. Such specialized instruction required for learning disabled children may be of value to other children. However, the population to be served with special education funds authorized for children does not include children with learning problems which are the result of poor instruction or economic or cultural deprivation, unless these children also have been identified as "specific learning disabled."

b. Mentally Retarded—Mental retardation is the limitation of mental ability which differs in both degree and quality to the extent that special assistance is necessary to aid the individual in the acquisition of understandings and skills for coping with environmental situations.

Each mentally retarded individual acquires a range of behaviors which he/she can use in order to perform on an independent basis in some situations, while he/she will require assistance and/or support to perform in other situations. Mental retardation occurs on a continuum range from independent performance through semi-independent, semi-dependent, dependent and totally dependent performance.

c. Gifted[4]—Intellectually gifted individuals are those who have potential for outstanding performance by virtue of superior intellectual abilities. The intellectually gifted are those with demonstrated achievement and/or potential ability. Individuals capable of outstanding performance include both those with demonstrated achievement and those with minimal or low performance who give evidence of high potential in general intellectual ability, specific academic aptitudes, and/or creative thinking abilities.

d. Emotionally Disturbed and Socially Maladjusted—The emphasis of earlier program planning focused on the child's behavior or emotional problem. Educational thought today attempts to utilize the more positive approach of studying the child's strengths and of adjusting the program to his/her needs. The goal of programming is to enable the child to function adequately in the educational mainstream.

Personal and social adjustment problems typically manifest themselves as marked behavior excesses and deficits which persist over a period of time. Behavior excesses and deficits include the following:

1. Aggressive and/or anti-social actions which are intended to agitate and anger others or to incur punishment.

2. Inappropriate and/or uncontrollable emotional responses.

3. Persistent moods of depression or unhappiness.

4. Withdrawal from interpersonal contacts.

5. Behaviors centrally oriented to personal pleasure.

e. Visually Impaired—For educational purposes, visually impaired children and youth shall be identified as those whose limited vision interferes with their education and/or developmental progress. Two divisions for the visually impaired shall be made:

1. Partially Seeing. Those whose visual limitation constitutes an educational handicap but who are able to use print as their primary educational medium.

2. Blind. Those who must depend primarily upon tactile and auditory media for their education. The group may include individuals who have some residual vision but whose vision loss is so severe that, for educational purposes, print cannot be used as the major medium of learning.

Legal blindness is a descriptive term, applying to the blind and to certain partially seeing. It is used solely for the purpose of qualifying the State for certain amounts of federal funds for each child so identified.

f. Language, Speech and Hearing Impaired—The inclusive term, communicative disorders/devia-

---

4. The "gifted" are not included in P.L. 94-142. However, they are recognized as exceptional students in Kansas.

tions/needs, is used to denote the continuum of problems and needs to be found in pupils requiring language, speech, and hearing services.

1. Pupils with communicative needs include the general school population for whom organized, sequenced curricular activities should be provided to promote the development of adequate communicative skills that will be beneficial to them as part of their overall educational program.
2. Pupils with communicative deviations include those with mild developmental or non-maturational problems in language, voice, fluence or articulation, as well as those with a hearing loss. These individuals need interventional measures in order to permit them to perform satisfactorily in the educational setting. Such measures may be programmed at different levels for those pupils with a more severe impairment.
3. Pupils with communicative disorders are those exhibiting impaired language, voice, fluency or articulation, and/or hearing to such degree that academic achievement and/or psycho-social adjustment are affected and are handicapping to the individual.

g. Multiply Handicapped/Deaf-Blind—Those with two or more conditions requiring special educational services designed to ameliorate the effects of the combined impairments are identified in this category. The multiply handicapped hearing and/or visually impaired refers to a child having significant physical, emotional, mental or specific learning disabilities in addition to or concurrent with a hearing and/or visual impairment. When communicative disorders/deviations/ needs are present, the provision of language, speech, and/or hearing services is considered essential.

h. Physically Impaired—Physically impaired individuals are those with physically impairing conditions so severe as to require special education and/or supportive services. These conditions include, but are not limited to, cerebral palsy, spina bifida, convulsive disorders, musculoskeletal conditions, congenital malformation and other crippling or health conditions.

If your school district is unable to provide services, that district may negotiate a contract for those services with an approved public or private educational agency.

The instructional program offered by an approved contracted agency must be of a quality at least equal to that offered by an approved public school program. Certification of such private programs and approval for contracts are made by the State Board of Education after investigation by the State Department of Education reasonably assures such quality.

It is the responsibility of the local district or special district of residence to have available a complete file of appropriate records for each student enrolled in a contractual program.[5]

RIGHTS AND SERVICES AVAILABLE TO PARENTS

Many parents of exceptional children are unaware of the rights and services available to them. Teachers can share the following rights and procedures with them.

Notification Of and Permission From Parents

Parents have rights as well as responsibilities in the implementation of Public Law 94-142. They must be notified and permission obtained from them in the following situations:

1. Before the child is tested to determine the extent of the child's handicap and educational needs
2. Before the child is placed in, transferred out, or refused a special education program
3. Before the child is transferred or excluded from a regular classroom "on the grounds that he/she is an exceptional child and cannot materially benefit from education in a regular classroom" (Kearns, p. 9)

If parents disagree with the placement of the child and wish to request a hearing, they should follow this procedure:

---

5. From Kearns, P. (Ed.). *Your child's right to a free public education: Parent's handbook.* Topeka, Kan.: Kansas Association for Children with Learning Disabilities, 1980, pp. 18–23.

1. The parents request the local school board of education for a hearing. (Check your area for time limitations.)
2. A hearing must be held within 15 to 30 days after the parents make the request.
3. An impartial hearing officer conducts the meeting.
4. Parents and their counsel have access to school reports, records, and files related to the case.
5. Parents may have counsels and witnesses to support their position.
6. The burden of proof is on the local education agency.
7. The meeting is closed unless an open meeting is requested.
8. The meeting is recorded.
9. A decision should be given to the parents by registered mail from the hearing officer within 7 days.
10. If a satisfactory solution is not reached in the hearing, the parents may appeal to the State Board of Education.

Review by State Board of Education

1. A written appeal to the Commission of Education must be made within 10 days. (Check the time limitation within your state.)
2. The appeal requires that the State Board of Education will examine the record of the meeting and determine if the hearing procedure was in accordance with due process.
3. Oral and/or written arguments will be requested at the discretion of the State Board.
4. The Board will give their decision within 5 days after completion of the review.
5. A written notice will be sent to the parent and the local board of education.
6. Should the decision be unacceptable to the parents, it can be appealed to district court. If it is acceptable, it must be upheld by the school and parents. (Modified from Kearns, 1980, pp. 9–11)

Although hearings tend to sound threatening, their purpose is not to create an adversary approach to parent-teacher interaction. They are a safeguard for the child. Parents and school personnel are the child's advocates. Both want what is best for the child.

PARENT INVOLVEMENT IN EDUCATION

In addition to an advocacy role, parents should also take an active role in the education of their children. Parent involvement in the regular classroom is an asset that is often overlooked or mismanaged. The parent is involved in planning the IEP and has the right of input and due process. Although parents are aware of these rights, many probably do not feel self-assured enough to fully capitalize on them. They rely on the teacher, the administrator, the psychologist, or whomever they are in contact with to keep them informed of what they, as parents, should be doing. Many parents feel that the teacher or person in the authority role knows what is best and that it is up to that person to decide if the parent can be of assistance. The counterpart is the teacher who is fearful of parent involvement, perhaps from misconceptions or a bad experience. Thus there is a lack of communication or overt action that prevents the use of an influential work force, the parents, for the education of the exceptional student.

Because implementation of Public Law 94-142 mandates that exceptional children be given a free and equal education, new programs have been installed in schools; certification programs have been quickly developed, and teachers and students have undergone many changes in a short time. From the passage of Public Law 94-142, which ensures that every child shall have a free education, to the recent emphasis on "mainstreaming," the teacher has been buffeted with rules, new demands, and concerns. In *Attitudes Toward*

Mainstreaming, Wheeler made the following statement:

In general, the regular classroom teachers indicated a lack of support for mainstreaming. Their responses tended to be slightly negative. Special education teachers, as a group, tended to respond more favorably toward mainstreaming. Regular classroom teachers were less willing to accept an educably mentally retarded student into their classrooms because they believed that they, as teachers, had inadequate knowledge and skills to be able to teach the student effectively.[6]

Both parents and teachers are uncertain as to how to go about helping the exceptional student fulfill his educational potential. "The law clearly states that the local school district must provide appropriate special education services. The responsibility for assuring that your child's rights are protected may fall upon you, the parents" (Kearns, p. 13). This responsibility is achieved more easily if the school provides sufficient educational alternatives to meet the varying degrees and different kinds of handicaps. Kearns describes a service continuum that provides several placement options for exceptional students. They may include the following:

1. Provide a continuous series of service levels as needed on a progressive scale from least to most intensive.
2. Provide for moving learners from one level to another in accordance with the least restrictive environment principle. This principle states that:
   a. Learners are placed where they benefit most at the least distance away from mainstream society.
   b. Exceptional learners are moved toward more intensive service levels only as far as necessary.
   c. All exceptional learners are moved toward the mainstream as soon as possible.[7]

The levels shown in Box 8–2, starting from an entry level that does not require a comprehensive evaluation, continue on to reach the most severely disabled and those who are temporarily incapacitated.

---

6. From Wheeler, J. *Attitudes toward mainstreaming.* Unpublished thesis, College of Emporia, Emporia, Kan., 1978.

7. From Kearns, P. (Ed.). *Your child's right to a free public education: Parent's handbook.* Topeka, Kan.: Kansas Association for Children with Learning Disabilities, 1980, p. 13.

BOX 8–2: Progressive Service Levels

Entry level services plan

Some learners require only special instructional materials or equipment for progress in the education mainstream. For example, a visually impaired student may need nothing more than large print reading materials. This is a minimal special education service. Periodic monitoring of pupil progress is necessary to ensure that the degree of support is sufficient.

The first two models, Special Instructional Materials and/or Equipment, and Consultant Teacher Plan are the level of least intensive special education services and are identified as entry level. Such services can be distinguished as "indirect" rather than "direct" services to children. These services may be initiated after an appropriate educational assessment and without completion of a comprehensive evaluation.

In addition, entry level services may include speech services provided after a diagnostic evaluation by an approved speech clinician and without completion of a comprehensive evaluation, if the child shows no accompanying academic problems.

No child shall be maintained on entry level services if the assistance given does not produce a satisfactory educational adjustment. Referral for a comprehensive evaluation shall be made whenever lack of progress in entry level services indicates the child may need more intensive special education.

Consulting teacher plan

The consulting teacher is a certified special education teacher whose role is to facilitate the maintenance of exceptional children in the educational setting most nearly approximating that of their normal peers. The consulting teacher functions as an instructional specialist who may work in several areas of exceptionality. The main thrust of this program is to assist classroom teachers in making their own educational diagnosis, prescriptive decision, and delivery of treatment. Direct service to children is limited to short-term instruction carried out with individual children in their classrooms for the purpose of demonstrating special skills to their teacher. No more than one-third of the consulting teacher's time is devoted to direct child instruction. Note: Because of the heavy responsibility placed on personnel serving as consulting teachers, this plan will be approved on an individual basis until definite guidelines are developed.

Itinerant teacher plan

The itinerant teacher provides direct service to learners enrolled in the regular classroom. The major role of the itinerant teacher is to provide specialized tutoring and small group instruction, although some time is devoted to consulting with regular teachers. Whenever possible, instruction should be done in the classroom setting in order to facilitate communication between the specialist and the regular teacher. Adequate facilities should also be available for instructional activities which cannot be appropriately carried out in the classroom.

Resource room plan

In the resource room program, the exceptional learner is enrolled in a regular classroom, but goes to a specially equipped room to receive part of his instruction from a special teacher. The resource room teacher is responsible not only for his/her own classroom, but also for maintaining communication with the student's regular classroom teachers.

Like the itinerant teacher, he/she provides both instructional and consultative services. This implies that scheduling must allow for work with other teachers. The amount of time spent by students in the resource room depends upon individual needs. However, the intent of the plan, which is to provide supportive assistance to exceptional learners in the educational mainstream, is violated if children spend most of their time in the resource room.

Integrated special classroom

In the integrated special classroom program, exceptional children are assigned to a special class, but receive most academic instruction in regular classes. The extent of integration is determined by the learner's individual capabilities. The special education teacher is responsible for monitoring the progress of his/her students in regular classes and providing appropriate support. The major difference between this program and the resource room plan is that in the resource room the pupil is enrolled in a regular education program.

Self contained special class

Students requiring a specialized curriculum are served in this program. They are enrolled in a special class and receive most academic instruction from a special education teacher. Like regular students, they engage in total school activities (such as school clubs, assemblies, and sports) and, whenever possible, participate in general education classes.

Special day schools

Special day schools are generally designed to provide specialized curricula; modified facilities and equipment; and/or interdisciplinary, ancillary, medical, psychiatric and social services for exceptional children. Day care centers, work activity centers or sheltered workshops are common types of special day schools.

School districts may contract with accredited special day schools for services to children or youth for whom the program is appropriate. School districts may also employ a teacher to work in the special day school setting.

Inasmuch as exceptional children enrolled in special day schools are segregated from their normal peers, this alternative should be used only when the unique needs of a learner cannot be met within the public school system. It is the responsibility of the district to monitor student progress and to facilitate reentry into the public schools whenever possible.

Residential schools

A few handicapped children profit most from intensive and comprehensive services provided by residential or boarding school facilities. The total residential treatment program should include educational experiences which optimize the learner's ability to cope with his environment. The ultimate goal should be to return learners to the community and the public schools. Cooperative agreements between residential centers and school districts can increase the program variations available to children and youth. Some learners may not require residential placement, but may benefit from the residential educational program. Others, who reside at the center, may be able to function successfully in the public school setting.

Hospital instruction

In this program students confined to hospitals or convalescent homes for psychiatric or medical treatment receive individual or group instruction from a special education teacher. Training requirements for the certified teacher utilized will depend upon the nature of the population served. This teacher serves both children with chronic disorders and those recovering from accidents or illness who are hospitalized for short periods of time. Satisfactory programming requires a team approach involving the physician, other hospital personnel, and the school to which the student will return when he has sufficiently recovered.

Homebound instruction

Homebound instruction is appropriate for children and youth whose health problems are so serious that school attendance is impossible, or for those temporarily disabled by an illness, operation or accident. In some cases, students with severe and/or unusual handicapping conditions may receive short-term homebound instruction as a temporary measure until more appropriate arrangements can be made. Instruction in the home is provided either by an itinerant special teacher or after school hours by the student's regular teacher. Frequent reevaluation of pupils in a homebound program is necessary. Inasmuch as this is the most segregated of all special education plans, discretion in its use is necessary.*

*From Kearns, P. (Ed.). *Your child's right to a free public education: Parent's handbook*. Topeka, Kan.: Kansas Association for Children with Learning Disabilities, 1980, pp. 14–18.

The challenge lies in three areas. First, a positive match between child and program is essential. In addition, the professional who works with exceptional children must be able to work with both the children and their parents. Third, parents must learn to exercise their right to understand their child's diagnosis and the reasons for special treatment or educational placement. They must be actively involved in the development of the IEP (Reynolds & Birch, 1977).

MASLOW'S HIERARCHY OF NEEDS

When schools become involved with parents, it is wise to list the basic needs that must be satisfied before parents can effectively assist in the education of their exceptional children. Coletta (1977) elaborates on Maslow's hierarchy of needs in *Working Together: A Guide to Parent Involvement*.

How does Maslow's hierarchy apply to exceptional children? When teachers or administrators work with parents, it is helpful if they understand the parents' feelings, motivations, and concerns. Maslow's hierarchy of needs serves as a guide to this understanding. Parents who are poor and struggling to provide the necessities of life have a different view of their problems than urban affluent parents. That is, physiological needs such as food and shelter must be satisfied before individuals can attend to higher order needs such as success and fulfillment. All parents' love and concern for their children will be the same. Therefore, all parents—regardless of economic standing—must be treated with dignity and respect.

The various levels of Maslow's hierarchy are discussed here:

Physical Needs. The needs for sustaining life, nourishment, protection from the elements, and sexual activity are physical. There must be protection from the cold, wind, and rain, which usually means a shelter, such as a house, and clothing. There must be food, and, to be effective, it must be nourishing. There is a need for companionship and sexual activity.

Psychologic Needs. One needs to feel secure in oneself. It is important to know that one will awake to have a job. It is difficult to handle change, conflict, and uncertainty. It is important to reduce these frustrations. Much emphasis is placed on norms and rules, which results in little flexibility at this level.

Emotional Love and Belonging. At this level there is a need to feel a part of a group where one is accepted, wanted, loved, and respected. When these needs are met or satisfied, then there can be love, respect for others, and consideration or helpfulness for others. When these needs are not being met, there may be self-defeating, attention-getting behaviors such as suspicion and aggression.

Self-esteem. It is wise to remember that basic needs must be met before one can satisfy the need for self-esteem. When one is regarded as valuable and competent by others, one has self-esteem. Growth in awareness of self-worth leads to less dependence upon another's judgment of one's worth. The key is for the professional to find ways to help parents see themselves as worthwhile contributors to their children's education.

Fulfillment. This is referred to as self-actualization and is achieved after all four of the previous levels have been reached. The person strives for self-development, directs energies for self-established goals, and takes risks willingly.

This hierarchy of needs is applicable to children, teachers, and administrators as well as parents. It is wise to mentally note where we are in the hierarchy as well as where the people are we would like to help. If there is an understanding of needs, then our expectations and suggestions for helping may be more valid.

SPECIAL PROBLEMS OF PARENTS OF EXCEPTIONAL CHILDREN

Parents react differently and sometimes unpredictably to the birth or the diagnosis of a child with a handicap. Reactions are a result of feelings; parents may experience frustration, hurt, fear, guilt, disappointment, ambivalence, or despair. In order for the professional to work effectively with parents of the handicapped, there must be an ability to recognize these feelings and a willingness to honor them (Chinn, Winn, & Walters, 1978).

It is usually easier for the professional to view the handicapped child objectively than it is for the parents. The professional deals with the child on a day-to-day basis or only occasionally, whereas the parents deal with the child before and after school and on weekends. Parents of severely handicapped children may be faced with a lifetime of care.

There is a need to offer parents relief from the constant care that is often required. Foster parents, substitute grandparents, and knowledgeable volunteers are becoming more available to give these parents helpful breaks (Chinn, Winn, & Walters, 1978).

PARENTAL REACTIONS

Parents usually go through definite steps in dealing with the problem of a child with a handicap. First, they become aware of and recognize the basic problem. They then become occupied with trying to discover a cause and later begin to look for a cure. Acceptance is the last stage (Chinn, Winn, & Walters, 1978).

Denial.   Parents who deny the existence of a child's handicap feel threatened. Their security is unsure, and they are defending their egos or self-concepts. This is a difficult reaction for the professional to deal with. Time, patience, and support will help these parents to see that much can be gained through helping children with handicaps realize their potentials.

Projection of Blame.   A common reaction is to project blame for the situation on something or someone else. It may be the psychologist, the teacher, or the doctor. They may or may not be the basis for criticism. Often parents' statements begin with "If only. . . ." Again, patience, willingness to listen to the parent, and tact will help the professional deal with a potentially hostile situation.

Fear.   The parents may not be acquainted with the cause of the characteristics of the handicapping condition. They may have misfounded suspicions or erroneous information, which causes anxiety or fear. Information, in an amount that the parent can handle, is the best remedy for fear of the unknown. A positive communication process helps the professional to judge the time for additional information to be added.

Guilt.   Feeling guilty, that perhaps if they had done something differently or that the handicapping condition is in retribution for a misdeed, is a reaction that is difficult to deal with. The professional will help by encouraging guilt-stricken parents to channel their energies into more productive activities after genuine communication has been established and continues throughout the relationship.

Mourning or Grief.   Grief is a natural reaction to a situation that brings extreme pain and disappointment. Parents who have not been able to accept their child as a child with a handicap but look upon the child as handicapped may become grief stricken. In this case it is necessary to allow the parents to go through a healing process before they can learn about their child and how the child can develop.

Withdrawal.   Being able to withdraw and collect oneself is a healthy, necessary action. It is when one begins to shun others, avoid situations, and maintain isolation that it becomes potentially damaging.

Rejection.   There are many reasons for rejection and many ways of exhibiting rejection. It may be subtle, feigning acceptance, or it may be open and hostile. Some forms of rejection are failing to recognize positive attributes, setting unrealistic goals, escape by desertion, or presenting a favorable impression to others while inwardly rejecting the child.

Acceptance.   Finally, the reaction of parents may be one of acceptance, acceptance that the child has a handicap, acceptance of the child and of themselves. This is the goal and realization of maturity. The parents and the child can grow and develop into stronger, wiser, and more compassionate human beings (Chinn, Winn, & Walters, 1978).

REACHING THE PARENT OF THE YOUNG EXCEPTIONAL CHILD

When parents are confronted with the task of rearing an exceptional child, they need both emotional support and specific information. One program for fathers of exceptional infants illustrates an innovative way to reach out to parents. Sam W. Delaney conducts classes for fathers and their special infants at Seattle Community College and the Model Preschool Center for Handicapped Children at the University of Washington. "What we need is a method for fostering and facilitating the awareness that a father can be spontaneous in his feelings of tenderness and love toward his infant son or daughter" (Delaney, 1980, p. 1). Early joyful interaction between parent and child facilitates the emotional bond. "The researchers suggest that early and sustained contact with the infant releases the father's potential for involvement with the child" (Delaney, 1980, p. 1). The model, therefore, is based on two concepts. The first is the establishment of attachment between father and infant. The second is the development of parenting qualities in the father. This ability is acquired when the father is able to read cues and understand the baby's behavior. The cues and behavior patterns of a handicapped child may not be the same as those exhibited by a normal infant. If misinterpreted by the parents, the behavior may cause parents to become confused, frustrated, and to eventually withdraw from meaningful relationships, "thereby impairing the attachment process and leaving the child at risk for a secondary handicap" (Delaney as cited in Delaney, Meyer, & Ward, p. 8).

The class for fathers and infants offers a support group, provides time for father-child interaction, shares appropriate child-rearing information, and fosters awareness of community resources (Delaney, 1980). The class meets each Saturday and follows this schedule.

Sharing, 10:00 to 10:15.   During the sharing period fathers discuss their observations of their children. "Fathers are able to develop a sense of community in which common concerns are made known, and each develops a sense of going through an experience similar to that of other fathers" (Delaney, Meyer, & Ward, p. 9). This period may also be used to bring up questions about the topic of the day.

Music and Exercise, 10:15 to 10:45.   Fathers join in song and rhythm exercises with their infants. Songs that greet are followed by songs pertaining to parts of the body, action songs, recorded music for dancing, and relaxing songs (lullabies and tender music) to bring the period to a pleasant ending.

Zingers, 10:45 to 11:00.   Zingers are distributed at the previous class so that fathers can discuss them during the week and can come to class ready for a lively discussion. Many zingers are controversial; others are thought provoking. Examples include:

The average American middle-class father spends 39 seconds per day with his children (as cited in Delaney, Meyer, & Ward, p. 11)

Parents should respond to a baby every time he or she cries (as cited in Delaney, Meyer, & Ward, p. 11)

Snack, 11:00 to 11:15.   Two fathers volunteer to bring snacks for the group each Saturday. Snacks must be nutritionally sound and appropriate for infants.

Guest Speaker: Child/Family Development, 11:15 to 11:55.   In an informal presentation a professional who is able to relate to the fathers shares expertise and knowledge about a variety of subjects, for example, physical therapy, health, nutrition, special education, and group care.

Preview, 11:55.   The last five minutes focus on the issues to be covered the next week.

Those fathers who must, leave, while others stay and socialize for a time. Delaney cautions that although there is a schedule, the class is not tied to a rigid plan. Mothers who are interested in a particular topic can join the group. Field trips, swimming, or a picnic can be substituted for the routine (Delaney, Meyer, & Ward).

This program illustrates how a small amount of time spent with parents of exceptional children can bring understanding and support. Although it is not meant to be a substitute for counselors and professionals in the health field, it serves as a model for reaching fathers (or mothers) with exceptional children.

EXCEPTIONAL CHILDREN IN HEAD START

In 1974, with the passage of the Community Services Act (Public Law 96-644), Head Start received a mandate from Congress that 10 percent of its children were to be handicapped. Handicapped children are defined as "mentally retarded, hard of hearing, deaf, speech-impaired, visually handicapped, seriously emotionally disturbed, physically handicapped, crippled, and other health impaired children or children with specific learning disabilities who by reason thereof require a special education and related services" (Riley, 1976, p. 9). Head Start procedures and policies were developed to respond to the needs of these exceptional children with individualized and appropriate education.

Mainstreaming of exceptional children resulted in the development of excellent materials for Project Head Start by the U.S. Department of Health, Education, and Welfare. The following are valuable resources for all parents and professionals working with handicapped children:

Mainstreaming Preschoolers: Children with Hearing Impairment
Mainstreaming Preschoolers: Children with Emotional Disturbances
Mainstreaming Preschoolers: Children with Health Disabilities
Mainstreaming Preschoolers: Children with Mental Retardation
Mainstreaming Preschoolers: Children with Physical (Orthopedic) Handicaps
Mainstreaming Preschoolers: Children with Speech and Language Impairment
Mainstreaming Preschoolers: Children with Communication Disorders
Mainstreaming Preschoolers: Children with Visual Handicaps

Copies of these manuals can be obtained from the regional Department of Health and Human Services or from the U.S. Government Printing Office.

TECHNICAL ASSISTANCE FOR PARENT PROGRAMS

Public Law 94-142 of 1975 recognized the need for an active and decision-making role for parents of the handicapped in helping to develop the IEP and in monitoring special education programs. In 1983 an amendment, Public Law 98-199, provided for parent training and information to increase parent effectiveness in working with the staff of their youngster's school. A network of regional centers known as the Technical Assistance for Parent Programs or TAPP has been set up throughout the nation (Gilles, 1986). For information about the TAPP project and its services, contact TAPP Project, 2nd Floor, 312 Stuart St., Boston, Massachusetts 02116; phone (617) 482-2915.

CHILD FIND PROJECT

Concern over reaching parents and their exceptional children resulted in the federal funding of the Child Find Project. Child Find is designated to locate handicapped children through using any feasible methods available such as door-to-door surveys, media campaigns, dissemination of information from the schools, and home visits by staff and/or volunteers (Lerner, 1981).

In recent years other logos such as Count Your Kid In and Make a Difference have been used to designate this program. In many cases this program is funded by both federal and state governments. Preschool screenings have been very successful in finding children in need and communicating to parents the help that is available.

ADVOCACY IN SPECIAL EDUCATION

Advocacy, pleading for the cause of another, is growing year by year. The need for informed advocates for the handicapped is great. Each state department of education will be able to inform you of their sponsored programs and of independent organizations' programs such as the Association of Retarded Children & Adults (ARC) or the Association for Children and Adults with Learning Disabilities (ACLD). The addresses and phone numbers may be found in local telephone directories and the *Encyclopedia of Associations,* which is available in public libraries.

INVOLVING PARENTS OF VERY YOUNG HANDICAPPED CHILDREN

Precise Early Education for Children with Handicaps (PEECH) involves parents through offering conferences, group meetings, home visits, classroom observations, and a lending library, as well as through being receptive to their questions and suggestions. This program integrates handicapped children in a classroom with children who have no special education needs. The children, age 3 to 6, attend the program half a day, 5 days a week (Far West Laboratory, 1983).

Merle Karnes, director of the project, emphasizes the importance of family involvement and the necessity of skillful staff interaction with parents. She finds that parents are interested in their handicapped children and want to become knowledgeable and skilled in working with them. To ensure success in your work with parents, give specific directions and objective feedback on their contributions. Respect them as individuals and be flexible in responding to their needs and value systems. If parents are included in decision making, if the program makes sense to them, if their goals and values are compatible with those of the school, if they are approached as individuals and are convinced that you, the professional, are interested in helping them, they will join with you in developing their abilities and contributing their time.

Parents can work effectively in the classroom, and they will extend their newfound understandings to other members of the family. They may become so knowledgeable and skillful that they can reach out to help parents of other handicapped children (Karnes, 1977).

NORMAL ACTIVITIES FOR PRESCHOOLERS

Normal activities for very young children are listed below. If young children cannot perform the activities for their age level, professional help should be sought.

Age Two. Children can run well, build a tower of six or seven blocks, walk up and down stairs alone, use three-worded sentences, use *I, me,* and *you* correctly. They know their name, and know approximately 270 words.

Age Three. They can put on shoes and button buttons, use four-worded sentences and give commands, stand on one foot for a moment, jump from a bottom stair, and build a tower with 10 blocks. They know and use about 900 words, speak rather fluently, feed themselves without too many spills, identify drawings, and know their own sex.

Age Four. Now the children can skip on one foot and walk down the stairs one foot at a time. They know front and back of clothes, wash themselves and dress with help, count to three, recognize colors, brush teeth, build a house with blocks, and stand on one foot for several seconds.

Age Five. Children can skip, draw human figures, count to 12 or more, use fingers to show how old they are, dress and undress without help, name four or more colors, and stand on one foot 8 to 10 seconds.

PLAY IS IMPORTANT

How do you teach play to an exceptional baby or small child? Play is especially important to the deaf and/or blind. These handicaps do not interfere with the natural phenomenon of learning about the world around oneself and growing and developing while doing so. Activities that are appropriate for normal babies are appropriate for the exceptional, too. Clapping hands, cooing, playing peek-a-boo, and cuddling are necessary and helpful. Provide the baby or small child with small objects to grasp and a large pillow to lay on. Rock children back and forth or play with them on a swing, so they will have the experiences needed to develop. Babies and small children must have the opportunity to think, to experiment, to investigate, and to learn about their environment.

A SHARED CONCERN

Suzanne Crane is the mother of a handicapped child. She has shared her feelings and thoughts about this so that others may benefit from her experiences.

Having a handicapped child was not what we expected. I remember the feelings likened to having run into a brick wall, the heartbreak of having a broken doll and no one able to fix her. The uncertainties were even more of a struggle due to fragmented medical care and follow-up on her development. We were told of the absolute and immediate necessity of finding special help for her and then sent home with no guidance as to who and where we could turn to for this help. However, through community support and the efforts of other parents we were able to secure services for our child. I do not believe our daughter would be walking or talking now if we hadn't persevered in this. She presently is 7 years old and being served by special education in the public school system. However, I will always crusade for the infants, toddlers, and preschoolers with special needs and their families who are faced with the overwhelming situation of no help available.

I feel that we are more like other families than set apart. I have seen other children accept her with open arms, bridging the gap. Our daughter's celebrative spirit, her love for music, her essence has affected us, her parents, and our second child in positive ways. She has shaped our perspective on the world and life. She has taught us to be happy. We hope that her future will enhance her internal spirit and allow her to be accepted by others. (Crane, 1986)

For Friends of the Handicapped

Blessed are you take the time
To listen to difficult speech
For you help me to know that
If I persevere, I can be understood.

Blessed are you who never bid me to "hurry
    up"
Or take my tasks from me and do them for
    me,
For I often need time rather than help.

Blessed are you who stand beside me
As I enter new and untried ventures,
For my failures will be outweighed
By the times I surprise myself and you.

Blessed are you who asked for my help
For my greatest need is to be needed

Blessed are you who understand that
It is difficult for me to put my thoughts into
    words

Blessed are you who never remind me
That today I asked the same question twice

Blessed are you who respect me
And love me just as I am.
(Reprinted by permission from Ann Landers,
author unknown; News America
Syndicate)

BURNOUT

Burnout is a term applied to the loss of concern and emotional feeling for those people you work with or live with (Maslach, 1976). Both teachers and parents experience burnout. It is felt most when what you are trying to do seems unproductive, or you may feel you have few alternatives that would change or improve the course of events. This is a frustrating situation, and it leads to a feeling of being trapped. It can happen to any teacher and any parent. The obligations of teaching and parenting are similar. The teacher or the parent is in the authoritarian role and is responsible for setting up the program. Balancing the student's needs with time constraints, the mechanical constraints of running a classroom or a home, and the constraints of the personal needs of the authoritarian figure is a role for a magician. Indeed, when parents and teachers are successful, the result does seem to be magical. No teacher or parent will agree that it is magical. They know it is hard work, good planning, cooperation, and perseverance.

Those who set high standards and aim for perfection are sometimes more likely to experience burnout. Also, those who feel a need to be in control may experience burnout. Feelings of anger, guilt, depression, self-doubt, and irritability are symptoms of burnout. When these occur, take a hard look at what is really going on and what needs to be going on. Are you neglecting yourself? Are the things you want to do essential? Do some things need to be changed? Learn to accept the fact that change can occur. Be willing to give yourself and others credit when credit is due.

Build in rewards so that you and others feel good about what you are doing. Always have some goals that are short term and accessible. There is nothing that feels better than having success. This is one of the best methods to combat burnout. Remember, burnout is reversible.

COMMUNICATING WITH PARENTS OF EXCEPTIONAL CHILDREN

Parents are receptive to open and direct communication. The message should be clear and in language the parents can understand. It is necessary to realize that the teacher or professional will deal with a wide variance of language efficiency. Professionals should acquaint themselves with the parents' backgrounds and be receptive to clues from the parents to determine if the message being communicated is indeed being received and accommodated. Ask a leading question to let the parents express what they understand about the topic being discussed. It may be a surprise to find that the interpretations are different.

It takes skill, tact, and ingenuity for a professional to communicate with all types of people who have different kinds of needs. Mistakes to avoid include "talking down" to the parents, assuming an understanding exists where in fact none may, and using jargon or technical language.

The professional should include the support and consultation of the medical and theological professions if the parents exhibit a need for these services. Be aware of the agencies and organizations that assist parents and professional workers in the local community as well as national organizations.

I recommend the book *Two-way Talking with Parents of Special Children, A Process of Positive Communication* (Chinn, Winn, & Walters, 1978) as a resource for learning more about communicating with parents. This book discusses in depth communication, semantics, transactional analysis, stroking, family interactions, and transactions.

Although two-way communication is essential, important tips and information can be relayed to parents through newsletters, personal letters, or charts. These can be used in conjunction with the conference, or they can be separate forms of communication.

Newsletter

Use a newsletter to offer tips for parents. There are things that all parents can do to help their children in school that are important to parents of both handicapped and average children. Select from the following tips.

Healthy Environment. First of all, it is important to provide an environment that will promote the good health of your child. Adequate housing, clothing, and food affect the development of every child. The disadvantaged child is handicapped, indeed, when these basic needs are not available.

Communicate With Children. It is important to talk with your children. This is the way children learn their language, and they must be given opportunities to practice using their skill. Talk naturally so the child can understand and be able to develop language. When your child talks, listen. How do you feel when you talk to someone who will not listen to what you are saying? Most adults don't waste time talking to people who do not listen to them. Children don't either. If you want your children to express themselves, then let them initiate conversations and respond by giving them your attention.

Praise, Praise, Praise. Praise reinforces learning and behaviors. Let children know when you are pleased with what they are doing. We all work for rewards, and praise is one of the most important rewards you can give. Be patient with your children. It takes many trials and errors to learn skills. Adults forget over the years how it was. If the situation gets out of hand and you do become impatient or angry, then leave the situation, do something else, and come back to it when you are in control of yourself.

No Comparisons. Don't compare your children. Allow for individuality. Every child is different with special characteristics that make up his personality and no one else's.

Good Work Habits. When it comes time for school, set the stage for good homework habits. A well-lighted place to study that is quiet with room for books, pencils, and papers helps. Schedule home study on a regular basis.

Sufficient Rest. Set a bedtime and stick to it. Children need a lot of rest to be able to do good mental work. Rest is necessary for proper growth.

Regular School Attendance. Do your part to see that your child attends school regularly and on time. Visit with teachers to learn how your child is getting along in school and listen to what they have to tell you about your child.

Enrichment Activities. Help increase your children's knowledge by taking them places such as zoos, libraries, or airports. Use television as a learning tool by selecting appropriate programs and discussing the program after it is viewed. Another learning experience that is often overlooked is the family mealtime. Sharing experiences, talking about interesting subjects, and improving conversational skills can happen around the dining table.

Read and Talk Together. Read to your children, have them read to you, and listen to them read. Let them tell you about what they have been reading. Magazines, newspapers, comics, and books can all be used to increase a child's knowledge and reading ability.

Letters

Letters are often effective means of communicating an idea or message to parents. Letters need to state the concern, then present a method or suggestion for dealing with or changing the situation, including any guidelines or datelines that are pertinent, and finally, end with a conclusion and an offer for assistance if needed.

There are as many ways to write the message you wish to convey as there are teachers. Each will need to adapt the contents to the concerns of the situation.

Charts

Charts are a valuable tool to communicate progress, to keep a graphic picture for easy reference, and to serve as a record of day-to-day or week-to-week events. There is as much variety in graphs and charts as there are situations, so it is important to learn to use the one that will complement your needs. It should clearly indicate the child's work so parents can immediately recognize their child's progress.

HOW PARENTS CAN HELP AT HOME

As a teacher or a parent the goal is to have all students or children perform to their full potentials.

It may become necessary to give exceptional students extra help at home in order for them to be able to keep up their schoolwork. Special tutoring by someone outside the family may be needed, and it can be very effective. If the parents are planning to work with their child, the following suggestions should help guide them in their endeavor.

Visit With the Teacher. Explain that you want to help your child at home with schoolwork. Ask the teacher to explain the material the class will be covering and how assignments should be done. Try to get a time sched-ule for assignments, or your student may already have one.

Set a Definite Time. Set a definite time to work with your child. Go over the day's experiences and listen to how your student felt about them. Discuss how the assignments can be completed and turned in on time.

Monitor Progress. Keep a record of the assignments handed in and the scores received. In this way you can tell how the student is doing. If the grades are low or you do not understand them, visit with the teacher so you will know exactly what the teacher expects.

Flashcards. Flashcards can be bought for times tables, word recognition, fractions, and many other skills. It is not hard to use tagboard to make cards that fit your child's specific needs. Use them in a consistent manner and review learned skills periodically to help establish skills that must be available for instant recall.

How to Promote Success. Your child will be more likely to succeed in the home-school program if you do the following:

1. Use a pleasant, firm approach, one that says, "Yes, this must be done, and we'll do it as quickly and pleasantly as we can."

2. Set up a reward system. None of us will work at a job we do not receive satisfaction from or get paid for. Our praise and approval is the students' pay for doing a job well. If they get scolded all of the time, they are unlikely to want to work for another scolding.

3. Work, play, and rest. There has to be some work, play, and rest in everyone's life. If we do too much of one, the other two will suffer. Parents are the best persons to determine how to keep this balance.

Name										Class				Sex				Birth																												Days on roll	Days taught	Days present	Days absent
	First week				Second week				Third week				Fourth week				Fifth week				Sixth week				Seventh week				Eighth week				Ninth week							
	M	T	W	T	F	M	T	W	T	F	M	T	W	T	F	M	T	W	T	F	M	T	W	T	F	M	T	W	T	F	M	T	W	T	F	M	T	W	T	F	M	T	W	T	F				
1st 9 wks																																																
2nd 9 wks																																																
3rd 9 wks																																																
4th 9 wks																																																
					Parent																	Address															Total											

FIGURE 8-3
A converted 9-weeks attendance chart can be used as follows: first 9 weeks for grades; second 9 weeks for attendance; third 9 weeks for behavior in class, positive or negative; and fourth 9 weeks for projects or extra work.

CHARTING

Keeping track of daily grades, attendance, and projects is a big task for student or parent. A converted 9-weeks attendance chart works very well (Figure 8-3). Place the grade earned in the line for the first 9 weeks. The attendance can be placed on the second 9-weeks line. Behavior or special projects can be placed on the next two lines. Encouraging children or students to keep track of their scores helps to build organizational skills. It also gives the parent a natural time for children or students to relate the day's events and discuss problems that may have come up. The chart gives a record of progress that can be used handily for a reward system.

To ensure success we should use every available aid, method, or technique that is effective. Many times the proper technique, the mechanical aid, or different method is not used because there is the fear of being different. Sometimes it is because of lack of familiarity. Whatever the reason, it must be put aside, and that which will help students learn to their potentials must be pursued with determination and compassion.

RULES OF LEARNING

When a teacher or parent is working with exceptional children, the rules of learning are the same as those for nonexceptional children. All

learning takes place in the same pattern, but there are differences in the ways individuals handle learning. Two approaches will be presented to give broader coverage and more adaptability to different levels.

Conceptual Levels

Readiness.   The readiness level represents the knowledge that already exists before one begins to teach. Therefore, all teaching should begin at the readiness level.

Motivation.   Motivation is the level of stimulating a desire or need on the part of the student to learn what is being taught.

Awareness.   Awareness is the actual teaching phase. According to scientific reference, something is learned when it is repeated once.

Assimilation.   Assimilation refers to the actual acceptance of the information by students. They now have the information for reference.

Accommodation.   Accommodation becomes a fact when students use the information they have learned in new circumstances.

With the learning accommodated, the student is using the information in new situations, yet the learning is still considered dependent. It is not until the learned information becomes automatic, without conscious thought, that it is called independent (Cochran, 1974).

PQ4R: A Reading Approach

PQ4R means

Preview	or set the stage for learning
Questions	arouse curiosity
Read	present your lesson
Reflect	discuss your lesson
Recite	give feedback—immediate response
Review	revisit and test

Both the PQ4R and the conceptual method are effective. It is easy to see the similarities of the two approaches. Either can be adapted to any learning situation. They do produce results (Thomas & Robinson, 1981).

A FEW THINGS TO REMEMBER

When teaching exceptional children, teachers and parents should follow these suggestions:

1. Encourage correct responses—wrong responses have to be relearned.

2. Use tests as learning instruments. More learning takes place when tests are answered and corrected soon after being given.

3. Learning occurs more effectively when more channels of learning are involved. If you involve the visual and hearing channels, it is more effective than involving just vision or just hearing.

4. Putting what has been learned into action through verbal or physical reaction increases the learning experience.

5. Learning is reinforced by repetition, that is, reviewing often at first and then again at varying intervals.

6. Begin with concrete items and move gradually to teaching abstract items.

7. When teaching motor skills, always begin with large muscle activities and gradually approach fine muscle activities.

HOW PARENTS CAN TUTOR AT HOME

Tutoring is one of the most effective and necessary tools in education. It is a skill that can be learned and developed. For some it seems to come easily, but for others it is difficult. It requires understanding another's rate of learning and being responsive to feelings and moods.

The cassette recorder is one of the most valuable instruments available in helping the student learn at home or at school. With a recorder parents (in this case, the tutors) can put exactly what they want in a lesson and determine its format. This means that parents are able to adapt the lesson to the student's level and are able to develop it in a way that will be most beneficial to the student. A set of headphones further enhances the learning situation. A carrel made from plywood or a cardboard box produces a one-to-one tutoring situation. This allows parents or teacher to go on with other duties.

What can the cassette recorder be used for? It is excellent for recording spelling words and for having children take spelling tests as they would in a classroom. If the children can read the words, then they should put the words on the tape and take them as in a spelling lesson. When the students listen to the words, they automatically monitor the sound of the word, the inflection, and the phrasing. Corrections are made unconsciously as the mind corrects errors that the ear hears.

The cassette recorder is valuable for taping messages to family members. It is particularly useful for giving directions to be followed. Directions for setting a table, making pudding, or making a bed can be put on tape to give a child valuable experience in learning to follow directions.

Another important use is letting the child put a reading lesson on the tape and then having the child correct errors. A chart of the time, number of words read, and errors made can be kept to show progress.

Suggestions for Putting Lessons on Cassettes

1. Limit the time of the lesson to 5 minutes less than the period you want the lesson to last. This allows a little flexibility for handling interruptions.

2. Arrange the tasks in sequential order. Check the order by doing the lesson once yourself.

3. Speak slowly, more slowly than your normal rate of conversation. Children with learning problems do not process words and thoughts as quickly as most people do. Check to see if the child knows what the tape is saying by asking him to repeat what he hears. Be careful not to ask if the child understands it. The student may think he does, but on your testing you may find out the child doesn't.

4. Include a set of questions at the end of the taped lesson for an immediate review of the material. This also is helpful for the teacher who has students who have missed reading lessons or lectures.

WHAT THE PARENT EXPECTS OF THE PROFESSIONAL

As a professional working with exceptional school-age children, it is important for you to remember what the parent looks for in a teacher. The parent will be on the lookout for the specialist who:

1. Understands his child's assets as well as his deficiencies.
2. Appreciates his child's accomplishments whenever and however they appear.
3. Helps the parent live without guilt or blame, both on the part of the child or himself.
4. Tells his child how it really is. The truth about himself may be difficult for a learning-disabled child, but not as difficult as the bewilderments and heartaches he experiences from half-truths and evasions.[8]

8. From Kratoville, B. L. Dealing with public schools. *Academic Therapy,* 1977, *3*(2), 231.

LEARNING IS HARD

For a period of years the popular philosophy has been that we could best motivate young people in pleasing and attractive settings. The lesson would stimulate interest, be fun, and be relevant to the learner; because one enjoyed doing it, one would be willing to learn. This is an excellent theory, and there is no quarrel with its premise. However, we have produced some youth who did not meet their potential because, in real life, work is not always pleasing.

Work involves diligence, tenacity, endurance, sacrifice, discipline, and repetition. It requires deep concentration and dedication. Work is *not* always fun. It is often boring! Most of us spend our lives doing work. We are willing to make this sacrifice not only for the extrinsic values of status, income, and fringe benefits but also for the intrinsic values of self-worth, dignity, and contribution to society. Our children have become confused because we gave them the impression that life should be fun and games. It is not, and we need to set them straight. Work is work.

The exceptional child works harder and longer to accomplish what other peers do easily and quickly. It is not easy always for them to accept this. It is hard for parents not to expect the school, the teacher to lighten the load, to not expect too much because the child is handicapped. This deprives the child of the feeling of accomplishment, of striving for and reaching his/her potential. The Individual Education Program provides for the appropriate level of accommodation. Use this effective tool to see that every exceptional child is given the opportunity to reach his/her goals.

KEEPERS OF THE FLAME

Parents are the keepers of the flame. Sometimes the flame flickers and almost goes out, and those are the hard days when clear heads, resolve, quick wits, and optimism must be pulled from reserve. Other times the flame burns brightly and steadily, a welcome and needed respite. But at all times the flame must be watched, with extra fuel and nourishment applied when indicated. It is not a thankless charge. That particular flame kindles a glow and warmth unlike any other and, if carefully tended, will one day burst into its own special radiance.[9]

Just as the parent feels warmth and joy with the development of a child with a handicap so, also, will you as a professional when your help and guidance has led to better family relations, improved schoolwork, and an ability to participate in life more fully for the child with a handicap. It is a worthy and mighty undertaking.

multiply handicapped/deaf-blind, and physically impaired. This law also provides for "due process," the right of a hearing if parents do not agree with the educational placement.

Parents have been effective forces in securing the legislation mentioned earlier. Parents should and do have an important role in the life and education of their exceptional children. The parent's role begins as one of nurturing in the home but can become an effective force in the school as the parent supports the teacher at home as a tutor or at school as a volunteer.

SUMMARY

Parents, teachers, and other professionals are effective forces in influencing the life of the exceptional child. It is important that each be able and willing to work together for the benefit of the exceptional child. Special educational terms, once crude, have been replaced with more inclusive, educational terms.

During the twentieth century the special education movement grew, and in 1971 the Pennsylvania Association for Retarded Children (PARC) won a case against the Commonwealth of Pennsylvania. This court decision assured the right of all children to a free and appropriate education. This includes the handicapped or exceptional child. The Rehabilitation Act of 1973, the Buckley Amendment, and the Education of All Handicapped Children Act of 1975 (Public Law 94-142) are some of the far-reaching legislations passed in the third quarter of the century.

From the Education of All Handicapped Children Act of 1975 came the Individual Educational Plan (IEP). It is a plan that involves the parents, child, teachers, administrators, special teachers, psychologists, and any who are involved with the child's education. The plan assures a continuum of services, appropriate to age, maturity, handicapping condition, past achievements, and parental expectations. The exceptional child or student includes the learning disabled, mentally retarded, emotionally disturbed, socially maladjusted, visually impaired, language, speech, and hearing impaired,

SUGGESTED ACTIVITIES AND DISCUSSIONS

1. Write a brief review of the development of special education.
2. List the five principles covering data collection systems for personal data. Which legislation provided these guidelines?
3. Describe in your own words exactly what "least restrictive" means.
4. Which "rights and services" are available to parents?
5. List and describe briefly the eight categories of exceptional students.
6. A staffing refers to the meeting that is held when an exceptional student's IEP is developed or changed. Who is included in such a meeting? What do they decide?
7. "Mainstreaming" is a misunderstood term. Read carefully about mainstreaming and write in your own words what you think mainstreaming means.
8. Using Maslow's hierarchy of needs, assess yourself and five other acquaintances. Try to select those from different professions. Use this as background material for a general class discussion to increase awareness of these needs.
9. Discuss the IEP, listing the six criteria each IEP must include. Conclude with a statement of your own opinion of the IEP. Is there more that should be added? Is there too much? If so, what?
10. Choose one of the problems a parent of exceptional children may encounter and describe how you as a professional would try to help that parent.

---

9. From Kratoville, B. L. Dealing with public schools. *Academic Therapy,* 1977, *3*(2), 231.

11. Develop lesson plans for teaching a specific skill using one set of the "Rules of Learning."

BIBLIOGRAPHY

Buck, P. S. *The child who never grew.* New York: John Day, 1950.

Chinn, P. C., Winn, J., & Walters, R. H. *Two-way talking with parents of special children: A process of positive communication.* St. Louis: C. V. Mosby, 1978.

Cochran, C. E. Class lecture. Assistant Professor of Educational Psychology, Mental Retardation Program, Wichita State University, Wichita, Kan., 1974.

Coletta, A. J. *Working together: A guide to parent involvement.* Atlanta, Ga.: Humanities Limited, 1977.

Crane, C. Personal communication, 1986.

Delaney, S. W. Fathers and infants class: A model program. *Exceptional Teacher,* March 1980, pp. 12–16.

Delaney, S. W., Meyer, D. J., & Ward, M. J. *Fathers and infants class: A model for facilitating attachment between fathers and their infants.* Paper from the Experimental Education Unit, Child Development and Mental Retardation Center, University of Washington, Seattle, Wash.

Far West Laboratory. *Educational programs that work, 1983.* San Francisco: Far West Laboratory for Educational Research and Development, 1983.

The Foundation Center. *The foundation directory* (9th ed.). New York: The Foundation Center, 1983.

Frost, S. E., Jr. *Historical and philosophical foundations of Western education.* Columbus, Oh.: Charles E. Merrill, 1966.

Gearheart, B. R. *Organization and administration of education programs for exceptional children* (2d ed.). Springfield, Ill.: Charles C. Thomas, 1979.

Gilles, C. Personal communication concerning the TAPP project. Boston, 1986.

Greenleaf, B. *Children through the ages: History of childhood.* New York: McGraw-Hill, 1978.

Hallahan, D. P., & Cruickshank, W. M. *Psychoeducational foundations of learning disabilities.* Englewood Cliffs, N.J.: Prentice-Hall, 1973.

Hallahan, D. P., & Kauffman, J. M. *Exceptional children: Introduction to special education.* Englewood Cliffs, N.J., 1978.

Haring, N. G., & Phillips, L. E. *Teaching special children.* New York: McGraw-Hill, 1976.

Johnson, D. J., & Myklebust, H. R. *Learning disabilities: Educational principles and practices.* New York: Grune & Stratton, 1967.

Karnes, M. B. Basic assumptions underlying the family involvement program. (PEECH Project. Institute for Child Behavior and Development). Urbana, Ill.: University of Illinois, 1977.

————. RAPYHT. *Journal for the Education of the Gifted,* 1979, *2*(3), 157–172.

Kearns, P. (Ed.). *Your child's right to a free public education: Parent's handbook.* Topeka, Kan.: Kansas Association for Children with Learning Disabilities, 1980.

Keller, H. *The story of my life.* New York: Grosset & Dunlap, 1905.

Kephart, N. C. *The slow learner in the classroom.* Columbus, Oh.: Charles E. Merrill, 1971.

Kirk, S. A. *Educating exceptional children* (4th ed.). Boston: Houghton Mifflin, 1983.

Kirk, S. A., McCarthy, J. J., & Kirk, W. D. *Illinois test of psycholinguistic abilities.* Urbana, Ill.: University of Illinois Press, 1968.

Kratoville, B. L. Dealing with public schools. *Academic Therapy,* 1977, *3*(2), 225–232.

Kroth, R. L. *Communicating with parents of exceptional children.* Denver, Colo.: Love Publishing, 1985.

Kroth, R. L., & Scholl, G. T. *Getting schools involved with parents.* Reston, Va.: Council for Exceptional Children, 1978.

Landers, A. For friends of the handicapped. (Ann Lander's column, author unknown, News America Syndicate.) In *Special Educational Instructional Paraprofessional Facilitator Program.* Topeka, Kan.: Kansas State Department of Education, 1986.

Lerner, J., Mardell-Czudnowski, C., & Goldenberg, D. *Special education for the early childhood years.* Englewood Cliffs, N.J.: Prentice-Hall, 1981.

Maslach, C. Burned-out. *Human Behavior,* September 1976, pp. 16–22.

McCarthy, J. J., & McCarthy, J. F. *Learning disabilities.* Boston: Allyn & Bacon, 1973.

O'Leary, K. D., & O'Leary, S. G. *Classroom management, the successful use of behavior modification.* New York: Pergamon Press, 1977.

Reinert, H. R. *Children in conflict: Educational strategies for the emotionally disturbed and behaviorally disordered* (2nd ed.). St. Louis: C. V. Mosby, 1980.

Reynolds, M. C., & Birch, J. W. *Teaching exceptional children in all America's schools: A first course for teachers and principals.* Reston, Va.: Council for Exceptional Children, 1977.

Riley, M. T. *Project LATON: The parent book.* Lubbock, Tex.: Texas Tech Press, 1976.

Seaberg, D. I. *The four faces of teaching: The role of the teacher in humanizing education.* Pacific Palisades, Calif.: Goodyear Publishing, 1974.

Smith, R. M. *Teacher diagnosis of educational difficulties.* Columbus, Oh.: Charles E. Merrill, 1973.

Spidel, J. *Exceptional students in the regular classroom, how we help them learn.* (Unpublished.) Presentation Showcase Kansas, Wichita State University, Wichita, Kan., March 15, 1980.

Sumner County Special Education Services. *Commentary regarding the Individual Educational Plan (IEP).* Wellington, Kan.: Sumner County Special Education Services, 1977.

Thomas, E. L., & Robinson, A. H. *Improving reading in every class.* Boston: Allyn & Bacon, 1981.

Turnbull, A. P., & Turnbull, H. R. III. *Parents speak out.* Columbus, Oh.: Charles E. Merrill, 1978.

Van Wyck, B. *Helen Keller.* New York: E. P. Dutton, 1956.

von Hippel, C., Foster, J., & Lonberg, J. *Civil rights, handicapped persons, and education, section 504, self-evaluation. Guide for preschool, elementary, secondary and adult education.* Washington, D.C.: Office of Program Review and Assistance, 1978.

Wallace, G., & Kaufman, J. M. *Teaching children with learning problems.* Columbus, Oh.: Charles E. Merrill, 1973.

Wheeler, J. *Attitudes toward mainstreaming.* Unpublished thesis, College of Emporia, Emporia, Kan., 1978.

CHAPTER NINE

The Abused Child

The physical or mental injury, sexual abuse, negligent treatment or maltreatment of a child under the age of 18 by a person who is responsible for the child's welfare under circumstances which indicate that the child's health or welfare is harmed or threatened thereby[1]

An aspect of parent-school involvement that requires an approach different from other parent-school relationships is the issue of child abuse and neglect. What are the obligations of the teacher and school (or child care center) to the child and family with abusive parents?

The responsibilities are great, and an affirmative response by schools is vital to the well-being of thousands of children throughout the United States. Because of required school attendance and an increase in the use of child care centers, caregivers and teachers have an expanded opportunity for contact with families and children. The professionals work closely with children and families over extended periods of time. In so doing, they are also the agencies most able to detect and prevent abuse and neglect. Schools have not al-

ways been recognized as an important agency in the detection of child abuse. Earlier it was believed that most cases of child abuse concerned battered infants. When infants are abused, they are vulnerable to serious injury or death, but it is now recognized that older children are also victims. Gil (1970) reported that 43.7 percent of reported cases involved children of school age. Children under age 2 made up 24.4 percent, while those over 2 and under 6 accounted for 29.3 percent (2.6 percent were in the age-unknown category). These figures indicate that over 70 percent of the children who are abused or neglected may have contact with schools or child care centers. Through Home Start, Head Start, and private and public preschool programs, the detection of abuse of 2- to 6-year-olds has become easier to achieve. Increasingly, the detection and prevention of child abuse and neglect is recognized as a concern and responsibility of the schools (*Report and Recommendations of the National Advisory Committee on Child Abuse and Neglect,* 1978; Shanas, 1975; *Teacher Education—Active Participant in Solving the Problems of Child Abuse and Neglect,* 1977). Schools should serve as a defense against child abuse: first, as an educational institution offering parent education to adults and students; second, as a referral agency

---

1. From the Child Abuse Prevention and Treatment Act of 1974. *United States Code, 1976, The Public Health and Welfare,* Section 5101, vol. 10. Washington, D.C.: U.S. Government Printing Office, 1977, p. 1826.

to child protection agencies; and third, as a support system for families.

BACKGROUND

Child abuse and neglect have been social phenomena for centuries. Childhood was described by DeMause (1975) as a "nightmare—the human track record on child raising is bloody, dirty, and mean" (p. 8). The child was considered property of the father to be worked, sold, loved, or killed as the father willed it. The child had no rights (Kempe, 1968; Nagi, 1977). Actions that would be called child abuse today were overlooked or considered to be the parent's right to discipline. In the 1800s it was common for children to work 12 hours a day under the threat of beatings. Children were cheap and useful laborers. It was not until 1874 in New York City that the first case of abuse was reported. It involved a 9-year-old girl, Mary Ellen, who was beaten daily by her parents and was severely undernourished when found by church workers. The only organization to which the workers could turn was the American Society for the Prevention of Cruelty to Animals. One year later the New York Society for the Prevention of Cruelty to Children was organized (Fontana, 1979). There were other early evidences of growing concern for children. A paper published in 1888 discussed acute periosteal swelling in infants (Nagi, 1977). National groups such as the Child Study Association of America and the National Congress of Parents and Teachers were formed. Mounting concern over working conditions and care of children culminated in the First White House Conference on Children, held in 1909, which resulted in the 1912 legislation that established the Children's Bureau—"an agency that reports all matters pertaining to the welfare of children and child life among all classes of people" (Nagi, 1977, p. 2).

During recent years, wide concern over and protective action for the child at risk has become a mandate to schools, and medical care agencies have recognized the prevalence of children who are abused. This relatively recent overwhelming concern over the tragedy of child abuse resulted in the nearly unanimous passage of the federal Child Abuse Prevention and Treatment Act of 1974 by a vote of 247 to 57 in the Senate and 354 to 36 in the House of Representatives (Besharov, 1976; Mondale, 1976). What transpired between 1913 and recent decades to focus attention on the child at risk?

Dr. John Caffey began collecting data that indicated child abuse in the early 1920s, but he was not supported in his beliefs by his associates. Thus, it was not until after World War II that he published the first of several studies relating to fractures in young children (Elmer, 1982; American Humane Association, 1978). Caffey's first medical paper, written in 1946, reported the histories of six traumatized infants and questioned the cause of their injuries. In it he reported that fractures of the long bones and subdural hematomas occurring concurrently were not caused by disease (pp. 163–173).

Dr. Frederick Silverman, a former student of Caffey's, followed in 1953 with an article that indicated that skeletal trauma in infants could be the result of abuse (Elmer, 1982; American Humane Association, 1978). Reports began appearing more frequently (Altman & Smith, 1960; Bakwin, 1956; Fisher, 1958; Silver & Kempe, 1959; Wooley & Evans, 1955), but it was an article by Kempe et al., *The Battered-Child Syndrome* (1962), that brought national attention to the abused child. They began their article with the following charge to physicians:

The battered-child syndrome, a clinical condition in young children who have received serious physical abuse, is a frequent cause of permanent injury or death. The syndrome should be considered in any child exhibiting evidence of fracture of any bone, subdural hematoma, failure to thrive, soft tissue swellings or skin bruising, in any child who dies suddenly, or where the degree and type of injury is at variance with the history given regarding the occurrence of the trauma. Psychiatric factors are probably of prime importance in the pathogenesis of the disorder, but knowledge of these factors is limited. Physicians have a duty and responsibility to the child to require a full evaluation of the problem and to guarantee that no expected repetition of trauma will be permitted to occur. (Kempe et al., 1962, p. 17)

The article went on to describe the status of child abuse in the nation and to point out the effectiveness of x-ray examinations in determining abuse. The term *battered* came from the description of bruises, lacerations, bites, brain injury, deep body injury, pulled joints, burns and scalds, fractures of arms, legs, skull, ribs, and other injuries that resulted from beating, whipping, throwing the child about, or slamming the child against something. Fontana (1973) described battering by parents as follows:

Parents bash, lash, beat, flay, stomp, suffocate, strangle, gut-punch, choke with rags or hot pepper, poison, crack heads open, slice, rip, steam, fry, boil, dismember. They use fists, belt buckles, straps, hairbrushes, lamp cords, sticks, baseball bats, rulers, shoes and boots, lead or iron pipes, bottles, brick walls, bicycle chains, pokers, knives, scissors, chemicals, lighted cigarettes, boiling water, steaming radiators, and open gas flames. (pp. 16–17)

The term *battered* and the picture it evoked aroused the nation. By 1967 all 50 states had mandated legislation to facilitate the reporting of incidences of child abuse. There was, however, no provision for the coordination of procedures, nor was there a standard definition of abuse and neglect. Other conditions that precluded standard reporting included the inconsistent ages of children covered by law, hesitation of professional and private citizens to report cases, different systems of official record keeping, and varied criteria on which to judge abuse.

One of the first comprehensive studies was completed by Gil (1970). He studied a sample, forwarded to him from central registries in the United States and territories of the United States, of 9563 cases in 1967 and 10,931 cases in 1968. After screening the reports, he reduced the number to 5993 subjects in 1967 and 6617 subjects who were abused in 1968.

Others placed the number of cases of child abuse much higher. Kempe (1977), a pediatrician who focused on child abuse, reported that of 300,000 suspected cases that are reported each year, about 60,000 result in significant injuries, including 2000 deaths and 6000 instances of brain damage to the child. Sussman and Cohen, after studying the 10 most populated states, projected 38,779 confirmed cases of abuse in 1973 (as cited in Nagi, 1977). Fontana, another pediatrician who works with abused children, believes that one or two children are killed and thousands are permanently injured by their parents each day. Although others may believe that the incidence of abuse is exaggerated, doctors who view children each day feel that child abuse occurs more often than data indicate and that what is revealed is merely the tip of an iceberg (Fontana, 1973; Gelles, 1977).

Gelles (1980) defined and operationalized violence in an effort to determine the extent of abuse in the United States. Violence was stated as "an act carried out with the intention of, or perceived intention of, physically injuring another person" (p. 875). The research included 2,143 participants who had at least one child, 3 to 17 years of age, living at home. The survey revealed that 3.8 percent of the children in the United States, aged 3 to 17, were abused each year. When this percentage is projected to the 46 million children in the United States, it means that between 1.5 and 2 million children are abused by their parents each year (Gelles, 1980).

Other statistics vary in their numbers, but the story is clear; there is a great amount of child abuse and neglect in our society. Violence has become an accepted mode of behavior by some persons. Physical punishment has long been condoned (Gil, 1970). Studies indicate that 84 to 97 percent of parents use physical punishment at some time during the rearing of their children (as cited in Gelles, 1977). Zigler (1977) warns that the long acceptance of physical abuse makes its detection and control more difficult, for the "long history of child abuse has left an historical residue that makes physical punishment of children an acceptable social form" (p. 30).

Fontana (1973) questions the use of physical force in rearing children. He suggests that it "springs not so much from the desire to discipline as to show 'who's boss around here' and the age-old concept that the child is the parent's property to do with as he pleases" (p. 39). Extreme cases of child abuse can be viewed as psychopathic deviations from the culturally approved and common physical forms of discipline.

Although we have made considerable progress since the 1700s and 1800s when child labor was rampant, our cultural values, socialization patterns, and resultant discipline still support the use of physical force with children; it is a "culturally sanctioned phenomenon in American society" (Gil, 1970, p. 14).

If I had to compare violence with a medical disease, I would compare it with cancer. Cancer can start insidiously in any part of the body . . . but it can spread all over the body. . . . When the environment tolerates, approves, propagates, or rewards violent expressions, violent behavior is more apt to happen. . . . It is a part of the harsh reality of our historically developed social life. (Wertham, 1966, pp. 3, 4, and 5)

In the 1970s there were concerted efforts to remedy this cancer. In 1974 the federal Child Abuse Act established the National Center on Child Abuse and Neglect in Washington, D.C. Subsequently, regional centers on child abuse were funded. Their purpose was to conduct research to determine the cause of child abuse and neglect, its identification and prevention, and the amount of child abuse in the nation (Besharov, 1977).

Working first with the Children's Bureau and then with the National Center, the American Humane Association, an organization that has focused on child protection since it was founded over 100 years ago, established a national clearinghouse in 1973 for reporting child abuse and neglect and analyzing reported data. Previously, in 1962, the American Humane Association completed one of the first surveys on child abuse by analyzing newspaper reports. It found 662 cases reported in 48 states and the District of Columbia. In 1983 the same organization disclosed 1,007,658 reports of child abuse (American Humane Association, 1985). From 1976 to 1983 reported child abuse cases have increased 142 percent (see Figure 9-1). The greatest growth came in 1977 and 1978 when 24.2 percent and 18.8 percent (43 percent) increase occurred. Reports of child abuse in general leveled out at approximately 9 percent per year during the 1980s, but reports of sexual abuse increased 54 percent between 1983 and 1984. The growth in reported cases reflects both better reporting and increase in abuse.

ABUSE AND NEGLECT

Just as all human behavior can be viewed as a continuum, so it is with maltreatment. The extremes of healthy development and serious maltreatment are easily identified; however, the difficulty arises when judgments must be made on situations that fall somewhere in between. (Halperin, 1979, p. 30)

The physically abused child shows signs of injury—welts, cuts, bruises, burns, fractures, and/or lacerations. Educators should be aware of repeated injuries, untreated injuries, multiple injuries, and new injuries added to old.

It is more difficult to identify emotional neglect and abuse, a situation in which the

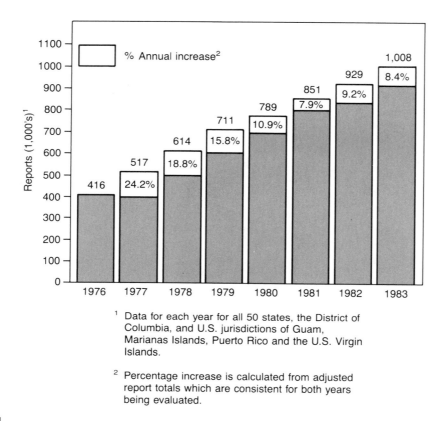

¹ Data for each year for all 50 states, the District of Columbia, and U.S. jurisdictions of Guam, Marianas Islands, Puerto Rico and the U.S. Virgin Islands.

² Percentage increase is calculated from adjusted report totals which are consistent for both years being evaluated.

FIGURE 9-1

Reports of child neglect and abuse have increased consistently since 1976. (*Source:* American Humane Association. *Highlights of official child neglect and abuse reporting, 1983.* Denver, Colo.: American Humane Association, 1985, p. 2.)

caretaker provides less of the warm, sensitive, nurturing environment than is required for the child's healthy growth and development (Steele, 1977). The parents are usually overly harsh and critical. They withhold love and acceptance and do not give the child either physical or verbal encouragement and praise. Although they expect performance, they do not support the child's endeavors.

Physical neglect refers to the parents' failure to provide the necessities—adequate shelter, care and supervision, food, clothing, and protection. The child shows signs of malnutrition, is usually irritable, and may be in need of medical attention. The child often goes hungry and needs supervision after school hours. The parents are either unable or unwilling to give proper care.

Medical neglect and educational neglect result in the child's inability to develop fully. Parents may not be indifferent; they may not recognize the importance of medical care or a developmental environment, or they may be incapable of furnishing them. Abandonment represents renunciation and total rejection of the child by the parent.

Multiple maltreatment often occurs in a child who suffers abuse or neglect. While emotional maltreatment can be isolated, incidences of physical abuse or neglect usually are accompanied by emotional abuse. "Multiple maltreatment is difficult to identify and is resistant to change" (Halperin, 1979, pp. 29–30).

IDENTIFICATION OF PHYSICAL ABUSE

What are the evidences of physical abuse? Although many bruises and abrasions are accidental, others give cause for the teacher to believe that they were intentionally inflicted. Bruises are the most common symptoms of physical abuse. Other symptoms include welts, lumps, or ridges on the body, usually caused by a blow; burns, shown by redness, blistering, or peeling of the skin; fractured bones; scars; lacerations or torn cuts; abrasions or scraped skin (U.S. Department of Health, Education, and Welfare, *A Self-Instructional Text for Head Start Personnel,* 1977).

Head Start personnel are given guidelines that give four criteria for identification of child abuse in the preschool child. These guidelines are useful for detection of abuse in any age child. The first is location of the injury. Bruises found on the knees, elbows, shins, and, for the preschool child, the forehead, are considered normal in most circumstances. "If these bruises were found on the back, genital area, thighs, buttocks, face or back of legs, one should be suspicious" (U.S. Department of Health, Education, and Welfare, *A Self-Instructional Text for Head Start Personnel,* 1977, p. 67). (See Figure 9-2.)

The second criterion is evidence of repetition of injury. A significantly large number of bruises or cuts and injuries that are at various stages of healing should be suspect. There are instances, however, when repetition could be accidental—the child could be accident prone, so criterion four needs to be kept in mind.

The third criterion is the appearance of the injury. If it is obvious that the bruise, cut, or burn was inflicted by an object such as a belt, stick, or cigarette, the teacher or caregiver should suspect abuse.

The fourth criterion is the correlation between the injury and the explanation given by the child or the parent. The accident as described should be able to produce the resultant injury. For example, could round burns shaped like cigarettes be caused by the child playing too near the stove?

In ascertaining the extent of suspected physical abuse, the teacher should not remove any of the child's clothing. Only personnel, such as a nurse or doctor, who would undress a child as part of their professional responsibilities should do so.

After reviewing the four criteria and checking school policy—the suspicious placement of injury, the severity and repetition of injuries, evidence of infliction by an object, and inconsistent explanation (or consistent if the child reports the abuse)—the educator must report the injury to the appropriate authorities.

IDENTIFICATION OF SEXUAL ABUSE

Sexual abuse ranges from exposure and fondling to incest and rape. It is very difficult to identify. Most of the offenders, approximately 75 percent, are known to the family or are family members. The victims are primarily girls, ranging from infants to adolescents.

Although historically most societies have had taboos against such behavior, sexual abuse and incest have always existed. But generally sexual abuse has been concealed, mythicized, or ignored. Not until the late 1970s and 1980s did its existence become realistically recognized and, even then, most persons gathering information on the problem felt that only the 'tip of the iceberg' had been revealed. Sexual abuse appears to be increasing. According to the American Humane Association, the sexual abuse reports increased by 54 percent from 1983 until 1984.

Incest and other sexual abuse occur in all socioeconomic groups, and therefore, teachers in all schools or child care settings should be

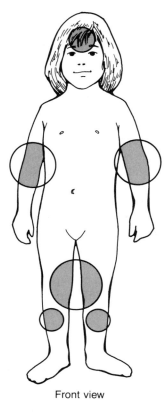

Front view

Normal bruising areas

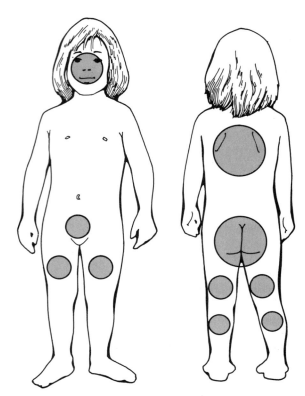

Front and back views

Suspicious bruising areas

FIGURE 9-2

Comparison of normal and suspicious bruising areas. The bruises children receive in normal play are depicted on the left. The bruises on the right would not normally happen in everyday play. (*Source:* Modified from U.S. Department of Health, Education, and Welfare. Head Start Bureau, Administration for Children, Youth, and Families, Office of Human Development and Children's Bureau. *A self-instructional text for Head Start personnel, child abuse and neglect.* Washington, D.C.: U.S. Government Printing Office, 1978.)

aware of the indicators since they have a legal and moral obligation to report suspected sexual abuse. Teachers and caregivers who report in good faith are immune from legal liability.

Signs for identifying sexual abuse include the following physical and behavioral characteristics (Riggs, 1982; Broadhurst, 1979; & Roth, 1979):

Physical Signs
- bruises or bleeding in external genitalia, vaginal, or anal area
- uncomfortable while sitting
- difficulty in walking
- pregnancy in young child
- torn, bloody, or stained underclothing
- sexually transmitted disease in young child

Behavioral Signs
- confides with teacher or nurse that she/he has been sexually mistreated
- reports by other children that their friend is being sexually mistreated
- displays precocious sexual behavior and/or knowledge

- unwilling to change for gym
- withdrawn, engages in fantasy
- depressed, sad, and weepy
- confused about own identity
- frequent absences justified by male caregiver or parent
- acts out in a seductive manner
- reluctance to go home
- young child regresses to earlier behavior by thumb sucking, bed wetting, difficulty in eating, sleeping, and being afraid of the dark
- older child turns to drugs, tries to run away, and has difficulty accomplishing school work

The teacher or child care giver who suspects sexual abuse must report his suspicions to proper authorities—ordinarily nurses, medical personnel, and social services agencies are the proper authorities to handle the situation. The teacher's role is a supportive one. Continue to have normal expectations for the child, keep a stable environment for the child, and do not make the child feel ostracized or different. Treat the child with understanding, be sensitive to the child's needs, and help build the child's self-esteem. Several programs have been developed to help the child develop defenses against personal abuse (see Chapter 11).

TALKING WITH FAMILIES

Just as there are varieties and levels of abuse and neglect, so also are there variations in your interaction with the parents. Child care workers and school personnel who want to help an abused child must exercise good judgment. Their first response may be to want to call the parent to determine how the injury occurred. In the case of violent abuse, the child may be in danger of being permanently damaged or killed. Calling the family to discuss the problem not only fails to help the family but may also precipitate more abuse. In addition, the family may become alarmed and move to an-

other area; the child may be abused for many more months before the new school or center identifies the problem. *With serious abuse do not call the parents or try to handle the situation by yourself. Contact the appropriate authorities immediately.*

When neglect rather than abuse is the problem, and a child comes to school hungry or inappropriately dressed, a supportive visit or call to the family is in order. The school can provide not only emotional support but clothing and food as well. Working *with* parents shows them they are not alone with their overwhelming problems. If providing services is beyond the capability of the school, or if the family needs professional help, social services should be called.

DEVELOPMENT OF POLICIES

School districts and child care centers need to develop the policies and training programs vital to successful child abuse intervention. If there is no policy, the teacher should see the school nurse, psychologist, director, counselor, social worker, or principal, depending on the staffing of the school. Even in the school district with a policy statement, each school or child care center staff should have one person who is responsible for receiving reports of child abuse. Making one person responsible results in greater awareness of the problem of abuse and facilitates the reporting process (U.S. Department of Health, Education, and Welfare, *Child Abuse and Neglect, Vol. 2,* 1975). It is also helpful to establish a committee to view evidence and support the conclusions of the original observer.

Suspected child abuse must be reported in all states. Evidence of violent physical abuse must be reported immediately. If school officials refuse to act, one can call social services, a law enforcement agency, or a family crisis center. The reporter should have the right to remain anonymous. When reporting in good faith, the person reporting is protected by immunity described in state legislation. Colorado law specifically states: "Any person participating in good faith in the making of a report or in a judicial proceeding held pursuant to this title shall be immune from any liability, civil or criminal, that otherwise might result by reason of such reporting" (Denver Public Schools' *Child Abuse Bulletin,* August, 1985, Appendix).

Needs Assessment

Schools and child care centers first have to determine the abuse and neglect delivery systems that are already available in the community. They should consider social service departments, child protection teams, child welfare agencies, law enforcement, juvenile court system, Head Start, day care centers, hospitals, clinics, public health nurses, mental health programs, public and private service groups, fund raising agencies such as United Way, and service organizations that might be unique to their community. Questions to ask include:

1. Which functions are being served by each agency?
   a. Identification
   b. Investigation
   c. Treatment planning
   d. Remediation
   e. Referral
2. Which preventive services are available in the community?
   a. Child development classes
   b. Prenatal counseling
   c. Self-help groups such as Parents Anonymous
3. Which groups are available for outreach?
4. Which training activities are available?
5. Are there crisis hot lines where help can be reached at all hours?
6. Which services are available for parents in the community?
   a. Lay therapists
   b. Parent aides
   c. Counseling

7. Which services are available for children?
   a. Crisis nurseries
   b. Therapeutic day care
   c. Residential and foster home care
   d. Play therapy

Following assessment of the community, the school and day care centers have to determine their role in an integrated approach to abuse and neglect. Communication lines must be kept open at all times. A representative of the schools should serve on the child protection team. One role that is mandated is identification of abuse and neglect. Other roles will be individualized according to the needs of the community, the resources in the schools and child care centers, and the commitment of the personnel (U.S. Department of Health, Education, and Welfare, *Planning and Implementing Child Abuse and Neglect Service Programs,* 1976).

Policy

"A child abuse and neglect reporting policy should embody a commitment and a course of action to protect and aid children whose health or welfare is threatened through nonaccidental injury or neglect by parents, guardians, or caretakers" (Education Commission of the States, 1978, p. 1). Child abuse is found in all socioeconomic groups in the United States, so all school districts must be prepared to work with interdisciplinary agencies in the detection and prevention of this national social problem.

The Education Commission of the States (1978), in its *Report and Recommendations of the National Advisory Committee on Child Abuse and Neglect* states:

An effective policy would spell out for school personnel their legal responsibilities and immunities with respect to reporting and would inform the community that educators are obliged to report suspected abuse and neglect, including any that might occur within the school setting itself. In essence, the policy gives those in education the information they need to make a report and to allay their fears that by reporting they might be overstepping their responsibility and jeopardizing their job . . . a school system can articulate its responsibilities with regard to child abuse and neglect, such as its commitment to cooperate with community efforts, to provide training or to conduct a public awareness program. (p. 13)

Policies should be written in compliance with the requirements of each state's reporting statute, details of which may be learned by consulting the state's attorney general. Because reporting is required in all states, the policy should include a clear statement of reporting requirements. The policy should also inform the school personnel of their immunity and legal obligations. (See Denver Public Schools' *Child Abuse Bulletin* in Appendix.) Dissemination of the policy should include the community as well as all school employees. Not only is it important that the community realize the obligation of the school or child care center to report suspected abuse or neglect, it is vital that the community becomes aware of the extent of the problem (Education Commission of the States, 1978).

Teacher's Role in Carrying Out Policy

Child Abuse and Neglect, Vol. 2, The Roles and Responsibilities of Professionals includes a special charge to teachers:

You should be aware of the official policy and specific reporting procedures of your school system, and should know your legal obligations and the protections from civil and criminal liability specified in your state's reporting law. (All states provide immunity for mandated, good-faith reports.)

Although you should be familiar with your state's legal definition of abuse and neglect, you are not required to make legal distinctions in order to report. Definitions should serve as guides. If you suspect that a child is abused or neglected, you

should report it. The teacher's value lies in noticing conditions that indicate that a child's welfare may be in jeopardy.

Be concerned about the rights of the child—the rights to life, food, shelter, clothing, and security. But also be aware of the parents' rights—particularly their rights to be treated with respect and to be given needed help and support.

Bear in mind that reporting does not stigmatize a parent as "evil." The report is the start of a rehabilitative process that seeks to protect the child and help the family as a whole.

A report signifies only the suspicion of abuse or neglect. Teachers' reports are seldom unfounded. At the very least, they tend to indicate a need for help and support to the family.

If you report a borderline case in good faith, do not feel guilty or upset if it is dismissed as unfounded upon investigation. Some marginal cases are found to be valid.

Don't put off making a report until the end of the school year. Teachers sometimes live with their suspicions until they suddenly fear for the child's safety during the summer months. A delayed report may mean a delay in needed help for the child and the family. Moreover, by reporting late in the school year, you remove yourself as a continued support to both the child protection agency and the reporting family.

If you remove yourself from a case of suspected abuse or neglect by passing it on to a superior, you deprive child protective services of one of their most competent sources of information. For example, a teacher who tells a CPS worker that the child is especially upset on Mondays directs the worker to investigate conditions in the homes on weekends. Few persons other than teachers are able to provide this kind of information. Your guidelines should be to resolve any question in favor of the child. When in doubt, report. Even if you, as a teacher, have no immunity from liability and prosecution under state law, the fact that your report is made in good faith will free you from liability and prosecution.[2]

---

2. From U.S. Department of Health, Education, and Welfare. *Child abuse and neglect (Vol. 2). The roles and responsibilities of professionals. The problem and its management.* Washington, D.C.: U.S. Government Printing Office, 1975, p. 71.

After a case is reported to the child protection agency, there should be a follow-up. If the agency does not provide feedback, the teacher should inquire about the disposition of the case. If the agency refuses to give information because of confidentiality, the teacher can still be supportive of the family and particularly sensitive to the child's needs. The teacher can give the child additional attention, talk with her, be warm and loving, and assure the child that someone cares. The pressure that the child is dealing with at home might make it necessary to individualize schoolwork. "Lower your academic expectations and make few demands on the child's performance" (U.S. Department of Health, Education, and Welfare, *Child Abuse and Neglect, Vol. 2,* p. 2).

Over time, the child protection agency in your district and the schools should be able to develop an excellent working relationship. This can be facilitated by joint meetings of school representatives and social workers. Each agency needs to understand the procedures and obligations of the other. Child abuse protection requires good communication and cooperative working relationships among all agencies involved in the child's welfare.

BREAKING THE ABUSIVE CYCLE

Professionals who work with the abusive parent must first understand themselves and their values so that they can come to peace with their feelings toward abuse and neglect of children. To help the family, professionals should not have a punitive attitude toward the parents. It helps to remember that the parents are probably rearing their child in the same way in which they were reared. It is a lifelong pattern that must be broken (Steele, 1977).

Although the parents may be resistant to intrusion or suggestion, they desperately need help in feeling good about themselves. They need support, comfort, and someone they can trust and lean on. They need some-one who will come when they have needs. Instead of criticism, they need help and assurance that they are worthwhile. Because they are unable to cope with their children, someone must help them understand their children without shaming them. Parents need to feel valuable and adequate (U.S. Department of Health, Education, and Welfare, *Child Abuse and Neglect, Vol. 2,* 1975).

WHAT PRECIPITATES CHILD ABUSE?

Helfer (1975), in a perceptive booklet published by the Department of Health, Education, and Welfare, relates three factors that must be present for child abuse to occur. The first is parents or caregivers who have the potential for abusing. The second, most obviously, is the child, but not just any child. This child is one who is seen by the parents as being different. The third factor is a stress situation that brings on a crisis.

According to Helfer (1975), abusive parents or caregivers have acquired the potential to abuse over the years. These parents usually had deprived childhoods. They lacked a consistent, loving, nurturing environment when they were young. They have a poor self-image, and their mates are passive and do not or are not able to give their spouses the emotional support that they need. It is probable that the family has isolated itself. The parents have no support system from neighbors or community. Since few of them understand child development, they have unrealistic expectations of their children (Steele, 1977).

Such parents are most likely to abuse children whom they see as being different. Child abuse also occurs against a child who actually is different from the norm: the mentally retarded, physically deformed, or hyperactive child.

Before the abusive act occurs, there is a precipitating event—one that does not directly cause the specific act against the child, but a minor or major crisis that sets the stage for the parent to lose control and abuse the child. This crisis may be physical (e.g., a broken washing machine) or personal (e.g., spouse desertion, death in the family). With these three factors the stage is set. The parent or caregiver loses control and abuses the child (Helfer, 1975).

WHO ARE THE ABUSED AND THE ABUSERS?

The abusive person is generally the natural parent; 81.5 percent of major physical injury is caused by the natural parent (see Table 9-1). Over 90 percent of the neglect cases is the result of the parent's inability to supply necessary care. The case is different for sexual maltreatment. Natural parents are responsible for 58.9 percent of sexual abuse, but over 30 percent can be attributed to adoptive, step, or foster parents, and 3 percent is caused by other relatives. From these data it is clear that incest is the largest cause of sexual abuse, while those outside of the family caused only 3 percent of the sexual abuse cases.

Neglect of children is reported more often than any other form of abuse. Both boys and girls are equally involved in reports. Forty percent of the reported families are headed by single mothers, which may be explained by the difficult financial condition in which single women find themselves. Insufficient income is cited as the greatest cause of neglect (see Figure 9-3). Deprivation of necessities is the most frequently cited type of neglect (58.4 percent) with minor physical injury represented by 18.5 percent. Major physical injury was indicated 3.2 percent of the time and sexual maltreatment, 8.5 percent (see Figure 9-4).

Young children from infancy through age 5 are the victims of the greatest number of major physical injuries. Child care centers need to be particularly alert for signs of physical damage. Table 9-2 shows that while the young children represent 34.5 percent of all children, they are overrepresented in all forms of abuse except sexual and emotional maltreatments. They account for 64.1 percent of major physical injury and 48.6 percent of deprivation of necessities. Children 6 years of age and older accounted for 75 percent of sexual maltreatment.

FIGURE 9-3
Comparison of selected factors for abuse and neglect reports (N = 16,040). Insufficient income causes the most neglect while lack of tolerance is most responsible for abuse. (*Source:* American Humane Association. *National analysis of official child neglect and abuse reporting.* Denver, Colo.: American Humane Association, 1978, p. 17).

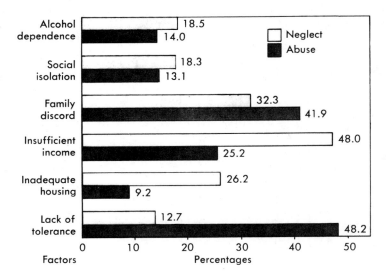

TABLE 9-1

Type of maltreatment and child relationship to perpetrator—caretakers (N = 85,039 children). The natural parent is most often responsible for maltreatment of the child.

Child-perpetrator relationship	Major or major with minor physical injury (N = 1,356)	Minor or unspecified physical injury (N = 15,339)	Sexual maltreatment (N = 3,683)	Deprivation of necessities (N = 44,591)	Emotional maltreatment (N = 6,311)	Other maltreatment[1] (N = 1,424)	Multiple maltreatment (N = 12,335)	Percent of all relationships
Natural Parent	81.5%	76.1%	58.9%	90.7%	80.0%	91.5%	80.8%	84.3%
Other Parent[2]	9.1%	13.5%	30.8%	1.2%	6.7%	2.4%	5.8%	5.9%
Natural and Other Parent	4.7%	5.7%	4.4%	4.8%	10.0%	4.8%	8.9%	5.9%
Other Relative	1.8%	2.3%	3.0%	2.1%	2.1%	0.9%	2.1%	2.1%
Nonrelative	1.6%	1.4%	2.3%	0.1%	0.5%	0.1%	0.4%	0.5%
Other Perpetrator Combinations	1.2%	1.1%	0.7%	1.1%	0.7%	0.3%	2.1%	1.2%
Total	100%	100%	100%	100%	100%	100%	100%	100%

1. Refers to relationships in which a child has more than one type of maltreatment indicated and "Major or Major with Minor Physical Injury" or "Minor or Unspecified Physical Injury" does not apply.
2. "Other parent" refers to adoptive, step and foster parents.

Source: American Humane Association. *Highlights of Official Child Neglect and Abuse Reporting, 1983.* Denver, Colo.: American Humane Association, 1985, p. 13.

TABLE 9-2

Type of maltreatment and age of involved child (N = 381,168 children). Children under 5 are most likely to receive physical injuries.

Age	Major or major with minor physical injury (N = 8,800)	Minor or unspecified physical injury (N = 71,884)	Sexual maltreatment (N = 27,714)	Deprivation of necessities (N = 192,223)	Emotional maltreatment (N = 24,808)	Other maltreatment (N = 15,917)	Multiple maltreatment (N = 39,822)	Percent of all involved children (N = 717,315)	Percent of all U.S. children (N = 62,580,000)
0–5	64.1%	37.3%	24.8%	48.6%	34.0%	47.0%	41.5%	43.3%	34.5%
6–11	19.8%	32.6%	34.3%	33.2%	34.2%	26.8%	31.7%	32.5%	30.7%
12–17	15.9%	30.0%	40.6%	18.2%	31.9%	26.2%	27.0%	24.1%	34.7%
Total	100%	100%	100%	100%	100%	100%	100%	100%	100%

Source: American Humane Association. *Highlights of Official Child Neglect and Abuse Reporting, 1983,* Denver, Colo.: American Humane Association, 1985, p. 16.

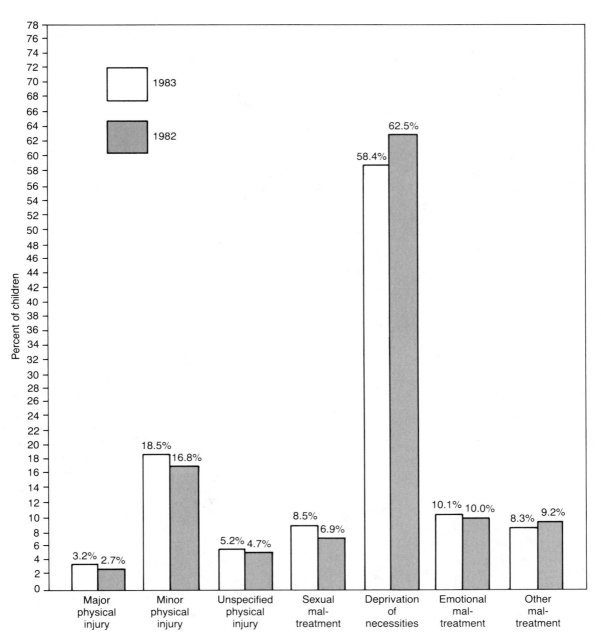

FIGURE 9-4

Type of maltreatment. Neglect, as shown through deprivation of necessities, is the most frequently reported form of abuse and neglect. (*Source:* American Humane Association. *Highlights of official child neglect and abuse reporting, 1983.* Denver, Colo.: American Humane Association, 1985, p. 11.)

FIGURE 9-5

Most cases of child abuse and neglect are reported by nonprofessionals—friends, neighbors, relatives, or sometimes the perpetrators or victims themselves. (*Source:* American Humane Association. *Highlights of official child neglect and abuse reporting, 1983.* Denver, Colo.: American Humane Association, 1985, p. 7.)

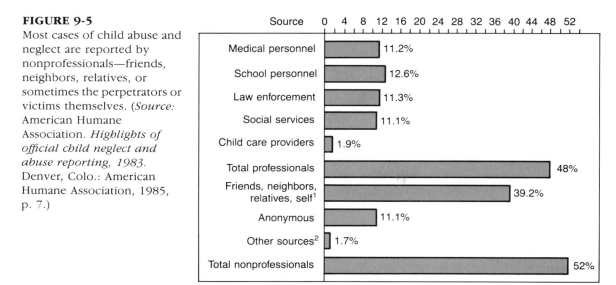

¹ "Self" includes both victims and perpetrators and accounts for about three percent of all reports.

² "Other Sources" includes, as examples, landlords and religious personnel, individuals not readily categorized by the other standard categories.

WHO REPORTS MALTREATMENT CASES

Cases of child maltreatment are reported by more nonprofessionals than professionals. The largest reporting group is friends, neighbors, relatives, and the abusers themselves, with 39.2 percent coming from that group. As Figure 9-5 illustrates, over 11 percent of the reporters are anonymous and probably contain some of the same group. The professional group is evenly divided among medical, school, law, and social services. Child care providers report only 1.9 percent of the cases.

BEHAVIORAL AND ATTITUDINAL TRAITS OF PARENTS AND CHILDREN THAT MAY INDICATE CHILD ABUSE

Specialists working with child abuse (Fontana, 1973; Kempe & Helfer, 1982) have developed some guidelines to help educators determine the existence of child abuse. The following are modified from these publications: *Child Abuse and Neglect, Vol. 1* (1975); *Guidelines for Schools* (1971); *What Everyone Should Know about Child Abuse* (1976); *A Self-Instructional Text for Head Start Personnel, Child Abuse and Neglect* (1977).

The Child of Preschool Age

1. Does the child seem to fear his or her parents?

2. Does the child miss preschool or the child care center often?

3. Does the child bear evidence of physical abuse? Are there signs of battering such as bruises or welts, belt or buckle marks, lacerations, or burns?

4. Does the child exhibit extreme behavior changes? Is the child very aggressive at times and then fearful, withdrawn, and/or depressed?

5. Does the child have sores, bruises, or cuts that are not adequately cared for?

6. Does the child come to school inadequately dressed? Does the child look uncared for?

7. Does the child take over the parent role and try to "mother" the parent?

8. Does the child seem to be hungry for affection?

The Child of Elementary School Age

1. Does the child exhibit behavior that deviates from the norm? Is the child aggressive, destructive, and disruptive or passive and withdrawn? The first may be a child who is shouting for help, demanding attention and striking out; whereas the second may be out of touch with reality, remote, submissive, and subdued, but crying for help in another way.

2. Does the child miss classes or is the child often late or tardy? Does the child come to school too early and stay around after school is over? In the first instance, the child's behavior suggests problems at home. In the second, the child may be pushed out in the morning and have nowhere to go after school.

3. Does the child bear evidence of physical abuse? Are there obvious signs of battering: bruises, belt or buckle marks, welts, lacerations, or burns?

4. Does the child lack social skills? Is the child unable to approach children and play with them?

5. Does the child have learning problems that cannot be diagnosed? Does the child underperform? If intelligence tests show average academic ability and the child is not able to do the work, there may be problems at home.

6. Does the child show great sensitivity to others' feelings? Does the child get upset when another person is criticized? Abused children often have to "mother" their abusive parents, and some are overly sensitive to the feelings of others.

7. Does the child come to school inadequately dressed? Is the child unwashed

and uncared for? This may be a signal of neglect.

8. Does the child feel tired and fall asleep in class?

9. Does the child seem to be undernourished? Does the child attempt to save food? Is there real poverty in the home, or are there just parents who do not care?

10. Does the child seem to be afraid of his or her parents?

The Secondary Level Student

Most of the traits just mentioned are relevant to detection of abuse in the junior and senior high child, but there are additional signs to watch for in the upper levels. In addition to evidence of physical abuse, neglect, truancy, and tardiness, the older student may experience the following:

1. Does the student have to assume too much responsibility at home?
2. Does the parent expect unrealistic and overly strict behavior?
3. Does the student have difficulty conforming to school regulations and policies?
4. Does the student have problems communicating with his or her parents?
5. Does the student have a history of running away from home and refusing to go home?
6. Does the student act out sexually?
7. Does the student lack freedom and friends?

Psychologic Characteristics of the Child

In addition to behavioral traits of the abused children, Martin and Beezeley (1976) investigated psychological characteristics and found the following commonalities in children's personalities.

1. Impaired capacity to enjoy life   66%
2. Psychiatric symptoms (e.g., enuresis, tantrums, hyperactivity, bizarre behavior)   62%

3. Low self-esteem   52%
4. School learning problems   38%
5. Withdrawal   24%
6. Opposition   24%
7. Hypervigilance   22%
8. Compulsivity   22%
9. Pseudo-mature behavior   20%
(p. 106)

Behavior and Psychologic Characteristics of the Child in School

Halperin (1979) cites some practical guidelines for teachers to follow in identifying the child who needs attention. He cautions against jumping to conclusions concerning maltreatment. Marks on a body may come from many circumstances. "Only when school personnel have gathered substantial information on the family and its internal functioning are they in a position to assess if a child is being maltreated at home" (p. 67).

If educators bear in mind that children are unique and may respond to the same treatment in opposite ways and that children display a wide range of behaviors, they will be cautious in labeling a child.

When educators recognize Halperin's clues for children who need attention, whether or not there is any thought of maltreatment, they will be doing a great service to all the children in their classrooms. Individualization of academic program as well as individualization for emotional needs will result in a well-rounded educational program for the child. As the teacher gets to know the child better and responds to the child with needed praise or reinforcement, as well as with an individualized curriculum, the results will be improved education. The following descriptions are modified from Halperin.

Aggressive child
Typical characteristics
   Defiant
   Domineering
   Blames others

Possible reasons for actions
   Little self-esteem
   Cannot control impulses
   Unhappy
   Little self-discipline

Show-off
Typical characteristics
   Extremely extroverted
   Answers questions without knowing the answer
   May appear hyperactive
   Wants to be center of attention
Possible reasons for actions
   Masks insecurity
   Little attention at home
   Shows off to compete for share of praise and love

Disobedient child
Typical characteristics
   Purposely breaks rules
   Impolite and insolent
   Struggles against authority
Possible reasons for actions
   Unhappy
   Disobeys to get attention
   Models parental attitude toward authority
   Inconsistent discipline at home
   Prefers punishment to indifference
   Has internalized feelings of worthlessness

Child who lies, cheats, and steals
Typical characteristics
   Lies
   Steals
   Cheats
Possible reasons for actions
   Lies to escape punishment
   Wants to get away with action without being caught
   Gains attention
   Little supervision at home
   Actions of dishonesty are condoned at home

Child nobody likes
Typical characteristics
   Sullen
   Depressed
   Jealous
   Blames others for acts
   Absent a lot
Possible reasons for actions
   Little warmth from parents
   Unable to establish healthy relationship with others

Lives an isolated life
Not fond of self
Poor self-concept

Unkempt child

Typical characteristics

Soiled clothes
Unkempt hair and body
General lack of care in work

Possible reasons for actions

Lack of adult supervision and concern
Poor self-image

Listless child

Typical characteristics

Unable to concentrate
Little energy
Daydreams
Slouches
Seldom volunteers

Possible reasons for actions

May be physically neglected at home
Nutritional neglect
Medical neglect
Cannot meet expectations of parents and teachers
May be bored
Leaves tasks incomplete to minimize parental rebukes

Careless child

Typical characteristics

Messy papers
Many errors in work
Personal appearance in disarray

Possible reasons for actions

Lack of structure at home
Too-great expectations at home so child gives up trying to satisfy

Accident-prone child

Typical characteristics

Hurts self
Poor coordination

Possible reasons for actions

Organic dysfunction
Wants attention
Feigns injuries as excuse
Low self-esteem
Self-destructive

Fearful child

Typical characteristics

Anxious
Uneasy
Emotionally unstable

Possible reasons for actions

Neurotic family life
Harsh punishment from caregivers
Unpredictable home environment

Shy child

Typical characteristics

Fearful in contacts with others
Sits quietly with lowered head
Seldom defends self
Seldom expresses self

Possible reasons for actions

Lacks encouragement and acceptance at school
Excessively critical parents
Fears failure
May share same timid characteristics as parents

Withdrawn child

Typical characteristics

Isolates self
Appears tense, nervous, and unhappy
Easily discouraged and frustrated
Abandons tasks if they prove difficult

Possible reasons for actions

Unsatisfactory experiences in past
Unsatisfactory experiences at school
Excessive demands from parents
Frequently lacks love, affection, and praise
Parents may be unpredictable and unable to establish relationships

Emotionally unstable child

Typical characteristics

Volatile and unpredictable
Attitude toward life is negative
Appears agitated, worried, or preoccupied

Possible reasons for actions

Little attention or affection
Inadequate supervision or psychologic support at home
Under tremendous pressure

Low-achieving child

Typical characteristics

Short attention span
Withdrawn from classroom activities
Disobedient and disruptive
Rarely completes assignments

Possible reasons for actions

Brain damage
Physically neglected
Medical problems
Educational neglect

If these characteristics and causes are kept in mind when working with children, along with the realization that typical factors may not affect a particular child, the educator can adapt the educational program to the needs of the child. The opportunity to raise a child's self-esteem will often improve the child's behavior. It is a safe beginning.

The Abusing Parent

School personnel and child care workers will attempt to make contact with parents of the suspected abused child. The following behavioral characteristics can help the professional to determine the possibility of abuse or neglect:

1. Do the parents fail to show up for appointments? Do they stay away from school? When they come to school, are they uncooperative and unresponsive?
2. Do the parents have unrealistically high expectations for themselves and the child? Do the parents describe the child as "different" or "bad"?
3. Do the parents have expectations for the child that are inconsistent and inappropriate for the child's age?
4. Do the parents become aggressive or abusive when school personnel want to talk about the child's problems?
5. Do the parents lose control or express fear of losing control?
6. Do the parents feel that beating the child is the correct way in which to discipline? Do the parents rationalize the punishment by saying it is necessary to keep the child in line?
7. Do the parents avoid others? Are they isolated? Do they know other parents in the school? Are they known by other parents?
8. Do they lack knowledge of child development and the child's physical and psychologic needs?
9. Do the parents report that they were abused or neglected as children?
10. Do the parents refuse to participate in school events?
11. Do the parents ignore the child and avoid touching?
12. Do the parents show little interest in the child's activities or concern for the child's well-being?

Psychologic Characteristics of the Parent

These parents also have personality traits that support their abusive behavior. School personnel need to understand the parents and recognize their need for supportive help in order to work effectively with them. Awareness of these psychologic factors will help the professional to understand the actions of the parents, even though they are not condoned. The personality factors include:

1. *Immaturity and dependence.* These parents did not have a childhood that allowed them to become independent, productive, functioning adults. Generally they had to disregard their own needs and desires for the wishes of an authority figure. They were unable to develop inner controls and looked to outside figures for direction. They also exhibit dependence on others in their search for love and affection. They are adults who are still affected by maternal deprivation.
2. *Sense of personal incompetence.* The parents do not feel competent, have difficulty planning for the future, and do not trust their own performances.
3. *Difficulty in experiencing pleasure.* Like their children, the parents do not enjoy life. Their social relationships are minimal and unrewarding.
4. *Social isolation.* Isolating oneself is a defense against being hurt and rejected. Although the abusive parents may act sure of themselves and self-sufficient, they are dependent, frightened, and immature.
5. *Misperceptions of the child.* The lack of nurturing in their own childhood leaves

the parents still looking for others to satisfy their needs for love. The parents may perceive the child to be acting out against them rather than giving love.

6. *Fear of "spoiling" the child.* Although this is a common element in child-rearing practices, the abusive parents go to extremes and believe that babies and children should not be allowed to "get away with anything."

7. *Belief in the value of punishment.* The problem lies in the parents' unrealistic perceptions of the child. The child does not live up to expectations and is considered bad. The parents are convinced that they have the moral duty to correct their child's behavior.

8. *Unawareness of the child's needs.* Abusive parents did not experience loving care when they were growing up, and they do not have a model to follow. They cannot change their own personality traits until they receive the support and love that they need. They do not recognize the child's needs (Steele, 1977; U.S. Department of Health, Education, and Welfare, *Child Abuse and Neglect, Vol. 1,* 1975).

The American Humane Association has developed a flyer that briefly describes parental attitudes, the child's behavior, and the child's appearance. This flyer succinctly focuses on the highlights of the foregoing discussion. Schools may purchase this flyer from the American Humane Association for a nominal fee and distribute it to staff and teachers. The flyer is illustrated in Box 9–1.

TRAINING

Tools for the training of school personnel may be obtained from a number of sources. The U.S. Department of Health, Education, and Welfare has published *A Curriculum on Child Abuse and Neglect* in a series of three books, *Leaders' Manual, Resource Materials,* and *Specialized Training for Child Protective Service Workers.* The child neglect and abuse series offers excellent data to use in training. (See Bibliography for U.S. Department of Education, *Child Abuse and Neglect, Vols. 1, 2, and 3,* Helfer, and Steele.)

A curriculum program for identification of child abuse and neglect was developed for Head Start personnel. *A Self-Instructional Text for Head Start Personnel: Child Abuse and Neglect* identifies child abuse, discusses treatment and prevention, and outlines procedures for reporting. As the title indicates, each person can study the text individually and at a self-determined rate.

Publications from the American Humane Association, the National Center for the Prevention of Abuse and Neglect, the Education Commission of the States and the Child Welfare League can supplement the training manuals.

Community resources should also be used. Social services, juvenile court, child protection teams, and law enforcement agencies have personnel who are actively involved in the detection, prevention, and remediation of child abuse. When the school works in close cooperation with these agencies, coordinated training is very beneficial.

After the trainees have an orientation to the identification and diagnosis of child abuse, seminars in which case studies are discussed enrich their understanding. Sample case studies may be obtained from the school's files. (Change identifying details so the family will remain anonymous.) Newspapers also give vivid descriptions and details. A recent article described a 9-year-old child who was subjected to neglect because the parents thought she was going to be different. She was kept in a confining closet and did not receive any emotional or cognitive stimulation. When found, she seemed to be a 3-year-old child in size, maturity, and development. After placement in a foster home, she has grown and begun to develop rapidly. The outcome of this case is not yet known. The parents epitomize the concept that abusing parents were themselves neglected and abused. Unwanted, unloved, and isolated people, they continue the pattern with their own children.

BOX 9-1: Indicators of a Child's Need for Protection*

The alert teacher

If teachers are alert to the signs and symptoms which point to the possibility of neglect or abuse they can take the first step to bring help to children whose needs are not being met at home. That first step is to involve the community's child protective services on behalf of the troubled child.

The protective program is charged with responsibility for bringing services to neglected and abused children and their neglecting parents. It is a non-punitive, helping, skilled social service. Its focus is on seeking to stabilize family life, on enhancing parental capacity for good child care and on maintaining family intactness where possible.

Children in troubled families

Teachers come into frequent contact with children who are physically or emotionally neglected or who are victims of physical or sexual abuse. Such troubled children may be found in families at any economic level or of any social status in the community. This is so because the motivating factors for child neglect or abuse may afflict any family. Common, underlying factors are emotional immaturity of parents, marital friction, alcoholism, drug usage, emotional disturbance or psychosis. These are families with problems, families under stress and, sometimes, families in crisis.

Importance of early casefinding

If children are identified when they show the earliest impact of their families' troubles, help can be made available at a stage when their problems can be more readily resolved. Too often referrals to protective services are not made until the conditions of neglect or abuse become acute and intolerable. Such referrals may come too late to salvage the home.

Here are some of the things to look for in the child.

The child's behavior

• Is the child aggressive, disruptive, destructive? Such a child may be acting out of need to secure attention. He may be shouting for help. His behavior may reflect a hostile or emotionally destructive climate at home, or he may be imitating destructive parental behavior.

---

*From the American Humane Association. *Guidelines for schools.* Denver, Colo. Copyright 1971 The American Humane Association.

The case history in Box 9-2 from the U.S. Department of Health, Education and Welfare's *A Curriculum on Child Abuse and Neglect, Resource Materials,* demonstrates case studies as a curriculum device.

As this case history demonstrates, families in which child abuse occurs have a variety of factors and problems that must be considered. The schools can contribute to the remediation and solution of the situation by working with the other agencies in a coordinated effort of support. In order to implement a coordinated plan, schools must first conduct a needs assessment and then develop a district policy.

HOW TO TALK WITH CHILDREN AND PARENTS

Care must be taken in talking with or interviewing children or parents. The conversation should take place in a private, relaxed, and comfortable atmosphere. Children should not feel threatened, nor should they be pressed for information or details they do not want to re-

- Is the child shy, withdrawn, passive or overly compliant? This child may be as emotionally damaged as the aggressive child. He has internalized his problem; his cry for help is a whisper instead of a shout. He may be inattentive; he may daydream; he may be out of touch with reality.
- Is the child an habitual truant—chronically late or tardy? Is he frequently absent for flimsy reasons and lame excuses? This behavior points to problems of adjustment—problems at home, in school, within the child, or in combination.
- Does the child come to school much too early? Does he loiter and hang around after school is dismissed? This child may be seeking to escape from home—he may lack normal satisfactions at home. On the other hand he may be "pushed out" in the morning and has no place to go after school because there is no one to supervise or care for him.

The child's appearance
- Is the child inadequately dressed for the weather? Is his clothing torn, tattered, or unwashed? Is the child not clean; is he unbathed? Do other children refuse to sit next to him because he smells? These are all signs of physical neglect, a condition not related to poverty. It reflects a breakdown in household management and in concern for the child.
- Is the child undernourished? Is he coming to school without breakfast; does he go without lunch? Again, this is often a problem unrelated to poverty.
- Is the child always tired? Does he sleep in class? Is he lethargic or listless? Such conditions are symptomatic of parental failure to regulate the child's routines, or of family problems which disrupt family routines.
- Is the child in need of medical attention? Does he need glasses or dental work?
- Does the child bear bruises, welts and contusions? Is he injured frequently? Does he complain of beatings or other maltreatment? Is there reason to suspect physical or sexual abuse?

Parental attitudes
- Are the parents aggressive or abusive when approached about problems concerning their child?
- Are they apathetic or unresponsive?
- Is parental behavior, as observed by school personnel, or as related by the child, bizarre and strange?
- Do the parents show little concern about the child? Do they fail to show interest in what he is doing?
  Do they fail to participate in school activities or to permit the child to participate?

veal. Parents should be aware of the school's legal obligation to report suspected neglect and abuse. If they feel that the school is supportive of the family, the interaction between parents and school will be more positive. Some guidelines to follow include:[3]

When talking with the child
DO:
Make sure the interviewer is someone the child trusts
Conduct the interview in private
Sit next to the child, not across a table or desk
Tell the child that the interview is confidential
Conduct the interview in a language the child understands
Ask the child to clarify words/terms which are not understood
Tell the child if any future action will be required
DON'T:
Allow the child to feel "in trouble" or "at fault"

---

3. From U.S. Department of Health, Education, and Welfare, *Child abuse and neglect: The user manual series. The educator's role in the prevention and treatment of child abuse and neglect.* Washington, D.C. U.S. Government Printing Office, 1979, p. 27.

BOX 9-2: Case History No. 3 and Discussion Questions/ The Heller Family

The presenting problem

On March 21, 1974, neighbors reported Mrs. Victoria Heller and her 7-year-old son, Terry, to the police. The investigating officer found Mrs. Heller incoherent, apparently unable to take care of her own needs, and afraid to stay in her apartment. He learned that she was extremely depressed over her brother's recent death from an overdose of heroin, and his wife's subsequent suicide. Believing that both Mrs. Heller and her son were in danger, he took her to the county hospital and had Terry placed in the juvenile detention center for the duration of his mother's recovery.

Family history

The family had first come to the attention of the police a year earlier, when Terry's teacher notified the police that Terry had not come to school for 2 days. The investigating officer learned from neighbors that Mrs. Heller did not reside at the address the school had reported, but rather next door in a duplex belonging to her boyfriend, David. Upon admittance there by Mrs. Heller, the officer found Terry with bruises all over his body. These bruises, Terry reported, were the result of a beating with a belt given by his mother 2 days before. Left alone in David's duplex while David and his mother had gone to New York, he had built a fire on the kitchen floor, because he was lonely and wanted something to do. When his mother and David returned, the fire had burned down, but his mother had become very upset and had beaten him. Terry told the officer that his mother and her boyfriend left him alone when they went out of town.

In subsequent investigations, a child protective services worker determined that this beating was an isolated incident, that Mrs. Heller appeared very remorseful, and was willing to cooperate in any way with the investigation. She had apparently not realized the serious consequences of leaving a 7-year-old boy unattended, and agreed to arrange for one of her brothers to take care of Terry whenever she went out.

In December 1973 (8 months after the beating incident and 4 months before she was found incoherent in her apartment), Mrs. Heller had attempted suicide by slashing her wrists, and was hospitalized for 3 days. Terry stayed with his uncle during this period, and Mrs. Heller began therapy with a psychiatrist at the county hospital. The doctor prescribed medication and attempted to get her into group therapy, which she refused. One month later, Mrs. Heller was beaten up by her boyfriend, David. Apparently a common occurrence, this time it caused Mrs. Heller to move out of his duplex and into her present apartment.

The investigation has produced the following information about Mrs. Heller and her son Terry:

Mrs. Heller. One of 11 children, Mrs. Heller comes from a very low-income and dysfunctional family. Her parents were divorced after her father was convicted of having an incestuous relationship

U.S. Department of Health, Education, and Welfare. *A curriculum on child abuse and neglect. Resource materials.* Washington, D.C.: U.S. Government Printing Office, 1979, pp. 42–44.

Disparage or criticize the child's choice of words or language
Suggest answers to the child
Probe or press for answers the child is unwilling to give
Display horror, shock, or disapproval of parents, child, or the situation

Force the child to remove clothing
Conduct the interview with a group of interviewers
Leave the child alone with a stranger (e.g., a CPS worker)
When talking with the parents
DO:
Select interviewer(s) appropriate to the situation
Conduct the interview in private

with one of her sisters. At a later time she and her brothers and sisters were removed from their mother's home and spent many years in foster homes.

Mrs. Heller married at 16, but was abandoned by her husband after a few months and re-referred to the probation department as incorrigible. She remained a ward of the court in foster homes until she was 18. She soon became pregnant with Terry, considered giving him up for adoption, but ultimately decided against it, since she was planning to divorce her first husband and marry again. Neither the divorce nor the marriage ever took place, but she kept the baby since she "really and truly" loved his father. She gave birth again in 1967 and 1968, but relinquished both babies at birth.

Between 1968 and 1970 she and Terry went back to live with her previous foster parents. In response to her request for training, the welfare department enrolled her in two different programs. She was dropped from the first because of poor attendance, and quit the second when she became emotionally unstable and made her first attempt at suicide. During this time Terry received adequate care from Mrs. Heller's foster parents.

In 1972 she terminated a fourth pregnancy by abortion.

Terry Heller. Mrs. Heller reports a normal pregnancy with Terry, and a normal delivery. He has been a healthy child, and his development is normal. At school, however, he does not do well. He reportedly is slow in English and spelling, and average or below average in his other subjects. However, he is well liked by his teachers and by his school counselor, who has visited him regularly. According to the investigator's report, Terry is confused and unhappy as a result of his mother's emotional breakdown, and this state has adversely affected his school performance.

According to the department's consulting psychologist who examined him, there is a "strong, healthy, loving attachment" between Terry and his mother, and it would be emotionally detrimental to separate them.

Discussion questions

1. What are the indicators of neglect in this case?
2. Is this a case of neglect? (If so, what kind?) (What defines it as such?)
3. What degree of certainty can be established that this is a case of neglect according to the following scale:
   0—certainty that neglect is not present in this case
   1—perhaps potential neglect, although the child is now receiving adequate care
   2—possible neglect, but more information is needed to be sure
   3—likely neglect, but the degree of risk is uncertain
   4—serious neglect, with the child in present danger
4. What additional information, if any, do you need to make a determination of this case?
5. What seems to be the Heller family's underlying problem?
6. Are there any contra-indicators in this case (factors which suggest an explanation other than neglect that would account for the conditions and behaviors of the family)?

Tell the parent(s) why the interview is taking place
Be direct, honest, and professional
Tell the parent(s) the interview is confidential
Reassure the parents of the support of the school
Tell the parents if a report has been made or will be made

Advise the parent(s) of the school's legal responsibilities to report
DON'T:
Try to "prove" abuse or neglect by accusations or demands
Display horror, anger, or disapproval of parent(s), child, or situation

Pry into family matters unrelated to the specific situation

Place blame or make judgements about the parent(s) or child

SUPPORT SYSTEMS FOR THE CHILD, PARENT, AND PROFESSIONALS

Working with the family after identification of abuse requires persons with exceptional sensitivity to others. Although the schools can provide help in parent education classes and other prevention and remediation programs and support, after the case has been reported to social services or a family crisis center, a case worker will be assigned to the family. It might be well for the teacher to be aware of the characteristics needed by these workers, for most of these characteristics are also needed by teachers. In *Child Abuse and Neglect: The Roles and Responsibilities of Professionals* (U.S. Department of Health, Education, and Welfare, 1979), the authors state:

Workers must be able to accept hostility and rejection without being devastated by it or needing to retaliate; they must be able to feel at ease with parents' criticisms, yet not be critical of the parents' behavior; share themselves, without sharing their problems; befriend while being aware of their helping role; think first of the parents' needs, rather than their own; avoid using the parents to increase their own feelings of self-worth; and have a sense of personal worth and achievement that will sustain them through demanding work that offers few immediate rewards. (pp. 5–6)

The responsibilities and demands are enormous, and case workers need reliable supportive services from other agencies as well as their own. Some communities have developed child protection teams where professionals can recommend procedures and give support. (In Colorado any county with 50 or more incidents annually must establish a child protection team.) The makeup of the team

may vary, but a typical team would include a physician, representatives of each of the following: the juvenile court, local law enforcement agency, county social services department, mental health clinic, public health department, and public school district, as well as an attorney and one or more members of the lay community. The case worker reviews the case with the team and indicates the treatment plan; the team advises the worker of resources available and comments on problems and strengths that it sees in the treatment plan.

Other supportive services aid the main case worker. There are medical and psychiatric services available for the abusive parent. In some areas there are crisis nurseries where the parent needing immediate assistance can take a child. Another emergency service for the parent is the crisis-intervention hot line, where assistance is as close as the telephone. Public health nurse visits are often well-received by the parents as are homemaking services. In some cases the children are taken from the parents for a short period and placed in foster homes or detention centers until the parents are in control of themselves. The availability of temporary foster homes or therapeutic day care centers helps the child as well as the family. Parent education is often a part of the therapeutic day care center; here the parents can learn to understand themselves and their children. These professionals, who are available to help the case worker in handling a family in need, are joined by a new group of lay persons who contribute yet another dimension (Kempe & Helfer, 1982).

PREVENTING ABUSE

Parents Anonymous, a self-help parent group, gives parents the chance to share their feelings with others who have had similar experiences. Parents can use Parents Anonymous and the crisis-intervention hot lines without the fear of public disclosure. The members help each other to avoid abuse by providing the opportunity to talk out problems. Groups vary according to the needs of the community, but their activities include meetings where the members remain anonymous if they desire, and they have a place where they can become actively involved with others, sharing feelings openly and developing trust. Positive ways of behaving and relating to others are learned as they sort through their pain and anger of the past (Holmes, 1982). The national organization has a booklet that describes how Parents Anonymous groups can be formed (Parents Anonymous, 1985). Some members also get involved in education, legislative action, and a crisis line (Rocky Mountain Parents Anonymous, 1978).

Many abusive parents want help. When they reveal their desires, they indicate that they want another parent to help them develop child-rearing skills through modeling and friendship. Professionals can give them psychiatric help and other support, but because these parents may have missed a childhood with nurturing parents, their greatest need is the opportunity to have an active experience with a nurturing model. The importance of bonding and of a close relationship between parent and infant has been recognized as necessary for the child's emotional and physical growth. Severe deprivation can result in failure to thrive and marasmus (Skeels, 1939; Spitz, 1945). Lack of development of close and trusting bonds as infants and children results later in parents who need special help in their ability to relate to their own child. These parents are still looking for someone to mother them. The supportive help of another parent can function as a nurturing model for both parent and child.

Researchers at the University of Colorado Medical School have been investigating mothers whom they have categorized as high risk for abnormal parental practices following observations made during and after labor and delivery. When identified as high risk, the family receives a pediatric follow-up by a physician, lay health visitor, and/or public health nurse. The study is a positive indicator that early intervention significantly decreases abnormal parent reactions and reduces subsequent physical injury to the child (Gray et al., 1976; Kempe, 1977).

RESPONSE BY SCHOOLS AND CHILD CARE CENTERS

Schools must do more than give lip service to the letter of the law. Even in the face of mushrooming curricula and increased parental demands, personnel need to become so actively involved in the prevention of child abuse and neglect that their efforts have great impact. The children, after all, are the persons at stake.

Standards that are applicable to the role of the educator include the following:

1. The State Department of Education should develop and implement child abuse and neglect reporting policies and procedures.
2. The State Department of Education and the Local Education Agency shoud ensure that the rights of all school personnel, students, and families are respected and protected.
3. The State Department of Education should participate on the State Child Protection Coordinating Committee, and the Local Education Agency should participate on the Community Child Protection Coordinating Council.
4. The Local Education Agency should offer programs to students and adults on parenting and child rearing.
5. The Local Education Agency, in cooperation with community organizations, should ensure the provision of child care services for school-age parents.
6. The Local Education Agency, in cooperation with community organizations, should ensure that child care services for children and families at risk are available.
7. The Local Education Agency, in cooperation with community organizations, should encourage the establishment of programs to identify and serve adolescents at risk.
8. All school personnel should know the indicators of child abuse and neglect and the effect

that abuse and neglect may have on the child's performance and behavior in school.

9. The Local Education Agency should participate on the community's multi-disciplinary case consultation team.

10. The Local Education Agency should provide annual in-service training for all school personnel on identifying and reporting suspected child abuse and neglect.

11. The State Department of Education and the Local Education Agency should conduct annual evaluations of their child abuse and neglect efforts.

12. The State Department of Education and the Local Education Agency, in cooperation with the State Child Protection Coordinating Committee and the Community Child Protection Coordinating Council, should develop, implement, and support public and professional education programs on child abuse and neglect.[4]

In addition to the active involvement of the school in the formation and implementation of child abuse programs, individual schools should respond to the needs of the families in their district. Supportive services, counseling programs, individual educational plans, and warm, understanding teachers can make the future brighter for the abused or neglected child. Financial support in the form of lunch programs, field trips, and extracurricular activities, provided free or at a reduced cost, may enable the child to participate more fully. Schools can also provide or work with agencies that provide glasses, hearing aids, and other equipment needed by the child.

Checklist for schools and centers

☐ Does the school have a policy statement for reporting child abuse and neglect?

☐ Did the school do a needs assessment that shows the resources in your areas and the status of child abuse and neglect in the school district?

☐ Does the school or center coordinate activities and resources with other social agencies?

☐ Does the school or center hold periodic meetings for improved communication and coordination among agencies?

☐ Does someone in the school district serve on the child protection team?

☐ Does the school or center have a training program?

☐ Do parents feel welcome in the school?

☐ Does the school or center have a parent education program for parents of preschoolers?

☐ Does the school or center have a parent education program for parents of infants and toddlers?

☐ Is the PTA or other parent group involved with the school or center in a meaningful way for parents?

☐ Is there a parent resource room in the school?

☐ Do parents feel welcome to visit the school?

☐ Is there regular contact with parents, the teacher, and school or center? Do the teachers have frequent communication with parents when there is something good to report?

UNITED NATIONS DECLARATION OF THE RIGHTS OF THE CHILD

In the International Year of the Child, 1979, the United Nations published the rights of children. These are appropriate for children of all nations, regardless of socioeconomic level, parentage, or status, and are particularly relevant to the abused child:

Affection, love, and understanding
Adequate nutrition and medical care
Free education
Full opportunity for play and recreation
A name and nationality

---

4. From U.S. Department of Health, Education, and Welfare. *Child abuse and neglect. The user manual series. The educator's role in the prevention of child abuse and neglect.* Washington, D.C.: U.S. Government Printing Office, 1979, pp. A-1 and A-2.

Special care, if handicapped

Among the first to receive relief in times of disaster

Learn to be a useful member of society and to develop individual abilities

Be brought up in a spirit of peace and universal brotherhood

Enjoy these rights, regardless of race, color, sex, religion, national, or social origin

SUMMARY

The rash of child abuse cases reveals a phenomenon that is not new. Child abuse has been with society since very early times, but it was not recognized as a problem until the second half of the twentieth century, and no concerted effort was made to stem the crisis until the 1960s.

Legislation was mandated that schools report cases of abuse and neglect. Schools work with children more than any other agency so they need to be in the foreground in preventing child abuse.

The chapter includes characteristics of families who tend to be abusive, ways to identify the abused or neglected child, and psychologic characteristics of abusive parents and abused children.

Training has been developed by the U.S. Department of Health, Education, and Welfare, based to a large degree on the work done by the National Center for the Treatment and Prevention of Child Abuse. Examples of training materials are given, and resources available for use are listed.

School district policy and responsibility are described and illustrated by a typical policy statement. Points useful for interviewing the child and/or parents are given, and suggestions that enable the school to be supportive of potentially abusive parents are discussed. Recognition of and response to the problem by financial support from the school, parent education groups, school curricula, resource rooms, crisis nurseries, and/or parent-to-parent support groups are necessary.

SUGGESTED ACTIVITIES AND DISCUSSIONS

1. Attend a Child Protection Council meeting. What is the composition of the council, for ex-

ample, doctors, educators, social workers, or a judge? How does the wide spectrum of specialists show the need for cooperation among agencies working with families?

2. Discuss the signs that teachers may observe in suspected child abuse and neglect cases.

3. What are the steps a teacher should take if child abuse or neglect is suspected?

4. Contact a school in your district and obtain a copy of their policy on child abuse and neglect.

5. Invite a social worker who is involved with child abuse cases to share experiences with the class. Investigate the policies, difficulties, and successes of child abuse programs.

6. Obtain a copy of the *Self-Instructional Text for Head Start Personnel*. Use it as a self-paced text.

7. Develop a policy for dealing with child abuse and neglect in a hypothetical school.

8. Visit with teachers and discuss how they feel about reporting child abuse. Which policies do they follow in reporting suspected child abuse or neglect cases?

9. Research material on bonding (see Chapter 1). Discuss the problems inherent in removing children from their homes.

10. Investigate the manner in which the courts handle child abuse and neglect cases. How do they manage out-of-home placements? Which rights are guaranteed the parents?

11. Obtain *A Curriculum on Child Abuse and Neglect* from the Department of Health and Human Services. Use the case studies for discussion.

12. Make a list of guidelines for identifying maltreated children. Base your discussion on Halperin's descriptions of these children. What are some of the ways that a teacher can give support to maltreated children?

BIBLIOGRAPHY

Altman, D. H., & Smith, R. L. Unrecognized trauma in infants and children. *Journal of Bone and Joint Surgery,* 1960, *42A,* 407–413.

American Humane Association, *National analysis of official child neglect and abuse reporting.* Denver, Colo.: The American Humane Association, 1978.

————. *Highlights of Official Child Neglect and Abuse Reporting 1983.* Denver, Colo.: American Humane Association, 1985.

Bakwin, H. Multiple skeletal lesions in young children due to trauma. *Journal of Pediatrics,* 1956, *49,* 7–15.

Besharov, D. The status of child abuse and neglect prevention and treatment. In *Proceedings of the First National Conference on Child Abuse and Neglect.* U.S. Department of Health, Education, and Welfare. (The National Center on Child Abuse and Neglect, Children's Bureau, Office of Child Development, Office of Human Development). Washington, D.C.: U.S. Government Printing Office, 1977.

Broadhurst, D. D. *The educators' role in the prevention and treatment of child abuse and neglect.* U.S. Department of Health, Education, and Welfare. (The National Center on Child Abuse and Neglect, Children's Bureau, Administration for Children, Youth and Families, Office of Human Development Services). Washington, D.C.: U.S. Government Printing Office, 1979.

Caffey, J. Multiple fractures in long bones of infants suffering from chronic subdural hematoma. *American Journal of Roentgenology,* 1946, *56,* 163–173.

DeFrancis, V. *Child abuse—preview of a nationwide survey.* Denver, Colo.: The American Humane Association, 1963.

DeMause, L. Our forebearers made childhood a nightmare. *Psychology Today,* April 1975, p. 85–88.

Education Commission of the States. *Education policies and practices regarding child abuse and neglect: 1978.* (Child Abuse Project Report No. 109.) Denver: Education Commission of the States, 1978.

————. *Report and recommendations of National Advisory Committee.* Denver: Education Commission of the States, 1978.

————. *Families and schools: Implementing parent education.* (Report No. 121). Denver: Education Commission of the States, 1979.

Elmer, E. *Children in jeopardy.* Pittsburgh: University of Pittsburgh Press, 1967.

————. Abused young children seen in hospitals. In Antler, S., Ed., *Child abuse and child protection: Policy and practice.* Silver Springs, Md.: National Association of Social Workers, 1982.

Fisher, S. H. Skeletal manifestations of parent-induced trauma in infants and children. *Southern Medical Journal,* August 1958, pp. 956–960.

Fontana, V. The diagnosis of the maltreatment syndrome in children. *Pediatrics,* 1973, *51,* 780–782.

————. *Somewhere a child is crying.* New York: Macmillan, 1973.

————. *Maltreated child.* Springfield, Ill.: Charles C. Thomas, 1979.

Gelles, R. *Violence towards children in the United States.* Paper presented at the American Association for the Advancement of Science, Denver, Colo., February 25, 1977.

————. Violence in the family: A review of research in the seventies. *Journal of Marriage and Family,* November 1980, *42,* 873–885.

Gil, D. G. *Violence against children.* Cambridge, Mass.: Harvard University Press, 1970.

Gray, J. D., Cutler, C. A., Dean, J. C., & Kempe, C. H. *Prediction and prevention of child abuse and neglect.* Denver, Colo.: National Center for the Prevention and Treatment of Child Abuse and Neglect, 1976.

Halperin, M. *Helping maltreated children: School and community involvement.* St. Louis: C. V. Mosby, 1979.

Helfer, R. E. *The diagnostic process and treatment programs.* U.S. Department of Health, Education, and Welfare. (Office of Human Development, Office of Child Development, Children's Bureau, National Center for Child Abuse and Neglect). Washington, D.C.: U.S. Government Printing Office, 1975.

Holmes, S. Parents anonymous: A treatment method for child abuse. In S. Antler (Ed.), *Child abuse and child protection.* Silver Springs, Md.: National Association of Social Workers, 1982.

Kempe, C. H. Predicting and preventing child abuse: Establishing children's rights in assuring access to health care through the health visitor concept. In *Proceedings of the First National Conference on Child Abuse and Neglect.* U.S. Department of Health, Education, and Welfare. (The National Center on Child Abuse and Neglect, Children's Bureau, Office of Child Development). Washington, D.C.: U.S. Government Printing Office, 1977.

Kempe, C. H., & Helfer, R. E. *The battered child.* Chicago: University of Chicago Press, 1982.

Kempe, C. H., Silverman, F. N., Steele, B. F., Droegemueller, W., & Silver, H. The battered-child syndrome. *Journal of the American Medical Association,* 1962, *181,* 17–24.

Martin, H. P., & Beezeley, P. Personality of abused children. In H. P. Martin, *The abused child.* Cambridge, Mass.: Ballinger Publishing, 1976.

Mondale, W. F. Symposium on prevention: Helping parents parent. In *Proceedings of the First National Conference on Child Abuse and Neglect.* U.S. Department of Health, Education, and Welfare. (The National Center on Child Abuse and Neglect, Children's Bureau, Office of Child Development, Office of Human Development). Washington, D.C.: U.S. Government Printing Office, 1977.

Nagi, S. Z. *Child maltreatment in the United States.* New York: Columbia University Press, 1977.

Packer, A. B., Resnick, M. B., Resnick, J. L., & Wilson, J. M. An elementary school with parents and infants. *Young Children,* 1979, *34,* 4–9.

Parents Anonymous. *The program development manual.* Los Angeles: Parents Anonymous, 1985.

Report and recommendations of the National Advisory Committee on Child Abuse and Neglect. Publication No. 108. Denver, Colo.: Education Commission of the States, 1978.

Riggs, R. C. Incest: The School's Role. *The Journal of School Health.* August 1982, *52,* 365–370.

Rocky Mountain Parents Anonymous. *General information.* Denver, Colo.: Rocky Mountain Parents Anonymous, 1978.

Roth, R. A. *Child sexual abuse: Incest, assault, and sexual exploitation.* U.S. Department of Health, Education, and Welfare. (Office of Human Development Services, Administration for Children, Youth and Families.) Washington, D.C.: Government Printing Office, 1979.

Shanas, B. Child abuse: A killer teachers can help control. *Phi Delta Kappan,* 1975, *61,* 479–482.

Silver, H. K., & Kempe, C. H. Problems of parental criminal neglect and severe physical abuse of children. *American Journal of Diseases of Children,* 1959.

Silverman, F. Roentgen manifestations of unrecognized skeletal trauma in infants. *American Journal of Roentgenology,* 1953, *69,* 413–427.

Skeels, H. M., & Dye, H. B. A study of the effects of differential stimulation on mentally retarded children. *Proceedings and Addresses of the American Association on Mental Deficiency,* 1939, *44,* 114–136.

Spitz, R. A. Hospitalism: An inquiry into the genesis of psychiatric conditions in early childhood. In A. Freud et al., (Eds.), *The Psychoanalytic Study of the Child* (Vol. 2). New York: International Universities Press, 1945.

Steele, B. F. *Working with abusive parents from a psychiatric point of view.* U.S. Department of Health, Education, and Welfare. Washington, D.C.: U.S. Government Printing Office, 1977.

Teacher education—active participant in solving the problems of child abuse and neglect. Child Abuse and Neglect Project No. 99. Denver, Colo.: Education Commission of the States, 1977.

U.S. Department of Health, Education, and Welfare. (Office of Human Development, Office of Child Development, Children's Bureau, National Center for Child Abuse and Neglect). *Child abuse and neglect: The diagnostic process and treatment programs.* Washington, D.C.: U.S. Government Printing Office, 1975.

_____. *Child abuse and neglect (Vol. 1): An overview of the problem. The problem and its management.* Washington, D.C.: U.S. Government Printing Office, 1975.

_____. *Child abuse and neglect (Vol. 2): The roles and responsibilities of professionals. The problem and its management.* Washington, D.C.: U.S. Government Printing Office, 1975.

_____. *Child abuse and neglect (Vol. 3): The community team. An approach to case management and prevention. The problem and its management.* Washington, D.C.: U.S. Government Printing Office, 1975.

_____. (National Center on Child Abuse and Neglect, Children's Bureau, Office of Child Development, Office of Human Development). *Planning and implementing child abuse and neglect service programs: The experience of eleven demonstration projects.* (Publication No. 30093). Washington, D.C.: U.S. Government Printing Office, 1976.

_____. (Head Start Bureau, Children's Bureau, Administration for Children, Youth and Families, Office of Human Development.) *Self-instructional text for Head Start personnel: Child abuse and neglect.* Publication No. OHDS 78-31103. Washington, D.C.: U.S. Government Printing Office, 1977.

———. *Child abuse and neglect. The user manual series. The educator's role in the prevention and treatment of child abuse and neglect.* Washington, D.C.: U.S. Government Printing Office, 1979.

———. *A curriculum on child abuse and neglect. Resource materials.* Washington, D.C.: U.S. Government Printing Office, 1979.

Wertham, F. *A sign for Cain.* New York: Macmillan, 1966.

Woolley, P. V., Jr., & Evans, W. A. Significance of skeletal lesions in infants resembling those of traumatic origin. *Journal of American Medical Association,* June 1955, pp. 539–543.

Zigler, E. Controlling child abuse in America: An effort doomed to failure. In *Proceedings of the First National Conference on Child Abuse and Neglect.* U.S. Department of Health, Education, and Welfare. (The National Center on Child Abuse and Neglect, Children's Bureau, Office of Child Development, Office of Human Development). Washington, D.C.: U.S. Government Printing Office, 1977.

Appendix

DENVER PUBLIC SCHOOLS
Department of Health and Social Services
Child Abuse Bulletin*
August 1985
To all principals, nurses, social workers,
psychologists and concerned personnel

Synopsis:
Updated Procedures (supersedes August 1980 Child Abuse Bulletin HE-47) for reporting child abuse and neglect:

Section

   I. Background Information
  II. Legal Responsibilities re: Abuse and Neglect
 III. *Reporting Procedures*
     A. Phone Reporting
       FAMILY CRISIS CENTER 893-6111
     B. Written Reporting
     C. Reporting to Denver Public Schools Social Work Office
 IV. The Family Crisis Center Investigation
  V. Additional Guidelines
     A. Child in Imminent Danger
     B. Neglect
     C. Unsupervised Children
 VI. Copy of Pupil Dismissal Form

I. *Background Information*

With each passing year, the importance and magnitude of the problem of child abuse and neglect becomes progressively more apparent. Child abuse is now being viewed as a major psychosocial and health problem by those concerned about the welfare of children. The scope of the problem is now being recognized to extend beyond "nonaccidental trauma" to physical and emotional deprivation, sexual abuse, and pervasive negative parental attitudes about children. The consequences of unremitting abuse are serious: disability, social deviance, death, and in virtually all cases, a lasting corrosion of self-esteem that both perpetuates child abuse from generation to generation and robs an individual of the opportunity to maximize his/her innate potentials.

The schools have become a major resource in the early identification of child abuse and neglect. During the 1984–1985 school year, 2967 reports of child abuse/neglect were investigated by the Denver Department of Social Services. Of these, 837 (28%) were initiated by Denver Public Schools personnel. The first year the present laws went into effect there were 161 cases referred by school district personnel.

This trend of better recognition and reporting of child abuse and neglect will not only help hundreds of children within the Denver

---

*Reprinted with permission from John M. Lampe, M.D.

Public Schools now, but untold numbers of future children will also be saved the personal misery and suffering that is associated with the ongoing perpetuation of abuse and neglect within families.

II. *Legal Responsibilities re: Child Abuse and Neglect*

In accord with Colorado statutes, Denver Public Schools has responsibilities in the area of child abuse. Both statutes and procedures have been revised several times since they were instituted in 1963. To clarify the roles and responsibilities of the school district and its personnel, the following sections of the law are stated:

Article 10 of Title 19, Colorado Revised Statutes 1973 as *Repealed and reenacted, with amendments,* in 1980.

A. *Definitions of Abuse and Neglect* (19-10-103)

   (1) (a) "Abuse" or "child abuse or neglect" means *an act or omission* in one of the following categories *which threatens the health or welfare of a child*:

   (I) Any case in which a child exhibits evidence of skin bruising, bleeding, malnutrition, failure to thrive, burns, fracture of any bone, subdural hematoma, soft tissue swelling, or death, and such condition of death is not justifiably explained, or where the history given concerning such condition or death, or circumstances indicate that such condition or death may not be the product of an accidental occurrence;

   (II) Any case in which a child is subjected to sexual assault or molestation, sexual exploitation, or prostitution;

   (III) Any case in which the child's parents, legal guardians, or custodians fail to take the same actions to provide adequate food, clothing, shelter, or supervision that a prudent parent would take.

B. *Persons Required to Report Child Abuse or Neglect* (19-10-104)

   (I) Any person specified in subsection (2) of this section who has reasonable cause to know or suspect that a child has been subjected to abuse or neglect or who has observed the child being subjected to circumstances or conditions which would reasonably result in abuse or neglect, shall immediately report or cause a report to be made of such fact to the county department or local law enforcement agency.

   (2) Persons required to report such abuse or neglect or circumstances or conditions shall include any:

   (a) Physician or surgeon, including a physician in training;

   . . .

   (i) Registered nurse or licensed practical nurse;

   . . .

   (l) School official or employee;

   (m) Social worker, or worker in a family care home or child care center, as defined in Section 26-6-102, C.R.S. 1973.

In addition, *any* citizen may report what he or she suspects to be child abuse or neglect by calling the Family Crisis Center at 893-6111. Anonymous as well as identified callers can be assured the complaint will be investigated.

C. *Penalty for Failure to Report* (19-10-104, subsection 4)

   Any person who willfully violates the provisions of subsection (1) of this section:

   (a) Commits a class 3 misdemeanor and, upon conviction thereof, shall be punished by a fine of $750.00 or 6 months in jail.

   (b) Shall be liable for damages proximately caused thereby.

D. *Role of Department of Social Services*

   By the revision of 1975, the implementation of this law, as of January 1976, becomes the responsibility of the Division of Services for Families, Children and Youth of the Denver Department of Social Services (DDSS-FCY) with the cooperation of reporting agencies. The initial investigation of all abuse reports is the responsibility of a division within DDSS-FCY, i.e., the *Family Crisis Center.*

E. *Protection for Persons Reporting*

   The law specifically states (19-10-110) "Any person participating in good faith in the making of a report or in a judicial proceeding held pursuant to this title . . . shall be immune from any liability, civil or criminal, that otherwise might result by reason of such reporting."

Ernest L. Boyer, U.S. Commissioner of Education stated that, "We agree that reporting of such incidents (child abuse, neglect) made in good faith, will not violate FERPA (Family Educational Rights and Privacy Act)."

F. *Required Teacher In-Service*

During the 1983–1984 session, the Colorado General Assembly passed a law reading as follows:

Board of Education—specific duties.

To provide for a periodic in-service program for all district teachers which shall provide information about the "Child Protection Act of 1975," article 10 of title 19, C.R.S., instruction designed to assist teachers in recognizing child abuse or neglect, and instruction designed to provide teachers with information on how to report suspected incidents of child abuse or neglect and how to assist the child-victim and his family.

III. *Denver Public Schools Procedures for Reporting Child Abuse*

To fulfill our obligations to pupils, in conformity with the law of the State, the following procedures have been developed for Denver Public Schools personnel:

A. *Telephone Reporting*

Family Crisis Center—phone 893-6111

When there is good reason to suspect that a child has been abused, the suspecting person should consult with the principal or his designee, social worker and nurse, if available. At this time, the decision will be made as to who will call to make the report. Please note that no one within the school district shall have the authority to "veto" the reporting of any suspected case of child abuse. Any *SUSPICION* of abuse *MUST* be reported to the Family Crisis Center.

The incident should be reported as soon as possible after discovery. This will help to facilitate additional investigations within the confines of the school day. Do not wait if the nurse, social worker, or principal is not available; rather, the suspecting

person or designee of the principal should make the call. In emergencies, the social worker and nurse may be contacted at their other schools of assignment. Time is of the essence!

Reporting a case to the Family Crisis Center does not mean you have labeled the family as perpetrators, as neglectful, or as abusers. It does mean that you are aware of injuries, maltreatment, or inadequate caring that has occurred to a child. Child Welfare and the court system determine if abuse or neglect has occurred. Remember that under the law, all suspected abuse must be reported!

1. *Steps In Telephone Reporting*

The caller should:

- contact the Family Crisis Center— 893-6111 (call as soon as possible. A call early in the school day will allow for adequate time for the Crisis Center worker to arrive at school and initiate the evaluation before school is dismissed.)
- identify self
- give location and telephone number of school
- provide identifying data pertaining to child
- provide information regarding suspected abuse
- note the name of the person who accepts the report and the time that the report was made
- ascertain at time of initial phone call whether Crisis Center worker will be coming before school is out for the day and if not, what course of action the worker recommends.

If the Family Crisis Center worker has not arrived by the time school is dismissed for the day, school personnel should:

- call the police if the child is afraid to go home, refusing to go home, or is felt to be in imminent danger
- send the child home if the abuse is minor and the child does not appear to be in imminent danger
- remain at school with the child to assist in the investigation if the police

and/or Crisis Center worker indicate they will be coming to school the day of the call.

2. *Reporting Of Abuse Inflicted By School Personnel*

Unfortunately, there have been a few instances where school personnel in their over-zealous use of discipline have bruised or physically injured students. Since the schools are functioning in loco parentis (in place of parents), abuse inflicted by school personnel must be reported to the Crisis Center. Follow the same reporting procedure outline in Section III–A–1, . . . except that the school administrator must immediately be made aware of any abusive situation involving school personnel.

B. *Written Reporting*

After reporting any abuse or neglect situation by telephone to the Family Crisis Center, the principal or his designee or reporting person *must* also write a Child Abuse Report using Form CAR 983 (available from Nursing Service, 837-1000, ext. 2615). The written Child Abuse Report should be completed and mailed as soon as possible, but in any event, no later than 24 hours after the telephone reporting. One original and three copies should be made.

1. Original (to be mailed within 24 hours of telephone reporting):
   Denver Department of Social Services
   Division of Services for Families, Children and Youth
   2200 W. Alameda
   Denver 80223
   (Do *not* hand the report to the worker responding to the crisis.)

2. Copy one—give to the nurse for inclusion in the student's Health Record

3. Copy two—give to the nurse for inclusion with her monthly report to Nursing Service

4. Copy three—give to the social worker for inclusion in the local social work record.

C. *Reporting to the Denver Public Schools Social Work Office*

The social worker (or in his/her absence, the nurse or reporting person) should call the Denver Public Schools Social Work Office to give information regarding the report so that it will be available to the person representing Denver Public Schools on the Child Protection Team. This is *very important* in order to assist the representative in clarifying and presenting any concerns of school personnel about specific cases. The Social Work Office should be called (837-1000, ext. 2611) to report the incident *before* the next weekly meeting of the Child Protection Team. (Usually on Thursday)

IV. *The Family Crisis Center Investigation*

A social worker will respond in person or by phone from the Family Crisis Center. It is the responsibility of the social worker from the Family Crisis Center, using whatever information school personnel can supply, to make an immediate judgement as to disposition.

A. THE FAMILY CRISIS CENTER ALTERNATIVES ARE:

1. to leave the child in school

2. to request the assistance of the police to
   (a) take the child to Denver General Hospital for medical examination, or
   (b) take the child into custody if it is felt that the child cannot safely return home at that time.

3. to obtain a verbal court order to arrange for care

4. There will be instances where the Crisis Center worker will accept the case but will decide that it is safe for the child to return to his home. It is important to determine if the Family Crisis Center worker or school personnel will notify the parents.

5. There may be other instances where the Crisis Center worker may decide to take no action. If this happens, each situation must be viewed individually to determine if parents should be notified.

B. *Facilitating Cooperation with Family Crisis Center*

1. *Family Crisis Center Investigation On School Grounds*

Our Denver Public Schools Office of Social Work Services is one of seven agencies serving on the Interagency Child Protection Team. The team meets weekly to review all cases of reported child abuse and neglect and makes recommendations for follow-up. It is critical that agencies work cooperatively in dealing with these cases.

The Denver City Attorney assigned to the Family Crisis Center points out that their social workers are required by law to interview or observe a child reported as having been abused or neglected, and occasionally these interviews cannot be conducted in the home for various reasons. As a result, a Family Crisis Center worker may request school authorities to allow a child abuse investigation (i.e., observation and/or interview) to take place on school grounds. This may occur even when the initial report came from outside the school district. It is important that the interview or observation be permitted at school when requested. However, it is suggested that the principal or his designee, usually the school social worker or nurse, sit in on the interview.

In such instances, the following procedures are recommended:

(a) The Child Welfare representative should produce identification.

(b) The principal or the principal's designee is to be present during any interview of a student.

(c) Notify the Child Welfare representative that the pupil's parent will be notified of the visit unless specifically requested by the representative not to do this.

(d) Unless specifically requested not to notify the parent, notify the parent of the details of the visit.

(e) Document the visit on your records.

The Child Welfare workers also will conduct interviews with the parents of these children where there is suspected abuse.

2. *Requests for Nurse Examinations*

Nurses may be requested and should comply with the request by Family Crisis Center to examine a child for signs of physical abuse. This should be done even if the report in question was not initiated by the Denver Public Schools. Generally, these examinations should take place on a day when the nurse is assigned to the building where the child is in attendance. Special arrangements may be made in case of emergencies.

V. *Additional Guidelines*

A. *Child in Imminent Danger*

1. *When To Notify Police:*

If a Family Crisis Center worker has not arrived at school to do the school investigation by dismissal time and the child is considered to be in *imminent danger,* the police should be called.

The law makes provision that if the child is considered in imminent danger, the police may be called immediately— 575-2011 or 911. Except in rare instances, we would not consider a child in the custody of school officials to be in imminent danger and hence this provision will be seldom used.

If a uniformed officer responds, his alternatives would be:

a. to leave the child in the school

b. to remove the child for medical examination or further investigation

c. to place the child in a receiving center.

In any event, once the officer considers the child to be physically safe, he will turn the investigation over to the Denver Department of Social Services, Services for Families, Children and Youth.

2. *When A Child Is Taken Into Police Custody*:

When it is necessary to place the child in the custody of the police, the following policy applies and must be strictly observed.

Denver Public Schools Policy 1206C

PUPILS, DISMISSAL OF DURING SCHOOL SESSION. Sections D and E

"D. *Custody requested by a Police Officer.* Whenever a police officer desires to take a child into temporary custody, the principal shall ascertain from the officer the reasons for the officer's action. The principal shall release the child to the police officer and shall immediately notify the child's parents of the action by telephone. If it is not possible to reach the parents by telephone, the principal shall prepare the notification memorandum (see attached form #01-1500-06). One copy shall be maintained in the school file, one copy taken to the child's home that day, and a third copy sent to the office of the appropriate Assistant Superintendent.

E. The principal will make every effort possible to insure that the taking of custody will be made in privacy, preferably in the principal's office."

Important: The notification memorandum (see attached form) shall be enclosed in a sealed envelope and the envelope properly addressed to the parent or guardian of the pupil involved. The envelope may be slipped under the door of the residence or otherwise put in a conspicuous place. It shall not be placed in the mailbox. (The placing of anything other than U.S Mail in residence mailboxes is contrary to regulations of the Post Office Department.) If a telephone exists in the home, but no contact has been made, the principal shall follow up at intervals until the parent has been advised. In case of uncertainties or situations which appear beyond the scope of this policy, principals shall request additional instructions from their supervisor or from the Department of Health and Social Services.

B. *Handling Nonemergent Problems—Neglect*

Many children are found in long-term neglectful situations which do not pose immediate danger, but will be to their detriment if not corrected. School social workers and/or nurses should counsel with parents. If after concerted effort, the situation has not been sufficiently improved or corrected, it may be reported. It is often helpful to discuss these situations with the social work supervisor or nursing coordinator before making the report. Nurses and social workers should use the CAR 983 form. Social workers should also use the Social Work Summary referral form (used for agency referrals) and send it to the Social Work Office for typing and forwarding. (Form CAR 983 available from Nursing Service, 837-1000, ext. 2615).

C. *Unsupervised Children*

1. *Children Under 12 Years of Age*

The Colorado Child Labor Law requires that children must be at least 12 years old in order to act as babysitters. It follows that children under 12 years should not be left alone. When children less than 12 years of age are left alone, the Family Crisis Center considers them unsupervised and neglected.

We know of the danger that children may be exposed to when left unsupervised, i.e., fire or harmful strangers. Parents are not always aware of the dangers and the existence of the law, and therefore many situations may be remediated by counseling with them. However, if this situation is not corrected, or young children are discovered alone, the situation should be reported. Judgement needs to be used in determining the action to take. When consultation is needed, contact the offices of Health (837-1000, ext. 2615) or Social Work Services (837-1000, ext. 2611).

To report these cases, call the Family Crisis Center at 893-6111, utilizing the same procedures as in Section III–A–1. Written report must also be made, as per Section III–B. . . .

2. *Handicapped Children*

Children with certain handicaps may need ongoing, direct supervision, regardless of their age and physical maturity level. When school personnel become aware of any handicapped student who appears to lack appropriate supervision, the same guidelines as above should be followed even though the child may be 12 years of age or older. If the child is over 18 the situation should be referred to the Adult Protection Unit of the Denver Department of Social Services (936-3666).

DENVER PUBLIC SCHOOLS
Notification Card

To _____
(Parent, Parents, or Guardian)

Address _____

Telephone Number _____

We have tried and were unable to notify you regarding your son _____

daughter _____, _____
(Name)

who was taken into custody by the following officer (or officers) of the Police Department at approximately _____ A.M./P.M. for _____ .

_____	_____
(Name and Division, Department or Bureau of Officer)	(Badge Number)
_____	_____
(Name and Division, Department or Bureau of Officer)	(Badge Number)

Please call the following number of the Police Department to secure information relative to

your child _____ .

_____	_____
(Signature of Officer taking custody)	(Signature of principal, or other school employee presently in charge of building)
_____	_____
(Date)	(School)
	_____
	(Date)

CHAPTER TEN

Rights and Responsibilities

G. R. Berger
Eugenia Hepworth Berger

Parents and students as well as professional educators have rights and responsibilities as members of the school community. Could mutual recognition of privileges and obligations provide guidelines for productive dialogue between schools and families? Today the school and the family, two of our most important social institutions, face a challenge to provide what is best for the child. The rapid pace of social change over the past 30 years has increased the importance of the schools, but it has also made the school system more vulnerable to outside criticism (Saxe, 1975).

Public education, particularly, has found itself the object of harsh criticism and earnest debate. No aspect of the public school has received more attention than that of the rights and responsibilities of students. (U.S. Department of Health, Education, and Welfare, 1979, p. v)

ORIGIN OF PARENTS' AND CHILDREN'S RIGHTS

Parents have long been recognized as having guardianship rights over their biological children. Parents of adopted children are guaranteed those same rights, which can be terminated only by court action or voluntary relinquishment. At the same time parents have responsi-

Children and their parents have responsibilities as well as rights.

bility toward their children. They have the right and responsibility to socialize their children, choose and provide health services for them, discipline and rear them, choose whether they will be educated in private or public schools, and give them care, shelter, and nourishment. It is only when they ignore or misuse these responsibilities that authorities have the right to interfere.

The rights and responsibilities of parents are derived from custom, legislation, and opinions of state and federal courts. The basis for these rights in the United States are based on the Bill of Rights and the Fourteenth Amendment of the Constitution. The First Amendment of the Constitution states that

Congress shall make no law respecting an establishment of religion, or prohibiting the free exercise thereof: or abridging the freedom of speech, or of the press: or the right of the people to peacefully assemble, and to petition the Government for a redress of grievances.

Thus, all citizens, including parents and their children, are guaranteed freedom of religion, freedom of speech, the right to assemble peacefully, a free press, and the right to petition for redress of grievances.

Constitutional Law

The Constitution forms the framework that guides the federal government. Each state also has its own constitution. Rights are prescribed by the federal Constitution and by individual state constitutions. The federal Constitution and the Supreme Court hold precedent over lower courts and states. Some powers, however, are delegated completely to the states. According to Amendment X of the Constitution,

The powers not delegated to the United States by the Constitution, not prohibited by it to the States, are reserved to the States respectively, or to the people.

Education was not included as a responsibility of the federal government and was designated as an obligation and right of the individual states. The federal Constitution provides basic rights that are common throughout the United States, but since regulations and laws vary in each state, persons concerned about their rights should check their state constitution.

Statute Law

The legislative branch of the government passes acts on statutes that affect individual rights. These laws extend from the United States Congress to state legislatures, down to county or city governments. These laws may be reviewed by the courts to determine their constitutionality.

Court Law

Court decisions handed down by judges at the federal, state, or local level are called court law, common law, or case law. The Supreme Court is the highest court in the land and its decisions are binding on all lower courts. Other court decisions are binding only within their own jurisdiction.

Administrative Law

Regulations and rules within federal and state agencies also affect the rights of parents and families. The Federal Register publishes the regulations of federal administrative agencies. Check in your state for specific regulations guiding your rights as a parent or teacher.

You can see by the descriptions of the rights and authority of the courts and administrative agencies, rights vary. The Supreme Court has jurisdiction over the nation. But because federal courts, state courts, and local courts have jurisdiction over their own areas, check with the attorney general's office or ask your legal counsel to find out the laws and regulations in your own state.

PARENTS' RIGHT TO SELECT THEIR CHILD'S EDUCATION

The fact that parents have the right to choose and guide their child's education is substantiated by several court decisions. In 1923 the *Meyer v. Nebraska* decision found that parents had the right to teach their own children. In 1925 it was found that parents had the right to choose parochial rather than public schools to teach their children. The Supreme Court in

Parents have the right to see their children's school records.

Pierce v. Society of Sisters of the Holy Name found that an Oregon law requiring children to attend public school was unconstitutional. The requirement for an educated citizenry could be met by acceptable private, parochial or secular, as well as public schools.

There are compulsory attendance laws in all states except Mississippi. Children usually must start school at the age of 5 or 6 and attend until they are 16 or 17. Parents have the responsibility to see that their children attend school. All states have free public schools. Children must attend them, or their parents must provide acceptable and approved schooling at home or in a private school.

STUDENT RECORDS—OPEN RECORD POLICY

In 1974 Congress passed the Family Educational Rights and Privacy Act (Buckley Amendment) which gives parents of students under the age of 18 and students 18 and older the right to see and control their school records, except for information placed in the file prior to January 1, 1975. These records, including health files, grades, school records, and other documents concerning the person and kept by the school, must be available within 45 days.

Directory information is given to newspapers and others who request it unless the parents or person over 18 years old request that their name or the child's name be removed from the directory information list. Directory information includes the student's name, address, telephone number, place and date of birth, dates of attendance, degrees and awards, participation in recognized activities of the school, height and weight of members of athletic teams, and the most recent previously attended educational agency. Some parents do not want their child's address and telephone number to be known. They should request that the school take their child's name off the list so that it will not be issued for news reports or similar reporting.

Privacy procedures
1. Schools must permit eligible students or parents to inspect student records.
    a. The teacher's gradebook is to be shared only with a substitute teacher. It is exempt from inspection.
    b. Parents or students may ask for explanations of the records. Explanation must be provided.
    c. Records may be destroyed prior to a request, but once a request has been made, the records may not be destroyed until the parent or eligible student has seen them.
    d. Psychiatric or treatment records may be available only to a medical doctor who can review them for the parent or eligible student.
    e. If parents are unable to come to school, the school should send the records to

them. The school may charge a reasonable amount for the copying, but not for the time spent preparing and obtaining the records.

2. Schools must let parents or eligible students correct misleading or false information.

   a. If the school administrator agrees with the parents' or student's request, the official may remove the data that is questionable.

   b. If the official refuses to change or remove the questionable information, a hearing may be requested. This hearing must be held within a reasonable time period, although no specific time period is required by law. Parents and students may bring a lawyer or friend to present evidence for them. Both sides may present evidence at a meeting presided over by an impartial hearing officer. If the decision is against the parents, they may insert a written statement about why they disagree with the information.

3. Schools must inform eligible students and parents of their rights of record disclosure and privacy.

4. Schools must obtain written permission from parents or eligible students before giving information to others, with the following exceptions:

   a. School officials and teachers with a legitimate educational interest.

   b. Federal and state officials for use in an audit or evaluation of state or federal supported programs.

   c. Accreditation associations doing accreditation work.

   d. Financial aid officials seeking information for processing financial aid requests.

   e. Administrators of another school district to which the student is transferring. Parents and eligible students have the right to review the file before it is processed.

   f. Persons doing research may use the material if the individuals are not identified.

   g. Emergencies where the information is necessary to protect the health of the individual.

5. No information on a student may be kept in secret.

If these requirements are met, eligible students and their parents can ensure that student records are accurate and that the records are not used for any purpose other than those stated above without their approval (Berger & Berger, 1985).

RIGHTS AND RESPONSIBILITIES OF STUDENTS

Students and their parents have rights and responsibilities while the child is attending school. The following excerpt from *The Rights and Responsibilities of Students: A Handbook for the School Community* (1979), developed by the Youth Development Bureau, explains the rights of students as well as expectations for behavior by students. Because laws change and vary, you should check the most recent law in your state if a specific incident occurs within your district. The handbook gives a general framework for understanding rights and responsibilities.

Speech and Expression[1]

RIGHT: Students have the right to express themselves, either orally or symbolically (through buttons, armbands, symbols on clothing, political salutes, etc.) however unpopular or critical of school or governmental policy they may be.

RESPONSIBILITY: When expressing themselves students must do so in a manner that does not

---

1. From U. S. Department of Health, Education, and Welfare. *The rights and responsibilities of students: A handbook for the school community.* Washington, D.C.: U.S. Government Printing Office, 1979, p. 5.

"materially or substantially" disrupt the operation of the school, or interfere with the rights of others.

In addition, students have the responsibility to exercise their First Amendment right to expression in a manner that does not slander or libel another person. The exact nature of these limitations is usually governed by the common law of individual States.

The decision on freedom of expression stresses the limitations imposed on authority of schools in *Tinker v. Des Moines Independent Community School District* (1969) as follows:

In our system, state operated schools may not be enclaves of totalitarianism. School officials do not possess absolute authority over their students. Students in school as well as out of school are "persons" under our Constitution. They are possessed of fundamental rights which the State must respect, just as they themselves must respect their obligations to the State.

Suspension and Expulsion[2]

RIGHT: Prior to a suspension for 10 days or less, a student must be given these procedural rights:
1. Oral or written notice of the charges
2. If the student denies the charges, an explanation of the evidence the authorities have to support them
3. An opportunity to tell his or her version of the events for which the suspension is proposed, or in emergency situations, has been imposed.

RESPONSIBILITY: Students have the responsibility to follow school regulations. The Constitution does not shield a student from a suspension "properly imposed" according to the above procedures. In addition, if a student's conduct is dangerous to other persons or continually threatens to disrupt school, he or she may be suspended immediately. In such cases, a hearing in which the above

procedures are followed should be given as soon as practicable after suspension.

The right to due process was established in the following Supreme Court cases. In *Dixon v. Alabama State Board of Education* (1961), students who participated in a sit-in were not given a hearing before they were suspended. The Supreme Court established the right to notice and a hearing prior to suspension. *Goss v. Lopez* (1975) involved 75 students who were suspended after a disturbance in the lunchroom; 9 filed a suit declaring lack of due process. The court decided that students were entitled to a public education and could not be suspended without due process.

Flag Salute and Pledge of Allegiance[3]

RIGHT: Students may not be forced to take part in the salute to the Flag or Pledge of Allegiance if doing so violates their beliefs or values.

RESPONSIBILITY: Students who refuse to participate in the salute to the Flag or Pledge of Allegiance may not disrupt the activity of others who wish to do so.

The Supreme Court in West Virginia, in *Barnette v. State Board of Education* (1943), found that students should not be forced to salute the flag if doing so violates their conscience and religious beliefs.

Religion[4]

RIGHT: Students have the right to observe any religion (or none at all, if they wish). The school shall not interfere with this right by requiring, establishing, or conducting religious exercises, nor by implementing policies that favor one religion over another or religion over nonreligion.

---

2. From U. S. Department of Health, Education, and Welfare. *The rights and responsibilities of students: A handbook for the school community.* Washington, D.C.: U.S. Government Printing Office, 1979, p. 8.

3. From U.S. Department of Health, Education, and Welfare. *The rights and responsibilities of students: A handbook for the school community.* Washington, D.C.: U.S. Government Printing Office, 1979, p. 6.

4. From U.S. Department of Health, Education, and Welfare. *The rights and responsibilities of students: A handbook for the school community.* Washington, D.C.: U.S. Government Printing Office, 1979, p. 3.

Students also have a responsibility to respect the freedom of others to observe the religion of their choice. Students who embarrass or harass others because of their religious beliefs may face the sanctions of the school disciplinary system.

RESPONSIBILITY: In enjoying this right, students may not interfere with the rights of others to observe their own particular religious beliefs.

In the case, *Epperson v. Arkansas* (1968), the Supreme Court restated the neutrality of United States government in religious concerns:

It (the government) may not be hostile to any religion or to the advocacy of nonreligion: and it may not aid, foster or promote one religion or religious theory against another or even against the militant opposite. The First Amendment mandates governmental neutrality between religion and religion, and between religion and nonreligion.

Racial Discrimination[5]

The *Brown v. Board of Education* decision on racial discrimination in 1954 set the stage for a process to implement racial equality in the schools. The court stated:

Today, education is perhaps the most important function of state and local governments. Compulsory school attendance laws and the great expenditures for education both demonstrate our recognition of the importance of education to our democratic society. It is required in the performance of our most basic public responsibilities, even service in the armed forces. It is the very foundation of good citizenship. Today it is a principal instrument in awakening the child to cultural values, in preparing him for later professional training, and for helping him to adjust normally to his environment. In these days, it is doubtful that any child may reasonably be expected to succeed in life if he is denied the opportunity of an education. Such an opportunity where

the state has undertaken to provide it, is a right which must be made available to all on equal terms.

RIGHT: The State, or other governmental body, may not establish racially segregated schools, thus depriving students of their right to an education, regardless of race.

This is one area of Federal law that has been extended to private schools, at least in the context of admissions policies. The Supreme Court has ruled that private institutions may not deny admission to prospective students on the ground of race (*Runyon v. McCrary, 427 U.S. 160,* 1976). The Court reached this conclusion through an interpretation of an 1866 Federal statute that prohibits racial discrimination in the making and enforcement of private contracts.

Congress enacted the Civil Rights Act of 1964 as an instrument to eliminate continued discrimination. Recipients of federal funds, including schools, have to meet the guidelines in order to receive government support. Title VI of the Act states:

No person in the United States shall, on the ground of race, color or national origin, be excluded from participation in, be denied the benefits of, or subjected to discrimination under any program or activity receiving Federal financial assistance.

Sex Discrimination[6]

Title IX of Educational Amendments (1972) provides:

No person in the United States, shall on the basis of sex be excluded from participation in, denied the benefits of, or subjected to discrimination under any education or activity receiving financial assistance.

In 1975 a federal regulation required schools to examine their programs to see if discriminatory policies were in effect. Exempted

---

5. From U.S. Department of Health, Education, and Welfare. *The rights and responsibilities of students: A handbook for the school community.* Washington, D.C.: U.S. Government Printing Office, 1979, pp. 9, 10, and 14.

6. From U.S. Department of Health, Education, and Welfare. *The rights and responsibilities of students: A handbook for the school community.* Washington, D.C.: U.S. Government Printing Office, 1979, pp. 17 and 18.

are military schools, religious organizations where the regulations are at variance with the religious beliefs, and single-sex colleges. Other than these, educational institutions receiving federal funds cannot do the following:

1. Exclude students of one sex from participation in any academic, extracurricular, research, occupational training, or other educational program or activity.
2. Subject any student to separate or different rules of discipline, sanctions, or other treatment.
3. Apply different rules of appearance to males and females (for example, requiring males to wear their hair shorter than females).
4. Aid or perpetuate discrimination against any person by providing significant assistance to any agency, organization, or person which discriminates on the basis of sex in providing any aid, benefit, or service to students.
5. Assign pregnant students to separate classes or activities, although schools may require the student to obtain a physician's certificate as to her ability to participate in the normal educational program or activity so long as such a certificate is required of all students for other physical or emotional conditions requiring the attention of a physician.
6. Refuse to excuse any absence because of pregnancy or refuse to allow the student to return to the same grade level which she held when she left school because of pregnancy.
7. Discriminate against any person on the basis of sex in the counseling or guidance of students or the use of different tests or materials for counseling unless such different materials cover the same occupation and interest areas and the use of such different materials is shown to be essential to eliminate sex bias.

Exceptions to the rules include:

1. Portions of classes in elementary and secondary schools which deal exclusively with human sexuality may be conducted in separate sessions for males and females.
2. The school may make requirements based on vocal range or quality which may result in a chorus or choruses of predominantly one sex.
3. The school may provide separate toilet, locker rooms, and shower facilities on the basis of sex,

Girls can participate in all noncontact sports offered by the school.

but such facilities provided for students of one sex shall be comparable to such facilities provided for students of the other sex.
4. The school may separate students on the basis of sex within physical education classes during participation in sports, the purpose of major activity of which involves bodily contact. (Wrestling, boxing, rugby, ice hockey, football, and basketball are used as examples in the regulation.)
5. The school may group students in physical education classes according to ability assessed by objective standards developed and applied without regard to sex.
6. The school may operate separate athletic teams for:
   a. Sports primarily involving body contact.
   b. Team sports in which members are chosen on the basis of competitive skill. The school, however, must allow members of both sexes to try out for a non-contact sport if there is only one team and members of one sex have been limited from participation on it in the past.

Minority Students[7]

Elementary or secondary schools cannot:

1. Separate students within the school by race, color, or national origin.
2. Provide different services or benefits to students because of their race, color, or national origin.
3. Use methods for deciding what services the student is eligible for which have the effect of discrimination. (For example, suppose some students have been transferred from an all minority school that did not offer a journalism course. Their new school could not prevent them from working on the student newspaper because they had not had such a course.)
4. On the ground of race, color, or national origin, deny a student the opportunity to participate as a member of a planning program.
5. Discriminate in any way against students because of their race, color, or national origin.

Handicapped and Special Education Students

The Rehabilitation Act of 1973 states that no person can be excluded or discriminated against on the basis of handicap in any program in a school that receives federal funds. Refer to Chapter 8 for a discussion of the Rehabilitation Act.

Selection of Texts

In general, schools choose text materials to achieve their educational objectives and goals. When parents object to the use of particular books, the courts make decisions based on each individual circumstance and how the book relates to the school's objectives. Courts determine the constitutionality of a position; legislatures may set curriculum requirements to be achieved by public schools. Private schools and early childhood centers that are not connected to the public school system

have autonomy in text selection. However, it is wise for both public and private schools to include parents in book selection. Including parents in evaluation of the texts can prevent later disagreements over text selection. When the issue becomes so heated that it ends up in court, the court will judge the material as a whole and by "contemporary community standards" (Schimmel & Fischer, 1977, pp. 78, 79).

DEVELOPING CRITERIA TOGETHER

When parents and teachers are working separately or at cross-purposes, education suffers (Newmark, 1976). Only when parents and teachers work together does the opportunity for optimum education exist.

A definition of three levels of involvement for home and school will clarify and help to delineate procedures that support positive home-school interaction:

1. Development and periodic review of a code of rights and responsibilities for each class, school, or local school district
2. Election of and active involvement with a parent or citizen advisory council
3. Implementation of the educational program in a classroom community

The first two levels can be accomplished by administrators and parents working together; however, individual classrooms can develop codes and advisory councils as well. The third level of teacher-parent involvement is that essential area where the benefits of positive relationships most make a difference—the classroom. The teacher-child-parent relationship nourishes the opportunity for learning. The clarification of issues and development of codes, a two-way communication system, and advisory councils are but means of supporting direct involvement with the classroom and its most important member, the child.

---

7. From U.S. Department of Health, Education, and Welfare. *The rights and responsibilities of students: A handbook for the school community.* Washington, D.C.: U.S. Government Printing Office, 1979, pp. 14 and 15.

This child is too young to be involved in developing a code, but his parents can help the schools develop a code that will protect him.

Development of a Code

An opportunity for participating in a democratic decision-making process exists in the formation of a school or classroom code. If parents and students join school staff in developing a code for their class or school, both rights and responsibilities are learned through a democratic process. *The Rights and Responsibilities of Students: A Handbook for the School Community* suggests a model code and a procedure for implementing a code. Recommended steps include:

1. *Identification of the level of interest.* Determine the interest in and awareness of codes with a questionnaire or informal survey of the school community. Include the teachers, administrators, students, parents, and interested community residents. If there is a lack of understanding of the purpose of a code, you must launch an awareness campaign to explain the code, its benefits, and why it is needed.

2. *Research.* Background information on the current rules and regulations should be gathered before writing a code. Samples of codes from other schools or states, legal groups, professional associations, and civil liberty organizations are helpful in the process. Key issues that need to be addressed in your individual area should be identified.

3. *Formulation of a draft code.* The actual writing of the code needs to be accomplished by a committee of parents, teachers, students, and administrators. Include the regulations that are important for your school and community. If guidance is needed, base your draft on the samples obtained.

4. *Feedback.* After the code is drafted, distribute copies or publish the document in the newsletter. Hold an open forum or ask for written comments on the code. The responses will reveal questions and areas of confusion or vagueness, which will enable the committee to revise the draft in final form.

5. *Approval and implementation.* The code should be approved by the student body as well as by the school staff. If the code is being developed for the entire district, the school board should review and approve the code. Their support is essential for implementation. At the preschool level the students will not need to approve the code, but their parents should be involved, and discussion of rules and regulations with the children is appropriate.

6. *Review.* Each year, the student body or governing committee should review the code. If needed, items may be revised. The review makes the code relevant to the current student body and is a learning as well as a decision-making process.

The three levels of involvement—the code, the parent advisory council, and the classroom—strengthen a school-home partnership. The parent advisory council is dis-

Parents are the prime advocates for their children from early childhood to young adulthood.

cussed in more detail in Chapter 4; good classroom relations are discussed in Chapters 4, 6, and 7. The code can be developed on a formal level in the entire school district, or individual teachers may modify it and use it in an informal way in their classrooms.

A SLEEPING GIANT: THE CHILD ADVOCATE

Only rarely have parent advocates—armed with facts, constructive complaints, and suggestions for improvement—demanded that principals and superintendents listen and respond to parental concerns (Jones & Jones, 1978). The majority of parents have not participated in the public school system. Advocate groups, taking advantage of their tremendous power, can be expected to involve themselves in decision making in the future. As an influential group, parents can become effective child advocates.

The Child Advocate

The advocate is a person, parent, teacher, or citizen, alone or in a group, who speaks for the child's welfare. The advocate has grasped the need of the child, the resources available within the school system, and the alternative resources outside the school system. The advocate then tries to create a workable match between the child's needs and available resources (Kappelman & Ackerman, 1977). Advocates face two situations: individual cases and class actions. The individual or case advocate works on behalf of a specific child. The class or social advocate works for a whole group of children who need special or basic services (e.g., Children's Defense Fund works for child rights). Lay advocates work to obtain services and help; when legal issues and court cases are involved, legal counsel from a lawyer is needed.

Qualifications

Qualifications for advocates are simple. Essentially what qualifies a person to be a good child advocate is the intrinsic quality of being truly motivated to help children. The help must be systematic and thorough. The advocate is committed to finding out all the needs of the child or children being helped. Although it is time-consuming and difficult work, advocacy, when supported by the best available data, is helpful to community, parents, and schools.

It must be remembered that each situation is different. The strategies that work vary, and the decision as to which strategy is most appropriate ultimately rests on two factors: (1) that the strategy accomplishes its objectives and (2) that it paves the way for long-range continuation of the practice of supplying the needed resources (Kappelman & Ackerman, 1977).

Procedure

To achieve their objectives, advocates must systematically study and proceed with a sound foundation. They first list the needs of the child and justify these needs by making certain they have been professionally determined. They read the literature and speak to experts in the field so that they are supported by reputable observations. Good advocates make sure that their positions are based not just on their own beliefs but on the true needs of the child, the group of children, and the society at large. Their positions are strengthened if the advocates are associated with a group. In fact, greater educational change and progress comes from advocacy groups than from the dedicated, but individual, parent or citizen. Proficient advocates set out to pursue all resources available (Kappelman & Ackerman, 1977).

An effective child advocate is a person who works very hard at discovering the full story behind children's needs, the total picture of the available resources, and the most appropriate method of blending the two. If a child advocate works well, he changes the system—for the better. (Kappelman & Ackerman, 1977, p. 329)

The following guidelines describe the steps to take when working on an individual advocacy case.[8]

8. From Fernandez, H. C. *The child advocacy handbook.* New York: The Pilgrim Press, 1980, p. 83.

1. *Know your facts.* Be sure they are correct. Find out: Who? What? Where? When? and Why?
2. *Know the rights* of the child, the parent, or other parties in the case. Contact an advocacy organization or lawyer if you have any questions.
3. *Know the policy* and/or procedures that relate to the problem. Get it in writing, don't just accept a verbal version.
4. *Keep accurate notes.* Document as much evidence as possible. Date everything.
5. *Discuss various options* with the child or parents you are assisting. Do not tell the young person or parent what to do. Rather let the person (child or parent) *choose* the option and course of action that is wisest and that he/she is willing to live with.
6. *Never go alone* (except in unusual circumstances) to a meeting with officials. Take the young person, the parent, or other concerned person with you.
7. In meeting with officials, *keep to the point,* be firm but not antagonistic, keep focused on the problem and the need for a resolution of the problem. Try to steer clear of personalities.
8. *Follow channels.* Don't go over a person's head until you have seen him/her about the problem. It is wise to let that person know you are dissatisfied with the result of your meeting and that you intend to go to the next person in authority.
9. If appropriate, send a letter to indicate your understanding of what took place at a meeting with officials or administrators.

AN EXAMPLE OF ADVOCACY AND COLLABORATION

A powerful collaboration can be achieved when parents and schools work together. Drug abuse is a social crisis in the United States that schools and parents must work together to solve. Many of the steps that are necessary for advocacy are also needed by parents and schools to form a united front to help with the drug crisis. Indeed, schools and parents must become advocates for their children. The first step is to gather facts and information.

Drug and Alcohol Abuse

The National Institute on Drug Abuse reports that there has been an increase in the use of higher-potency marijuana by younger children; the greatest increase occurred among students, 8 to 14 years of age. The American Medical Association revised its 1972 position which stated that there seemed to be insufficient evidence of adverse effect over long-term use of marijuana. In its 1977 report, the AMA warned about the effects of drugs on the young:

The effects of drugs on the young, who are in early stages of both physiological and psychological development, can be more pronounced and persistent than effects on mature persons. . . . Marijuana is potentially damaging to health in a variety of ways, but it can be especially harmful when used by a person who is immature, unstable, or already ill. (as cited in Manatt, 1981, p. 36)

In 1982 56 million persons had tried marijuana. Of that number 27 percent, or 7 million of them, were between the ages of 12 to 17. The largest group, 21 million or 64 percent, were between the ages of 18 to 25 (Cohen, 1985). Most studies also show that early use of drugs is associated with greater use of drugs later, greater probability of use of more dangerous drugs, more deviant activities, and lower performance by the users (U.S. Department of Health and Human Services, 1981; Hendin et al., 1981; Manatt, 1981).

After observing a slight decline in the use of drugs and alcohol, a University of Michigan study found that there was a significant rise in cocaine snorting. In the 1985 survey of new high school graduates it was found that 4 out of 10 students used marijuana at least once a year and more than 1 in 8 students used cocaine.

In 1975 daily marijuana use by high school seniors was 1 out of every 17. In 1978 this ratio increased to 1 out of every 9 who smoked marijuana daily (Manatt, p. 35). The ratio returned to a lower level in 1984 when 1 out of every 20 used marijuana. Of the class of high school seniors who used drugs, 4.3 percent had tried it first in 6th grade, 14.1 percent tried marijuana in the 7th and 8th grades, 13.6 percent in 9th grade, 11.2 percent in 10th grade, 7.3 percent in 11th grade, and only 4.4 percent in 12th grade (Johnston et al., 1985, pp. 33 & 66). The problem of drug use is not going away.

Problem Behavior

At-risk children usually display a variety of problem behaviors, for example, rebelliousness, impulsiveness, truancy, vandalism, theft, and irresponsibility. The National Institute on Drug Abuse classified the following three correlates as most related:

- Cognitive/emotional correlates significantly related to a variety of problem behaviors include low self-esteem, impulsiveness, negative attitudes toward school, low cognitive development, and low academic aspirations.
- Behavioral correlates most frequently associated with other problem behaviors are school discipline problems, delinquent behavior, all types of antisocial behavior, and frequent use of cigarettes, alcohol, and other drugs.
- Social network correlates most strongly associated with involvement in problem behavior include a variety of forms of family disorganization, inadequate parenting, poor parent-child relationships, and peer models (U.S. Department of Health and Human Services, 1981, p. 25).

The three variables that most often relate to problem behavior are stress, skill deficiencies, and situational constraints. These variables are described by the National Institute on Drug Abuse:

Stress
Youth experience stress in a variety of forms—for example, loss (of a parent or friend), rejection, abuse (sexual or physical), and failure in varying degrees of severity and across different aspects of their experience. At-risk youth are highly stressed;

although all youth inevitably experience some stress, those with lower levels of stress appear to be less inclined toward problem behavior.

Skill Deficiency

Young people vary according to the kinds of skills they have for coping successfully with stress when it occurs. Important developmental skills relate to such tasks and life events as problem solving, communication, accurate self-assessment, and constructive processes for interpreting and understanding experiences. At-risk youth are often characterized by low attainment of such skills. Some youth who have adequate life-coping skills can deal effectively with high degrees of stress; others who lack such skills are more vulnerable.

Situational Constraints

At the situational level the influence of the peer group is particularly important. Many teenagers' peers or role models encourage experimentation with high-risk behaviors such as substance abuse, precocious sexual activity, and vandalism. At-risk youth often find themselves in situations where problem behavior is expected and supported. (U.S. Department of Health and Human Services, 1981, pp. 25, 26)

Drugs That Are Abused

Knowledge of what is happening to children is the first data needed. Next, the advocate needs to know what drugs are involved and what they do. Last, the advocate needs to develop the plan of action.

The following list from the National Institute on Drug Abuse describes the major drugs of abuse:

Stimulants, known as "uppers" and "speed," are drugs which speed up the central nervous system. In strong doses, they produce a mood of euphoric well-being often followed by a sudden withdrawal ("crashing").

Barbiturates, known as "downers" and "reds," are among the most commonly abused and dangerous prescription drugs, primarily because of their interaction with alcohol, in which the effects of both drugs and the possibility of dangerous overdose are greatly increased. Barbiturates are often prescribed as sleeping pills, but they are used nonmedically to produce a "mellow" high.

Other sedatives, generally called "tranquilizers" and similar in their effects to barbiturates, are commonly prescribed in order to quiet people's nerves or relax their muscles. The tranquilizers Valium and Librium are among the best selling prescription drugs made.

Cocaine, a white powder usually sniffed through the nostrils, is a drug taken from the leaf of the coca plant that grows in South America. It produces a high similar to that of synthetic stimulants. . . .

Heroin is usually injected into the bloodstream and is highly addictive. Although the actual percentage of Americans who use heroin regularly is small—less than one-half of one percent for all age groups—the social and financial costs of heroin addiction are disproportionately high.

Inhalants are much more likely to be used by young people than by adults. This category includes glue, aerosol propellants and other chemicals with strong vapors, such as gasoline. Eight percent of the youth and three percent of the adults surveyed have used inhalants.

Hallucinogens, another major category of drugs that are commonly abused, include LSD, peyote, and PCP (used more among youth than adults and known as "angel dust"). All the hallucinogens are categorized as those that are manufactured artificially—LSD, "STP," and others—and those that are derived from plants and mushrooms—like peyote, mescaline, and psilocybin. The synthetic hallucinogens are much more dangerous than the natural ones, since often it is impossible to know exactly what chemicals are in a drug being sold "on the street" as a hallucinogen. Five percent of both the youth and the adults in the survey have used hallucinogens other than marijuana. (Resnick, 1979, p. 11)

Marijuana

Although marijuana was formerly considered innocuous, its effect on young people and long-term users, as well as its high rate of usage among students starting at the age of 8, makes it of prime importance to educators and parents.

Of the 350 chemicals in marijuana, 50 are cannabinoids, found only in marijuana. THC (delta-9 tetrahydro cannabinol) is the major mind-altering chemical in marijuana, but at least three other psycho-active cannabinoids interact with THC. Marijuana plants and the parts of the plant vary in the amount and strength of chemicals found in them and the effects they have on the user. In the 1960s most of the marijuana used here was grown in the United States, and the THC content was low—0.2 to 1.5 percent. In the 1970s and 1980s marijuana has been increasingly smuggled from Columbia, Jamaica, and Mexico with an increase in THC potency—2.5 to 5 percent. In addition, seeds from high-potency plants grown in the United States have produced THC as high as 6 to 8 percent. This escalation of the amount of psycho-active chemicals ingested makes the problem of marijuana as a drug even greater than previously (Manatt, 1981).

The effect of marijuana on the user is related to the dose per body weight. A person with slight build may get a double dose by taking the same amount as someone with a large build; think what this means to a small child. The cannabinoids are fat-soluble chemicals that accumulate in fatty linings of the body and brain. Thirty to 50 percent of the THC remains in the body a week after the cigarette is smoked. Although the high experience may seem to go away after a few hours, the effects of irritability and edginess may continue throughout the week and influence school performance. It is estimated that 4 to 6 weeks are needed before all the THC is out of the body. Repeated accumulation may affect the following physical and psychological characteristics of the users (Manatt, 1981).

Hormone Change. The National Institute of Drug Abuse (NIDA) warns that marijuana's depressant effect on the endocrine or hormonal system may interfere with normal physical and emotional development—a high risk for growing children and adolescents. Studies on long-term effect of marijuana suggest that THC may cause genetic mutations—a very real crisis for young adults who plan to have children.

Lungs. The NIDA cited studies that indicated smoking 3 to 5 marijuana cigarettes a week is equivalent to smoking 16 tobacco cigarettes a day. Five marijuana cigarettes equal 112 cigarettes, and marijuana has more cancer-causing chemicals. It takes fewer marijuana cigarettes to cause precancerous changes in lung tissue.

Heart. Marijuana has an adverse effect on the heart. After smoking a marijuana cigarette, the user's heart accelerates. It is not known what consequences smoking has on the heart's condition later in the child's life.

Brain Function. The chemical action of marijuana on the brain causes changes in the functioning of the brain. The user may experience difficulty in concentration, impaired memory, inconsistency in verbal communication, and preoccupation with internal visual imagery. Although most of these conditions are seen during the period of intoxication and are reversible, in long-term heavy users the neurological changes may become permanent. While persons are intoxicated with marijuana, their motor agility is reduced, thus reducing their ability to drive a car safely.

Psychological and Emotional Effects. Most users of marijuana do not recognize that the drug has affected their behavior or personality. Parents may notice that their child is lethargic, withdrawn, depressed, uninterested in activities, fatigued, and moody. Users have a tendency toward paranoia and believe that everyone is against them.

These changes in the child, especially during this period of growth and development, make it absolutely necessary for parents and schools to accept the challenge of working with the children to provide a drug-free environment in which they may grow (Manatt, 1981).

Developing an Advocacy Approach

After you have decided to change the environment to help children cope with the drug and alcohol problem, it is necessary to involve others. Each community has its own special needs and background, so each program should be geared to the individual problems. A two-pronged approach is one way of getting started. First, begin a series of seminars, workshops, and presentations that inform the total community. Second, simultaneously find out how the community, including adults and children, views the crisis.

Determining Needs. In order to respond to the problems of a community, you first need to know what the needs are. In the area of drug abuse the problems of the parents and schools are different from those of the students, so each group should have an opportunity to respond to the request for information. To set up a needs assessment, gather representatives from each group, brainstorm about the problems in their areas, list these concerns, and construct a questionnaire for use with a larger population.

Organizing the Parent Community. In some communities parents are very aware of the problem and want to get involved in the solutions. In other communities they avoid the issue, hoping the problems will go away. Under both circumstances it is better to have an informed community, and a series of community meetings, school seminars, and articles in the newspapers will start the education process. Once the community is informed, it is easier to get involvement and cooperation.

Informing the community takes time. Many communities spend a great deal of time and effort in establishing community seminars and out-reach to the schools before they feel the groundwork is established for developing alternatives and programs to combat the drug abuse problem in the community. Working through PTA, PTO, parent education groups, and community task forces, many communities have educated their citizens and brought the situation out into the open with seminars given by authorities in the field.

Student/Parent Rap Sessions. Students are generally better informed on drug and alcohol abuse than their parents are. Opportunities for students to talk about the problems in their lives can be very helpful to them and very informative to those who are able to listen to them. A very effective method of communication is school exchanges. Students rap while parents from another school are able to listen and join into the discussion. Parents learn what is happening in young peoples' lives. Students get an opportunity to share and explore. No value judgments are made, but parents go home much wiser and students have had an opportunity to express their frustrations and desires. Later, in an open and non-blaming atmosphere parents may be able to rap with students from their own school area. This exchange is an opportunity for parents to become more aware of the social world their children face.

Parent Peer Groups. A movement that is helpful for parents and, subsequently, their children is parent peer involvement. Parents need to be able to express their concerns and talk with others who have similar concerns. Communicating with parents lets them know that they are not alone in the challenges of rearing children.

Parent peer groups may evolve from different needs and reasons. Parents may get involved in a peer group just for the opportunity of knowing the parents of some of their own children's friends. Others get involved because they have been exposed to the increased use of drugs by their own or neighborhood children.

Peer groups may be established by the PTO, PTA, or parent education groups, or they may evolve from a concern by a single parent in a neighborhood. When a single parent attempts to organize a parent peer group, that parent may get mixed reactions from the parents contacted. Reports show that parents are often resentful if it is suggested that their children are involved with drugs. This barrier is sometimes very difficult to break. If great care is taken to establish a nonblaming campaign to inform parents of the problem, many parents may accept the true situation. Establishment of a parent group to establish common guidelines for their young children gives parents an opportunity to get acquainted before serious issues such as delinquency or drug use enter into the discussions.

Parent peer groups vary according to their needs. They may serve as support groups, as well as action groups. Develop them according to the needs of your specific community.

Organizing Student Groups.   Involving students is a necessary step for working with the drug and alcohol abuse problem. Nothing can be accomplished without their cooperation and support. In order to promote student involvement, do the following:

1. If students do not initiate a student group on their own, select a representative group and try to include those who are involved and interested. Students who volunteer are more likely to be committed to the problem. Initiating a student group may be accomplished by one of the following:
a. Ask for volunteers via bulletin boards or school newspapers.
b. Request that the student council solicit and appoint a committee.
c. Work with teachers of social studies or family life education and use their classes as a forum for discussion of the drug abuse issue.
d. Request that counselors or administrators appoint a committee.
2. At an initial meeting encourage the students to brainstorm on the following issues:
a. The drug problem
b. Reasons why students resort to drugs
c. Information and activities that make the community, school, and parents more aware and responsive to student needs

d. Alternative that would be welcomed by them
3. At a subsequent meeting encourage the students to evaluate the ideas discussed at the initial meeting and to develop a questionnaire for other students to complete.
4. Test the questionnaire on a few students. Rework it if the questions or statements are not clear. Add to it if new ideas are important and relevant.
5. Ask teachers of required classes at each level to allow their students to answer the questionnaires.
6. Tabulate the answers to the questionnaires. Share the information with the school, task force, and other students.
7. Make plans to implement requested changes. Share student plans and desires with the parent group and school.

Parent-school Teams

Parent-school teams, formed in each school, keep parents informed. The groups can reflect the needs of each school. Students serve on each team allowing the team to have an ongoing awareness of student needs from elementary through junior and senior high school.

Alternative Programs

The most crucial part of the drug and alcohol abuse program is the development of alternatives—a change in the environment. As students, parents, and community work together, the needs of the students are addressed. Students take the lead with support and backing from the parents and community.

A new code is developed. (A suggested format for the development of a behavior code was discussed earlier in this chapter.) Rules and plans for social get-togethers are established and followed.

Instead of focusing on past negative behavior, a positive approach should be used. "We are serving cider, apples, and cookies. If you wish alcohol tonight, come back another time." If the adolescents counter with "My parents drink, why shouldn't I?" the students are informed that their parents' behavior is not the concern. The concern is to have healthy children grow to productive adults. The facts demonstrate that drugs and alcohol are detrimental and injurious to growing bodies.

Just as important as eliminating drugs and alcohol are the increased opportunities for students and adolescents to develop meaningful relationships, to feel competent, and to have a chance to contribute in a significant way. Review the needs assessment completed by the students. What do they say that their needs are?

First, what facilities in the community provide a wholesome environment for young people? Does the community reflect a recognition of the needs of their adolescent population?

Second, how can schools, recreational districts, and parents help provide alternatives the children would enjoy? Is there an active after-school program? Are tutors available to help students who have difficulty in school? Are there rap times available for students during the school day? Are there activities such as crafts, auto mechanics, and art that fit the needs of all? *Advocate for the children's needs!*

Until alternatives are available and drug and alcohol information is believed, the problem will not go away. Think, however, of all the good that can come from recognizing and attacking the problem. Families may start communicating more. Schools and parents will start working together to solve the problem. The whole community can become involved. You will live where people care about each other and where they are willing to advocate for needed change.

SUMMARY

Rights and responsibilities of parents, students, and professional educators are explored in this chapter.

Criticisms of schools make cooperation between home and schools even more essential than in previous periods.

Rights and responsibilities of parents and students are expressed on the following topics: suspension and expulsion, speech and expression, flag salute and Pledge of Allegiance, religion, racial discrimination, sex discrimination, handicapped and special education students, and the Buckley Amendment on open record policy.

Three levels of involvement between home and school help clarify and delineate procedures that support positive home-school relationships. These include: (1) development and periodic review of a code of rights and responsibilities for each class, school, or local school district; (2) election of and active involvement with a parent or citizen advisory council; and (3) implementation of the educational program in a classroom community. Development of a code involves identification of interests, research and gathering of background material, formulation of a draft code, feedback, approval, implementation, and review.

The child advocate, a sleeping giant, has begun to have an effect on children's rights. Working as both case advocates and class advocates, individuals and groups are being heard. Parents who advocate for a drug-free environment for their children need to learn about drug abuse. This should be followed by organizing, planning, and advocating for a more caring and healthy environment. Parents and schools working together can provide a wholesome, intellectually stimulating, and challenging environment for families and children.

SUGGESTED ACTIVITIES AND DISCUSSIONS

1. Develop a code of conduct for students in a hypothetical school. What would the differences be between an elementary school code and a secondary school code?
2. Who should be involved in the development of a conduct code? Discuss.
3. Discuss the changes in sex stereotyping. Go to the library and skim textbooks of the 1960s and the 1980s. Can you find a difference in the subliminal messages about sex roles? Devise a test about sex roles. Have the class

test their own beliefs about the roles of each sex.

4. What is free speech? How are the boundaries defined? Discuss.
5. Which rights do parents and students have to see school records?
6. Discuss the concept that rights are also accompanied by responsibilities.
7. How have schools responded to the need to eliminate racial discrimination? Investigate the changes that have occurred in schools in your area as a result of affirmative action.
8. Which changes were needed in schools to accommodate handicapped children? Visit a school and note which changes were instituted for the handicapped child. Discuss.
9. Contact a school in your area and find out what programs exist for the reduction of drug abuse.
10. Follow the legislative action in your state, choose a bill that you strongly support, and advocate for its passage.
11. Brainstorm and come up with a list of needs that should be addressed by an advocate or advocacy groups.

BIBLIOGRAPHY

Barnette v. West Virginia State Board of Education, 319 U.S. 624 (1943).

Berger, E. H., & Berger, G. R. Parents and law: Rights and responsibilities. In L. Sametz & C. S. McLoughlin (Eds.), *Educators, children and the law.* Springfield, Ill.: Charles C. Thomas, 1985.

Cohen, M. *Marijuana: Its effect on mind and body.* New York: Chelsea House Publishers, 1985.

Dixon v. Alabama State Board of Education, 368 U.S. 930 (1961).

Fernandez, H. C. *The child advocacy handbook.* New York: The Pilgrim Press, 1980.

Goss v. Lopez, 419 U.S. 565 (1975).

Hendin, H., Pollinger, A., Ulman, R., & Carr, A. C. (Department of Health and Human Services, Public Health Service, Alcohol, Drug Abuse, and Mental Health Administration, National Institute on Drug Abuse.) *Adolescent marijuana abusers and their families.* Washington, D.C.: U.S. Government Printing Office, 1981.

Johnston, L. D., O'Malley, P. M., & Bachman, J. G. (U.S. Department of Health and Human Services, Public Health Service, Alcohol, Drug Abuse, and Mental Health Administration, National Institute on Drug Abuse). *Use of licit and illicit drugs by America's highschool students: 1975–1984.* Washington, D.C.: U.S. Government Printing Office, 1985.

Jones, P., & Jones, S. *Parents unite: The complete guide for shaking up your children's school.* New York: Wideview Books, 1978.

Kappelman, M., & Ackerman, P. *Between parent and school.* New York: Dial Press, 1977.

Manatt, M. (National Institute on Drug Abuse, U.S. Department of Health and Human Services, Public Health Services, Alcohol, Drug Abuse, and Mental Health Administration.) *Parents, peers, and pot.* Washington, D.C.: U.S. Department of Health and Human Services, 1981.

Meyer v. Nebraska, 262 U.S. 390, 399 (1923).

National Institute for Drug Abuse. (U.S. Department of Health and Human Services, Public Health Service, Alcohol, Drug Abuse and Mental Health Administration.) *Drug abuse prevention.* Washington, D.C.: U.S. Government Printing Office, 1980.

Newmark, G. *This school belongs to you and me.* New York: Hart Publishing, 1976.

Pierce v. Society of Sisters of the Holy Name, 268 U.S. 510 (1924).

Resnik, H. S. (U.S. Department of Health, Education, and Welfare, Public Health Service, Alcohol, Drug Abuse, and Mental Health Administration, National Institute on Drug Abuse) *It starts with people; Experiences in drug abuse prevention.* Washington, D.C.: Department of Health, Education, and Welfare, 1979.

Saxe, R. W. *School-community interaction.* Berkeley, Calif.: McCutchan Publishing, 1975.

Schimmel, D., & Fischer, L. *The rights of parents in the education of their children.* Columbus, Md.: National Committee for Citizens in Education, 1977.

U.S. Department of Health and Human Services. (Office of Human Development Services, Public Health Service, Alcohol, Drug Abuse, and Mental Health Administration, National Institute of Drug Abuse). *Adolescent, peer pressure: Theory, correlates, and program implications for drug abuse or prevention.* Washington, D.C.: U.S. Government Printing Office, 1981.

U.S. Department of Health, Education, and Welfare. (Office of Human Development Services, Administration for Children, Youth and Families, Youth Development Bureau). *The rights and responsibilities of students: A handbook for the school community.* Washington, D.C.: U.S. Government Printing Office, 1979.

Appendix
Constitutional Amendments

Amendment I Congress shall make no law respecting an establishment of religion, or prohibiting the free exercise thereof: or abriding the freedom of speech, or of the press: or the right of the people peaceably to assemble, and to petition the Government for a redress of grievances.

Amendment IV The right of the people to be secure in their persons, houses, papers, and effects against unreasonable searches and seizures, shall not be violated, and no Warrants shall issue, but upon probable cause, supported by Oath or affirmation, and particularly describing the place to be searched, and the persons or things to be seized.

Amendment V No person shall be held to answer for a capital, or otherwise infamous crime, unless on a presentment or indictment of a Grand Jury, except in cases arising in the land or naval forces, or in the Militia, when in actual service in time of War or public danger: nor shall any person be subject for the same offense to be twice put in jeopardy of life or limb: nor shall be compelled in any criminal case to be a witness against himself, nor be deprived of life, liberty, or property, without due process of law: nor shall private property be taken for public use, without just compensation.

Amendment IX The enumeration in the Constitution, of certain rights, shall not be construed to deny or disparage others retained by the people.

Amendment X The powers not delegated to the United States by the Constitution, not prohibited by it to the States, are reserved to the States respectively, or to the people.

Amendment XIV All persons born or naturalized in the United States, and subject to the jurisdiction thereof, are citizens of the United States and of the State wherein they reside. No State shall make or enforce any law which shall abridge the privileges or immunities of citizens of the United States; nor shall any State deprive any person of life, liberty, or property, without due process of law: nor deny to any person within its jurisdiction the equal protection of the laws.

CHAPTER ELEVEN

Resources for Home and School Programs

Establishment of a resource center or library is necessary for effective school-based and home-based programs. Compile references that discuss the issues of communication, child development, health, and other topics concerning parents. Collect books, pamphlets, magazines, and media materials that cover the many aspects of working with par-

ents. This chapter is designed to furnish lists of resources for the basic parent education program.

Books form a basis for reference in a resource center, but pamphlets and short articles are very practical for parent groups. Refer to the section on organizations that furnish free or inexpensive pamphlets to obtain materials

The innovative plans for this playground reflect the creative ideas that can help all children grow into productive and happy adults.

that can be loaned on a wide scale. The size of a handout or pamphlet is less intimidating than a large book to parents who are very busy. In addition, books are expensive; you cannot have copies for everyone. Buy books for a basic library but supplement them with pamphlets and copies of articles (abide by copyright regulations). Government publications can generally be duplicated freely. Permission to make copies of articles from professional magazines can usually be obtained by writing the publisher. After copies of articles are duplicated, staple each into a file folder or back each with a piece of construction paper. Mark the folder with the name of the resource center. Classify and file the articles for easy retrieval and subsequent loan. With reference books, pamphlets, and articles you can plan and develop many diverse parent meetings.

MAJOR ANNOTATED LISTS OF MATERIALS FOR PARENT EDUCATION AND CHILD REARING

One of the best first steps a person can take when developing a school-home or home-based program is to obtain a comprehensive listing of available materials and organizations. This chapter gives an overview of materials and organizations, but annotated bibliographies devoted exclusively to the subject are more complete. The Administration for Children, Youth, and Families contracted Dingle Associates to prepare the following bibliography. It is quite complete and very useful. Check for revised editions when ordering.

An Annotated Bibliography for Child and Family Programs (U.S. Department of Health, Education, and Welfare. Administration for Children, Youth, and Families)

- Obtain from: Superintendent of Documents, U.S. Government Printing Office, Washington, DC, 20402, Stock No. 017-060-001310-3, DHEW Publication No. (OHDS) 78-31118

Parenting in 1977: A Listing from PMIC

- Obtain from: Parenting Materials Information Center, Southwest Educational Development

Laboratory, 211 East Seventh Street, Austin, TX 78701 or check your library.

For current information, write to National Center for Education in Maternal and Child Health, 38 and R Street, NW, Washington, DC 20057. For a complete listing of new books available, check *Books in Print* under subject titles, such as child development. This reference may be found in your public library. It lists books that are currently available, but you will have to determine whether the books are appropriate.

PROGRAMS HELPFUL IN DEVELOPING PARENTING SKILLS

Numerous formats have been developed to help parent educators teach parenting skills. These range from books to sound or video cassettes. The following selections illustrate the types of programs available.

Abidin, R. R. *Parenting skills workbook and training manual* (2nd ed.). New York: Human Services Press, 1982.

- A trainer's manual accompanies the workbook. The text guides parents in their behavior with children, emphasizing that the parent has an impact on the child's development. The author includes parent-child relationships including a discussion on feelings. The book is based on behavior modification principles.

Dinkmeyer, D., & McKay, G. D. *STEP (systematic training for effective parenting)*. Circle Pines, Minn.: American Guidance Service, 1982.

- This very usable set, which includes a trainer's manual, parent's manual, 10 charts, 9 posters, and 5 cassettes, can be used as a training program for parents. The authors emphasize reflective listening, problem ownership, logical and natural consequences, and "I" messages in the solving of parent-child communication (see Chapter 5).

American Guidance also has sets concerning the following:

STEP/Teen—Systematic Training for Effective Parenting of Teens

TIME—Training in Marriage Enrichment

Responsive Parenting Partners in Developing Human Potential

Strengthen Stepfamilies
PREP for Effective Family Living—Preparenting materials for students in marriage and family living classes

Ferguson-Florissant School District. *Parents as teachers project (NPAT).* Ferguson, Mo.: Ferguson-Florissant, 1985.

- This project developed excellent curriculum materials for children from birth through age 3. Described in Chapter 7, the project has been evaluated and found to be effective in increasing the very young child's aptitude. It includes guides for parents to use with their children at home. The books may be ordered from Early Childhood Education Section, Missouri Department of Elementary and Secondary Education, Box 480, Jefferson City, MO 65101 or Ferguson-Florissant School District, Parent-child Early Education Program, 1005 Waterford Drive, Florissant, MO 63033.

Frede, E. *Getting involved: Workshops for parents.* Ypsilanti, Mich.: The High/Scope Press, 1984.

- Frede developed workshops to be used by leaders in parent education programs. There is a wide range of programs, based on attitudes toward learning, play, language, reading, writing, math, science, TV, and problem solving. These programs may be used as developed or modified for use by other parent groups. The book was developed through a federal grant, so reproduction should not be a problem.

Gordon, T. *P.E.T.: Parent effectiveness training.* New York: New American Library, 1975.

- Gordon uses active listening, "I-messages," and a "no-lose" method in his program for parents. The program has been helpful for many parents in the development of communication with children (see Chapter 5).

    _____. *Leader Effectiveness Training.* New York: Bantam Books, 1980.

- In this program Gordon stresses leadership development.

Patterson, G. R. *Living with children.* Champaign, Ill.: Research Press, 1976.

- Based on a social learning theory, this text was written using a programmed format to help parents develop parenting skills.

Popkin, M. H. *Active parenting.* Atlanta, Ga.: Active Parenting, 1985.

- This parent education format contains videotapes for six sessions: (1) The Active Parent, (2)

Understanding Your Child, (3) Instilling Courage, (4) Developing Responsibility, (5) Winning Cooperation, and (6) The Democratic Family in Action. A *Parents' Handbook* and *Action Guide* accompany the tapes.

Stratton, C. *Parent and children series.* Carrboro, N.C.: Health Sciences Consortium, 1985.

- Stratton developed a series of 10 videotapes to teach parents about *Play:* (1) How to Play with a Child, (2) Helping Children Learn; *Praise and Reward* (1) The Art of Effective Praising, (2) Tangible Rewards; *Effective Limit Setting* (1) How to Set Limits, (2) Helping Children Learn to Accept Limits (3) Dealing with Noncompliance; *Handling Misbehavior* (1) Avoiding and Ignoring Misbehavior, (2) Time Out and Other Penalties, (3) Preventive Approaches.

    This program may be ordered from the Health Sciences Consortium, 103 Laurel Avenue, Carrboro, NC 27510.

PARENT-SCHOOL RELATIONSHIPS

The importance of positive parent-school relationships has been emphasized throughout this book. Other publications that discuss similar concerns and give ideas for specific issues are included here.

Bell, T. H. *Active parent concern: A new home guide to help your child in school.* Englewood Cliffs, N.J.; Prentice-Hall Publishing Co., 1976.

- Bell gives tips for strengthening families and for the education of children at home and at school.

Boehm, A. E., & White, M. A. *The parents' handbook on school testing.* New York: Teachers College Press, 1982.

- Parents need a book that helps interpret the results of tests taken by their children. Boehm and White have written that book.

Bradley, R. C. *Parent-teacher interviews.* Wolfe City, Tex.: University Press, 1971.

- This comprehensive book on parent-teacher conferences includes a series of short articles by experts on conferring with parents as well as a systematic plan for preparing for parent-teacher interviews.

Brandt, R. S. *Partners: Parents and schools.* Alexandria, Va.: Association for Supervision and Curriculum Development, 1979.

- This booklet is a compilation of articles on parent-school relationships.

Brigham Young University Press (Ed.). *How to involve parents in early childhood education.* Salt Lake City: Brigham Young University Press, 1982.

- Brigham Young publishes quite a number of books on early childhood, parenting, and parent involvement. They offer good material on parent education.

Brim, O. G., Jr. *Education for child rearing.* New York: Free Press, 1965.

- Brim wrote this classic on parent education for Russell Sage Foundation in the 1950s. The material is still quite relevant for professionals concerned with parent education. The appendix includes the history of education for child rearing. The main body of the book discusses the nature and aims of parent education, influence of parent on child, causes of parent behavior, and methods for education programs.

Canady, R. L., & Seyfaith, J. T. *How parent teacher conferences build partnerships.* Bloomington, Ind.: Phi Delta Kappan, 1979.

- This is a short book on parent-teacher conferences and their ability to be used to develop working partnerships with parents.

Chinn, P. C., Winn, J., & Walters, R. H. *Two-way talking with parents of special children: A process of positive communication.* St. Louis: C. V. Mosby, 1978.

- This book contains an excellent discussion of the communication process and its importance in education.

Croft, D. J. *Parents and teachers: A resource book for home, school, and community relations.* Belmont, Calif.: Wadsworth Publishing, 1979.

- This book fills the need for a practical guide for the early childhood educator. It contains program ideas and information and suggestions for improving communication with parents of young children.

Curran, D. *In the beginning there were the parents. Discussion guide.* Minneapolis: Winston Press, 1980.

- This book is an inexpensive guide to discussion of parenting.

D'Evelyn, J. *Individual parent-teacher conferences.* New York: Bureau Publications, Teachers College Press, 1963.

- Parent conferences are illustrated through conference narratives with suggestions included for improved communication.

Gordon, I. J., & Breivogel, W. *Building effective home-school relationships.* Boston: Allyn & Bacon, 1976.

- This book systematically shows how a home-based program for young children was established and directed.

Hefferman, H., & Todd, V. E. *Elementary teachers' guide to working with parents.* West Nyack, N.Y.: Parker Publishing, 1961.

- This book discusses conferences, handling different conference situations, securing parent involvement, and working with socioeconomically disadvantaged children.

Honig, A. *Parent involvement in early childhood education.* Washington, D.C.: Association for the Education of Young Children, 1979.

- Honig discusses parent involvement and parent education based on research projects and demonstration programs that involve parents in the education of their young children.

Hymes, J. L. *Effective home-school relations.* Sierra Madre, Calif.: Southern California Association for the Education of Young Children, 1974.

- This easily read book discusses elementary school parents and the schools. There is a resource list for materials in the bibliography.

Kawin, E. *Basic concepts for parents: Parenthood in a free nation.* New York: Purdue University, 1969.

- Kawin wrote a series of books including the *Basic concepts for parents, Early & middle childhood* and *Later childhood & adolescence.* All are designed for parent education courses. These well-written guides stress the responsibilities of raising children in a democracy.

Kroth, R. L. *Communicating with parents of exceptional children.* Denver: Love Publishing, 1985.

- The title depicts the theme of the book, but many of the ideas can be used with parents of average children as well.

Kroth, R. L., & Simpson, R. L. *Parent conferences as a teaching strategy.* Denver: Love Publishing, 1975.

- Communication, conferences, and preparing reports for parents are emphasized. Although the book is directed to parents of exceptional children, many of the suggestions are relevant to teachers and parents of the average child.

Lane, M. B. *Education for parenting.* Washington, D.C.: National Association for the Education of Young Children, 1975.

- Lane's work with the Cross-cultural Family Centre in San Francisco was the impetus for this book devoted to parent education. She stresses the need to approach each parent and parent group according to locality and socioeconomic needs. With "self insight and human relations" parent groups can overcome barriers of ethnic, social, and economic differences.

Larrick, N. *A parent's guide to children's reading* (6th ed.). New York: Westminister Press, 1983.

- This is an inexpensive paperback that teachers and administrators can give parents to guide them in home activities. Written first in 1958, this book is a classic and is as good as when it was first written.

Lyons, P., Robbins, A., & Smith, A. *Involving parents: A handbook for participation in schools.* Ypsilanti, Mich.: The High/Scope Press, 1983.

- The authors did a study on parent involvement and federal programs. From this study, they chose ideas and findings, divided into five functional areas—project governance, instruction, noninstructional support, community-school relations, and parent education. They prepared a book that discusses activities, forms, and information based on the various programs.

Miller, M. S., & Baker, S. S. *Straight talk to parents.* New York: Stein & Day, 1976.

- This book provides guidance to parents in their relationship with schools.

Morrison, G. S. *Parent involvement in the home, school, and community.* Columbus, Oh.: Charles E. Merrill, 1978.

- This book on home-school relationships is primarily geared for young children and Home Start programs.

Nedler, S. E., & McAfee, O. D. *Working with parents.* Belmont, Calif.: Wadsworth Publishing, 1979.

- This book gives an overview of parent involvement in elementary and early childhood programs. It discusses both school-parent involvement and home delivery programs.

Newmark, G. *This school belongs to you and me.* New York: Hart Publishing, 1976.

- Newmark gives many tips on establishing schools where administrators, teachers, and parents work as effective teams.

Rich, D., & Mattox, B. *101 activities for building more effective school-community involvement.* Washington, D.C.: Home and School Institute, Trinity College, 1976.

- Each page of the book gives an idea or activity that schools and parents can use to build more effective relationships. Sample suggestions include a book swap, museum visit, cross-age tutoring, and class cookbook.

Swick, K. *Inviting parents into the young child's world.* Champaign, Ill.: Stipes, 1984.

- Swick clearly discusses children's need to have continuity and support from all those around them. Swick relates his discussion to the realities of today's society and the child's world.

Turnbull, A. P., & Turnbull, H. R. (Eds.). *Parents speak out.* Columbus, Oh.: Charles E. Merrill, 1984.

- Parents, who are also professionals, write of their experiences with their mentally retarded, autistic, or otherwise handicapped children.

BOOKS ON CHILD REARING

As teachers and parents work together, questions concerning child development and child rearing arise and need answers. This occurs in parent-teacher conferences and during school visits, as well as in parent education groups. Schools should have a library in their resource center that relates to parent education. Parent resource centers, libraries for parent education, and school libraries need to be well stocked with literature, pamphlets, and books relating to parenting and "questions parents ask." Suggested resources follow:

Child Rearing

Abraham, W. *Living with preschoolers.* Phoenix, Ariz.: O'Sullivan Woodside, 1976.

- Advice on many questions that affect parents is given in this easily read book. Topics include the single-parent family, the only child, television viewing, and discipline.

Beaty, J. J. *Observing development of the young child.* Columbus, Oh.: Charles E. Merrill, 1986.

- The author includes child skills checklists in the study of child development. Written in conversational style, this child development book may be used by parents as well as teachers.

Bettelheim, B. *Dialogues with mothers.* New York: Avon, 1971.

- Bettelheim reflects psychoanalytic theories in his answers to parents.

Bigner, J. J. *Parent-child relations*. New York: Macmillan, 1985.

- Bigner's book, attractively illustrated, explores the process of interaction between parents and children during the child-rearing period.

Brazelton, T. B. *Toddlers and parents*. New York: Dell Publishing, 1975.

- Brazelton includes a discussion of working parents, single parents, and the problems of coping with demanding, hyperactive, and withdrawn toddlers. Written in an easily read style, this book allows parents of toddlers to identify with the situations.

_____. *Infants and mothers*. New York: Dell Publishing, 1983.

- Brazelton describes three infants—quiet, active, and average—as they interact with their parents. The book is written in a descriptive style that enables inexperienced parents to gain a feeling for the newborn and the variations that occur in child rearing.

Briggs, D. C. *Your child's self-esteem*. Garden City, N.Y.: Dolphin Books, 1975.

- This book supports parents in their approach to child rearing and illustrates how they can build self-esteem and self-respect in their children.

Chess, S., Thomas, A., & Birch, H. G. *Your child is a person: A psychological approach to parenthood without guilt*. New York: Penguin, 1977.

- The authors are supportive of parents in their roles of caregivers. Child development is studied in nine stages, from infancy on. The child's personality develops during the interaction of the unique individual and the environment. The parents, as a part of the child's environment, are important in the child's development, and methods to help the parent provide a nurturing environment are provided.

Comer, J. P., & Poussaint, A. F. *Black child care, how to bring up a healthy black child in America: A guide to psychological and emotional development*. New York: Simon & Schuster, 1975.

- This book is a practical book on child rearing for black parents. The format uses questions and answers to cover the material. The book is good for parents and professionals of all ethnic backgrounds.

Dodson, F. *How to parent*. New York: Signet Books, 1973.

- The book, based on psychologic theories, discusses child rearing and gives practical advice to parents on parenting practices.

Duvall, E. M. *Handbook for parents*. Nashville, Tenn.: Broadman Press, 1974.

- Duvall bases her book on goals and responsibilities of parenthood. The issues that face families as they rear children, infancy through adolescence, are explored.

Fraiberg, S. H. *The magic years: Understanding and handling problems of early childhood*. New York: Scribner's, 1968.

- This book concentrates on the child from infancy through 6 years of age. Emotional issues that arise during this period are discussed in an easily read manner. Issues include imagination, reality, sex education, and development of a conscience.

Ginott, H. G. *Between parent and child. New solutions to old problems*. New York: Avon, 1969.

- Ginott emphasizes reflective listening and open communication lines as necessary ingredients to productive child-parent relationships.

_____. *Between parent and teen-ager*. New York: Avon, 1973.

- The author writes in a style that promotes understanding on the part of parent and teen-ager. Communication that is open establishes an understanding that allows parent and teen-ager to develop a process of cooperation and/or coping behavior.

Gordon, I. J. *Baby learning through baby play*. New York: St. Martin's Press, 1970.

- This book is restricted to infancy through toddlerhood. Games and activities for parents to use with their infants are described. The author recommends that the activities be enjoyed by both parents and child.

Harrison-Ross, P., & Wyden, B. *The black child*. New York: Berkeley Publishing, 1974.

- The subtitle, *A parent's guide to raising happy and healthy children*, illustrates the tone of the book. It is a guide to help black parents rear their children to be liberated emotionally and socially.

Kelly, J. *Solving your child's behavior problems*. Boston: Little, Brown & Co., 1983.

- Kelly advises parents on techniques for reducing unacceptable behavior in young children. Praise and encouragement are suggested with easy-to-follow directions that help parents implement behavior modification.

Klein, C. *The myth of the happy child.* New York: Harper & Row, 1975.

- The author interviewed children ages 3 to 13 about their feelings. From the interviews and findings in psychology it is shown that emotions such as guilt, anger, shame, and loneliness are common in all children.

Leach, P. *Your baby and child.* New York: Knopf, 1978.

- The book discusses the stages of development in young children, birth to 5 years of age. The author gives very clear and specific guidance for helping the parent answer questions related to children.

_____. *The child care encyclopedia: A parents' guide to the physical and emotional well-being of children from birth to adolescence.* New York: Knopf, 1984.

- Leach wrote this book to include the whole stage of childhood. She covers a longer period of the child's life, from birth to adolescence, and discusses the emotional as well as the physical well-being of the child.

Markun, P. M. *Parenting.* Washington, D.C.: Association for Childhood Education International, 1973.

- A booklet published by ACEI on death, divorce, television, and grandparents focuses on child rearing as a community responsibility.

Pearce, J. C. *Magical child.* New York: Bantam, 1977.

- The author looks at the child's life from the child's point of view, beginning with the birthing process. He examines the child's rights and needs and discusses how a child feels and reacts to life's experiences.

Salk, L. *What every child would like his parents to know.* New York: Warner, 1973.

- This title sets the tone for the book. Salk discusses how parents can help their children develop emotional health.

_____. *Preparing for parenthood.* New York: Bantam Books, 1980.

- Salk writes a book for new parents. In it, the reader finds clarification of feelings about pregnancy, childbirth, and new babies.

Schickedanz, J., Schickedanz, D., & Forsyth, P. *Toward understanding children.* Boston: Little, Brown & Co., 1982.

- This book on human development covers infancy through adolescence. It is written from a contemporary point of view.

Spock, B. *Dr. Spock talks with mothers.* Boston: Houghton-Mifflin, 1955.

- If written today the book's title would probably be *Dr. Spock Talks with Parents.* This book is easily understood and relevant to questions parents ask. This type of book helps parent groups as they search for answers to specific problems.

_____. *Problems of parents.* New York: Fawcett, 1962.

- This book addresses itself to problems of child rearing.

_____. *Rearing children in a difficult time* (rev. ed.). New York: W. W. Norton, 1985.

- Spock responded to the troubled times of the 1960s and 1970s with a book that helps parents with difficult decisions. Included are control of children, adolescence and rebellion, sex education, drugs, divorce, and discussion of families and family values.

Spock, B., & Rothenberg, M. B. *Baby and child care* (rev. ed.). New York: Pocket Books, 1985.

- Spock's classic on child rearing covers everything from health to discipline.

Stone, L. J., & Church, J. *Childhood and adolescence.* New York: Random House, 1979.

- This classic, first written in 1957, was revised in 1979, and the material within is both comprehensive and updated. Discussions on children range from the newborn to the adolescent and after, but the book focuses primarily on the infant and young child. This book is most useful as a reference.

Swick, K., & Duff, R. E. *Involving children in parenting-caring experiences.* Dubuque, Iowa: Kendall/Hunt Publishing Co., 1982.

- Swick and Duff wrote a pleasant book that brings out the importance of a caring and sharing relationship between parent and child.

U.S. Department of Health, Education, and Welfare. Washington, D.C.: U.S. Government Printing Office.

- Send for the most recent publication list from the government and order a series of booklets on child rearing. Include these in your resource library for parents. The booklets are written in a clear and concise style. Some current publications include: *Infant care/elcuidado el su bebe; Prenatal care; Your child from 1 to 6; Your child from 1 to 3; Your child from 6 to 12;* and *Your child from 3 to 4.*

White, B. L. *The first three years of life.* Englewood Cliffs, N.J.: Prentice-Hall, 1975.

* White divides the first 36 months into seven development stages. Within each stage he gives a comprehensive discussion of intellectual, emotional, and physical development. The book also includes advice on child rearing based on social learning theory and appropriate toys and materials that enrich the child's world.

Zimbardo, P., and Radl, S. *The shy child.* New York: McGraw-Hill, 1981.

* The authors discuss the parenting style that encourages self-confidence in a child. Based on the causes of shyness, the book provides methods for helping build the child's self-esteem and reducing shyness.

Raising Children in the United States

Curran, D. *Traits of a healthy family.* Minneapolis: Winston Press, 1983.

* This book has become a best seller. It focuses on the strengths of the family, listing and discussing 15 traits that healthy families have. Parent groups enjoy discussing the traits of the healthy family, and they learn in the process.

————. *Stress and the healthy family.* Minneapolis: Winston Press, 1985.

* Curran's easy-to-read book discusses the stress the average family faces in everyday living.

LeMasters, E. E. *Parents in modern America.* Homewood, Ill.: Dorsey Press, 1977.

* Written in an easy style, the book documents the factors that influence families as they rear children and the ensuing relation to the children's personalities and health.

Swick, K. *Involving children in parenting/caring experiences.* Dubuque, Iowa: Kendall/Hunt Publishing Co., 1982.

* Swick has written a number of books that relate to children, families, and society. Check for his other books as well as this. He writes in an easy-to-read style, and this book could be used with parent groups.

Talbot, N. B. *Raising children in modern America.* Boston: Little, Brown & Co., 1976.

* The subtitle, *What parents and society should be doing for their children,* tells the tale. Talbot analyzes needs that are not being met by society.

Vaughn, V. C., III, & Brazelton, B. T. (Eds.) *The family—Can it be saved?* Chicago: Yearbook Medical Publishers, 1976.

* This book covers television, violence, medicine, education, and philosophy as they impinge on child rearing.

The Working Mother

Harrell, J., & Pizzo, P. (Eds.). *Mothers in paid employment.* Washington, D.C.: Day Care and Child Development Council, 1973.

* The Day Care and Child Development Council produced a book of readings dealing with the everyday issues of working and caring.

Kuzma, K. *Working mothers: How to have a career and be a good parent, too.* Los Angeles: Stratford Press, 1981.

* This source book for working mothers offers suggestions for solving many problems such as finding child care and handling fatigue and family disruptions.

The Stepparent

Maddox, B. *The half-parent experience.* New York: M. Evans & Co., 1975.

* The author discusses the issues involved in being a stepparent as well as those connected with caring for children other than one's own.

Visher, E. B., & Visher, J. S. *How to win as a stepfamily.* Chicago: Contemporary Books, 1983.

* The Vishers, recognized authorities on stepparenting, have written a book on the positive methods to use to have a winning stepfamily.

Discipline—Behavior or Misbehavior

Association for Childhood Education International. *Toward self-discipline: A guide for parents and educators.* Wheaton, Md.: ACEI, 1981.

* This booklet gives pointers on effective discipline.

Becker, W. C., & Becker, J. W. *Parents are teachers.* Champaign, Ill.: Research Press, 1971.

* *Parents Are Teachers* is a child management program that tells parents how to use positive reinforcement and punishment to change behavior problems.

Cherry, C. *Please don't sit on the kids: Alternatives to punitive discipline.* Belmont, Calif.: Pitman Learning, 1982.

- Cherry, author of many excellent children's books, talks about discipline. She has workable alternatives to punitive discipline.

Dodson, F. *How to discipline—with love.* New York: New American Library, 1978.

- This book was recommended by parents who felt it was very helpful to them.

Dreikurs, R. *Discipline without tears.* New York: Dutton, 1974.

- Dreikurs uses a system of consequences based on Adlerian psychology with the result of making children become responsible for their actions. Logical and natural consequences related to a child's actions form a basis for discipline and guidance.

Dreikurs, R., & Soltz, V. *Children: The challenge.* New York: Dutton, 1964.

- This book offers parents an approach to working with children. It supports parents in their development of guidelines for children's behavior.

Krumholtz, J. D., & Krumholtz, H. B. *Changing children's behavior.* Englewood Cliffs, N.J.: Prentice-Hall, 1972.

- This book guides parents and teachers in the process of changing the child's behavior. Many examples of behavior and misbehavior are used as illustrations.

Macht, J. *Teaching our children.* New York: Wiley & Sons, 1975.

- This is an easily read book that emphasizes behavior modification as a tool to teaching.

Simon, S. B., & Olds, S. W. *Helping your child learn right from wrong: A guide to values clarification.* New York: Simon & Schuster, 1977.

- Value clarification and understanding one's own motives and attitudes helps in the development of responsibility. Children learn to examine problem solving and develop their own system of values.

Fathers

Biller, H., & Meredith, D. *Father power.* New York: David McKay, 1974.

- This book discusses the father's role in the home and the ways in which a father can be a strong contributing member of the family.

Dodson, F. *How to father.* New York: Signet Books, 1975.

- Dodson, who wrote *How to Parent* in 1970, added this publication to cover the father's role more adequately. Practical material on fathering and information on older children are included in this book.

Green, M. *Life without fathering.* New York: McGraw-Hill, 1976.

- Green supports the father as a significant caregiver in the rearing of children.

Lamb, M. E. (Ed.). *The role of the father in child development.* New York: Wiley & Sons, 1976.

- Based on research and studies on children, articles were selected from many authorities in the field. They conclude that fathers are important to the psychologic development of children.

Lynn, D. B. *The father—his role in child development.* Monterey, Calif.: Brookes/Cole Publishing, 1974.

- Lynn's book covers controversial and significant research as it relates to the father's role. Sex-typing, social adjustment, and socialization of children are examined.

Divorce and the Single Parent

Arnold, W. V., Baird, D. M., Langan, J. T., & Vaughn, E. B. *Divorce: Prevention or survival.* Philadelphia: Westminister, 1977.

- This small book discusses ways to thoroughly examine options before divorce. Suggestions are also offered for those who are divorced.

Cherlin, A. J. *Marriage, divorce, remarriage.* Cambridge, Mass.: Harvard University Press, 1981.

- This book does not solve all the problems of divorce, but it analyzes the trends of families in the United States by discussing social change and social thought.

Despert, J. L. *Children of divorce.* New York: Doubleday, 1953.

- Although his is not a new book, Despert's discussion of the impact of divorce on children is still relevant and meaningful.

Gardner, R. A. *The boys and girls book about one-parent families.* New York: Putnam, 1978.

- Gardner has written several books about divorce, one-parent families, and fairy-tales for today's families. All are designed to help the child survive today's turmoil and change.

Greif, C. L. *Single fathers.* Lexington, Mass.: Lexington Books, 1985.

- Greif includes case studies and family profiles to describe the life of the single father, the family before the divorce, the divorce, custody, balancing work and child rearing, and relationships.

Grollman, E. *Talking about divorce and separation.* Boston: Beacon Press, 1976.

- This book has an illustrated story that is to be read with the children along with a guide that helps the adult be responsive to the child's responses.

Klein, C. *The single parent experience.* New York: Avon, 1974.

- Single parents need a support system and a means of coping with child rearing alone. This book discusses these issues.

Spilke, F. *What about the children?* New York: Crown Publishers, 1980.

- Spilke wrote three books on divorce. This one is a divorced parent's handbook. The other two are for the children. *The Family That Changed* is a primer for the very young; *What About Me?* is a guide for young people.

Weiss, R. S. *Going it alone.* New York: Basic Books, 1979.

- Weiss examines the social situation of the woman or man who is the custodial parent. He discusses how custodial parents can establish a new life in the community and also develop a satisfactory personal life for themselves and their children.

Parenting for Teen-agers

Gordon, S., & Wollin, M. *Parenting: A guide for young people.* New York: William H. Sadler, 1975.

- This text discusses the issues involved in parenting. Written for young people, it is easily read and geared for high school parenting courses.

Howard, M. *Only human: Teen-age pregnancy and parenthood.* New York: Seabury Press, 1975.

- The author wrote this book to fill a need for young parents in their quest for answers. The questions are explored through three kinds of parental situations.

Health and Nutrition

American Academy of Pediatrics. *Standards of child health care.* Evanston, Ill.: American Academy of Pediatrics, 1972.

- This reference was produced by the academy and contains the knowledge and approved practices of that prestigious organization.

Castle, S. *The complete guide to preparing baby foods at home.* New York: Doubleday, 1973.

- Parents may use this reference to help in preparing food for infants.

Davis, A. *Let's have healthy children* (rev. ed.). New York: Signet, 1981.

- This book focuses on nutrition for children.

Deutsch, R. M. *Realities of nutrition.* Palo Alto, Calif.: Bull Publishing, 1976.

- Deutsch considers questions about nutrition and discusses basic principles related to diet. The book includes special chapters on carbohydrates, proteins, amino acids, fats, vitamins, minerals, and the scientific art of eating.

Endres, J. B., & Rockwell, R. E. *Food, nutrition, and the young child* (rev. ed.). Columbus, Oh.: Merrill Publishing, 1985.

- This practical book examines nutrition and dietary guides and standards. It focuses on the role of nutrition in early childhood programs and provides basic concepts about food and nutrition, suggestions for menus, methods of interrelating curriculum and basic nutrient concepts, and suggestions for working with parents.

Feinbloom, R., & Boston Children's Medical Center. *Child health encyclopedia.* New York: Delacorte Press, 1975.

- If you do not find this book under Feinbloom, look for it under the Boston Children's Medical Center. It is a comprehensive book, 561 pages in length, that answers many questions about rearing children. It describes illness, childhood diseases, and preventive health care for the parent's use.

Feingold, B. F., & Feingold, H. S. *The Feingold cookbook for hyperactive children.* New York: Random House, 1979.

- Although parent groups must keep in mind the differences surrounding Feingold's theories, they might also like to discuss these controversies about food and hyperactivity. This book is filled with recipes and ideas for additive-free and salicylate-free meals.

Green, M. I. *A Sigh of relief: First aid handbook for childhood emergencies* (rev. ed.). New York: Bantam Press, 1984.

- This handbook gives needed information on first aid, good for everyday care and emergencies.

Hatfield, A., & Stanton, P. *How to help your child eat right: A fun cookbook and guide to good nutrition.* Washington, D.C.: Acropolis Books, 1978.

- This book includes ideas for fixing attractive meals for children.

Lansky, B., et al. *Free stuff.* Wazzata, Minn.: Meadowbrook Press, 1980.

- This booklet gives recipes and lists 250 companies to which you may write for free or inexpensive booklets about nutrition and food preparation.

Reuben, D. *Everything you always wanted to know about nutrition.* New York: Avon Books, 1979.

- In a question-answer format, Reuben discusses many of the controversial concerns about nutrition—vitamins, fats, carbohydrates, proteins, minerals, and sugar.

Salk, L. *Dear Dr. Salk: Answers to your questions about your family.* New York: Warner Books, 1980.

- Dr. Salk uses a question-answer format to inform parents about their children's health and development needs.

Samuels, M., & Samuels, N. *The well child book.* New York: Summit Books, 1982.

———. *The well pregnancy book.* New York: Summit Books, 1985.

- *The Well Child Book,* a popular book on health and staying well, has been followed by *The Well Pregnancy Book.*

Smith, L. *Feed your kids right.* New York: Dell Books, 1980.

- Smith, a pediatrician, writes for parents about nutrition and preventive diets. He includes the nutrient connection, allergies, metabolism, and energy in his easy-to-read discussions.

U.S. Department of Health and Human Services and U.S. Department of Education. *Food.* Pueblo, Colo.: Consumer Information Center, 1979.

- A guide to better diet with information about snacking, recipes, calorie counter, and nutritional information. These departments also furnish many other booklets concerning health and nutrition. Write to the Consumer Information Center, Pueblo, CO 81009 for a copy of the Consumer Information Catalog. Educators, libraries, and consumer and other nonprofit groups who wish 25 copies of their quarterly catalog on consumer information may get on the mailing list. Articles and booklets cover information from 30 agencies of the federal government. More than half of these articles are free.

CHILD ABUSE

The increasing amount of child abuse and neglect in the United States makes it necessary for all parents to recognize the problems. Parents who abuse need to know the resources available to them. All parents need to understand the realities of the times and the programs available to help them cope with abuse problems.

Sexual Abuse

Adams, C., & Fay, J. *No more secrets: Protecting your child from sexual assault.* San Luis Obispo, Calif.: Impact Publishers, 1981.

- Parents have found this to be a valuable book because it offers an approach to use in the prevention of the sexual abuse of their children.

Committee for Children. *Prevention of child abuse: A trainer's manual.* Seattle: Committee for Children, 1984.

- Committee for Children is a nonprofit organization designed to provide training and information that will help reduce violence against children. It has developed training material that gives a complete list of available resources, in-service training, preventive education, identification and reporting. Two curricula, *Talking about Touching* and *Talking about Touching with Preschoolers,* use laminated photographs and accompanying lessons to teach children how to handle situations. Information may be obtained by writing Committee for Children, 172 20th Avenue, Seattle, WA 98122.

Herman, J. L. *Father-daughter incest.* Cambridge, Mass.: Harvard University Press, 1981.

- This book analyzes the sexual abuse problem based on clinical experience with incest victims.

Kempe, C. H., & Kempe, R. *The common secret: Sexual abuse of children and adolescents.* San Francisco: W. H. Freeman, 1984.

- Kempe was one of the first to inform people about the prevalence of child abuse. In this book, he and his wife discuss the concerns and issues of sexual abuse.

Kent, C. *Child sexual abuse prevention project: An educational program for children.* Minneapolis: Sexual Assault Services, n.d.

- A program entitled *Child Sexual Abuse Prevention Project: An Educational Program for Children* was tested on 800 children in the Minneapolis public schools. The training manual is available from Sexual Assault Services, Hennepin County Attorney's Office, C-2100 Government Center, Minneapolis, MN 55487.

Kraizer, S. K. *The safe child book.* New York: Health Education Systems, 1985.

- The author has developed a training program, *Children Need to Know,* that has been presented to thousands of children and was featured in the television program, *Saying No to Strangers.* This program can be obtained by writing P.O. Box 1235, New York, NY 10116.

May, G. *Understanding sexual child abuse.* Chicago: National Committee for Prevention of Child Abuse, 1979.

- This book describes the offender and the victim. It also describes the various types of abuse that may be perpetrated against a child.

U.S. Department of Health and Human Services. (Office of Human Development Services, Administration for Children, Youth and Families, Children's Bureau, National Center on Child Abuse and Neglect.) *Child sexual abuse: Incest, assault and sexual exploitation.* Washington, D.C.: U.S. Government Printing Office, 1981.

- This government publication provides an overview of techniques for prevention and treatment of sexual abuse on children.

Physical Abuse and Neglect Resources

American Humane Association. *National analysis of official child neglect and abuse reporting.* Denver: American Humane Association, 1986.

- Each year the American Humane Association publishes a report of the incidence of reported child abuse cases in the United States.

Antler, S. (Ed.) *Child abuse and child protection; Policy and practice.* Silver Springs, Md.: National Association of Social Workers, 1982.

- This book, published by social workers, contains a series of articles pertaining to child abuse, ranging from the definition of the problem to strategies for dealing with the violence. It discusses treating the abused and the abuser as well as protecting the child protective worker.

Ebeling, N. B., & Hill, D. A. (Eds.). *Child abuse and neglect.* Littleton, Mass.: John Write PSG, 1983.

- This book is intended for social workers and those who give service to families. Written by professionals from the Boston area and the British Isles, it covers a wide range of information from home visits to assessment and treatment. It includes case studies, treatment of the child, and integration of individual and family therapy.

Fontana, V. J. *Somewhere a child is crying: Maltreatment—causes and prevention.* New York: New American Library, 1976.

- Fontana has written several excellent books on the subject of child abuse. They give good background information.

Green, M. R. (Ed.). *Violence and the family.* Boulder: Westview Press, 1981.

- The American Association for the Advancement of Science held a symposium on which this book was based. It includes material that is not found in other texts such as television viewing, family style, and cultural differences.

Kempe, C. H., & Helfer, R. E. (Ed.). *The battered child* (3rd rev. enlarged ed.). Chicago: University of Chicago Press, 1982.

- Kempe and Helfer were early pioneers in the field of child abuse. Their books are excellent references.

Newberger, E. H. (Ed.) *Child abuse.* Boston: Little, Brown and Company, 1982.

- Newberger selected 14 professionals to write chapters for this book on child abuse. The information ranges from the social context of child abuse to principles and ethics of practice. Information based on medical expertise is included.

U.S. Department of Health, Education, and Welfare (Office of Human Development Services, Administration for Children, Youth and Families, Children's Bureau, National Center on Child Abuse and Neglect). *A curriculum on child abuse and neglect.*

Leader's manual. Washington, D.C.: U.S. Government Printing Office, 1979.

- The U.S. Government Printing Office has published an enormous amount of excellent materials on child abuse and neglect. This leader's manual is a comprehensive text on teaching others about child abuse and neglect.

U.S. Department of Health, Education, and Welfare (Office of Human Development Services, Administration for Children, Youth and Families, Head Start Bureau). *Child abuse and neglect: A self-instructional text for Head Start personnel.* Washington, D.C.: U.S. Government Printing Office, 1980.

- This self-instructional text is excellent to use with anyone who works in a child care center or school. It is easily used, self-correcting, and easily read.

Centers and Associations Concerned with Child Abuse

American Humane Association
9725 East Hampden Avenue
Denver, CO 80231

C. Henry Kempe National Center for Prevention and Treatment of Child Abuse and Neglect
1205 Oneida
Denver, CO 80220

National Center on Child Abuse and Neglect
Children's Bureau, ACYF
Department of Health and Human Services
P.O. Box 1182
Washington, DC 20013

National Coalition against Domestic Violence
1500 Massachusetts Avenue NW #35
Washington, DC 20005

National Center for Prevention of Child Abuse
332 South Michigan Avenue, Suite 1250
Chicago, IL 60604

NCCAN Child Abuse Clearinghouse
Aspen Systems
1600 Research Boulevard
Rockville, MD 20850

Parents Anonymous
7120 Franklin Avenue
Los Angeles, CA 90046

PUBLICATION SOURCES FROM ORGANIZATIONS AND AGENCIES ON CHILD REARING AND PARENT EDUCATION

The following organizations and government agencies publish periodicals, pamphlets, and booklets that can be used for a parent resource center. Articles range from prenatal care to adolescent motherhood. Write to these agencies for current publications lists.

Alexander Graham Bell Association for Deaf
3417 Volta Place
Washington, DC 20007

American Academy of Child Psychiatry
3615 Wisconsin Avenue
Washington, DC 20016

American Academy of Pediatrics
P.O. Box 927
141 Northwest Point Road
Elk Grove Village, IL 60007

American Alliance for Health, Physical Education, Recreation, and Dance
1900 Association Drive
Reston, VA 22091

American Association for Adult and Continuing Education
1201 16th Street, NW, Suite 230
Washington, DC 20036

American Association for Maternal and Child Health
233 Prospect
La Jolla, CA 92037

American Association of Psychiatric Services for Children
1001 Connecticut Avenue
Washington, DC 20036

American Foundation for the Blind
15 West Sixteenth Street
New York, NY 10011

American Home Economics Association
2010 Massachusetts Avenue NW
Washington, DC 20036

American Humane Association
9725 East Hampden
Denver, CO 80231

American Library Association
50 East Huron Street
Chicago, IL 60611

American Montessori Society
175 Fifth Ave
New York, NY 10010

American Speech and Hearing Association
10801 Rockville Place
Rockville, MD 20852

Appalachian Educational Laboratory
P.O. Box 1348
Charleston, WV 25325

Association for Childhood Education International
11141 Georgia Avenue, Suite 200
Wheaton, MD 20902

Association for Children and Adults with Learning
Disabilities
4156 Library Road
Pittsburgh, PA 15234

Association for Retarded Children
P.O. Box 6109
Arlington, TX 76011

C. Henry Kempe National Center for Prevention
and Treatment of Child Abuse and Neglect
1205 Oneida
Denver, CO 80220

Children's Defense Fund
1520 New Hampshire Avenue NW
Washington, DC 20036

Child Welfare League of America
67 Irving Place
New York, NY 10003

Council for Basic Education
725 Fifteenth Street NW
Washington, DC 20005

Council for Exceptional Children
1920 Association Drive
Reston, VA 22091

Council on Interracial Books for Children
1841 Broadway, Room 500
New York, NY 10023

Department of Education
400 Maryland Avenue SW
Washington, DC 20202

Education Commission of the States
300 Lincoln Tower Building
1860 Lincoln Street
Denver, CO 80295

Educational Resources Information Center, Early
Childhood Education (ERIC/ECE)
805 West Pennsylvania
Urbana, IL 61801

EPIE Institute
P.O. Box 839
Water Mill, NY 11976

Families in Action
3845 North Druid Hills Road, Suite 300
Decatur, GA 30033

Family Service Association of America
44 East Twenty-third Street
New York, NY 10010

High/Scope Educational Research Foundation
600 North River Street
Ypsilanti, MI 48197

Home and School Institute
Trinity College
Washington, DC 20017

Institute for Responsive Education
704 Commonwealth Avenue
Boston, MA 02215

International Association of Parents of the Deaf
814 Thayer Avenue
Silver Springs, MD 20910

International Reading Association
P.O. Box 8139
800 Barksdale Road
Newark, DE 17714

La Leche League International
9616 Minneapolis Avenue
Franklin Park, IL 60131

Mental Health Association
1021 Prince Street
Arlington, VA 22314

Mental Health Materials Center
30 East 29th
New York, NY 10016

National Association for the Education of Young
Children
1834 Connecticut Avenue NW
Washington, DC 20009

National Association for Hearing and Speech Action
10801 Rockville Place
Rockville, MD 20852

National Black Child Development Institute
1463 Rhode Island Avenue NW
Washington, DC 20005

National Center for Prevention of Child Abuse
332 South Michigan Avenue, Suite 1250
Chicago, IL 60604

National Center on Child Abuse and Neglect
Children's Bureau, Administration for Children,
Youth, and Families
Department of Health and Human Services
P.O. Box 1182
Washington, DC 20013

National Committee for Citizens in Education
(NCCE)
10451 Twin Rivers Road
Columbia, MD 21044

National Congress of Parents and Teachers
700 North Rush Street
Chicago, IL 60611

National Council on Family Relations
1910 West County Road B., Suite 147
St. Paul, MN 55113

National Education Association
1201 16th Street NW
Washington, DC 20036

National Institute on Drug Abuse
5600 Fishers Lane
Rockville, MD 20857

National Institute of Health
9000 Rockville Pike
Bethesda, MD 20205

National Institute of Mental Health
5600 Fishers Lane
Rockville, MD 20857

National Maternal and Child Health Clearinghouse
38th and R Streets NW
Washington, DC 20057

National Mental Health Association
1021 Prince Street
Arlington, VA 22314

National School Board Association
1055 Thomas Jefferson Street
Washington, DC 20007

National School Volunteer Program
16 Arlington Street
Boston, MA 02116

Pacer Center (handicapped child's education)
Parent Advocacy Coalition for Educational Rights
4826 Chicago Avenue South
Minneapolis, MN 55417

Public Affairs Committee
181 Park Avenue South
New York, NY 10016

Science Research Associates
259 East Erie Street
Chicago, IL 60611

Southwest Educational Development Laboratory
211 East Seventh Street
Austin, TX 78701

Superintendent of Documents
U.S. Government Printing Office
Washington, DC 20402

Sample Pamphlets from Publication Sources

The American Humane Association
9725 Hampden Avenue
Denver, CO 8231
Discipline, your child and you. This publication on
discipline and how children grow and learn is

written by a pediatrician and a psychologist, R. Blum, M.D., and L. Blum, M.A.

Guidelines for schools. This leaflet is available for schools and agencies to use in the identification of child abuse. Indicators include the child's behaviors, child's appearance, and parental attitudes. (L-5)

Neglecting parents. A study of psychosocial characteristics of neglecting parents by M. Cohen, R. Mulford, and E. Philbrick identifies problem characteristics. (No. 37)

Selected readings. This booklet includes eight selected excerpts and an annotated bibliography concerning child protection. (SR 501)

American Library Association
50 East Huron Street
Chicago, IL 60611

Information on everyday survival: What you need and where to get it (1976). A book crammed full of information compiled by P. Gotsick, S. Moore, S. Cotner, and J. Flanery, Appalachian Adult Education Center; it is included here because it gives much information that would be helpful to a parent education program.

Association for Childhood Education International
1141 Georgia Avenue, Suite 500
Wheaton, MD 20902

Bibliography of books for children (1983). Titles of books arranged by subject and age level; annotated; excellent reference.

Bits and pieces—imagination used for children's learning (1967). Creativity in the classroom developed from recycling of leftovers and throwaways.

Children and stress: Helping children cope (1982). Articles by psychologists that discuss the internal and external factors that cause stress. Edited by A. S. McNamee.

Children and TV II mediating the medium (1982). Recommends the use of TV for education purposes. Written by M. P. Winick and J. S. Wehrenberg.

Creative dramatics for all children (1973). Six principles for using creative dramatics explored by Emily Gillies; chapters on working with physically handicapped, emotionally disturbed, and second-language speaking children.

Excellent paperbacks for children (1979). Joint publication of ACEI and American Association of School Librarians; selects and annotates paperbacks for children ages 2 to 14.

Films for childhood educators (1977). Reviews films on teaching and parenting.

Growing free: Ways to help children overcome sex-role stereotypes (1976). Explores the questions and concerns of sex-free child rearing; resource list included.

On families and the re-valuing of childhood (1983). An ACEI position paper that recommends a commitment by the home/school/community to revalue the child and the family. Written by Warren Umansky.

ERIC Clearinghouse on Elementary and Early Childhood Education
College of Education
University of Illinois
Urbana, IL 61801

Cerebral dominance and its psychological and educational implications: an ERIC abstract bibliography (1978). Catalog No. 173; 22 pages.

Family/school relationships: An ERIC abstract bibliography (1978). Catalog No. 178; 30 pages.

Fathering: A bibliography (1977). Compiled by A. S. Honig; catalog No. 164; 70 pages.

Parent involvement in education (1979). A bibliography compiled by M. Henniger; catalog No. 184; 92 pages.

The visual arts and cognitive development: An annotated bibliography (1979). Compiled by W. Ives; catalog No. 185; 42 pages.

Family Service Association of America
44 East Twenty-third Street
New York, NY 10010

Family life today: Crucial issues and lasting values (1976). An issue of *Social Casework* that covers the Centennial Symposium held in May 1975; focuses on value conflicts affecting family life today.

Parent-child communication (1977). A book by D. P. Riley, K. Apgar, and J. Eaton designed to help leaders of parent education groups teach problem-solving skills and communication to parents of adolescents.

National Association for Mental Health
1800 North Kent Street
Arlington, VA 22209

Child alone in need of help. This pamphlet describes the mentally ill child, the kind of help available, and where to find it.

Depression: Dark night of the soul. This 20-page booklet describes depression, its origin, its symptoms, and its treatment.

How to deal with your tensions. This pamphlet, part of the *Learning to Cope* film package, suggests 11 ways to deal with tension. It helps people recognize when life situations have assumed crisis proportion and gives guidance on how to obtain professional help.

National Association for the Education of Young Children
1834 Connecticut Avenue NW
Washington, DC 20009

The American family: Myth and reality (1980). A. Eugene Howard describes families of today and emphasizes that the strong basis for families is connectedness. 33 pages.

Language in early childhood education (1981). C. Cazden, editor; includes a critical analysis of language programs and suggestions for helping children develop oral language; 170 pages.

More than the ABCs: The early stages of reading and writing (1985). Reading starts long before a child enters school. J. Schickedanz gives sound techniques for starting children to read.

What is quality child care (1985). In order for child care to provide for the child properly, it must be thought of as a necessary priority. Is the public willing to pay for it? Written by Bettye M. Caldwell and Asa G. Hilliard III.

National Council on Family Relations
1219 University Avenue SE
Minneapolis, MN 55414

Black families. M. Peters, guest editor. This special issue of *Journal of Marriage and the Family*, November 1978, examines the issues concerning being black and family strengths. (No. 273)

Fatherhood. J. Walters, editor. The Family Coordinator (October 1976) devoted an issue to the subject of fatherhood. (No. 271)

Non-traditional family forms in the 1970's. M. B. Sussman, editor. This paperback discusses alternate family styles. (No. 251)

NEWSLETTERS

Newsletters provide current information and ideas. Since they are concise and easy to read, they can supplement the parent education curriculum.

Active Parents
4669 Roswell Road, NE
Atlanta, GA 30342

Center for Parent Education Newsletter
55 Chapel Street
Newton, MA 02160

Citizen Action in Education
Institute for Responsive Education
605 Commonwealth Avenue
Boston, MA 02215

Cooperatively Speaking
P.O. Box 90410
Indianapolis, IN 46290-0410

CWLA Newsletter
Child Welfare League of America
67 Irving Place
New York, NY 10003

ERIC/ECE Bulletin
ERIC Clearinghouse on Early Childhood Education
Publications Office/ERIC
University of Illinois
805 West Pennsylvania Avenue
Urbana, IL 61801

Family Resource Coalition Report
230 North Michigan Avenue
Chicago, IL 60601

High Scope Resource, A Magazine for Educators
The High/Scope Press
600 North River Street
Ypsilanti, MI 48198

Home and School Institute Newsletter
1201 16th Street NW
Washington, DC 20036

IRC Newsletter (Information Resources Center)
Mental Health Materials Center
30 East 29th
New York, NY 10016

Micronotes on Children & Computers
Publications Office, ERIC/EECE
University of Illinois
805 W. Pennsylvania Avenue
Urbana, IL 61801

Newsletter of Parenting
2300 W. Fifth Avenue
P.O. Box 2505
Columbus, OH 43216-2505
Editorial address:
803 Church Street,
Honesdale, PA 18431

Nurturing News
187 Caselli Avenue
San Francisco, CA 94114

Parents-As-Partners Series
National Association for the Education of Young
Children
1834 Connecticut Avenue, NW
Washington, DC 20009-5786

Parent Talk
c/o Sunshine Press
6402 East Chapparal Road
P.O. Box 572
Scottsdale, AZ 85252

Preventing Sexual Abuse
ETR Associates, Coordinators
1700 Mission St., STE. 203
Santa Cruz, CA 95060

Prevention Notes
Committee for Children
172 20th Avenue
Seattle, WA 98122

Protecting Children
An American Humane Publication
P.O. Box 1266
Denver, CO 80201

School Age NOTES
P.O. Box 120674
Nashville, TN 37212

MAGAZINES AND JOURNALS

Magazines and journals are important because
of their relevancy and the up-to-date informa-

tion that can be found in them. The magazines,
*Beginnings, Child Care Quarterly, Children
Today, Pro-Education, Parents' Magazine
and Learning* can be purchased through sub-
scriptions or can be found at a library. The other journals are provided as part of membership
in professional organizations. They can also be
found in public libraries.

Beginnings
P.O. Box 2890
Redmond, WA 98073
• Published four times a year, this magazine focuses
  on concerns of interest for teachers of young
  children.

Black Child Advocate
National Black Child Development Institute
1463 Rhode Island Avenue NW
Washington, DC 20005
• Concerned primarily with issues of public policy
  related to black children, this monthly magazine
  also includes articles on curriculum and other subjects related to the development of the black child.

Child Care Quarterly
Behavioral Publications
72 Fifth Avenue
New York, NY 10011
• Published four times a year, this publication discusses issues concerned with providing good
  day care for children.

Child Development
Society for Research in Child Development
University of Chicago Press
5801 Ellis Avenue
Chicago, IL 60637
• This professional journal is concerned with re-
  search related to various topics in child develop-
  ment.

Childhood Education
Association for Childhood Education International
11141 Georgia Avenue, Suite 500
Wheaton, MD 20902
• Assorted articles containing information on education of young children, materials, and activities
  that encourage optimal development in children
  are included. Many of the articles contain theory
  and educational philosophy.

Children Today
Childrens' Bureau
Administration for Children, Youth, and Families
Office of Human Development

Superintendent of Documents
U.S. Government Printing Office
Washington, DC 20402

- This government magazine includes a wide selection of articles on children, birth through adolescence. The articles range from mental health, education, child care, health, and handicapped to social services and crime prevention.

Child Welfare
67 Irving Place
New York, NY 10003

- It contains both research and applied articles related to children and examines social services and policies as well as practical implementation of programs for children.

CIBC Bulletin
Council on Interracial Books for Children
1841 Broadway
New York, NY 10023

- The *CIBC Bulletin* is concerned with abolishing sexism, racism, and other forms of discrimination in reading and learning materials.

Exceptional Children
1920 Association Drive
Reston, VA 22091

- The journal for the Council for Exceptional Children contains articles related to special education and exceptional children. It provides information on materials, books, films, and legislation concerning exceptional children.

Gifted Child Quarterly
National Association for Gifted Children
4175 Lovell Road, Box 30
Circle Pines, MI 55014

- This journal for the National Association for Gifted Children contains articles on gifted children and research in the field.

Learning: The Magazine for Creative Teaching
Education Today Company
530 University Avenue
Palo Alto, CA 94301

- *Learning* includes many suggestions for implementing a creative learning environment in the school or home. It features a swap shop, ideas for learning centers, articles on innovations and strategies, and a potpourri of suggestions, concepts, and creative activities.

Mailbox
The Education Center
P.O. Box 9753
Greensboro, NC 27429

- *Mailbox* is filled with practical ideas for teaching elementary aged children with reproducible worksheets, bulletin board ideas, and games.

Parents Magazine
Bergenfield, NJ 07621

- *Parents Magazine* is a publication with a long history of providing child development articles for parents. Many of the articles pertain to young children and ways to respond to their development (e.g., discipline, sibling rivalry, and health). The format has varied during the years and in 1980 includes special features for children called "As They Grow," with articles on each age level, prenatal through age 13.

Pro-Education
5000 Park Street North
St. Petersburg, FL 33709

- *Pro-Education* is a magazine about partnerships with education. It discusses issues concerning parents, schools, and organizations concerned with education. The articles cover a wide range of interests and contributors include the Education Commission of the States, National Education Association, etc.

The Single Parent
Parents Without Partners
7910 Woodmont Avenue, Suite 1000
Bethesda, MD 20814

- Parents Without Partners publishes a journal concerned with special problems and issues confronting the single parent.

Teacher
Macmillan Professional Magazines
262 Mason Street
Greenwich, CT 06830

- *Teacher* includes articles for all age-groups and many features that are adaptable for all ages. Special departments include a creative calendar, book bonanza, television talk, early education workshop, and the creative classroom. The wide variety of ideas and discussions makes this a magazine that can be used by teachers or parents of children of all ages.

Young Children
National Association for the Education of Young Children
1834 Connecticut Avenue NW
Washington, DC 20009

- The National Association for the Education of Young Children publishes *Young Children*. In keeping with the organization's goals, the magazine is geared to parents of children (birth to 8 years) and includes a wide selection of articles related to child rearing and education.

LEARNING ACTIVITIES FOR HOME AND SCHOOL

Curriculum ideas, whether they are play activities for an infant or learning activities for an older child, are essential in a parent education program. There are many new books on the market that join the ones written earlier. Both groups have many helpful ideas. Encourage parents to develop their own library and select a cross-section of books for the parent education library.

Adcock, D., & Segal, M. *Play together, grow together.* White Plains, N.Y.: Mailman Family Press, 1983.

Baratta-Lorton, M. *Workjobs.* Menlo Park, Calif.: Addison Wesley, 1975.

————. *Workjobs for parents.* Menlo Park, Calif.: Addison Wesley, 1978.

Behrman, P., & Millman, J. *EXCEL Experience for children in learning, 1968. EXCEL II Experience for children in learning, 1976.* Cambridge, Mass.: Educators Publishing Services.

Bell, T. H. *Your child's intellect: A guide to home-based preschool education.* Salt Lake City: Olympus Publishing, 1973.

Belton, S., & Terborgh, C. *Sparks: Activities to help children learn at home.* New York: Behavioral Publications, 1972.

Bernard, J. *Joyous motherhood.* New York: Evans Publishing, 1979.

Board of Cooperative Educational Services of Nassau County. *While you're at it: 200 ways to help children learn.* Englewood Cliffs, N.J.: Prentice-Hall, 1976.

Braga, J., & Braga, L. *Children and adults: Activities for growing together.* Englewood Cliffs, N.J.: Prentice-Hall, 1978.

Burtt, K. G., & Kalstein, K. *Smart toys.* New York: Harper & Row, 1981.

Caldwell, B., et al. *Home teaching activities.* Little Rock, Ark.: Center for Early Development in Education, 1972.

Canfield, J., & Wells, H. C. *100 ways to enhance self-concept in the classroom.* Englewood Cliffs, N.J.: Prentice-Hall, 1976.

Carson, J. *The role of parents as teachers.* Philadelphia: Temple University (The Recruitment Leadership and Training Institute), 1975.

Cole, A., Hass, C., Bushness, F., & Weinberger, B. *I saw a purple cow and 100 other recipes for learning.* Boston: Little, Brown & Co., 1972.

Cole, A., et al. *Recipes for fun.* Northfield, Ill.: Parents As Resources, 1970.

Cratty, B. J. *Active learning games to enhance academic abilities.* Englewood Cliffs, N.J.: Prentice-Hall, 1971.

Croft, D., & Hess, R. D. *An activities handbook for teachers of young children* (4th ed.). New York: Houghton Mifflin, 1984.

D'Audney, W. *Calendar of developmental activities for preschoolers.* Omaha, Neb.: Meyer Children's Rehabilitation Institute, University of Nebraska Medical Center, 1975.

Dumas, E., & Schminki, C. W. *Math activities for child involvement.* Boston: Allyn & Bacon, 1971.

Fleming, B. M., Hamilton, D. S., & Hicks, J. D. *Resources for creative teaching in early childhood education.* New York: Harcourt Brace Jovanovich, 1977.

Ferguson-Florissant School District. *Parents as first teachers.* Ferguson-Florissant, Mo.: Ferguson-Florissant School District, 1985.

Gordon, I. *Baby learning through baby play: A parent's guide for the first two years.* New York: St. Martin's Press, 1970.

————. *Child learning through child play, learning activities for two and three year olds.* New York: St. Martin's Press, 1972.

Gotts, E. E. (Ed.). *Classroom learning activities. (Vol. I) Physical and social development. (Vol. II) Personal and emotional development. (Vol. III) Language and conceptual development.* Miami, Fla.: Educational Communication, n.d.

————. *Home visitor's kit.* New York: Human Science Press, 1977.

Hendrick, J. *Total learning for the whole child: Holistic curriculum for children ages 2 to 5.* St. Louis: C. V. Mosby, 1980.

Home and School Institute. *Success for children! Teaching ideas from the home and school institute.* Washington, D.C.: Trinity College, 1972.

Honig, A. *Playtime learning games for young children.* Syracuse, N.Y.: Syracuse University Press, 1982.

Jenkins, P. D. *Art for the fun of it.* Englewood Cliffs, N.J.: Prentice-Hall, 1980.

Karnes, M. B. *Helping young children develop language skills: A book of activities.* Reston, Va.: Council for Exceptional Children, 1977.

———. *Creative art for learning.* Reston, Va.: Council for Exceptional Children, 1979.

———. *Learning mathematical concepts at home.* Reston, Va.: Council for Exceptional Children, 1980.

———. *You and your small wonder: Book 1 and book 2.* New York: Random House, 1984.

Larrich, N. *A parents' guide to children's reading.* New York: Bantam Books, 1975.

Levy, J. *The baby exercise book for the first fifteen months.* New York: Pantheon Books, 1973.

McElderry, J. S., & Escobedo, L. E. *Tools for learning activities for young children with special needs.* Denver: Love Publishing, 1979.

Marzollo, J. *Supertot.* New York: Harper & Row, 1979.

Marzollo, J., & Lloyd, J. *Learning through play.* New York: Harper & Row, 1974.

Moreno, S. *Parents—teach your children to learn before they go to school.* San Diego: Moreno Educational Co., 1975.

Newman, S. *Guidelines to parent-teacher cooperation.* New York: Book-Lab, 1971. (Series of workshops for early childhood.)

Orlich, T. *The cooperative sports and game book.* New York: Pantheon Books, 1978.

Parent-Child Early Education. *Parent-child home activities for threes, some fours. A curriculum on cards for kindergarten. Learning activities for fours and fives. Skill and concept activities for threes and fours.* Ferguson, Mo.: Ferguson-Florissant School District.

Portage guide to early education. Portage, Wis.: Portage Project, CESA (Cooperative Educational Service Agency) 12, 1976.

Recruitment Leadership and Training Institute. *The role of parents as teachers.* Washington, D.C.: U.S. Government Printing Office, 1975.

Rich, D., & Jones, C. *A family affair: Education.* Washington, D.C.: Home and School Institute, Trinity College, 1977.

Stein, S. G. *New parents' guide to early learning.* New York: New American Library, 1976.

Turner, T. N. *Creative activities resource book for elementary school teachers.* Reston, Va.: Reston Publishing, 1978.

U.S. Department of Health and Human Services. Office of Human Development Services, Administration for Children, Youth and Families, Head Start Bureau. *Getting involved.* Washington, D.C.: U.S. Government Printing Office, 1981. *Getting Involved* is a series of books that includes titles such as *Your Child and TV, Your Child and Reading, Your Child and Language, Your Child and Math, Your Child and Writing,* and *Your Child and Science.*

Wile, E. M. *What to teach your child.* Elizabethtown, Pa.: Continental Press, 1978.

New Materials

There has been a wealth of new pamphlets and books developed in the last few years. These are distributed by publishers and distribution centers.

Gryphon House
3706 Otis Street, P.O. Box 275
Mt. Rainier, MD 20712

- Gryphon House sends a resource catalog that lists the new books that they distribute. There are home learning ideas galore!

Toys 'n Things Press
906 North Dale Street
St. Paul, MN 55103

- Toys 'n Things Press, a division of Resources for Child Caring, supplies a catalog with learning activities books.

FILMS ON CHILD DEVELOPMENT AND PARENTING

Films are valuable sources of information and can serve as catalysts of discussion and questions. Because humans learn through all the senses, a multisensory approach to teaching reaches more of the audience. A follow-up workshop after a film encourages even more sensory involvement with touch and smell available to reinforce the learning concepts. Films should not be used as a substitute for preparation. In order to achieve the most from films, they should be previewed, and program plans should be developed. The leader should prepare some questions and interesting comments for use prior to and after the film presentation. Have a short discussion prior to the showing of the film to point out important concepts to look for and arouse interest. It is sometimes valuable to be able to stop the film during the presentation in order to discuss particular points. A discussion following the film helps clarify any questions and solidify the learning.

Modern Talking Picture Films

During the 1960s many films were developed for use by Head Start. These films were distributed on a free-loan basis through the libraries of the Modern Talking Picture Services to schools, child care centers, colleges, and other groups working with children. Some of these films may still be available for distribution, but MTP has stopped issuing them. At present MTP has the following films available. Write Modern Talking Picture Services, 5000 Park Street North, St. Petersburg, FL 33709 or call (813) 541-7571 for information on these films and a list of MTP distributors.

Becoming a Family
(Color, 25 minutes, MTP No. 16419)
* This film portrays the way it feels for a couple to become parents for the first time. Through interviews with first-time parents the film probes the changes in lifestyle that occur after the birth of the first child.

Newborn
(Color, 28 minutes, MTP No. 20156)
* The infant's world during the first 3 months of life is viewed through the eyes of the child. The film shows a first-time mother and father as they nurture their newborn.

The Special Journey
(Color, 22 minutes, MTP No. 16713)
* Six women are portrayed. Their approaches to infant feeding, nutrition, and mother-child relationships illustrate their choices in making informed decisions regarding the rearing of their children.

How Children Learn

Child's Play
(Color, 20 minutes, CRM Films)
* This lovely film of multiethnic children involved in play explains the importance of play in a young child's life. It is narrated by Goldenson and Croft.

Development of the Child: Cognition
(Color, 30 minutes, Harper & Row)
* Research into the way a child develops intellectually and the differences between the young child's cognitive development are shown.

Foundations of Reading and Writing
(Color, 26 minutes, Campus Films)
* This beautiful film is an excellent means of illustrating to parents, teachers, and students that learning occurs while young children are involved in activities and play. Use it for parent meetings early in the school year to explain the early childhood curriculum. The film focuses on painting, building with blocks, clay modeling, and other activities that form a basis for reading and writing, eye-hand coordination, perceptional development, and coordination.

What Do You Think?
(Color, 32 minutes, Parents Magazine Films)
* Dr. David Elkind explores the way children think with six children who reveal their concepts of the physical, moral, and religious world. This film clarifies and illustrates Piaget's three stages of cognitive development, for ages 4 to 11 years.

Parent-child Relationships

Adapting to Parenthood
(Color, 20 minutes, Polymorph Films)
* Focused on the new parent, this film can be used to bring forth discussions of parents' feelings.

Days of Discovery
(Color, 20 minutes, Olympus Publishing Co., 1975)
* Parent education is described, with the emphasis on parents as the prime educators and caregivers of their children. Parenting is illustrated as an art. It shows parents how to support and guide their children more effectively.

Footsteps
(Color, half-hour television programs, National Audio Visual Center National Archives and Records Service, General Services Administration Reference Section, Washington, DC 20409)
* The films and study guides (University Park Press, 233 East Redmond Street, Baltimore, Maryland 21202) were produced for public television. Footsteps is a complete curriculum on parenting. Five families were illustrated in the 20 films that discuss all aspects of family living, in-

cluding identity, discipline, attachment, TV parenting styles, and 16 other topics.

On Being an Effective Parent
(Color, 45 minutes, American Personnel and Guidance)
- If you are using Parent Effectiveness Training, you are aware of the program developed by Dr. Thomas Gordon. This film demonstrates Gordon's method of active listening and communication between parent and child.

Parental Roles: Don and Mae
(Color, 25 minutes, Encyclopedia Britannica Films)
- The film was taken inside a home where a family is shown unable to communicate with one another. The parents are not able to reach their sons. After family counseling, the family's problems are left unresolved, ready for the audience's interpretations.

Parenting: Growing with Children
(Color, 22 minutes, Film Fair Communications, 1976)
- The film describes four families: a young couple, a large family, working parents, and a single mother. It focuses on the responsibilities, rewards, and realities of parenting.

Step Parenting: New Families, Old Ties
(Color, 25 minutes, Polymorph Films)
- This film is directed toward a large part of the population—the divorced and remarried. It deals with the problems and satisfactions of developing new relationships.

Child Development

The Child: Part I, The First Two Months
(Color, 29 minutes, CRM Films)
The Child: Part II, 2–14 Months
(Color, 28 minutes, CRM Films)
The Child: Part III, 12–24 Months
(Color, 29 minutes, CRM Films)
The Child: Part IV, Three Year Olds
(Color, 28 minutes, CRM Films)
The Child: Part V, Four to Six Years Old
(Color, 30 minutes, CRM Films)
- These films are from the National Film Board of Canada series and are documentary style with emphasis on filming normal children and family action without elaborate narrative. Each film focuses on a time period within the life of the infant through the 6-year-old.

Development of the Child: Language
(Color, 24 minutes, Harper & Row)

- This film explains the development of language in the child.

Development of Feelings in Children
(Color, 50 minutes, Parents Magazine, 1974)
- The film examines the child's emotional makeup and illustrates how to cope with fear, love, joy, sadness, and anger as you interact with the child.

Emotional Development: Aggression
(Color, 19 minutes, CRM Films)
- Aggression is studied from a social-learning viewpoint, learned primarily in a social context. It discusses the manner in which aggression is learned and how it can be changed.

In the Beginning
(Color, 15 minutes, Davidson Films)
- This film examines early infant development and the stages of growth. It is narrated by Bettye Caldwell.

Individual Differences
(Color, 18 minutes, CRM Films, 1979)
- The film examines individual differences and the wide variety of normal characteristics. Included is a discussion of the Denver Developmental Screening Test and the Gesell Infant test.

Infancy
(Color, 19 minutes, CRM Films)
- An infant's abilities, innate and learned, are examined. As the child develops socialization skills, language, cognition, and motor abilities, independent functioning of the child becomes possible.

Infant Development in the Kibbutz
(Color, 27 minutes, Campus Films)
- The film visually explores a kibbutz and the infant's development in an infant house. Care of children by the metapelet and the parents' involvement with their children are depicted. The children interact with each other, the metapelets, and the parents in a positive manner, reflecting excellent motor, social, and cognitive development.

Nurturing
(Color, 15 minutes, Davidson Films)
- *Nurturing* describes the role of the caregiver in the development of the young child. The commentator is Bettye Caldwell.

On Their Own/With Our Help
(Color, 14 minutes, Bradley Wright Films)
- Film showing examples of selective intervention.

Our Prime Time
(Color, Bradley Wright Films, 1980)

- This is an important film for parents because it shows how ordinary events of each day can be prime time for learning and developing human attachment.

Personality: Early Childhood
(Color, 20 minutes, CRM Films, 1979)
- Dr. Paul Mussen explains emotional and instrumental dependency, and Dr. Robert Liebert discusses identification and modeling. Aggressive behavior tied to television violence and family aggression illustrate aggressive modeling.

Prenatal Development
(Color, 23 minutes, CRM Films, 1974)
- This well-produced film examines the biologic and psychologic impact on the fetus during pregnancy. The film shows the developing fetus and explains the prenatal development by interviewing researchers and doctors. Nutrition, drugs, maternal emotional influence, and developmental processes are examined.

Rock-a-Bye Baby
(Color, 30 minutes, Time Life Multimedia)
- This beautiful film shows the importance of human attachment through examination of research on premature babies, institutionalized children, and monkeys.

The Sleeping Feel Good Movie
(Color, 6 minutes, Churchill Films)
- A short movie that shows children getting out of bed and then going to school. Those who had enough sleep are rested; others are not. The film is good for illustrating the importance of rest for the child.

The Way We See Them
(Color, 17 minutes, Bradley Wright Films)
- Learning to observe infants is depicted.

Child Development Training Films

Exploring Childhood Films is a series of films collected or developed for the Exploring Childhood program in high schools.

Module One: Working with Children
Michael's First Day (Black and white, 6 minutes)
Water Tricks (Color, 13 minutes)
Storytime (Color, 5 minutes)
Teacher, Lester Bit Me (Color, 9 minutes)
Helping Is . . . (Color, 12 minutes)
Sara Has Down's Syndrome (Color, 16 minutes)

Module Two: Seeing Development
Half a Year Apart (Color, 12 minutes)
Gabriel Is Two Days Old (Black and white, 15 minutes)
Bill and Suzi: New Parents (Black and white, 13 minutes)
From My Point of View (Color, 13 minutes)
Little Blocks (Color, 8 minutes)
Painting Time (Color, 7 minutes)
Racing Cars (Color, 7 minutes)
Clay Play (Color, 8 minutes)
All in the Game (Color, 22 minutes)

Module Three: Family and Society
Craig at Home (Black and white, 13 minutes)
Jeffrey at Home (Black and white, 11 minutes)
Howie at Home (Black and white, 13 minutes)
Rachel at Home (Black and white, 11 minutes)
Oscar at Home (Black and white, 10 minutes)
Michelle at Home (Hi, Daddy!) (Color, 10 minutes)
Seiko at Home (Color, 12 minutes)
Howie at School (Black and white, 7 minutes)
Rachel at School (Black and white, 11 minutes)
Oscar at School (Black and white, 6 minutes)
Seiko at School (Color, 7 minutes)
At the Doctor's (Black and white, 10 minutes)
Around the Way with Kareema (Color, 18 minutes)
Girl of My Parents (Color, 8 minutes)
Young Children on the Kibbutz (Black and white, 25 minutes)
Broken Eggs (Color, 10 minutes)
Raising Michael Alone (Color, 17 minutes)
Raising a Family Alone (Daniel) (Black and white, 9 minutes)
Families Revisited: Jenny is Four: Rachel Is Seven (18 minutes)

These films were developed for use with the program, Exploring Childhood, and may be obtained from Exploring Childhood, EDC School and Society Programs, 55 Chapel Street, Newton, MA 02160. They vary in quality from excellent to fair.

Issues that Affect Family Life

Crime of Innocence
(Color, 27 minutes, Paulist Communication, 1974)
- The issue of mentally retarded persons moving into community neighborhoods is explored in this film. Peter and his "family" of eight mentally retarded children move into a middle-class area.

The film shows reactions from homeowners who fear for their property values and their safety. The film explores these feelings and illustrates the plight of the mentally retarded.

First Year AD

(Color, 12 minutes, Tele, 1975)

- A hospitalized asthmatic child's visit by his divorced parents reveals the conflict and misunderstandings in the family. A nurse's counseling reveals to the parents that the parents' actions are not helpful to the child's development.

John Baker's Last Race

(Color, 33 minutes, Brigham Young University, 1976)

- This is the heart-rending story of an athlete, John Baker, who had great hopes for running the mile in the Olympics when he found that he had cancer. He continued working with children, helping them to do their best in spite of the odds. His remaining life was spent working with children at Aspen Elementary School, handicapped children, and a group of girls known as the Duke City Dashers. The children do their best for John Baker.

Married Lives Today

(Color, 19 minutes, BFA Educational Media, 1975)

- Three couples work at their marriages in different ways. One couple works together operating a business and considers themselves equal partners; a second couple has a traditional relationship; and a third, separated, couple shares the responsibilities for their child.

Peege

(Color, 28 minutes, Phoenix, 1974)

- This is a sensitive film about a senile grandmother in a nursing home who is visited by her family at Christmas. After the rest of the family leaves, Peege stays with his grandmother and talks with her about old times and his memories of times with her. After he leaves, she manages to smile.

What Color Is the Wind?

(Color, 26 minutes, Allan Grant Productions)

- Perhaps this film belongs under a different heading, but as a film that treats the issue of blindness, it is listed here. It is an excellent film that portrays a family with twins, one blind and the other with sight. It illustrates the parents' positive attitudes and their child-rearing abilities as they treat both sons as equals.

When a Child Enters the Hospital

(Color, 16 minutes, Polymorph Films)

- This film discusses the issue of hospitalization of children. The child's fears and how parents and hospital staff can lessen these anxieties are discussed.

Special Children

Early Intervention

(Color, 30 minutes, Stanfield Film Associates)

- *Early Intervention* stresses the importance of working with the young child. It recommends effective programs that should be implemented as early in the infant's life as feasible.

Hidden Handicaps

(Color, 23 minutes, McGraw-Hill Films)

- Early programs that meet the needs of young children can benefit the special child who is yet unrecognized. Parents, teachers, and counselors have roles in preparing curricula that meet the needs of children with learning disabilities.

It's Cool to Be Smart

(Color, 23 minutes, McGraw-Hill Films)

- This film examines a variety of programs for the gifted child. It focuses on the child's feelings and the teacher's role.

Nicky: One of My Best Friends

(Color, 15 minutes, McGraw-Hill Films)

- The mainstreaming of Nicky, a blind, cerebral palsied 10-year-old is illustrated.
  McGraw-Hill has issued a number of films to help with mainstreaming. These include *Fulfillment of Human Potential, Mainstreaming Techniques: Life Science and Art, First Steps, Token Economy: Behaviorism Applied,* and *Special Education Techniques: Lab Science and Art.*

What Was I Supposed to Do?

(Color, 28 minutes, Stanfield Film Associates)

- This documentary film illustrates the emotional impact on families who have handicapped children and points out the problems and the support systems.

A Matter of Expectations

(Color, 23 minutes, Stanfield Film Associates)

- This film accompanies *What Was I Supposed to Do?* and focuses on practical issues of raising the handicapped child. Included are suggestions for using the latest knowledge and techniques in working with the handicapped child.

Child Abuse

Physical Abuse

Barb: Breaking the Cycle of Child Abuse
(Color, 28 minutes, Motorola Teleprograms)
- This film shows a case history of child abuse, including the police investigator who comes to the home and the mother's treatment in group sessions.

Child Abuse and the Law
(Color, 22 minutes, Perennial Education)
- This film familiarizes teachers and others working with children with the signals of child abuse and their responsibility according to the law.

Child Abuse: Cradle of Violence
(Color, 20 minutes, MTI Teleprograms)
- This film discusses the cause of abuse and what can be done to reduce it. Actual child abusers discuss the problems of abuse.

Children in Peril
(Color, 22 minutes, Xerox Films)
- This film was an ABC special that went to different parts of the country to analyze child abuse. Dr. C. Henry Kempe discusses the cause of abuse. Women in therapy also reveal their feelings toward themselves and to the abuse they had forced on their children.

Cipher in the Snow
(Color, 24 minutes, Brigham Young University)
- This is a story about a young boy who is ignored until his death in the snow makes those who knew him examine their feelings toward him. The film brings about the point that every child has the need for a nurturing relationship.

War of Eggs
(Color, 27 minutes, Paulist Productions)
- A drama that points out that we can only love others if we love ourselves.

Sexual Abuse

Incest: The victim nobody believes
(Color, 23 minutes, MTI Teleprograms)
- Incest is a taboo that has not been openly discussed, but in this film three women discuss their experiences as incest victims.

No more secrets
(Color, 13 minutes. ODN Productions)
- This is a film to help prevent sexual abuse. It encourages no more secrets and teaches children to believe in themselves and their own reactions to good or bad touching.

FILMSTRIPS

Filmstrips and slide presentations, either accompanied by a cassette or narrated by the presenter, are an inexpensive method of using both sight and sound in the teaching process. Reinforcement of the discussion by a visual aid is more effective than relying solely on auditory reception. Most programs are able to purchase filmstrips or capture the message on slides for use in parent education meetings, inservice and preservice training, or formal presentations.

Filmstrips or slides are often used to initiate a discussion. Be sure to review the filmstrip before using it; its content may need additional data and information.

The following filmstrips include child development concepts, family life education, and home-based training sets for use by parents, paraprofessionals, and professionals.

Exceptional Children

Hello Everybody (A mainstreaming package that has 6 color/sound filmstrips. In the filmstrips you meet Danny who has a hearing and speech impairment; Toni, who has a visual impairment; Jed, who is orthopedically handicapped; Sheila, who is developmentally disabled; Matt, who has learning disabilities; and John, Laura, and Ken, who have behavior disorders.)
James Stanfield Film Associates,
P.O. Box 1983, Santa Monica, CA 90406

Coping with Family Change

Redefining the Family
Single Parent Families
Step-parents and Blended Families
Sunburst Communication
39 Washington Avenue
Pleasantville, NY 10570

Parents Magazine Films

Obtain from: Parents Magazine Films
685 3rd Avenue
New York, NY 10017

Children in Crisis
    Set 1: *Child Abuse and Neglect* (V. Fontana)
    Set 2. *Death* (R. Obsershaw)
    Set 3: *Illness* (M. Wessel)
    Set 4: *Divorce and Separation* (J. L. Despert)
The Effective Parents (D. Bert)
    Set 1: *The Parent As Teacher*
    Set 2: *Learning in the Home*
    Set 3: *Learning Away from Home*
    Set 4: *Learning through Play*
Even Love Is Not Enough: Children with Handicaps
    Set 1: *Behavioral and Emotional Disabilities*
    Set 2: *Physical Disabilities*
    Set 3: *Intellectual Disabilities*
    Set 4: *Educational and Language Disabilities*
What Do I See When I See Me? Emotional and Social Growth in Children
    Set 1: *"I See Hope." The Importance of Emotional and Social Development*
    Set 2: *"I See Smiles. I see Frowns" Expressing Emotions*
    Set 3: *"I See Strength." Building Self-Confidence*
    Set 4: *"I See Love." Parent-child Relationships*
Children with Handicaps
    Set 1: *Support from the Family*
    Set 2: *Support from Educators*
    Set 3: *Support from the Community*
    Set 4: *Support from the Helping Professions*
Bringing up Children—A "How To" Guide for Parents and Caregivers
    Set 1: *Feeding to Nourish and Love*
    Set 2: *Bathing, Dressing, and Toilet Training*
    Set 3: *Health Care*
    Set 4: *Day to Day with Your Child*
With Pride to Progress: The Minority Child
    Set 1: *The Black Child* (J. Comer)
    Set 2: *The Puerto Rican Child* (A. Figueroa)
    Set 3: *The Chicano Child* (N. Archuleta)
    Set 4: *The Indian Child* (W. Sample)
Developing Creative Thought in Children (D. Singer and J. Singer)
    Set 1: *Imagination and the Creative Process*
    Set 2: *Growing Through Make-Believe*
    Set 3: *Exercises in Creativity*
    Set 4: *The Parents' Role in Creative Play*

FILM DISTRIBUTORS

AIMS Instructional Media Services
626 Justin Avenue
Glendale, CA 91201

BFA Educational Media
Division of Phoenix Films
468 Park Avenue
New York, NY 10016

Bradley Wright Films
1 Oak Hill Drive
San Anselmo, CA 94960

Brigham Young University
Educational Media Center
Provo, UT 84602

Campus Films
24 Depot Square
Tuckahoe, NY 10707

Carousel Films
241 East 34th
New York, NY 10016

Churchill Films
662 North Robertson Boulevard
Los Angeles, CA 90069

CRM Films (McGraw-Hill)
Box 641
Via de la Vall
Del Mar, CA 92014

Davidson Films
164 Turnstead Avenue
San Anselmo, CA 94960

Education Development Center
Distribution Center
55 Chapel Street
Newton, MA 02160

Encyclopedia Britannica Films
425 North Michigan Avenue
Chicago, IL 60611

EPIE Institute
463 West Street
New York, NY 10014

Film Flair Communication
10900 Ventura Boulevard
P.O. Box 1728
Studio City, CA 91604

Harper & Row
10 East 53rd Street
New York, NY 10022

High/Scope Educational Research Foundation
600 North River Street
Ypsilanti, MI 48197

International Film Bureau
332 South Michigan Avenue
Chicago, IL 60604

Learning Corporation of America
1350 Avenue of America
New York, NY 10019

McGraw-Hill
1221 Avenue of Americas
New York, NY 10020

Modern Talking Picture Services
Film Scheduling Department
5000 Park Street North
St. Petersburg, FL 33709

Motorola Teleprograms
3710 Commercial Avenue
Northbrook, IL 60062

MTI Teleprograms
3710 Commercial Avenue
Northbrook, IL 60062

New York University Film Library
26 Washington Place
New York, NY 10003

O.D.N. Productions
75 Varick Street, Suite 304
New York, NY 10013

Olympus Publishing Company
1670 East 13th South
Salt Lake City, UT 84105

Parents Magazine
685 3rd Avenue
New York, NY 10017

Paulist Productions
17575 Pacific Coast Highway
Box 1057
Pacific Palisades, CA 90272

Perennial Education
930 Pitner Avenue
Evanston, IL 60202

Phoenix
468 Park Avenue South
New York, NY 10016

Polymorph Films
118 South Street
Boston, MA 02111

Pyramid Films
Box 1048
Santa Monica, CA 90406

Roche Laboratories/Association Films
600 Grand Avenue
Ridgefield, NJ 07657

Stanfield Film Associates
P.O. Box 1983
Santa Monica, CA 90406

Sunburst Communication
39 Washington Avenue
Pleasantville, NY 10570

Third Eye Films
12 Arrow Street
Cambridge, MA 02138

Time-Life Video
1271 Avenue of the Americas
New York, NY 10020

Xerox Publishing
1 Pickwick Plaza
P.O. Box 6710
Greenwich, CT 06836

REFERENCES TO BE USED IN THE DEVELOPMENT OF A HOME-BASED PROGRAM

If you plan to develop a home-based educational program for children, use some of the following resources. They describe programs that were developed and tested. Some of these are no longer being published and will have to be found in a library, but the material is still relevant and helpful.

Day, M. C., & Parker, R. K. *The preschool in action: Exploring early childhood programs.* Boston: Allyn & Bacon, 1977.

- An entire section of this text is devoted to home-based programs for preschoolers and infants. These include chapters by Merle Karnes and R. Reid Zebrbach, Glen Nimnicht, Phyllis Levenstein, Earl Schaeffer, Alice S. Honig, and J. Ronald Lally.

Gordon, I. F., & Breivogel, W. F. (Ed.). *Building effective home-school relationships.* Boston: Allyn & Bacon, 1977.

- Ira Gordon and William Breivogel edited this text which illustrates the successful home-based program in Florida. It includes chapters that describe the roles and duties of teachers, administrators, home visitors, and parents.

Gotts, E. E. (Ed.). *The home visitor's kit: Training and practitioner materials for paraprofessionals in family settings.* New York: Human Sciences Press, 1977.

- This kit, developed by the Appalachia Educational Laboratory, includes a Home Visitor's Notebook, Parents Notes, and resource materials for use in training paraprofessionals to work in home-based programs.

Grogan, M., et al. *The homesbook: What home-based programs can do with children and families.* Cambridge: Abt Associates, 1976.

- Abt Associates developed a book that demonstrates activities and curriculum that can be used in home-based programs.

Hewett, K. D., Jerome, C. M., Grogan, M., Nauta, M., Rubin, A. D., & Stein, M. *Partners with parents: The Home Start experience with preschoolers and their families.* U.S. Department of Health, Education, and Welfare (Office of Human Development Services, Administration for Children, Youth and Families, Head Start Bureau). Washington, D.C.: U.S. Government Printing Office, 1978.

- This book describes many of the Home Start programs that were funded during the 1970s. It includes suggested training plans and reports that can be used by persons interested in starting a home-based program.

Lambie, D. Z., Bond, J. T., & Weikart, D. *Home teaching with mothers and infants.* Ypsilanti, Mich.: High/Scope Educational Research Foundation, 1981.

- Developed by the Ypsilanti-Carnegie Infant Education Project, this book summarizes the curriculum used with mothers and infants in the program.

Massoglio, E. T. *Early childhood education in the home.* Albany, NY: Delmar Publishers, 1977.

- This is a textbook that describes the steps for implementing a home-based program.

Portage Project. *The portage guide to early education.* Portage, Wis.: The Portage Project, 1976.

- This book contains the complete developmental curriculum used in the Portage Project. The curriculum has three components: (1) Checklist of Behaviors, (2) Card File, and (3) Manual of Instruction.

U.S. Department of Health, Education, and Welfare. (Office of Human Development, Office of Child Development, Home Start). *A guide for planning and operating home-based child development programs.* Washington, D.C.: U.S. Government Printing Office, 1974.

- This guide was developed to be used in assisting in the implementation of a home-based program. It draws from the experience of 16 funded Home Start demonstration projects and gives information, methods, and procedures for setting up a home-based program.

ADVOCACY

The following organizations form a base from which to obtain information on legal rights, responsibilities, and advocacy. Because addresses and telephone numbers change with regularity, some will be outdated. Check with your library for the yearly update on associations and organizations in the United States if you find an address has changed.

Children's Defense Fund

122 C Street NW
Washington, D.C. 20001

- Long-range advocacy of children was the goal of the Children's Defense Fund when founded in 1973. Since that time, it has monitored areas of education, child care, health, and juvenile justice. The agency works with individuals, agencies, or community groups.

Child Welfare League of America

67 Irving Place
New York, NY 10003

- The League, a privately supported organization with 376 affiliate groups, works for the benefit of dependent and neglected children and their families. They have also published a *Parenting Curriculum* by Grace C. Cooper for adolescent mothers.

Institute for Responsive Education

605 Commonwealth Avenue
Boston, MA 02215

* Founded in 1973 to assist citizen involvement in educational decision making, the Institute believes that parents and community, in collaboration with school officials and teachers, can make a difference. To foster parent and community involvement in the schools, the Institute publishes a quarterly journal, *Citizen Action in Education.*

National Coalition of ESEA Title I/Chapter I Parents

1314 14th Street NW, Suite 6
Washington, DC 20005

* The federal Title I program has made great strides in involving parents in the education of their children. Its findings and suggestions are appropriate for parents and schools in any economic area. Currently called Chapter I, the Coalition supports Chapter I parents as well as others. The organization established the National Parent Center.

National Congress of Parents and Teachers

700 North Rush Street
Chicago, IL 60611

* The PTA is the oldest organization devoted to improving relations between home and school on behalf of children. Founded in 1897, this organization has fluctuated in the acceptance of its role as the spokesperson for parents and teachers but has consistently furnished educational information through the following publications: *PTA Today, PTA Communique,* and pamphlets on parent education, juvenile protection, safety, parent-teacher relationships, and improvement of the quality of education in schools.

National Resource Center for Child Advocacy and Protection

American Bar Association
1155 East 60th Street
Chicago, IL 60637

National School Board Association

1680 Duke Street
Alexandria, VA 22314

* This association, founded in 1940, furnishes information on curriculum development and legislation that affects education and school administration. Members of school boards are familiar with their publications, *Insider's Report,* a weekly newsletter, and the *American School Board Journal,* a monthly journal. These publications are also informative for parents concerned about schools.

National School Volunteer Program

701 North Fairfax Street, Suite 320
Alexandria, VA 22314

* Volunteers have made great strides in opening schools to parent involvement. They have state groups, some of which give six training sessions to volunteers. Housewives, professionals, and young people are typical volunteers.

National Committee for Citizens in Education (NCCE)

Suite 410, Wild Lake Village Green
Columbia, MD 21044

* NCCE has established a Parents' Network and has developed a series of pamphlets to help parents advocate for their children.

INDEX